'*Fashion Management* is a much-needed addition. The book
aspects of the topic with a clear strategic focus. It is written i
to incorporate a good level of critical analysis, making it suit
students. The book offers a broad and exciting range of material, making good use of relevant examples and
case studies from around the world to illustrate the concepts discussed. It is great to see such an informative
and inspiring book about contemporary practice in fashion management.'

– Barbara Waters, *Senior Teaching Fellow in Fashion Marketing, School of Design,
University of Leeds, UK*

'Fashion is bigger than you think and the new textbook *Fashion Management* hits all the right notes. This
comprehensive text, with its varying contributing authors who are both academics and industry practitioners
alike, provides the reader with a global perspective on the fashion industry. Fashion Management transcends
borders and can be adapted in any college or university setting regardless of location. The chapters are well-
formulated, from the introduction to the references, and packed with relevant information that students can
utilize to develop a deeper understanding of the inner workings of the global fashion industry. Suitable as a
standalone text for fashion management and product development courses, and as a supplemental text on
courses from visual merchandising to supply chain.'

– Michael Londrigan, *Vice President for Academic Affairs, LIM College, USA*

'This is a timely, detailed and comprehensive book which is a must-read for anyone interested in the business
and management of fashion. Suitable for undergraduate and postgraduate students, it covers the whole
spectrum of fashion business and management issues, with diverse industry examples and case studies used
to provide useful illustrations and prompt further discussion. Featuring a balance of theoretical concepts and
detailed explanations of industry practices and challenges, this book enables the reader to develop an in-depth
and critical understanding of today's fashion industry from multiple perspectives.'

– Dr Patsy Perry, *Senior Lecturer in Fashion Marketing, The University of Manchester, UK*

'As an academic who teaches both undergraduate and postgraduate Fashion Management and Business, I
found this book not only insightful but a practical teaching tool. Full of online resources which point you
to the companion website as well as contemporary case studies hitting the right mark! Challenges and
conversations further explore each chapter and allow one to open discussion and debate around each topic. A
real collaboration of fashion minds who have created an in-depth strategic approach to fashion business which
will not only support those studying but also those starting out in fashion business. I expect all my students to
be reading this!'

– Katherine Boxall, *Deputy Director, Business School for the Creative Industries,
University for the Creative Arts, UK*

'A comprehensive and structured guide to fashion management and to the changing factors that are impacting
the strategic fashion environment. Cases and mini-cases showcase emerging tools for innovation and new
business models. An ideal textbook for degree students to improve their understanding about the new
directions of contemporary fashion management and strategy and for potential managers entering the fashion
industry.'

– Cabirio Cautela, *Design School, Politecnico di Milano, Italy*

'This book provides an excellent, thorough assessment of management practices in the fashion industry. In
particular it will help students contextualise key concepts and to challenge existing approaches in a highly
dynamic industry. *Fashion Management* will prove to be a very valuable addition to teaching and learning on
fashion business courses.'

– Anthony Kent, *Professor of Fashion Marketing, Nottingham Trent University, UK*

FASHION MANAGEMENT

A STRATEGIC APPROACH

Rosemary Varley

Ana Roncha

Natascha Radclyffe-Thomas

Liz Gee

First published 2019 by
RED GLOBE PRESS

Red Globe Press in the UK is an imprint of Springer Nature Limited, registered in England, company number 785998, of 4 Crinan Street, London, N1 9XW.

Red Globe Press® is a registered trademark in the United States, the United Kingdom, Europe and other countries.

ISBN 978–1–137–50818–8 paperback

This book is printed on paper suitable for recycling and made from fully managed and sustained forest sources. Logging, pulping and manufacturing processes are expected to conform to the environmental regulations of the country of origin.

A catalogue record for this book is available from the British Library.

A catalog record for this book is available from the Library of Congress.

Dedication

The author team would like to thank our co-authors and contributors, as well as industry and academic colleagues, and our students, past and present, for the shared experiences that have informed our writing. We would also like to thank our families for their continued support and understanding of academic life and endeavours:

Sam and Sophie Varley

Mathew Bayliss and Thomas Roncha-Bayliss

Tommy, Babette and Beau Radclyffe-Thomas

Anthony, Tom, Will and Ellie Gee

BRIEF CONTENTS

LONG CONTENTS

LIST OF FIGURES

LIST OF TABLES

LIST OF BOXES

LIST OF CASE STUDIES

Case Studies

Mini Case Studies

CASE STUDY GRID

Challenges relating to chapter	1	2	3	4	5	6	7	8	9	10	11	12	13	14	15
Case study															
1 Di$count Universe	*	*	*	*	*										
2 Kering		*	*												
3 Armani		*	*			*		*							
4 L'Oreal		*		*		*									
5 Etiko					*	*	*		*						
6 Acne						*	*					*			
7 Havianas				*		*	*								*
8 John Smedley				*		*		*	*						
9 H&M		*				*			*			*			
10 Burberry 1						*		*		*					
11 Burberry 2		*									*				
12 M&S Plan A		*										*			
13 Shanghai Tang				*		*				*			*		
14 Toms				*		*	*							*	
15 Vigga		*		*								*			*

Although we are confident that readers will find the Case Studies of general interest, we have indicated chapters that are particularly applicable to the case and will help to frame answers to the Case Challenges and Conversations.

THE AUTHOR TEAM

Rosemary Varley, Liz Gee, Natascha Radclyffe-Thomas and Ana Roncha

BIOGRAPHIES AND PHOTOS

Editor and Author: Rosemary Varley

Rosemary Varley is Subject Director for Retail and Marketing at the Fashion Business School at London College of Fashion (LCF), University of the Arts London. She has many years of teaching experience and has written well-respected textbooks and articles on retailing. Rosemary is responsible for teaching and curriculum development at both undergraduate and postgraduate level. She also coordinates the Centre for Fashion Business Innovation and Research at LCF and through research and student projects Rosemary maintains links with the fashion industry. Rosemary has taken the role of lead editor for this project. She wrote the chapter on marketing and co-authored chapters on strategic product management, supply chain management and retail management, as well as the introductory chapter.

Author Team

Dr Ana Roncha

Ana Roncha leads the MA Strategic Fashion Marketing course at LCF, having previously been a post-doctoral research fellow in Enterprise and Innovation at the Fashion Business School. Ana holds a PhD in Design and Marketing Management for the Fashion Industry and lectures in the fields of Fashion Business Strategies, Strategic Branding, Marketing Communications and Marketing Management.

Building on over 12 years of experience creating high-impact strategic programmes for international fashion, beauty and lifestyle brands in the USA, UK and Portugal, Ana's research explores how innovation drives business development and value creation in the fashion sector. She has published in academic journals on the topics of strategic brand management, business model innovation for fashion and co-creation of value through sustainability.

Ana wrote the chapters on brand management, integrated marketing communications and the future of fashion and co-authored chapters on corporate strategy, international growth, social responsibility, as well as the introductory chapter.

Dr Natascha Radclyffe-Thomas

Natascha Radclyffe-Thomas is an internationally recognized researcher and educator working at the Fashion Business School. She leads LCF's acclaimed BA (Hons) Fashion Marketing course, and her research focuses on how culture, heritage, city-branding and social enterprise manifest themselves in contemporary fashion marketing in the West and Asia. Natascha is a Senior Fellow of the Higher Education Academy and became a Fellow of the RSA to further her work in education for sustainability. In 2017 Natascha was awarded an HEA National Teaching Fellowship and was recognized as a University of the Arts London Senior Teaching Scholar for her teaching and pedagogic research in the field of e-learning and internationalizing the curriculum. Before embarking on her academic career Natascha was partner in the award-winning directional luxury children's fashion label, Miss Fleur.

Natascha co-wrote the chapter on corporate responsibility and contributed the case studies of Kering, Armani, H&M, Burberry Parts 1 and 2, Shanghai Tang and Toms and many of the images. She also acted as pedagogic design consultant for the book.

Liz Gee

Liz Gee is Associate Dean of the Fashion Business School at LCF. Liz is a Fellow of the Institute of Chartered Accountants in England and Wales, having trained with EY, and as a Chartered Manager is also a Fellow of the CMI. Liz has fashion industry financial experience at a senior level: as Treasurer of Debenhams plc and as a Corporate Banker for retail and wholesale businesses at Barclays plc. The recipient of two University of the Arts London (UAL) awards for teaching excellence, Liz completed her MA in Academic Practice at UAL and is a Senior Fellow of the HEA. With an interest in finance coaching for start-ups she is currently researching the pedagogy of financial competence in enterprise and employability. This background finds her in the ideal position to contribute the chapters on financial management and risk. She also co-wrote the chapters on corporate strategy and international growth with Ana Roncha.

Chapter Contributors:

Chapter 14 Lisa Henderson

Lisa Henderson is a Lecturer in Human Resource Management at LCF, teaching on undergraduate and postgraduate courses. She has an MSc in International Human Resource Management, is accredited to the Chartered Management Institute as Chartered Manager and is an associate member of the Chartered Institute of Personnel and Development. In her twenty-year industry career she has worked globally in Retail Operations, gaining an extensive experience in leading, managing and developing people. She is currently undertaking a PhD in strategic leadership and culture within the fashion industry. She also has a strong research interest in the generational challenges and well-being of the future workforce.

Chapter 11 Francesca Bonetti and Matteo Montecchi

Francesca Bonetti is a Lecturer in Fashion Marketing at undergraduate and postgraduate level at London College of Fashion and a PhD researcher in fashion marketing, consumer-facing technology and retailing. Her academic research interests also include luxury fashion retailing in China and the consumption of fashion goods by Asian consumers. She has international industry experience in marketing communications and business development in the fashion and apparel sector (and consults for fashion brands and retailers on retailing and wholesaling, communications strategies and the use of consumer-facing technology across retail channels).

Matteo Montecchi is Programme Director for Fashion Management at the London College of Fashion. His expertize is strategic marketing for fashion, lifestyle and luxury products, digital and social media marketing for luxury brands and online retailing. He has extensive experience in teaching at undergraduate and postgraduate level, including MBA and executive courses. Currently registered for a PhD, Matteo's research investigates how digital technologies and emerging social platforms influence the creation, development and management of fashion and luxury brands.

Contributors

In addition to the chapter authors, the expertize of three other colleagues made significant contributions in the respective chapters on product management, supply chain management and retail management, working alongside Rosemary Varley to produce a distinctive fashion orientation in these significant subject areas.

James Clark (Chapter 8)

James Clark is the course leader of the Executive MBA (Fashion) and a senior lecturer specializing in fashion product management at London College of Fashion, UAL. His teaching within the Fashion Business School currently covers fashion merchandising, supply chain management and entrepreneurship. Prior to joining UAL, he held substantive product management positions within mass market UK-based fashion retailers including Debenhams and House of Fraser.

Heather Pickard (Chapter 9)

Heather Pickard is Dean of the Fashion Business School, London College of Fashion (LCF), UAL. Her previous roles at LCF include Associate Dean for the School, Programme Director Fashion Management and Course Leader for BA (Hons) Fashion Management. Her academic expertize is in buying and merchandising, sourcing and supply chain management. Prior to joining academia Heather was a buying and merchandising controller with several large-scale fashion retailers.

Dr Mirsini Trigoni (Chapter 10)

Mirsini is a lecturer at London College of Fashion, University of the Arts London at undergraduate and postgraduate level. She completed her MA in Art in Architecture and PhD in set design, styling, target audiences and visual communication. Mirsini has worked as an interior designer and display designer in Athens and London. Her expertize lies in the field of interior design and visual communication, the relationship between commercial spaces and target audiences: how to use retail design, display design and visual merchandising, set design and styling so as to effectively target market segments and enhance a brand and its identity. Her current research interests include retail design, visual merchandising, fashion branding, print and social media, photography and visual communication.

ACKNOWLEDGEMENTS

We would like to additionally acknowledge the contribution of the following people who have helped us to complete the book.

We would like to thank Professor Frances Corner OBE, Head of London College of Fashion, Pro Vice-Chancellor, University of the Arts London, for her enthusiasm for the project and for the Foreword. We would also like to thank Heather Pickard, and her predecessor Andrew Hughes, Dean of LCF Fashion Business School for their encouragement to undertake the project. We would also like to acknowledge the contribution of our additional case study authors: Bethan Alexander, Course Leader MA Fashion Retail Management, LCF, for the John Smedley case; Michael Beverland, Professor of Fashion Enterprise, RMIT University for the Di$count Universe and Etiko case studies; and Jeanne Nielsen, Associate Lecturer in Fashion Management, LCF for the Vigga case study. We would also like to thank James Clark, Course Leader Executive MBA (Fashion), LCF for the worked through WSSI Model which can be found in the Companion Website (Chapter 13) and Bill Webb, Associate Lecturer in Fashion Retail, LCF for the Hub and Spoke Conceptual Model featured in chapter 10. We would also like to thank our anonymous reviewers for their constructive and enthusiastic guidance.

We would like to thank the Red Globe Press Editorial Team (Isabelle Cheng, Peter Atkinson, Andrew Malvern and Milly Weaver), the Design Team and the Production Team for their expertize and support.

PUBLISHER'S ACKNOWLEDGEMENTS

The publisher is grateful to the following organizations and people for kindly granting permission to reproduce, or use adaptions of, figures, tables, images, photographs or text that appear in the book: Oxford University Press; Emerald Publishing; Mansur Gavriel; Prada; Zalando – Zalon; Oioba; Anisa Sojka; Taylor & Francis; knowtheorigin.com; Jewel; A. T. Kearney; Armine Linke; Primark; SAGE Publications; Springer; Redress; Elvis & Kresse; Kokoon; Birchbox; Etiko; VIGGA; TOMS; Shanghai Tang; Acne; Valerie Wilson Trower; London College of Fashion.

For the full page photos found at the start of each chapter, the publisher would like to give credit to the following:

Chapter 1
46968 London College of Fashion BA16 catwalk show, June 2016, Nicholls and Clarke building, Shoreditch. Photography by Roger Dean.

Chapter 2
Photograph by Natascha Radclyffe-Thomas.

Chapter 3
46615 Case study, BA (Hons) Illustration, London College of Fashion. Courtney Burnan, BA (Hons) Fashion Illustration, London College of Fashion. Photographer Alys Tomlinson. Copyright University of the Arts London.

Chapter 4
46930 London College of Fashion BA16 catwalk show, June 2016, Nicholls and Clarke building, Shoreditch. Photography by Roger Dean.

Chapter 5
Photograph by Natascha Radclyffe-Thomas. Reproduced by permission of Shanghai Tang.

Chapter 6
Photograph by Natascha Radclyffe-Thomas. Reproduced by permission of Shanghai Tang.

Chapter 7
Clutch bag by Maria Sokolyanskaya, MA Fashion Artefact. London College of Fashion. Copyright University of the Arts London.

Chapter 8
Photograph by Natascha Radclyffe-Thomas. Reproduced by permission of Shanghai Tang.

Chapter 9
Case study, BA (Hons) Bespoke Tailoring. India Heaversedge, BA (Hons) Bespoke Tailoring, London College of Fashion. Photographer Alys Tomlinson. Copyright University of the Arts London.

Chapter 10
Photograph by Natascha Radclyffe-Thomas. Reproduced by permission of Shanghai Tang.

Chapter 11
47047 London College of Fashion BA16 catwalk show, June 2016, Nicholls and Clarke building, Shoreditch. Photography by Roger Dean.

Chapter 12
35320 moss dress. Tara Baoth Mooney, MA Fashion and the Environment 2011, London College of Fashion. Photography Sean Michael. Image courtesy of Centre for Sustainable Fashion.

Chapter 13
46925 London College of Fashion BA16 catwalk show, June 2016, Nicholls and Clarke building, Shoreditch. Photography by Roger Dean.

Chapter 14
Photograph by Valerie Wilson Trower.

Chapter 15
Photograph by Valerie Wilson Trower.

TOUR OF THE BOOK

INTRODUCTION

Introductory sections provide you with an overview of the structure and major themes of each chapter.

LEARNING OBJECTIVES

Learning objectives outline the knowledge and understanding you should gain from reading the chapter.

 INTRODUCTION

An overview of the fashion industry is imperative as a starting point for strategic analysis in this context, and without it the nuances of a strategic approach to fashion management would not be understood. The fashion industry is vast and global, generating huge economic value through the conversion of natural resources into sophisticated end-use products. It is complex in its interwoven structures, from the supply chains that link to produce fashion goods, to the distribution and communication channels

organizations that conceive, design and produce fashion and those who buy and wear it.

The chapter begins by considering what the term 'fashion' means as a concept and provides some boundaries around it as a descriptive term. The second part of the chapter uses a number of dimensions to describe the fashion industry in terms of its structures and networks, and the relationships between the different types of organizations within it, to give a broad understanding of how the fashion

 LEARNING OBJECTIVES

After studying this chapter, you should be able to understand:

- The overview of the global fashion industry, appreciating its economic, social and cultural importance;
- The characteristics and dimensions of the fashion industry in terms of organizational players and market levels;

- The structural and technological changes which have shaped the contemporary fashion industry;
- The importance of trends and business models that will continue to influence the evolution of the fashion industry in the future.

CASE STUDIES

Mini case studies appearing throughout the text and key case studies found at the end of each chapter offer you an insight into how the theory and topics discussed apply in practice to real world organizations and situations.

CASE STUDY 1 - Di$count Universe: A new type of luxury defined by brand culture

Di$count Universe (www.discountuniverse.com) is a small luxury fashion label founded in Melbourne, Australia, by Cami James and Nadia Napreychikov. It is an interesting case of a growing brand that differentiates on the basis of a strong brand culture and a rejection of the norms of the luxury fashion industry.

The choice of the brand name 'Di$count Universe' is the first striking example of the founders' beliefs about authenticity, given that the name is hardly consistent with traditional luxury category codes. Rejecting the idea that clothes are only made for one season, the brand is staunchly anti-seasonal: 'Clothes aren't just made seasonally to go out of fashion the next season. If something has resonance with people over and over again we will keep releasing it' (Nadia Napreychikov). Describing their look, Cami James states, 'It's obviously excessive in style ... it's anti-industry, that's part of the DNA of the brand. There's a lot of messages and certain innuendo and humour in the brand.'

Rather than striving to produce a catwalk show or opening a static retail outlet, Cami and Nadia were early adopters of the blog as a legitimate place to display their garments. This quickly generated an online community and a large and engaged fan base. The brand's big break came when Miley Cyrus was photographed in one of their tops. At the time, Cyrus was transitioning from her Hannah Montana character to a more mature performer,

and Nadia and Cami were initially reluctant to use the endorsement as Cyrus didn't fit their perceived identity. Cyrus's photograph featuring Di$count Universe was printed on her tour T-shirts and brought the awareness of the nascent brand to the global stage. Other high-profile brand adopters such as Katy Perry, Lady Gaga and most recently Kylie Jenner have driven sales and built awareness of the brand.

The brand culture approach is a direct assault on the perceived elitism of the luxury fashion industry, in which just a few privileged insiders get to attend shows and launches. In contrast, Di$count Universe shows give priority to the brand's online fan base and are set up like rock shows or giant parties where cheering and hedonistic expressions are encouraged, and content is available to any fan who wishes to blog, post, or tweet about the collection. 'It's about having that relationship with the people who got us to where we are, more so than someone who might have come up through [a magazine] nurturing them' (Cami James, Founder).

Source: Parts of this case are based on Beverland, M., Brand Management, SAGE, London, UK, Copyright © 2018.

Case Challenge

How would you classify Di$count Universe in terms of the levels of the industry (see Figure 1.2)? How does this brand illustrate change and trends within the fashion industry?

industry are: adult clothing (including outerwear), accessories (including handbags) footwear, jewelry, make-up (cosmetics). Categories that are increasingly fashion orientated include children's wear, home furnishings, and stationery while perfume is related because of the dominance of fashion brands in this category. According to Corner (2014), fashion is, at its heart, about self-adornment and the visual presentation of ourselves to the external world, reflecting how we want the world to view us and how we view the world ourselves.

Category A group of products that broadly perform a similar function, satisfying similar consumer needs, from which further sub-categories might evolve.

capacity and a sales turnover (Inditex, 2017). Quantitati to understand and frequer company size. and impact ca sizeable and a sm like Victoria Be owned stores, r and a relatively be considered industry becaus impact; the epo was awarded D

KEY CONCEPTS

Definitions and explanations of important ideas are provided throughout the text by an on-page glossary. Other key terms are also highlighted to aid your navigation through the book.

ONLINE RESOURCES

Additional teaching and learning materials, including extended case studies and case challenges, can be found on the book's companion website at: www.macmillanihe. com/companion/Varley_Fashion_ Management.

ONLINE RESOURCES

A longer version of this case study, with additional challenges, can be found on our companion website: https://www.macmillanihe.com/companion/Varley_Fashion_Management.

CHALLENGES AND CONVERSATIONS

Engaging questions and exercises at the end of each chapter invite you to check your understanding of the topics you've read about and to further develop and apply your knowledge of the subject matter.

 CHALLENGES AND CONVERSATIONS

1. What is your own interpretation of the word 'Fashion'? How do you see the fashion world changing and what do you think will be the most challenging aspects of managing a fashion brand in the future?

2. Consider the fashion brands that you like. How would you describe them in terms of their market level? Consider the challenges and opportunities of maintaining a brand over different market levels.

3. A strategic approach to fashion management requires the acknowledgement of, understanding of, and response to change. What characteristics of the fashion industry make the management of change complex?

4. Debate the idea of the consumer omni-channel journey. Is it as complex as Figure 1.4 shows? What is your own experience? Has your journey changed in the last 5 years; if so how and why?

SUMMARY AND CONCLUDING THOUGHTS

These sections bring together the main points discussed in each chapter and reinforce the learning objectives.

 SUMMARY AND CONCLUDING THOUGHTS

This chapter has provided an overview of the fashion industry in an attempt to contextualize the sphere in which strategic decisions are made. Building an appreciation of what characterizes fashion businesses and the environment in which they operate helps us to understand what is relevant to fashion consumers and the organizations that connect with them. The influence of technology has caused a great impact on consumers' behaviour with greater demands for experiences, interaction and personalization. It could be argued that the current situation presents a tipping point for many companies in the fashion industry, with a significant share of retailers and brands in need of significant realignment of their business models as

a prerequisite to sustain growth. Understanding the full capabilities of new technologies as well as their applications is essential to attract, engage and satisfy consumers.

The rapidly changing business landscape makes long-term strategic planning difficult; over time nevertheless, a set of theoretical concepts, frameworks and tools have become established, which help fashion managers in their strategic thinking and decision-making. The next three chapters provide a tailored discussion of a selection of these models, before we move on to subsequent chapters that explore in more detail the implementation of strategy in specific organizational contexts.

REFERENCES AND FURTHER READING

A list of sources for further study.

 REFERENCES AND FURTHER READING

Abnett, K. (2015) *Will mass customization work for fashion.* Available at: https://www.businessoffashion.com/articles/intelligence/mass-customisation-fashion-nike-converse-burberry [accessed 12/01/2016].

Agins, T. (1999) *The End of Fashion: How Marketing Changed the Clothing Business Forever.* New York: Harper Collins.

Barnard, M. (2002) *Fashion as Communication,* 2nd edn. Abingdon: Routledge.

Barthes, R. (1983) *The Fashion System* (English translation). Now available through Berkeley, CA: University of California Press (2010 paperback edition).

Bazilian, E. (2014) *Derek Lam Believes in Fashion for the Masses.* Available at: http://www.adweek.com/brand-marketing/derek-lam-believes-fashion-masses-157455/ [accessed 12/01/2016].

Bogoviyeva, E. (2011) *Co-branding: Brand development: The effects of customer co-creation and self-construal on self-brand connection.* AMA Summer Educators' Conference Proceedings. Chicago, IL: American Marketing Association (AMA), p. 371.

Braham, P. (1997) 'Fashion: Unpacking a cultural production', in Du Gay, P. (ed.) *Production of Culture/Cultures of Production.* London: SAGE.

British Fashion Council (2013) *Facts & Figures SS14.* Available at: http://www.britishfashioncouncil.co.uk/pressreleases/Facts--Figures-SS14 [accessed 06/07/2016].

Clara Lionel Foundation (2017). Available at: http://claralionelfoundation.org.

Corner, F. (2014) *Why Fashion Matters.* London: Thames & Hudson.

FOREWORD

Fashion is defined by change, and this is true now more than ever. As production cycles get faster, and the demands of the consumer grow, fashion is becoming an ever more uncompromising industry. Styles, brands, and business come and go as they struggle to adapt to the pace of change. Yet, in spite of all the churning within the industry there are fashion names and brands that have been with us for decades, centuries even, that survive this change, maintaining desirability. They are still with us because they are managed strategically; enabling fluidity in the operational process to respond to changing commercial landscapes yet disciplined by thoughtful and considered leadership.

This book offers you the chance to understand the strategic approach to managing fashion businesses. Fashion businesses have unique challenges, dynamic opportunities, and are hugely influenced by the power of creativity. Creativity in product output, creativity in customer and community engagement, creativity in organizational structures, and company cultures; but also, creativity in thinking; building on the tried and tested, and not afraid to break rules and challenge the norm. Through the chapters, you will come to understand how the established theoretical knowledge of strategic management can be applied to fashion orientated companies, but also where it has limitations in its application and requires adaptation to this fascinating industry. The text covers all the well-established frameworks and concepts that form the foundation of strategic thinking from a corporate perspective, but it also provides contextualized discussions on specific aspects of strategic planning and considers what future directions strategic thinking will need to move in to maintain pace and manage divergence.

The Fashion Business School which is situated within London College of Fashion (LCF), part of University of the Arts London, was established in 2015; however, fashion management as an academic discipline was pioneered by the London College of Fashion back in the 1980s. The author team has emerged from this world-renowned institution, whose relationship with the fashion industry started over a century ago, as a provider of dedicated vocational training to the local economy of London's fashion scene. Now LCF graduates make a huge contribution to the global fashion industry, but while the cat-walked collections, and the head-turning campaigns are often the more visible results of the endeavours of our alumni, it is those who become buyers, marketing managers, visual retail and supply chain directors, and above all, self-starting entrepreneurs, that energize the industry internally and who make up much of the LCF graduate network. The Fashion Business School faculty team are uniquely positioned to write this book, using their combined teaching experience, subject expertize and global outlook through the London lens, to bring lively and comprehensive chapters that will facilitate learning and provide a backbone of academic relevance in this growing and important discipline.

Fashion means business. The fashion industry contributes £28 billion to the UK economy and supports over 880,000 jobs. Globally the industry is worth an estimated US$2.4 trillion to US$3 trillion per annum. However, with fashion's economic significance comes responsibility. There is much to be concerned about within our industry and its relationship with society, the environment, and natural resources. This is impacting strategic thinking in a deeply significant way and is reflected in this book, not only in a specific chapter on responsible management but also in the critical approach taken throughout the book.

The publication of this book is timely and welcome, and I am proud to endorse it as a specialist and extensive resource that I am confident fashion business and management students, teachers and practitioners will enjoy.

Professor Frances Corner OBE
Head of London College of Fashion
Pro Vice-Chancellor, University of the Arts London

PREFACE

Strategic management for fashion is fun and fast-paced, combining creativity with a constantly changing environment for doing business. Long range, systematic planning may not spring to mind when thinking about the way fashion companies are managed and a certain degree of serendipity has always played a part in shaping fashion brand appeal because of the fashion industry's highly visible and consumer-centric orientation. Fashion companies that are not flexible and responsive to opportunities, quickly and troublingly appear out of date. Maintaining a vision and direction, while remaining relevant and desirable, is challenging. Yet many successful fashion companies have found a formula that allows for flexible decision-making within a clear and considered organizational direction. As such, fashion management is a challenging discipline and this book has been created to help build frameworks for a strategic approach to it. We hope that you, the reader, will grasp fashion management in all its complexity and take away those frameworks so that you too can start to manage strategically in this fascinating and turbulent industry.

Although fashion strategy has been central to the curriculum at specialist institutions such as our own for decades, this is the first comprehensive text to be written about strategic management entirely in the context of the fashion industry. The book aims to fill a resource gap that has been getting wider and deeper. The fashion industry is global and substantial, yet it is often overlooked in business and management texts from the point of view of its global economic contribution and its societal status. Fashion business and management education continues to grow in its ability to engage students, encourage recruitment to courses and produce highly employable graduates all over the world. Studying fashion management with a strategic approach will help students to grasp transferrable knowledge and apply established theory.

As researching academics at London College of Fashion, within the University of the Arts London, our combined expertize and experience brings a unique perspective and deep understanding of strategic management within fashion corporations. This text goes further than contextualizing and applying tried and tested strategy theory to the fashion industry; it places emphasis on what really matters to fashion companies and fashion consumers, highlighting and expanding the discussion of pertinent theoretical concepts, while critiquing those that don't quite 'fit' in the case of inputs and outputs of fashion organizations, and developing new models that do.

We collaborated to produce this book for a number of reasons; perhaps the most compelling being that we all have a vested interest in the project. We are colleagues who teach fashion management at both undergraduate and postgraduate level, and who have been conscious of the need for a comprehensive text in this subject area for many years. More specialist fashion texts are available, for example on aspects such as marketing, design, buying, and visual merchandising, but these tend to be focused on operational detail rather than the longer-term and bigger-picture managerial approach. Likewise, there is a rich vein of excellent books on strategy, and we are collectively very familiar with many of them, but we find our students are frustrated by the lack of specificity to fashion within these. By collaborating we are proud to have produced an interesting and current book, with a plethora of examples and illustrations; some well known and others that we hope will encourage curiosity. We have used our own areas of research interest and academic expertize to bring a level of critical analysis that has not been offered before in a fashion business textbook at this level. We hope you enjoy reading it and find it useful. As this is a collection of chapters by multiple authors, we have worked hard to achieve a consistent tone of voice, resulting in a clear writing style with suitable approaches for the subjects covered in each chapter.

One final note: defining a fashion company is difficult. Fashion and clothing are often considered synonymously but cars and food can be fashionable and clothing can be something different from fashion, as in the case of protective garments. It is not our intention or purpose to enter a debate about the definition and purpose of fashion. We intend to concentrate our attention on those companies for whom consumer and product trend and style are core to their values and operations, and in that sense, are different from non-fashion organizations where this consideration is irrelevant, such as the healthcare or energy industries.

CHAPTER PATHWAY

The pathway devised for this book was to introduce fashion management at the strategic level, making it accessible to those who have not studied management in the context of the fashion industry before, while making it interesting for those of you who may already be familiar with it. Chapter 1 therefore provides a concise overview of the fashion industry to set the scene and begins the process of learning the unique requirements of a strategy for a fashion organization. Chapter 2 then moves into some of the key concepts associated with strategic thinking to provide an overview of fashion strategy, including business environment analysis, the nature of competitive forces and the ways fashion companies can use their capabilities to seek advantage. Given the consumer orientation of the fashion industry, marketing strategy comes next, providing a backbone for later chapters on brand management, marketing communications management, and managing customer relationships. This chapter concentrates on the STP (segmentation, targeting and positioning) process and considers how product and market development can contribute to strategic goals. After marketing strategy, we explore the concept of strategic growth and development, with an emphasis on international strategy, covering different approaches to international growth, and the necessity for adaptation when operating in markets with different cultural norms. The importance of resource management in a competitive industry is reflected in the inclusion of a chapter on financial management early on in the book (Chapter 5) covering sources of funding and financial analysis while appreciating some of the complex issues surrounding the valuation of fashion businesses.

Chapter 6 focuses on the management of one of the most important assets for fashion companies – the brand. We introduce key concepts and frameworks for brand analysis and focus on the strategic role of brands, and brand collaborations within fashion organizations. Chapter 7 extends this discussion

in terms of how fashion brands communicate and engage with fashion consumers, with an emphasis on the growing importance of digital marketing communications. Given that the product is absolutely central to all fashion businesses, Chapter 8 provides a detailed insight into merchandise management from a strategic perspective, including range planning, brand extension considerations, pricing architecture and resourcing implications. The related subject of supply chain management is covered in Chapter 9, with an emphasis on the challenges of global sourcing, including sustainability, and the relationship between the strategic aims of a fashion organization and supply chain decisions. In contrast, but very much related in terms of organizational integration, retail management is the subject of Chapter 10, given that retail activity is the basis of much strategic growth and development and that the retail environment plays such an important part in fashion brand–consumer engagement.

In Chapter 11 we delve even deeper into the relationship between fashion companies and consumers, by focusing on customer relationship management and the growing use of data analysis to inform strategic decisions. In the era of the conscious consumer and political and economic uncertainty, we explore in detail how strategies need to address the social and environmental responsibilities of corporations in Chapter 12, and manage risk, whether financial or corporate brand risk, in Chapter 13. The part people play in strategic fashion management, as leaders, implementers and influencers of organizational goals, is the subject of Chapter 14. The book finishes by considering what the future holds for fashion strategy, questioning the effects of disruptive technology, new ways of thinking and modelling business organizations, and the introduction of innovative management approaches such as shared value, brand communities and co-creation.

The fashion industry is creative and visual, with innovation and novelty in the way products are created, presented and delivered. To reflect this, relevant and interesting examples, illustrations, diagrammatic models and learning stories in the form of mini case studies abound in this book. In addition a Case Study at the end of each chapter will introduce you to a wide variety of managerial practice, and help you to understand through application how theoretical approaches to strategy can help with managerial decision-making. Case companies include Acne Studios, Armani,

Burberry, H&M, Havaianas, The Kering group, Marks and Spencer, Shanghai Tang and TOMS. We have tried to remain as true to life as possible with our case studies, but stress that the purpose of them is for learning, and in most cases, we highlight practices that are relevant to particular situations.

Supplementary material such as additional resource suggestions, worked-through examples and longer versions of case studies are included on our companion website: https://www.macmillanihe.com/companion/Varley_Fashion_Management. In an effort to keep this book affordable we have opted for a simple but chic approach to presentation. Given the universal accessibility of full colour digital images we make no apology for taking the decision to use black and white images, which maintains the focus on visual research and analysis.

INTRODUCING A STRATEGIC APPROACH TO FASHION MANAGEMENT

Rosemary Varley and Ana Roncha

INTRODUCTION

An overview of the fashion industry is imperative as a starting point for strategic analysis in this context, and without it the nuances of a strategic approach to fashion management would not be understood. The fashion industry is vast and global, generating huge economic value through the conversion of natural resources into sophisticated end-use products. It is complex in its interwoven structures, from the supply chains that link to produce fashion goods, to the distribution and communication channels that move finished product towards the fashion consumer. The fashion industry follows particular patterns and cycles, which have shaped the way the industry has evolved, and it reflects sociological, cultural and economic situations directly because of the very personal relationship between the fashion consumer and the outputs of the fashion industry. It has also, like most other industries, been disrupted by technological innovations that are changing the way fashion goods are made and, above all, presented to fashion consumers, resulting in new relationships between those people and organizations that conceive, design and produce fashion and those who buy and wear it.

The chapter begins by considering what the term 'fashion' means as a concept and provides some boundaries around it as a descriptive term. The second part of the chapter uses a number of dimensions to describe the fashion industry in terms of its structures and networks, and the relationships between the different types of organizations within it, to give a broad understanding of how the fashion world operates. Relevant industry terminology is introduced to provide a framework for further discussion and analysis of strategy within this context. In the third section of the chapter specific characteristics of the industry that influence strategy formation are highlighted, to start an appreciation of some of the important strategic constraints and opportunities inherent within fashion. The final section of the chapter considers how technological trends and evolving business models have shaped the contemporary fashion industry, and the experience of the fashion consumer.

LEARNING OBJECTIVES

After studying this chapter, you should be able to understand:

- The overview of the global fashion industry, appreciating its economic, social and cultural importance;

- The characteristics and dimensions of the fashion industry in terms of organizational players and market levels;

- The structural and technological changes which have shaped the contemporary fashion industry;

- The importance of trends and business models that will continue to influence the evolution of the fashion industry in the future.

---

1. 46968 London College of Fashion BA16 catwalk show, June 2016, Nicholls and Clarke building, Shoreditch. Photography by Roger Dean.

THE CONCEPT OF FASHION

Although it is not the intention of this text to provide an extended debate on the meaning of fashion, it is necessary to give an introduction to this elusive term as a concept as well as a descriptor of a product.

The sociologist Georg Simmel (1957: 544) referred to fashion as '… a product of social demands …' and the term generally means the process that identifies certain design, products or social behaviours as '*in*' for a limited period and then replaces them regularly with new design, new products and new forms of behaviour. A sociological approach to fashion represents it as an expression of social interaction and of status seeking. This viewpoint sees brands as a way to provide consumers a feeling of shared well-being and common interest. Barthes' *The Fashion System*, originally published in French in 1967, is one of the most notable studies of the fashion industry and it suggests that people constitute an identity through clothing, and that the meaning of clothes is socially constructed. In the English translation the author states, 'the semiology of fashion is directed toward a set of collective representations' (1983: 10).

The term 'fashion' can be related to any object or phenomenon that changes in style over time and is based upon individuals' collective preferences (Barnard, 2002). In economic and business analysis, fashion can be defined as a cycle that allows mature industries, such as clothing, footwear or even food, to be dynamic and maintain profitability over time. For most purposes, the main product categories that constitute the fashion industry are: adult clothing (including outerwear), accessories (including handbags), footwear, jewelry, make-up (cosmetics). Categories that are increasingly fashion orientated include children's wear, home furnishings, and stationery while perfume is related because of the dominance of fashion brands in this category. According to Corner (2014), fashion is, at its heart, about self-adornment and the visual presentation of ourselves to the external world, reflecting how we want the world to view us and how we view the world ourselves.

> **Category** A group of products that broadly perform a similar function, satisfying similar consumer needs, from which further sub-categories might evolve.

THE DIMENSIONS OF THE FASHION INDUSTRY

Globally the fashion industry is estimated to be worth 3 trillion dollars in terms of apparel alone (Fashion United, 2017), accounting for 2 per cent of the world's gross domestic product (GDP). In its diversity the fashion industry provides a range of organizational entities, which vary according to a number of dimensions:

- Size, from large conglomerates to sole trading artisans;
- Function orientation, from production, through wholesaling to retailing;
- Market level and quality orientation, from luxury to discount;
- Product specialization, from single category specialist brands to generalist retailers.

A comprehensive economic analysis of this vast and dynamic industry is beyond the scope of this text and has been provided by other writers and sources (for example, Kunz et al., 2016; Fashion United, 2017); however, the dimensions above provide a framework for an overview of the fashion industry to help understand the strategic context in which fashion management takes place.

SIZE AND IMPACT OF FASHION ORGANIZATIONS

The size of fashion organizations can be measured in a number of ways. For example, fashion conglomerate Inditex is one of the very largest fashion companies with over 7000 outlets, a substantial production capacity and a sales turnover of over 23 billion Euros (Inditex, 2017). Quantitative statistics are easy to understand and frequently-used measures of company size. Yet, industry influence and impact can also be considered sizeable and a small design-led company like Victoria Beckham with only two owned stores, no production facilities and a relatively modest turnover may be considered significant within the industry because of its media and social impact; the eponymous celebrity brand was awarded Designer of the Year at the British Fashion Awards in 2011 and was the most talked about designer collection on Twitter during New York Fashion Week in 2012 (Kamali, 2012). In the fashion industry, this type of public affirmation is an important evaluation of success.

Fashion-related organizations can also have particular emphasis in terms of their historical and geopolitical context, and may have a specific relevance to a part of the fashion **supply chain**. For example, many large international luxury brands have their roots in Italy and France, while much of the world's cotton fibre production is centred on India, China and the US; more recently, Scandinavia has built a reputation for ethical fashion and sustainable supply chains.

FUNCTION ORIENTATION AND ORGANIZATIONAL STRUCTURES

The **fashion system** is made up of a wide and complex network of closely interconnected sub-industries, all influential to a certain degree. While our attention tends to focus on finished products, we must understand that these are the result of a long chain of stages, activities and technologies whose

> **Supply chain**
> The processes and organizations involved in manufacturing and supplying a product to a consumer, from raw materials to end use, and increasingly considered to include disposal.

> **Vertical integration**
> A supply chain in which all entities involved are connected and co-dependent, usually through business ownership, although the term is sometimes used when separate supply chain business entities work so closely that they are dependent on one another.

interaction is largely responsible for a product's success in the market.

Fashion supply chains are long and complex, and fashion retailing structures are fragmented. Some fashion organizations are only concerned with a single function, such as garment production, but many cover a diverse range of business activities. Some companies operate principally as manufacturers of fibres, yarns, fabrics and garments, while others operate as intermediary selling organizations such as wholesalers and retailers. Some fashion organizations are **vertically integrated**, owning, for example, production operations at various stages of the supply chain and often retailing facilities in addition. The complexity of such chains can be seen in the process map shown in Figure 1.1. This identifies the key stages within the production of a fashion garment such as a dress. Production and supply process maps often use the concept of industry tiers, which represent key stages in the chain.

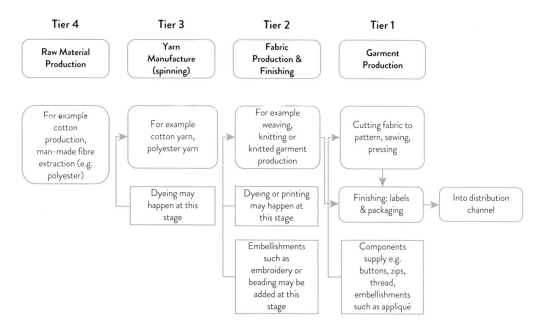

Figure 1.1 *Process map for the production of a dress*

What fundamentally and inextricably links all fashion organizations is design and style input. Whether this is shape, colour, texture, pattern or

seam detail it is the blending of these elements that helps to create a fashion product. The organizational structure and the strategic management of fashion organizations reflect one another; for an organization that manufactures, supply chain management and production management are likely to predominate, whereas for a fashion retailer, merchandise management and customer relationship management may take precedence. In both types of organizations human resource management and financial management will underpin strategic decision-making. These supporting, underpinning and absolutely crucial aspects of strategic management will be explored in Chapters 5 (Financial Management in Fashion) and 14 (People Management) within this book.

FASHION MARKET LEVELS

Historically fashion has been seen as a concern of the 'elite'. The famous trickle-down theory (originally proposed by Simmel in the 1905 book *Philosophie der Mode*) refers to a fashion system where high-fashion designers, their affluent clients and fashion magazines dictated the way everyone dressed. The late 20th century, however, witnessed changes that would transform the fashion industry forever (Agins, 1999). The old model where the couture houses set the trends and the rest of the industry followed this lead was transformed by a shift in consumer expectations, demanding more frequent fashion changes, which has resulted in an internal restructuring of the industry.

> ... fashion moves up, down and along from a variety of starting positions and in several directions, rather than a single system in which fashion only moves in one direction, 'trickle-down' from the elite to the majority. (Braham, 1997: 360)

In addition, the rise of street wear as a major fashion influence and driver of trends has not only transformed the way collections are developed and presented but also inverted the power of brands and consumers and the dynamics between these constituents. This shift will be explored further in Chapter 6 (Fashion Brand Management). The marketing strategies used by many of the mass-market or 'high street' fashion companies have become increasingly similar to those of the more exclusive and premium fashion brands. Mass produced casual clothes have claimed the title of 'designer' items or even 'high fashion', paving the way for innovative strategies such as collaborations, capsule collections and celebrity brands. This has led to the concept of fashion democracy, whereby 'ordinary people' are able to consume and influence high fashion. Figure 1.2 visualizes the different levels that can be seen in today's global fashion market.

Figure 1.2 *The levels of the fashion market*

Haute Couture luxury brands

The highest level in the fashion market is Haute Couture. These brands are highly priced, luxurious and exclusive, targeting a small consumer group (the elite and celebrities) who lead a lifestyle of high profile events and social engagements, including the red carpet of film premiers and media awards, which are of particular interest to the creative community. Made-to-measure items with a high level of craftsmanship, these pieces are works of art and keep the dream of the fashion industry alive, building high levels of awareness for the limited number of brands that operate at this level.

Ready-to-wear designer brands

Haute Couture is followed by the level traditionally referred to as 'Ready-to-wear' (RTW). A mixture of creativity and industrialization characterizes this market sector, made possible by the technological advances in the textile and clothing pipeline. Most Haute Couture houses also own an RTW line (Chanel and Dior, for example), which produces higher profits due to greater availability on global markets and a higher volume of sales. Not all RTW designers operate at the Haute Couture level and in this case, they might be described as accessible luxury brands. RTW collections are usually presented twice a year during Fashion Weeks all over the world. These take place on a city-by-city basis; historically the most relevant ones have been Paris, Milan, New York and London. During recent years we have seen the decentralization of such events, with fashion shows being held in different and unexpected locations as well as the introduction of cruise and pre-fall collections to offer more consumer choice and more opportunities for brands to sell through the year.

> **Fashion Week** A short period of time in a specific location where new fashion collections are presented, often via a catwalk show, traditionally to the media and business-to-business buyers, but in some instances to the consumer market.

Diffusion designer brands

Diffusion lines are usually targeted at a younger audience and constitute more accessible ranges from well-established luxury fashion brands. They are characterized by higher volume in terms of production and wider distribution. RED Valentino and DKNY for Donna Karen exemplify this level. A successful diffusion line must adhere to the crucial principle of maintaining a strong and consistent brand identity. The benefits of diffusion lines extend beyond profitability as they increase brand awareness and synergies for the main line. A diffusion line can be seen as a cost-effective strategy to grow a company.

Although diffusion lines can be a successful strategy in terms of brand development, there is a danger that this might lead to the weakening of the parent brand; if not properly managed, these lines can cannibalize the parent brand as well as dilute its value because of lower quality products and wider market coverage. These aspects of strategic brand marketing will be explored further in Chapters 3 (Fashion Marketing) and 6 (Fashion Brand Management).

Bridge brands and premium brands

After diffusion brands and accessible luxury brands, we can identify bridge and premium brands as those connecting the high-end market with the mass market. These brands intend to give consumers augmented value for money by delivering a higher level of quality and design than in the mainstream mass market. Brands such as Max Mara, Coach, Tory Burch, Acne and The Kooples would be examples of this level.

Mass market and value brands

Mass market is the 'lower' level of the fashion market and includes brands that are often associated with the fast fashion movement. Big chains such as H&M and those within the Inditex Group (Zara's parent company) offer high fashion products at very reasonable prices. Making use of economies of scale and effective consumer targeting, Zara is a well-known example of a highly successful mass market fashion brand. Fast product design development, efficient and accurate product forecasting, combined with a flexible supply chain and logistics, are notable aspects of this leading international fashion retailer's success. 'Value brands' is an expression used for those operating at a very low price or discount level; examples would be Primark, Target or TK Maxx, although H&M is sometimes referred to as a value brand.

In the fashion market the relationship between price and demand is often unclear from an economic viewpoint because other product attributes such as brand, or style, can add value and therefore raise the price. This leads to the concept of the value chain, which helps us to understand that value can be added to fashion products at many different stages between raw materials and finished goods at retail. For example, colour and pattern can be added at the fibre and fabric production stage; while style and fit can be added at garment production stage. Quality value can be added at any point of production, along with brand value, which can be added at any stage but is particularly associated with marketing and retailing activities. The value chain is essentially the set of activities performed to design, produce, market, deliver and support products; geared towards the generation of value for the consumer as defined by the consumer. This concept will be explored in more depth in Chapter 2 (Strategic Planning for Fashion Organizations).

> **Value chain** The idea that value (from a buyer's perspective) can be added at any point in the transformation of raw materials to end product delivery and use, which that buyer is willing to pay a premium price for.

As mentioned before, the fashion marketplace is characterized by ever growing complexity and dynamic change. Fashion trends are more volatile than ever, the consumer is better informed and more confident and no longer pays attention to narrow levels of the market. Instead, consumers mix and match designer pieces with mass-market and premium ones. This move towards eclectic consumption was accelerated by the phenomenon of online retailing, enabling a virtually unlimited choice of products available anytime and anywhere; these converging changes are making it harder for brands to have a sufficient competitive advantage for guaranteed year-on-year growth.

SPECIALIZATION, GENERALIZATION AND DIVERSIFICATION

This refers to the extent to which a fashion organization operates as a specialist or a more diverse company. Some fashion companies have a very precise mission, concentrating on a particular type of product, and focusing their efforts in one section of the supply chain. An independent men's wear shop, for example, may operate in one location, and purely operate as a retailer. In contrast, H&M is a company that designs, sources and retails women's wear, men's wear, children's wear, accessories and homewear globally. Many large fashion companies operate as conglomerates. The Kering Group, for example, encompasses 19 luxury fashion and lifestyle brands, some of which own manufacturing operations (see Case Study 2 in Chapter 2). Given the wide scope of the term 'fashion', the industry covers every possible degree of specialization, and this is what gives the industry endless scope in terms of business model.

CHARACTERISTICS OF THE FASHION INDUSTRY

The fashion industry and the organizations within it can be described up to a certain point of understanding using familiar economic and business descriptors; however, in order to fully grasp how the industry works, an appreciation of those characteristics that make it unique is also needed.

Concentration of the market

Although there are some very strong players in the fashion market, both internationally and nationally, the industry overall can be seen as fragmented with many companies each having a small market share. In the UK fashion retail market, for example, the largest six companies have a combined market share of only 29% (Mintel, 2016a), contrasting this to the UK grocery market where the top six retailers dominate two-thirds of the sector value (Mintel, 2016b). In fashion supply markets, the situation is broadly similar, with some large manufacturing firms spanning the globe, but also a plethora of smaller companies at various points in the supply chain. Where particular firms have specific manufacturing capability, pockets of concentration can arise in supply chains, which can influence the competitive dynamic of a part of the industry. The fragmentation of the supply market in mass fashion manufacturing, however, is one of the most problematic features of the industry in terms of sustainable supply chain transparency. This will be explored further in Chapters 9 (Fashion Supply Chain Management) and 12 (Managing Fashion Responsibly). The structure of the fashion industry makes it highly competitive, sometimes referred to as **hyper-competitive**, with large and global players that lead and dominate and compete with each other yet are surrounded by a vast and ever-changing set of alternative brands that vie for the attention of the notoriously promiscuous fashion consumer.

Labour intensity

It is very difficult to establish accurately how many people work in the fashion industry globally, as any total employment figure would include people working in designing, manufacturing and retailing, all of which are labour intensive. In 2014, Fashion United estimated that almost 58 million people worked in the global textile and clothing manufacturing sector alone, and the dependence on human capital has had a significant influence on the global development of the industry. Volume production has moved from one country to another as large fashion intermediaries have searched out the lowest labour cost. Garment production is generally the most labour intensive part of the fashion supply chain; fibre, yarn and fabric manufacturing requires sophisticated and expensive machinery to produce in volume, but it is difficult to standardize the production of fashion garments and so the industry still relies on individual sewing machines for individual garments operated by individual workers. Craft textiles also can be labour intensive, produced by a web of small makers and suppliers that are often geographically clustered and based on indigenous materials and skills.

The retail industry also generally relies on people rather than high capital intensity, although the operation of stores in high footfall locations in international city centres requires considerable capital investment. Around half a million people work in the UK fashion retail sector (Fashion United, 2017). As online retailing grows in popularity more people are employed in distribution centres, but these can be highly automated, resulting in a lower labour cost structure overall.

Creativity and enterprise

Many elements of the fashion industry are part of what is frequently referred to as the 'creative industries'. In the UK, for example, the creative industries, which include not only fashion design but related aspects such as advertising, marketing and craft, were reported to be worth £76.9 billion per annum (Gov.uk, 2015). Design is important to all fashion brands and many fashion companies are 'design-led'. This means design and creativity is at the heart of what the company does and leads the company in its operations. One of the principal differences between fashion companies and other organizations is the rate of change in the offer. Product ranges are constantly evolving to offer something new to consumers. Newness and change and their importance to the fashion consumer mean that creativity, innovation and enterprise have a large part to play in the industry. The fragmented structure of the industry allows room for small enterprises to establish and flourish, although not without challenge. Larger enterprises provide the resources for creativity to flow and the 'intrapreneur' (the idea of an entrepreneur working inside a large organization) to work flexibly and experimentally.

Social and cultural influence

Many aspects of the fashion industry are highly visible. **Celebrity culture** has always had an influence on fashion, with the styles of the rich and famous being interpreted and adopted by the masses. Digital communication has enabled this influence to happen more frequently and faster than ever before. The use of social media is also making changes to the way fashion companies communicate with their customers, bringing the relationship closer, and making it more personal, three-way (company, customer and community), and dynamic. Fashion ideas are exchanged in volume and more quickly, regarding not just celebrity style, but all aspects of style and trend, making the industry fluid and responsive.

The fashion industry, with its emphasis on personal adornment, is influenced by social subcultures, which can have a strong influence on the emergence of fashion trends. This is one of the aspects of the fashion industry that makes it so fascinating; it is also an area that is well documented and beyond the scope of this text (for further reading, see Welters and Lillethun, 2011, and Kaiser, 2011). The term 'fashion zeitgeist' is sometimes used to summarize the understanding that an idea, or the combination of ideas, can emerge, become adopted and influential and thus create 'fashions' (Vinken, 2005). As such, this is a useful expression for explaining influences that are more difficult to rationalize but may nevertheless be eventually monetarized (Mini Case Study 1.1). In the age of digital marketing communications, style influence is becoming increasingly diverse, complex and

fast moving, as we shall see in Chapter 7 (Fashion Marketing Communications).

 ## MINI CASE STUDY 1.1 - Rihanna and fashion

Rihanna (often called RiRi) is a globally revered music artist, making her album debut in 2005. Her sense of style and interest in fashion is almost as well known as her chart success. Rihanna has collaborated with fashion brands operating at different market levels. She also is a powerful endorser of fashion brands, both formally in advertising campaigns, and informally as a confident woman who enjoys pushing her own style boundaries.

In 2008, when she was only 20, Rihanna became the face of Gucci's UNICEF limited edition collection and, like many other trend-aware people, has recently demonstrated her continued interest in wearing the brand. Another early foray into fashion was a collaboration with Armani Jeans after she appeared in a promotional campaign for Armani Jeans and Emporio Armani underwear in 2011. She followed this with a collaborative collection with UK mass-market young fashion retailer River Island in 2013, which not only improved the brand's sales performance, but also helped to raise its profile internationally.

In 2014 Rihanna wore a two-piece Stella McCartney outfit at one of the most prestigious fashion events of the calendar, the Met Gala in New York, and she continues to support the designer by wearing her brand on the red carpet. She has also

supported other young designers including Craig Green. In 2014 she became creative director of Puma, which has resulted in several sell-out shoe collections and the development of a ready-to-wear collection for the brand.

A sunglasses range for Dior, a beauty range for luxury conglomerate LMVH under the name Fenty Beauty by Rihanna (whose full name is Robyn Rihanna Fenty), a denim footwear range for Manolo Blahnik, a collection for Stance socks, and six perfumes of her own, paved the way to her Fenty x Puma collection being shown at Paris Fashion Week.

Now a philanthropist, as well as an A-list superstar and fashion guru, Rihanna hosted her 3rd Annual Diamond Ball in New York City in September 2017 in aid of the Clara Lionel Foundation, named after her grandparents and founded to benefit impoverished communities across the globe with healthcare and education programmes. The event was attended by Cardi B, Lil Kim, JAY-Z, Beyoncé, and other hip-hop stars. As a celebrity who is always in touch with the fashion zeitgeist, Rihanna seamlessly moves across a variety of fashion industry networks.

Sources: Various, including Ruddick (2013), Clara Lionel Foundation (2017), and Pike (2017).

FASHION INDUSTRY TRENDS

The preceding sections have given an insight into some of the characteristics of the fashion industry to highlight how it differs from other industries. Understanding these characteristics informs the application of strategic management theory to this specific context. The shaping of the fashion industry has also been affected by technological and other more general business trends, and these are explored in the following sections.

Evolving business models

At one time the route from fashion manufacturer to consumer was a relatively straightforward one. Manufacturers would sell in large quantities to wholesalers, or directly to large retailers. Wholesalers would sell to retailers, and retailers would sell to consumers through their shops or catalogues. However, digital communications and e-commerce have changed and continue to shape the business structural landscape. For example, ASOS has grown into one of the most successful fashion retailers, globally, but operates entirely from an online platform. Manufacturing brands can now easily reach consumers directly, which makes them less reliant on their network of retail customers. Wholesalers and retailers use e-commerce sites such as Amazon to sell directly to consumers, and with the facility of a transactional website, the independent retailer can become a direct global operator. Consumers themselves are also becoming proficient retailers; the success of eBay has spawned alternative consumer to consumer platforms such as Depop, and now vast online entities such as We-Chat enable an almost boundary less and fluid consumption network where everyone can talk, share, buy and sell.

> **Omni-channel** The idea that a consumer's interaction with a brand can start from a number of alternative brand touch-points and involve multiple interactions via different retail channels and media platforms during the journey to purchase.

Channel structural change

As a consequence of more complex and flexible consumer purchasing behaviour, the traditional channel structures are becoming obsolete, giving rise to a hybrid structure whereby consumers can connect with producers directly as well as indirectly through third party intermediaries.

- **Direct:**
  Producer to consumer

- **Indirect:**
  Producer to intermediaries to consumer

- **Hybrid:**
  Producer to consumer + producer to intermediaries to consumer

The roles in both direct and indirect channels were assumed to be static, mutually exclusive and corresponding to a specific set of functions. In a hybrid structure, channels become more flexible and consumers choose how, when and whom to interact with.

The main driver facilitating this change is technology and its patterns of use by both fashion organizations and consumers. The influence of technology in fashion consumer behaviour and the way fashion brands interact with those they sell to cannot be overstated. The challenge for fashion companies is to maintain a strategic approach to management while adapting to and embracing the opportunities that

technological innovation affords. Brands are conscious that in order to survive it is crucial to actively and strategically adapt to the changing environment and turn this to their advantage.

Changes in the consumer journey

Digital media allow users to have more control, to access more information more often and more accurately than with conventional media (Jackson and Shaw, 2009). The 'omni-channel age' is a new business environment enabling fashion brands to provide seamless experiences simultaneously across multiple touch-points (physical stores, online, mobile, social media), resulting in holistic and consistent consumer–brand interactions (see Figure 1.3).

Single Channel	Multi-Channel	Cross-Channel	Omni-Channel
Customers experience a single type of touch-point	Customers see multiple touch-points acting independently	Customers see multiple touch-points as part of the same brand	Customers experience a brand, not a channel within a brand
Retailers have a single type of touch-point	Retailers' channel knowledge and operations exist in technical and functional silos	Retailers have a single view of the customer but operate in functional silos	Retailers leverage their single view of the customer in coordinated and strategic ways

Figure 1.3 *Evolution from single, multi-, cross- to omni-channel*

According to Rigby (2011: 67), who is credited with introducing the term, omni-channel retailing is 'an integrated sales experience that melds the advantages of physical stores with the information-rich experience of online shopping'. The author acknowledges that the integration of the advantages of the physical experience with digital convenience was the way to better meet the expectations of consumers as well as create higher profit margins. The integration of the physical with the digital is therefore the core focus of this approach, but the aim is to provide the consumer with a seamless experience where multiple touch-points are used interchangeably and simultaneously. Rather than taking a linear journey from website to store to home, consumers are free to make cross-media journeys involving social media (where posts are seen, liked and shared), mobile apps (for detailed perusal), physical stores (for real-life sensory appreciation and advice), online owned website space (for purchase and delivery tracking), and then back to social media or apps (for posting and reviewing). This reinforces the concept of the consumer–brand experience, which will be explored in detail in Chapter 6 (Fashion Brand Management).

Fashion consumer power

The blurring of the physical and digital world has been made possible by the rapid spread of mobile devices and internet connectivity, eliminating the boundaries between time and space for consumers to experience a holistic overview of fashion brands. This challenges the fashion company to integrate every aspect of its business and information provided about it. Price transparency as well as a consistent and active interaction between consumers and brands has been the main effect so far, driven by consumer behaviour based on the ability to easily and quickly compare prices, product features, reviews and order facilities. In-depth analysis of the consumer journey, which considers how they start, where they look for information, where they finish and complete transactions and where they go in between, are all new areas of research that can help to build an understanding of the omni-channel shopper. This subject will be developed further in Chapter 10 (Fashion Retail Management).

Fashion consumers and their relationships with brands

Developing a strong connection with the consumer may be the only solution to address the more and more crowded landscape of global fashion markets. Most fashion consumers are well-informed about brands and products and have sophisticated and complex needs and wants. The consumer's relationship with brands has also changed: strongly connected to brands of choice, engaging in conversations and acting as spokespeople for them. Consumers are now interested in more than a product

and its utility or quality; it is also about the story behind it (Olenski, 2012). Whether this story is about integrity of design, innovation, exclusivity, brand heritage, sustainability or trend setting, consumer interest is triggered by the story. This engagement is defined by a combination of rational and emotional bonds and so the need for strong and effective brand management is crucial in fashion marketing. The discipline of creating and sustaining a brand requires the whole company to be engaged with this purpose, following integrated marketing programmes geared towards that aim.

Personalization of the consumer experience

Over time, consumers are becoming more demanding and wanting greater levels of personalization in their consumption experience (Prahalad and Ramaswamy, 2000), providing the opportunity for brands to provide customers with more effective responsiveness. This can be translated into the growing importance of the consumption experience, with consumers increasingly seeking not only to purchase products and meanings, but also to participate in unique, memorable consumption experiences (Gouillart and Ramaswamy, 2010). This idea was introduced by Pine and Gilmore (1999), who predicted the growth of an 'experience-based economy', where consumers would seek full immersion in unique contexts and experiences which confirm the meanings, cultures, symbols and identities behind their chosen brands. The basis of the experience is brands promising not only the product and value set announced by marketing communications, but also places, spaces, and contexts within which the 'potential world' of the brand can be experienced. In this environment, the consumer can act out a part in creating stories and experiences, exploring the brand's deepest values and meanings. As we will see, this is especially relevant in the context of fashion consumption. A company can differentiate itself by creating a unique, customized and personalized customer experience and by doing so improve its ability to retain customers, target specific customer segments and enhance profitability. The concept of differentiation in the fashion industry is explored in the next chapter and is one of the most important aspects of strategy formation for fashion companies.

> **Differentiation** The ability of a company or brand to be perceived as distinctive by its customer, by offering a combination of functional and/or emotional attributes that are considered different, better or additional to those of competitors.

Consumer-centricity and the co-creation of value

The traditional perspective on customer engagement views value creation and innovation as a firm-centric activity, where information flows from the customer to the firm (Prahalad and Ramaswamy, 2004). This has changed to a customer-centric perspective, where the consumer actively participates in the value creation process. Customer-centricity is intrinsically connected to Customer Relationship Management (CRM), which is a comprehensive strategy that includes acquiring, retaining, and partnering with selected customers to create superior value for the company and the customer. It involves the integration of areas of a company such as marketing, sales, customer service and the supply chain to achieve greater efficiencies and effectiveness in delivering customer value. The strategic importance of CRM is analyzed in depth in Chapter 11 (Managing Fashion Customers).

Co-creation is a concept that is central to the consumer-centric perspective and can be described as a 'collaborative activity in which customers actively contribute to the creation of brand identity and image as well as ideas, information, product, service and experience offered under a particular brand' (Bogoviyeva, 2011: 371). The personal nature of fashion preferences means that this is a highly relevant concept, and some examples of its application can be seen in Chapters 6 (Fashion Brand Management) and 8 (Fashion Merchandise Management).

Globalization

The fashion industry is truly global. Historically, luxury fashion and youth brands have been adept at skimming markets in new geographical locations, and 'western' fashion has recently experienced opportunities for profitable sales growth in regions of vast population explosion and high economic growth as they industrialize and urbanize. Simultaneously, improvements in logistics have enabled fashion companies to view the world as their sourcing base, rather than use suppliers closer to home as they once did. The Fashion Weeks of Paris, Milan, New York and London continue to dominate the publicity machine for fashion; yet, in a digital age, fashion promotion is moving closer to the consumer, with the see-now-buy-now approach (where new collections appear in retail outlets simultaneously with being shown on the catwalk) beginning to change the established industry cycles. The Internet provides the means by which consumers can peruse fashion from all corners of the earth, and there is a growing global interest in 'non-western' fashion as populations and fashion markets become more diverse. Globalization within the fashion industry alters the forces of competition, and fashion companies are faced with increased complexity when strategically managing this opportunity. In Chapter 4 we concentrate on international development as an important growth strategy for fashion companies.

Sustainability

The fashion industry has been condemned many times for what is sometimes referred to as its dark side. Human atrocities concerning unsafe and unfair factories, environmental damage and waste, and consumer psychological damage are all issues that are real and unfortunate features of fashion production and consumption. In order for retailers to compete on price in the selling of high-volume low-cost fashion, production has to take place in countries where labour costs are at their lowest. Poor regulation and lack of law enforcement mean the survival of bad practice, in terms of treatment of workforces, and in terms of water, earth, and air pollution. The fashion manufacturing industry is the second most polluting industry on earth, second only to oil, and the contributions of discarded fashion to landfills across the world are truly shocking. In addition, aspects of communicating fashion can be psychologically damaging to consumers, such as the emphasis on unhealthily thin models and the early sexualization and gender stereotyping of children.

The conscious consumer

Increased awareness of sustainability issues has led to what is known as 'conscious consumption', a movement of people who seek out ways to make positive decisions about what they buy and are engaged in finding solutions to the negative impact of consumerism. There is evidence that the will to slow down fashion consumption is being translated into brand strategy. The premium UK-based fashion brand Jigsaw, for example, used the strapline 'for life not landfill' in their 2015 advertising campaign.

We also see governments getting more involved in regulating environmental hazards that originate from clothing production. Sustainability is now an integral part of the industry and can form a key component in the strategy or a pillar of the business model, and it has been developed by different sections of the fashion industry (see, for example, the Case Studies on Marks and Spencer in Chapter 12, Etiko in Chapter 5, H&M in Chapter 9, TOMS in Chapter 14, and Kering in Chapter 2). An interesting consequence of this trend has been the development of business models that question and rethink the concept of ownership. For example, companies such as Rent the Runway (Mini Case Study 6.4), and Vigga (see Case Study 15, in Chapter 15), give consumers the option to rent pieces instead of buying them. Chapter 12 (Managing Fashion Responsibly) will explore sustainability in the fashion industry in more detail.

STRATEGIC THINKING AND PLANNING

The fashion industry provides a unique context for strategic thinking and planning, and so this text makes an attempt to find a path through this complexity to foster an understanding of why it may be necessary to have a strategic plan at all, and how the leaders of a fashion organization, whatever its size or shape, might go about the task of forming one and then implementing it. The fashion landscape demands constant updating, improvement and innovation to remain relevant to the personal digital ecosystems of fashion consumers. By embracing complexity, fashion brands can turn the dynamics of the market into competitive advantage, a concept we will return to in Chapter 2 (Strategic Planning for Fashion Organizations). This may require a substantial change to their business models and a readiness to adapt to change, and to ensure the development of key capabilities in terms of structures, processes and technologies to maintain competitiveness and to support market growth.

We have adapted the idea of a digital eco-system (Kurt Salmon, 2014) to demonstrate how fashion management can adopt a strategic approach in the digital age (see Figure 1.4). Although it is hard to model visually in two dimensions, an ecosystem is based on the connectivity between elements. It is increasingly apparent that for better or worse, the fashion industry is driven by marketing activity, using data analysis to inform and evaluate all processes and initiatives, such as range planning and social media communication. Operational decisions such as the blending of routes to customers, and which supply sources to use, are informed by the detailed understanding of consumer preferences and behaviours, which are in turn informed by quantitative and qualitative data analysis. Supporting operations concerning resource management, whether human, finance, buildings,

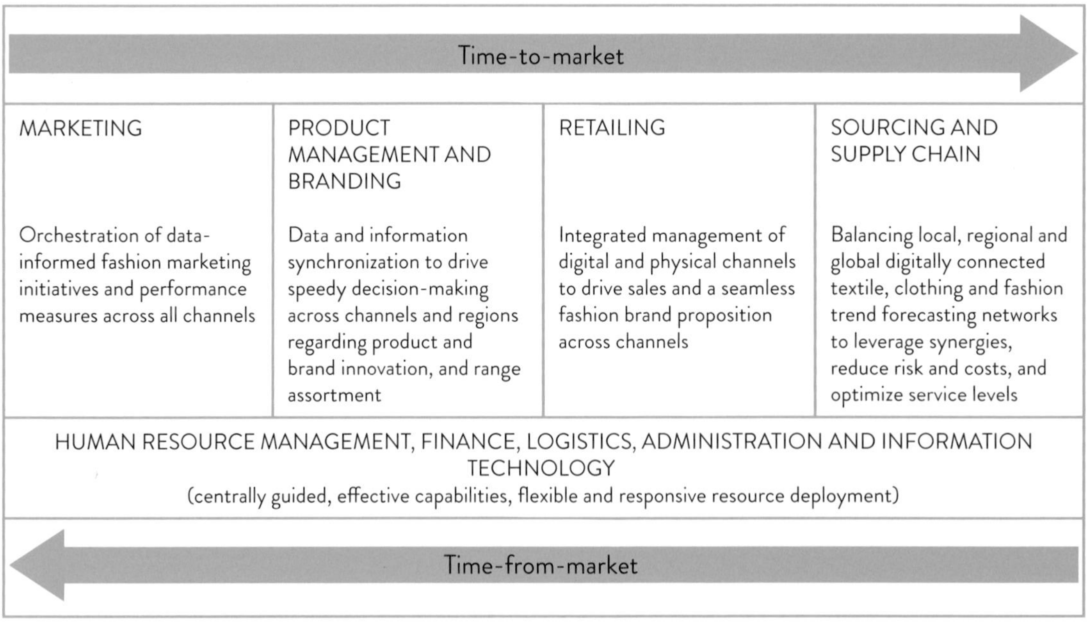

Time-to-market →			
MARKETING	PRODUCT MANAGEMENT AND BRANDING	RETAILING	SOURCING AND SUPPLY CHAIN
Orchestration of data-informed fashion marketing initiatives and performance measures across all channels	Data and information synchronization to drive speedy decision-making across channels and regions regarding product and brand innovation, and range assortment	Integrated management of digital and physical channels to drive sales and a seamless fashion brand proposition across channels	Balancing local, regional and global digitally connected textile, clothing and fashion trend forecasting networks to leverage synergies, reduce risk and costs, and optimize service levels
HUMAN RESOURCE MANAGEMENT, FINANCE, LOGISTICS, ADMINISTRATION AND INFORMATION TECHNOLOGY (centrally guided, effective capabilities, flexible and responsive resource deployment)			
← Time-from-market			

Figure 1.4 *Strategic fashion management within the digital eco-system*

transport, or information technology resources, contribute to the ecosystem and become responsive to its needs. The ecosystem embraces a network of entities that can be internal or external to the fashion organization, but connectivity, communication and fast data flow are the operational basis of it. Rather than planning schedules and rigid organizational structures dominating management approaches, the digital ecosystem is informed, fluid and flexible, which, for an industry like fashion, is ideal.

CASE STUDY 1 - Di$count Universe: A new type of luxury defined by brand culture

Di$count Universe (www.discountuniverse.com) is a small luxury fashion label founded in Melbourne, Australia, by Cami James and Nadia Napreychikov. It is an interesting case of a growing brand that differentiates on the basis of a strong brand culture and a rejection of the norms of the luxury fashion industry.

The choice of the brand name 'Di$count Universe' is the first striking example of the founders' beliefs about authenticity, given that the name is hardly consistent with traditional luxury category codes. Rejecting the idea that clothes are only made for one season, the brand is staunchly anti-seasonal: 'Clothes aren't just made seasonally to go out of fashion the next season. If something has resonance with people over and over again we will keep releasing it' (Nadia Napreychikov). Describing their look, Cami James states, 'It's obviously excessive in style ... it's anti-industry, that's part of the DNA of the brand. There's a lot of messages and certain innuendo and humour in the brand.'

Rather than striving to produce a catwalk show or opening a static retail outlet, Cami and Nadia were early adopters of the blog as a legitimate place to display their garments. This quickly generated an online community and a large and engaged fan base. The brand's big break came when Miley Cyrus was photographed in one of their tops. At the time, Cyrus was transitioning from her Hannah Montana character to a more mature performer, and Nadia and Cami were initially reluctant to use the endorsement as Cyrus didn't fit their perceived identity. Cyrus's photograph featuring Di$count Universe was printed on her tour T-shirts and brought the awareness of the nascent brand to the global stage. Other high-profile brand adopters such as Katy Perry, Lady Gaga and most recently Kylie Jenner have driven sales and built awareness of the brand.

The brand culture approach is a direct assault on the perceived elitism of the luxury fashion industry, in which just a few privileged insiders get to attend shows and launches. In contrast, Di$count Universe shows give priority to the brand's online fan base and are set up like rock shows or giant parties where cheering and hedonistic expressions are encouraged, and content is available to any fan who wishes to blog, post, or tweet about the collection. 'It's about having that relationship with the people who got us to where we are, more so than someone who might have come up through [a magazine] nurturing them' (Cami James, Founder).

Source: Parts of this case are based on Beverland, M., *Brand Management*, SAGE, London, UK, Copyright © 2018.

Case Challenge

How would you classify Di$count Universe in terms of the levels of the industry (see Figure 1.2)? How does this brand illustrate change and trends within the fashion industry?

 ## ONLINE RESOURCES

A longer version of this case study, with additional challenges, can be found on our companion website: https://www.macmillanihe.com/companion/Varley_Fashion_Management.

SUMMARY AND CONCLUDING THOUGHTS

This chapter has provided an overview of the fashion industry in an attempt to contextualize the sphere in which strategic decisions are made. Building an appreciation of what characterizes fashion businesses and the environment in which they operate helps us to understand what is relevant to fashion consumers and the organizations that connect with them. The influence of technology has caused a great impact on consumers' behaviour with greater demands for experiences, interaction and personalization. It could be argued that the current situation presents a tipping point for many companies in the fashion industry, with a significant share of retailers and brands in need of significant realignment of their business models as a prerequisite to sustain growth. Understanding the full capabilities of new technologies as well as their applications is essential to attract, engage and satisfy consumers.

The rapidly changing business landscape makes long-term strategic planning difficult; over time nevertheless, a set of theoretical concepts, frameworks and tools have become established, which help fashion managers in their strategic thinking and decision-making. The next three chapters provide a tailored discussion of a selection of these models, before we move on to subsequent chapters that explore in more detail the implementation of strategy in specific organizational contexts.

 ## CHALLENGES AND CONVERSATIONS

1. What is your own interpretation of the word 'fashion'? How do you see the fashion world changing and what do you think will be the most challenging aspects of managing a fashion brand in the future?

2. Consider the fashion brands that you like. How would you describe them in terms of their market level? Consider the challenges and opportunities of maintaining a brand over different market levels.

3. A strategic approach to fashion management requires the acknowledgement of, understanding of, and response to change. What characteristics of the fashion industry make the management of change complex?

4. Debate the idea of the consumer omni-channel journey. Is it as complex as Figure 1.4 shows? What is your own experience? Has your journey changed in the last 5 years; if so how and why?

 ## REFERENCES AND FURTHER READING

Abnett, K. (2015) *Will mass customization work for fashion.* Available at: https://www.businessoffashion.com/articles/intelligence/mass-customisation-fashion-nike-converse-burberry [accessed 12/01/2016].

Agins, T. (1999) *The End of Fashion: How Marketing Changed the Clothing Business Forever.* New York: Harper Collins.

Barnard, M. (2002) *Fashion as Communication,* 2nd edn. Abingdon: Routledge.

Barthes, R. (1983) *The Fashion System (English translation).* Now available through Berkeley, CA: University of California Press (2010 paperback edition).

Bazilian, E. (2014) *Derek Lam Believes in Fashion for the Masses.* Available at: http://www.adweek.com/brand-marketing/derek-lam-believes-fashion-masses-157455/ [accessed 12/01/2016].

Bogoviyeva, E. (2011) *Co-branding: Brand development: The effects of customer co-creation and self-construal on self-brand connection.* AMA Summer Educators' Conference Proceedings. Chicago, IL: American Marketing Association (AMA), p. 371.

Braham, P. (1997) 'Fashion: Unpacking a cultural production', in Du Gay, P. (ed.) *Production of Culture/Cultures of Production.* London: SAGE.

British Fashion Council (2013) *Facts & Figures SS14.* Available at: http://www.britishfashioncouncil.co.uk/pressreleases/Facts--Figures-SS14 [accessed 06/07/2016].

Clara Lionel Foundation (2017). Available at: http://claralionelfoundation.org.

Corner, F. (2014) *Why Fashion Matters.* London: Thames & Hudson.

Fashion United (2017) *UK fashion industry statistics.* Available at: https://fashionunited.uk/uk-fashion-industry-statistics [accessed 10/12/2017].

Global Poverty Project (2013) *Time for the High Street to Come Clean, say UK Consumers.* Available at: http://www.globalpovertyproject.com/wp-content/uploads/2013/12/PRESS-RELEASE-STF-APPROVED.pdf [accessed 10/12/2017].

Gouillart, F. and Ramaswamy, V. (2010) *The Co-Creation Effect.* Blog. Available at: http://francisgouillart.com/ [accessed 04/07/2018].

Gov.uk (2015) *Creative Industries worth £8.8 million an hour to UK economy.* Available at: https://www.gov.uk/government/news/creative-industries-worth-88-million-an-hour-to-uk-economy [accessed 05/07/2016].

Inditex (2014) *Annual Report.* Available at: https://www.inditex.com/documents/10279/246651/AnnualReport_2014.pdf/60eef29d-7a6c-43f5-b811-e63a9f7786fe [accessed 20/06/2016].

Inditex (2017) *Group Consolidated Annual Accounts at 31 January 2017.* Available at: https://www.inditex.com/documents/10279/342486/Inditex+Group+Consolidated+Annual+Accounts+2016.pdf/f09cfd0d-9bd3-44d3-ab34-eb7e992228b3 [accessed 10/01/2018].

Jackson, T. and Shaw, D. (2009) *Mastering Fashion Marketing.* Basingstoke: Palgrave Macmillan.

Kaiser, S. B. (2011) *Fashion and Cultural Studies.* London: Berg.

Kamali, S. (2012) *Victoria Beckham Is Top On Twitter.* Available at: http://www.vogue.co.uk/article/victoria-beckham-most-talked-about-designer-on-twitter-new-york-fashion-week [accessed 12/12/2016].

Karimzadeh, M. (2014) *Marc by Marc Jacobs Gets Social with Fall Campaign.* Available at: http://wwd.com/business-news/media/real-time-7775379/ [accessed 12/12/2016].

Kunz, G. I., Karpova, E. and Garner, M. B. (2016) *Going Global: The Textile and Apparel Industry*, 3rd edn. New York: Fairchild Books.

Kurt Salmon (2014) Retail 2014. Available at: https://www.retail-week.com/topics/technology/multichannel/report-retail-2014-industry-leaders-business-priorities/5056911.article [accessed 05/07/2016].

Mintel (2016a) UK Fashion Retailing Report. Available at: https://store.mintel.com/clothing-retailing-uk-october-2016

Mintel (2016b) UK Grocery Retailing Report. Available at: https://store.mintel.com/grocery-retailing-in-uk-2016-market-sizes-59260.

Olenski, S. (2012) *Dear Brands, Tell Us A Story – Love Consumers.* Available at: https://www.forbes.com/sites/marketshare/2012/10/30/dear-brands-tell-us-a-story-love-consumers/#1ec67682770a [accessed 05/07/2016].

Pike, N. (2017) *Rihanna's Fashion Forays.* Available at: http://www.vogue.co.uk/gallery/rihanna-fashion-collaborations-puma-dior [accessed 10/09/2017].

Pine II, B. J. and Gilmore, J. H. (1999) *The Experience Economy: Work is Theater and Every Business a Stage: Goods are No Longer Enough.* Cambridge, MA: Harvard Business School Press.

Prahalad, C. K. and Ramaswamy, V. (2000) 'Co-opting customer competence'. *Harvard Business Review*, 78(1), pp. 79–90.

Prahalad, C. K. and Ramaswamy, V. (2004) 'Co-creating unique value with customers'. *Strategy & Leadership*, 32(3), pp. 4–9.

Rigby, D. K. (2011) 'The Future of Shopping', *Harvard Business Review*, December.

Ruddick, G. (2013) 'River Island plots international expansion after Rihanna tie-up'. *The Telegraph.* Available at: http://www.telegraph.co.uk/finance/newsbysector/retailandconsumer/10319048/River-Island-plots-international-expansion-after-Rihanna-tie-up.html [accessed 10/09/2017].

Simmel, G. (1905) *Philosophie der Mode.* Berlin: Pan-Verlag.

Simmel, G. (1957) 'Fashion'. *The American Journal of Sociology*, 62(6), pp. 541–558.

Tsjeng, Z. (2014) *Check out Marc by Marc Jacobs' Instagram-cast campaign.* Available at: http://www.dazeddigital.com/fashion/article/20587/1/check-out-marc-by-marc-jacobs-instagram-cast-campaign [accessed 12/12/2016].

Vinken, B. (2005) *Fashion Zeitgeist: Trends and Cycles in the Fashion System.* Oxford: Berg.

Welters, L. and Lillethun, A. (eds) (2011) *The Fashion Reader.* Oxford: Berg.

STRATEGIC PLANNING FOR FASHION ORGANIZATIONS

2

Liz Gee and Ana Roncha

⊛ INTRODUCTION

Given the complexity and challenges of the industry itself, all fashion organizations need a strategic plan in order to ensure their success. This chapter aims to give you an overview of strategic planning tools and techniques and is structured by thinking about each of the 3Cs of strategic analysis in turn. It will take you from consideration of the external environment (Context), through analysis of the organization itself (Capability), to look at the Choices to be made. Fashion organizations with a clear strategy are usually the winners as the process of formulating this strategy helps them to identify their strengths and weaknesses so they can exploit advantages and avoid any threats emanating from competitive or industry changes.

Context	Capability	Choice

Figure 2.1 *The 3Cs approach to strategic analysis*

👕 LEARNING OBJECTIVES

After studying this chapter, you should be able to understand:

- The evolution and meaning of strategy and its role within organizations;

- The need for and implications of an environmental analysis at both a macro- and a micro-level;

- What competitive advantage is and how it is achieved by fashion organizations;

- The competitive forces that impact fashion organizations and that leverage competitive advantage; and

- Drivers of innovation and new market creation at different levels within the fashion industry.

WHAT IS STRATEGY?

Many academics have tried to define strategy and these debates can fill entire textbooks in their own right. Michael Porter, who is considered to be the grandfather of strategic planning, defined it as follows:

> Competitive strategy is about being different. It means deliberately choosing a different set of activities to deliver a unique mix of value. (Porter, 1996)

The authors of one of the key business school strategy texts provide a fuller definition focusing on the importance of stakeholders in a business:

> Strategy is the direction and scope of an organization over the long term, which achieves advantage in a changing environment through its configuration of resources and competences with the aim of fulfilling stakeholder expect-ations. (Johnson, Whittington and Scholes, 2011)

2. Photograph by Natascha Radclyffe-Thomas.

This definition summarizes many of the key terms of strategic analysis which will be discussed throughout this chapter, and highlights that strategic decisions are about the long-term direction of the fashion organization and the scope of its activities; hence strategic decisions are likely to be complex and have far-reaching effects through to the operations of the organization. It also tells us that the whole aim of strategy is to gain advantage over the organization's competitors to help it achieve its goal; not just by doing things better but by doing things differently.

For most fashion organizations the main long-term goal will be to generate more income than is spent in costs, because most require profit as reward for investment by the shareholders. This is the traditional profit motive of business. Organizations which are run on a 'not-for-profit' basis still need to generate a surplus of income over their costs; the surplus is then applied to their defined purpose.

In either case, generating income requires the organization to offer something that its customers value and want to buy, and that has many external influences, but before exploring those influential factors, let's think about who the stakeholders could be in a fashion organization. These are individuals or groups who depend on the fashion organization to fulfil their own goals, and conversely the organization itself depends on stakeholders to reach its own goals. Internal and external stakeholders in a fashion business care about the performance of that business, and the revenue and profit that is generated (see Table 2.1). Stakeholders are also interested in the stability and liquidity (financial health) of the company, whether it is likely to stay in business for the foreseeable future (is a going concern) or, indeed, whether it may be an acquisition target. All of these issues will impact the value of the company and are explored from a financial perspective in Chapter 5.

Type of Stakeholder		Why do they care?
Internal	Employee/ Management	Job security and income levels Training and career progression Management may have incentive schemes linked to company performance
	Shareholders	Value of company and their shareholding, revenue stream from dividends or realization of capital growth via potential exit
External	Government	Tax revenues
	Local Community	Job creation; regeneration of/impact on local area and environment
	Customers	Pricing and availability of goods/services
	Competitors	Competitive pressures on market share and pricing impacting their revenue and profit
	Suppliers	Continuing revenue streams impacting their own business
	Banks	Likelihood of loan repayments and servicing costs being met. Opportunities for business expansion

Table 2.1 *Stakeholders in fashion businesses*

Organizations often articulate their goals in a mission statement that provides their vision of where the business is going and its ultimate ambition. As Box 2.1 shows, some of these can be complex but the best are simple, straightforward and easy for every stakeholder in the business to remember. Mission statements embody the aims and values that underpin all the activities of the business. Business values are further explored in Chapter 6 from a brand perspective and in Chapter 12 from the perspective of corporate responsibility.

Box 2.1 - Mission statements from global fashion businesses

'Lifestyle merchandising is our business and our passion. The goal for our brands is to build a strong emotional bond with the customer. To do this we must build lifestyle environments that appeal emotionally, and offer fashion-correct products on a timely basis. Our customers are the reason and the inspiration for everything we do.' (Anthropologie)

'The mission of the LVMH group is to represent the most refined qualities of Western "Art de Vivre" around the world. LVMH must continue to be synonymous with both elegance and creativity. Our products, and the cultural values they embody, blend tradition and innovation, and kindle dream and fantasy.'

(LVMH)

'Changing clothes. Changing conventional wisdom. Change the world.'

(Fast Retailing; owners of Uniqlo)

'Fashion and quality at the best price'

(H&M)

Source: Company websites and reports, 2015–2016.

So, in practice, business strategy sets a goal and influences the choice of activities that an organization will pursue to reach that goal. Strategy will therefore dictate the operational decisions and can be seen as the umbrella that holds together all the strategic and operating decisions a company makes: for example, the organization structure (human resources strategy), the way the organization will raise and spend money (financial strategy), the way the organization will identify itself and communicate with its customers (marketing strategy, retail strategy), and the way the organization will provide its customers with what they want (supply chain strategy). All these areas of strategic management are explored in detail in their dedicated chapters.

Obviously organizations will have different strategic priorities at different points in their lifecycle. A small start-up business will be much more concerned with establishing funding and growth strategies, whereas a large mature business will be concerned more with its geographical scope and control.

Returning to the (Johnson et al., 2011) definition, it gives a sense of dynamism, helping us to see that the business world is constantly changing and the business must use its resources and competences to give it capability to succeed in reaching its goal. This notion of change in the business world leads to the first of our 3 Cs – Context.

> **Drivers of change** The strategist in a business must understand those factors that can bring about change in the business environment to understand the context in which strategy is formed.

STRATEGIC CONTEXT

The starting point for the formulation of any successful strategy has to be gaining an understanding of the external context within which the organization is operating. As Figure 2.2 shows, the business environment is complex and multi-layered with many inter-connected factors. Every organization needs to understand what is changing in the business environment, the drivers of change, and how this is affecting the organization not only now but in its potential impact in the future.

The environment is the source of both opportunities that can be exploited in pursuit of strategic goals and also the threats that the organization must seek to avoid or protect itself against. It is useful to use a framework to ensure that all elements of the business environment context are considered. Two important frameworks are useful here and will be discussed in turn: the PESTEL and the 5 Forces frameworks.

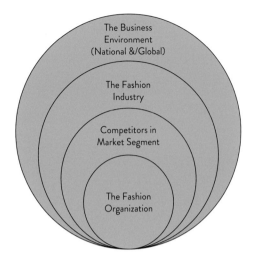

Figure 2.2 *The layers of strategic context*

Analyzing the business environment

This type of analysis has many different names: PEST, PESTLE, PESTEL, STEEPLE, but all of these are essentially the same and refer to the outermost layer of the strategic context 'onion' in Figure 2.2. Factors external to the organization should be examined in turn and the impact on the fashion industry considered. A framework like this helps organization of the analysis and ensures that no areas are overlooked. Do remember, however, that one factor may impact different segments of an industry to different extents so perspective is important; for example, a restriction on Russian national travel may have a positive effect on luxury fashion in Russia but will reduce the Russian tourist spend abroad. In performing an analysis of such external factors it is important to keep asking 'So what?' to ensure that this is not just a list of factors but that the implications for the present and future industry are captured. Table 2.2 is a starting point for some contextual issues to consider.

This analysis can be rather messy as it is not easy to isolate factors, many overlap and are inter-connected; however, it does not particularly matter how factors are classified in this analysis, merely that their impact on the industry segment in which the fashion organization operates is considered. The analysis will also be different for each territory the organization operates in. We will return to this framework in Chapter 4 to see how it needs to be further developed when an organization is looking to expand into new markets.

Factor	Consider the issues and their likely impact on fashion organizations …
Political	Government stability, policy effects on all other factors, austerity measures. Impact of global political issues; the status and composition of free trade areas such as the EU.
Economic	Macro-economic: global economic factors, such as an economic slowdown that has a potential impact on cost and demand. Micro-economic: those factors specific to a country/region, such as productivity, interest rates, inflation, unemployment, minimum/living wage, all impact both the cost of doing business and the consumer's disposable income.
Social	Ageing population, increasing compulsory education and social mobility all impact consumers wants and needs. Long-term fashion trends, such as casualization of dress.
Technological	The constantly connected society and big data impact ways of doing business and consumer expectations.
Ethical	More than environmental impact considerations, businesses must now consider ethics and sustainability to ensure they are responsible in all areas of their business activities.
Legal	Complex legislation to protect consumers and businesses; for example, the Sale of Goods Act, Intellectual Property Protection (IPP) legislation.

Table 2.2 *Starting to use a PESTEL framework*

Analyzing the competitive forces

Moving into the second layer and thinking about the context of the industry itself, Porter (1980) devised a model to help analyze the attractiveness of a particular industry or, indeed, segment of that industry. His model considers the perspective that within any industry there is a pot of profit to be shared out, and that a 'tug of war' is played out between the participants of the industry in order to maximize their shares of that profit. It is the strength of the five forces within an industry that determines how the players compete with each other for a share of the available profit. We can consider how these forces are constantly changing in the mass market fashion industry segment in the UK for a company such as Topshop.

1. **Rivalry between competitors** is high. There are many competitors jostling for position and market share in a mature market with a low growth rate. Topshop's competitive rivals include H&M, New Look, ASOS, Zara, River Island, and all of these firms are competing for the discretionary income of a defined customer segment.

2. **Bargaining power of customers** is quite high. Thinking about the average Topshop customer, she is young, pursues shopping as a leisure activity, browses, shops and communicates constantly online and probably has little loyalty to these brands, wanting only to find on-trend pieces at the right price. She can easily switch to one of the other similar brands, should Topshop not fulfil her needs at the right price.

3. **Threat of alternatives** that may act as substitutes is also high. Such a customer will switch easily between brands as direct substitutes and will trade off all of her fashion and social needs within her limited budget; for instance, she may not be able to buy a new dress in Topshop because she needs to repair her cracked phone screen, or she may choose to spend on a big night out this month instead (indirect substitutes).

4. **Bargaining power of suppliers** at the other end of the spectrum could be conceived as quite low. A business like Topshop will be a large customer to certain suppliers. Topshop will therefore be in a strong position to be able to dictate the cost prices it pays, always conscious of the price the consumer will be willing to pay, and it will be prepared to switch to other suppliers to achieve lower cost prices to protect its profit margins.

5. **Threat of upstarts** is quite high in this segment. The market is attractive to new entrants and relatively easy to penetrate if there is some capital backing. The fashion industry appears to have fairly low barriers to entry; particularly in comparison with highly capital-intensive industries such as the automotive or petrochemical industries where extensive investment in production facilities is required. To enter the fashion market, some investment is needed in either a physical or an online presence, but the real barrier to entry is brand awareness and loyalty. Fashion companies use many resources developing their brand to enhance their points of difference and protect their position from the threat of upstarts who try to enter the market.

The competitive forces model helps us to understand not only the competitive pricing dynamics in a market but also the need to be different from competitors and for the business to keep the promises it makes to its customers. It also helps to see how a business can make strategic decisions to reduce the strength of a force. For example, in this segment, to reduce the strength of the threat of new entrants, expenditure on marketing and brand building is justified. The American-based brand Forever 21 entered the UK market in 2012 with big ambitions for expansion, but they underestimated the strength of established players like Top Shop, Zara and H&M and the growing threat of online players such as Boohoo.com and Missguided.com.

Environmental scanning and strategic drift

It is important to remember that the business environment is constantly changing and so the process of analyzing it needs to be ongoing. A continual process of environmental scanning will help any organization remain current and help to ensure that there is no strategic drift. This happens when senior management set a strategic course of action without properly understanding the environment. A good example of this was seen in the 1990s when the management of the dominant UK clothing retailer Marks & Spencer lost touch with their customers and failed to give the customers the contemporary styling they wanted, and consequently lost the high levels of customer loyalty that they are still battling to regain. So in a dynamic industry environment we can expect the balance in the five forces tug-of-war to be constantly changing; but it is important that businesses are able to gain and retain some advantage over their competitors and make a profit.

STRATEGIC CAPABILITY

The environmental analysis has provided the external context in which the business is operating. The next step in a strategic analysis is to look inside the business to consider how well placed it is to exploit the external opportunities and defend itself against the identified threats within the external context. Every business has a key set of resources that it uses; in other words, the 'what' of the business. The resources can be human, financial and

> **Strategic capability**
> Those internal resources that help a business win the long-term game it is playing.

physical tangible assets (sometimes known as the 3Ms – men, money and machines). A fourth 'M', minds, refers to the intangible assets of a brand and intellectual property, as shown in Table 2.3. Resources are important to a business because if they are unique and are not easily imitated by competitors then they are probably good bases for competitive advantage.

Just having resources is not enough, it is the way they are used that can influence whether this competitive advantage can actually be realized. Competitive advantage is one of the most commonly used terms in discussions about strategy and we will return to it later in the chapter. The 'how' of the use of these resources is called strategic competence. There are some competences that are so fundamental to survival amongst competition that they are called 'core competences'. If a business has a particular unique resource and uses it effectively, it can be said to have a strategic capability. We will return to strategic competences and capabilities later.

Resources "what we have"	'M'	Competences "how we use it well"
Employees Suppliers Customers	**Men**	Employee engagement, reward and motivation Relationships Understanding and communicating
Finance Cash flow	**Money**	Raising funds and controlling spend
Buildings Factories Shops	**Machines**	Efficient and effective product sourcing and distribution
Brand Intellectual Property	**Minds**	Engagement, reputation and protection

Table 2.3 *The 4Ms applied to fashion businesses*

The concept of a value chain

The value chain is a useful conceptual framework for gaining an understanding of an organizational context. It was first introduced by Michael Porter in 1985 and attempts to identify particular capabilities and assets being used by a company to see whether they are adding value to the product or service being created. The value chain also identifies the critical resources being used and key linkages between them.

Porter's original value chain model distinguishes between two levels of activity within a business: primary and support. Primary activities are those directly involved in delivering the products or services to the customer, and support activities are those that contribute indirectly by supporting the primary activities and improving their effectiveness or efficiency. Primary activities are those that transform goods and services to provide additional benefit (value). Primary activities could be production or retailing, and they revolve around inputs, transformational operations and outputs.

- **Inbound logistics**
  Activities concerned with receiving, storing and distributing inputs to the product or service, including materials handling, stock control and transport (for example, in fashion retailing a variety of suppliers may be involved).

- **Operations**
  Transforming inputs into the final product or service (for example, in garment production – machining, assembly, packaging, testing and so on).

- **Outbound logistics**
  Concerned with collecting, storing and distributing the product to customers (for example, warehousing, distribution).

- **Marketing and sales**
  Related to how consumers are made aware of the product or service and how they are able to purchase it (for example, customer sales service and online and offline marketing communications).

- **Service**
  Concerns the activities that enhance or maintain the value of a product or service (such as returns, repair, after sales and loyalty programs).

Support activities can be considered the more static aspects of an organization that are there to guide the primary activities, such as the infrastructure of the organization, including people, technological support (information technology, relevant research and development activities) and procurement, which sources general and product-specific supplies.

- **Firm Infrastructure**
  Concerned with the system of planning, finance, quality control, information management and structures part of the company's culture.

- **Human Resource Management**
  Concerned with the activities involved in recruiting, managing, training, developing and rewarding people within the company.

- **Technology Development**
  The knowledge that can be directly connected either to the product (for example, R&D (research and development) investment, product design) or to processes (for example, production systems and processes) or to a particular resource.

- **Procurement**
  Related to the processes that occur in the company in acquiring resource inputs to the primary activities. Includes general business needs as well as those relating to products and service offers, for example, a supply chain management system.

In principle the way value chain activities are performed determines costs and therefore affects profits. The classification of secondary and primary activities can help to better understand the sources of value of a specific company.

From an internal perspective, applying value chain concepts can be used to:

- Facilitate an internal analysis of business operations;

- Assess where capabilities lie and which functions could be outsourced to gain better efficiencies;

- Understand and analyze the value chains of other related companies and identify possible areas of integration;

- Identify better linkages between activities in order to create efficiencies.

From the customer perspective, applying value chain concepts can improve the effectiveness of customer value and enhance differentiation for brands, as it helps businesses:

- Select and enhance best practices and technologies that lead to innovation, improved design and enhanced creativity;

- Understand and implement best practices in providing customer service;

- Reallocate resources that will devote more to activities with the biggest impact on the value delivered to the customer and those that address the customer's most important purchase criteria;

- For intermediate buyers (for example, in the case of a fashion manufacturer supplying retail companies), understand how the activities the company performs impact on the buyer's value chain;

- Signal and adopt best practices for recognizing the value in a product/brand and enhance customers' perceptions of that value.

Contemporary thought on the creation of value suggests that internal operations of a fashion organization might be more helpfully viewed as a network, rather than a chain, with less clear distinctions between primary and support activities. In addition, it is common for external organizations to be part of this network as outsourced activities. We return to this in chapter 15 where we discuss the concept of the digital ecosystem for fashion brands.

STRATEGIC CHOICE

Identifying resources and competences not only helps define what the business has and does, but it can also point out competence gaps. Putting this internal perspective together with the environmental analysis may reveal areas where action must be taken to fill these gaps lest the business be adversely impacted.

A useful summarizing framework for this insight is the TOWS matrix as shown in Table 2.4. This is an extended version of the traditional SWOT analysis that many readers will be familiar with. A SWOT analysis, while useful, tends to produce a static list, whereas the more active TOWS matrix suggests the strategic action that needs to be taken to build on strengths, combat weaknesses, take advantage of opportunities and avoid threats; thus the TOWS matrix is more useful in bringing together the external and internal perspectives.

	Internal Strengths	Internal Weaknesses
External Opportunities	Use strengths to capitalize on identified opportunities	Take advantage of identified opportunities by addressing identified weaknesses
External Threats	Use strengths to overcome identified threats	Take action to avoid threats and minimize weaknesses

Table 2.4 *The TOWS matrix: An active SWOT analysis*

The identification of weaknesses to be combated will lead an organization to look at how to stretch, add or change strategic capabilities, resulting in the need to make strategic choices. Adding competences can be done internally or by external acquisition. There is a trade-off, however, between the time it takes to develop an internal competence versus the costs and risks incurred by acquiring them from external sources, even if this is faster. If sustainable competitive advantage is achieved by developing durable strategic capabilities that provide advantage over time, then in rapidly changing environments organizations need the capability to be dynamic: to change, innovate, flex, adapt and learn.

In an external environment that is changing rapidly, the only way a business can hope to gain competitive advantage and survive in the long term is by building distinctive resources and competences (Hamel and Prahalad, 1990). This is the resource-based view of strategy, taken further by Barney (1991) who proposed that for strategic capabilities to confer sustainable competitive advantage, the capability must be:

> **Strategic choice** The options for action available to a business depending on the stage in its business cycle, including the valid choice to do nothing.

- **Valued:** by target customers
- **Rare:** not currently possessed by competitors
- **Inimitable:** not easily copied by competitors, and
- **Non-substitutable:** not easily replaced by another capability.

This framework was further developed into the VRIO framework for analysis (Barney and Hesterly, 2014), where the idea of non-substitutability is replaced by the importance that the Organizational processes (O) are aligned, to ensure the competitive advantage can be realized.

A fashion business needs to bear in mind what stakeholders' expectations may be. In Table 2.1 we saw that there are many different stakeholder perspectives to consider. The purpose of the business, its values and culture are all important in shaping strategic direction, decision and implementation. The impacts of all of these elements of analysis need to be considered when making strategic choices.

Choosing how to compete

So we have seen that strategic choice is based on the decisions that are made about how a fashion organization uses its resources, to get ahead of the competition, while considering the constraints of the internal and external business landscape. The important and elusive concept of competitive advantage is vital to understand, particularly in a fragmented and competitive industry such as fashion. Many theorists have attempted to capture the essence of what competitive advantage is, in different ways (see Box 2.2).

Box 2.2 - Definitions of competitive advantage

'Competitive advantage grows out of value a firm is able to create for its buyers that exceeds the firm's cost of creating it. Value is what buyers are willing to pay, and superior value stems from offering lower prices than competitors for equivalent benefits or providing unique benefits that more than offset a higher price.' (Michael Porter, *Competitive Advantage*, 1985, p. 3)

'A firm is said to have a competitive advantage when it is implementing a value-creating strategy not simultaneously being implemented by any current or potential player.' (Barney, 1991; cited by Clulow et al., 2003, p. 221)

'A specific advantage one firm/brand may have over competitors within the market.' (Posner, 2015)

As well as being centred on the concepts of being better/higher/greater in value to the customer or user, competitive advantage can also refer to the idea of being the first to do something, and thus value lies in newness, as we see in fashion all the time. According to Porter (1980), at the most fundamental level, companies can create competitive advantage by perceiving or discovering new and better ways to compete in an industry and innovate in how they bring them to market. When competitors fail to perceive the new way of competing or are unable to respond, innovations shift competitive advantage and bring significant advantages to early movers. These are especially evident in industries with significant economies of scale and/or when customers are more concerned about replacing suppliers, both relevant factors in the fashion industry, as shown in Box 2.3.

Box 2.3 - Fashion industry innovations that have shifted competitive advantage (CA)

- **New technologies**
  Technology developments that create new possibilities for the design, production, marketing and delivery of products. Examples of this are 'smart watches' and the rising market for 'wearables' (wearable technology).

- **New or shifting buyer needs**
  CA can be achieved when new competitors perceive new needs before established competitors do so, or when established players are unable or unwilling to respond. For example, the entry and sustained growth of online retailer ASOS within the saturated young fashion market; its offer of free and fast shipping, a wide product assortment and flexible returns policy was a combination highly valued by the growing online shopper market.

- **The emergence of a new industry segment**
  CA is created when a new segment of the industry emerges. The 'athleisure' trend is an example of this; brands such as Sweaty Betty and Lululemon have successfully exploited the trend of wearing fashion-orientated 'workout' clothing all day.

- **Shifting input costs or availability**
  When a significant change occurs in the absolute or relative cost of inputs (such as labour, raw materials, machinery or communication) that leads to CA. International fashion retailer Zara is able to operate truly global production systems, benefiting from the optimization of its own facilities, its suppliers and global logistics.

- **Changes in government regulations**
  Environmental regulations, product control or trade barriers may stimulate innovation. For example, Levis Water<Less™ products significantly reduce the use of water in the finishing process.

Competitive advantage is implemented through the way companies perform activities and conceive new ways to conduct those same procedures, technologies or other inputs. The fit between these internal activities is the key component to alienate competitors. The value chain analysis (as explored above) can be useful to reflect on how activities build competitive advantage. The value chain maps out all the strategically relevant activities of the company so as to understand the behaviour of costs and the existing or potential sources of difference. The activities within the value chain contribute to buyer value and its cumulative costs determine the difference between buyer value and producer cost. This means that competitive advantage can come from anywhere in the value chain and not necessarily just from the product or service provided to the end consumer.

Porter (1980) suggested there are three possible generic strategies capable of delivering superior performance for an organization through the arrangement and coordination of its value chain activities. Adopting one of these strategies confers the ability to achieve competitive advantage, which may in turn lead to market share gain.

Cost leadership

Pursuing a cost leadership strategy requires that a company becomes the lowest cost producer of a specific product or service. The goal is to earn above-average profit even though the price charged for the product is below the price charged by competitors. Emphasis is placed on cost reduction in every activity within the value chain. The company increases efficiency and lowers production and operational costs to gain the ability to offer its specific products or services to its target market at a lower price (see Mini Case Study 2.1).

To sustain the competitive advantage, a company needs to regularly improve its product and services while maintaining cost leadership. Ways by which a company can acquire cost advantages are:

- Improving process efficiencies
- Gaining access to lower-cost materials or lower production costs
- Making optimal outsourcing decisions
- Vertical integration
- Avoiding some costs altogether, such as advertising.

 ## MINI CASE STUDY 2.1 - H&M: Leading on price

H&M was founded in 1947 in Sweden and currently operates across 62 countries with over 4000 stores worldwide. The brand is part of the Hennes & Mauritz AB Group, which also owns COS, & Other Stories, Monki, Weekday, Arket, and Cheap Monday. It is one of the leading fast fashion companies (the company ranked number 21 in the top 100 global brands by Interbrand in 2015). Their competitive advantage is reflected in their strapline, as reinforced by H&M's head of design, Ann-Sofie Johansson (in Walker, 2010): 'At the beginning it was only "fashion at the best price" but several years back we added the term "quality". We are working really hard on that and we always have the customer as the focus. Our goal is to satisfy them with great collections every year.' H&M create value for customers by offering fashion and quality at the best price.

H&M do not own factories, but instead produce ranges using around 850 independent suppliers, mainly in Asia (for products with longer lead times) and Europe (for products with shorter lead times). This close relationship with suppliers allows H&M to guarantee quality at a low cost. H&M rely on a well-developed IT system that gives access to vital information to allow for high efficiency. Not only can H&M restock stores quickly but they can also monitor the trends from sales in each store and use this information to develop products tailored to their customer through shorter lead time manufacturing across Europe.

The company has used customer data to inform decisions about the release of new products, and the agile supply chain allows the brand to deliver collections at a price that customers will pay, making it a core player in the trend-driven fast fashion industry sector. Recently H&M have been facing increasing pressure from competitors, not only on price and quality, but also on service and styling.

Sources: Various, including
http://about.hm.com/en.html
http://www.independent.co.uk/life-style/fashion/features/swede-shop-how-do-hm-stay-on-top-2026039.html

Differentiation

A **differentiation strategy** is one of developing products and services that offer unique attributes that are valued by customers; requiring that the customer perception of similar products or services is higher in value than that of other similar brands. Differentiation can be based on design, brand image, customer service, quality, or performance, for which a premium price can be justified and which is hugely relevant in an industry where such nuances can be sophisticated and specific to particular customer groups (see Mini Case Study 2.2).

A differentiation strategy of a company can be underpinned by specific strengths in:

- A well-established research and design development department
- Access to scientific research
- Skilled product developers and manufacturers
- Strong marketing and selling departments
- Reputation of the company for innovation and quality
- Reputed brand name.

Differentiation is often the most relevant strategy for fashion organizations, so we will return to this later in the chapter for a deeper exploration of the concept.

 ## MINI CASE STUDY 2.2 - Hermès: Enhancing differentiation

Hermès is perceived as one of the most exclusive luxury brands in the world, valued for its traditional craftsmanship, brand exclusivity and cultural values. Founded in 1837 by a French harness maker, the company grew by extending different product categories such as ready-to-wear, silk, fragrances and watches. As stated by Alex Dumas, CEO of the brand (in Thomas, 2011), 'the main strength of Hermès is the love of craftsmanship. We see ourselves as creative craftsmen. The philosophy of Hermès is to keep craftsmanship alive.' According to the Interbrand 2015 ranking, Hermès held position 41 in the Top 100 Global brands in the world, up 22 places from the previous year.

Hermès maintains a high level of control over its development, production and distribution, focusing on superior quality; Hermès' vision, creativity and dedication to rigour, sets the brand apart from its competitors. Its brand strategy values the longstanding history of producing ultra-quality distinguishable products requiring high levels of craftsmanship, elegance, creativity and superior service.

Capacity constraints are the core of the brand's strategy, making it difficult for people to buy its most coveted products or, in some cases, making consumers believe that that is the case. As mentioned by Dumas (in Thomas, 2011), 'Our business is about creating desire. It can be fickle because desire is fickle but we try to have creativity to suspend the momentum.'

Sources: Various, including
http://lesailes.hermes.com/gb/en/#history
https://www.businessoffashion.com/articles/intelligence/the-secret-to-hermes-success

Focus

If opting for a **focus strategy**, companies can use either a differentiation or cost leadership strategy but in a narrower market segment. For that purpose, companies develop uniquely low-cost or well-specified products for that market. A focus strategy includes the splitting of the target market into specific sections and the development of business strategies for each niche. The theory behind the focus strategy has been criticized for the lack of information on what is a focused market in terms of how broad/narrow the segment should be. In addition, a niche or specialist approach runs the risk of that market segment disappearing over time. The focused differentiation strategy is, however, probably the most frequently implemented competitive strategy for fashion brands. Mini Case Study 2.3 highlights the focused strategy of the innovative fashion brand Bonobos.

MINI CASE STUDY 2.3 - Bonobos: Leading through focus

Bonobos is a multi-channel retailer that aims to create the ideal shopping experience for men. It was founded at Stanford Business School, US, in 2007 as an e-commerce platform, but has recently opened physical showrooms referred to as 'guideshops'. The brand predominantly sells business-casual trousers to male millennials, expanding its offer to ties, shorts, swimwear, outerwear and accessories.

The company provides quality products and high-touch consumer service at an affordable price. Their business model is simple: targeting male millennial shoppers with a value proposition of well-fitting apparel, maximum convenience during the shopping experience and at an affordable price.

Fit and convenience were key determinants for developing brand loyalty with male shoppers since they typically enjoy shopping less than women. The brand set out to create a shopping experience that is quick, painless and stress-free with a focus on customer service. Employees (or 'ninjas' as Bonobos calls them) are deeply immersed in the brand culture to better assist consumers.

Sources: Various, including
https://bonobos.com/about
http://uk.businessinsider.com/how-bonobos-is-maturing-into-a-major-brand-2015-8?r=US&IR=T

CONTEMPORARY APPROACHES TO STRATEGIC CHOICES

Porter's original work in 1980 proposed that if a business tried to achieve differentiation and low cost it would become 'stuck in the middle', pursuing neither strategy well and leading to failure. There are many instances in the fashion world, however, where businesses have proven highly successful competing with a combination of low cost and differentiation. H&M (see Mini Case Study 2.1) blend a general low-cost approach to fast fashion but use their famous designer collaborations to maintain customer interest by providing something different in the market. This is referred to as an integrated low-cost differentiation strategy by Hitt et al. (2007), acknowledging that a company can gain advantage by offering products with unique features at a lower price. Other theorists have developed Porter's ideas and proposed that there are shades of grey in the choices of bases for competition. We will examine some of these important contemporary perspectives next.

Bowman's (1995) Strategy Clock

This model reflects customer *perception* of the value that is offered by a brand and so is particularly useful for the fashion industry. The model is adapted and explained in Figure 2.3 and Table 2.5. The arrows show that because this is based on customer perception, strategies are not static and brands can move between quadrants and clock face positions. The darker arrows show the danger of moving into the zone of doom where the business could fail.

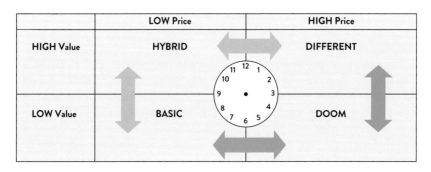

Figure 2.3 *Fashion strategies*

Source: Based on Bowman (1995).

Bowman's clock considers the **customer value proposition (CVP)** as perceived by product benefits, with perceptions influenced by service and experience. The key to successful differentiation lies in the price/value equation. When a firm is offering the customers something unique that they value highly enough, they will be willing to pay more for it, resulting in a price premium, and hence a profit can be justified. For this equation to endure over time there must be consistency in all aspects of a firm's relationship with its customers. Differentiation can be tangible, such as the product itself, its packaging or services offered with it; for example, in a Hermès handbag the tangible aspects of differentiation are sumptuous leather, hand crafted by artisans with exclusivity in design, luxurious packaging and personal repair services. In addition, the intangible differentiation elements such as the heritage story of the brand, the associations of wealth and the tribal belongingness accrued to a customer carrying such an exclusive bag add to customer value. So, differentiation advantage is not just about the product but embraces the whole relationship with the customer, underpinned by design, service and quality considerations, where consistency is key.

Clockface Position	Name of Strategy	Price	Value	Characteristics	Fashion Example
6 – 7	Basic	**Low**	**Low**	Commodity-like product sold to price-sensitive customers with low switching costs.	Value players, e.g. Primark
8 – 10	Basic Hybrid	**Low**	**Mid**	Need to achieve a low cost base in ways that competitors cannot match, to sustain this.	Low cost but more trend led, e.g. H&M
10 – 11	Hybrid	**Low**	**High**	Achieving differentiation and a low price at the same time by investing in low cost base.	Zara
11 – 1	Hybrid Different	**Mid**	**High**	Offer benefits different from competitors that are valued by customers so product perceived as better. Must know customer well.	Mid-Market and Premium Brands, e.g. Ted Baker
1 – 3	Different	**High**	**High**	As above but a more focused customer base, usually with a price premium.	Luxury Brands, e.g. Hermès
3 – 6	Doom	**High**	**Low**	Do not provide perceived value for money, either not cheap enough to be basic or not different enough to warrant the price premium.	Arguably no brands here as they are failed businesses!

Table 2.5 *Applying Bowman's Strategy Clock to the fashion industry (based on Bowman, 1995)*

Blue Ocean strategy

In 2004, Kim and Mauborgne proposed a new **value innovation** model, which helps to identify where a company can outperform its competitors by creating demand in an uncontested market space. The authors propose the concept of value innovation as the basis for their 'Blue Ocean strategy', using an 'Eliminate – Reduce – Raise – Create' (ERRC) grid that intends to develop a four-action framework in the pursuit of a new value curve. This value curve allows managers to see how their strategy works in relation to competitors and assess the factors that they need to work further on. A brief explanation of the ERRC grid is displayed below:

- **Eliminate:** Which factors can you eliminate that your industry has long competed on?

- **Reduce:** Which factors should be reduced well below the industry's standard?

- **Raise:**   Which factors should be raised well above the industry's standard?

- **Create:**   Which factors should be created that the industry has never offered?

According to the authors, if the brand creates an added value for customers, then new markets are opened and new models for demand would be created, making competition an outdated concept. They identify Ralph Lauren as an example of a brand within the fashion industry that falls into this concept, due to the creation of what the authors call 'high fashion with no fashion' – taking over classical elements from established high-end or premium brands, investing in elegant retail locations and store interiors and selling products at a reasonable price (Kim and Mauborgne, 2015). The premises behind this theory are indicated below.

'Red Ocean strategy' refers to the traditional approach to strategy that focuses on current customers and makes little effort to attract new buyers into the existing market space. In terms of competition, the focus of companies here is always to beat their competitors, sometimes by duplicating ideas and value propositions. Instead of creating added value, demand is exploited and attention is on the supply side. Also, in a red ocean, companies are supposed to align the whole system of a company's activities with the strategic choice of differentiation or low cost (as discussed above under Porter's theory). The underpinning vision is that the industry's structural conditions are as given and therefore have little or no scope for change.

Blue Ocean strategy takes the opposite approach by looking at non-existing customers and focusing on creating uncontested market space. Companies in a blue ocean never use competition as a benchmark and, in fact, focus on increasing the size of the industry by attracting people who have never purchased in that industry. Competition is deemed irrelevant because under this new approach a leap in value for both buyers and the company itself is created, through creating and capturing new demand. Contrary to Porter's theory of competitive advantage, blue oceans are intended to align the whole system of a company's activities in pursuit of differentiation and low cost, making sure that any unnecessary costs are removed and that anything that does not create value is eliminated or reduced (as shown in the ERRC grid application to online fashion platform Farfetch, see Box 2.4). Contrary to red oceans, in blue oceans, market boundaries and industry structure are considered versatile and flexible and able to be shaped by the actions and beliefs of players within the industry.

Box 2.4 - Applying ERRC to Farfetch

Farfetch owns an online marketplace that connects sellers (boutiques and brands) to buyers (shoppers) of luxury fashion around the world. It was founded in 2007 by José Neves, a Portuguese entrepreneur. Applying the ERRC approach demonstrates the value innovation model created by the platform:

Eliminate	Reduce
Inventory risk	**Working capital requirements**
Farfetch's boutiques act as individual warehouses and fulfil the order directly whenever a consumer makes a purchase through the platform.	By developing partnerships with boutiques all over the world, Farfetch is able to have a global business without the overhead costs, while redirecting funds to grow their platform.

Raise	Create
Convenience of purchase	**A highly differentiated business model with unique positioning mixing creativity and technology**
Consumers want products as fast as possible, at the best price and with the most convenience (i.e. free shipping, duties and taxes included). The platform makes it easy for consumers to access products they like while shopping on a site in their own language, with local payment solutions and customer service that addresses their needs.	By aggregating some of the best independent luxury boutiques across 30 countries, Farfetch has been able, through a curated selection, to build a unique business model stocking a wide range of brands and designer pieces.

Product accessibility

Through cross-border commerce and ease of shipping items fast and reliably from one country or continent to another, Farfetch embodies a truly global perspective, connecting fashion lovers anywhere in the world to unique products and shops, wherever they may be, and thus creating value for small-scale retailers as well.

Data intelligence & use of IT

Inventory management analytics are in place to help boutiques manage across online and in-store purchases

Consistency of experience

The platform ensures a consistent shopping experience across boutiques as well as premium customer service.

Farfetch is in charge of photographing all merchandise displayed on the website to ensure consistency.

The platform also provides the same packaging to all customers from all boutiques and offers a standardized return policy.

A truly omni-channel retailing strategy

By using technology and analytics in order to integrate online and in-store shopping experiences in new ways.

An innovative technology system

Farfetch's technology is also an asset when convincing boutiques to join the platform.
The content is API-based, which enables stores to easily integrate the shopping channel with their pre-existing website.

Sources:
https://www.farfetch.com/uk/
https://medium.com/@fcourt/farfetch-s-journey-to-a-1bn-valuation-blending-creativity-technology-to-form-a-european-unicorn-f6626df48bd#.56ln6z3kp
https://www.businessoffashion.com/community/voices/discussions/is-fashion-missing-the-technology-revolution/farfetchs-global-platform-play
https://www.fastcompany.com/3029848/like-a-high-fashion-etsy-farfetch-puts-the-worlds-rarest-fashion-at-your-fingertips

Transient competitive advantage

In 2013, Rita McGrath proposed that the whole idea that a company could achieve and retain competitive advantage was misleading and even dangerous as it encouraged complacency. She advocated that in a fast-moving competitive environment such as fashion, brands should look to ride the waves of transient competitive advantage, with agility being key. She found any competitive advantage, whether lasting two seasons or two decades, goes through a similar lifecycle to that of brands. A deep understanding of the five stages of this cycle allows fashion companies to move through them quickly and effectively, when advantages are not long lasting:

- **Launch:** Identify an opportunity and direct resources to capitalize on it.

- **Ramp up:** Bring that business idea to a larger scale.

- **Exploit:** Capturing market share and profits, which forces competitors to react.

- **Reconfigure:** Explore actions to keep the advantage and transition assets, people and competencies from one advantage to another.

- **Disengage:** When the advantage is fading, know when to extract resources and reallocate to the next advantage.

This approach recognizes a need for speed and instead of slow, precise decisions advocates fast and 'good enough' decisions. Although this changes some of the premises of strategy, it still requires a company to choose what to do and what not to do. For this purpose, it is still relevant to define where to compete, how to win and how to move from advantage to advantage, maintaining strategy as a fundamental aspect of managing fashion businesses in a time-pressured era.

THE IMPORTANCE OF DIFFERENTIATION IN FASHION

The thing that is going to decide whether it gets talked about is: is it remarkable. Is it worth making a remark about. (Seth Godin, 2011)

As mentioned earlier, differentiation is at the heart of the strategic management of many fashion companies, brands and products. It is used as a way of finding a place to successfully operate in a large, fragmented, dynamic and competitive industry. Company profit is not only dependent on good products, advertisements, branding or prices; being memorable is a requirement of any successful business strategy. In the fashion world, like many other business sectors, a strong brand adds significant value to a product offering. Fashion is a field that allows for social distinction and activates concerns that can become the basis for differentiation.

Differentiation is also a fundamental concept in fashion marketing. When the elements of differentiation are pursued correctly, within the core values of the brand, competitive advantage is created and the brand will stand out. Most fashion brands, whether mass market, premium, niche or luxury, rely on differentiation to ensure distinction from competitors whether related to the product design, marketing communication, and/or customer service, to justify their market and price positioning.

Alternative ways to differentiate

We have highlighted that the fashion marketplace is characterized by constantly changing customer demands and by a dynamic competitive environment, where brands are urged to be flexible and apply differentiation in order to stay ahead of competition. Due to the wide spread of online business models such as those used by Farfetch, ASOS and Net-a-Porter, the traditional value chain concept has needed some rethinking. The emergence of new competitive obligations has prompted a revision of the traditional paradigms of business strategy. Differentiation, for example, can be considered as a concept with a wider scope than the one introduced by Porter in 1980, as part of his generic strategies model discussed above.

Given that differentiation is defined by Kotler (2003: 315) as 'the process of adding a set of meaningful and valued differences to distinguish the company's offering from competitors' offerings', a company can differentiate its offering along five broad dimensions: product, services, personnel (people), channel (route to customer), and image (Table 2.6).

Product	Services	Personnel	Channel	Image
Aesthetics	Ordering ease	Competence	Coverage	Visual identity
Features	Delivery	Courtesy	Functionality	Media
Performance	Installation	Credibility	Performance	Offline atmospherics
Innovation	Customer training	Reliability	Integration	Online atmospherics
Quality	Customer consulting	Responsiveness	Easiness	PR & Events
Reliability	Personal stylists	Communication		
Reparability	Maintenance and repair	Empathy		
Design				
Comfort				

Table 2.6 *Dimensions of differentiation*
Source: Based on Kotler (2003).

Product differentiation

Product differentiation is the process by which a product is distinguished from those of other competitors by making it more attractive to a particular target market, and can be enhanced by different packaging, advertising campaigns, sales promotion or distribution. The difference can also be through the product itself: in the product's functional aspects, in quality and/or in price (Hoyle, 2005).

Availability of the product can also be relevant, for example, restricted availability in stores enhances exclusivity. The goal of differentiation is to position a product (or more usually a brand in the case of fashion) as unique and to be valued by customers. This will enhance a brand's competitive advantage and a strategy can be devised around the uniqueness of its product range, often called the 'unique selling proposition' or USP (see Mini Case Study 2.4).

 MINI CASE STUDY 2.4 - Product differentiation: Bottega Veneta

An example of a brand that has achieved differentiation via product uniqueness is Bottega Veneta. The Italian luxury house founded in 1966 uses a very distinctive leather weave design – *intrecciato* – on the exterior of many of its products, in particular the handbags. This product characteristic accounts for one of the most recognizable and identifiable elements of the brand, leading to the communications tag line 'When your own initials are enough' in a clear allusion to the visible product differentiation, which negates the need for a prominent brand logo.

Source: Bottega Veneta website, various dates.

 MINI CASE STUDY 2.5 - Service differentiation: ASOS

ASOS is an example of a company successfully delivering on style, affordability and accessibility. Their business model is built on trend-driven fashion and the company is conscious of the importance of getting their brand and channels integrated into the everyday lives of their customers. They are committed to being the best in user experience, which is evident by how they engage with their consumers on social media and are highly responsive to their questions.

The ASOS experience is collaborative, entertaining and personalized. Fashion-lovers come to us for inspiration and conversation, and to create their own fashion collections, not just for shopping. (...) we are working to deliver a seamless experience on our website, across social networks and devices from phones and iPads to laptops. It will be increasingly personalized, available in all places, and at all times. We are investing in mobile and digital innovation and services to make us faster and ever more desirable as a destination for twenty-somethings. (ASOS website)

Source: ASOS.com various dates.

Service differentiation

When goods cannot be easily differentiated on the basis of their tangible product characteristics, adding valued services can be a way to ensure competitive success (Kotler, 2000). Bruhn and Georgi (2006) characterize services as intangible, perishable, not transportable, produced and consumed simultaneously, different from one customer to the other, and co-produced by the customer. They also state that service differentiation strongly influences a consumer's loyalty. Different factors can be blended to achieve service differentiation: ordering ease, delivery, installation, customer service training, customer consulting, maintenance and repair. Attention to detail in the service offer has helped to differentiate ASOS from other fashion retailers (see Mini Case Study 2.5).

Personnel differentiation

In today's fashion market, products can be easily copied by competition, so companies need to embrace differentiation by focusing on better-trained people for sustainable superior performance. People who represent a brand must be reactive, flexible and responsive to customers' changing needs. The sales force is one of the major resources of a company and is responsible for the direct contact with customers in commercial activity; they represent a powerful driver of revenues due to the significant impact they have on a company's success.

The way a service is delivered impacts on the quality of the services itself. Consumers will be more likely to be satisfied if the sales force are trained to listen to their expectations. According to Kotler (2000), sales people need to develop the following specific skills in order to provide the best service quality: competence, courtesy, credibility, reliability, responsiveness, and communication.

Channel differentiation

The way brands design their distribution channels (routes to customer markets) in terms of coverage, expertize, and performance can also impact competitive advantage. Channel differentiation explores the different ways a company or brand distributes, sells or offers its products to customers. It also includes expertize of the channel management and the performance of the channel in terms of the ease of ordering, service and personnel. Being concerned with the logistics aspects as well as the marketing aspects, it is an important factor in achieving differentiation in the market. According to Kotler and Keller (2007), standing out in the way you offer your products in the market can be an excellent way to gain customers' attention. The choice of channels involves consideration of which product will be available to which customers. Channel differentiation is increasingly important with the advent of omni-channel retailing, as discussed in Chapter 1. The John Lewis department store group has continued to be successful by focusing on channel management (see Mini Case Study 2.6).

 MINI CASE STUDY 2.6 - Channel differentiation: John Lewis

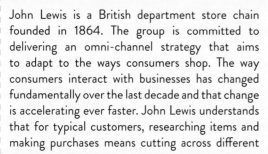

John Lewis is a British department store chain founded in 1864. The group is committed to delivering an omni-channel strategy that aims to adapt to the ways consumers shop. The way consumers interact with businesses has changed fundamentally over the last decade and that change is accelerating ever faster. John Lewis understands that for typical customers, researching items and making purchases means cutting across different channels. The department store estimates that at least two-thirds of its customers are already omni-channel shoppers, extending their purchase journey across online, in-store, phone and mobile devices.

Sources: Various, including https://www.marketingweek.com/2015/10/16/john-lewis-predicts-the-rise-of-the-master-shopper-as-digital-gives-consumers-ever-greater-control/

Image differentiation

A brand's image is the overall perception that consumers have of the brand. An image can be built through promotional activities, external business environmental factors, competitors' actions and/or through non-paid-for activities like word of mouth. It is formed out of the experiences, values and impressions that consumers share with the brand and about the brand. A strong brand is a company's most powerful asset (Aaker, 1991) and its importance is likely to be actively recognized by competitors; for this reason, designing and managing brands to achieve sustainable competitive advantage is of great strategic impact. Branding is a powerful way of attaching an identity and delivering emotional power to a product or service, and in this way differentiates the product from competing products. A brand's image should represent the product benefits and should reflect its market positioning, through a strategic mind-set that delivers customers' expectations. It needs to be conveyed consistently through all the communication tools used. A brand image can be regarded as an intangible asset for the company and can possess different functions: information provider, identity keeper, personality creator (see Mini Case Study 2.7) and/or risk reducer.

MINI CASE STUDY 2.7 - Image differentiation: The Kooples

The Kooples is a French brand founded in 2008 by three brothers. Their strategy from the outset relied on word of mouth as a tool to gain brand awareness. Even before the opening of the first store, the brand launched an advertising campaign featuring couples, with no mention of the brand name. The goal was twofold: to gain attention and create a buzz for the brand, and to display the concept – one brand that would suit both men and women, with mixed collections. Couples represented were heterosexual and homosexual, young and old, all with one thing in common: style. The brand targets urban and trendy consumers who use fashion as a way to reinforce their personality and image to their peers. 'We wanted to offer an androgynous look. Women like borrowing their men's clothes, their styles reflect a 'rock' and 'free' personality. (...) We really wanted to be precursors for men who want to have an image as thought-out as their girlfriends' (Alexander, Co-founder of The Kooples).

Sources: Various, including
http://www.thekooples.com
https://www.theguardian.com/fashion/2014/apr/13/perfect-kooples-fashion-brothers-paris

SUSTAINING COMPETITIVE ADVANTAGE IN THE CONTEMPORARY FASHION INDUSTRY

The fashion world is one that constantly requires an equilibrium; as described by Schultz (2010), the balance to achieve is between enough supply to meet demand, but not too much to create a glut; optimal distribution in the right markets to fill customer needs at the right time; pricing that provides value for the user, but some level of profit for the seller. This continuous balance of the market is destabilized through branding and marketing. It is only by making the product or service different from those of competitors, that a differential advantage for a company is created. There is a constant search for some marketplace disturbance that will offset the naturally occurring marketplace equilibrium, to the advantage of the marketer and the disadvantage of the competitor (Schultz, 2010).

Corporate response to competition

The competitive environment is not static and to maintain competitive advantage requires constant scanning for threats and opportunities. Brands such as those in the luxury market with clearly differentiated products and services are rarely concerned by the moves of their competitors. If the global luxury market continues to grow, all luxury brands should be able to position themselves for a share of that growth. It is a completely different story in a crowded market such as the mass-market fashion retail sector in the UK, where there is little absolute market growth and the only way that individual players will see their revenue and profits grow is at the expense of their competitors. The strategic moves of competitors become very important; for example, the prevalence of 'price match events' across the UK department store sector is an indication of high levels of competition in this low-growth market.

Copycat moves are not just in the pricing arena. When innovation is not easy the temptation is to imitate; indeed, most of the mass-market fashion industry is based on imitation and bringing the designs, colours and trends of designer fashion in a more accessible form to the mainstream consumer market. Thus, much of the fashion offer in mature markets tends to be similar to that of competition. In spite of this, fashion businesses that do find a point of differentiation are more protected from threats from competition than those that don't.

McGrath's (2013) ideas again resonate as it is now rare for a fashion company to maintain a truly lasting market advantage, due to the unpredictability of consumers and the changing nature of industries. The digital revolution, globalization, and the volatility of markets and the changing needs of consumers, lead to the need to exploit and build transient competitive advantages to stay ahead of the competition. This perspective views strategy in a more fluid and customer-centric manner and uses different approaches to define and evaluate it, to engage in innovation and develop new business opportunities.

CASE STUDY 2 - Kering: Leveraging centralized resources to support diverse directional growth

Kering is an example of an international fashion business that has successfully grown across markets and products by leveraging the advantages of a strong centralized management structure balanced with differentiated brand strategies. In 2017, the Kering luxury group comprised the following brands: in the soft luxury category, Gucci, Bottega Veneta, Saint Laurent, Balenciaga, Alexander McQueen, Stella McCartney, Christopher Kane, and Brioni. In hard luxury (jewellery and watches), Boucheron, Pomellato, Dodo, Qeelin, Girard-Perregaux, and Ulysse Nardin. In sport and lifestyle, Puma and Volcom. Kering employs over 40,000 people and operates in over 120 countries.

Having group-level roles and functions means Kering takes advantage of specialist knowledge and acquired experience as well as the economies of scale afforded to larger organizations. The benefits of a centralized management structure headquartered in Paris are realized through back-end functions and services such as compliance, human resources, property, strategic marketing, product development, sourcing, logistics, IT and invoicing systems, and retail strategy and management. As an experienced luxury group, Kering uses its expertize in retail real estate to locate and negotiate on the best store locations and terms, ensuring each of their brands has a presence in the appropriate retail districts and malls worldwide. Centralized management also helps optimize product assortment for differing retail formats as well as supporting recruitment for retail and store managers, who will be the public face of the brand.

In terms of marketing strategy, Kering has developed a multi-brand model in order to move into new segments through brand acquisitions, expanding the business without compromising the brand DNA of their flagship brand Gucci or their pillar brands Bottega Veneta, YSL and Balenciaga. By building a brand portfolio to include established brands with diverse aesthetics, such as Alexander McQueen and Stella McCartney, Kering is able to support its distinct creative visions and gain new customer bases for the group.

An important strand of the group's strategy is the ability to pair each of the brands' independent designers or creative directors with strong business executives, aiming for a perfect blend of design creativity with financial sustainability. Gucci's current success is attributed to its clarity of creative vision guided by its Creative Director Alessandro Michele, and its strong communication strategy. Although each brand has its distinctive brand identity and customer, lessons learned by one brand can benefit other Kering brands; for example, Gucci's digital innovation was ranked number one in the L2 Fashion Digital IQ Index in 2016.

Case Author: Natascha Radclyffe-Thomas

Case Challenge

Analyze the strategic capability that the Kering group companies have benefited from as a result of the holding group's ownership and organizational structure. Use Table 2.3 as a guide for this.

 ## ONLINE RESOURCES

A longer version of this case study, with additional challenges, can be found on our companion website: https://www.macmillanihe.com/companion/Varley_Fashion_Management.

 ## SUMMARY AND CONCLUDING THOUGHTS

We have used the simple concept of three Cs, context, capability and choice, to provide a framework for the complex idea of strategy. We can reflect on a fourth C, change, which is always present in strategic planning. We have seen that competitive advantage can emerge from external change agents, for example, changing consumer shopping patterns leading to greater customer engagement with online shopping. We can see that some firms who foresaw this trend and had more technology investment and more agile approaches were able to take advantage of change and gain competitive advantage. It is often the new entrants (like ASOS) who more easily exploit advantages as they are unencumbered by existing relationships and expectations. It is also clear that some firms have greater creative and innovative capabilities and will gain their competitive advantage in that way, for example, by reconfiguring design or supply chain processes (like Zara).

Perhaps competitive advantage as a concept is outdated and unachievable, perhaps even damaging as it encourages complacency. Instead, businesses could focus on riding a wave of temporary or transient advantage (McGrath, 2013), exploiting short-lived opportunities with speed and decisiveness to build the capabilities of people in knowledge and skills. The idea of doing things differently, however, underpins strategy and indeed underpins fashion itself. This fast moving industry is restless and reactive by its very nature. There is a debate about whether organizations do consciously make strategy or whether it just emerges as a reaction to the environment and actions of competitors (Porter and Kramer, 2006).

Pragmatically speaking, the Pareto principle applies here; probably 80% of realized strategy (what actually happens) is 'emergent' with around 20% being planned and intended by senior management.

Certainly fashion by its very nature is cyclical and some industry segments are fast moving, even exhibiting conditions of hyper-competition (D'Aveni, 1994), lending more importance to the need for strategic analysis. Ultimately the purpose of strategy is to direct the fashion business towards a successful future. By their long-term nature, all strategic decisions will have far reaching consequences so they must be carefully managed and implemented to ensure the organization is aligned to reduce risk (a concept we explore in depth in Chapter 13). A strategic plan helps the business use its resources efficiently to create value for its customers, leading to the end result of 'beating' their competition. Engaging in a process of strategy formulation is rather like a personal reflection, it helps the fashion business understand its strengths and weaknesses, allowing it to react to and change its environment, avoiding threats and exploiting advantages. In avoiding rigidity and allowing itself to be a learning organization, a fashion business can be successful.

CHALLENGES AND CONVERSATIONS

1. For a fashion brand of your choice:

    a. conduct an analysis of the macro- and micro-business environment in which it operates;

    b. consider the strength of the 5 competitive forces;

    c. provide a 4Ms analysis to assess key competences and capabilities;

    d. summarize your findings using a TOWS matrix to recommend the future strategic direction of your chosen brand.

2. Identify a fashion company that has successfully launched in the last 5 years. Apply the ERRC framework to analyze its successful formula in the market in which it operates.

3. Choose a fashion retailer that you consider to be successfully using a focused differentiation strategy. Suggest how the configuration of activities in its value chain supports this type of competitive advantage.

REFERENCES AND FURTHER READING

Aaker, D. (1991) *Managing Brand Equity: Capitalizing on the Value of a Brand Name*. New York: The Free Press.

Barney, J. (1991) Firm resources and sustained competitive advantage. *Journal of Management*, 17(1), pp. 99–120.

Barney, J. B. and Hesterly, W. S. (2014) *Strategic Management and Competitive Advantage: Concepts and Cases*, 4th edn. Upper Saddle River, NJ: Prentice Hall.

Bowman, C. (1995) *The Essence of Competitive Strategy*. Upper Saddle River, NJ: Prentice Hall.

Bruhn, M. and Georgi, D. (2006) *Services Marketing: Managing the Service Value Chain*. Harlow: Pearson Education.

Clulow, V., Gerstman, J. and Barry, C. (2003) The resource-based view and sustainable competitive advantage: The case of a financial services firm. *Journal of European Industrial Training*, 27(5), pp. 220–232.

D'Aveni, R. A. (1994) *Hypercompetition. Managing the Dynamics of Strategic Maneuvering*. New York: The Free Press.

Godin, S. (2011) Differentiating your brand in the digital world. Available from: http://fashionscollective.com/FashionAndLuxury/07/differentiating-your-brand-in-the-digital-world/ [accessed 24/09/2015].

Grant R. (2012) *Contemporary Strategic Analysis*, 8th edn. London: Wiley.

Hamel, G. and Prahalad, C. K. (1990) The core competence of the corporation. *Harvard Business Review*, 68(3), pp. 79–91.

Hitt, M. A., Hoskisson, R. E. and Ireland, D. (2007) *The Management of Strategy: Concepts and Cases*. Cincinnati, OH: Thomson/South Western.

Hoyle, D. (2005) *Automotive Quality Systems Handbook*. Oxford: Butterworth-Heinemann.

Johnson, G., Whittington, R. and Scholes, K. (2011) *Exploring Strategy*, 10th edn. Harlow: Pearson.

Kim, W. C. and Mauborgne, R. (2004) Blue Ocean strategy. *Harvard Business Review*, 82(10), pp. 76–84.

Kim, W. C. and Mauborgne, R. (2015) Red Ocean traps: The mental models that undermine market-creating strategies. *Harvard Business Review* (March), pp. 68–73.

Kotler, P. (2000) *Marketing Management – The Millennium Edition*, 10th edn. Upper Saddle River, NJ: Prentice Hall.

Kotler, P. (2003) *Marketing Management*, 11th edn. Upper Saddle River, NJ: Prentice Hall.

Kotler, P., Armstrong, G., Wong, V. and Saunders, J. (2008) *Principles of Marketing*, 5th European edn. London: Financial Times/Prentice Hall.

Kotler, P. and Armstrong, G. (2016) *Principles of Marketing*, 16th edn. Harlow: Pearson.

Kotler, P. and Keller, K. (2007) *A Framework for Marketing Management*, 3rd edn. Harlow: Pearson Education.

Law, K., Ming, Z., Ming, Z. and Leung, C. S. (2004) Fashion change and fashion consumption: The chaotic perspective. *Journal of Fashion Marketing and Management*, 8(4), pp. 362–374.

McGrath, R. (2013) Transient advantage. *Harvard Business Review*, 91(6), pp. 62–70.

Porter, M. E. (1980) *Competitive Strategy: Techniques for Analyzing Industries and Competitors*. New York: Free Press.

Porter, M. E. (1985) *Competitive Advantage*. New York: Free Press.

Porter, M. E. (1996) What is strategy? *Harvard Business Review*, November–December, p. 60.

Porter, M. E. and Kramer, M. R. (2006) Strategy and society: The link between competitive advantage and corporate social responsibility. *Harvard Business Review*, 12, pp. 78–92.

Posner, H. (2015) *Marketing Fashion: Strategy, Branding and Promotion*, 2nd edn. London: Laurence King.

Schultz, D. E. (2010) Battle-based marketing terminology: It's dead, dude! *Marketing News*, 44(15), p. 14.

Thomas, D. (2011) The battle for Hermès. Available at: https://www.wsj.com/articles/SB10001424053111903596904576517151602728260 [accessed 10/01/2017].

Walker, H. (2010) Swede Shop: How do H&M stay on top? Available at: https://www.independent.co.uk/life-style/fashion/features/swede-shop-how-do-hm-stay-on-top-2026039.html [accessed 14/12/2016].

West, D., Ford, J. and Ibrahim, E. (2010) *Strategic Marketing: Creating Competitive Advantage*, 2nd edn. Oxford: Oxford University Press.

FASHION MARKETING

3

Rosemary Varley

 INTRODUCTION

The term 'marketing' is somewhat ubiquitous these days, and in some cases used rather disparagingly in association with some of the negative issues associated with consumerism, but it is a fundamental concept when it comes to the strategic management of organizations; and for the fashion industry, which is so deeply connected to consumers in their thinking and their behaviour, a marketing orientation has proved to be a success factor. This chapter reinforces the underlying principles of marketing and builds them into a discussion of fashion marketing strategy and its link to the overall strategy of a corporation. It starts with an overview of the STP (segmentation, targeting and positioning) process, as the foundation of marketing strategies. It then suggests the blend of marketing operations (the marketing mix) that have relevance for fashion organizations today. The chapter moves on to consider the contributions that strategic product and market developments make to corporate strategy in the context of long-term business aims and concludes by suggesting that marketing innovation can drive fashion strategies. Very often, marketing activity, whether a campaign or a particular way of connecting with customers, is a route to competitive advantage via differentiation. This chapter lays the foundation for related chapters that follow in the book, including brand management in Chapter 6, marketing communications in Chapter 7 and customer management in Chapter 11.

 LEARNING OBJECTIVES

After studying this chapter, you should be able to understand:

- How marketing strategy is situated in the context of the overall strategic direction of a fashion corporation;

- The three key stages of the strategic marketing process: segmentation, targeting and positioning;

- The connection between corporate strategic direction and strategic marketing opportunities;

- Tools of analysis for marketing management (such as the marketing mix) within a strategic marketing plan for fashion organizations;

- How effective marketing can add strategic value and differentiate a fashion business.

3. 46615 Case study, BA (Hons) Illustration, London College of Fashion. Courtney Burnan, BA (Hons) Fashion Illustration, London College of Fashion. Photographer Alys Tomlinson. Copyright University of the Arts London.

FASHION MARKETING CONCEPTS

Many readers will be familiar with the fundamental concepts and principles of marketing. The American Marketing Association (AMA) approved the following definition in 2013: 'Marketing is the activity, set of institutions, and processes for creating, communicating, delivering and exchanging offerings that have value for customers, clients, partners, and society at large' (AMA, 2013), while the UK Chartered Institute of Marketing offers 'marketing is the management process responsible for identifying, anticipating and satisfying customer requirements profitably' (CIM, 2015). The AMA definition is wider and has value rather than profits as a central purpose, reflecting the acceptance and importance of a marketing orientation in organizations that are not solely profit motivated; however, the CIM definition more concisely maintains the customer at the heart of marketing and includes the idea of anticipating their requirements, which is a helpful concept when applying marketing theory to the fashion industry. The CIM goes on to state that marketing 'is a key management discipline that ensures producers of goods and services can interpret consumer desires and match, or exceed them'. Marketing has moved from an operational department to a central and strategic management aspect of companies of all sizes 'a frontline business attitude for all employees' (CIM, 2015).

The well-known concept of a marketing mix suggests that a successful marketing strategy requires the considered management of products, prices, places, promotions, people, processes and physical evidence. How the marketing mix elements might translate within the fashion context is discussed in detail later on in this chapter; it is the purpose of the mix to bring planning into action in order to achieve marketing aims and objectives.

As we discussed in Chapter 1, the relationship between fashion consumers, fashion producers, brands and fashion marketers is complex and sophisticated, and it may come as no surprise that fashion companies sometimes disrupt marketing principles

> **Marketing** 'Marketing is the activity, set of institutions, and processes for creating, communicating, delivering and exchanging offerings that have value for customers, clients, partners, and society at large' (AMA, 2013).

> **Target customer** The customer for whom goods and services should be matched against their wants, needs and desires.

> **Market segment** Groups of consumers who have identifiable similarities in their wants, needs, desires, and preferences.

with varying levels of success. Easey (2009: 7) suggests that fashion marketing is different because of the 'very nature of fashion, where change is intrinsic', and also because of the emphasis on design both in product development and in defining customer needs. For example, a picture of a dress worn by a celebrity on social media or a coat in a new season's colour featured in a window display can create demand surges that would normally only be possible by implementing a major advertising campaign or a significant price reduction. Nevertheless, established strategic marketing theory provides a starting point for understanding the contribution marketing makes to strategic fashion management and the development of fashion organizations.

THE STP (SEGMENTATION, TARGETING AND POSITIONING) PROCESS

One of the backbones of a marketing strategy is the STP (Segmenting, Targeting, Positioning) model, conceptualized by marketing guru Kotler in 1997. This three-stage planning process is based on the well-known and often quoted premise that if you try to please all customers all of the time, you end up pleasing no-one. In their description of marketing as a management discipline, CIM introduces the idea of a target customer, for whom goods and services should be matched against their wants, needs and desires. If groups of consumers who have similarities in their wants, needs, desires, and preferences can be identified, working with those customers (the market segment) to bring satisfactory and viable marketing relationships through the creation of 'offerings of value' (AMA, 2013) becomes a more effective and efficient way of doing business. Many commentators would argue that no one 'needs' fashion; however, in most societies clothing satisfies the need to be clothed and therefore physiologically comfortable. In addition, consumer wants and desires for fashionable clothing can be related to the more complex motivation to belong to social groups (Maslow, 1954: 236). These social groups can therefore be useful when considering fashion market segments.

West et al. (2015) provide a 'visual blueprint' to demonstrate the STP process within the wider context of strategic marketing, planning and implementation (see Figure 3.1).

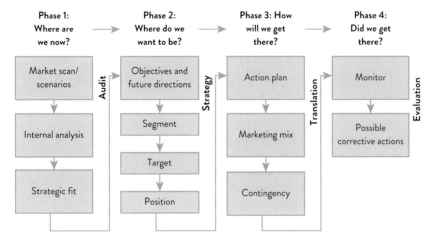

Figure 3.1 *Competitive Marketing Strategy Blueprint*

Source: West, D. C., Ford, J. and Ibrahim, E., Strategic Marketing: Creating Competitive Advantage. 2nd edn. Oxford, Oxford University Press, © 2015. Figure 1.8 'Marketing Strategy Blueprint' (p. 20). Permission of Oxford University Press.

SEGMENTATION

It has become common practice for fashion companies to use a variety of characteristics on which to base the process of breaking down, or segmenting, a market population into smaller consumer groups. Once a group has been identified and understood (not a small task), then a marketing mix can be devised that will appeal to this group, resulting in the fashion brand becoming **positioned** in the customer's mind as one that is 'right' for them. In the context of strategic management, Quinn et al. (2007) suggest that by focusing on those buyers that fashion brands have the greatest chance of satisfying, segmentation can enhance marketing effectiveness and the benefit from marketing opportunities.

Segmentation of fashion markets

In a fast moving and fragmented market such as fashion, grouping customers is challenging. In addition, fashion consumers, by their very nature, can be fickle and unpredictable in their purchasing behaviour. Quinn et al. (2007) suggest that if this market context is ignored in the strategic approaches used, then marketing initiatives are likely to be unsuccessful. Figure 3.2 summarizes the theoretical and rationalized strategic segmentation process. It begins with the identification of market segments, for whom organizational resources are allocated (in the form of a marketing mix, for example). Segment performance is then measured and the identified segments can be analyzed, tracked, and fine-tuned as required.

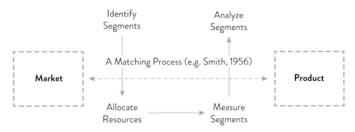

Figure 3.2 *A summary of the strategic segmentation process*

Source: Quinn, L., Hines, T. and Bennison, D. 'Making sense of market segmentation: a fashion retailing case', European Journal of Marketing, Vol. 41/5–6 pp. 439–465, 2007, Emerald Insight, https://doi.org/10.1108/03090560710737552.

Demographic and psychographic segmentation

Traditional demographic bases for segmentation can work as a starting point for identifying similar fashion consumers; Solomon and Rabolt (2009) use the term 'subcultures' in their extensive discussion of fashion consumer groups and break these down into demographic subcultures that have evolved around age, race and ethnicity and demographic subcultures that relate to income and social class. However, many brands have found that a rigid use of demographic factors does not work well enough to be useful to a fashion company for consumer grouping. At least two generations can happily shop together in fast fashion retailers like Topshop or Zara; wealthy people love finding a bargain in Primark or Target; a young graduate with low disposable income may save up for weeks to buy a luxury handbag, while octogenarians feature in fashion magazines. Segmentation bases such as the way consumers like to shop are therefore very relevant for fashion brands when attempting to 'profile' (identify and understand) their customers. The use of psychographic segmentation, made famous by the VALS (values and lifestyles) consumer groupings (Mitchell, 1983), suggests that customers' purchasing of preference is based on a combination of measurable and intangible consumer attributes, and this would appear to make sense in the fashion industry where both tangible and emotional attributes are blended in product offerings.

> **Gender fluidity** The acceptance that people do not necessarily conform to the male and female gender divide, but that gender is more like a spectrum along which people can be placed and can move.

> **Psychographic segmentation** The use of psychological variables such as attitudes, values, and fashion orientation combined with behavioural differences such as lifestyle, to group consumers.

Gender segmentation

It may be obvious to state that gender is a useful basis for fashion segmentation; although unisex and androgyny are both well understood in fashion trends and product development, gender is often important in terms of providing parameters in shape or silhouette, fit, style and colour. Gender is not only influential in terms of product attribute, but in attitudes towards shopping processes and environments (Yurchisin and Johnson, 2010), and therefore may be important in the management and styling of retail outlets. Nike's flagship stores, for example, have been criticized for being masculine and aggressive and off-putting to female customers (Warner, 2002), which resulted in Nike opening specific stores for women and more recently an increased emphasis on fashionable 'athleisure'. The acceptance of gender fluidity is a growing societal phenomenon in many regions across the globe, which has been reflected in fashion collections, catwalk shows and media campaigns.

Geographical segmentation

Another way of segmenting consumers is by using geographical regions or location; in particular, this has been historically important in a retail marketing context. Geographical segmentation can contribute to the broader strategic aim of managing geographical expansion, where understanding consumers is part of a wider accumulation of knowledge about how markets in different regions or countries operate. Again, whilst this is useful to consider for fashion companies, many fashion brands, particularly those in the luxury sector, are international in their outlook, referred to by Solomon and Rabolt (2009: 68) as an 'etic perspective'. In addition, online fashion marketers have reduced the impact of distance as an influencing factor. The locational preferences of omni-channel consumers are an area of shopping behaviour research that will continue to have relevance in the context of geographical segmentation of fashion consumers. Ko et al. (2007) refer to the emergence of a global fashion consumer culture with groups of consumers exhibiting similarities to people in other nations in terms of lifestyle and consumption patterns, leading to fashion segments that cut across national boundaries. In particular, global digital marketing communications are likely to influence a converging of preferences in fashion products, brands and shopping behaviour, as discussed further in Chapter 7.

Fashion lifestyle segmentation

The use of lifestyle segmentation is often seen in practice in the fashion industry. In such a crowded and fragmented market, differentiating on the basis of a finely tuned understanding of lifestyle preference has produced successful brands such as Ralph Lauren, Hollister, Top Shop, and Seasalt. Fashion lifestyle segmentation uses consumer attitudes, interests, and opinions related to the purchase of fashion products as a basis for consumer grouping (Ko et al., 2007). An early study by Shim and Bickle (1994) purported three fashion lifestyle segments. These were described as the 'symbolic and instrumental segment', who were deemed to be young, innovative, and fashion-conscious; the so-called 'practical and conservative segment' motivated by comfort and function and who show little enjoyment of fashion shopping; and finally, the 'apathetic segment', whose shopping habits show a preponderance for discount stores.

Kim and Lee (2000) suggested that fashion lifestyle was influenced by the consumer characteristics of price-consciousness, fashion-consciousness, information seeking, self-confidence, attitudes toward local stores, and time-consciousness, while Lee et al. (2004) divide shoppers into four segments based on fashion lifestyle – the aesthetic group, the economic fashion innovator group, the showy uncritical group, and the fashion-uninterested group. Both of these studies were conducted in the context of home shopping and although there is no agreement yet about fashion lifestyle segment definition, the concept seems to be prevalent in practice. For example, in spring 2016, the brand Hollister made reference to the travelling lifestyle in the content of their online shop; for males the message was 'carve your own path in vibrant travel-inspired trends' whilst for women it was 'wish and wander – endless possibilities lie just over the horizon'.

The fashion consumer as an innovator

Although the scope of this text does not allow for an in-depth study of consumer behaviour in fashion (see, for example, Solomon and Rabolt, 2009, or Yurchisin and Johnson, 2010), it is perhaps worth noting the theory of the diffusion of innovations in the context of segmentation and targeting in the fashion industry. This well-established theory (the Diffusion of Innovations model, see Rogers, 2003) acknowledges that not all consumers adopt new or innovative products and ideas at the same rate. It is suggested that there are five different categories into which consumers can be placed according to their

likelihood of adopting an innovation: innovators, early adopters, early majority, late majority and laggards. As the fashion industry depends, rightly or wrongly, on the continual adoption of new shapes, colours and styles, the identification of consumers that conform to the early categories of Innovators and Early Adopters, who the theory suggests account for 2.5% and 13.5% of a population respectively, is important for targeting the fashion enthusiast. The context of the adopter profile should be specific as consumers may not adopt innovations in different product categories at the same rate, but generally innovator consumers and early adopters tend to be risk takers, to have higher education and income levels and to be socially active. They are also likely to be opinion leaders, and therefore in today's society, where vast amounts of visual information are shared, these consumers will be influential in the process of introducing and popularizing new looks. According to Marr (2015: 70), more than 45 million pictures are uploaded to Instagram every day and although fashion products will not be in all of them, those fashion images endorsed by innovators and early adopters can be valuable to marketers for identifying the adoption of new trends and looks.

> **Innovator consumer**
> Likely to be a risk taker, have higher education and income levels, be socially active and opinionated.

TARGETING

The concepts of market segmentation and customer targeting go hand in hand. By identifying customers who have particular needs, wants and desires, a segment of the wider consumer market can be made the target of a marketing mix (see later section in this chapter). This means that offerings are developed with that customer in mind at a price that will appeal; the target customer becomes the focus of communications, and the offering is delivered in a place or by a process that the target customer enjoys. Using research to more accurately portray the target customer group will lead to a more effective allocation of resources in order to reach that customer. In a study on the UK bridge brand Reiss, Quinn et al. (2007) found 'the identification and pursuit of the market potential for a women's wear product range represented an effort to increase the company's targeting precision, which is argued to be particularly useful to design teams and in-store sales staff'.

The practice of systematic segmentation and targeting is perhaps more widely referred to in theoretical sources than it is used in practice in the fashion industry. Quinn et al. (2007) uncovered the use of intuition and tacit knowledge in fashion segmentation, combined with the use of a strongly defined brand identity (see Chapter 6) to which consumers can relate. A more pragmatic approach to segmentation and targeting, allowing for an intuitive understanding of a brand and its competitors, and flexibility in the light of the dynamic nature of the industry, is likely to be more beneficial for fashion brands. At the heart of this practice is the concept of positioning.

POSITIONING

Positioning, as the final stage of the STP process, is considered a very important concept in strategic fashion marketing and it is one of the most creative aspects of fashion marketing management. It can become the focus of decision-making at corporate level because it may be part of a directional strategy, for example, to reposition a brand or reinforce a position which has become unclear. Positioning is therefore at the heart of strategic fashion management. It is not an easy concept to define, however, and is used in a number of different ways in the context of market analysis.

One of the most accessible aspects of positioning to grasp is the idea of price positioning. In the fashion market, prices are used to position different companies against each other in the same product category. Jeans is a good category to use as it is very obvious that jeans can range from budget basics at a few dollars to very carefully detailed jeans which sell for a few hundred dollars. Between these two extremes, other mainstream and luxury jeans brands are positioned at different price levels. However, price and detail are not the only attributes that customers use to decide which jeans are of interest. What also matters in this purchase is what brand is attached, and it is the emotional qualities that go with a brand (such as 'cool', or 'hip' or 'tough') that most effectively separate out different jeans that may look very similar in terms of price or detail. Positioning is therefore about what is done inside a customer's mind (Ries and Trout, 2001) and setting an offering in a mental space that is appealing in a multi-dimensional way to the target customer. It is the particular blend of tangible and intangible attributes that appeals and

> **Positioning** Setting an offering in a mental space that is appealing in a multi-dimensional way to the target customer, using a blend of tangible and intangible attributes.

when successfully applied, particularly in fashion markets, the positioning appeal can actually define a customer segment.

As effective positioning is often achieved by layering emotional benefits onto tangible brand aspects in order to be held in a unique place in a consumer's mind, it therefore concerns how a brand is perceived by the consumer, which may in turn be heavily influenced by how a brand is communicated. Positioning also concerns the identity and image of a brand, where customers' experiences inform and sculpt the mental space.

Positioning in a fragmented market such as fashion clothing is a highly relevant strategy; the concept of fashion itself is ethereal, emotive and leans towards the intangible. Small details can position a fashion product as hip and cool, in contrast to something similar, which might be considered quite basic. Fashion brands therefore use a vast range of features and benefits to etch out a position that is appealing and relevant to the targeted consumer segment. These might be, for example, aspects of the merchandise itself (quality, styling, uniqueness), prices, personality (derived from brand identity and brand communication, see Mini Case Study 3.1), and service. These will vary according to the market level of the fashion company and its organizational structure; for example, positioning on the basis of service may have most relevance for a retail orientated fashion brand. Figure 3.3 demonstrates the use of two positioning attributes; in this hypothetical case, the appeal to different age groups and the styling of the brand in terms of formality and informality. The figure demonstrates some white space where a viable gap in the market may exist, and the clustering of the circles suggests which brands are closest to each other and therefore competitive in terms of their perceived brand appeal.

Positioning is not only a multi-dimensional concept, but it is also a relative one, as can be seen in Figure 3.3. The consumer mind-space is crowded with other brands; therefore positioning also needs to be used to differentiate the brand from competitors by creating and maintaining a distinctive and valued image in the target customer's mind relative to them. According to Aaker and McCloughlin (2007: 223), a strategic position is 'the face of the business strategy, [which] specifies how the business aspires to be perceived (by its customers, employees and partners) relative to its competitors and market'.

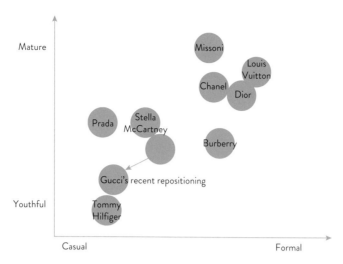

Figure 3.3 *A positioning map demonstrating attributes of selected luxury fashion brands*

Source: Based on author's own perception, for illustrative purposes only.

 MINI CASE STUDY 3.1 - The strategic positioning of Diesel

Diesel describes itself as an innovative international lifestyle company. Born in 1978, Diesel set the precedence for premium denim-wear, and has since expanded to offer a wide range of men's and women's casual clothing and accessories. Strikingly innovative and often provocative advertising has been the handwriting of the Diesel brand and this has helped to differentiate Diesel in an ever increasingly crowded market. A strong brand message is at the heart of their marketing strategy, used to communicate what the founder Renzo Rosso believes the brand stands for: passion, individuality and self-expression (diesel.com, 2016).

In 2010, Diesel launched a campaign called 'Be Stupid', which was run on posters, in magazines and via digital media. Although the campaign won a top award at the Cannes advertising festival, the UK Advertising Standards Authority (ASA) banned one of a series of images from being used on a poster, although it was cleared to be printed in magazines. The image showed a young woman at the top of a ladder lifting her top up to a security camera to create surprise in anyone viewing the CCTV footage! The ASA received complaints that the images were offensive and unsuitable to be seen by children, and condoned or encouraged antisocial behaviour. Diesel defended the campaign by describing it as 'a very strong and unexpected image of femininity'.

More recently in 2013, Diesel was innovative again by using photographic portraits of up and coming creatives in the world of art and fashion, instead of professional models, in their advertising. The creative director Nicola Formichetti expressed his idea as follows: 'Visually I wanted to highlight the individual beauty of our community. It was less about capturing fashion and more about getting an insight into these people's souls' (Formichetti, cited in www.wonderlandmagazine.com, 23 August 2013 [accessed 05/02/2016]). This campaign was part of a wider brand 'reboot', acknowledged to be necessary by Rossi, who admitted in 2014 that the brand had become 'tired'.

The new strategic direction in 2013 included revamping the product range to focus more on quality and style, with an increased emphasis on women's wear, which was said to have suffered because Diesel is perceived to be a brand skewed towards the male consumer. The sub-brand Diesel Black Gold was also given a central role in unlocking the potential to grow the women's side of the business. Attention has also been paid to the retail side of the business with refurbishment of key stores in order to help refresh the brand image. According to Bogliolo (Diesel's Chief Executive), the campaign is part of a strategy to reboot rather than 'reposition', which is considered to be too corporate a term for Diesel; aiming to recreate the unique brand aura that Diesel had in the past. In the words of Rosso, 'we think to be cool is better than to be big' (Rosso, cited in businessoffashion.com, 2014).

Diesel continues to make provocative cultural and societal references in advertising content. In spring 2017 the use of the campaign straplines 'Make Love Not Walls' and 'You got walls? We got wrecking balls' was a commentary on an era 'where fear is making the world divided by walls' (Rosso, quoted in Zargani, 2017).

Sources: http://www.creativeadawards.com/diesel-be-stupid-advertising-campaign/
Zargani, L. (2017) 'Diesel Promotes Love, Not Walls in Spring Ads'. WWD, 14 February 2017.

LIMITATIONS OF THE STP CONCEPT FOR FASHION

The STP process is a useful framework for fashion marketing management; however, fashion consumers often fail to behave predictably and rationally and so a rigid approach to segmentation, targeting and positioning may cause a fashion organization to overlook some marketing opportunities. External influences such as serendipitous endorsement can provide unchartered opportunities that should be grasped and developed. The intuitive approach to segmentation and customer understanding mentioned earlier fits well with the concept of emergent strategy discussed in the previous chapter and is very relevant in the context of fashion marketing. Furthermore, it is suggested that the generation of 'big data' for marketers to drill into could provide the opportunity to discover 'gems' about customers. 'In data discovery you just look at data with no questions or agenda to see what the data tells you about your business' (Marr, 2015).

The Ansoff matrix A summary of alternative ways in which companies can grow and develop, based on strategic decisions concerning products offered and markets targeted.

STRATEGIC MARKETING OPPORTUNITIES

The relationship between corporate strategy and marketing strategy is often so close that it can be difficult to separate the two; especially as most fashion companies have a high level of marketing orientation in their philosophy. Strategic decisions at the level of the marketing function can be broadly classified as those concerning products, those concerning markets, and the relationship between the two (positioning). One of the reasons why the marketing function within organizations has grown to be of such relevance to an overall corporate strategy is that decisions that concern the direction and orientation at corporate level are very often those that also concern products, customer markets and positioning. Marketing departments are therefore instrumental in both implementing and guiding strategy.

One of the best-known strategy models is Ansoff's (1988) product/market matrix, which was originally devised to provide a clear and easily understood summary of alternative ways in which companies could grow and develop (see Figure 3.4). These alternatives are based on strategic decisions concerning the products that are offered and markets that are targeted. The original **Ansoff matrix** delineates between existing and new in terms of products and markets. Over time and with increasingly numerous applications and iterations, the delineation between existing and new products has been found rather prescriptive. For example, the introduction of a new product for a fashion company is rarely strategically significant; fashion product ranges change regularly and frequently and it is only when a fashion organization is considering the introduction of a new product *category* that this becomes a decision of strategic significance. The idea of a new market is also rather a blunt tool for strategic decisions about customers because market development can often be about adopting new ways of reaching additional customers with existing needs, wants and desires, as well as finding completely new customer markets.

In spite of these limitations, this matrix has endured over time for its conceptual logic and, as a framework for a marketing strategy that involves customers and products in the context of the product/market framework, it is suitable for most fashion organizations. Without this level of planning, a company can lack direction and purpose, which may result in stakeholder disenchantment.

Figure 3.4 *Ansoff's product/market matrix*
Source: Based on Ansoff (1988).

Market development strategy

Identifying viable groups of customers in a global context means that segmentation concepts have to be blended with a wider analysis of market variables in order to assess how attractive an international market is as a growth opportunity. This analysis is considered in more detail in the next chapter.

Maintain position and penetrate the market

The Ansoff matrix suggests that, in terms of strategic intent, one alternative course of action could be to maintain a current market position; with a product/ service offer that is already familiar and successful and appeals to a market segment which is viable, and possibly growing naturally due to external factors, this would appear to be a sensible and resource-efficient strategy. The danger associated with this course of action is the threat of competitive behaviour whereby alternative brands will attempt to steal market share. It follows therefore that protection of this position is likely to require some marketing activity simply to maintain it. This is vital for fashion brands, where customer loyalty is rarely strong and easily broken. Marketing communication activity that reiterates and reinforces brand benefits and promotes loyalty is continuously required. In

an overall healthy product market, a strategy of 'no change' may still present considerable operational challenges, such as maintaining availability and customer service standards, but in a stagnant product market situation a defensive, possibly aggressive stance may be necessary to consolidate and protect existing business or steal the market share of weak competitors.

Product development

Given the dangers of a 'no change' plan, it is no surprise that fashion companies will choose some form of growth plan even if with that intent comes risk and the need for new resources. For example, launching new ranges in previously unoccupied complementary product categories is a very common way for fashion companies to attempt to make additional sales. Strategic analysis and auditing will provide the input to a risk assessment of such a move, because the launch of a new range normally requires resource input in terms of design and/or buying expertize, the establishment of a new supplier base, the investment of selling space and so on, all of which will take resources from existing operations or require additional investment. The extent to which a fashion company remains a product category specialist or extends a brand depends on the ambitions of a brand strategy. The simple product development box of the Ansoff matrix does not adequately represent the complexity of some fashion brand development and extension strategies such as those of Armani, where brand stretching has gone hand in hand with customer market extensions and entirely new product market entries that suggest diversification (see Case Study 3 on Armani, below).

Product development in new markets

As mentioned previously, identifying and profiling a customer is part of the STP process; if the existing targeted customer segment is not sufficient to provide the desired rate of growth, a course of action that could be taken is that of appealing to more customers with the same product range. Although this sounds like a logical plan, this is often difficult to achieve for a fashion brand or company without additional product development. A fashion retailer could embark on a store expansion programme or develop new channels to reach customers further afield. However, geo-political boundaries and cultural differences can make what might appear to be similar segments unviable due to operational difficulties or nuanced differences in consumer preference. This can make market development very challenging without some adaptations to the product and/or service offer.

A common approach to market development in fashion companies is to launch specific ranges to appeal to new customer segments; for example, women's wear, men's wear, children's wear, more fashion forward, outsize, petite and so on. The extent to which this might be considered product development, market development or even diversification depends on the extent to which new resources are required to service the new customer group. For example, if a women's wear brand was able to design a men's range without the need for a new designer and supply base, and/or was able to sell the range through the same outlets or channels, this would be considered product development for the company. If, on the other hand, the development of a fashion forward range required a new product development team and dedicated retail outlets then this would probably be considered a diversification for that company.

> **Marketing mix** The blending of marketing activities according to a chosen product/market strategy.

Diversification

The Ansoff matrix suggests that diversification is where an organization enters new customer markets with new products. Traditionally diversification is considered to be a high-risk strategy due to unfamiliarity of customer preference and behaviour and the need to invest in new resources to produce new products. Some fashion organizations appear to have diversified widely, such as Armani into hotels and eating establishments. However, the customer for these additional Armani products and services is likely to have similar characteristics to the Armani customer for fashion clothing. The fact that successful product/market strategies can vary so much in terms of what they mean for individual companies again makes the delineation of the Ansoff matrix difficult to apply in the context of the fashion industry; however, we expand our discussion of the matrix in Chapter 4 in the context of corporate growth, as a base from which to explore strategies for growth and development in more detail.

MANAGING FASHION MARKETING: THE MIX

Marketing management is concerned with the coordination of marketing activities within the strategic marketing plan. Many readers will already be familiar with the concept of a marketing mix, which is the blend of those marketing activities under the operational guidance of a chosen product/market strategy. Most marketing texts acknowledge Borden (1965) as the first writer to use the idea of a mix of marketing activities that are blended to create a viable marketing plan; whereas the articulation of what these component activities comprised was famously encapsulated by McCarthy (1964) in the 4P framework – the blend of product, pricing, promotional and place/distribution plans. In a short space of time three further aspects of a marketing strategy were added with particular reference to the marketing of service orientated offers: people, physical evidence and process (Booms and Bitner, 1981). In the fashion context this was especially relevant because retail orientated brands have been so dominant in the fashion industry, and this extended services mix could be successfully applied to them. Although the concept of 'the mix' is a little dated, it does provide a systematic way of thinking through marketing offers. In particular, the idea of 'promoting' a product has become a narrow concept, overtaken by the idea of marketing communications, and as more and more of these communications have become digital the practice of managing active and dynamic marketing relationships between brands and consumers is how the modern fashion industry operates (Kotler et al., 2017).

Table 3.1 provides a marketing mix framework, devised in particular for fashion companies or brands. For some readers this may be a revision exercise because the marketing plan is a familiar concept to many students of business and management; however, inclusivity and details are vital ingredients in fashion marketing plans, and so we make no apology for including such a framework at this point in this text.

Product	Brand names, including the designer's name, sub-brands, range planning, categories, design handwriting, quality level, specialization, product and brand lifecycles, sustainability aspects
Pricing	Price level (luxury, bridge, mass market, value, discounter), range entry and exit prices, markdown (price reduction) timing and extent, price/value relationship
Promotions/Communications	Direct to consumer (internet, mail), through media (TV, print, internet, owned and public space), messages and content, reach and frequency, planned and unplanned endorsements, social networks
Place/Distribution	Own retail, wholesale, concessions, online and physical, national, international
People	Sales personnel, company ambassadors, spokespeople (including corporate leadership), advocates, creative direction
Process	Retail and wholesale sales process, online and personal sales process, multi-channel options
Physical evidence	The augmented product (labelling carrier bag, wrapping and packaging), store design, retail atmospherics, visual merchandising

Table 3.1 *The fashion marketing mix*

MARKETING CHANNELS – THE VERTICAL CHANNEL CONCEPT

Many fashion products have long and complex supply and demand chains in the transformation from raw materials to finished goods for consumption. A marketing strategy can involve brand aspects that can add consumer value at many points in this process, as shown in Figure 3.5.

Traditionally, what can be thought of as a 'manufacturing brand' designs and makes a product and this set-up can still be seen frequently in the fashion industry. The producer may also sell their product through their own retail outlets, or they may alternatively rely on a network of retail partners to get their products to consumers. John Smedley, for example, produce high quality knitwear in their own factory, claimed to be the oldest in the world (www.johnsmedley.com, 2016). Their products are sold through their own stores, department stores, online multi-brand retailers and specialty boutiques (see Case Study 8 in Chapter 8). Many fashion brands, however, do not actually manufacture products, and do not own a factory. Huge organizations like Nike, H&M, and Michael Kors, for example, do not own any factories but design and engineer their products to the finest detail, commission factories selected from a global supply base to make them, and then retail through their own and/or other retail outlets. The variety of combinations of organizations, skills, and networks that feature within fashion marketing channels is

Raw Materials value e.g. organic cotton, cool-wool, luxury fibres	Design Process value e.g. skill and vision of designers, engineering to price points, co-creation with customers	Production Process value e.g. fast style turnaround, flexible factories, craftsmanship	Retail Outlet value e.g. best locations, designed environment, window and in-store display, sales service interactive website	Communications value e.g. branding via emotive imagery, strong relationships via social media	Relationship Marketing value e.g. after sales service; customer relationship management

Figure 3.5 *Adding marketing value in the fashion supply and demand chain*

perhaps one of the most interesting aspects of the fashion industry. Fashion companies are amongst those with the highest values of brand equity, much of which is built on the strength of branding and marketing expertize, rather than functional activities such as producing or retailing. In fact, innovative marketing concepts are often the cornerstones of successful fashion organizations, particularly in the digital era. Companies such as Asos, Net-a-Porter, FarFetch, Fabletics and Vigga (see Case Study 15) started up using non-traditional marketing channel models which found easy acceptance and adoption by the fashion-orientated and innovative consumer.

CASE STUDY 3 - Armani: The stretching and extending of a fashion brand empire

Fashion businesses, particularly those at the luxury level, rely on the 'halo effect' or power of their founder's name and the associated brand heritage to retain established clients and engage new customers; Giorgio Armani is one such company. The Armani stable of brands serves as an interesting example of the power of a designer name brand, whereby a fashion designer has been able to leverage a strong brand identity and to increase their market reach through lucrative brand expansions across a wide range of product categories.

Following a stint as a buyer and window dresser at Milan's iconic La Rinascente department store, Giorgio Armani launched the eponymous brand in 1975, starting with a men's wear collection, and growing this over 40 years into a global luxury fashion lifestyle conglomerate. As early as 1979 Armani launched the diffusion lines Giorgio Armani Le Collezioni or 'white label', Mani the line for professional dress, as well as the Borgonuovo label also known as 'black label'. Armani was an early practitioner of celebrity endorsement and has established close links with Hollywood, whether it is designing costumes for screen idols such as Richard Gere in the 1980s film 'American Gigolo' or becoming a regular red-carpet choice for Hollywood actors including Julia Roberts and Michelle Pfeiffer. Subsequently, Armani expanded the fashion offer and established himself as a master of mass luxury retailing with extensions across women's wear, men's wear and children's wear as well as the premium sportswear label EA7.

It is said that Giorgio Armani, now in his eighties, maintains a tight control over every manifestation of the Armani brand in his brand stable, which is no mean feat when each of the brand extensions has its own marketing mix. The Armani brand is built on three pillars: class, quality and exclusivity, while a whole array of sub-brands has been designed under the parent umbrella brand, which catered to different market segments and product specialisms.

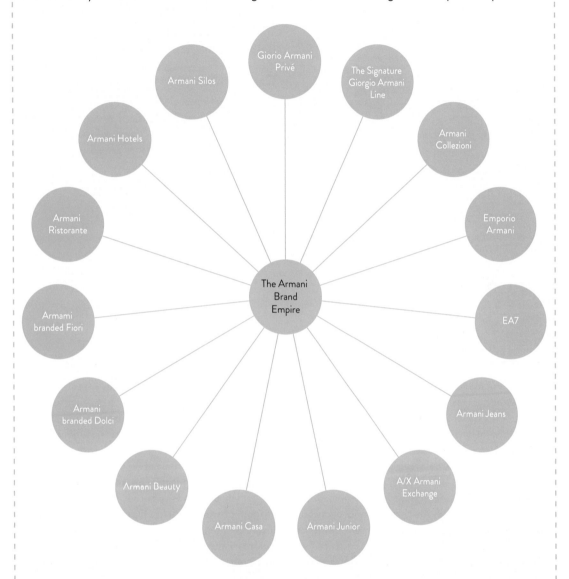

Although Armani remains in private ownership, it had, in common with other fashion businesses, entered into joint ventures and licensing agreements in order to develop its product offer and market reach. Maintaining core brand identity through brand aesthetic and variations of the Armani name and logo, each new line was targeted at a specific segment and was supported by its own distinct brand communications and retail experience. Locations such as Hong Kong's Chater House showcased the total Armani brand portfolio, seeing not only the fashion lines Giorgio Armani and Emporio Armani for men and women, but also Giorgio Armani Cosmetics, Armani Junior childrenswear, Armani Fiori florists, Armani Dolci confectionery created in collaboration with Venchi, a specialist Italian chocolate manufacturer, the Armani Acqua restaurant and Armani Privé. Elsewhere, in Dubai, the world's first Armani Hotel opened in Burj Khalifa in partnership with Dubai-based Emaar Properties. Closer to home, Armani opened the Armani Hotel Milan in the same 1930s building on the via Manzoni that houses the Armani flagship store. Milan is the spiritual home of the

Armani brand and as well as its retail and hotel properties, it is the location of the Teatro Armani and the Armani Silos creative arts spaces and home to the Armani archives.

In 2017 a restructure of the Armani brand portfolio was announced with the intention of simplifying product offer and communications for its contemporary customers. The new brand portfolio proposal targets three distinct customer groups: the primary line Giorgio Armani will now encompass the brand's luxury offer, comprising the haute couture Armani Privé collection, Women's, Men's as well as Armani Casa design, and the interiors line. Emporio Armani will now include Armani Collezioni and Armani Jeans. The A/X Armani Exchange line continues to provide fashion products aimed at the younger, urban customer.

Case Author: Natascha Radclyffe-Thomas

Case Challenge

Using the Product/Market Matrix (see Figure 3.4), plot the brand extensions within the Armani portfolio to show how product and market development has taken place. Would you consider any of the Armani sub-brand developments to be a diversification strategy?

ONLINE RESOURCES

A longer version of this case study, with additional challenges, can be found on our companion website: https://www.macmillanihe.com/companion/Varley_Fashion_Management.

SUMMARY AND CONCLUDING THOUGHTS

Marketing management plays a very significant part in strategic fashion management. It is often difficult, especially in more recent years where digital innovations drive marketing practice, to separate marketing strategy from strategic marketing, and in many ways it makes no sense to do so. Strategic marketing planning stops a fashion company losing sight of customers being at the centre of long-term thinking and decision-making. This will then guide the direction of marketing strategy and resource allocation to marketing activity. Most fashion companies would describe themselves as marketing-led, and insist that 'customers are at the heart of everything we do', but if this were the case, why do so many companies have problems with unwanted stock, and why do successful fashion brands appear to lose their desirability? A deeper understanding of the fashion industry reveals that the drive, ambition and intuition of marketers (as well as owners, leaders and designers) can sometimes fizzle out and what began as positive forces can become misguided and hubristic. Having organizational and resource-management structures in place that help the marketing function remain entirely relevant and central to strategic fashion management is vital for the smooth development and especially international growth of fashion brands.

CHALLENGES AND CONVERSATIONS

1. Use the STP framework to analyze the marketing strategy of a chosen fashion brand.

2. Consider growth options that have been taken by a fashion company of your choice in recent (for example 5) years and demonstrate how strategic marketing campaigns have supported this. (You could use the L'Oréal Case Study, Case Study 4 in Chapter 4, for this challenge.)

3. Review the benefits and drawbacks of the marketing mix concept and apply it to a fashion lifestyle brand of your choice.

4. Define the concept of positioning and, using examples, suggest why this is such an important aspect of strategic fashion marketing.

5. To what extent do you agree that fashion companies need to be marketing-led to be successful? You could use the definitions of marketing given at the start of this chapter to help you frame this discussion.

 REFERENCES AND FURTHER READING

Aaker, D. A. and McCloughlin, D. (2007) *Strategic Market Management*, European Edition. New York: Wiley.

Alexander, N. and Doherty, A. M. (2008) *International Retailing*. Oxford: Oxford University Press.

AMA (2013) American Marketing Association. Available at: https://www.ama.org/aboutama/pages/definition-of-marketing.aspx [accessed 06/07/2016].

Ansoff, I. (1988) *The New Corporate Strategy*. New York: John Wiley & Sons.

Booms, B. H. and Bitner, M. J. (1981) 'Marketing strategies and organization structures for service firms', in Donnelly, J. H. and George, W. R. (eds) *Marketing of Services*. Chicago, IL: American Marketing Association, pp. 47–51.

Borden, N. H. (1965) 'The concept of the Marketing Mix', in Schwartz, G (ed.) *Science in Marketing*. New York: Wiley.

CIM (2015) Chartered Institute of Marketing. Available at: http://www.cim.co.uk/files/7ps.pdf [accessed 06/07/2016].

Easey, M. (2009) *Fashion Marketing*, 3rd edn. Chichester: Wiley.

Ebeltoft (2014) Retail Internationalization Report. Available at: www.ebeltoftgroup.com [accessed 15/04/2015].

Kim, Y. K. and Lee, J. (2000) 'Benefit segmentation of catalog shoppers among professionals'. *Clothing and Textiles Research Journal*, 18(2), pp. 111–120.

Ko, E., Kim, E., Taylor, C. R., Kim, K. H. and Kang, L. J. (2007) 'Cross-national market segmentation in the fashion industry'. *International Marketing Review*, 24(5), pp. 629–651.

Kotler, P. (1997) *Marketing Management: Analysis, Planning, Implementation and Control*, 9th edn. Upper Saddle River, NJ: Prentice Hall.

Kotler, P., Kartajaya, H. and Setiawan, I. (2017) *Marketing 4.0: Moving from Traditional to Digital*, Hoboken, NJ: Wiley.

Lee, S. I., Park, H. J. and Chung, H. Y. (2004) 'The impact of TV-home shoppers' fashion lifestyle on fashion goods purchasing'. *Journal of the Korean Society of Clothing & Textiles*, 28(1), pp. 54–65.

Marr, B. (2015) *Big Data*. Chichester: Wiley.

Maslow, A. (1954) *Motivation and Personality*. New York, NY: Harper.

McCarthy, J. E. (1964) *Basic Marketing. A Managerial Approach*. Homewood, IL: Irwin.

McDonald, M. and Dunbar, I. (2004) *Market Segmentation*. Oxford: Butterworth-Heinemann.

Mitchell, A. (1983) *The Nine American Lifestyles: Who We Are and Where We're Going*. New York, NY: Macmillan.

Quinn, L., Hines, T. and Bennison, D. (2007) 'Making sense of market segmentation: A fashion retailing case'. *European Journal of Marketing*, 415/6, pp. 439–465.

Ries, A. and Trout, J. (2001) *Positioning: The Battle for your Mind*, 2nd edn. New York, NY: McGraw-Hill Professional.

Rogers, E. M. (2003) *Diffusion of innovations*. 5th edn. New York: Free Press.

Shim, S. and Bickle, M. L. (1994) 'Benefit segments of the female apparel market: Psychographics, shopping orientations, demographics' *Clothing and Textiles Research Journal*, 12(2), pp. 1–12.

Solomon, M. R. and Rabolt, N. (2009) *Consumer Behavior in Fashion*, 2nd edn. Upper Saddle River, NJ: Prentice Hall.

Warner, F. (2002) 'Nike's Women's Movement'. *Fast Company*, 31 July. Available at: https://www.fastcompany.com/45135/nikes-womens-movement.

West, D. C., Ford, J. and Ibrahim, E. (2015) *Strategic Marketing: Creating Competitive Advantage*, 2nd edn. Oxford: Oxford University Press.

Yurchisin, J. and Johnson, K. K. P. (2010) *Fashion and the Consumer (Understanding Fashion)*. Oxford and New York: Berg.

Zargani, L. (2017) 'Diesel Promotes Love, Not Walls in Spring Ads'. *WWD*, 14 February 2017.

INTERNATIONAL GROWTH STRATEGY IN FASHION MARKETS

4

Ana Roncha and Liz Gee

 ## INTRODUCTION

There is normally an expectation from stakeholders that businesses should grow. In particular this is the case in large public corporations, where dividends and capital growth are demanded by the corporate investors. Even if fast growth is not expected, for example in a well-established private business operating in mature markets, development is required both to meet the challenges of the changing business environment and to exploit the competences of the business whilst all the time meeting the expectations of stakeholders such as employees and suppliers. This chapter aims to explore the challenges and rewards of pursuing growth strategies in fashion. In particular we devote an extended discussion on international growth because this has become one of the most important opportunities for fashion organizations in the last two decades and will continue to be an important strategy for many in the future.

 ## LEARNING OBJECTIVES

After studying this chapter you should be able to understand:

- Why growth underpins most fashion strategies;

- The risks and opportunities of growth strategy alternatives;

- The different approaches to international growth, including globalization, localization and glocalization;

- The necessity for strategic adaptations when pursuing growth in markets with different cultural norms;

- The meaning of place and origin in relation to international fashion strategies;

- The concept of strategic portfolio management for large fashion organizations.

CHARACTERIZING GROWTH AMBITIONS

Strategic choices at a corporate level can be seen as the 'big decisions' taken by a company in terms of both the direction and the scope of the corporation, and the methods by which growth ambitions may be realized – the growth strategy.

> **Growth strategy**
> Strategies designed to grow the business by increasing sales and profits as well as expanding brand reach according to different directions, focusing on new/existing products and new/existing markets.

The decisions about the markets a business should be operating in and how these markets will be accessed are key. Also important here are decisions about which business units should be included in the scope of the company as a whole and how resources should be allocated amongst them. In complex business models this becomes the role

---

4. 46930 London College of Fashion BA16 catwalk show, June 2016, Nicholls and Clarke building, Shoreditch. Photography by Roger Dean.

of the parent company, and the giant luxury houses of Kering and LVMH are excellent examples of the role of parenting strategy steering complex groups to dominate the luxury fashion market.

Parent Company		
WHAT? Decisions of product scope/diversity	**WHERE?** Decisions of geographical scope/ diversity	**HOW?** Resource allocation & value creation: managing the portfolio

Figure 4.1 *The role of the corporate parent*

We will return to this later, but first we will revisit the seminal work of Igor Ansoff (1988) introduced in Chapter 3, which conceptualizes the directions in which a business can be grown. The Ansoff matrix is a simple way to think about the strategic options available to any business by looking at the products and markets it operates in and the opportunities available to it. As with any of the analytical matrices it is important to remember that strategies change over time and there can be arguments over which quadrant a particular strategic decision resides in.

Figure 4.2 represents an application of this matrix to the hugely successful global sports apparel brand Nike, to demonstrate how their business has grown over time. Protecting and building a position in current markets and products is often the first strategy adopted. Then the push and pull factors of globalization see the business ambitious to move into new markets with new or existing products. The arrows show the easiest developments to make, with diversification being seen as a risky leap.

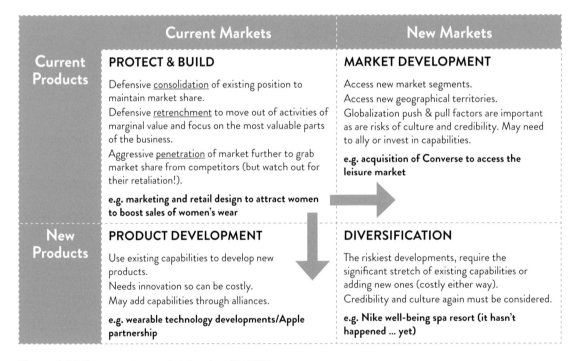

	Current Markets	New Markets
Current Products	**PROTECT & BUILD** Defensive <u>consolidation</u> of existing position to maintain market share. Defensive <u>retrenchment</u> to move out of activities of marginal value and focus on the most valuable parts of the business. Aggressive <u>penetration</u> of market further to grab market share from competitors (but watch out for their retaliation!). **e.g. marketing and retail design to attract women to boost sales of women's wear**	**MARKET DEVELOPMENT** Access new market segments. Access new geographical territories. Globalization push & pull factors are important as are risks of culture and credibility. May need to ally or invest in capabilities. **e.g. acquisition of Converse to access the leisure market**
New Products	**PRODUCT DEVELOPMENT** Use existing capabilities to develop new products. Needs innovation so can be costly. May add capabilities through alliances. **e.g. wearable technology developments/Apple partnership**	**DIVERSIFICATION** The riskiest developments, require the significant stretch of existing capabilities or adding new ones (costly either way). Credibility and culture again must be considered. **e.g. Nike well-being spa resort (it hasn't happened ... yet)**

Figure 4.2 *Nike strategic growth (after Ansoff, 1988)*

Growth via product development

As noted in the previous chapter, when Ansoff developed his growth matrix he was not thinking of the fashion industry where new products are developed on a continual basis, and introduced to customers on a monthly, weekly or even daily basis. For fashion, therefore, we need to consider growth via product development in terms of the introduction of new categories or perhaps a capsule collection designed in collaboration with a celebrity of some kind, which adds freshness to the existing product range. In the fashion context there is a fine line between product development and related diversification and it is the extent of risk that would suggest which 'box' a particular strategic development would fall into. A fuller discussion of product related strategies is given in Chapter 8.

Diversification as a growth strategy

Diversification is a form of growth strategy where the main purpose is to allow a company to grow by moving into new businesses, by developing new products for new markets. This can pose a high investment and risk because it requires both product and market development outside the company's core competencies.

Diversification can be *related* or *unrelated* in relation to the existing market (Hunger and Wheelen, 2011), either *forwards* or *backwards* in relation to the value chain, and *horizontal* or *vertical* in relation to the market, as shown in Table 4.1. Consider here a simple supply chain of fabric suppliers, garment manufacturers and apparel retailers.

Company	Acquires	Motive	Horizontal or Vertical?	If Vertical: Forwards or Backwards?
Fabric Supplier	Garment Manufacturer	To secure distribution	Vertical	Forwards
Fabric Supplier	Fabric Supplier	To remove a potential competitor and grow market share	Horizontal	N/A
Garment Manufacturer	Fabric Supplier	To secure sourcing	Vertical	Backwards
Garment Manufacturer	Garment Manufacturer	To remove a potential competitor and grow market share	Horizontal	N/A
Garment Manufacturer	Apparel Retailer	To secure distribution	Vertical	Forwards
Apparel Retailer	Garment Manufacturer	To secure sourcing	Vertical	Backwards
Apparel Retailer	Apparel Retailer	To remove a potential competitor and grow market share	Horizontal	N/A

Table 4.1 *Related diversification directions in a fashion supply chain*

Related diversification aims to achieve strategic fit and increased synergies. It is the most common and least risky as it is seen as less of a leap in terms of competence and credibility, such as a men's wear brand moving into women's wear. Unrelated diversification occurs when a company enters completely new business areas either through technology or through market needs (Ansoff, 1988). There might be synergies in place resulting from the application of management expertize or financial resources; however, the goal is to acquire valuable assets that will increase profitability. For example, some luxury fashion brands have moved into 'lifestyle' product markets, such as spas and hotels (see the Armani Case Study, Case Study 3, in Chapter 3). Just how far brands can diversify before their credibility is damaged is explored in Chapter 6 (Fashion Brand Management). Adopting a diversification strategy can be as a reaction to push factors (see Table 4.2 below), for example to escape a declining market, but more often it is as the result of opportunities offered in an attractive market segment that promise earnings growth and allow some risk spreading. We will return to financial debates around risk and diversification in Chapter 13.

Growth via market development

As indicated in the preceding chapter, growth via market development has always been an important strategy for fashion companies. For fashion retailers opening outlets in new locations, whether in the same country or internationally, is a natural way to grow, and has provided significant opportunities for many. For non-retail businesses, selling to business markets further afield has been part of the history and culture of the textiles, clothing and fashion industries for centuries: forming what is now referred to as the global supply chain. Market development can also refer to strategies closer to home, by finding a new, but related customer market segment in which to offer existing products. In reality and particularly in fashion, attracting a new market segment (such as a different age group) will require some new product development, such as a new design approach; therefore again we see that the Ansoff (1988) matrix boxes need to be viewed with flexible boundaries. Given that market development, and in particular

international market development has been the source of successful growth for both large and small fashion companies, this chapter continues with an in-depth exploration of international marketing as a growth strategy.

INTERNATIONAL GROWTH

Fashion brands have been searching for new markets to sell their products into for well over a century; for example, Louis Vuitton opened a shop in London in 1855 and Burberry opened a store in Paris in 1909. Historically the drive to internationalize has come in waves, driven by factors in the external environment such as political and economic conditions driving cost and demand dynamics (see Table 4.2). More recently digital technology has shrunk the world for both brands and consumers, reducing communication and cultural barriers. International growth is therefore relevant to the majority of fashion businesses, and

Push Factors _forcing_ brands to seek overseas opportunities	Pull Factors _enticing_ brands to try doing business overseas
• Saturated home market with intense competition meaning there are limited opportunities to grow revenues	• Growing middle classes emerging as consumers with similar needs • World shrinking as cultural and language barriers are reduced • Perceived less developed home fashion brands offering weak competition
• The need to escape challenging economic conditions impacting revenues	• Growing global economies that are often countercyclical to home economies so allowing risks to be spread • Host government incentives and global trade support agencies to ensure reduced financial and legal trade barriers (e.g. tariffs and quotas)
• The need to reduce costs through economies of scale in overheads	• Country-specific cost drivers, e.g. lower costs of labour, raw materials, and/or logistics
• The need to be seen as an international brand keeping pace with the competition.	• Appetite for new revenue streams from potential trading partners, consultants and property agents • Technology developments enabling digital communication, and transferable marketing.

Table 4.2 _Push and Pull factors driving internationalization in fashion_

the orientation of company growth for many has moved from domestic to international in order to satisfy stakeholders.

International expansion as a growth strategy

So if international growth is the answer to stakeholders' demands for long-term growing profits then how is this achieved? The fastest way for any business to grow is to 'take out' the competition, by acquiring a rival for its market share. The problem with this is that the price paid for the whole business can result in paying for duplication of effort and resources, which is rarely worthwhile. This horizontal consolidation will increase the scale and market power of the business but there are likely to be issues in realizing predicted synergies. It may be assumed, for example, that support activities such as human resources and product development might be easy to manage on a global basis; however, it is often difficult for key personnel to be as geographically flexible as the organization would like.

Pursuing any strategic option whether diversification, innovation or internationalization will require the business to acquire new competences. A business can do this itself through developing its own expertize slowly and organically, or by moving faster to take the more extreme path of acquisition of entities for their competences. Often capabilities are best developed through some form of strategic alliance. Alliances exist in many forms from a key supplier relationship, through formal contractual licensing and franchising agreements to joint ventures and mergers. No matter how the alliance is characterized, and whatever the control and ownership structure, the strategic aims should remain the same, which is to add value to the existing business. Often avoiding the problems that can result from acquisition such as overpayment, inflexibility and culture clash, the dynamic current fashion business will look to form mutually

> **Internationalization**
> A strategic option that sees brands expanding towards new markets so as to add value to the existing business and pursue growth. There are various approaches and different entry mode strategies that brands need to consider in terms of how to approach these new markets, depending on profile, level of investment, challenges and risks.

beneficial partnerships, to learn from its partners and develop its own capabilities. As we consider different types of business combinations we can also apply this to thinking about the best modes to access new markets for fashion businesses of all sizes.

THE PROCESS OF INTERNATIONALIZATION

According to Hollensen (2007), internationalization occurs when companies expand their business activities across geo-political boundaries. This can refer to research and development, production or selling into international markets, making the competition wider than in the initial local market. As Kotler et al. (2005) indicate, management must consider their entry strategy carefully as each involves different levels of financial and management commitment, financial and brand risks, control, and potential profit.

Like any other growth strategy, an international strategy needs to address key strategic questions. According to Akehurst and Alexander (1996) these are:

- Why? We know the answer to that one ... to grow

- Where are the most attractive territories with the least chance of local retaliation?

- What are our most suitable brands/ product lines for global markets?

- Who does it? Do we go it alone or do we need to find a partner? Do we send people from our domestic headquarters to preserve our brand integrity or recruit internationally to gain local knowledge?

- When is a realistic timescale?

- How to do it ... with several options this is a key decision and is to a greater or lesser extent dependent on all of the above.

There are several business models that can be used to access a new market: direct online selling and e-commerce, wholesaling and licensing, franchising

ONLINE RESOURCES

Our companion website explores the advantages and disadvantages of each of these routes to market and provides examples of fashion companies that have used them: https://www.macmillanihe.com/companion/Varley_Fashion_Management.

and joint venture (JV), and direct investment into permanent or temporary stores.

The 'right' mode to adopt depends on how quickly the market is changing and the resources available to the brand, and early theories of internationalization suggested that brands progressed through each business model in stages. This assumption is challenged by contemporary small, agile businesses that rapidly expand by building transferable competences and leveraging digital technologies; sometimes described as 'born global'. The influence of external and internal parameters on the level of control and pace of retail expansion is shown in Table 4.3. In order to develop an effective international expansion strategy, fashion brands should consider all these parameters, which when viewed in aggregate should lead towards a preferred business model.

Parameter	Internal or External	Effect on Control	Effect on Speed	Comment
High Level of Investment	Internal	High	N/A	Access to capital and the materiality of the investment will affect the retailer's choices. The greater the investment, the more control the retailer will want to retain.
Longer payback	Internal	N/A	Slow	The longer an investment takes to payback and the capital being released for reinvestment, the slower the pace. May also influence control.
High Risk Market	External	Low	N/A	There is an inverse correlation between market risk and exposure. Retailers will want to distance themselves from high risk markets and will be prepared to give up control to achieve that.
Strong brand image/ customer experience	Internal	High	N/A	N/A
Low business model complexity	Internal	Low	Fast	Formulaic retail concepts require less control and can be rolled out faster than highly specialized concepts.
Low levels of required capabilities	Internal	Low	N/A	If the retailer is reliant on a partner to provide relevant resources and competences then risk will need to be shared and control relinquished.

Table 4.3 *Method of entry parameters*

Source: Based on Deloitte (2012).

Although some fashion companies tend to have preferred methods of entry for new markets, many of them employ multiple methods of entry, varying them by market (see Table 4.4). In some countries, there may be little choice as local laws dictate permissible forms of foreign direct investment and the level of control that may be exerted by foreign entities.

Fashion Retailer	Wholly Owned	Joint Venture	Franchise
Mango	Asia Europe (West) Europe (East) Americas	Europe (West) Americas	Asia Europe (West) Europe (East) Americas Middle East/ Africa
Marks & Spencer	Asia Europe (West)	Europe (West) Europe (East)	Europe (West) Europe (East) Middle East/ Africa
Nike	Asia Europe (West) Europe (East) Americas		Asia Middle East/ Africa
Zara	Asia Europe (West) Europe (East) Americas		Asia Europe (West) Europe (East) Americas Middle East/ Africa

Table 4.4 *Method of international market entry by selected fashion retailers*

Source: Based on Deloitte 2012.

INTERNATIONALIZATION AND GLOBALIZATION – THE CHALLENGES

The very nature of fashion gives specific problems when trying to grow internationally. Fashion products themselves are not necessities, especially at the luxury end of the market, and are strongly commoditized with little differentiation at the mass-market level. Global consumers can be fickle when it comes to fashion; they may care where a product is designed and made one week but then want something completely different the next. For a fashion brand, this adds complexity to the supply chain, which needs to be flexible and fast moving.

Thinking about expansion into any new territory should prompt a fashion company to review the business environment in an extended PESTEL analysis and think about the characteristics of the fashion industry in that territory using a competitive forces analysis (see Chapter 2). Global fashion markets have by their nature fairly low barriers to entry, being open to business models that require little resource commitment (such as e-commerce or wholesale), but as alluded to earlier, there can be some real local pitfalls around cultural norms, taste, religion, climate and so on, and so consumer and competitor intelligence from the target territory is important here.

The concept of distance is useful for brands embarking on an international strategy. A CAGE analysis (see Figure 4.3) considers the most important elements of an extended PESTEL which impact distance.

Cultural Distance	Administrative Distance
Similar/different in demographics and social structure	Political regime and risks (e.g. corruption, terrorism)
Similar/different cultural norms, conventions, values and beliefs	Government policies and trade barriers/incentives
Language barriers	Local policies regarding planning, consumer protection, counterfeiting and so on
Levels of education	
Use of credit cards	
Internet speed and available platforms	
Geographic Distance	**Economic Distance**
Not just the physical distance; the further away, the more likely to be differences in weather, in risk of natural hazards, and even in the size and shape of consumers	Distribution of wealth and domestic market conditions (GDP and disposable income indicate potential market size)
Geographic factors include urbanization trends and national infrastructure (transport and communications)	Financial stability (exchange rates, restriction on repatriation of funds)
May have natural resources that may be relevant to the supply chain, or that influence the level of wealth generally	

Figure 4.3 *CAGE factors characterizing distance considerations for successful internationalization*

INTERNATIONAL MARKETING STRATEGIES

International marketing can be defined as 'the performance of business activities that direct the flow of the company's goods and services to consumers or users in more than one nation' (Cateora and Graham, 2007: 9). These business activities can include research and development, marketing intelligence, as well as the transfer of goods and so international marketing is of great importance to both country and company. Companies must be fully aware of consumers' ways of life before taking decisions on

what to produce, for whom to produce and how to approach price, promotion and distribution strategies. The relevance and importance of culture in international marketing can never be overemphasized, Awoniyi (1999).

The 12C Analysis Model is a tool to help companies identify the information to be collected while planning a marketing strategy to enter an overseas market and helps to evaluate the attractiveness of that market (see Table 4.5).

For fashion, the fourth C (culture) can become a make or break factor, as we will discuss in the next section.

Country	• Business environmental factors, • country's policy to import, • business customs, • business laws, • the country's marketing • business infrastructure.
Choices	• Competition, • strengths and weaknesses of competitors • consideration of the marketing mix choices available in the target market.
Concentration	• Structure of market segments, • geographical spread showing age distribution, income distribution, access to channels of distribution, access to decision makers, density of population and so on.
Culture	• Consumer behaviour, • decision-making style, • norms and values, • language, • behaviour,

	• aesthetics, • arts, • music, • technology, • ethics.
Consumption	• Existing and future demand, • growth potential, • demand patterns.
Capacity to pay	• Costing, • pricing, • prevailing payment terms, • ability of the consumer to pay – payment methods and credit facilities, • capacity of clients to reach contractual agreements, • price–quality interpretation.
Currency	• Presence of exchange controls, • degree of convertibility, • acceptability and stability of local currency.
Channels	• Distribution costs, • existing distribution infrastructure, • direct or indirect marketing channel, • mode of transportation and warehousing, • channel relationships.
Commitment	• Market access, • tariff and non-tariff barriers, • commitment to quality and service.
Communication	• Available communication media, • channel media, • language and style, • choice of promotional media, • available social media, • values and ethics in message.
Contractual obligations	• Business practices, • insurance, • legal obligations, • payment terms and conditions, • credit terms and period, • warrantees, guarantees of delivery, • penalties for late delivery or failure to deliver.
Caveats	• Special precautions to be taken regarding: • Company's reputation; quality of products, delivery time, long-term presence in the market. • Motivation of export sales people. • Local risk and political stability. • Economic trends. • Modes of doing business in the target country.

Table 4.5 *Understanding overseas markets: The 12C Analysis Model*

Source: Based on Doole, Phillips and Lowe (1997), and Usunier (1998).

THE GLOBAL – LOCAL – GLOCAL DEBATE

> Quite often, a lot of British high street brands are almost too fashionable for international markets. They're very dress-based, very catwalk-based, moving very quickly, which doesn't necessarily work for a US market or a French market. But we're much more about a stylishness and longevity, which works really well internationally. Peter Ruis, CEO Jigsaw (see Just Style, 2014)

Globalization has had a huge impact on fashion and on the branding strategies of fashion brands. Since the 1990s many fashion companies have moved from a multi-domestic to a global marketing approach, making use of global branding strategies (Schuiling and Kapferer, 2004). As the global marketplace becomes more competitive, brands see both local and international consumers as an integral part of their strategy. The **global consumer culture** is one where people are united by a common devotion to brand name consumer goods, movie stars or celebrities (Solomon, 2009). For some products, including fashion, preferences and choices of the consumers in different geographic locations have started to converge towards a global norm, helped by the rising accessibility and influence of social networks. The emergence of new markets means that fashion brands now find valuable consumers far from their home country (Jansson and Power, 2010).

When deciding to go international, a fashion brand may choose to adopt a **standardized** or a **localized** approach to target different consumers and cultures (Solomon, 2009). Standardization allows a brand to benefit from economies of scale, as it does not have to incur the substantial time and costs of developing a separate strategy for each culture. On the other hand, a localized strategy, focusing on variations between cultures, may require brands to incur product changes so as to better fit the needs and wants of a specific market (Solomon, 2009).

> Adaptation often allows you to go faster, but it might also take you away from your equity. You might have to twist your brand a little to be successful and go faster as you adapt to consumers as opposed to consumers adapting to your brand. Some other times, especially when it pertains to luxury brands, you just need to be patient and allow time for consumers to discover your brand. Serge Jureidini, former president of Lancôme and CEO of Arcade Marketing, in Spencer Stuart, *Crossing borders Internationalizing brands* (2013)

Establishing a compromise between global and domestic marketing strategies is what is often referred to as a *glocal* strategy, '**glocalization**', which standardizes certain core elements and localizes others. On a corporate level, global strategic directions are given while local units focus on the local customer differences.

> **Glocalization** A strategy employed by brands where core elements of the brands are standardized across markets while others are localized. Born from the awareness that brands must adapt certain aspects of their strategy and identity to better suit the needs and demands of local consumers in a specific market.

Kotler (2009) suggested that by acting on a glocal perspective, brands gain higher market share, because consumers feel that the brand is of relevance to them and tailored to their needs, while harmony is maintained between marketing activities on the strategic, tactical and operational levels (see Table 4.6).

Adaptation

In a localized strategy a company aims to fully understand the markets it intends to serve, the culture of the people, consumer behaviour, taste and preferences, business customs, and laws, and use them to guide all business activities in the host country. The case study of L'Oréal (Case Study 4, at the end of the chapter) demonstrates one of the most successful brands in adopting **cross-cultural marketing** strategies to suit the different markets they cover. However, in a glocalized strategy adaptation is made to some rather than all aspects of the business. When deciding how far to adapt, a fashion company will be steered by the need for consistency in terms of brand marketing across markets, the resources available to adapt (such as an extra product development or marketing communications teams) and the extent to which customers would accept an offer without adaptation.

It is a paradox that the trend towards **personalization** is becoming increasingly important in a world of global brands. Advances in technology have not created a global consumer but have created a global culture, and that has not come at the expense

Type of Strategy and Brand Examples	Key Aspects of the Strategy
Standardized strategy Examples: Michael Kors, Abercrombie & Fitch	• Proponents of standardized marketing strategy argue that many cultures have become so homogenized that the same approach will work throughout the world. • By developing one approach for multiple markets, a company can benefit from economies of scale, since it does not have to incur the substantial time and expense of developing a separate strategy for each culture. • This approach is objective and analytical – it reflects the impressions of cultures as viewed by outsiders. • Usually applied in vertically integrated companies and those that sell under private labels, to prevent brand dilution.
Localized strategy Example: L'Oréal (see Case Study 4)	• Multinational strategy – which focuses on variations within a culture. Each culture is considered unique, with its own norms, value system, conventions, and regulations. • This perspective argues that each country has a national character, a distinctive set of behaviour and personality characteristics. • An effective strategy is tailored to the sensibilities and needs of each specific culture. • A subjective and experiential approach – attempts to explain a culture as it is experienced by insiders. • Can involve modifying a product or the way it is positioned to make it acceptable to local tastes.
Glocalized strategy Example: Bottega Venetta	• A combination of the words 'globalization' and 'localization' used to describe a product or service that is developed and distributed globally but is also fashioned to accommodate the user or consumer in a local market. • The offer is tailored to conform to local laws, customs or consumer preferences. • Products or services that are effectively 'glocalized' are usually going to be of much greater interest to the end user.

Table 4.6 *Summarized standardized and localized strategies for fashion brands*

of local culture. Instead, technology has actually made local culture more vibrant. Fashion consumers enjoy brands with character, with style, and a connection to community and culture. The rise of business models such as notonthehighstreet.com, made.com and etsy.com offers good examples of this, where local culture has become a creative multiplier for global brands; by combining global and local elements these companies can go further than locally orientated brands. Similarly, the rise of community stores is another interesting trend; some global brands have started to open physical stores that aim not only at driving sales, but also at providing a social benefit to the surrounding local community.

> **Culture** A set of values, formed out of invisible and visible parts that act as a collection of learned behaviour. How consumers do things, how they respond to stimulus, how they interact with each other and with various entities.

EXPLORING THE INFLUENCE OF CULTURE ON INTERNATIONAL FASHION MARKETING

When businesses expand their operations internationally, culture and its consequences become more relevant. Culture acts as a set of values that add to a brand's universe and to its identity. According to Kapferer (2008), brands can simultaneously be derived from culture and also convey that same culture. The notion of culture entails a variety of constructs but at its utmost means the way, and why, we do things. We are not born with a culture yet we learn it and it will influence the majority of our decisions as we grow and develop as a consumer. 'Culture is the collective mental programming of the people in an environment. Culture is not a characteristic of individuals; it encompasses a number of people who were conditioned by the same education and life experience' (Hofstede, 2001).

Understanding local culture is of strategic importance for fashion brands, allowing for an understanding of the variations that motivate people and making it easier to position brands and tailor communication messages to consumers from a specific cultural background (De Mooij, 2010; Hofstede 2001). There are invisible and visible parts of culture as shown in Figure 4.4.

Culture can relate to a country (national culture), be linked to a part of the community (sub-culture) or to an organization (corporate culture). Culture includes everything we have learned about values and social norms, customs and traditions as well as religions and beliefs. One of the ways to explore culture and its implications is to use a framework designed by Terpstra and Sarathy in 2000, which distinguishes between 8 different constructs; these are considered for their relevance to fashion organizations in the next sections.

Values and attitudes

Values are important as they have the potential to be translated into consumption vehicles (Doole and Lowe, 2008) but are also relevant to the running of fashion organizations. An example of how this can impact on business is the difference in the number of paid holidays across different countries. Managing employees across the world means dealing with such complex and diverse approaches to HR policies and benefits. Values and attitudes can also make it necessary to change brand communication messages and content.

Education

Education affects all aspects of culture, from economic development to consumer behaviour, in terms of how skills, ideas and attitudes are transmitted. Education can also be used for cultural change (Czinkota et al., 2009). Levels of education vary across international markets and can impact on the type and medium that brands use to communicate. When countries have low literacy levels, for example, brands might choose to opt for messages that are mostly visual or audio.

Social organizations

Social organization relates to how a society is organized. Social institutions such as schools, churches, agencies, and peers influence the behavioural pattern of consumers. The role of women, the influence of class or casts, social mobility, and the presence of trade unions are all part of social organization. This

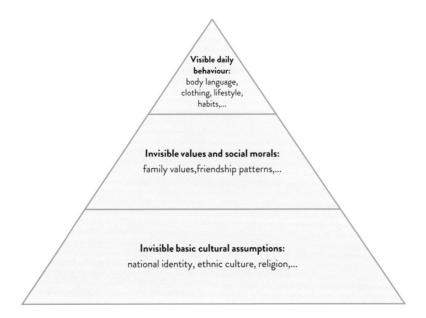

Figure 4.4 *Invisible and visible parts of culture*

factor may influence how brands communicate their messages. For example, the European version of the *Guy Laroche Drakkar Noir* advertising campaign showed a female hand assertively grabbing a bare male arm holding the product; in Saudi Arabia the image showed a female lightly caressing a suited male arm holding the product.

Technology and material culture

This concerns transport infrastructure that can have a direct impact on logistics and distribution. It also concerns how quickly innovation diffuses and how consumers value the consumption of material goods.

The International Product lifecycle model (Vernon, 1966) shows how countries, whether emerging or established, are at different stages of development and therefore acceptance of products. For example, wearable technologies would be irrelevant in countries where nearly all income goes towards basic needs such as food.

Law and politics

The underpinnings of social culture drive the political and legal landscape for the majority of countries. They are often a codification of the norms deemed acceptable by local culture. Cultural sensitivity to political issues is of high importance. Fashion advertisements should comply with local laws and be sensitive to the political environment.

Aesthetics

Aesthetics is an important factor in product design, packaging and advertising, and generally revolves around colour, quality and product use. It relates to the senses and appreciation of what should be a pleasant experience. Consumers respond to images and metaphors that help them define their personal and national identities and relationships within the context of culture and product benefits (Baisya, 2008). Colours have a high degree of symbolism in international markets. For example, in the US and Europe, black is the colour of mourning, whereas in Japan and the Far East, white has the same symbolic value; contrasting with the colour associated with weddings, which is traditionally red in China, whereas in western countries white is the conventional option of

brides. Another example can be seen in what is referred to as 'Scandinavian Style' and the notoriously famous and distinct concept of 'Hygge'. This word symbolizes the cosy, warm feeling derived from being indoors, by a fire, or around a group of friends with flowing conversation and wine. The use of Scandinavian-style pieces and how they translate to interior, jewellery and fashion trends is widely acknowledged (Vogue, 2017). The fashion brand COS was created in 2007 to cater for women and men who want modern, functional, considered design. It offers reinvented classics and wardrobe essentials, where traditional methods and new techniques merge to form timeless, understated collections. The brand has a central thread of Scandinavian aesthetics that can be seen across their imagery (http://www.cosstores.com/).

Language

Language defines a culture – when a country has several different languages, it implies several cultures.

When looking into language we must consider if national culture is a high or low context culture (Hall, 1976), which indicates the balance between verbal and non-verbal communication. In low context culture spoken language carries the emphasis of the communication – what you say is what you mean (for example, in the Netherlands). In high context culture, verbal communication may not carry a full message, but is supplemented with hidden cultural meaning such as body language (for example, in Japan).

Language therefore entails verbal and non-verbal expressions of culture and is a crucial factor in communicating effectiveness in marketing especially in packaging, labelling and promotional materials. An example of this factor can be seen in a NIVEA campaign launched in South Africa. The brand makes use of the sentiments and learning specific to the country to make a deep, emotional impact on consumers, exploring the concept of Ubuntu, which translates as 'I am because you are, and you are because of me' and inspires kindness in a community.

Religion

Companies need to ensure their products and campaigns are not offensive, unlawful or against the tastes of the local country. In 2005, Marithe and François Girbaud lost an injunction to the Catholic Church in France brought about because of an advertisement inspired by Leonardo da Vinci's painting of Christ's Last Supper. The brand used mostly women in a billboard and portrayed the character of John as the only man, wearing only jeans. The Catholic Church in France and Italy claimed the advertisement trivialized the iconic moment of the Last Supper and that it was not a suitable appropriation of the religious symbols.

In contrast, H&M's use of model Mariah Idrissi wearing a hijab in one of their images for the Close the Loop campaign was seen as an emblematic shift in the way Islam is portrayed in mainstream marketing, entertainment and society (JWT, 2015) and an acknowledgement of the value of the Muslim fashion consumer market that spent $266 billion on clothing and footwear in 2013, more than the total fashion spending of Japan and Italy combined (Petrilla, 2015). Mini Case Study 4.1 demonstrates how Net-a-Porter has also appealed to the Muslim fashion consumer.

A global mind-set and awareness are important when developing global brands that are strong yet rooted in local cultures. Sensitivity and willingness to get under the skin of the local culture and to scan the differences and similarities are crucial for success; this can be done through immersion to sharpen deep understanding and insight. Fashion companies nowadays have to deal with much shorter cycles and increased flexibility. This means they have to gain agility, not just in operations but in intellectual, cultural, social and emotional dimensions. They also need to apply learning to different situations and to sort through a variety of data and advance the right strategic decisions quickly. How culture impacts on brands and their image also relates to the widely spread concept of country of origin (brand origin), which has a direct influence on consumers' perceptions of quality, and behaviour towards brands.

 ## MINI CASE STUDY 4.1 - Net-a-Porter: Modest marketing

In 2015, online retailer Net-a-Porter launched a Ramadan version of *The Edit*, its weekly online magazine, in celebration of the Muslim holy month. The brand was mindful of its global consumers' needs by carrying pieces specifically for this season. A selection of modest dressings and wardrobe staples in a range of skin-coloured tones was introduced in

an attempt to court the consumer. The importance of this season was highlighted by Euromonitor in 2012: 'Like Christmas, a religious context serves as a reason for families and friends to come together. A typical "Ramadan consumer" is likely to emerge in the same way as the Christmas shopper as a global phenomenon.'

THE RELEVANCE OF THE COUNTRY AND BRAND ORIGIN EFFECT

It is widely acknowledged that consumers perceive global brands to have higher quality, higher credibility and prestige. When brands fail to deliver on perceived and intended quality, however, their reputation can be damaged and further brand development hindered. In a globalized and highly international industry such as fashion, the role of the perceived country and brand origin in influencing brand evaluations and buying behaviour is, therefore, a crucial construct.

Brand origin can be defined as 'the overall perception consumers form of products from a particular country, based

Country of origin
The associations and perceptions consumers hold of different countries that impact on how they view and evaluate brands from those same countries. Country of origin has proven to be an important intangible and intimately associated with a brand's performance.

on their prior perceptions of the country's production and marketing strengths and weaknesses' (Roth and Romeo, 1992: 480). It is related to brand strategy in a number of ways: as an information cue (Insch and McBride, 2004), and as an influence on consumer perception of product quality and performance (Chuang and Yen, 2007) and the price consumers are willing to pay (Aaker, 1991). On the other hand, inaccurate country of origin can lead to confusing and negative impacts on a brand (Paswan and Sharma, 2004).

Associating brands with their country of origin means tapping into a network of associations such as national stereotypes, beliefs, experiences, reputation, and specific country imagery (Chattalas et al., 2008). This may be leveraged by some companies through adopting the imagery and cultural positioning in order to transfer the attributes associated with the country to the brand. Anholt (2007) regards brands as increasingly important drivers of national image and reputation, even of culture. In turn, countries and cities can be branded and used as a differentiating strategy to achieve competitive advantage, as evident in the association between New York and fashion brands portrayed in the TV series *Sex and the City*. The images and myths underlying brands anchored to the city of New York are a product of the many image-producing agents based in that city as well as the people that consumed the programme (Jansson and Power, 2010).

A product's production country can affect consumers' decision-making because consumers can hold stereotyped images of countries that affect their perception; for example, products made in developed countries are evaluated more positively than products from developing countries

(Elliott and Cameron, 1994). Unlike product specialists and manufacturers who have adequate knowledge to accurately evaluate quality and level of craftsmanship, consumers base their evaluation on external design, price or the value of the brands, and the country of production. Luxury fashion brand Prada challenged these perceptions by highlighting the origin of production alongside the brand origin in a high quality woven labelling system (see Mini Case Study 4.2).

An interesting insight into the evolution of the country of origin (COO) concept was undertaken by Insch and McBride (2004), who looked at the effect of country-of-assembly (COA), country-of-design (COD), and country-of-parts. With globalization, this concept has shown to be quite controversial and ever more complicated as country of origin *can* refer to brand origin, country of manufacture or assembly, or a value-creation process that takes place separately in various countries (Hamzaoui-Essoussi et al., 2011). A consumer's evaluation of a

---

MINI CASE STUDY 4.2 - Prada 'Made In ...' Project (2010)

Reproduced with permission of Prada.

Prada developed a collection of globally produced clothing and accessories that was labelled according to the region where it was produced. The collection was a tribute to Mario Prada, current design director Miuccia Prada's grandfather, who travelled around the globe for inspiration in creating the Prada collection as well as scouting the most exotic skins, decadent fabrics, and craftsmanship that revolutionized his designs. To develop the collection, Prada collaborated with artisans around the globe to produce 'modern, innovative designs utilizing the traditional craftsmanship, materials,

and manufacturing techniques of a specific region using Mario Prada's time-honed strategy' (Prada. com).

There were 4 labels within this collection:

- 'PRADA Made in Scotland' – A collection of traditional tartan wool kilts from the original UK workshops that utilize centuries-old manufacturing and weaving techniques.

- 'PRADA Made in Peru' – A collection of alpaca wool knitwear using artisanal techniques from the most traditional workshops of the Peruvian 'campesinos'.

- 'PRADA Made in Japan' – Jeans produced by Dova (referred to as the world's most sophisticated denim manufacturer). These jeans could be custom ordered in four different varieties of cloth and seven different washes, making each piece unique.

- 'PRADA Made in India' – Entirely handmade garments from the factories that specialize in Chikan (an ancient type of Indian embroidery) as well as handmade ballerina flats, sandals and handbags that employ an equally sophisticated traditional weaving technique.

This spirit of the curious connoisseur remains at the heart of Prada, especially in the age of globalization, where geographic and cultural borders disappear. Remaining faithful to these ideals, the company continues to identify those specialized crafts people that represent an unrivalled standard of excellence ... In an unceasing quest for excellence, Prada continues to transcend geographical boundaries. Rather than restrictive, such 'barriers' offer new ways to think and work.

Source: Prada.com.

product is likely to decrease if there is a lack of fit between a product's brand origin and the country of manufacture (Johnson et al., 2016).

FASHION TOURISM

A further link between fashion and the global consumer is that of the fashion tourist. The increased tendency for consumers to link leisure and fashion shopping has provided opportunities to target global shoppers by offering more personalized shopping experiences. Linked to the growing demand for experiences, this has led several retailers to try to strike an emotional chord with customers rather than focusing too heavily on product. An interesting take on this was developed by luxury Hong Kong retailer Lane Crawford in 2016 (see Mini Case Study 4.3), who targeted the fashionable traveller.

THE ROLE OF THE CORPORATE PARENT

This chapter has demonstrated why internationalization as a growth strategy is central to strategic fashion management yet remains challenging in its complexity. Very often the most successful international fashion brands are supported by a parent or holding company which provides the resources and manages the risk associated with moving down the various avenues for growth. The holding company of a group has two main roles, as a coordinator of the businesses in the group and to manage the contents of the corporate portfolio. The idea of the corporate portfolio can be illustrated by using the well-known BCG (Boston Consulting Group) Matrix. This useful tool characterizes four types of business units by relating their market share to market growth. This analysis can usefully be applied

MINI CASE STUDY 4.3 - Lane Crawford and the new global traveller

The Hong Kong based department store Lane Crawford aimed to empower a cultural connection through travel in partnership with Luxe Guides (the guidebook publisher) by designing itineraries for five luxury trips – each built around a theme tying into the destination: 'Fashion in New York', 'Culture in Paris', 'Wellness in Los Angeles', 'Design in Tokyo' and 'Culinary Delights in Bangkok'. These custom trips included business class flights, five-star hotel accommodation and a HK$10,000 Lane Crawford gift card.

Each destination featured a unique set of exclusive activities: for example, the LA trip allowed travellers to meet 'notable photographers' and the Paris trip included a tour of 'hidden underground clubs'. Lane Crawford promoted the trips by offering customized city guides plus a range of merchandise that would tie well into each destination; a black leather Alexander Wang backpack for New York, the Adidas X Kolor Nylon Hood jacket for LA or a Comme Des Garçons Homme hood jacket for Tokyo.

Sources:
http://wwd.com/fashion-news/fashion-scoops/lane-crawford-luxe-guides-offer-themed-trips-10435307/.
WGSN (2016) The new global traveler.

Relative Market Share	Rate of Market Growth	BCG Character	Cash flow	Profits	Strategic Action	Kering Example
Low	Low	Dog	-ve	Falling	Divest	Puma
Low	High	Question Mark	-ve	Growing	Analzse	Christopher Kane
High	Low	Cash Cow	+ve	Stable	Milk	Gucci
High	High	Star	Neutral	Growing	Invest	Stella McCartney

Table 4.7 *Applying the BCG Matrix*

to different business units, product categories or sub-brands depending on how the business in question is organized. Although performances may change over time this analysis gives an idea of the actions that need to be taken with a brand/business for the good of the corporation as a whole. It might also be applied to analyze market potential in different international locations. Table 4.7 shows what this looks like for the Kering group (see also the Kering Case Study, Case Study 2 in Chapter 2).

The rate of market growth and the brand's relative share of that market will dictate the share of profits available to it. Brands in a Low/Low position will not always be ruthlessly divested if there is a possibility that investment in the brand could reposition it as a star. By keeping the portfolio under review as the conglomerate changes to respond to the market, the group may conclude divestment would in the end achieve a better outcome for the brand itself, and the business can apply the realized funds to other purposes. In an analysis such as this it must be remembered that brands can move quadrant but this does usefully highlight the brands needing strategic action. This corporate portfolio analysis also highlights

> **Corporate portfolio analysis** A process that evaluates each unit within a company's portfolio, categorizes these and identifies business opportunities towards growth potential. A diversified portfolio allows companies to evolve and grow their business, and corporate portfolio analysis is a productive manner of channelling investment and allocating resources.

the need for balance across the portfolio. Not all of the corporate group's brands should be stars; cash cows are essential to fund the development of the question marks and the maintenance of the stars.

Managing the corporate portfolio means taking decisions over diversification, acquisition and divestment of brands within the portfolio to achieve balance and overall profitability. It also sees such groups acting like incubators for small businesses where potential is seen. For a small successful designer such as Christopher Kane the financial investment and management resources provided on acquisition by the Kering group have allowed him to realize the potential of his brand; for Kering the brand is a question mark so will need to have expertize and resources applied, to realize the potential. Conglomerates will move financial resources between businesses by cash pooling and move human resources across businesses to share talent and expertize. In managing the business strategy formulation, as well as monitoring and controlling the performance of each of the businesses, the conglomerate parent can add real value not just layers of bureaucracy, which is in itself a risk.

 CASE STUDY 4 - L'Oréal: International brand diversity and innovation for global growth

L'Oréal was founded in 1909 by the chemist Eugène Schueller and is now a well-established group of brands, represented in 140 countries across five continents, with an international marketing model based on innovative skill, knowledge and an unshakeable reputation. L'Oréal's brand values are expressed in its tagline, created in 1971: '*Because I'm Worth It*'. The brand celebrates beauty and the intrinsic self-worth of consumers around the world, providing beauty products in four major categories: hair colour, haircare, skincare and cosmetics. L'Oréal Paris's iconic cosmetics collections include the sub-brands Infallible, True Match, Color Riche, Voluminous, and Visible Lift. The brand has been at the forefront of technology and in 2014 introduced 'Makeup Genius' – an app that allows users to scan a L'Oréal Paris product or advertisement to try products and looks virtually. Acquiring dynamic and leading local brands to reinforce international status is a key strategy for the brand. In the United States, L'Oréal purchased Gemey (1974) and Maybelline (1994); Jade in Germany (1995); and Shu Uemura (2000) in Japan. The company's unique approach to distribution strategy is another factor of its success. By operating across all distribution chains (including department stores, pharmacies, supermarkets, hypermarkets, independent stores and hair salons) it achieves a much wider market coverage than competitors.

L'Oréal's strategy has focused on innovation as a key factor in brand development. 'L'Oréal's strategy consists of being present across all markets in the industry, becoming the world leader and, in order to achieve this, constant innovation' (Collin and Rouach, 2009). The company has six research and innovation regional hubs worldwide: the latest one opened in South Africa with the aim to expand its knowledge of the specific needs of African hair and skin, in order to successfully adapt the group's products for this market. They work on consumer insights, advanced research, product development, and product evaluation teams, and partner with the region's scientific ecosystem, including universities and dermatologists. This is an important dimension of the group's strategy that aims to help the brand get closer to target markets by adapting to specific cultural differences in the beauty market: 'For a Brazilian woman, hair and body are most important, for a Chinese woman facial skin is the priority, for an Indian woman it's make-up. Our approach is the "universalization" of beauty, i.e. globalization without uniformisation' (Jean-Paul Agon, CEO of L'Oréal; www.usinenouvelle.com).

L'Oréal has been able to maintain a strong cultural grounding despite local adaptation to different countries and regions, being widely recognized as a leading and expert French beauty brand. The group ensures brand heritage by keeping part of its production in France and takes advantage of the 'Made in France' dimension and the perceived quality associated with it. This label is particularly relevant and of added value for some of the group's brands such as Lancôme, Yves Saint-Laurent, Vichy and La Roche-Posay. In 2017 the brand launched the 'Your Skin, Your Story' campaign for its True Match foundation range – inspired by the 33 shades available it addresses a universal beauty, celebrating diversity and difference, with individuals sharing their unique heritage and skin story.

Case Challenge

On what basis does L'Oréal aim to achieve differentiation in crowded international consumer markets?

ONLINE RESOURCES

A longer version of this case study, with additional challenges, can be found on our companion website: https://www.macmillanihe.com/companion/Varley_Fashion_Management.

SUMMARY AND CONCLUDING THOUGHTS

Growth and development are usually signs of a healthy fashion organization and are therefore usually central to strategic aims and goals. Strategy concerns the pace, direction and scope of growth and development at company and/or brand level. Supporting growth within the organization is what drives operations and channels resources. The final 'box' in the Ansoff matrix refers to market penetration, reinforcement and consolidation as a way to maintain a position in existing markets with an existing product range. Small, specialist and private organizations may be content with low levels of overall growth but in an increasingly competitive fashion market it is likely that some development at least is required to prevent erosion of sales and profits.

Many organizations in today's fashion market are global in their ambition and seamlessly operate in many international markets, which in turn makes them increasingly dependent on market extension and development to provide a good rate of return on investment. They are constantly seeking opportunities, responding to drivers of growth and evaluating the attractions while dealing with the complexity and subtlety of international markets, preserving brand integrity and values while creating desire and demand to make it all worthwhile.

Global marketing strategies become more important as companies around the world try to achieve success in various markets, develop products and services that appeal to consumers as well as differentiate their offer. The notion of place in an era of globalization has changed with glocal companies creating new and improved products by using locally sourced materials derived in local culture. New technologies are an essential part of global competitiveness and drivers of economic growth, productivity and innovation. In order to manage this digital revolution, understanding cultural differences is crucial.

CHALLENGES AND CONVERSATIONS

1. For a fashion brand of your choice:
   a. Apply the Ansoff matrix to determine the strategies used in the brand's history.
   b. Conduct an analysis of its international presence – what territories is it present in, and what format does the presence take?
   c. Where do you see its future growth coming from? Justify your answer.

2. Consider applying the BCG matrix to LVMH. Can you identify where the brands are located in the matrix? Have the brands' positions changed over time? What evidence can you find for strategic actions taken by the group in reaction to brand positions in the matrix?

3. What examples of international brand expansion failure can you think of? Using American Apparel as an example, apply the 12Cs to help you analyze what went wrong for this brand.

REFERENCES AND FURTHER READING

Aaker, D. (1991) *Managing Brand Equity: Capitalizing on the Value of a Brand Name*. New York: The Free Press.

Akehurst, G. and Alexander, N. S. (1996) 'The internationalisation process in retailing', in Akehurst, G. and Alexander, N. S. (eds) *The Internationalisation of Retailing*. London and New York: Routledge, pp. 1–15.

Alexander, N. and Doherty, A.-M. (1997) *International Retailing*. London: Blackwell.

Anholt, S. (2007) 'Competitive identity: A new model for the brand management of nations, cities and regions'. *Policy & Practice: A development education review*, 16, pp. 3–13.

Ansoff, I. (1988) *The New Corporate Strategy*. New York: John Wiley & Sons.

Awoniyi, M. A. (1999) The Emergence of Common Market in West Africa: An Examination of Cross Culture and Ethnographic Marketing System of Alaba International Market, Lagos-Nigeria. *American Journal of Industrial and Business Management*, 6(2), pp. 136–154.

Baisya, K. R. (2008) *Aesthetics in Marketing*. New Delhi: Sage Publications.

Bowman, J. (2015) 'The cream of the crop: How Nivea's universal focus gets local treatment'. *WARC*. Available at: https://www.warc.com/content/article/the_cream_of_the_crop_how_niveas_universal_focus_gets_local_treatment/105792 [accessed 26/10/2016].

Cateora, P. R. and Graham, J. L. (2007) *International Marketing*. Boston, MA: McGraw-Hill.

Chattalas, M., Kramer, T. and Takada, H. (2008) 'The impact of national stereotypes on the country of origin effect: A conceptual framework'. *International Marketing Review*, 25(1), pp. 54–74.

Chuang, S. and Yen, H. (2007) 'The impact of a product's country-of-origin on compromise and attraction effects'. *Marketing Letters*, 18, pp. 279–291.

Collin, B. and Rouach, D. (2009) *Le Modèle L'Oréal*. Paris : Pearson.

Czinkota, R. M., Ronkainen, I. A. and Moffett, M. H. (2009) *Fundamentals of International Business*, 2nd edn. New York: Bronxville.

De Mooij, M. (2010) *Global Marketing and Advertising, Understanding Cultural Paradoxes*, 3rd edn. Thousand Oaks, CA: Sage Publications.

Deloitte (2012) *From Bricks to Clicks: Generating Global Growth through eCommerce Expansion*. London: Deloitte.

Doole, I. and Lowe, R. (2008) *International Marketing Strategy: Analysis, development and implementation*, 5th edn. London: South-Western Cengage Learning.

Doole, I., Phillips, C. and Lowe, R. (1997) *International Marketing Strategy: Contemporary Readings*. London: International Thomson Business Press.

Elliott, G. and Cameron, R. (1994) 'Consumer perception of product quality and the country-of-origin effect. *Journal of International Marketing*, 2, pp. 49–62.

Euromonitor (2012) *Ramadan and Consumers*. Available at: http://blog.euromonitor.com/2012/07/ramadan-and-consumers-2012-trends.html [accessed 18/04/2017].

Hall, E. T. (1976) *Beyond Culture*. New York: Anchor Books.

Hamzaoui-Essoussi, L., Merunka, D. and Bartikowski, B. (2011) 'Brand origin and country of manufacture influences on brand equity and the moderating role of brand typicality'. *Journal of Business Research*, 64(9), pp. 973–978.

Hofstede, G. (2001) *Culture's Consequences – Comparing Values, Behaviors, Institutions and Organizations Across Nations*, 2nd edn. Thousand Oaks, CA: Sage Publications.

Hollensen, S. (2007) *Global Marketing: A Decision-oriented Approach*. Harlow: Pearson Education.

Hunger, D. and Wheelen, T. (2011) *Strategic Management and Business Policy: Toward Global Sustainability*, 13th edn. Englewood Cliffs, NJ: Prentice Hall.

Insch, G. S. and McBride, J. B. (2004) 'The impact of country-of-origin cues on consumer perceptions of product quality: A binational test of the decomposed country-of-origin construct'. *Journal of Business Research*, 57(3), pp. 256–265.

J. Walter Thompson Intelligence (JWT) (2015) The imperfect aesthetic, boutique thrift and more. Available at: https://www.jwtintelligence.com/2015/08/the-imperfect-aesthetic-boutique-thrift-and-more/ [accessed 16/04/2017].

Jansson, J. and Power, D. (2010) 'Fashioning a global city: Global city brand channels in the fashion and design industries'. *Regional Studies*, 44(7), pp. 889–904.

Johnson, Z. S., Tian, Y. and Lee, S. (2016) 'Country-of-origin fit: When does a discrepancy between brand origin and country of manufacture reduce consumers' product evaluations?' *Journal of Brand Management*, 23(4), pp. 403–418.

Just Style (2014) Available at: https://www.just-style.com/interview/peter-ruis-chief-executive-of-jigsaw_id121567.aspx [accessed 10/06/2016].

Kapferer, J.-N. (2008) *The New Strategic Brand Management, Creating and Sustaining Brand Equity Long Term*. London: Kogan Page.

Khondker, H. H. (2004) 'Glocalization as Globalization: Evolution of a sociological concept'. *Bangladesh e-Journal of Sociology*, 1 (July).

Kotler, P. (2009) *Marketing Management*. Harlow: Pearson Prentice Hall.

Kotler, P., Wong, V., Saunders, J. and Armstrong, G. (2005) *Principles of Marketing*, 4th European edn. Harlow: Prentice Hall.

Levitt, T. (1983) 'The globalisation of markets'. *Harvard Business Review*, May–June.

Moore, C. et al. (2000) 'Brands without boundaries: The internationalization of the designer retailer's brand'. *European Journal of Marketing*, 34(8), pp. 919–937.

Paswan, A. K. and Sharma, D. (2004) 'Brand-country of origin (COO) knowledge and COO image: Investigation in an emerging franchise market'. *Journal of Product & Brand Management*, 13(3), pp. 144–155.

Petrilla, M. (2015) The next big untapped fashion market: Muslim women. Available at: http://fortune.com/2015/07/15/muslim-women-fashion/ [accessed 12/06/2016].

Roth, M. S. and Romeo, S. B. (1992) 'Matching product category and country image perceptions: A framework for managing country-of-origin effects'. *Journal of International Business Studies*, 23, pp. 477–497.

Schuiling, I. and Kapferer, J.-N. (2004) 'Real differences between local and international brands: Strategic implications for international marketers'. *Journal of International Marketing*, 12(4), pp. 97–112.

Solomon, M. (2009) *Consumer Behavior: Buying, Having, and Being*. Upper Saddle River, NJ: Prentice Hall.

Spencer Stuart (2013) *Crossing borders: Internationalizing brands*, Spencer Stuart. Available at: https://www.spencerstuart.com/research-and-insight/crossing-borders-internationalizing-brands [accessed 17/04/2015].

Terpstra, V. and Sarathy, R. (2000) *International Marketing*, 8th edn. Fort Worth, TX: Dryden Press.

Treadgold, A. (1989) 'Pan-European retail business: Emerging structure'. *European Business Review*, 89(4), pp. 7–12.

Usunier, J.-C. (1998) *International and Cross-Cultural Management Research*. SAGE series in Management Research. London: Sage Publications.

Vernon, R. (1966) 'International investment and international trade in the product cycle. *The Quarterly Journal of Economics*, MIT Press, USA.

Vogue (2017) *What is Scandinavian Style now?* Available at: http://www.vogue.co.uk/article/what-is-scandinavian-style-now-christina-exsteen [accessed 18/11/2017].

WGSN (2016) *The new global traveler*. Available at: www.wgsn.com [accessed 19/12/2016].

Wigley, S., Moore, C. M. and Birtwistle, G. (2005) 'Product and brand: Critical success factors in the internationalization of a fashion retailer'. *International Journal of Retail & Distribution Management*, 33(7), pp. 531–544.

5

FINANCIAL MANAGEMENT IN FASHION

Liz Gee

⊛ INTRODUCTION

For any fashion business to be able to pursue strategic objectives like those outlined in the previous chapter, it must have funds available. Money is one of the three internal business resources alongside men and machines, and some would argue *the* most important. This chapter looks at the different sources of funding available and what a business must do to obtain and retain finance as the consequences of failing to manage this resource effectively are serious. Financial management is a key strategic competence, indeed a threshold capability as without a degree of proficiency it is impossible to compete at all let alone achieve competitive advantage. The role of managing finances may fall to different people depending on the size of the fashion business; there may be a dedicated Finance Director or Financial Controller but regardless of job role it is important that all fashion business people have a good understanding of this important discipline. This chapter starts by introducing some of the underpinning concepts of financial management and then takes a logical path through financial research and analysis, which underpins the understanding of company valuation, and the development of a strategic approach to financial management within fashion organizations.

👕 LEARNING OBJECTIVES

After studying this chapter, you should be able to understand:

- The inextricable link between the strategic aims and the financial capability of a fashion organization;

- The key sources of long- and short-term funding used in fashion businesses of all sizes;

- The importance of published financial information as a rich research source that can aid understanding of a fashion business;

- The application of basic financial analysis skills to financial statements to assess the position and performance of a fashion business;

- Some of the complex issues around valuing fashion businesses of different sizes.

THE CONCEPT OF RISK AND RETURN

This basic concept underpins the rational decisions of all finance-minded professionals. The underlying premise of all business is that money has to be put at risk in order to make more money from it, that is, to make a 'return'. At a basic level it dictates that all investors behave rationally and will not take any risk with their money unless they get something in 'return' for taking that risk, usually in the form of more money. The compensation dynamic going on here is – take an increased risk only if compensated by increased return.

---

5. Image credit Natascha Radclyffe-Thomas. Reproduced by permission of Shanghai Tang.

The rational investor dislikes uncertainty because it increases risk:

- For a given level of return they will *always* choose the least risky investment.

- For a given level of risk they will *always* choose the investment giving the highest level of return.

- Risk/return trade-off: they will accept greater risk only if it is compensated for by greater return.

We will come back to defining, measuring and controlling business risk in much greater detail in Chapter 13 but first it is necessary to consider what risk actually is in terms of a financial concept. In purely financial terms, risk is about fluctuations in returns; that is, traditionally getting less profit than we expected. It may seem strange that getting more profit than expected is still a risk, but it is the fact that it is not what we expected that is important. From a mathematical perspective risk is measured using standard deviation from the mean, which denotes the 'spread' of results.

> **The rational investor**
> This investor dislikes risk and will demand increased return as a trade-off for accepting increased risk.

> **Sources of finance**
> These differ in cost and availability to businesses depending on their stage in the business cycle. It is therefore important to consider the purpose of the funds.

SOURCES OF LONG-TERM FUNDING

Where the money comes from very much depends on the size of the fashion business in the first instance and secondly its legal structure. In theory, six different sources of funding exist (see Figure 5.1, and a summary in Table 5.1) but not all may be available to the business nor appropriate for the funding requirement; matching sources to purpose is an important consideration. Long-term funding relates to a large amount of capital for a strategic investment which may last several years. We will come back to short-term funding requirements in the section on 'Short-term funding requirements'. Small businesses, particularly start-ups, have fairly limited options as they have no track record and no reason for external entities such as banks or institutional investors to trust that their money is safe and will earn a return. It is the Finance Manager's job to find the most efficient combination of capital from these sources, balancing the benefits and drawbacks of each.

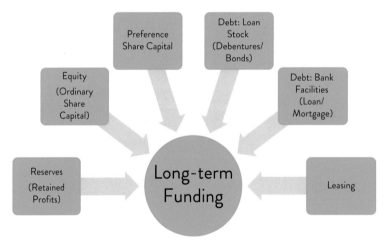

Figure 5.1 *Sources of finance for matching to long-term purposes*

Reserves (Retained Profits)

When a business makes a profit there are two options for what it can do with it at the end of its financial year. The business could pay some to shareholders as a form of return (a dividend) on their share of investment. We examine the complex decision-making behind

paying dividends later. On the other hand these profits could be retained in the business to be used for growth purposes in subsequent financial years. As they are an internal source of finance there is no need to obtain permission to use these profits for growth (unlike bank funding) and hence retained profits tend to be the most common source of finance. There is of course a major snag; the need to be making a profit to generate reserves; fluctuations in annual profit levels may mean that the level of retained profits available for investment is not wholly reliable (see Figure 5.2). Another technicality applies here, that the reserves must be real. That sounds rather strange but a company balance sheet may note reserves that are created by applying accounting principles; reserves such as a 'revaluation reserve' arising from property revaluations are not 'real' and hence cannot be used; only the reserve labelled 'profit and loss brought forward' (or similar) can be used. There are similar restrictions around the use of reserves for paying dividends, as we will see later.

Equity (Ordinary Share Capital)

Equity is the foundation of the financial structure of all businesses and is also known as Ordinary Share Capital. When a decision is made to start a business, it is inevitable that some money must be put at risk by being invested with the aim of generating more money. Consequently, small business owners normally invest their own money in their businesses and it is this injection of funds that becomes the capital of the business, and hence is owed back to the owners of the business.

Ordinary shares carry a Nominal Value (e.g. £1) which is detailed as part of the legal documents issued at the time of company formation, the Memorandum and Articles. These documents detail the rules and legal constitution of the company and the maximum number of shares that the company can ever issue (the Authorised Share Capital). When shares are issued they are sold at this Nominal Value or at a premium; they can never be sold at a discount. This only refers to the issue of shares; obviously the value of an investment may go up or down as we will see when we consider stock markets later in the section on 'Accessing long-term sources'.

In return for putting their capital at risk by investing in a company, ordinary shareholders become part owners of the company, and get to vote on decisions tabled by the directors. The principle of the 'divorce of ownership and control' means that the directors have a 'fiduciary duty' to act in the best interests of the shareholders. Directors may or may not be shareholders although share ownership is a useful incentive to ensure alignment of company and personal objectives.

If a company wishes to raise additional capital to fulfil strategic objectives it is common to make a Rights Issue where existing shareholders are offered the *right* to acquire more shares in proportion to their existing shareholding, usually at a discounted price. If the Rights are taken up, the ownership structure of the company will remain the same. Alternatively, the company can also issue new shares to the market, in which case there is a risk that new shareholders will buy these shares. This would *dilute* the % shareholding of existing shareholders. This could result in a change in ownership, for example in a takeover situation, as any one shareholder that owns 51% of the ordinary shares can take control of the company. Because of these control impacts, the issuance of shares is governed by complex rules enshrined in law (Companies Act 2006). For example, there are legal requirements for shareholders to declare an interest and their intentions towards a listed company once their shareholding reaches certain triggers. The intricacies of share issues are further governed by the rules of the stock market on which a particular share is listed. The website of the London Stock Market has some good detailed guides (www.londonstockexchange.com).

Once issued, shares exist permanently, as parts of the separate legal entity that is a company. A shareholder who no longer wants to hold shares in a company must find another investor to buy the shares so that s/he can realize their investment. Most commonly this is facilitated in public companies by the Stock Exchange, which allows buyers and sellers of shares to come together. This is a problem for small companies because there is not an active market in their shares and so these have to rely on personal investors, or sometimes venture capital or private equity firms (see section on 'Accessing long-term sources' for more details on investors). The digital-age phenomenon of crowd-funding can help small companies to sell their shares. Things can go wrong for an ordinary shareholder and this is where the risk becomes apparent. Under Insolvency Law, ordinary shareholders are the last priority for payment on winding up a company; the Government is first. This risk dynamic is explored in more depth in Chapter 13.

The debate around the merits of a public listing of shares versus remaining a private limited company could warrant a chapter of its own, but simply put it is a question of being willing to comply with enormous amounts of regulation and to disclose your business model, in return for a more liquid market for your shares. The global fashion industry sees an interesting split opinion over this. One view is – if you don't need the money then don't do it; Arcadia, New Look, and

River Island are three highly successful UK-based young fashion retail groups where secrecy and lack of disclosure is an aid to their competitive advantage. In contrast, fashion retailers who are PLCs, such as Debenhams and Marks & Spencer, are subject to a high level of press scrutiny and criticism. Those in the middle ground who may have an Alternative Investment Market (AIM) listing – on the London 'baby' stock market – are subject to less scrutiny and regulation and whilst this listing is supposed to be a short-term springboard to the main market, they tend to stay there; Mulberry and ASOS are examples of companies who are sizeable but have remained listed on AIM. Companies will often list on the stock market which has appetite for their shares; hence the Italian Prada group's 2011 listing on the Hong Kong Stock Exchange, reflecting the Asian appetite for luxury goods. The high-profile luxury conglomerate LVMH remains in private ownership yet discloses significant information about its business as a source of financial PR to make a market for its shares.

The Initial Public Offering (IPO) process, which launches a company onto the open market for ownership, is fraught with risks, costs and guesswork. Setting the share price, valuing the business and finding buyers for shares can be aided by a Merchant Bank, at a price. Global trends in financing drive appetite for shares and in different business sectors so there is an important role of

timing as conditions have to be acceptable for sensible valuations to be achieved. For example, New Look, and Fat Face have had many false starts to their IPO ambitions.

Once listed shares have been sold to the public in an IPO and the cash proceeds of the sale banked, there is no further income to the company until new shares are issued; however, that is by no means the end of the story as the fortunes of the company are inextricably linked to fluctuations in its share price. Fashion retailer Supergroup plc suffered heavily from not being fully prepared for the regulatory demands of being a public company, yet others like Ted Baker have had a long track record of success. We will return to the issue of share prices and the minefield of business valuations again in the section on 'Business valuation'.

Preference Share Capital

There is a second type of share capital, which is also technically equity, but its special features mean it behaves more like debt capital. Preference shareholders are not owners of the business, consequently they cannot vote at meetings nor take decisions, and so one or more of the following special preference rights are attached to these shares to make them attractive to investors:

- **Dividend Priority**:   preference share dividends are paid before ordinary share dividends.
- **Capital Priority**:   preference shareholders rank above ordinary shareholders in the priority of capital repayment in a winding-up scenario.
- **Cumulation**:   if the full amount of dividend cannot be paid one year, due to the poor performance of the business, then the balance of the dividend is carried forward for payment in the following year before the ordinary shareholders can receive a dividend.

These rights reduce the risk for the holders. Preference shares are uncommon and issued where there is a need to increase the attractiveness of a new share offer for a company wishing to raise additional funds. For example, preference shares were used in the restructure of India's largest fashion retail group, Birla, in May 2015.

Loan capital (Debt)

This is different in nature from equity and it can be fixed-interest debentures or loan stock ('bonds') issued in a company. For example, Nike plc recently had over $1.1bn of bonds in an issue with a staggered maturity profile to 2043 at fixed interest rates

ranging from 5.15% to 3.625%. More commonly loan capital takes the form of a fixed-term bank loan, which if taken over a long term (say 25 years) and secured against property is termed a mortgage. This is a common form of capital for small businesses, where the entrepreneur will often put their house at risk to raise funds for a new venture. Loan capital carries very little risk for the holder, as the holder is always paid interest annually (as demonstrated in Figure 5.2) and the investment principle (original lend amount) must either be repaid over time or in a lump sum 'bullet' at the end of the loan term. This is true of long-term bank loans too, and the mechanisms of security and covenant monitoring put into place by the banks to further reduce the risk are explored further in the section 'Short-term funding requirements'. Term loans are commonly used in private equity deals; for example, the 2015 refinancing of Fat Face by its private equity owner Bridgepoint Capital was backed by a £210m syndicated loan provided by a group of banks forming a 'syndicate' led by lead investment banks, in this case Citibank & Goldman Sachs.

Leasing

Leasing is a common form of finance for Fixed Assets which lose value when used in a business and need regular replacement. Commonly leased assets include fleet vehicles which are rented from a specialist leasing company (lessor), often part of a High Street bank. The lessee does not own the asset but the lease will require the lessee to fund the upkeep and maintenance to preserve the residual value of the asset. Lease contracts may take the form of Hire Purchase contracts where title passes to the lessee on the final payment. The lease payments will have interest payments built in but are a fairly easy form of debt to obtain because the asset itself is the security for the loan and would be seized in the event of payment default.

Source of Long-Term Finance	Advantage	Disadvantage
Retained Profit (Reserves)	• No external permissions required • Readily available in a profit-making business	• Business must be making a profit • Retaining profit in the business will reduce profits available for dividend pay-out to ordinary shareholders
Ordinary Share Capital (Equity)	• Large sums available	• Dilution of existing shareholding and control issues possible, e.g. takeover • Expensive for business to raise • Lowest priority in event of winding up
Preference Share Capital	• Preferences make these shares attractive to investors	• Preference dividend pay-out will reduce the profits available for dividend pay-out to ordinary shareholders • Preference dividend often cumulative
Loan Capital	• No impact on business ownership or control • Interest payments are tax deductible	• Security required • Onerous covenants and monitoring procedures • Interest payments must be met even when business is not profitable
Lease Agreements	• Readily available, as leased asset effectively provides loan security	• Built-in interest payments are often higher to reflect administration costs and risk to the lessor

Table 5.1 *Summary of the advantages and disadvantages of different sources of long-term finance*

THE COST OF CAPITAL

It could be assumed that all money costs the same; however, this is not the case because different forms of funding carry different levels of risk and, knowing about the trade-off between risk and return, it makes sense that riskier funding should be more expensive. Thinking that a business should be wholly funded by the least risky type of capital and therefore have the lowest funding costs is not quite right either. Risk must be considered from the viewpoint of the funder such as a bank providing a loan or a shareholder investing capital in turn for a share.

Figure 5.2 shows the legal order of distributions in a fictional company 'Mirage plc', which has three different sources of long-term capital and fluctuating profits over a five-year horizon. This illustrates the risk profiles of the different forms of long-term finance. From an investor's viewpoint it is best to be a debt holder as they are always paid out first and regardless of the amount of profit that is made.

Preference shareholders, because of the nature of cumulation, will get their full pay-out eventually until the worst happens. Ordinary shareholders can have good and bad years; their returns are unpredictable hence this is a risk. Figure 5.2 also illustrates how unpredictable retained profit is if the

Mirage plc has the following capital structure:

	£
Ordinary share capital	500,000
9% cumulative preference shares	200,000
6% debenture stock	100,000

Profits (before interest charges and dividends but after tax) over 5 years have been:

Year	1	2	3	4	5
Profit £	30,000	40,000	20,000	50,000	25,000

The practice is to distribute half of available amounts to ordinary shareholders.

Year	1	2	3	4	5
	£	£	£	£	£
Profit	30,000	40,000	20,000	50,000	25,000
Debenture Interest (1)	6,000	6,000	6,000	6,000	6,000
	24,000	**34,000**	**14,000**	**44,000**	**19,000**
Preference Interest (2)	18,000	18,000	14,000	22,000	18,000
	6,000	**16,000**	**0**	**22,000**	**1,000**
Ordinary Dividend	3,000	8,000	0	11,000	500
Retained Profit	3,000	8,000	0	11,000	500
Rate of Ordinary Dividend (%)	0.6	1.6	0	2.2	0.1

Figure 5.2 *Distributing profits in a fictional company*

business relies on this as a source of funding for a growth programme.

This risk profile influences the cost of each type of capital because of the risk and return trade-off. Also influencing this cost is the concept of 'servicing' this capital.

Servicing debt is most straightforward to understand: if you have a bank loan, as we will see later, you repay the principal amount but must also pay interest and arrangement fees to the bank, so the loan costs more than the amount borrowed. The bank must get a 'return' for lending to you. The bank also has great power over a business it lends to. If the business is unable to meet its interest payments the bank can 'call in' the loan and insist it is repaid immediately, and the business may be forced into administration. This great power gives the bank certainty; it bears very little risk and as such will not require a large return.

Servicing equity is a harder concept to understand as the business is effectively 'borrowing capital' from shareholders. We know that the shareholders have injected money into the business and put it at risk (they may lose it) in the hope of getting returns. Returns can be in the form of capital growth (for example, the share price grows so their £1 share is worth £2) or in the form of income (annual dividend). From the company's perspective they must provide capital growth and/or dividend to keep the shareholders happy and the share price high (if listed), so that is the 'cost' of having equity funding. There are additional costs of being a publicly quoted company too. There is less certainty in returns on equity so servicing costs are higher than in the case of debt. Greater dividend growth and/or share price is demanded by investors to balance out the risk of this uncertainty.

Servicing dynamics generally result in the cost of equity being higher for a company than the cost of debt. This means that the optimal capital structure of a company should have some element of relatively cheaper debt to keep the cost of capital down. Whilst an element of debt is a good thing from a cost perspective, too much is a bad thing from a risk perspective. The issue here is that you have to be making profits or at least cash flow to fund the interest payments or else the bank could call in the loan. This pressure introduces risk (fluctuations) to profit streams for the ordinary shareholders (see figure 5.2). This is the concept of "gearing" and the optimal capital structure will have some level of debt, but not too much. The gearing ratio can be calculated by relating the amount of debt capital in a company to its total capital (that is, debt + equity capital).

This simplified view of the concept and its calculations can be expanded by researching the Weighted Average Cost of Capital (WACC) in any good Corporate Finance text (see suggestions at the end of the chapter). The WACC calculation is the effective cost of funding for a business made up of the cost of each type of capital in its capital structure weighted according to the proportion of each type of funding contributes to the overall capital structure. The WACC can be a useful benchmark against which

you can assess the profitability of future investment strategies (see p268) after all if your new strategy cannot bring you in as much return as the cost of the capital you will be using to pursue it, then it probably is not a good idea.

A STRONG BALANCE SHEET AND THE DIVIDEND DECISION

The closing sections of a plc's annual report and accounts discloses the major shareholders. You may be surprised for example to see that the majority of share capital is in the hands of only a small proportion of shareholders who are investment trusts and pension funds.

Investors will hold shares for one of two reasons. They may have a growth motive and buy the share at a low price, expecting the price to rise so they make a capital gain when they sell it on (potentially taxable). Investment trusts will actively manage their share portfolio, moving in and out of investments to maximize their capital gain and hence the size of their capital pool for further investment. Pension funds conversely are a good example of an investor holding a share for the other motive of revenue generation. They need an income from to fund their pension payments so will hold shares which pay out a regular and relatively high stream of dividends.

Since the 2008 financial crisis there has been a trend for companies to preserve cash, stockpiling it on their balance sheet. Initially this was in reaction to liquidity in the financial markets due to the crisis, and only the best companies were being lent to. At one stage even Next plc, which then had an AAA credit rating was not able to borrow against its existing arranged bank facilities. Keeping cash on the balance sheet means that a company does not pay it out to ordinary shareholders in the form of dividends. It is questionable how long a company can continue to hoard cash on the balance sheet before investors demand its investment in strategic initiatives, its payment in dividends or the buy-back of shares.

 ONLINE RESOURCES

To examine motivations for companies to pay dividends or retain cash in further depth you can visit our companion website at: https://www.macmillanihe.com/companion/Varley_Fashion_Management.

ACCESSING LONG-TERM SOURCES

There are a number of 'institutions' that may play a part in the process of accessing long-term funding for a fashion business.

The Stock Exchange

This is a marketplace for shares. It does not contribute funds to businesses but allows exchange of investment funds between companies, hence encouraging the movement of funds to the most desirable companies.

Merchant banks

These provide a professional service to companies seeking to raise long-term funds. They will be retained to advise and administer a share issue. They may even be required to 'underwrite' the issue, in which case the bank undertakes to buy any unsold shares to ensure that the company raises its target funding. All of these services are offered at a high price. A share issue may be an issue to the general public, a rights issue to existing shareholders or a placing to a limited number of investors, who are clients of the bank. The advantage here is that banks will know how likely their clients are to be receptive to the offer and be able to price and market the share offer appropriately.

Commercial banks

High Street banks such as Barclays or HSBC are used mainly for provision of short-term funds such as an overdraft or medium-term secured loans of around 5–10 years. Beyond that horizon, banks will issue mortgage loans secured on property.

Institutional investors

We noted earlier that the largest investors in any publicly traded fashion entity, such as Marks & Spencer plc, Debenhams plc, or Supergroup plc, are not private individuals but instead are the pension funds and investment houses. A return on their investment and the timescale over which this return is required will drive their investment motivation rather than a concern for fashion trends! A pension fund will have an income requirement to fund its regular outgoings in the form of payments to its pensioners, and therefore will expect the company to pay a steady stream of dividends. Unit and Investment trusts will have different profiles and return requirements, which will drive the fund managers to actively buy and sell shares in response to market and company performance.

Private investors

Grassroots private investors can be of great importance to some fashion companies. The increasing popularity of crowd-funding for entrepreneurial ventures taps into the consumer community for business funding. Private investors range in size from the individual 'Angel' Investor through to the Private Equity firms and the Venture Capitalists.

Crowd-funders

The age of social media has had an important impact on small business funding opportunities. Platforms such as Kickstarter have enabled small fashion businesses to raise money to grow. For example, a successful campaign by Strathberry bags provided the investment to produce their next range. Crowd-funding taps into the trend of building communities and belongingness, and consumers can get involved in the businesses they like through rewards-based crowd-funding. Hard core financiers are more likely to be involved in equity-based crowd-funding, in it for the size of the profit opportunity rather than the love of the product. This is an important consumer trend discussed further in Chapter 15 (Fashion Futures).

Angel investors

Before crowd-funding, the way to access individual investors, often called 'Angels', was through an organized networking event. This would give the entrepreneur an opportunity to pitch their idea and business plan to a gathering of local High Net Worth Individuals (HNWIs) with spare cash to invest in a business opportunity that appears lucrative, in a local version of the popular BBC TV programme Dragons' Den.

Angels	Bonmarché, a women's wear chain catering for the 50 plus market, was bought in a pre-pack administration in January 2012 from the wreckage of the Peacocks group. A motivated management team were parachuted in by the new Private Equity owners Sun European Partners, who spotted an opportunity in this growing demographic. A focus on rejuvenating the product and retail format resulted in a real turnaround of fortunes. It was floated on AIM raising £40m and made a solid start to life as a listed company amid accusations that it was valued too cheaply. Shares rose 10 per cent to 220p on day one. The company saw a transformation under its new management with a step change in profitability and not one of its 264 stores making a loss. The product improved in fashionability and quality; prices and multi-channel operations improved in this lucrative market where mature shoppers are focused on quality and value alongside price. With little direct competition, loyal customers, and expansion prospects in this flourishing demographic, the business initially went from strength to strength.
Devils	Debenhams plc in the 1990s was a solid department store business with steady if rather unexciting turnover and profit growth. It also had significant property assets and little debt, rendering it vulnerable to the promise of increasing efficiencies and increased profitability. So when a Private Equity (PE) consortium comprising Texas Pacific Group and Permira bought up all the shares, delisted it and took it into private ownership the results were not surprising. The PE consortium installed a strong retailer with a good track record as Chief Executive, sold off the property and leveraged up the balance sheet. Profitability and cash flow improved as overheads were slashed, store refits cancelled and store staff reduced. The PE consortium sought an exit to realize their investment so they could move on to the next opportunity, by re-floating the business. The price of the IPO was high but as there was little growth potential left in the business, the share price struggled to increase resulting in disgruntled shareholders. This has since resulted in stock market investors being rather wary of the floatation of a retail PE exit.

Table 5.2 *Two perspectives on private equity in UK mass-market fashion*

Private Equity houses

These play an important role in funding fashion. Their motivation is to spot opportunities to make themselves money so not surprisingly they have been characterized as both angels and devils on the UK fashion high street, as Table 5.2 explains.

Corporate venturing

This covers a wide range of entity funding including Venture Capital firms. We referred to the luxury conglomerate houses of LVMH and Kering in their incubator role in Chapter 4; their vast funds allow them to invest in order to turn around struggling brands in their portfolio (such as Gucci) or invest in new small brands for growth (such as Stella McCartney). Individuals often front investment houses; such as Tom Hunter fronting West Coast Capital, which invested in many UK mass-market fashion retailers in the early 2000s.

Incubators

Whilst not providing funding directly, incubators are of great importance at the entrepreneurial/ SME end of the fashion business spectrum. The traditional fashion business model of making a range then selling it requires significant investment in product before demand can be gauged. The Centre for Fashion Enterprise and the British Fashion Council both provide valuable practical support for new small fashion businesses, such as advice in finance, production, legal and marketing, and have helped designers such as Richard Nicoll, Peter Pilotto and Mary Katrantzou to achieve great success.

SHORT-TERM FUNDING REQUIREMENTS

Aside from looking at the need for large sums of new money to finance growth, fashion businesses require everyday financing called Working Capital. This can be seen on their balance sheet as the net worth of current assets and current liabilities: the sum of everything that is cash or nearly cash (including stock and debtors) less everything that the business owes in the short term (to creditors). Remember, the balance sheet only shows a snapshot position of the company on that one day in its year – it could be in a very different position the following day.

There are bound to be times of year when there is a short-term cash requirement. This is a very common issue for fashion retail businesses with seasonal trade patterns overlaid by monthly wages bills and quarterly rent payments (see Table 5.3). Matching the source of funding to use is important, mainly for cost reasons – for example, whilst you would use an overdraft to cover a supplier payment you need to make before your next sale period, it would be inappropriate to use an overdraft to buy a new distribution facility because other sources of funding are cheaper in the longer term.

High Street bank lending

If a cash shortfall is anticipated it cannot be ignored, and action is needed. A one-off benefit could be gained by changing the working capital cycle but usually it is best to approach the bank to put a short-term facility in place because unauthorized overdrafts are charged heavily. A credit profile will be built, which may allow a bank to offer a bank overdraft, often termed a multi-option facility (MOF). High Street banks are able to create large sums of money by careful lending of the funds they care for. Most banks will use similar considerations to the 'CARPE DIEM' model in Table 5.4 to help them decide to lend. Whilst a fashion business may want to 'seize the day' and take an opportunity, its bank will undertake a lengthy process of analyzing financial projections, which *may* result in a facility being granted at a negotiable price (I and E) with conditions attached (D and M).

Working with a bank manager is all about trust and building a relationship. The company therefore needs to show that it has a competent and committed management team (C) who understand their business model and business environment (E) and who appreciate the importance of cash flow (R).

From the bank's perspective it is considering allocating a portion of its own balance sheet for the business to draw down against and therefore put some of its funds at risk. To compensate for this risk the bank will want several things in return including insurance provisions to reduce the risk of default (D). This usually takes the form of security; a specific asset of a value similar to the loan amount, which the bank

	January	February	March	April	May	June
Capital	60,000					
Sales				12,000	16,000	28,000
Sub total	60,000			12,000	16,000	28,000
Purchases		48,000	16,000	18,000	20,000	14,000
Equipment			6,000			6,000
Premises		30,000				
Wages	800	800	800	800	800	800
Directors' salaries	2,400	2,400	2,400	2,400	2,400	2,400
Other expenses		600	600	600	600	600
Sub total	3,200	81,800	25,800	21,800	23,800	23,800
Net Cash Flow	56,800	-81,800	-25,800	-9,800	-7,800	4,200
Balance B\F	0	56,800	-25,000	-50,800	-60,600	-68,400
Balance C\D	56,800	-25,000	-50,800	-60,600	-68,400	-64,200

Table 5.3 *Cash flow forecast shows a short-term working capital requirement*

Competence	How competent are the management at delivering the promised results? What is the track record of the management?
Amount	How much are they asking for?
Repayment	How will they generate the extra cash to repay? Is this supported by realistic cash flow forecasts?
Purpose	What will the facility be used for? Have alternative funding sources been considered?
Entity	Does the bank have an understanding of the business model and the sector it operates in to assess its competitive advantage, resilience, flexibility, growth potential?
Default	What is the bank's security in case things go wrong, e.g. are there substantial physical assets or personal guarantees available?
Interest	What is the appropriate margin over base rate to be charged for amounts drawn on the facility to compensate for the risk?
Expenses	There will be an arrangement fee to be paid upfront for arranging the facility. There will also be fees charged for using the facility (utilization fees) or not using the facility (non-utilization fees) or both.
Monitor	What covenant monitoring can be put in place to act as an early warning of default?

Table 5.4 *CARPE DIEM: The types of questions a bank will ask when assessing whether to lend to a fashion business*

has the right to seize should the company default on its loan payments. Directors of small companies will often give personal guarantees that they will step in to repay their business loan should the business fail, which effectively means they are risking their family home. Less common is the lending of a fixed amount against the liquid assets of a company in a debenture. This forms a floating charge which can crystallize on default. Think of this as a net floating over all the assets of the company. Once the company fails to meet an interest or principle repayment, the net falls on the assets, the company can no longer trade and the bank can sell off the assets to make sure the loan is repaid. Before getting to this stage the bank will put extensive monitoring (M) processes in place to provide an early warning of default. The company makes promises with regards to its financial health and performance, called Covenants. The bank monitors these levels using ratio analysis commonly of Interest Cover, Profitability and Gearing (explored further in the Ratio Analysis section).

Banks *will* lend to companies who are making a profit with credible, achievable performance forecasts. They also want to see that a company matches funding sources to funding requirements (long term and short term). For example, overdrafts should be temporary, fully fluctuating and being cleared down so the account goes into credit at least once every month. If there appears to be a hard-core element of debt then the bank will demand that element of debt is rescheduled over a longer period, for example as a medium term loan, with more fees attached and increased security required.

Banks will also want to see that the business has considered alternative sources of long-term finance, for example hire purchase and leasing. If after negotiation the bank is not willing to support the business then there are alternatives.

Alternative short-term funding sources

Depending on the business model there may be options available to a company for maximizing the working capital cycle but many of these benefits are 'one off'.

A one-off benefit can be gained by manipulating cash flow in the business to help get you through a problem time. Supplier payment can be delayed but stretching creditors in this way can be risky; doing it too often can damage goodwill and lead to suppliers withholding goods. It is common to alternate which suppliers are made to 'wait' from one month to the next. The company may also be hit with lost early settlement discounts or see a price rise from suppliers if credit worthiness is damaged.

Fast collection from debtors can maximize the efficiency of working capital. Factoring of debtors is common, where specialist providers allow borrowing against the promise of future collections. The outstanding invoices are 'sold' and title assigned across to the specialist, passing on the risk of default. Not surprisingly the company does not get paid the full amount of the invoice to allow for the risk. This *invoice discounting* is common practice for small firms, where the specialist provider will pay around 85% of invoice value; they then bear all the responsibility for money collection, bad debts and financing.

A fashion business could also seek to release funds tied up in stock, or assets, but this may take time and investment. Some special providers are in the market to provide asset based lending against a basket of business resources as security, including stock, plant, and vehicles. In fashion, stock is seen as fairly worthless due to its speed of obsolescence and difficulty in realizing any value and hence is a risky asset and not often good security.

Another alternative for new ventures could be government loan schemes such as the UK's Enterprise Finance Guarantee.

> **Published financial statements** These are a treasure trove of information about public companies. There may be charts and graphs to help you understand the Key Performance Indicators (KPIs) of the business.

USING PUBLISHED FINANCIAL STATEMENTS

In Chapter 2 we considered all the different stakeholders in a fashion business and their differing perspectives. These different perspectives and information demands of stakeholders have contributed to the increasing length and complexity of disclosure in the Annual Reports and Accounts of public companies.

The 'Annual Report' at the front of the document interprets the numbers and puts a story around the numbers, written by the directors to comment on the year that has passed and strategic priorities going forwards. This part of the document can be considered as a brand congruent piece of financial PR to help analysts and investors understand the story of the brand (see, for example, Supergroup plc); or it can merely document the statutory minimum (see, for example, Mulberry plc) with no glossy photos or infographics. This document is a good place to start to get an overview of the company but it is necessary go a little deeper to gain a real understanding.

There are two key published financial statements to focus on when trying to analyze what is happening in a public company. First a word of warning: when looking at a complex group of companies it is important to ensure you are consulting the results of the whole group, which is the *consolidated* income statement. This statement shows all the group company results added together in a process accountants call 'consolidation'. Note also that there is little detail shown on the face of the accounts as all the detail and analysis is shown behind the face of the statement, in the *Notes to the accounts*. It is suggested you read this section alongside an exploration of the investor website of a brand such as Ted Baker, a successful British fashion brand with a fairly simple structure and hence not too complex a set of accounts.

There are differences in accounting and reporting regimes across the globe. UK company disclosure is enshrined in the Companies Act 2006 which sets out the formats and details of published financial information; add to this, the additional reporting requirements of the London Stock Exchange and the non-statutory accounting conventions called UK GAAP (Generally Accepted Accounting Principles). US companies are governed by US GAAP which means their presentation and disclosure are different. There is some convergence of these approaches in the IAS (International Accounting Standards).

ONLINE RESOURCES

Our companion website at: https://www.macmillanihe.com/companion/Varley_Fashion_Management provides an learning activity to help you understand published accounts.

The income statement

It is important to understand when it is most appropriate to analyze at the level of *operating profit* and not *profit before tax* or even *profit for the period*. This is an issue of comparability and controllability. From *operating profit* the income and expenses of the way the company is financed are taken – so stripping out the effects of capital structure allows businesses to be compared. It is advisable to compare operating profit because as we saw earlier, businesses are financed by different proportions of several sources of debt and equity. It is also here that the effect of currency movements will be seen, again something to be stripped out of the analysis of the underlying business. We will return to currency risk in Chapter 13.

Without getting too deep into financial complications it is possible to discover an awful lot about a business by asking some basic questions:

- Is revenue growing year on year and by what percentage?

- If revenue is growing then gross profit should be growing too (by a similar percentage). If not, why not?

- Does the increase in operating profit match the increase in gross profit? If not, then what are the additional business costs that are eroding the operating profit?

Published financial statements tell you very little detail about the expenses incurred in running the plc. All these costs tend to get lumped into SGA (Selling and General Administration) costs. Rarely are *administration costs* and *distribution costs* separately identified. A little digging in the notes to the accounts can yield details of staff costs and directors' benefits, which have to be separately disclosed. The answers to crucial questions may be nowhere to be found and you have to make do with an educated guess. For example, just how much do businesses spend on marketing? Remember also that types and amounts of expenses incurred will differ depending on the business model; for example, a bricks and mortar retailer with a large store estate will pay lots of rent and rates, salaries, heat, light and power bills, in contrast to a pure-play e-retailer that has no stores to run.

The statement of position

A company's performance is interesting when looking for a return on financial investment but many stakeholders are more concerned about the stability of the company. Has it got cash and assets, and is it likely to continue to trade? How is the business funded? The answers to these questions can be determined by looking at the *balance sheet* or *statement of position*. The column labelled 'Company' shows the position of a holding company; the 'Group' position consolidates all the positions of all the group companies into one column.

ONLINE RESOURCES

Our companion website at: https://www.macmillanihe.com/companion/Varley_Fashion_Management provides a learning activity to help you to read a statement of position (balance sheet).

When looking at this statement remember the key difference between this and the *income statement*. Whilst the income statement is a statement of flows, the statement of position is a snapshot of the business taken on the last day of its accounting period. This statement shows what the company *owns* (its assets) in the top half and what it *owes* (its liabilities) in the lower half. The statement *must balance* and it is structured around the accounting equation which holds that all the assets that a business owns are financed either by liabilities or by equity so:

Assets = Liabilities + Equity

Different fashion business models will have different balance sheets. For example a retailer has few debtors, a wholesaler has many; a retailer will have more fixed assets in the way of store fixtures and fittings than a wholesaler, while an online-only retail business will have few fixtures and fittings but more computer related assets.

We saw earlier that disclosure and the application of accounting rules is often prescribed but one choice companies do have is the date of their financial year end on which the balance sheet snapshot is taken. Commonly the year end date of 31st March is chosen for administrative ease as it coincides most closely with the tax year running to 4th April (examples include Mulberry plc). Some companies choose a calendar year end (for example the Kering Group report on 31st December) and others have seemingly odd dates (such as Nike on 31st May). For a seasonal, cyclical business like fashion the date of the balance sheet snapshot may have a bearing on the shape and valuation of the business particularly from a stock and cash perspective, so be aware of this when comparing competing businesses. Ted Baker plc's financial year ends 31st January when stock is potentially low; similarly Debenhams issue their balance sheet on 30th August before the stock build into Christmas trading.

This section has provided a *very* brief overview of the key financial statements. It is no substitute for personal research and analysis of a full set of Report and Accounts as they really are a treasure trove of information about a company's strategy and performance. Reading these in conjunction with one of the many good texts on financial accounting for non-specialists listed in the 'Further reading' section could provide further insight. The brief discussion here alludes to the many rules, jargon and terms that accountants use. Time would be well spent understanding some of these to improve financial literacy. This section has also focused on the accounts of PLCs as these are available for public analysis. Sole trader financial statements look different from the plc accounts under scrutiny here, particularly with reference to the treatment of directors' payments. Entrepreneurs running their own fashion business and who need to prepare accounts are directed to the many good reference books that can help (see Further Reading section).

Key Performance Indicators (KPIs)

Financial KPIs tend to be very similar for all businesses and the focus on performance means these are the key headlines from the Profit and Loss account; namely revenue and margin (see the section on 'Using published financial statements') but also with focus on working capital on the balance sheet and the all-important cash flow. Look for examples of these headlines in Report and Accounts.

A company may also choose to shine a spotlight on some *non-financial* KPIs which illustrate its strategic priorities such as space growth. In 2014 Marks &

Spencer plc began a strategic priority in international expansion and so reported the annual growth in number of international stores. In addition, Marks & Spencer's strategic priorities around sustainability led them to monitor performance around their 'Plan A' objectives and produce separate reports on sustainability targets (see Case Study 12 at the end of Chapter 12).

The financial and fashion trade press pay particular attention to two particular KPIs; *'like for like sales growth'* is a common metric frequently referred to in the fashion trade press which tries to measure underlying growth of a business by stripping out the effect of new space. Retailers, however, may use inconsistent definitions, rendering this metric somewhat out-dated, especially considering the effect of digital channels on sales growth. The other popular metric in the financial press is EBITDA (*earnings before interest, tax, depreciation and amortization*). The terms *earnings* and *profit* are interchangeable so EBIT and PBIT (*profit before interest and tax*) are referring to the same number. EBITDA attempts to remove some of the arbitrariness from the measure of earnings to facilitate greater comparability across businesses, sectors and even across the same business over time where there may have been changes in accounting policies. On the income statement EBIT (or PBIT) is the profit remaining after all the expenses of running the business are removed but before taking out Interest or Tax. If comparisons are made on the performance of businesses with different funding structures then it is right to look at the level of profit generated before interest is paid, because businesses with less debt will pay less interest. It may also be appropriate to compare businesses at the level of earnings that they can control, looking at earnings before tax is paid, as it should follow that a profitable business will pay some tax in the country in which it mainly trades. Businesses with shrewd accountants and complex offshoring arrangements may pay less (the ethical debate about this is another matter). All this justifies comparing businesses at the EBIT level.

We saw earlier that fixed assets are reduced in value on the balance sheet over the period they are held in the business, with this process termed *depreciation* for tangibles and *amortization* for intangibles. There is some flexibility in the accounting rules around these processes, aside from the fact that they are not actual movements of cash in a business, so for comparability purposes they should be removed from the EBITDA metric. These amounts have already been charged to expenses in arriving at PBIT so we add them back to get to the super-comparable metric of EBITDA.

RATIO ANALYSIS

It is possible to tell a lot about a business from asking some simple questions and looking at the changes in the financial headlines. The next level of financial analysis involves relating some of these key numbers together in what is called by accountants, *ratio analysis*. There are many different ratios and even different ways to calculate the same ratio, but here we focus on those ratios that are most useful when looking at fashion companies. Ratios can be used internally and externally to a business and they are often used as warning signs of financial trouble ahead, with banks using ratios to set covenants to monitor debt facilities (see section 'Short-term funding requirements'). The three types of relevant ratios are listed in order of importance in Figure 5.3. The fourth category of investor metric, solvency, is touched upon here and revisited in Chapter 13.

Liquidity

The first priority in any business is not its ability to make profit but its ability to generate cash. A business cannot survive without cash, whilst it can survive in the short term without making a profit.

A fashion business should always have sufficient current assets (stock, debtors, and cash) to be able to pay its current liabilities as they fall due (bank overdraft, trade creditors). Liquidity ratios measure this ability. The *current ratio* simply relates current assets to current liabilities and a healthy level is anything above 1.5:1 (i.e. £1.50 of current assets for every £1 of liabilities). A current ratio below 1:1 could mean that the business is unable to meet its debts as they fall due; hence the business is technically insolvent. A high current ratio could also raise concerns that too much money is tied up in current

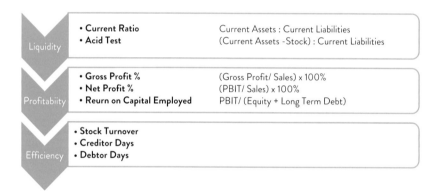

Figure 5.3 *Ratio analysis categories*

assets; for example, sitting in unproductive cash or uncollected debt.

In fashion retail businesses a healthy current ratio can give a false sense of security. We saw earlier that often the largest number on a fashion retailer's balance sheet is stock, but stock is not that easy to convert to cash if we need cash to pay a bill; so it would be more prudent to exclude stock from our liquidity calculation. The *acid test* (also called the *quick ratio*) removes the stock number from the total of current assets and compares this with current liabilities. In a fashion retailer this is often well below the safe level of 1:1 and can get as low as 0.5:1 without undue concern as it is important to look at timings of cash flows and remember that ratio analysis uses a snapshot position.

Performance

Once the solvency of the company has been established we can look at its trading performance. The concept of margins is used at a product level in a fashion business (see Chapter 8) and is the same underlying principle here although in this case we are interested in margins at a business level. Obviously this is an oversimplification of the underlying departmental and stock keeping unit (SKU) complexity, but it is a useful benchmark for target setting.

At the business level the *gross profit margin* simply expresses gross profit as a percentage of sales revenue. Gross profit is what is left once the direct costs of a product are subtracted from the sales revenue. A fashion business needs to make sure that it makes sufficient gross profit to cover the costs of running the business and preferably leave some net profit either to distribute to the business owners or to reinvest in growing the business.

Most businesses will set targets for absolute growth in gross profit year on year but they will also want to see improvements in gross margin as this reflects efficiencies in the supply chain. Gross margin percentages can also be compared across competing firms in the sector. A fall in a gross margin percentage year on year may mean that there are supply chain issues that need to be addressed, or perhaps a rise in raw material prices such as cotton that could not be passed on to the consumer in price rises. More worryingly, falling margin could indicate that selling prices are falling due to excessive markdown to achieve sales volume.

Profit margins lower down the Income Statement can be calculated either at Operating Margin or Net Profit Margin levels, the latter using Profit before Interest and Tax (PBIT), again expressed as a percentage of sales revenue. Sometimes banks use Profit After Tax in this calculation so it is important to ensure comparability of metrics.

Another popular performance metric is Return on Capital Employed (ROCE). There are lots of similar but slightly different metrics all looking at return generated on the assets used in a business (for example, Return on Equity, or Return on Assets) so it is important to ensure the same calculation is used when comparing across businesses. For ROCE here, Capital Employed in a business is the equity and the long-term debt added together and the Return is taken at PBIT level.

Efficiency

There are many different efficiency ratios that can be used depending on the business model and sector under scrutiny. What is being measured here is the efficiency of using working capital – so there is a focus on the middle part of the balance sheet – but it also gives insight into management processes. For fashion businesses, stock is the most important current asset so it would make sense to look at the efficiency of the use of this asset. Stock turnover can be measured in two different ways by essentially the same calculation.

Whilst absolute levels of stock would be expected to increase to support a growing retail business there is a danger that too much cash could be tied up in stock which goes out of fashion and cannot be sold

or needs to be heavily discounted to shift it. So the rate at which stock turns over through the fashion business is important and impacts the business's ability to meet demand. Stock turn ratio is calculated by dividing the Cost of Sales by the Average Stock (closing stock + opening stock / 2) to give the number of times per year the stock is effectively sold. This can be expressed in days if you take (Stock / Cost of Sales) x 365 and here, obviously, the faster the better. You will see great variation in stock turn between fast fashion (higher number of times per year, lower number of days) and luxury fashion business models (lower number of times per year stock turn, higher number of days of stock held).

For a wholesaler, where sales are made on credit, it is important to monitor how quickly outstanding debts are collected by the business. Here the average debtors figure (opening debtors + closing debtors /2) should be used and expressed as a percentage of sales revenue made on credit. It may be necessary to make an assumption about the proportion of sales that is made on credit. Note also that sales revenue on the Income Statement is stated VAT exclusive, but the debtors figure on the balance sheet is stated VAT inclusive so therefore needs to be reduced (for example, by dividing the debtors figure by 1.2 where the VAT rate is 20%). It may be useful to know how efficient the business is at collecting outstanding debts and comparing this against credit policies; here divide debtors' turnover ratio by 365 days to get an average collection period in days.

A similar calculation can be performed looking at creditor days in both retailers and wholesalers. Here the business wants its creditor's collection to be as long as possible, without upsetting the goodwill of suppliers, jeopardizing product availability or affecting a credit rating. Again VAT should be excluded from creditor collection calculations.

Solvency

There is a fourth category of ratios that needs to be touched on briefly, as these are used particularly by banks in setting covenants but are also important for internal monitoring by management. A business is technically insolvent when its total liabilities are greater than its total assets (resulting in it having negative net worth) and it cannot repay its creditors. We will see in Chapter 13 that the directors commit an offence under the Companies Act 2006 if they allow a business to become insolvent.

The *gearing ratio* shows the proportion of debt funding in a company – usually Long-Term Liabilities / Capital Employed (but beware as there are variants) – and provides a good indicator of its solvency. We saw earlier that a certain amount of debt is good as it is a cheaper form of funding but that debt brings with it the requirement to pay interest and principle repayment at regular, set intervals. Banks will want to see low gearing whereas shareholders will want it to be as high as possible (they will benefit from the leverage effect of the ROCE exceeding the cost of borrowing). Ideally, the gearing ratio should not exceed 50% although it often does in small businesses.

Banks will also want to see that a business can comfortably meet the interest payments due on its loans. The interest cover ratio hence shows how many times the interest payments can be covered by profits (calculated as PBIT/ Interest) and a healthy ratio is 4 times; a worrying ratio being 2 times.

To summarize therefore, ratio analysis can be used internally for a business to help manage financial performance and the financial position. We have also seen that banks use ratios as the basis of covenants on lending facilities. Ratios can also be a good starting point when we try to put a value on a business if the owners are looking for an exit, either as an outright private sale or as an IPO on a stock market.

BUSINESS VALUATION

The age-old problem of assigning a value to a business is more art than science; a range of different approaches can be taken depending on the purpose of the business valuation and the type and size of business, with this being a particular problem for small businesses. Whilst the true value of anything can only be what the buyer is willing to pay, there are several different approaches that can narrow down the value of a business to a sensible range.

The balance sheet would appear to be a good place to start, as the 'net assets' is the worth of the business; however, we saw earlier that assets are carried on the balance sheet at book value, being a historic cost reduced over time by depreciation. That in no way reflects the market value of the assets or indeed the replacement value if you wanted to start the business from scratch. Secondly, missing from most balance sheets is a hugely important part

Business valuation An art within the science of financial management. Various analytical tools can be used yet stock markets are the ultimate valuation tool and are subject to many rational and irrational influences.

of a business that helps generate revenue, retain loyal customers, and on which huge amounts of money are spent trying to build, especially in many fashion businesses. We are talking about '*the brand*', which does not appear in the book value of most businesses. From an accounting viewpoint that makes perfect sense although it causes huge debates in the accounting profession. For example, we saw earlier the accounting rule that the balance sheet shows tangible and intangible assets at a value that is the lower of their cost or their net realizable value. Brands have no net realizable value until another business is willing to pay for them. International Accounting Standards (IAS) do not allow companies to recognize the value of assets they have generated themselves on their balance sheets. Conversely, if a brand has been acquired then that brand value can be shown on the group's balance sheet, as an intangible asset of goodwill, and tested each year for impairment.

So in thinking about where the value lies in any business, it is not in the assets it owns but in what it does with them. A business valuation has to consider not only past profit performance but also future profit potential, which is the big unknown. There is also the conflicting perspective that a seller will believe his business is worth more than the buyer, who is out to minimize the amount paid. Net asset value reflects the position if all the tangible assets in the business were sold off, and the liabilities paid off, then this would be the remaining value in the business. This provides us with a minimum baseline valuation but certainly not a fair value.

It is possible to factor in investor ratios, considering multiples of net earnings using the P/E (Price/ Earning) ratio – see the next section, on Share price performance. For example, a small fashion retailer might be valued at around '5 times earnings'. Here a small business which has generated an average net profit (PAT) of £30,000 over the past 5 years would therefore be priced at around £150,000. P/E ratios for fashion PLCs are published and can vary widely, with star performer Ted Baker at 36 times, and an out-of-favour Debenhams at 10 times (September 2015). Private companies usually have something like a quarter of the P/E ratio of their quoted equivalent due to the lack of a market for their shares, and hence increased perceived risk.

A market valuation will give often a top end to a valuation range. Quoted company value takes into account the value of the brand in generating future cash flows. Financial analysts will use sophisticated models and techniques including discounted cash flow (DCF) models to value businesses. The corporate finance texts listed at the end of this chapter provide more detail in this area. A further source of information is a specialist agency such as Interbrand, which publishes its own methodologies and rankings each year.

SHARE PRICE PERFORMANCE

A share price is a reflection of the current stock market valuation of a share in a publicly traded business. It is important to think about how the stock market behaves and what affects the market's perception of a business's value.

There are two opposing schools of thought about how the Stock Market behaves. *Fundamentalists* believe that every business has a long-term intrinsic value that is independent of the market's valuation (the share price) and you can determine this intrinsic value by analyzing the company's financial statements to see the trends in the common investor metrics (see Figure 5.4). This school believes that if an analysis of the metrics shows the intrinsic value of the share is above current market value then you should BUY this share. They believe that in the long term the market will reflect this intrinsic value and the share price will rise. As an investor you will have made a profit.

These metrics are comparators when an investor looks at the efficiency of a share portfolio in terms of return (only applies to ordinary shares):

Dividend Cover – How many times could the Dividend have been paid out of Profit after Tax (PAT/ Dividend)

Dividend Yield – relates the income from the share to the market price i.e. return on investment (Dividend per share/ Market Price)

Earnings Per Share – How much could the dividend pay-out have been if all profit paid out (PAT & Preference Dividend/ Number of Ordinary Shares)

Price/Earnings Ratio – Market Perception (Price per share/ EPS)

Remember the comparability and utility of these metrics may be affected by changes in accounting policies, such as share buy-back schemes.

Figure 5.4 *Common investor metrics*

Opposed to this view are the *Chartists*, the market analysts who take the view that the company's share price depends purely on the interaction of market forces, regardless of trends in the metrics found in a company's accounts. They believe that the share price represents a consensus view arrived at by considering a company's financial statements in the context of the general economic environment and investors should buy early in a rising period and sell early in a fall to maximize their profit. In reality the Stock Market is a mix of both of these views; it is a 'semi-strong efficient market' assimilating all new information rapidly and reflecting news in share prices. Rappaport (1987) argues that the Stock Market gives powerful signals to the management of a company in terms of what the investors think about their strategic direction and performance.

The factors that can affect share prices can be categorized into the environment, the industry context and the company itself.

ONLINE RESOURCES

For a detailed summary of factors that affect share prices see our companion website at: https://www.macmillanihe.com/companion/Varley_Fashion_Management.

It is difficult to know whether the broader picture, the industry sector or the company itself has the most influence on changes in share price movement. The share market can react dramatically to a change of management within a company. On 14 October 2013 it was announced that Burberry's CEO Angela Ahrendts was moving to Apple. The share price of Burberry took a dramatic tumble as a large volume of shares were sold following this news. As the share price 'bottomed out' there was further buying activity, as investors were heartened at the reassurances that Christopher Bailey would be a safe pair of hands to take the company forward.

THE FICKLE FASHIONS OF THE STOCK MARKET

A successful IPO (Initial Public Offering) needs a good story and that story is often around financing growth ambitions. Michael Kors and Prada (December 2011) are examples of great IPO success stories in fashion.

Michael Kors' IPO raised $1bn on the New York Stock Exchange to fund its global growth ambitions. Launch day saw a 25% increase in share price, valuing the company at $3.8bn (44 times its net earnings). It continued to exceed expectations and enjoy a buoyant share price but public visibility can have its downsides when plans are not met and expectations are not managed accurately. Kors forecasted sales growth of 19% in 2014 but when quarterly trading update reported a healthy (but lower than predicted) growth of 16.4% its share price fell 8%. Why? Well the lower than expected result raised concerns around the accuracy of management predictions and prompted the thoughts that perhaps the once stellar growth rate was starting to plateau.

It was a different story at Prada, which targeted a new investors' market by listing its shares on the Hong Kong Stock Exchange. A healthy rise in share price followed, driven by sustained net profit growth; but then in December 2014 the economic slowdown in Asia led to a 12.5% fall in its share price. The influences here were completely outside of the company's control.

The financial press coverage around the possibility of a company's IPO can provide free marketing communications. For example, Jimmy Choo, Moncler, and New Look have all benefited from press interest in their financial news. Conversely, there are downsides not only to the visibility and potential overexposure in the financial media, but more harmful can be the short-termist behaviours that management must pursue in order to keep announcing sales growth every quarter. It is no wonder that many luxury companies such as Chanel prefer to stay private to retain control and protect their distinctive heritage and story, which is at the heart of their competitive advantage. If a company has access to private equity funding and does not need external bank funding (Tory Burch for example) then why go public with all the associated burdens of disclosure?

At the end of the day, where the money comes from does not influence a company's performance. What matters is the strength of the management team, creative talent and ultimately a product that meets the needs of customers (see Mini Case Study 5.1).

MINI CASE STUDY 5.1 - Mulberry

In 2011 the leather accessories brand Mulberry was doing very well under creative director Emma Hill, who tapped into a young aspirational market with accessibly priced 'it' bags such as the Alexa bag named after the fashion blogger-icon Alexa Chung. Revenue rose 69% and pre-tax profit was up by 358% in the year ending March 2011. It all started to go wrong, however, when a new CEO, Bruno Guillon, was brought in from Hermès with a remit to move the brand upmarket. In raising prices and reducing distribution he succeeded in alienating the brand's core customers, but without the heritage and credibility, Guillon was unable to establish the brand in the higher echelons of luxury. Sales worldwide plunged, leading to a profit warning and then, in 2013, Emma Hill left too. Guillon had managed to preside over a 72.4% fall in share price between May 2012 and February 2014 and so he left. In November 2014, Mulberry appointed a new creative director, Johnny Coca from Céline, in the hope of turning around their fortunes.

Source: Various, including Mulberry Published Accounts.

CASE STUDY 5 - Etiko: How to generate funds for growth

Etiko (etiko.com.au) founder Nick Savaidis has long been passionate about ethical issues in manufacturing, and fashion in particular. Growing up in Brunswick, Melbourne's historic garment production area, he had seen the disparity between the piece rates his hard-working mother had received for her garments versus the retail prices of these clothes in Melbourne's designer stores. Moving through university he lived in second-hand clothes as a protest against worker exploitation in offshore garment factories and also became a involved with Oxfam's Community Aid Board. Graduating as a teacher, he had worked in many outback communities, helping aboriginal communities earn money through social enterprise. Nick had been instrumental in setting up local supply chains that were able to make clothing featuring prints by Aboriginal artists. This ensured consumers received an authentically Aboriginal item, and that the funds spent went to communities of creators rather than to large firms who often used stylized versions of these designs without paying the creators anything.

These formative years paved the way for Nick's own ethical brand, Etiko, which has become a recognized leader in Fair Trade sourcing, sustainable fibre use, and transparency. Etiko originally emerged from Nick's desire to make footballs from sustainable materials, and then evolved into a range of footwear and now clothing. The main product lines are casual footwear, ostensibly inspired by the design of Converse's famous Chuck Taylor high-top and low-rise sneaker, and a range of thongs (flip-flop sandals, an everyday facet of Australian life) using sustainable rubber and co-branded with a range of charity groups including Animals Australia, Free the Bears, and Sea Shepherd. Recently the brand has expanded into underwear made from sustainable Fair-trade cotton.

Etiko footwear. Reproduced by permission of Etiko.

The brand's vegan friendly status has ensured it has a strong following within this community, featuring widely on social media and in specialist stores such as the local chain Vegan Wares.

However, the brand is also at a turning point. Nick aims to grow the business and needs to raise funds for expansion. To grow, he knows he must expand beyond his current loyal, vegan/ethical fan base and appeal more widely to a health and sustainability lifestyle segment. Etiko products are competitively priced, and available through specialist channels and through the brand's own web-store. The brand has strong moral credentials, being recognized in an industry fashion report as the only A+ awarded ethical producer in Australia, and this is stressed in much of the brand's communications.

Case Author: Michael Beverland

Case Challenge

Explore the alternative sources of funding outlined in this chapter (see Figure 5.1) and suggest with justification which one(s) might be the most suitable for Etiko.

 ONLINE RESOURCES

A longer version of this case study, with additional challenges, can be found on our companion website: https://www.macmillanihe.com/companion/Varley_Fashion_Management

 SUMMARY AND CONCLUDING THOUGHTS

Successful fashion businesses have good financial managers who balance managing external expectations with an internal focus on strong business fundamentals, which helps to support overall corporate aims. Having a small number of relevant KPIs that can be benchmarked against the competition reinforces a company's market positioning, from both a marketing and a financial perspective. Constantly monitoring where the business is and where it is going ensures synergy between trading performance, cash flow and strategic direction. Good financial management helps a company to avoid waste and non-essential spending whilst fighting the urge towards short termism. Having an efficient working capital cycle, the so-called 'sweating' of assets, will help a company achieve the most out of its capability, whilst giving investors confidence with a strong, cash-rich balance sheet. We will return to many of these considerations when we consider risk management in fashion in Chapter 13.

 CHALLENGES AND CONVERSATIONS

1. Financial Information Research

   Explore the investor relations websites for fashion PLCs such as Next plc, Supergroup plc, or M&S plc. Look at the wealth of information that is provided there. Review the contents of the most recent Annual Report and Accounts. Compare and contrast the KPIs each company chooses to focus on and consider how this aligns with their strategy.

   Then explore the corporate website for a private company such as River Island, New Look or John Lewis. Observe the differing depth of detail offered by these companies and consider how their ownership structure affects their information disclosure.

2. Financial Analysis

   Choosing one of the companies you have researched, perform some basic financial analysis to gain an understanding of the company. If you have access to a database such as FAME (Financial Analysis Made Easy), extract your data from that source. If not, then complete the table using their Annual Report and Accounts.

   (i) Performance – From the Income Statements (P&L – profit and loss) extract a table of KPIs. Choose to focus on 3–5 years of history and ensure you are extracting full year results. Complete a table such as the one shown, computing year on year change in the KPIs.

	2017	2016	% Change
Sales Revenue (Turnover)			
Gross Profit			
Operating Profit			
Profit Before Tax			
Profit After Tax			

Use a spread-sheet package to draw a graph comparing some of these metrics. Compare the rate of growth of each and consider what this is telling you about the business.

Consider also using ratio analysis to calculate gross margin, net margin and ROCE.

(ii) Position – From the Statements of Position (Balance Sheet) extract a table of the key components of value for the business. For a fashion business the interplay between stock and cash is most important. Consider how the accounting date and business model impact the company position.

Again use ratio analysis, focusing on liquidity and stock turn in particular. Relate these observations to any increase in turnover/store numbers etc.

Look also at the sources of funding the business uses and the balance between debt and equity. Explore the relevant notes to the accounts to find out more. Calculate Gearing.

(iii) Consider the investors' perspective. Extract a share price graph and explore any significant share price movements. Can these be related to company events or market impacts?

Using ratio analysis to calculate EPS and Dividend yield, consider investor motives for holding shares in this business.

(iv) Put all the analysis together to consider what you now know about this business. Press reports can help you gain a greater understanding. Remember, all you have done here is compare the business to itself – you also need to compare it with its peers. When you have done that, consider whether, at its current share price, you would buy/sell/ hold.

REFERENCES AND FURTHER READING

Attrill, P. and McLaney, E. (2014) *Accounting and Finance for Non-Specialists*, 9th edn. Harlow: Pearson.

Brealey, R., Myers, S. and Allen, F. (2010) *Principles of Corporate Finance*, 10th edn. London: McGraw-Hill.

Interbrand (n.d.) Brand Valuation Methodology. Available at: https://www.interbrand.com/views/brand-valuation-a-versatile-strategic-tool-for-business/ [accessed 23/07/2018].

Moles, P., Parrino, R. and Kidwell, D. (2011) *Corporate Finance: European Edition*. Chichester: John Wiley & Sons.

Rappaport, A. (1987) 'Stock market signals to managers'. *Harvard Business Review*, 65(6), pp. 57–62.

Ted Baker Annual Report and Accounts (2015). Available at: http://www.tedbakerplc.com/~/media/Files/T/Ted-Baker/results-and-reports/report/2015/2015-Annual-report.pdf [accessed 10/04/2018].

Watson, D. and Head, A. (2013) *Corporate Finance: Principles and Practice*, 6th edn. Harlow: Pearson.

6

FASHION BRAND MANAGEMENT

Ana Roncha

INTRODUCTION

Perhaps the most distinctive skill of professional marketers is their ability to create, maintain, protect, and enhance brands. In the competitive marketplace, new products, service and channel options make the decision-making process highly complex. Brands are a part of an offer that helps consumers make a decision. They help to identify the source and quality of a product and signal specific attributes and credible benefits. A brand name can be one of the most valuable assets of a company and for fashion brands in particular a strong motivation for purchase. Brands can differentiate, and this can drive consumers to evaluate virtually identical products differently. Several concepts contribute to brand differentiation: identity and brand image, brand values and promise, brand personality and brand positioning, and in the competitive global fashion industry, branding is an area where companies can actually achieve meaningful and sustainable competitive advantage.

This chapter provides the foundation for an analysis of strategic brand management in the fashion context. It begins by considering the meaning of brand management and introduces conceptual terms including brand identity, brand image, brand personality, brand purpose and brand equity that will help to develop a strategic approach to this vital aspect of fashion marketing management. The chapter then gives an extensive discussion on important aspects of brand management, specifically relating these to fashion brands and their corporate objectives. It explores the opportunities for and risks of specific brand strategies in the context of organizational development and growth, including extensions, collaborations, and repositioning. The chapter concludes by highlighting consistency and integration as routes to sustained brand lifecycles.

LEARNING OBJECTIVES

After studying this chapter, you should be able to understand:

- The scope and complexity of fashion brand management;

- The value of brands as strategic assets and how they bring value to customers and equity to fashion companies;

- Key terminology and concepts to analyze brand strategies, including brand identity, brand image, brand personality and brand positioning;

- How brand relevance and engagement can be built within the fashion brand lifecycle;

- The strategic role of brands within a fashion organizational structure, referring to concepts of brand architecture, brand portfolios and brand collaborations.

---

6. Photograph by Natascha Radclyffe-Thomas.

WHAT IS A BRAND?

According to the American Marketing Association (AMA) (1995), a brand is a name, term, sign, symbol, or design, or a combination of these, intended to identify the goods or services of one seller or group of sellers and to differentiate them from those of competitors. Brands span the product-to-service spectrum from tangible products such as physical goods (clothes, bags, shoes) to services (such as hairstyling, and hospitality), where consumers are likely to transfer the perception of assets of the brand into a perception of service quality. In addition, people can be considered brands (from celebrities like David Beckham or Beyoncé to digital influencers like Chiara Ferragni); organizations (such as the British Fashion Council or the World Economic Forum) can also be brands, and even geographic locations such as cities or shopping destinations can be branded in the same manner as other entities (as discussed in Chapter 4). In fashion the concept of retailers as brands is an important one; having an overarching 'own brand' helps retailers position themselves and explore a set of associations regarding the quality of their service, product assortment, merchandising, pricing and loyalty programmes. The department store John Lewis, for instance, not only sells a wide range of products under the John Lewis brand name, but also has introduced successful sub-brands in its fashion department, for example 'Modern Rarity' and 'KIN'.

David Ogilvy (quoted in Randall, 2000) described a brand as 'the intangible sum of a product's attributes: its name, packaging, and price, its history, its reputation, and the way it is advertised', and according to Kotler (2000) a brand is a complex symbol that can convey up to six levels of meaning (Table 6.1).

Meaning	Description
Attributes	A brand brings to mind certain attributes
Benefits	Attributes are translated into functional and emotional benefits
Values	The brand says something about the producer's value
Culture	The brand may represent a certain culture
Personality	The brand can project a certain personality
User	The brand suggests the kind of customer who buys or uses the product

Table 6.1 *Levels of brand meaning*

Source: Based on Kotler (2000).

Although the origins of branding can be traced back to the times when whiskey distillers burned their names onto wooden shipping crates to ensure the correct identification of their product (Aaker, 1991), the 1980s decade was a turning point in branding history, when managers began to realize that brands were a company's main asset. The concept of brand equity was discovered (Kapferer, 2008), understanding that qualities beyond tangible attributes could drive consumer preference and profit margins.

Although the fashion industry was a late adopter of these principles, fashion brands soon realized that a strong brand could encourage a consumer to pay more to acquire a particular product, even if other similar quality products at lower prices were available.

'In a world where it takes less than 6 months on average to replicate any true product innovation, a brand is often the only barrier to competition' (Steve Hayden, Ogilvy & Mather; cited in Miller and Muir, 2005: 29).

Key terminology in branding

Wally Olins, sometimes referred to as the 'godfather of branding', suggested that for brands to be successful and to differentiate themselves from competitors, they need to find a way to talk about themselves within an emotional context (Courier, 2014). For Olins, the power of a brand comes from a mixture of its functional performance with its emotional meaning. Emotion has acquired a growing importance in fashion brand management and is intimately connected to the concept of competitive advantage achieved by differentiation, explored in Chapter 4.

Figure 6.1 summarizes the main conceptual themes within branding academic literature, and the discussion that follows further develops the nature and impact of this terminology within the context of the fashion industry.

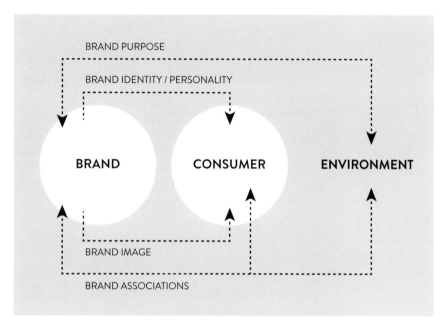

Figure 6.1 *Key branding terminology and its interconnections*

Brand identity

One of the basic building blocks for brand strategists is brand identity, which is the set of visual brand associations (Aaker and Joachimsthaler, 2000). The concept of 'identity' is largely confined to the visual expression of a specific company, often consisting of visual identification cues like symbols and distinctive typography that together create recognition (for example, Lacoste's crocodile and Nike's Swoosh). However, Reizebos (2003) argues that it is crucial to distinguish between brand identity and visual identity, with visual identity being regarded as a natural extension of the chosen brand identity but representing it through visual form. This is sometimes referred to as a brand's 'handwriting' in the fashion industry.

Aaker and Joachimsthaler (2000) suggest that brand identity is supported by brand architecture,

> **Brand identity** A set of visual associations created and maintained to establish a strong relationship with the consumer.

brand building programmes, organizational structure and organizational processes. According to Aaker's (1996a) Model of Brand Construction, brand identity should interact with brand image, in order to produce an efficient brand communication.

Brand identity represents the company's ideas of what its brand should stand for and it also represents what the company wants its consumers to perceive it to be. It serves as a well-orchestrated corporate branding system, a valuable communication tool acting as an indication and endorsement of quality, value and reliability; assets that can turn a brand into a powerful strategic weapon that will differentiate products in an increasingly competitive marketplace. Kapferer's Brand Identity Prism (2012) is one of the best known conceptual models among fashion scholars and practitioners. It considers six dimensions, as shown in Table 6.2.

Dimension	Relates to	Description	Example
Physique	Sender	All the tangible aspects that come to mind when we think of a brand. Can include the logo, packaging, a particular shape or a colour.	Levi's: Red tab YSL: Black tuxedo
Personality	Sender	Personality is often described as a set of human characteristics associated with a brand. It can also be defined in terms of communication tone and style, and identification with a specific person (use of brand ambassadors).	Victoria Secret: Sexy, glamorous, young Dove: Authentic, real
Culture	Internal Environment	The values and ethos of the brand. This dimension can also communicate the brand origin (see Chapter 4) and draw on positive associations with a specific country/culture.	Chanel: French and timeless sophistication Hermès: Craftsmanship and exclusivity. Made in France.
Relationship	External Environment	How consumers feel when purchasing or engaging with the brand. The value of exchange beyond a transaction.	L'Oréal: Trust and commitment Zara: Fair exchange of value
Self-Image	Recipient	The internal mirror that portrays how the consumer wishes to be seen.	Diesel: I am young, provocative and irreverent and want to show it. COS: Individual, quality seeker
Reflection	Recipient	The external mirror that shows how others perceive the consumer when wearing the brand.	Bulgari: Elegant, rich and with a distinct social position Nike: Sporty, energetic, young and competitive

Table 6.2 *Brand Identity Prism*

Source: Based on Kapferer (2012).

Identity is seen here as a concept that resides in the sender, who is responsible for specifying the meaning and aim of the brand. These should be based on the core competences of the company, coming directly from their superior skills and resources (Alsem and Kostelijk, 2008). The model indicates that a brand's physique (physical attributes) works alongside its personality. A brand's relationship(s), for example with its customers and its culture (by association, for example to music, art, lifestyle and so on), are aspects of a brand that surround its core identity and help to strengthen it. The base of the prism is where the recipient (for example, a customer or brand advocate) interprets a brand identity according to

their own self-image, which in turn reflects back into the identity prism.

Brand identity is a highly important concept because it can help to position a brand (Kapferer, 2008). In a saturated market like fashion, where the consumer is overloaded with information and communication messages, brand identity is of crucial importance. Alsem and Kostelijk (2008) believe that identity can be a stable point of reference for consumers; and it can help maintain a relationship with customers who have a connection with the brand values promoted.

When discussing the identity of a brand it is important to consider its 'core ID' and 'extended

ID' (Aaker, 1996a). The core ID is intimately connected to the brand essence, its soul, beliefs and values, while the extended ID adds brand texture by referring to associated product categories, experiences, personality, logo, brand origin and so on. Aaker integrates these into a wider framework called the brand identity planning system (see Figure 6.2). It includes the strategic brand analysis stage (inputs), brand identity system (the stage where the brand provides a value proposition and credibility, with the focus on enhancing brand–customer relationships), and the identity implementation system (outputs). The purpose of this system is to help brand managers consider the different elements and patterns of behaviour that can help to achieve clarity and differentiate an identity. This planning model is aligned to the more general strategic planning model outlined in Chapter 2, and demonstrates the importance of brands within a corporate strategy.

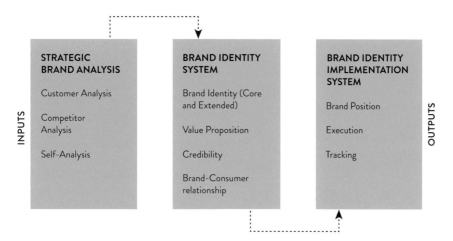

Figure 6.2 *Brand identity planning system*

Source: Adapted from Aaker (1996a).

Brand image

'Brand image' refers to the perception of a brand in the mind of the consumer, usually working as a mirror reflection of the brand personality or of a product association. It is what people think about a brand, the feelings and expectations it creates. It is said that a brand image does not belong to the company, but to those individuals who have knowledge and experience of the brand.

A consumer's image of a brand is based on many sources of information, often beyond the control of marketers. Its formation lies in a unique interpretation and understanding of the brand, which is usually guided by cultural context. Brand images are strongly influenced by reports in the media, by consumers' experiences with a brand, and by word-of-mouth (Schultz and De Chernatony, 2002) and are therefore a subjective, perceptual phenomenon reflected by a network of associations in the memory of consumers. A positive brand image is intrinsically connected to a consequently positive attitude and increased loyalty towards the brand and is understood as a long-term, committed and affect-laden partnership. Two important components of brand image are the associations that consumers attach to the brand and brand personality.

> **Brand image** Brand image is the perception of a brand in the mind of the consumer, what people think about a brand, the feelings and expectations it creates. This construct is the result of various sources of information and unique interpretations, strongly influenced by media and past experiences.

Brand associations

According to Keller (1993), brand associations are defined by attributes, benefits and attitudes. Attributes are the descriptive product- and non-product-related features, benefits are the functional, experiential and symbolic personal value attached to the brand, and attitudes are the overall evaluation of the brand that often forms the basis of consumer behaviour. Associations can be intended and unintended and are what gives meaning to the brand (Till et al., 2011). Aaker (1996a: 8) refers to them as 'the heart and soul of the brand' and Hsieh (2004) considers them to be fundamental in understanding customer-based brand equity because they help consumers retrieve and process information. If positive, the associations create beneficial attitudes and feelings and provide a reason to buy. They can also be explored to create effective brand extensions as we will see later in this chapter.

In Chapter 4 we saw that fashion brands can use country of origin to tap into a network of associations and stereotypes. One clear example of these benefits lies in the notion of 'heritage'. Brands with a heritage are perceived to be more credible, trustworthy and reliable resulting in higher brand loyalty as well as the ability to charge a premium price. The brand heritage may be leveraged by adopting an imagery and/or culture positioning strategy in order to transfer the attributes associated with the country to the brand.

By attaching references to historical, tangible aspects of the brand, intangible brand associations are created and contribute to reinforcing the heritage factor. Examples of this include Burberry with its London/UK heritage, Ralph Lauren with American classics, and Dolce & Gabbana with Italian colour extravaganza.

Brand personality

Brand personality can be defined as the set of human characteristics and traits that are associated with a given brand (Aaker, 1996b; Keller, 1998). Brand personality traits provide self-expressive and symbolic aspects for the consumer (Aaker, 1999). According to Grime et al. (2002), brand personality is a strategic dimension of high importance, helping companies achieve enduring differentiation and sustainable competitive advantage. For that reason, to develop a clearly defined brand personality is an important strategic objective of fashion brand management. Once a brand holds the desired personality, consumers' feelings towards that brand are enhanced and they become loyal to it, because consumers usually choose brands that are similar to their self-concept (Keller, 2003; Kressman et al., 2006). If brand managers have a deep understanding of these reflections, they can determine the symbolic use of brands by consumers and thereby target them effectively.

Aaker (1997) establishes five dimensions of brand personality: (1) sincerity – representing warmth and acceptance, (2) excitement – indicating sociability, energy and activity, (3) competence – as in responsibility, (4) sophistication – for class and charm, and (5) ruggedness – indicating masculinity and strength. Many of these dimensions can be seen in the illustrative examples of fashion brands later on in this chapter. Multi-sensory experiences help to drive the emotional experience of a brand and have an important role in the definition and development of a fashion brand personality (Berry, 2000).

Brand equity

One of the core concepts in brand marketing, brand equity is defined as the 'marketing effects uniquely attributable to the brand' (Keller, 1993: 1); with the 'effects' being based on the following aspects: price premium attained, increased efficiency, effectiveness of marketing programmes, increased margins, increased customer demand and satisfaction, brand extension facilitation, negotiation leverage, and lower vulnerability to competitors (Aaker, 1992; Bendixen et al., 2004).

According to Aaker (1991) brand equity is created via **five categories of assets**:

- brand loyalty,
- brand awareness,
- perceived quality,
- brand associations,
- other proprietary brand assets.

Aaker's perspective is brand-focused and assumes that these five factors will drive value recognition in the consumer's mind, so that the consumer will be more attracted to that particular brand and will become brand loyal, leading to the establishment of competitive advantage for the brand.

Keller's (1993) conception of brand equity is more consumer-focused and is regarded as 'the differential effect of brand knowledge on consumer response to the marketing of the brand' (Keller, 1993: 8). Keller's model of customer-based brand equity is built by sequentially adding brand building blocks in the brand–consumer relationship (Keller, 2003). The foundation of the model is brand salience, indicating the level of awareness of the brand; built on this is brand performance relating to the satisfaction of customers' functional needs, and imagery indicating the satisfaction of customers' psychological needs. Feelings are customers' emotional responses and reactions to the brand, while judgements focus on customers' opinions based on performance and imagery. At the top level, resonance indicates the brand–customer relationship and the level of identification a customer holds with a brand. For Keller (1993) brand equity is directly related to the consumer's perspective and their level of awareness and image of a particular brand, whereas Aaker's perspective considers the assets of the brand itself as the generator of brand equity. With both perspectives it is the ability of a brand to generate strategic returns that an unbranded offer cannot that is at the heart of this concept.

Brand purpose

Although it is a relatively new construct, brands with a strong sense of purpose are able to transform and innovate better (Kapferer, 2012), and have higher levels of employee satisfaction (Roderick, 2016). Consumers increasingly want companies to demonstrate a purpose beyond profit and show a commitment to making the world a better place.

According to Meehan (2016), 87% of global consumers believe that business needs to place at least the same weight on society's interests as on businesses' interests and only 6% of people believe the singular purpose of business is to make money for shareholders. Kapferer (2012) has demonstrated this by placing brand vision and purpose at the top of his brand management process model. This indicates a top-down reading of the brand with the vision and purpose guiding further stages of the brand management process. An example of a brand guided by a strong vision and purpose is Nike with their mission to bring innovation and inspiration to every athlete in the world. For the brand, anyone can be an athlete – if you have a body, you are an athlete (www.nike.com). The brand TOMS (see Case Study 14, Chapter 14) also places brand purpose (in the form of charitable giving) at the heart of its strategy.

We increasingly see consumers wanting to ascribe meaning to their consumption, which can be regarded as an added value. Meaning can be achieved through telling a story or situating consumption in a ladder of immaterial values. 'Brand management emerges as an ongoing dynamic and social process in which the entire firm's stakeholders

> **Brand purpose** A brand orientation that sees companies demonstrate a purpose beyond profit and show a commitment to making the world a better place. Its relevance comes with consumers increasingly wanting to ascribe meaning to their consumption.

participate, to co-construct brand meaning and to establish a network of relationships with the brand and interact with each other socially' (Santos-Vijande et. al., 2013). Purpose can be a way for brands to differentiate themselves and achieve a sustainable market positioning. This was mentioned previously in Chapter 4 and will be explored in terms of the scope of purpose in Chapter 12.

THE FUNCTION, SCOPE AND CHARACTERISTICS OF BRANDING IN FASHION

In his well-known brand system model, Kapferer (2008) highlights three main constructs: (1) the product or service experience, (2) the brand concept, with its tangible and intangible benefits, and (3) the brand name, symbols or variations of these using semiotics. These three different sources of cumulative brand experience co-exist to form the brand system. This system is an effective tool in helping managers structure most of the issues around brand management, such as choosing the right concept and balancing tangible and intangible benefits; choosing and differentiating the product/service and identifying the products through a set of graphic visual signs and symbols. Thus, a brand is unified not only by external signs, but also by values, vision and ideals.

Brand relevance for both consumer and company

When consumers frequently and repeatedly choose a brand, their commitment evolves to form a brand relationship (Oliver, 1999). Customers come to expect that all interactions with the brand should provide them with known benefits. For fashion brands in particular customers will choose brands because they are associated with a particular lifestyle, which can increase the customers' willingness to pay a price premium. The value of the brand comes from its ability to gain an exclusive, positive and prominent meaning in the minds of its consumers. The extent to which companies recognize the relevance of brands determines their level of brand orientation, which is a mind-set and organizational culture that will strongly influence the overall strategy. In the case of the well-established UK department store John Lewis, all their employees are partners in the organization, which helps to achieve higher degrees of employee satisfaction and customer service. This internal buy-in is crucial in bringing the brand culture to life and supporting a consistent delivery of the brand at every customer touch-point.

ONLINE RESOURCES

The companion website at: https://www.macmillanihe.com/companion/Varley_Fashion_Management provides a short case study on the John Lewis Partnership to demonstrate this.

THE BRAND LIFECYCLE

A well-designed and coherent plan followed by a well-coordinated implementation of the action programme is crucial to ensure the success of a brand wherever it happens to be in its lifecycle.

The concept of brand life can be described as the distinguishing of separate stages: an introduction stage, the growth stage, maturity and the revival or decline stage. Groucutt (2006) emphasizes the links between the cycles of the product life and the brand life. It is important to take a holistic perspective as a brand lifecycle is based not only on a product(s), but also on customers and their behaviour, as well as external opinion. Each stage needs to be underpinned by a relevant strategy. We can distinguish the main characterizing factors that feature in each stage.

> **Brand lifecycle** The various stages a brand goes through from introduction, growth, maturity to the revival or decline stage, giving an indication of the strategies needed at each stage.

1. The **introduction stage** is when a brand is launched. It includes the planning, strategizing, and investing that brings the brand to life. Consumers know little, if anything about the brand, and habits of consumption have not been developed. The purpose is to enter a long and durable relationship with the consumer but the challenge is to achieve differentiation to find a market entry point. A brand therefore usually narrows its focus to attract early adopters with the story of the brand's unique difference. In fashion, new designers graduate every year with their final collections, many hoping to grow that collection into a desirable and successful brand.

2. The **growth stage** is when a wider range of consumers recognize the brand and its products. Growth begins among niche consumer groups, presenting the first opportunity to make use of brand reputation. Being aware of consumers and their consumption habits is crucial to achieve growth. In this stage, the brand becomes known; however, its loyal consumer base is only just forming. Brands need to consider the need for long-term recognition and carefully manage their value proposition in order to achieve this. Clarity of brand messages, tone of voice, values and mission become important at this stage.

   The early adopters, by their very nature, will eventually abandon a growing brand because they identify themselves as 'discoverers of the new' so the core values need to be established at this stage to separate a resonant brand from a fad. In fashion, brands can become 'hot' at this stage, which means supply chain and distribution decisions become crucial in order to keep up with demand.

3. The **maturity stage** is when the sales of the brand stabilize, or even decrease as competing brands that address similar needs appear on the market. The brand already has a base of customers at this stage; however, it now needs to foster long-time attachment and engagement. At this stage growth becomes difficult to maintain due to the high level of awareness, and marketing efforts should be focused on refreshing and reinforcing the brand. This is when a company should seek new ways to increase brand relevance, for example by changing

its target or finding new revenue streams, possibly through expanding into new niches, markets, and brand extensions.

4. The last stage is the **revival stage** where sales of the brand are decreasing due to new products/brands appearing on the market. Change in societal values and consumer habits can require a brand to adapt to survive. At this stage, the brand has become a household name with a broad generational fan base and shows little sign of differentiation. In order to maintain relevance, strategies such as brand extension, new sources of differentiation, or repositioning are required. The challenge is to regain relevance in a new, updated context, so that the brand becomes a growth engine again (see the Burberry case study, Case Study 10).

A thorough understanding of the brand at its various stages in the lifecycle serves as the starting point for companies to develop effective strategies that will foster long-term survival, profitability and consumer engagement. In the next section we will look at these four stages in the context of well-orchestrated fashion brand strategies.

THE BRAND-BUILDING PROCESS: FROM CONCEPT TO IMPLEMENTATION

Given that the first two stages of the brand lifecycle (introduction and growth) are the most crucial to its long-term success, this section will concentrate on the brand-building process from conception to a fully-fledged brand that instils meaning to consumers through identity and values. Management of a brand and its interrelations is the focus of fashion brand strategy, including its direction and resource management, with the overall aim of maintaining brand equity. This section is underpinned by the brand-building process theory developed by Urde (1999); Johnson, Scholes and Whittington (2011), and Aaker and Joachimsthaler (2000). Figure 6.3 illustrates the various stages we will be discussing in detail.

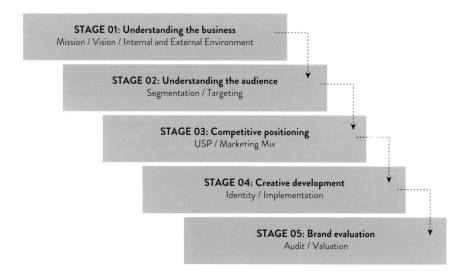

Figure 6.3 *Stages of the brand-building process*

STAGE 01: Understanding the business

The first stage of brand building involves defining the mission and vision of the brand clearly. For example, what does the brand do and what future does the brand seek to create? This is the time to reflect on the goals for the brand and the strategies to be used to accomplish them, including the metrics used to help understand how the brand is doing. We have used the example of Tiffany & Co. to showcase the importance of understanding mission and vision as the first step of brand strategy (see Mini Case Study 6.1).

MINI CASE STUDY 6.1 - Tiffany & Co.

Founded in 1837, this famous jewellery brand has as its mission to celebrate the world's great love stories. Very consistent across all the touch-points, the brand's clear vision and mission guides all the brand activities and deepens the associations with luxury, love, engagement and family. Tiffany's mission and values embody the celebration of universal feelings such as love and friendship and this can be seen across all the brand's activities.

We believe the authenticity – capturing meaningful emotions and real relationships –

will increasingly resonate with our broad international audience. The joy is not only in our blue box, but also in the deep feelings people share. (Caroline Naggiar, Tiffany's chief marketing officer, in WWD, 2015)

The brand has successfully been able to manage its intangible and tangible assets, capitalizing on its logo, design, and above all the trademarked blue box.

STAGE 02: Understanding the audience

This is the stage where a brand becomes clear about the target market and being in touch with their attitudes, beliefs, values and behaviour. By knowing the target customer, a brand can develop a unique value proposition that will enhance consumers' relationship

with the brand as well as effectively position it. In fashion, this stage can involve some very deep and subtle analysis, to really understand consumers, as shown in the example of handbag brand Mansur Gavriel (see Figure 6.4), who identified their customers as fashion-forward and 'brand agnostic' and use individuality to define themselves as cool; embracing a style that is not recognizable or status-driven.

 ONLINE RESOURCES

The companion website provides a short case study about the Mansur Gavriel brand, at: https://www.macmillanihe.com/companion/Varley_Fashion_Management.

Figure 6.4 *Mansur Gavriel, appealing to the brand agnostic consumer. Reproduced with permission from Mansur Gavriel.*

STAGE 03: Competitive positioning

The essence of this stage was explored in detail in Chapter 2 in relation to strategies companies can opt for to achieve a sustainable differentiation in the marketplace. Of crucial importance is the ability to translate a Unique Selling Proposition (USP) across the marketing mix programme. Being conscious of what a brand is particularly good at and what makes it different or better than the competition is the basis of this stage. The development of the fashionable eyewear brand Warby Parker illustrates this (see Mini Case Study 6.2).

MINI CASE STUDY 6.2 - Warby Parker

This American start-up brand emerged in Philadelphia in 2010 and disrupted the eyewear industry with an innovative selling proposition and unique vision. Facing well-established competition from other eyewear brands such as Luxottica, the brand was created with the desire to offer a unique retail experience, which was more welcoming and fun, yet with superb customer service and distinctive products, and with a lower price point achieved by investing in online sales.

> We just love glasses. But we didn't love the process of buying glasses: we thought that was something you could just do better. Category-after-category was moving online. So we thought, 'Of course: eyewear as a category is going to eventually be sold online. Whoever does that is going to make a tonne of money.' (Neil Blumenthal,

Warby Parker's CEO/Co-founder, in *WARC*, 2014)

Their differentiation aspect came from the simple idea of their Home-Try-On programme – sending customers five chosen frames free of charge, so they could try them on at home and get feedback from friends and family. At the end of the try-on, customers would return the frames (no cost) and finalize their purchase. At that time Warby Parker's business model was unique – from the point of view of pricing, design, customer service, distribution and marketing strategy. This online brand moved to multichannel a few years later with the brand operating 30 stores in locations across 16 US States plus 2 stores in Toronto by the end of 2016.

Sources: https://www.warbyparker.com, and Whiteside (2014).

STAGE 04: Creative development

A unique identity supports effective branding and differentiates a brand from competition; therefore brands must control their verbal and visual identity by maintaining consistency. Most recognizable fashion brands are very efficient at controlling their identity in order to maintain a consistent brand image to achieve fast recognition. Bridge casualwear brand Acne, for example, has a consistent, understated brand identity (see Case Study 6, at the end of this chapter). Other notable examples include Valentino with its consistent use of red, and Chanel's monochromatic tones across its various channels of communication.

STAGE 05: Brand evaluation

Within this stage, it is extremely important to assess the brand's internal alignment to ensure a proper fit between image and identity. It also includes tracking the awareness of consumers and assessing the brand's business performance. One of the most famous companies engaged in brand evaluation is Interbrand.

> A strategic tool for ongoing brand management, valuation brings together market, brand, competitor, and financial data into a single framework within which the performance of the brand can be assessed, areas for growth identified, and the financial impact of investing in the brand quantified. Interbrand was the first company to have its methodology certified as compliant with the requirements of ISO 10668 (requirements for monetary brand valuation) and has played a key role in the development of the standard itself. There are three key components to all of our valuations: an analysis of the financial performance of the branded products or

services, of the role the brand plays in purchase decisions, and of the brand's competitive strength. (Interbrand, 2016)

The company publishes a list of the Top 100 Global Brands annually, with Nike at number 18, Louis Vuitton at 19, H&M at 20 and Zara at 27. A total of 13 fashion/beauty brands appeared in the list in 2016.

BRANDING STRATEGIES FOR GROWTH

The next section explores various ways in which brands are managed within a growth strategy. Referring to the Ansoff matrix discussed in Chapters 3 and 4, brand management can often be considered as a blend of market and product development strategies, and includes the management of brand portfolios and architecture, brand extensions, co-branding, collaborations, and partnerships.

Brand portfolio

A brand's portfolio is an indication of a company's desire to better fit the needs of market segments by offering different brand identities and branding strategies. Pursuing a portfolio strategy helps to position individual (but associated) brands more accurately in consumers' minds while generating possible synergies from product-development, sourcing, HRM, finance and marketing. The search for growth is often the main impetus to launch new brands; however, this is a risky strategy, imposing complexity costs from product development, sourcing, distribution and marketing communications.

Assessing the financial attractiveness of new brands as well as understanding how they fit with existing one(s) is crucial when deciding whether or not to increase the portfolio value by making strategic decisions about restructuring, acquisition, divestiture, or launch of brands (Mycoskie, 2016). The classic fashion example is Giorgio Armani (see Case Study 3, Chapter 3), which at the time of writing is facing

the challenge of reorganizing their brand portfolio to achieve better clarity.

Brand architecture

Brand architecture organizes and structures the brand portfolio by specifying brand roles and the nature of relationships between brands and between different product-market contexts. A well-conceived and managed brand architecture can generate clarity, synergy, and brand leverage and thus avoid a diffused focus, marketplace confusion, and brand-building waste. By allocating resources to brand building in a strategic way, the brand architecture can help an organization create effective and powerful brands and support future growth (Aaker and Joachimsthaler, 2000). The Kering Group demonstrates a clear brand architecture with their portfolio of luxury fashion brands (see Case Study 2 on Kering, in Chapter 2).

Brand extension

> ... Having a perfume and license in general is a financial necessity. A designer must reap back the money spent on prototypes and all that sort of thing. (Vivienne Westwood, in Johnson, 2014)

Brand extension is a strategy that sees brands using the name of one of their existing brands, instead of using a new brand name, for the purpose of entering new product markets.

The luxury goods sector was an obvious adopter of such a strategy as this helped to spread the aspiration and dream across product categories to enhance profitability. As Posner (2015) suggests, the cosmetic and fragrance target market have completely different characteristics from the main target of luxury brands. They are intended to help the brand achieve higher degrees of recognition and awareness as well as extend their customer reach. Luxury fashion brands have extended to accessories, eyewear, leather goods, jewellery, watch-making, tableware and cosmetics, with perfumes becoming the most visible. The hospitality business has been a preferred category

Brand extension A brand management strategy that sees brands using the name of one of their existing brands for the purpose of entering new product markets. The purpose of extensions is to help brands achieve higher awareness and extended consumer reach.

for fashion brand extensions for some time. Giorgio Armani's first restaurant was opened in 1989 and was seen as innovative at the time, but it is now a natural progression with brands such as Bulgari and Versace having multiple restaurants. Burberry launched a café called Thomas's at its Regent Street store with the aim of keeping customers in-store for longer to maximize purchasing opportunities and dwell time. The location also features its own gifting section.

> I wanted to create a space where our customers *can* spend time relaxing and enjoying the world of Burberry in a more social environment. By blending our new café, Thomas's, with a gifting area, we are trying something new. (Christopher Bailey, Burberry, referring to Burberry's Thomas café in Regent Street; Prynn, 2015)

According to Kapferer (2012), a successful brand extension needs three elements:

- **Fit:** the extension needs to create a good alignment with the parent brand, having in consideration the brand's concept and the internal resources of the organization;

- **Relevance:** the proposed extension needs to show good understanding of consumers' needs and desires;

- **Sustainable competitive advantage:** the extension should bring a differentiating factor, to enhance competitive advantage and contribute to the brand's positioning.

When evaluating brand extensions, it is important to consider 8 fundamental questions (Kapferer, 2012; Keller, 2012):

- What is the attractiveness of the new market?

- What advantage does this product bring to the existing products in this category?

- What needs does it satisfy – what benefit (if any) does it supply?

- How can this product advantage be made durable?

- What would be the level of defence or retaliation by the competition?

- How does the brand make those products superior?

- What would it bring to the parent brand?

Brand extensions can be a viable option for growth because of the high failure rate of brand introduction, and because building brand awareness can be a very expensive strategy to pursue. They can be used as an opportunity to enter a new and/or growing product market that may have a more favourable profitability and cost structure. They can also be used to reposition brands or re-establish obsolete brands by introducing new products that will help the brand regain its relevance and interest and also demonstrate an updated image. Net-a-Porter is now a well-established online luxury fashion retailer and provides a good example of an innovative organization that has grown via brand extension (see Mini Case Study 6.3). See also chapter 8 for further discussion on brand extensions within a product strategy.

 MINI CASE STUDY 6.3 - YOOX Net-a-Porter group

In 2015, Net-a-Porter and YOOX merged to become YOOX-Net-a-Porter, the leading online luxury fashion retailer group, bringing together two companies that had been major players in the online luxury market since 2000. The group is the leading destination for the world's most famous designer brands. Net-a-Porter has grown using two major brand extensions. In 2009, **The Outnet** was launched; a fashionable outlet platform that became a go-to destination for designer products at discounted prices. That was followed in 2011, when **Mr Porter** was introduced and quickly established itself as the global retail destination for men's style. Tapping into the growing market for luxury men's wear and accessories, the platform combines the world's best men's wear brands, watchmakers and specialist grooming brands. Editorial content is a key feature of the contemporary e-commerce experience and the group's media division creates relevant and remarkable content for its titles: *PORTER*, *The EDIT*, *The Daily* and *The Journal*.

Source: http://www.ynap.com/pages/about-us/who-we-are/company-dna/.

Co-branding

Co-branding is another strategy for growth that sees a collaborative venture of two or more independent parties working to create something new (product, service or enterprise). This something new often falls outside their individual areas of capabilities or expertize; however, when joining forces, it becomes attainable by capitalizing on the unique strengths of each contributing brand.

> **Co-branding** A brand management strategy where two or more independent parties work together to create something new. It can help brands to increase market share, reinforce positioning and enter new markets.

Co-branding is a tool for moving brands on, taking them into new markets and generally providing the refreshment needed to remain relevant (Blackett and Russell, 1999). There needs to be a clear rationale for the collaboration so as to ensure the right fit in terms of values, capabilities, and goals, as well as an appropriate balance of brand equity. In 2017 a surprising but highly successful co-branding strategy was introduced by Louis Vuitton and streetwear brand Supreme, appealing to the younger luxury consumer and their propensity for on-selling of 'hot' branded goods. 'Co-branding strategies can offer a viable opportunity for luxury brands to increase their market share, while they maintain their market position' (Luck et al., 2014).

Co-branding helps brands to address new audiences, by borrowing needed expertize for product development. It can also generate increased publicity and word-of-mouth brand communications (see Chapter 7). It improves perceptions and brand image by attaching positive associations from a partner brand, and also reduces the cost of new product introduction due to synergies established between both brands. Some of the risks associated with co-branding are the loss of control, risk of brand equity diffusion or negative feedback effects. It can also become an organizational distraction when there is a lack of brand focus and clarity.

Retailers very often use co-branding to provide interest and an opportunity to communicate brand activity. One of the most renowned co-branding strategies is the annual H&M designer collaboration. This supports H&M's positioning as trendy and fashionable while offering exclusive co-branded items for a limited time. Recent collaborations have included high fashion brands: Jimmy Choo (2009), Martin Margiela (2012), Marni (2012), Isabel Marant (2013), Alexander Wang (2014), Balmain (2015), Kenzo (2016) and Erdem (2017). According to Forbes, the designer brands are moved by a desire to expose their brand name to a new generation of potential consumers, who will increasingly aspire to owning more pieces from the high-end collection. Target is another mass-market retailer that has successfully co-branded with luxury brands including Missoni, Prabal Gurung and Victoria Beckham.

Retail platform collaborations

Another way that retailers collaborate is by blending different formats or sales platforms. Fuelled by the conscience that no brand can be an island (WGSN, 2016a), retail brands from different spheres have started to merge into each other's universe. This brings customer interest and an augmented experience in retail stores, helping both parties achieve higher brand awareness as well as extend their customer reach. By aligning with different but similar-minded brands from different categories or market segments, brands are tapping into the trends for new retail experiences (see Mini Case Study 6.4).

🖪 MINI CASE STUDY 6.4 - Neiman Marcus and Rent the Runway ✂

Neiman Marcus entered into a partnership with online fashion rental company Rent the Runway as a way to increase store space productivity. The Rent the Runway space displays a rotating selection of clothes and accessories from more than 400 brands that consumers can rent. This offers consumers the possibility to buy or rent in one store, attracting new potential customers to both parties while showing a clear direction towards the future by acknowledging changes in shopping behaviour. 'Partnering with Rent the Runway's innovative model combined with their affinity amongst millennials provides an exciting opportunity for us. Together we're helping the next generation of luxury consumers discover and fall in love with designer fashion' (Karen Katz, CEO Neiman Marcus).

Inter-industry collaborations

A strategy frequently adopted by fashion brands is to leverage art and design to foster cultural collaborations. This move is a significant shift from the more typical sponsoring of artistic events. By working directly with artists, fashion brands establish themselves as creative, culturally relevant and trendy. Louis Vuitton has been active with this type of collaboration for many years, dating back to 2001 when they partnered with New York designer Stephen Sprouse, resulting in a line of neon graffiti monogram bags. This was followed in 2003 with a line of white multicoloured accessories designed in collaboration with artist Takashi Murakami and, in 2012, LV collaborated with 83-year-old artist Yayoi Kusama for one of the most visually captivating collections to date, with stores being transformed into a polka dot fantasy world (Cadogan, 2017).

With a wider brand-building strategic aim, fashion and beauty brands have started creating content platforms that showcase little or no branded product push, but that build a creative community around a category (such as beauty, fashion or art) that drives authentic conversation and engagement (WGSN, 2016b). Examples include L'Oréal's FAB (Flair, Artistry, and Beauty) – an online beauty platform showcasing global trends and influencers, including competitor brands – and Nowness – a platform set up in 2010 by LVMH as an unbranded content hub that quickly became a source of cultural inspiration for the creative industry. Other types of inter-industry collaborations include fashion and food, and fashion and home interiors.

ONLINE RESOURCES

Our companion website at: https://www.macmillanihe.com/companion/Varley_Fashion_Management gives some interesting examples of fashion-food, and fashion-home interior collaborations.

BRAND DILUTION

The major trap to avoid when pursuing brand extensions is the risk of brand dilution. Achieving a balance between increasing sales and preserving image is not always easy and some brands might encounter a loss of distinctiveness and brand value in this journey. A study from *Harvard Business Review* on luxury brand extensions suggested Diane von Furstenberg and Pierre Cardin as examples of upmarket fashion brands that over-expanded in the 1970s and 1980s (Reddy and Terblanche, 2005). Both brands launched extensions by licensing to third party manufacturers and distributors in markets that were far from their original scope. This led to damage of the brand's image and loss of exclusivity and therefore diminished brand value.

To avoid dilution a brand should normally be extended into categories adjacent to the core brand. It is not wise for luxury brands to translate into pens or keyrings – as in the Pierre Cardin case. It is possible, however, for brands to extend outside their adjacent categories, as demonstrated earlier in this chapter, if their symbolic power has enough appeal to cross categories. Success or failure are dependent on whether or not the extension lines have an affinity with the core brand values of the 'umbrella brand'. Without this, consumers feel the company is attempting to take undue advantage of its name (Keller and Sood, 2003). An important point to note is that brand dilution is not always based on how well adjusted extensions are in terms of product, but can also be affected by retail distribution strategy, pricing decisions, overall brand performance, and in particular, customer experience (Keller and Sood, 2003).

BRAND POSITIONING

As we saw in Chapter 3, a way to distinguish a fashion brand is by positioning; designing offerings that will occupy a distinctive place in their consumer's mind (Kotler, 2000; Ries and Trout, 2000). Positioning a brand is to emphasize the distinctive characteristics that make it different from its competitors and appealing to the public (Kapferer, 2008). It relates to competitors in the market and is likely to change over time, due to changing consumer needs, expectations and perceptions. Ries and Trout (2000) see positioning as a creative exercise done with an existing product or brand. 'When you think of the blur of all the brands out there, the ones you believe in and the ones you remember ... are the ones that stand for something' (Ralph Lauren, in CNN, 2007).

Using Jobber's (2010) model of 'The anatomy of brand positioning' we have highlighted all the components of a fashion brand that help to position it effectively:

- **Brand domain**: Where it competes in the marketplace and who it targets. For example, Zara competes in the mass market and targets a youthful and trendy consumer base while Michel Kors competes in the affordable luxury segment.

- **Brand heritage**: This relates to a brand's background and its culture. For some brands, especially in the luxury sector, this dimension provides a key differentiation factor. Tradition and heritage are dimensions that help 'define these brands today and add value, especially when they are re-interpreted in a contemporary light' (Aaker, 2004: 7). Brands like Hermès that date back to 1837 can still hold relevance and high brand value. Although the brand makes use of tradition and authenticity as part of its brand USP, it is able to maintain an aura of constant innovation in the ultra-luxury segment: 'We see ourselves as creative craftsmen' (Forbes, 2016). They have been able to leverage this innovation with the introduction of products such as the Apple Watch Hermès.

- **Brand values**: An example is the strong value and purpose guiding the actions of the brand TOMS: using business to improve lives, whether through shoes, eyewear or coffee. Having clear and unique values guides the brand and helps to position it (see the TOMS Case Study, Case Study 14).

- **Brand assets**: Attributes that make a brand distinct from competitors (such as symbols, features, images). These can be easily recognizable and over time, if well managed, become a feature of it, such as the Nike Swoosh. Some brands are able to achieve this by having a unique way of doing things, for example Bottega Veneta's 'intreccio' woven leather.

- **Brand personality**: As described earlier, the character of the brand is described in terms of human or even animal traits. This helps to position a brand as an entity that possesses a set of characteristics that help to define and guide its actions. Ted Baker, for example, has used the idea of a sense of humour to enhance brand personality.

- **Brand reflection**: This refers to how a brand relates to a consumer's self-concept (how consumers perceive themselves and how they would like others to see them). This is crucial in today's market, characterized by a growing desire to use brands as an expression of the self and as enhancers of a person's own values. The case of active-wear retailer Sweaty Betty exemplifies this (see Mini Case Study 6.5).

MINI CASE STUDY 6.5 - Sweaty Betty

The brand Sweaty Betty was founded in 1988 and named as 'one to watch' only 2 weeks after its introduction. It was launched to redefine the way women dress, transforming active wear into clothing that makes them feel powerful and beautiful. The brand promotes a sporty and healthy lifestyle, selling items geared towards a diverse range of activities. They instil quality, performance and a feminine style in garments with a desire to 'inspire women to find empowerment through fitness' (http://www.sweatybetty.com/meet-tamara/?#meettamara), using high-quality, cutting-edge fabrics, fashion-forward designs and outfit-building. The brand has been able to stand out in the saturated fitness industry by building its own social community and actively engaging loyal followers who wear Sweaty Betty products as an expression of themselves and their life choices.

This is an example of a successful business built around a brand community, using social networks as the primary vehicle for promotion, brand narratives and engagement. The brand has used a variety of campaigns on social media including: the 30-day sweat challenge; posts that highlight nutrition and fitness; filmed interviews with models; and filmed fitness advice. The brand's message appears seamlessly spread across all customer touch-points.

Another key differentiating factor for the brand is the experiential approach towards brand building. The brand hosts regular yoga classes in store, running clubs and other fitness events, and makes use of innovative technology by creating a social community with content and context that appeals to its audience. It fits closely with the trend of experiential retail and the rise of well-being and healthy lifestyles. By using the brand, customers express themselves and the brand becomes the vehicle for doing so.

BRAND REPOSITIONING

Referring back to the fourth stage of the brand lifecycle (renewal), some brands are faced with challenges that lead to a repositioning strategy. These challenges might include pursuing a new audience/segment, adapting to competitive forces, changes in consumer attitudes, or internal changes.

Repositioning involves:

- Audit – understand the current state of the brand and what it stands for, review the marketplace and its competitors and assess key challenges and opportunities. Clarify consumer equity drivers, what they value and their current relationship with the brand;

- Research and insights – obtain a clear understanding of what the brand means to consumers, consumer perceptions and image of the brand, key areas of growth, best target markets and their potential, brand positioning assessment (current and desired);

- Strategy formulation – design a clear strategy, focusing on key elements such as: brand vision and mission, brand values and purpose, personality and tone of voice;

- Brand activation – allow for channels of distribution and communication to follow the developed strategy so as to implement the new positioning effectively.

When awareness is high, a brand is harder to reposition due to increased levels of familiarity. Brand repositioning focuses on changing the associations consumers have with a brand and usually entails work on a brand's promise, personality and identity elements, to secure the desired positioning.

Recently a number of well-established fashion brands have re-evaluated their values and adopted bold repositioning strategies for evolution and revolution (WGSN, 2017) in order to adapt to social, political and economic change. This kind of strategy can also be referred to as a reboot; a brand that has been through this process is Gucci. According to Kering (2017), the strategies used were broken down into 3 sections: product positioning, brand perception and brand experience. In terms of product positioning, the brand has simplified the product offering, concentrated on high-impact product identity, reinvented its merchandising and engaged in a gradual renovation according to its product categories. Regarding brand perception, Gucci developed a new and energetic creative vision (led by creative director Alessandro Michele), focused on contemporary design, and shaped their message and communication so as to enhance desirability. The last section, brand experience, consisted of a new and more integrated online presence, a new store and window display concept, and a clearer focus on the clientele's retail excellence (Kering, 2017).

An indication of the changing times is that repositioning is often communicated on social media content before expanding to other brand touch-points. This is an indication of how much marketing has changed and demonstrates the role and influence of social media in fashion business (this will be explored further in Chapter 7). With 'legacy' brands, the big question is how to preserve consistent and authentic brand heritage while maintaining relevancy and freshness in the digitally influenced landscape. Although a high-risk strategy, repositioning can provide a high-reward opportunity for brands, as demonstrated by the revival of Gucci.

Brand identity in the retail environment

Retail design is the physical representation of a brand and its identity, values and promise and includes all aspects of the store: entrance, windows, signage, displays, fixtures, walls and floor. Along with visual merchandising it is an essential tool in brand positioning or renewal as it reinforces the brand's relationship with consumers and also excites and innovates. Visual merchandising engages the senses – touch, sight, hearing and smell, and again stimulation of these with consistent cues can add to a brand's identity. Lighting, music, scent, colour and texture can all feed into the visual representation of the brand in a store; 'consumers experience this environment with all their senses creating a very powerful impetus' (Lea-Greenwood, 2012).

A concept that has arisen to enhance the topic of branded retail environments is that of the brandscape. 'Brandscape' refers to the space where experiences provide a consistent message of a given brand and where strong experiences are created, which will meet the expectations raised by the brand promise and improve consumer satisfaction. An important element of branded retail space is the store window, offering the chance to attract and entice the consumer inside. Although window designs should always communicate the brand's positioning and the products available in the stores, they also provide the opportunity to link to a creative brand-orientated seasonal or cultural theme.

Store interiors are the visible expression of the concept of atmospherics, which refers to 'the conscious design of the space to create certain effects in buyers' (Kotler, 1973: 3). The holistic store environment can be analyzed in terms of three different types of cue:

- design cues (internal and external), materials, shape and space;
- ambient cues (store layout, lighting, music, temperature);
- social cues (employees and customers).

When translating the retail experience into online space, we can use the concept of web atmospherics to describe how online retailers provide an 'atmosphere' through their website which can affect shoppers' image of and experience with the online store (Eroglu et al., 2005). Web atmospherics can be defined as 'the conscious designing of web environments to create positive effects in users in order to increase favourable consumer responses' (Dailey, 2004: 76). Evidence suggests online atmospherics impact aspects of consumer behaviour (Manganari et al., 2009) with images of the merchandise, music, icons, colour, background patterns, animation, and fonts influencing feelings of pleasure and sense arousal, which might in turn encourage purchase in a similar way to atmospherics in physical stores (Eroglu et al., 2001). Online visual merchandising therefore aims to provide experiences that are as close to the in-store experience as possible so as to reduce the perceived risk related to the lack of physical contact with the store and product. 'The best and most successful brands are completely coherent. Every aspect of what they do and what they are reinforces everything else' (Olins, 2004). The brand COS, for example, demonstrates common traits such as a neutral colour palette and understated brand aesthetics across retail channels making it a coherent brand experience. The ability to manage identity and image across channels within a global context is one of the biggest challenges of brands, as we saw in Chapter 4. A brand that has been successful at this is the Brazilian footwear brand Havaianas (see Case Study 7, Chapter 7).

CASE STUDY 6 - Acne Studios: The understated cool of a Nordic brand

Acne Studios premises. Reproduced by permission of Acne Studios.

Acne Studios is a Swedish fashion house with a multidisciplinary approach, offering ready-to-wear, magazines, furniture, books and exhibitions (Garced, 2017). The brand was set up in Stockholm in 1996 and was initially part of the creative collective ACNE – Ambition to Create Novel Expressions – founded by four creatives, that operated in the areas of film, production, advertising and graphic design. At that time, it was called Acne Jeans and gained attention in 1997 when the founder and Creative Director Jonny Johansson created 100 pairs of raw denim jeans and gave them to 100 influential and creative friends in Stockholm (Acne Studios, 2018). These quickly became popular, and featured in magazines such as Wallpaper and Vogue Paris.

The brand's collections are defined by a signature style juxtaposing design and attention to detail, with an emphasis on tailoring and an eclectic use of materials and custom-developed fabrics. The collections cover men's and women's ready-to-wear, footwear, accessories and denim. The core market segment is 'bridge', which indicates that the brand sits between mass market and high-end luxury. Acne has established itself as a socially responsible brand that values art and creative expression and their customers value the brand's integrity, 'principled aesthetic decisions' and transparency (Acne Studios, 2016).

The brand tries to provoke new ways of blending fashion with their values and beliefs. Its identity and personality are deeply influenced by a 360° world of simplicity and clean lines in the aesthetic. Underpinning this unique identity is a consistent and coherent verbal and visual identity including a clear and recognizable logo and the use of a trademark soft pink in all their packaging and online/physical retail spaces. The Acne stores build on a belief in the 'studio' as an open and developing space for creativity (Moore, 2013).

The brand's innovative and fresh approach to fashion is translated in their communications activities. Between 2005 and 2014, the brand published ACNE Paper, the brand's bi-annual magazine. Originally printed in larger format it carried forth the ethos of the brand and replaced other forms of traditional advertising. 'We started the magazine because we thought it was a way to express our world without talking about our own brand' (Johansson, in Moore, 2013). For Spring 2017, Acne Studios commissioned Italian photographer Paolo Roversi to photograph a range of artists and writers wearing their looks, in a celebration of international diversity (Garced, 2017). The brand chose not to work with models but with women in creative professions such as art and music to celebrate strength, openness and inner reflection.

Sources:

Acne Studios (2016) Acne Studios Social Report 2015–16. Available at: https://www.acnestudios.com/on/demandware.static/-/Library-Sites-acne/default/dwad56197f/csr/acnestudios-social-report-2015-2016.pdf.

Acne Studios (2018). Available at : https://www.acnestudios.com/uk/en/about/about.html.

Garced, K. (2017) Acne Studios Unveils Spring Campaign. Available at: http://wwd.com/fashion-news/fashion-scoops/acne-studios-spring-campaign-10775768/.

Moore, B. (2013) Acne Studios opens 5,000 square foot store in downtown LA. Available at: http://www.latimes.com/fashion/alltherage/la-ar-acne-studios-opens-5000-square-foot-store-in-downtown-la-20131218-story.html.

Case Challenge

Apply the Brand Identity Prism (Table 6.2) to Acne Studios to analyze how the brand creates a unique identity that differentiates it in a crowded market.

 ## ONLINE RESOURCES

A longer version of this case study, with additional challenges, can be found on our companion website: https://www.macmillanihe.com/companion/Varley_Fashion_Management.

⌐⊙ SUMMARY AND CONCLUDING THOUGHTS

Within this chapter we have introduced key terminology and concepts in strategic brand management, demonstrating their interconnections and discussing the associated challenges in the pursuit of a consistent brand strategy. The brand mix wheel brings these together in one framework (see Figure 6.5). The successful establishment of strong and long-lasting fashion brands depends on integration and achieved consistency across the 4 dimensions: core, elements, dynamics and activation.

Figure 6.5 *The fashion brand mix wheel*

Fashion brands operate in a global context with changing customers, competitors, and business models, and face disruption at every stage of the value chain. This means they need to be managed in this dynamic context and build the following characteristics:

- **Adaptive** – those brands willing to change quickly and be responsive to opportunity are more likely to be successful;

- **Purposeful** – brands must be clear about what they stand for and seek ways of delivering value to ensure relevancy, yet be guided by their ultimate purpose;

- **Networked** – brands should be shaped and sustained by ongoing conversations in a world of co-creation. They should use their network of stakeholders and engage in collaborations to ensure relevance and novelty;

- **Leading** – brands must seek new possibilities to refine priorities and increase value, in other words, being active rather than reactive;

- **Seamless** – brands must work consistently across various platforms and touch-points, adapting to the context of the medium while being true to themselves;

- **Global** – every brand has the potential to be global, bringing opportunities to reach new consumers, learn from a global marketplace and show relevancy to the needs of local markets;

- **Open** – given the dynamics of today's market, brand management can never be finished and needs constant improvement and evolution;

- **Consistent** – consistency should be the biggest goal in brand building and the guiding principle in all brand management activities;

- **Experiential** – the most successful brands deliver a promise across platforms, geographies, and audiences through their actions.

With the rapid growth of emerging markets and change within established ones, product choices are extending and communication channels are growing in complexity (McKinsey, 2012). Understanding the industry structure helps brand managers to extend the possibilities for strategic action, such as positioning a brand to better cope with competitive forces, anticipating market shifts and even creating a new industry structure that might be more favourable to the company (Porter, 2008). A brand strategy that is orientated well towards its market is one that understands the dynamics of the networks that consumers belong to and with that knowledge comprehend current, and anticipate future, customer demands.

Fashion concerns business philosophies centred on customers and their fashion needs and desires and, because of its fast pace, there is a need for a different emphasis to be placed on fashion marketing activities than those usually regarded for other industries (Easey, 2009). Fashion brand managers need to identify market opportunities in line with the company's experience and core competencies. They should also observe competition and look for market segments where they believe brands can be profitable. Putting all elements together in order to achieve a brand's long-term aim is the ultimate task of a brand marketing strategy.

In order to survive today's hypercompetitive, fast-moving world, fashion brands need to be agile and able to adapt and react quickly to the market. According to Jacobs and Ordahl (2014) this is both the best time and the worst time to be a brand as a result of branding becoming a mainstream business activity, and the fact that everyone has (and potentially is!) a brand.

CHALLENGES AND CONVERSATIONS

1. Select a fashion brand. Then conduct the following tasks using this brand:
   A) Apply the brand identity prism and evaluate the advantages and the limitations of this framework;
   B) Discuss the brand's image and identity and evaluate their alignment;
   C) Identify the brand's positioning and consider how it differs from that of its competitors, evaluating points of parity (sameness) as well as points of differentiation.

2. For a chosen fashion brand, analyze its extendibility and make a recommendation for a possible brand extension or collaboration, identifying its leverage points and any barriers to success.

3. Role play challenge centring on Louis Vuitton (LV).
   In advance of this session: Participants should research market reports about trends in the athleisure category. Research should be focused to ascertain:

   - Overall information about the LV brand and its target audience;
   - Key players of the athleisure category and their market performance;
   - Previous collaborations of the LV brand, and their success factors.

   Context and the objectives of role play: In the last year, the athleisure trend has dominated the global apparel market, stealing market share from non-athletic apparel as more people globally choose active wear whether they work out or not. A modern 'super trend', athleisure is now in the dictionary, defined by Merriam-Webster as 'casual clothing designed to be worn for both exercising and for general use'. You will take part in a role play to assess the viability of a brand collaboration between luxury brand Louis Vuitton and a sportswear brand. *LV wants to arrive at an agreement on whether or not it should consider a collaboration and how this would take place.*

   Scenario: The Louis Vuitton board meets at the brand's headquarters in Paris, France, to consider whether or not they should undertake a collaboration with an athleisure/sports brand (to be decided).
   Roles to play:

   - a group representing LV's board;
   - a group advising on why a collaboration is the best strategy to enter this market;
   - a group advising on why this is not a good strategy for the brand at this stage.

Aspects to consider:

- which brand to collaborate with, and target audience;
- the attractiveness of the new segment/category and the advantages it could bring to the LV brand as well as the needs it will satisfy;
- how this collaboration should take place to enhance positioning.

 REFERENCES AND FURTHER READING

Aaker, D. A. (1991) *Managing Brand Equity: Capitalizing on the Value of a Brand Name*. New York: The Free Press.

Aaker, D. A. (1992) 'The Value of Brand Equity'. *Journal of Business Strategy*, 13(4), pp. 27–32.

Aaker, D. A. (1996a) *Building Strong Brands*. New York: The Free Press.

Aaker, D. A. (1996b) 'Measuring brand equity across products and markets'. *California Management Review*, 38, pp. 102–120.

Aaker, D. A. (2004) *Brand Portfolio Strategy*. New York: The Free Press.

Aaker, D. A. and Joachimsthaler, E. (2000) *Brand Leadership*. New York: The Free Press.

Aaker, D. A. and Keller, K. (1990) 'Consumer evaluations of brand extensions'. *Journal of Marketing*, 54(1), pp. 27–41.

Aaker, J. L. (1997) 'Dimensions of brand personality'. *Journal of Marketing Research*, 34, pp. 347–356.

Aaker, J. L. (1999) 'The malleable self: The role of self-expression in persuasion'. *Journal of Marketing Research*, 36, pp. 45–57.

Adams, E. (2015) *How Mansur Gavriel plans to handle demand in 2015*. Available at: http://www.racked.com/2015/1/5/7562403/mansur-gavriel-bags [accessed 12/05/2016].

Alsem, K. J. and Kostelijk, E. (2008) 'Identity-based marketing: A new balanced marketing paradigm'. *European Journal of Marketing*, 42(9/10), pp. 907–914.

AMA (1995) *Dictionary*. Available at: https://www.ama.org/resources/pages/dictionary.aspx?dLetter=B [accessed 10/08/2015].

Assouline (2015) *Farfetch Celebrate The Launch of Farfetch Curates: Food at Maison Assouline*. Availabe at: http://www.assouline.com/Farfetch-celebrate-the-launch-of-Farfetch-Curates-Food-at-Maison-Assouline.html [accessed 22/5/2016].

Banks, L. (2014) *Designing a handbag niche*. Available at: http://www.nytimes.com/2013/09/18/fashion/Sophie-Hulme-and-Her-Handbag-Niche.html?_r=0 [accessed 21/05/2016].

Bendixen, M., Bukasa, K. A. and Abratt, R. (2004) 'Brand equity in the business-to-business market'. *Industrial Marketing Management*, 33(5), pp. 371–380.

Berry, L. L. (2000) 'Cultivating service brand equity'. *Journal of Academy of Marketing Science*, 28, pp. 128–137.

Blackett, T. and Russell, N. (1999) 'What is co-branding', in Blackett, T. and Boad B. (eds) *Co-Branding: The Science of Alliance*. Basingstoke: Macmillan, pp. 1–21.

BoF (2014) *What's the Difference Between Prada and Miu Miu? Miuccia Speaks*. Available at: https://www.businessoffashion.com/articles/intelligence/miuccia-prada-unravels-difference-prada-miu-miu [accessed 10/08/2015].

Cadogan, D. (2017) *Louis Vuitton's best cult art collaborations*. Available at: http://www.dazeddigital.com/fashion/article/35567/1/louis-vuitton-art-collaborations-yayoi-kusama-richard-prince-cindy-sherman [accessed 25/11/2017].

Carlotti, S. J., Coe, M. E. and Perrey, J. (2004) Making brand portfolios work. *McKinsey Quarterly*. Available at: https://www.mckinsey.com/business-functions/marketing-and-sales/our-insights/making-brand-portfolios-work [accessed 13/08/2015].

Clarke, J. (2017) John Lewis, BBC and Sony seen as best quality brands in the UK. Available at: http://www.independent.co.uk/news/business/news/john-lewis-bbc-sony-best-quality-brands-uk-yougov-brandindex-amazon-samsung-heinz-boots-a7859886.html [accessed 21/12/2017].

CNN (2007) *That look of Ralph Lauren*. Available at: http://edition.cnn.com/2007/LIVING/homestyle/10/15/is.ralph.lauren/ [accessed 13/08/2015].

Colon, A. (2015) *Stop what you're doing: Mansur Gavriel just Restocked*. Available at: http://www.refinery29.com/mansur-gavriel-spring-bucket-bags#slide [accessed 12/05/2016].

Correia, R. (2016) Vera Wang gives an exclusive look at her new David's Bridal wedding dresses. Available at: https://www.brides.com/story/vera-wang-davids-bridal-interview-2017 [accessed 11/12/2016].

Coscarelli, A. (2016) *Start saving now – Mansur Gavriel shoes coming spring 2016*. Available at: http://www.refinery29.com/mansur-gavriel-shoes-fashion-week-spring-2016#slide [accessed 12/05/2016].

Courier (2014) *Five lessons branding startups*. Available at: http://www.courierpaper.com/2014/05/five-lessons-branding-startups-wally-olins-daren-cook/ [accessed 10/08/2015].

Dailey, L. (2004) 'Navigational web atmospherics: Explaining the influence of restrictive navigation cues'. *Journal of Business Research*, 57(7), pp. 795–803.

Dewhurst, M., Harris, J. and Heywood, S. (2012) The global company's challenge. *McKinsey Quarterly*. Available at: https://www.mckinsey.com/business-functions/organization/our-insights/the-global-companys-challenge [accessed 12/0820/15].

Easey, M. (2009) *Fashion Marketing*, 3rd edn. Chichester: Wiley-Blackwell.

Eroglu, S. A., Machleit, K. A. and Davis, L. M. (2001) 'Atmospheric qualities of online retailing: A conceptual model and implications'. *Journal of Business Research*, 54, pp. 177–184.

Eroglu, S. A., Machleit, K. A. and Chebat, J. (2005) 'The interaction of retail density and music tempo: Effects on shopper responses. *Psychology & Marketing*, 22(7), pp. 577–589.

Farm Rio (n.d.). Available at: http://www.farmrio.com.br [accessed 12/08/2016].

Forbes (2016) *The World's Most Innovative Companies*. Available at: http://www.forbes.com/companies/hermes-international/ [accessed 21/12/2016].

Grime, I., Diamantopoulos, A. and Smith, G. (2002) 'Consumer evaluations of extensions and their effects on the core brand. Key issues and research propositions'. *European Journal of Marketing*, 36(11/12), pp. 1415–1438.

Groucutt, J. (2006) 'The life, death and resuscitation of brands'. *Handbook of Business Strategy*, 7(1), pp. 101–106.

Harris, F. and De Chernatony, L. (2001) 'Corporate branding and corporate brand performance'. *European Journal of Marketing*, 35, pp. 441–456.

Hsieh, M. H. (2004) 'Measuring global brand equity using cross-national survey data'. *Journal of International Marketing*, 12(2), pp. 28–57.

Interbrand (2016) *Best Global Brands 2016* Available at: http://interbrand.com/best-brands/best-global-brands/2016/ranking [accessed 21/12/2016].

Jacobs, L. and Ordahl, T. (2014) *The agile brand*. Available at: https://landor.com/thinking/the-agile-brand [accessed 19/12/2016].

Jobber, D. (2010) *Principles and Practice of Marketing*, 6th edn. London: McGraw-Hill.

John Lewis Partnership (n.d.). Available at: https://www.johnlewispartnership.co.uk/about.html [accessed 21/12/2017].

Johnson, F. (2014) *The Very Best of Vivienne Westwood*. CreateSpace Independent Publishing Platform.

Johnson, G., Scholes, K. and Whittington, R. (2011) *Exploring Strategy*, 10th edn. Harlow: Pearson.

Kapferer, J.-N. (2001) *(Re)Inventing the Brand*. London: Kogan Page.

Kapferer, J.-N. (2008) *The New Strategic Brand Management: Creating and Sustaining Brand Equity Long Term*. London: Kogan Page.

Kapferer, J.-N. (2012) *The New Strategic Brand Management: Creating and Sustaining Brand Equity Long Term*, 5th edn. London and Philadelphia, PA: Kogan Page.

Keller, K. L. (1993) 'Conceptualizing, measuring, and managing customer-based brand equity'. *Journal of Marketing*, 57, pp. 1–22.

Keller, K. L. (1998) *Strategic Brand Management: Building, Measuring, and Managing Brand Equity*. Upper Saddle River, NJ: Prentice Hall.

Keller, K. L. (2003) *Strategic Brand Management: Building, Measuring, and Managing Brand Equity*. Upper Saddle River, NJ: Prentice Hall.

Keller, K. L. (2012) *Strategic Brand Management*, 4th edn. Harlow: Pearson.

Keller, K. L. and Sood, S. (2003) Brand Equity dilution. Available at: http://sloanreview.mit.edu/article/brand-equity-dilution/ [accessed 29/11/2015].

Keller, K. L., Apéria, T. and Georgson, M. (2008) *Strategic Brand Management: A European Perspective*, 1st edn. Harlow, England, and New York: Prentice Hall/Financial Times.

Kering (2017). Available at: http://www.kering.com/en [accessed 19/02/2017].

Kotler, P. (1973) 'Atmospherics as a marketing tool'. *Journal of Retailing*, 49(4), pp. 48–64.

Kotler, P. (2000) *Marketing Management – The Millennium Edition*, 10th edn. Upper Saddle River, NJ: Prentice Hall.

Kotler, P. (2003). *Marketing Management*, 11th edn. Upper Saddle River, NJ: Prentice Hall.

Kotler, P. and Keller, K. L. (2009) *Marketing Management*. Harlow: Pearson Education.

Kressman, F., Sirgy, M. J., Herrman, A., Huber, F., Huber, S. and Lee, D. J. (2006) 'Direct and indirect effects of self-image congruence on brand loyalty'. *Journal of Business Research*, 59(6), pp. 955–964.

Lea-Greenwood, G. (2012) *Fashion Marketing Communications*, 1st edn. Chichester: John Wiley & Sons.

Luck, E. M., Muratovski, G. and Hedley, L. (2014) 'Co-branding strategies for luxury fashion brands: Missoni for Target', in Hancock, J., Muratovski, G., Manlow, V. and Peirson-Smith, A. (eds) *Global Fashion Brands: Style, Luxury and History*. Bristol: Intellect, pp. 41–56.

Manganari, E. E., Siomkos, G. J. and Vrechopoulos, A. P. (2009) 'Store atmosphere in web retailing'. *European Journal of Marketing*, 43(9/10), pp. 1140–1153.

Mansur Gavriel (n.d.). Available at: https://www.mansurgavriel.com [accessed 12/05/2016].

McKinsey (2012) *Building brands in emerging markets*. Available at: https://www.mckinsey.com/business-functions/marketing-and-sales/our-insights/building-brands-in-emerging-markets [accessed 03/12/2015].

Meehan, M. (2016) *The Top Trends Shaping Business for 2017*. Forbes. Available at: https://www.forbes.com/sites/marymeehan/2016/12/15/the-top-trends-shaping-business-for-2017/#5760062c6a8a [accessed 28/12/2016].

Miller, J. and Muir, D. (2005) *The Business of Brands*. Chichester: John Wiley & Sons.

Moore, B. (2014) *Mansur Gavriel finds success with stealth luxe*. Available at: http://www.latimes.com/fashion/alltherage/la-ar-mansur-gavriel-finds-success-with-stealth-luxe-20140818-story.html [accessed 12/05/2016].

Mycoskie, B. (2016) *The founder of TOMS on reimagining the company's mission*. Available at: https://hbr.org/2016/01/the-founder-of-toms-on-reimagining-the-companys-mission [accessed 12/07/2016].

Neff, J. (2012) *Revlon counts on 'selling hope' to make up for its small size*. Available at: http://adage.com/article/cmo-interviews/revlon-counts-selling-hope-make-size/236961/ [accessed 12/08/2015].

Nielsen (2015) *Understanding the power of a brand*. Available at: http://www.nielsen.com/us/en/insights/news/2015/understanding-the-power-of-a-brand-name.html [accessed 12/08/2015].

Olins, W. (2004) *On Brands*. London: Thames & Hudson.

Oliver, R. (1999) 'Whence consumer loyalty?' *Journal of Marketing*, 63(1), pp. 33–44.

Porter, M. E. (2008) 'The five competitive forces that shape strategy. *Harvard Business Review*, January.

Posner, H. (2015) *Marketing Fashion: Strategy, Branding and Promotion*, 2nd edn. London: Laurence King.

Prynn, J. (2015) *Burberry invites customers to check out its all-day cafe in the flagship Regent Street store*. Available at: https://www.standard.co.uk/fashion-0/burberry-invites-customers-to-check-out-its-all-day-cafe-in-the-flagship-regent-street-store-10315921.html [accessed 12/08/2015].

Randall, G. (2000) *Branding: A Practical Guide to Planning your Strategy*, 2nd edn. London: Kogan.

Reddy, M. and Terblanche, N. (2005) *How not to extend your luxury brand*. Available at: https://hbr.org/2005/12/how-not-to-extend-your-luxury-brand [accessed 12/08/2015].

Reizebos, R. (2003) *Brand Management*. Harlow: FT Prentice Hall.

Ries, A. and Trout, J. (2000) *Positioning, the Battle for your Mind*. New York: McGraw-Hill Professional Publishing.

Roderick, L. (2016) *Why brand purpose requires more than just a snappy slogan*. Available at: https://www.marketingweek.com/2016/02/15/why-brands-must-prove-their-purpose-beyond-profit/ [accessed 29/12/2016].

Roll, M. (2016) *Hermès – The Strategy Insights Behind the Iconic Luxury Brand*. Available at: http://bbf.digital/hermes-the-strategy-insights-behind-the-iconic-luxury-brand [accessed 29/12/2016].

Samotin, P. (2014) *Mansur Gavriel: Why a simple bucket bag became Fashion's most-wanted piece*. Available at: http://stylecaster.com/mansur-gavriel [accessed 12/05/2016].

Santos-Vijande, M., Río-Lanza, A., Suárez-Álvarez, L. and Díaz-Martín, A. M. (2013) 'The brand management system and service firm competitiveness'. *Journal of Business Research*, 66, pp. 148–157.

Schultz, M. and De Chernatony, L. (2002) 'Introduction: The challenges of corporate branding'. *Corporate Reputation Review*, 5(2/3), pp. 105–112.

Sherman, L. (2015) *How Mansur Gavriel created the first post-recession it bag*. Available at: https://www.businessoffashion.com/articles/intelligence/mansur-gavriel-created-first-post-recession-bag [accessed 12/05/2016].

Smith, P. R. and Zook, Z. (2016) *Marketing Communications: Offline and Online Integration, Engagement and Analytics*. London: Kogan Page.

Sowray, B. (2013) *Best of the High Street's collections*. Available at: http://fashion.telegraph.co.uk/article/TMG10256918/One-to-watch-Mansur-Gavriel.html [accessed 12/05/2016].

Supply, N. (2013) *Interview: Mansur Gavriel*. Available at: https://blog.needsupply.com/2013/10/31/interview-mansur-gavriel/ [accessed 13/05/2016].

Sweaty Betty (2016). Available at: http://www.sweatybetty.com.

Till, B. D., Baack, D. and Waterman, B. (2011) 'Strategic brand association maps: Developing brand insight'. *Journal of Product & Brand Management*, 20(2), pp. 92–100.

Urde, M. (1999) Brand orientation: A mindset for building brand into strategic resources. *Journal of Marketing Management*, 15(1–3), pp. 117–133.

Urde, M. (2013) 'The corporate brand identity matrix'. *Journal of Brand Management*, 20(9), pp. 742–761.

Urde, M., Greyser, S. and Balmer, J. (2007) 'Corporate brands with a heritage'. *Journal of Brand Management*, 15(1), pp. 4–19.

Wahba, P. (2016) *Neiman Marcus taps Rent the Runway in search of younger shoppers*. Available at: http://fortune.com/2016/11/16/neiman-marcus-rent-the-runway/ [accessed 15/06/2016].

Warby Parker (n.d.). Available at: https://www.warbyparker.com [accessed 12/06/2016].

WARC (2014) *Warby Parker challenges norms*. Available at: https://www.warc.com/NewsAndOpinion/News/32673/ [accessed 12/06/2016].

WARC (2016) *Abercrombie & Fitch plans revival*. Available at: https://www.warc.com/NewsAndOpinion/news/Abercrombie__Fitch_plans_revival/03715ef8-482c-42b8-a386-ce251a3ab639 [accessed 12/09/2016].

WGSN (2016a) Brand Partnerships. Available at: www.wgsn.com [accessed 21/01/2017].

WGSN (2016b) Unbranded content hubs. Available at: www.wgsn.com [accessed 23/01/2017].

WGSN (2017) The rise of Unbranding. Available at: www.wgsn.com [accessed 10/11/2017].

Wheeler, A. (2009) *Designing Brand Identity: An Essential Guide for the Whole Branding Team*, 4th edn. Hoboken, NJ: John Wiley & Sons.

Whiteside, S. (2014) 'How Warby Parker disrupted the eyewear category'. *WARC*, March. Available at: www.warc.com [accessed 12/06/2016].

Wood, Z. (2012) The John Lewis model and what others could learn from it. Available at: https://www.theguardian.com/business/2012/jan/16/john-lewis-model-lessons [accessed 21/12/2017].

WWD (2015) *Tiffany & Co. Holiday Campaign Features Anja Rubik, Brad Kroenig*. Available at: http://wwd.com/accessories-news/jewelry/tiffany-holiday-campaign-anja-rubik-brad-kroenig-10271265-10271265/ [accessed 29/05/2016].

YOOX NET-A-PORTER (n.d.). Available at: http://www.ynap.com/pages/about-us/who-we-are/company-dna/ [accessed 28/05/2016].

FASHION MARKETING COMMUNICATIONS

Ana Roncha

INTRODUCTION

Communicating about fashion is not like communicating about other consumer goods. Since fashion in itself is already a form of communication (Saviolo and Testa, 2002), fashion brands must ensure the correct narrative is delivered when they engage in conversations with their consumers. Technological and societal change has resulted in a desire from consumers to be heard, interact and build seamless and effortless relationships with brands. The effectiveness of communication in a strategy depends on the clarity and consistency of the message and the definition of the target consumer. An integrated communication strategy is one that provides for the synergetic use of all the tools available to achieve a particular objective. In this chapter we will be uncovering marketing communications, its characteristics, processes and scope and we will demonstrate how integrated marketing communication plans help fashion brands implement successful strategic ventures.

Today's connected and informed fashion consumer is surrounded by a vast array of messages in the media and by a complex and competitive retail environment. In this environment, innovation and originality in the way fashion brands communicate is needed to grab the attention of consumers. Many new opportunities to communicate have been prompted by the rise of social media, which has democratized the communication process, switching it from a top-down process to a multi-way conversation. The dialogue between brands and consumers is now more open, with people wanting to feel connected and brands better understanding the pace and intention of fashion. This interactive process can be seen clearly with the proliferation of user-generated content (UGC) and in the growing part played by digital influencers who fully embrace Barthes's (1973) vision that 'there is no law, whether natural or not, which forbids talking about things'. This chapter considers these developments from the strategic viewpoint.

LEARNING OBJECTIVES

After studying this chapter, you should be able to understand:

- The marketing communications process within the strategic context;

- How marketing communications can be used to support strategic objectives such as building brand awareness and engagement;

- The choices available when planning fashion marketing communications, including the variety of tools, media, and content types;

- The impact of the changing digital landscape on the way fashion consumers receive and respond to marketing communications;

- The significance of consistency and integration when communicating across multiple brand touch-points.

---

7. Clutch bag by Maria Sokolyanskaya, MA Fashion Artefact. London College of Fashion, © University of the Arts London.

THE PRINCIPLES OF MARKETING COMMUNICATIONS

Marketing communications is an important discipline in brand building (see Chapter 6) since customer-based brand equity is determined by the brand knowledge created in consumers' minds and this can be done through a marketing campaign. 'Marketing Communications are the means by which firms attempt to inform, persuade, incite, and remind consumers – directly or indirectly – about the brand they sell' (Keller, 2001: 819). There have been numerous definitions of marketing communications (Fill, 2013); however, we can define it as the way an organization represents itself to and engages with its audiences. Although engagement is a concept that also holds different definitions, it has strong ties with the analysis of consumer–brand relationships and brand personality, and according to Hollebeck (2011), it is a priority in marketing communication strategy. Brand engagement extends beyond involvement, encompassing an interactive relationship with the engagement object, and for that purpose, requires the emergence of an individual's perceived experiential value (Mollen and Wilson, 2010). It is a concept strongly rooted in the domain of relationship marketing, which emphasizes interactivity and customer experience (Vivek et al.,

> **Brand engagement**
> The process that takes place between brands and consumers and the main purpose of marketing communications. Engagement is a concept that goes beyond involvement as it aims to enhance the interactive relationship with the engagement object.

2011), and as a psychological process it comprises cognitive and emotional aspects (Bowden, 2009).

Historically, marketing communications were used to persuade people to buy products using mass media, with an emphasis placed on rational and product-based information. In the current communications landscape, resources are used in a more effective and efficient manner enabling consumers to have a clear vision of the brand's value propositions, with emphasis being placed on strategy and a balance between rational and emotional communication. The goal is to achieve mutual value as well as meaning and recognition across various stakeholders.

Communication models – a new take on the process

Although early models of communication see it represented in a two-way exchange between two parties (Figure 7.1), our understanding of the complexity of the communication process has evolved, and this is represented in later models. Fill (2013: 42, quoting Theodorson and Theodorson, 1969) states that the linear model emphasizes the 'transmission of information, ideas, attitudes, or emotion from one person to another, primarily through symbol'.

Although the model appears quite simple, it is the quality of the linkages between the various elements (sources, messages and receivers)

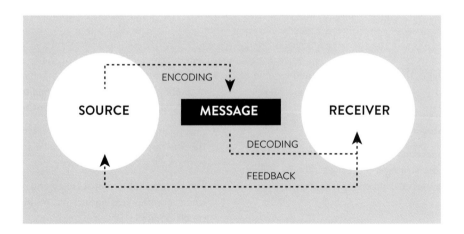

Figure 7.1 *The linear model of communication*

Source: Based on Baines, Fill and Page (2011); Schramm (1955); and Shannon and Weaver (1964).

that determines whether a communication will be successful. Within this communication process, the concepts of encoding and decoding are fundamental because regardless of the model, they form the basis of communication. Encoding means putting thoughts, ideas, or information into symbolic form while decoding implies transforming the sender's message back into thought (Belch and Belch, 2012). There can be two types of message or content: information-based messages and emotion-based messages. The first makes use of factual and rational content while the second focuses on senses, feelings and lifestyle content.

The interaction model of communication that followed (see Figure 7.2) considers the interaction between various entities and how communications move from one member to another in a communication network, making interaction a key component of the communication process and the basis for dialogue. Underpinning the interaction model of communication is the concept of co-creation of value, created by information flowing from the consumer to the company (Prahalad and Ramaswamy, 2004). The consumer (receiver) is now an active partner in the communication process, mainly due to technological innovations providing new ways to connect.

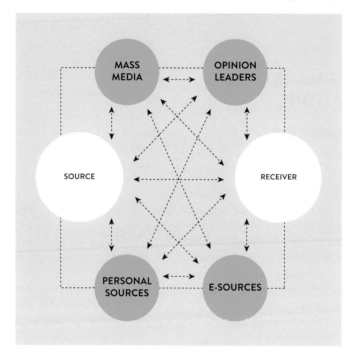

Figure 7.2 *The interactive communication process*

During an interaction all parties are involved in the communication process, with messages moving through media channels and opinion leaders. Between the brand (source) and the consumer (receiver) there are multiple aspects that can influence the final message. This impacts on the brand image and associations (see Chapter 6) and it can lead to different receiver interpretations.

Disruption in the communication sphere – the rise of opinion leaders and creative consumers

The opinion leaders mentioned above include journalists, celebrities, bloggers, consultants, style leaders and so on, who influence other members in a marketplace. We have identified below some global and local influencers relevant to the fashion industry at the time of writing (see Table 7.1).

Opinion leaders were classified by Malcolm Gladwell (2000) as 'socially contagious connectors' and their power is so strong that it is worth brands identifying and partnering with them to target messages at the market more efficiently. This idea is revisited by Smith and Zook (2016), who studied how communications are accelerated by word of mouth, viral messages, and opinion leaders communicating to consumers and brands, and vice versa. In the fashion industry the idea of the consumer as brand advocate and co-creator of brand value is important. This will be discussed further, later on in this chapter.

Global fashion influencers	Local fashion influencers
Gigi Hadid (American model) 33.8 million followers	**Fan Bingbing (Chinese fashion icon, actress and singer)** 3.1 million followers
Chiara Ferragni (Italian blogger) 9 million followers	**Lu Han (Chinese pop star)** 8.3 million followers
Selena Gomez (American singer and actress) 119 million followers	**Helena Bordon (Brazilian blogger)** 971K followers

Table 7.1 *Fashion influencers – global and local*

Source: Instagram (April 2017).

INTEGRATING MARKETING COMMUNICATIONS

Marketing communications and its role in the strategic context

The strategic context of brands and the current landscape of marketing communications impact strongly on each other. The various tools available can be used to support strategic objectives such as building awareness and engagement, promoting brand loyalty, and helping the brand to achieve higher value and equity. In the process of marketing communications planning, it is important that all aspects of promotional activity work in conjunction with other components of the marketing mix. In sum, an effective marketing communication strategy is one that allows consumers to engage with brands and to develop a relationship with them (Fill and Jamieson, 2011); the roles that communication can play in this strategic process are demonstrated by Fill and Jamieson's (2011) DRIP framework:

- D – to Differentiate: make a brand stand out;

- R – to Reinforce: remind, consolidate and strengthen the previous messages and experiences, such as reinforcing why a brand is different or superior;

- I – to Inform: make consumers aware and educate them about features and availability, in particular

> **Integrated marketing communications**
> A marketing communications strategy that uses all tools available to communicate a brand message consistently, informing consumers about the brand's purpose and products, and leading to higher brand equity.

when products or brands are new to market and need explanation;

- P – to persuade: encourage further positive purchase-related behaviour, such as visiting the website, reading about a brand, sharing opinions or requesting a trial.

Integrated marketing communications (IMC) and a shift in focus

The marketing communications mix represents the incorporation of several 'tools' that can be used and blended together to reach a target audience (Fill, 2013). These tools overlap and jointly contribute towards the same goal, becoming part of what is known as integrated marketing communications (IMC) (Scott, 2017).

IMC allows the company to communicate more effectively with a unified voice across all communication platforms, creating synergy and consistency (Rehman and Ibrahim, 2011). It can be defined as 'a concept of marketing communications planning that recognizes the added value of a comprehensive plan that evaluates the strategic roles of a variety of communications disciplines – for example, general advertising, direct response, sales promotion and public relations – and combines these disciplines to provide clarity, consistency and maximum communications' impact through the seamless integration of discrete messages' (American Association of Advertising Agencies, n.d.).

Decisions regarding the mix of disciplines or tools should consider:

- Control required over the message to be delivered;
- Cost related to the financial resources available;
- Audience size and geographic dispersion;
- Media preferences in relation to the message and content delivery;
- Behaviour of target audience in terms of media consumption;
- Tasks and goals to be achieved by the programme.

The role of media typologies

Paid, owned and earned media (POE) (Pessin and Weaver, 2014) is a model of media planning that has emerged in the digital age. Media planning evolved to include the many stages of the consumer journey, with a complex ecosystem of media activity at each stage. Consumers now interact with brands and media in a non-linear way, making it harder to evaluate the true effect of POE, and so marketing plans, resources and capabilities should adapt and evolve accordingly.

Paid media are those that a brand pays for in order to leverage a channel of communication, such as PPC (pay per click), PPP (pay per post), search ads, sponsored links, affiliate marketing, and blogging marketing, as well as traditional paid for space (print, TV, billboard and so on). All of these can be a catalyst to feed owned media and create earned media. Owned media relates to those channels that are either owned or fully controlled by a brand. Examples would include their own website, mobile sites and official social media accounts. Earned media refers to the customer as the media channel, usually in the form of user-generated content. It includes word of mouth, viral marketing, consumers' social media posts, reviews, online communities, influencer outreach, and publisher editorial. These different types of media represent different costs and benefits; in particular earned media has the benefit of being both low cost and the most credible but is difficult to control, and to measure in its effectiveness.

More recently, two types of media were added to this model: sold, and hijacked (McKinsey, 2010). Sold media relates to what occurs when the company/brand invites others to place their content on its owned media channels, for example when an e-commerce retailer sells advertising space on its own website or when a consumer creates an online community and sells advertising space. Hijacked media occurs when a brand's asset or campaign is taken hostage by those who are opposed to it – examples of this can be found when consumers create and distribute their own negative version of a campaign or advertisement.

MARKETING COMMUNICATIONS TOOLS – AN OVERVIEW

The range of marketing communication tools available, sometimes referred to as the marketing communications mix, has been extended substantially by the introduction of digitally based tools (see Figure 7.3). Previously, emphasis was placed on tools that could be planned well in advance of the fashion selling season, like advertising, and most of the tools used were those that delivered a one-way message to consumers. These tools are placed on the right-hand side of the diagram. Those tools on the left-hand side are ones that have proliferated in the digital era. It is not within the scope of this text to give a detailed discussion of all of these tools, which can be found in other texts (see Further Reading), but we will relate our discussion of communication tools to their particular use in fashion marketing communications and highlight some emerging trends in this important aspect of strategic fashion management. The retail environment (both physical and online) acts as a focal point for brand communication, and is explored in Chapters 6 and 10. An IMC plan should also consider how the tools set out in Figure 7.3 can be translated onto the various touch-points, including the retail space, so as to guarantee a cohesive image and message.

 ONLINE RESOURCES

Our companion website provides an overview of the generic advantages and disadvantages of the various marketing communication tools in this chapter: https://www.macmillanihe.com/companion/Varley_Fashion_Management.

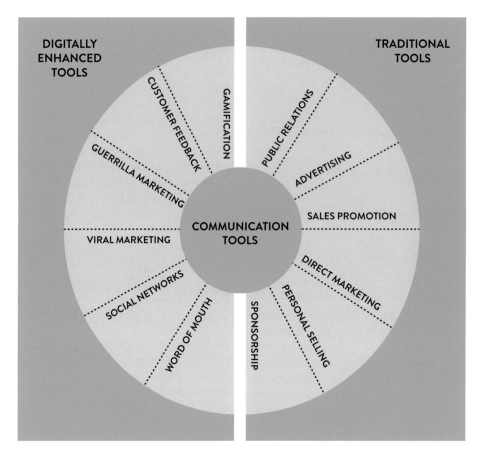

Figure 7.3 *Communication tools – from traditional to digitally enhanced tools*

Public relations

Public relations (PR) is the discipline that looks after the corporate image, aiming to earn a good reputation, which supports and influences opinions and behaviours. It integrates with public affairs, corporate and community affairs, community and corporate relations as well as corporate communications. It concerns building relationships with the various publics, such as media and key stakeholders, and allows for a direct and closer contact with journalists, bloggers and influencers. It has grown in impact over the years due to rising media interest in fashion business, new investor criteria and more demanding consumers and pressure groups. PR was once seen as a natural tool for fashion communications, with PR companies acting as gatekeepers of the information flow between fashion brands and the mainstream media, but in the digital age many of the PR-type messages are now delivered via owned media space. Nowadays PR is less measured by press clippings (coverage) and more by web traffic, sales, brand awareness and engagement (Smith and Zook, 2016). PR can be split into two areas: Corporate PR, which is concerned with company image enhancement and is usually the responsibility of a corporate communications director; and Product PR, which is concerned with promoting a product or a brand and is the responsibility of a marketing manager.

Publicity generating activities that can be relayed by PR are:

- Press releases (for example, about new ranges or campaigns)
- News conferences
- Publicity stunts
- Events
- Exhibitions
- Sponsorship
- Sales promotions
- Product launches

- Press days
- Fashion shows
- Private shopping evenings
- Designer guest appearances
- Product placement.

Advertising

Advertising is a paid form of mass communication that incorporates television, radio, print, as well as digital media. Although the costs of advertising are high, it is one of the most effective tools in shaping a brand's image and building awareness and engagement. The use of storytelling in advertisements is very effective and the repetition of messages cements brand positioning, meanings and associations into the consumer psyche.

There are six main components of an advertising campaign:

- **The message** What is the most important message it needs to convey? Is it to raise awareness, inform, reinforce brand values or provoke action? How will the message be communicated? Is the message clear and direct or indirectly implied? Through the use of text, image or both?

- **The medium** The vehicle by which an advertisement is presented and reaches the public, such as TV, radio, magazines, billboards, social media, internet search engines.

- **Timing and exposure considering the target audience** Which media are most suitable to attract desired customers and when are they engaged with that media?

- **Reach and frequency** How many people will be exposed to the advertisement and how many times are they likely to be exposed in a particular period?

- **Impact** Which media or combination of media will provide most impact, considering, for example, the size, colour and movement opportunities?

- **Cost** Consider the cost implications of each medium and how to best use advertising investment for the required returns.

The well-known AIDA model (Strong, 1925) was devised to evaluate the effectiveness of advertising in relation to the consumer decision-making process. The model traces how the receiver of the campaign communication is taken through four stages: the first stage, Attention, concerns learning or cognition about a product or brand; the creation of affective feelings occurs in the Interest stage; the building of preference in the Desire phase; and purchase Action in the final stage is the successful outcome of the advertisement. The AIDA process model can be adapted to consider the effectiveness of many other types of fashion marketing communications.

More recently, fashion brands have been looking at advertising from a different perspective; they have used provocation, humour, and irony as ways to make themselves noticed in a crowded landscape (see Mini Case Study 3.1 about jeans brand Diesel).

> Great advertising stimulates desires consumers don't even realize they have. Increasingly more campaigns veer in this direction. Noticeably this happens more often with mature brands or 'bold' emerging brands that are comfortable in their positioning and identity; brands that can afford the luxury of taking the 'odd' and completely owning it without damaging their market share. (Asma Ali, Associate Creative Director, McCann World group, in WGSN, 2016b).

Authenticity, attainability and relatability are pillars of successful engagement in advertisement messages: for example, the (role) models used to create more realistic and engaging marketing content (see Mini Case Study 7.1).

MINI CASE STUDY 7.1 - Lane Bryant

Lane Bryant has been able to build a brand narrative based on being authentic by celebrating beauty in real bodies. Their 2015 '#ImNoAngel' campaign was the result of consumer opposition to Victoria Secret's 'The Perfect Body' campaign, which used exclusively very slim models. Lane Bryant's '#ImNoAngel' hashtag was used in over 100,000 Instagram posts, serving as a call for action. The company has also used brand ambassadors such as plus-size models Ashley Graham and Precious Lee to promote its products. In the words of Lane Bryant's CMO, Brian Beitler, 'the brand aims to reflect and amplify the thoughts and feelings of its customer' (Saunter, 2016).

Sales promotion

This is an inclusive term used for short-term incentives that encourage trial or purchase by influencing at or near the time of the purchase decision. It often refers to discounts, but also includes competitions, premiums, loyalty cards, samples, limited editions and so on. Sales promotions affect the later stages of the buying process as they trigger actions such as purchase or repeated purchase or they increase usage of a brand. Within loyalty schemes, they may refer to extra benefits or services, engagement in the brand's activities, brand activation and the building of loyalty points.

Sales promotions integrate with other communication tools such as point-of-sale materials, visual merchandising, advertising (including via social media) and PR. These activities are effective in the young fashion sector where brand loyalty is generally low, and consumers can be persuaded to switch to competitors. Although they originated from the US, sales promotion events such as Black Friday and Cyber Monday are now present in the majority of global markets and have proved to be very popular with fashion consumers (see Box 7.1).

Box 7.1 - Uniqlo and Singles Day

An interesting example of how sales promotion has been used in the digital sphere is Singles' Day Campaigns. Global brands have been joining this promotional day of sales across the Asian market. Evolving from a purely discount shopping festival to a much more creative opportunity to engage with consumers, we have seen many international brands encouraging engagement prior to the event and using event marketing and virtual reality as strategies for higher customer participation. In 2016, Uniqlo became the top-selling women's wear brand on Tmall, selling all its discounted merchandise before noon. Heavy promotion on WeChat prior to the day as well as styling tips shared on social media were some of the reasons for this (Chen, 2016).

Direct marketing

Direct marketing accompanies the shift in communication messages from mass to personalized messages. This strategy is used to create a personal and intermediary-free dialogue with customers and is therefore aimed at creating and maintaining one-to-one relationships. Enhanced by big data, database technology, and personalization-enabling technology, digital direct marketing is providing a cost-effective means of mass customization of marketing communications. Direct marketing can take the form of: postal mailshot, telemarketing, email or text (SMS), and content via mobile apps. Fashion brands should choose the medium to be contextually relevant, and to differentiate their customer experience, as well as use it as a personalization vehicle.

> We make sure that everything is fully optimized to work on a mobile device. It is very important that the customer has a seamless experience with the brand on any channel. It has really been just about having very striking imagery, and then being slightly tongue-in-cheek but still intelligent with the wording to go around it; that is what we really focus on with our tone of voice, and the content that's in them. (Nickyl Raithatha, CEO Finery, in WGSN, 2016a)

The tone of voice and the type of message should resonate with the target customer in the environment where the reading of digital messages takes place. For example, according to a survey by Adobe in 2017, millennials spend six hours a day on their emails, 70% check their emails in bed (in the morning or evening), 57% check them in the bathroom, and 27% browse emails while driving (Naragon, 2017). Email fatigue is a constraint and so brands should consider how frequently they get in touch. Many fashion brands have found it more effective to send fewer, targeted emails, indicating what is new and what is happening, without being too intrusive.

Personal selling

This is the face-to-face communication process that occurs between a customer and a sales representative, and normally takes place in physical retail stores. It can encourage trial and purchase and can lead to long-term relationships with the consumer. It can have a deep impact on how consumers view a brand, as the experience in store is crucial to forming the brand image (as explored in Chapter 6). The use of personal shoppers can provide guidance on trends, offer individual and tailored advice based on suitability and body shape, and ultimately remove risk from the shopping experience.

In the online store environment the use of virtual or digital personal assistants can contribute to higher engagement and personalization. Driven by the need for convenience and by the growth in messaging platforms with demand-aggregation approaches, virtual assistant apps promise to reduce the purchase journey, facilitate requests and increase conversion as they can provide a more personalized and consistent service. They become a new touch-point between brands and consumers and one that has access to a

large amount of data on consumers' preferences and behaviours that can be leveraged. This can be addressed as the 'third phase of commerce' with messaging experience taking centre stage and messaging-based mobile shopping assistants being able to serve and respond to consumers' queries and requests. For example, Operator, GoButler, Scratch and SMS-based assistant Magic are services that offer on-demand request services that handle the path-to-purchase from initial intent through to transaction. '(...) no one wants to have to install a new app for every business or service that they interact with. We think you should be able to message a business; in the same way you would message a friend' (Mark Zuckerberg, CEO of Facebook, in Luckerson, 2016). The ever-evolving mobile landscape drives new touch-points, ways of connecting to, and shopping from, brands. Online retailer Zalando, for example, set up the styling and advice service through WhatsApp, called Zalon.

 ## MINI CASE STUDY 7.2 - Zalon by Zalando, curated shopping service

Reproduced with permission of Zalando – Zalon.

Zalon is the curated shopping service implemented by Zalando, focusing on style advice for different occasions and for both female and male customers. The service is currently available in Germany, Austria, Switzerland, the Netherlands and Belgium. Zalon works with a stylists' community of about 500 fashion experts, who advise customers and create fashionable looks that are then shipped in

an eye-catching Zalon box. A personal and close contact between the stylists and customers is key for this type of service. In order to better succeed at this personal contact, they have also implemented a messenger service on the website as well as within the app. This free service is available at all times and the customer only needs to pay for the items she/he keeps.

'Conversational commerce' is the term used to describe retailing through messaging apps. It is enabled by artificial intelligence bots that suggest products and services to the customer and can be seen as an evolution of personal shopping as it offers personalized and direct advice on shopping as well as information on brands (see Mini Case

Study 7.3). Leveraging big data to enable accurate voice recognition as well as highly contextual results are the two main objectives of this type of marketing communication tool. China has been at the forefront of these initiatives with consumers being able to order taxis, book laundry services, pay bills or order fashion goods through apps like WeChat.

MINI CASE STUDY 7.3 - Sephora on Kikservice

Kik is a messaging platform launched in 2009 in Ontario, Canada. Having 300 million users over 195 countries worldwide, it works as a way to connect with friends and video chat in a one-on-one conversation or group of up to six people. Brands such as Sephora (a beauty brand) are using this platform to talk to and share content with their consumers. Using a Chabot, rather than humans, to feed its communications, it takes a route of education and product discovery. When Kik users enquire about a particular product, Sephora directs them to video and image tutorials on how to use the product, or to see the latest innovations in a product category. This allows the brand to communicate to their target audience in a more conversational manner using relevant content and product reviews, and it avoids turning users off with a hard sell.

Sponsorship

'Brands have found that the best way to get our attention is to identify the passions of new communities and align with them through sponsorship' (Collett and Fenton, 2011). Sponsorship refers to the association of a brand with a specific entity (property) such as:

- Event
- Team
- Cause
- Art exhibition
- Cultural attraction
- Entertainment
- Celebrity (endorsement).

It helps to extend brands beyond their tangible attributes and attaches associations that add depth, richness and a contemporary feel to the brand. It also allows for greater exposure to particular audiences and makes them more willing to participate in brand experiences. Sponsorship allows the target audience to perceive the sponsor indirectly through a third party, so both benefit from this association. Sponsorship plays an important role in today's fashion marketing communications mix in terms of brand activation. Special attention should be paid to the selection of the right entity to sponsor (see Box 7.2).

Box 7.2 - Coachella Festival

Coachella is one of the biggest festivals in the United States and presents itself as a golden opportunity for brands to take part in an experience by associating themselves with top influencers that drive fashion, beauty and lifestyle. The strategies at Coachella go well beyond having banners at the back of a stage – brands engage in a fully immersive experience (from renting houses to host parties, to sponsoring air conditioned tents), focusing on brand activation and influencer marketing opportunities.

Why is Coachella relevant?

- 32 million people attend one or more music festivals in the United States every year.
- 8 in 10 Coachella attendees bought something before Coachella to prepare for the festival.

- Coachella drew 99,000 attendees each day of the six-day festival in 2016.
- Between consumers and businesses, an estimated $704 million was spent in Coachella Valley in 2016.
- The multi-day ticket for Coachella costs $375, which, in 2015, had festival goers paying $1.74 per artist.
- Coachella's Snapchat Story reached over 40 million people worldwide.
- Tweets about Coachella during the first weekend of the festival totalled 3.8 million.

H&M and Sephora have been amongst the sponsors for Coachella for a couple of years, with the intention to make their brands more appealing and meaningful for their target audience, who are engaging in experiences in a live setting. Research shows that consumers who engaged in a branded music experience came away with a 37% better perception of the brand in terms of it being more authentic and trustworthy. These are attributes that resonate well with the target audience of the festival.

Brands are finding alternative ways of connecting with their audience, before, during and after the event; for example, all Coachella ticketholders were sent Google cardboard headsets for VR purposes. H&M allowed consumers to try Oculus VR headsets and use a 360-degree mirrored 'selfie station' (in 2016), while Sephora created a make-up bar with its private-label brand and set up a vending machine that would give free products in exchange for photos posted on Instagram (Mediakix, 2017). In 2017, H&M created a 'see now, buy now' fashion collection in the third year of its co-branded 'H&M Loves Coachella' line. The brand has exclusive rights to use the festival name in its collection name and marketing materials, as it is the only fashion brand that is an official partner of the festival. The brand also partnered with 15 Instagram influencers to promote the collection (H&M, 2017).

Celebrity endorsement

According to Social Media Week (2015), endorsing the right celebrity can increase sales by 4% and while it does not necessarily influence consumer brand loyalty, it is a powerful tool to magnify the effects of a campaign and grab consumers' attention (Olenski, 2016).

Sometimes, endorsements can go wrong when brands are damaged by the behaviour of people they sponsor. After pictures of fashion model Kate Moss consuming cocaine emerged in the press in 2005, Chanel, Burberry and H&M cancelled their contracts with her. In a statement by Burberry, the company said: 'We are saddened by her current circumstances and hope she overcomes her problems as soon as possible' (Burberry, in Dodd, 2005). As testament to her personal brand strength this incident did not cause irreparable damage to the career of Kate Moss.

Word of mouth (WOM)

Word of mouth (WOM) is the process of sharing information about the ownership, usage and characteristics of a particular product or service person-to-person and has been shown to influence and shape consumer behaviour (Chevalier and Mayzlin, 2006; Kotler and Keller, 2007). Traditional WOM involves personal communications with family and friends, while eWOM in social media platforms such as Facebook and Instagram involves users without any definite border (Reinhard et al., 2012). The impact, main drivers and influences of eWOM, and the considerations about international differences in consumer usage, are all important areas for research to gain a better understanding of this important communication tool (Goodrich and de Mooij, 2013).

There are three main typologies of WOM:

- **Voluntary** – this encompasses the most natural form of interpersonal conversation, the ones free from external influences;

- **Prompted** – when brands convey information to opinion leaders, aiming to deliberately encourage them to share the information with their followers;

- **Managed** – when brands target and reward opinion leaders for recommending their offerings to their network of followers. In this case, opinion leaders become ambassadors of the brand and, if not properly managed, might lead to a diminish of credibility.

The role of bloggers and digital influencers and their relevancy has been an on-going discussion for some time, with traditional editors questioning their authenticity and role in the industry. 'Note to bloggers who change head-to-toe, paid-to-wear outfits every hour: Please stop. Find another business. You are heralding the death of style' (Sally Singer, Vogue, 2016). Word of Mouth has a strong impact on customer acquisition and brand management (Trusov et al., 2009) because of consumers' desire for social interaction, economic incentives and the chance to develop their self-worth (Hennig-Thurau et al., 2004). Rather than being mere recipients of marketing messages, more and more consumers are using the web to express their knowledge or opinions about fashion products and brands (Valck et al., 2009).

The two main dimensions of eWOM are: opinion seeking and opinion giving. Opinion seeking can be understood as 'the extent to which individuals seek opinions and information about a particular product category from personal sources, such as friends, neighbours, relatives and acquaintances' (Pornpitakpan, 2004: 92). This is usually done through social media, where opinion giving also takes place. Digital influencers give advice and recommend particular brands and products using social networks. The rationale behind these dimensions can be attributed to users' willingness to connect and maintain social relationships within personal networks.

Social networks

Social media can be defined as 'a group of Internet-based applications that build on the ideological and technological foundations of Web 2.0, and that allow the creation and exchange of User Generated Content' (Kaplan and Haenlein, 2010: 61). An effective use of social media channels presents itself as an alternative route for collaboration and innovation. Social networks are touch-points to engage communities, start conversations, recruit employees and develop new and innovative ideas.

Social media platforms such as Facebook, WeChat and Instagram allow for one-to-one marketing or relationship marketing strategies to happen as well as creating space for the implementation of two-way relationship marketing (Lamb et al., 2009). This closely connected relationship allows brands to establish a mutual relationship with the consumer. By treating customers as individuals and tailoring products and services to meet customer needs, fashion brands can achieve online brand loyalty (see Box 7.3).

On social media platforms, brands need to be authentic, transparent, and to engage in an informal dialogue. According to Smith and Zook (2016) the 10 steps towards integrating social media into the business are:

1. Listen

2. Create a presence

3. Join the conversation

4. Identify communities, the burning issues within them, and opinion formers

5. Develop a content strategy

6. Implement social media guidelines

7. Grow the community

8. Socialize the team

9. Socialize the business process and workflow

10. Measure and report.

Box 7.3 - WeChat

WeChat is China's leading digital instant messaging service. Its users can video chat, microblog, play games as well as shop. It has an estimated 800 million active users, the majority being between 15 and 40 years of age, with the penetration in tier-one cites in China being 93%. Chinese women's wear brand JNBY uses Wechat extensively to communicate brand updates or content about collaborations (such as their Vice series). The brand uses shoppable hyperlinked icons to link it to the WeChat store. The JNBY group generated 1.3 billion yuan revenue in the first half of 2017, of which 63.6% was instigated from WeChat (WGSN, 2017).

Viral marketing

The moving image has been embraced by fashion brands as a promotional tool with digital runway shows, promotional pieces and interviews used as part of an IMC strategy. Videos involve more senses in terms of information gathering than other media and this accounts for a more extended evoke of emotions (Shaw and Ivens, 2002), and for that purpose videos can be qualified as more engaging and more likely to strengthen brand attachment (Safko and Brake, 2009).

Viral Marketing can be defined as the form of communication that creates informative messages designed to be passed along electronically in an exponential way. It is a cost-effective marketing strategy that drives sales and facilitates interconnection between brands and consumers. Viral videos are becoming an important element of promotional campaigns as they have potential to reach millions of viewers; YouTube is one of the most dramatic beneficiaries, accounting for 56% of all consumer Web traffic in 2012 (Fox, 2013). Kiss and Bichler (2008: 1) define viral marketing as 'marketing techniques that use social networks to produce increases in brand awareness through self-replicating viral diffusion of messages, analogous to the spread of pathological and computer viruses'. Viral marketing aims to build awareness and generate a buzz around a brand, leading to positive WOM, trial and acquisition. Its main characteristics are that it:

● Needs to be good enough so people feel compelled to share

● Should be on trend and authentic

● Needs to create a shared experience

● Builds on emotional aspects

● Should have the 'wow factor'.

Guerrilla marketing

Guerrilla marketing can be defined as an 'unconventional way of performing marketing activities in non-traditional media on a very low budget' (Levinson, 1984). These non-traditional campaigns often include controversial methods (Dahlén and Edenius, 2007) and are developed with the purpose of developing a positive 'buzz' around the brand (Marciniak and Budnarowska, 2009). In this type of campaign, the consumer becomes the primary means of 'brand dissemination' (Catalano and Zorzetto, 2010). Guerrilla marketing campaigns are usually flexible, low cost, focused and targeted, innovative and simple. This means they are important for smaller businesses with limited resources.

 MINI CASE STUDY 7.4 - Oioba

Swimwear and active-wear brand Oioba rolled out a campaign in the summer of 2017 where their logo (a passion fruit) was printed in large format and plastered in various locations all over the city of Porto (Portugal). After a couple of weeks, the brand unveiled that they were the entity behind the logo and the sunset parties taking place in the city. By opting for a less conventional approach in terms of brand activation, Oioba cemented itself as a brand deeply rooted in the city's artistic environment and thus increased their loyalty levels and reach amongst the target audience.

Reproduced by permission of Oioba, Tropical Intuition LDA.

Customer reviews

Recommendations and reviews have proven to be effective marketing communications tools, as they create a new level of personalization. They can impact largely on consumers' choice of product, brand or service, a well-known example being Amazon's 'if you liked that, you might like this' recommendation service. The influence of reviews has grown exponentially through the use of digital communications, with social media playing a major decision-making role, resulting in businesses needing to organize themselves around the consumer and not the channel. Good reviews are a positive consumer response to good business practice, but perhaps more importantly, unfavourable reviews point to areas of concern that need to feed into strategic decision-making. For example, an increasing level of bad reviews on quality and fit may lead to a review of supply chain activities, whereas bad reviews of customer service may relate to retail strategy.

Gamification

Some forward-thinking brands have begun to explore the world of gamification as a new form of brand building and communicating. It can be defined as the use of game thinking in a non-game context so as to engage users and solve problems. It explores the characteristics of reward, recognition and process (Smith and Zook, 2016). Using social media vehicles such as Snapchat, Instagram and Twitter, gamified marketing provokes a dialogue and entertaining engagement, in particular with a younger audience. Examples of gamification marketing used by fashion brands are included in Box 7.4.

Box 7.4 - Gamification marketing examples

Bally teamed up with graffiti artist André Saraiva for a capsule collection of footwear and leather goods. The collection was introduced through Instagram and consumers were encouraged to follow the brand's Snapchat to win an exclusive poster from the artist. Alexander Wang's Adidas collection followed a very similar strategy of provoking online dialogue. The brand created a treasure hunt with a phone number being posted to Instagram and Snapchat and fans were able to call the number to find the pop-up shop.

THE DIGITAL MEDIA LANDSCAPE

Digital marketing can be defined as 'achieving marketing objectives through applying digital technologies' (Chaffey and Ellis-Chadwick, 2012:10) and usually refers to the management of both online presence and communication through digital media. As highlighted before in this chapter, fashion brands have shifted their focus from traditional forms of media to online and digital media like social networking sites and viral marketing to allow for more interactive opportunities to occur. These are inexpensive platforms on which to implement marketing campaigns, allowing smaller brands to gain notoriety in the competitive fashion market (Anjum, 2011).

The growth of social networking has resulted in UGC (user-generated content) and this change in relationship has affected and altered customers' interaction with a brand (Singh and Sonnenburg, 2012). These types of platforms are allowing brands to uncover consumers' drivers and give brands a deeper understanding of what moves customers, by listening to them and communicating directly with them. The digital landscape, which we will return to in Chapter 15 (Fashion futures) has had a disruptive effect on fashion marketing communication and distribution. Box 7.5 focuses on one of the most effective social media platforms for fashion brands – Instagram.

Box 7.5 - Instagram for fashion

Instagram is a social network platform for sharing photos and videos on mobile devices with other users (followers), where users can 'like' each other's photos and comment on them. It was launched in October 2010 by Kevin Systrom and Mike Krieger and named App of the Year by Apple in 2011 (Goor, 2012). In 2017, Instagram had 600 million monthly and 400 million daily users and it has become the number one tool for fashion brands to connect with young customers. In the US, 48.4% of women engage with influencer-sponsored marketing posts on the platform (WGSN, 2017).

Instagram has proved to be a very effective way of connecting brands and consumers, with 53% of Instagram users following their favourite brand; more than any of the other main social platforms (Cohen, 2015). More than 90% of the 150 million people on Instagram are under the age of 35, making it an attractive platform for fashion, entertainment and media brands focused on the 18 to 34-year-old consumer (Mancuso and Stuth, 2015). Female consumers in particular are prone to impulse purchasing due to connection to brands and beliefs (Hassan, 2014), and are therefore more likely to respond to campaigns on this platform. Instagram has also been instrumental as a tool to discover under-the-radar brands, first seen by bloggers and digital influencers.

Anisa Sojka (http://anisasojka.comhttps://www.instagram.com/anisasojka/) is a micro-influencer blogger who operates on Instagram. Reproduced by permission.

Going live on Instagram Stories allows followers to directly connect with bloggers – as if they are actually hanging out with them or are part of their everyday lives. It's that connection that builds up a follower's loyalty – bringing them back to engage by liking/commenting on photos as well as buying the products the blogger wears. Bloggers are relatable to their audience and that's why their brand recommendations and style tips are impactful. Followers are aware of the big-shot names (ex. Gucci, Prada) so when an unknown designer is introduced I feel as though they are curious to discover the newness. It's an excellent way for emerging designers to get their foot in the door and introduce themselves to a new audience.

▶ ONLINE RESOURCES

A longer version of this Box can be found on our companion website: https://www.macmillanihe.com/companion/Varley_Fashion_Management.

EVOLVING FORMS OF MARKETING COMMUNICATIONS

Content marketing

While content and message have always been fundamental aspects of the marcoms mix, the importance of the quality and quantity of message means that content marketing has grown to be a marcoms activity in its own right. Content marketing is about creating and distributing the most relevant content at the right time. The choice of content and format (video, tweets, posts, advertisements) is dependent on a fashion brand's mission, values and personality and highly related to what the target values and desires. It constitutes an on-going process requiring internal or external resources with new skills and mind-sets.

> **Content marketing**
> A strategy that aims to create and distribute the most relevant and valuable content at the right time. It involves a wide array of formats and should be related to the brands' target and mission. The driving force behind this strategy is for brands to think as a publisher and engage in conversations.

'Content marketing is a marketing technique of creating and distributing valuable, relevant and consistent content to attract and acquire a clearly defined audience – with the objective of driving profitable customer action' (The Content Marketing Institute, in Headworth, 2015).

The main driver behind this strategy is to think like a publisher: how to engage in conversations, hot topics, create concepts, where best to distribute them and how to measure their impact. Brands are expected to integrate content and commerce in a 'migration of retail and content meshing' (Patrick Bousquet-Chavanne, M&S's executive director of Customer and Marketing, in Ridley, 2014). Most brands try to build trust through their content and narratives in a bid to engage in a friendly and conversational tone which is not deemed to be pushy. The consultancy Smart Insights developed a planning tool to help brands generate ideas for the most engaging content and act as a guide through the dimensions of each content, based on how the target customer might think and the goals and aims defined for the brand (Bosomworth, 2015). Their content marketing planning matrix identifies four quadrants; we have identified a series of examples to apply this planning tool in the fashion context (see Table 7.2).

Dimension Type	Examples
Entertain Emotional content used to generate awareness and reach	Diesel's recent social media-driven campaign 'Wanted: Diesel Chair Executive Office' asking applicants to demonstrate they are good at sitting in an important chair – the CEO chair. The video is driving awareness of the brand through using an emotional and innovative campaign.
Inspire Emotional content chosen with the intention to influence and convert	Topshop's blog offers consumers original and trend-driven content including styling tips, cultural opinions and industry news. Also, by linked content with commerce, the brand has established an effective shoppable editorial allowing users to shop straight from images.
Educate Rational content to generate awareness	NastyGal's #GirlBoss is woven into all of the brand's marketing campaigns. #GirlBoss is the name of the brand's content hub, where alongside articles on fashion and lifestyle, the founder has also implemented a podcast where she interviews successful women entrepreneurs. The brand educates the consumer into the values that are core to the brand.
Convince Rational content to influence purchase	Everlane, known for ethical fashion and radical transparency (a concept discussed further in Chapter 12) launched six different styles of cashmere sweaters in various colours with the price point of US$100. Due to a drop in the cost of raw cashmere the brand was able to lower their costs and provide a luxury material at an affordable price-tag. Reinforcing their price transparency resulted in a waitlist for the new collection and a countdown to release on the website.

Table 7.2 *Content marketing planning with examples*

Co-creation and user-generated content (UGC)

Co-creation has been defined as a 'collaborative activity in which customers actively contribute to the creation of brand identity and image as well as ideas, information, product, service and experience offered under a particular brand' (Bogoviyeva, 2011: 371). It can also involve collaboration with customers to develop new products and services, involving customers or end users in the process of innovation. According to SunIdee (2010) there are

> **User-generated content** A type of co-creation that happens when consumers create their own content shared via a given platform. It builds on the fact that consumers are not passive recipients of the brand but work collaboratively to give a contribution and allow for interactions.

five types of co-creation: co-creation workshops, crowdsourcing, open sourcing, mass customization, and user-generated content. For the purpose of this chapter, we will focus on the last type.

User-generated content (UGC) happens when customers create their own 'products', which are shared through the company platforms. Instead of being passive recipients of brand information, customers that are engaging with brands make active contributions to these brand interactions (Hollebeck, 2011) and this leads to UGC; a powerful and interactive strategy for narrative building and brand advocacy.

Fashion brands have used UGC in a variety of ways. For example, Marc Jacobs cast models for his campaign using Instagram; Burberry developed a platform called 'The Art of the Trench' where consumers could upload photos of themselves wearing the famous trench coat (see Case Study 10 in Chapter 10); Jimmy Choo took a similar approach with the 24/7 platform and Tiffany & Co. created the 'What makes love true' platform, where users can once again contribute with photos and narratives around the topic of love and romance. Another example was TOMS' 'One Day Without Shoes' event (see Case Study 14), where participants were invited to upload photos, and for each one posted, a pair of shoes was donated.

Ramaswamy and Gouillart (2010) suggest that value is increased when brands and customers work together because consumers want to feel a sense of freedom in their interaction. UGC campaigns are also a way to collect creative material for marketing purposes as well as drive sales and brand engagement.

UGC can assume the following types:

- Informal discussions about products and services;

- Structured reviews and evaluations in text or video;

- Involvement in the promotion or demotion of brands through self-created advertising (Berthon et al., 2012);

- Involvement in the modification of proprietary products and services and the distribution of these innovations (Berthon et al., 2012).

Storytelling

Storytelling is the art of using words and actions to unfold elements of a story and at the same time encourage the audience's imagination to engage with its narrative. Digital storytelling is when 'real people' use digital tools to share their story. Storytelling conveys expectation and reality, and involves sensory and emotional aspects which play between brands, their customers and their audiences.

The reason for the success of storytelling in communicating a brand's value messages is due to the way 'Individuals are more trustworthy than brands. Storytelling amplifies your message. With social media, the storytellers aren't always controllable' (Geoffroy de la Bourdonnaye, president of Chloé, in Hemsley, 2016). This content strategy helps brands to differentiate themselves in a creative, unfiltered and original way in the saturated space of digital media (see Box 7.6).

> **Storytelling** A marketing communications strategy that uses words, photos or moving images to tell a story and engage the audience in a narrative. It involves sensory and emotional aspects that embrace brands, consumers and audiences in a mixture of content and emotion through an amplified message with the capacity to become viral and shared across social media.

Box 7.6 - Storytelling content

Nike used storytelling in their 'Margot vs Lily' eight-episode series on YouTube to inspire fans to work out. The series is about a pair of interracial, adopted sisters with very different characteristics. 'Great product is featured in the series. But I think for us it is a way to show the full breadth of all kinds of athletes. By doing longer form, we got to show all the emotions that are a part of the personal fitness journey' (Kerri Hoyt-Pack, VP of Nike Women Brand Marketing, in Jacoby, 2016).

The Kate Spade #missadventure series is another good example of storytelling by turning campaigns into a sequence of episodes. These episodes look at modern Millennial problems and their narratives have an original and sassy tone; '... It is all about entertainment over an advertisement – we really want to create engaging content that people just want to watch like a TV series' (Mary Beech, CMO of Kate Spade & Co., in Johnson, 2016).

MARKETING COMMUNICATIONS PLANNING

In the era of media proliferation, increased transparency and interaction across touch-points afforded by digital communications, fashion companies, like other organizations need a way to manage their marketing communication operations effectively within the context of the overall corporate strategy and organizational resources. One of the most effective tools that can be used in the process of formulating a marketing communications plan is the SOSTAC™ framework. It was introduced in the 1990s by P. R. Smith and became one of the most popular frameworks amongst marketers due to its ability to provide an outline/structure for a detailed plan. This framework is important for fashion strategy as it relates operational activities to corporate and marketing strategy. The planning process is presented as a series of stages, although in reality the process may be more fluid.

The first stage is a **S**ituation analysis (see Chapter 2) to fully understand the strategic context. **O**bjective setting is the next stage, when it is vital to ensure the objectives of the campaign are aligned to the company's overall strategy and the brand strategy within that. The more realistic and focused the objectives are in terms of being measurable within a time frame, the more likely the campaign is to achieve its aims. The next phase is devising the campaign **S**trategy, which is the detailed plan that reflects the preceding analysis and decision-making that frames the plan. This will guide the selection of tools, media, message, content, associations, with integration and engagement as key considerations. The **T**actics stage is where the level of detail comes into operation, including costs and timing for all communication channels selected, and this is followed by **A**ction, where the campaign project is implemented and managed. The last stage, **C**ontrol, refers to the evaluation of the campaign, reflecting on the objectives set in the second stage, and considering the resources used. Qualitative evaluation such as reputation enhancement or social media conversations may be as important to evaluate as quantitative measures such as sales over a time period.

 ONLINE RESOURCES

Our companion website provides a more detailed expansion of the SOSTAC™ model, at: https://www.macmillanihe.com/companion/Varley_Fashion_Management.

 CASE STUDY 7 - Havaianas: The brand appeal of a simple product enhanced by Brazilian creativity

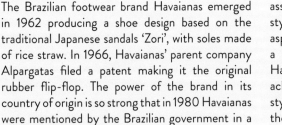

The Brazilian footwear brand Havaianas emerged in 1962 producing a shoe design based on the traditional Japanese sandals 'Zori', with soles made of rice straw. In 1966, Havaianas' parent company Alpargatas filed a patent making it the original rubber flip-flop. The power of the brand in its country of origin is so strong that in 1980 Havaianas were mentioned by the Brazilian government in a list of inflation-controlled goods, alongside rice and beans (Havaianas.com).

Whilst widely known in its home country, the brand was originally positioned as a staple, associated with lower-class consumers and a boring style. Alpargatas cleverly shifted this to a more aspirational customer proposition and started a repositioning strategy that would transform Havaianas into a truly global brand. This was achieved by hiring leading designers to reinvent the styles, with striking patterns and colours. In 1995 the brand launched its first printed 'Havaianas Floral', a pattern featuring hibiscus flowers and expanded into more than 15 different colours. Later in that decade the brand began its international expansion, thanks to tourists taking home the famous flip-flops, which had become a symbol for Brazil.

Although the core of the product is simplicity, the Havaianas team works daily to identify new technologies and shapes that can be integrated into their new styles. The brand maintains a clear product focus, releasing more than 500 styles every year. Havaianas is also exploring ways to incorporate innovation into their products so as to increase occasions for usage of the flip-flops – they are not just to be used on the beach but also in the city.

Portraying the Brazilian culture and its positivity has always been the core of the brand's communication strategy, and the campaigns rolled out were flexible enough to be adaptable to other countries, without losing the key message. The brand opted for a consistent marketing communications strategy, making the most of its

partnerships and celebrity/influencer events as well as leveraging PR and social media (both paid and organic). They have also sponsored fashion events such as São Paulo Fashion Week and were included in the Oscars gift bag in 2003.

Havaianas is an example of a company whose success is based on a very simple product concept which has been enhanced over time using the key drivers of innovation and creativity while maintaining a strong and consistent brand identity.

Sources: Various, including Havaianas.com.

Case Challenge

Develop a marketing communications plan to further enhance the positioning of the Havaianas brand in the UK market. Consider the target audience and the most appropriate communication tools to do so.

 ONLINE RESOURCES

A longer version of this case study, with additional challenges, can be found on our companion website: https://www.macmillanihe.com/companion/Varley_Fashion_Management.

 SUMMARY AND CONCLUDING THOUGHTS

The SOSTAC™ framework provides a central path by which to navigate the complex world of marketing communications and it acknowledges that initiatives and campaigns are only worthwhile if there is a clear strategy behind them. Creative marketing communications expertize is a valuable resource that can be overlooked; all too often it is assumed that bigger marketing communications budgets guarantee success, whereas innovative approaches are often the most engaging. Evaluation of marketing communications success is not straightforward and what a brand is trying to achieve must be clear from the start of the marketing communications planning process.

Digital now represents a significant proportion of media spend and it is widely acknowledged that 2017 was the year when advertising expenditure (ad-spend) on digital media surpassed TV for the first

time. Brands use social networks, dedicated content, forums and blogs, and are faced with the challenge of deciding what measurement techniques to employ to analyze the overwhelming amount of information they have access to.

The traditional measures of return on investment (ROI) – such as the direct effects of advertising on sales – do not measure the indirect effects of interaction between channels. This is crucial to understand in order to improve the way media are planned and how content is managed. The complexity of the digital sphere means that brands are turning to innovative and diverse tactics to fully own the changing landscape. Measuring the impact of digital marketing communications is still an on-going discussion with the most effective methods so far being identified as cost-per-click (CPC) and cost-per-engagement (CPE). By using predictive analytics and big data, brands will be able to make better recommendations to their customers and that will lead to higher conversion rates, which will impact ROI.

Companies are increasingly focusing on a longer-lasting customer experience instead of standalone campaigns or interactions. One of the metrics of engagement in this new scenario is the fostering of a community. Smaller communities may be more profitable, as we have become aware that influencers with smaller followings that are more active and engaged drive higher sales than more widely connected influencers. The use of influencers allows a brand to appear favourable to its customers and to generate positive associations and conversations. These so-called soft metrics – brand awareness, recognition and favourability – are not easy to measure but impact strongly on a brand's ROI. In the era of digital marketing there is a tendency for data science to overwhelm the artistic and creative aspects of brand engagement and this is highly inadvisable in fashion marketing communications.

CHALLENGES AND CONVERSATIONS

1. Select a couple of advertising images from a brand of your choice.
   What is the single most important point/message they are communicating?
   How is this transmitted through imagery and copy? How is this message relevant to the overall strategic objectives of the brand/owner of the brand?

2. Select a fashion brand of your choice. Discuss the traditional tools that have been used by the brand. Then discuss the digitally enhanced tools they have used. To what extent are these two sets of tools integrated as part of an overall marketing strategy? You should focus on addressing consistency of message and tone of voice as well as effectiveness.

3. Discuss the effectiveness of using fashion bloggers as part of a brand's digital strategy. How can brands identify the right influencers – the ones that align with their overall communication strategy?

4. Select a fashion brand of your choice. Using the content marketing matrix, design a content marketing strategy for that brand and discuss how it should be implemented across the various touch-points the brand uses. Also suggest how content marketing could relate to the company's overall strategic aims.

REFERENCES AND FURTHER READING

American Association of Advertising Agencies (n.d.) Available at: http://www.aaaa.org [accessed 08/12/2016].

Anjum, A. H. (2011) *Social Media Marketing*. Munich: GRIN Publishing.

Baines, P., Fill, C. and Page, K. (2011) *Marketing*, 2nd edn. Oxford: Oxford University Press.

Barthes, R. (1967) *The Fashion System*, translated by M. Ward and R. Howard. New York: Hill and Wang.

Barthes, R. (1973) *Mythologies*. London: Jonathan Cape.

Belch, E. G. and Belch, M. A. (2012) New York, NY: McGraw Hill.

Berthon, P. R., Pitt, L. F., Plangger, K. and Shapiro, D. (2012) 'Marketing meets Web 2.0, social media, and creative consumers: Implications for international marketing strategy'. *Business Horizons*, 55, pp. 261–271.

Bogoviyeva, E. (2011) *Co-branding: Brand development: The effects of customer co-creation and self-construal on self-brand connection*. AMA Summer Educators' Conference Proceedings, 22, p. 371.

Bosomworth, D. (2015) *The content marketing matrix*. Available at: http://www.smartinsights.com/content-management/content-marketing-strategy/the-content-marketing-matrix-new-infographic/ [accessed 22/01/2018].

Bowden, J. (2009) The process of customer engagement: A conceptual framework. *Journal of Marketing Theory and Practice*, 17(1), pp. 63–74.

Catalano, F. and Zorzetto, F. (2010) *Temporary Store. La Strategia Dell'effimero*. Milan: Franco Angeli.

Chaffey, D. (2012) *The difference between paid, owned and earned media – 5 viewpoints.* Available at: http://www.smartinsights.com/digital-marketing-strategy/customer-acquisition-strategy/new-media-options/?new=1/?new=1 [accessed 27/05/2016].

Chaffey, D. (2017) *Global social media research summary 2017.* Available at: http://www.smartinsights.com/social-media-marketing/social-media-strategy/new-global-social-media-research/ [accessed 22/01/2018].

Chaffey, D. and Ellis-Chadwick, F. (2012) *Digital Marketing: Strategy, Implementation and Practice.* Harlow: Pearson.

Chaffey, D. and Smith, P. R. (2017) *Digital Marketing Excellence: Planning, Optimizing and Integrating Online Marketing.* Abingdon: Routledge.

Chen, Y. (2016) *$17 billion in one day: How Alibaba turned China's Singles' Day into a shopping bonanza.* Available at: https://digiday.com/social/17-billion-one-day-alibaba-turned-chinas-singles-day-shopping-bonanza/ [accessed 15/04/2017].

Chevalier, J. A. and Mayzlin, D. (2006) The effect of word of mouth on sales: Online book reviews. *Journal of Marketing Research,* 43(3), p. 9.

Cohen, D. (2015) *More Than Half of Instagram Users Follow Brands (Infographic).* Available at: http://www.adweek.com/digital/gwi-instagram-brands-infographic/ [accessed 08/12/2016].

Collett, P. and Fenton, W. (2011) *The Sponsorship Handbook: Essential Tools, Tips and Techniques for Sponsors and Sponsorship Seekers.* Chichester: John Wiley & Sons.

Dahlén, M. and Edenius, M. (2007) 'When is advertising advertising? Comparing responses to traditional and non-traditional advertising media'. *Journal of Current Issues and Research in Advertising,* 29(1), pp. 33–42.

Dodd, V. (2005) *Chanel and Burberry drop Moss as police start inquiry.* Available at: https://www.theguardian.com/uk/2005/sep/22/drugsandalcohol.vikramdodd [accessed 22/05/2012].

Fashion targets breast cancer (n.d.) *Our history.* Available at: http://fashiontargetsbreastcancer.org.uk/our-history [accessed 22/01/2018].

Fill, C. (2013) *Marketing Communications: Brands, Experiences and Participation.* Harlow: Pearson.

Fill, C. and Jamieson, B. (2011) *Marketing Communications.* Edinburgh: Edinburgh Business School, Heriot-Watt University.

Fill, C. and Turnbull, S. (2016) *Marketing Communications: Discovery, Creation and Conversations.* Harlow: Pearson.

Fox, Z. (2013) *17.4% of Global web traffic comes through mobile.* Available at: http://mashable.com/2013/08/20/mobile-web-traffic/#bvXbPsxE5gq4 [accessed 24/05/2016].

Gladwell, M. (2000) *The Tipping Point.* New York: Little Brown.

Goodrich, K. and De Mooij, M. (2013) 'How "social" are social media? A cross-cultural comparison of online and offline purchase decision influences'. *Journal of Marketing Communications,* June, pp. 1–14.

Goor, M. A. (2012) *Insta-marketing: A Content Analysis into Marketing on Instagram.* Amsterdam: Amsterdam University.

Hassan, A. (2014) 'Do brands targeting women use Instamarketing differently: A content analysis', *Marketing Management Association Spring 2014 Proceedings.* Mankato, MN, 21 April 2014. Marketing Management Association, pp. 62-65. Available at: https://cornerstone.lib.mnsu.edu/urs/2014/poster_session_B/28 [accessed 24/07/2018].

Headworth, A. (2015) *Social Media Recruitment: How to Successfully Integrate Social Media into Recruitment Strategy.* London and Philadelphia, PA: Kogan Page.

Hemsley, S. (2016) *Why brand storytelling should be the foundation of a growth strategy.* Available at: https://www.marketingweek.com/2016/02/28/why-brand-storytelling-should-be-the-foundation-of-a-growth-strategy/ [accessed 22/01/2018].

Hennig-Thurau, T., Gwinner, K. P., Walsh, G. and Gremler, D. D. (2004). 'Electronic word-of-mouth via consumer-opinion platforms: What motivates consumers to a rticulate themselves on the Internet?' *Journal of Interactive Marketing,* 18(1), pp. 38–52.

Hollebeck, L. (2011) 'Demystifying customer brand engagement: Exploring the loyalty nexus'. *Journal of Marketing Management,* 27(7–8), pp. 785–807.

H&M (2017) *H&M loves Coachella collection: Get the festival spirit with the atomics.* Available at: https://about.hm.com/en/media/news/general-2017/h-m-loves-coachella.html [accessed 22/01/2018].

Jacoby, S. (2016) *Nike's New Web Series Will Make You Feel Great About Your Burpees.* Available at: http://www.refinery29.com/2016/01/101992/nike-better-for-it-web-series [accessed 30/05/2017].

Johnson, L. (2016) *Kate Spade New York Wants People to Watch Its Ads Like TV Shows.* Available at: http://www.adweek.com/digital/kate-spade-wants-people-watch-its-ads-tv-shows-170402/ [accessed 19/11/2017].

Kaplan, A. M. and Haenlein, M. (2010) 'Users of the world, unite! The challenges and opportunities of social media'. *Business Horizons,* 53(1), pp. 59–68.

Keller, K. L. 2001. 'Building customer-based brand equity: A blueprint for creating strong brands'. *Marketing Management* (July/August), pp. 15–19.

Kiss, C. and Bichler, M. (2008) *Identification of Influencers – Measuring Influence in Customer Networks.* Available at: http://citeseerx.ist.psu.edu/viewdoc/download?doi=10.1.1.92.6410&rep=rep1&type=pdf [accessed 02/11/2017].

Kotler, P. and Keller K. (2007) *A Framework for Marketing Management,* 3rd edn. Harlow: Pearson Education.

Lamb, C., Hair, J. and McDaniel, C. (2009) *Essentials of Marketing*, 6th edn. Mason, OH: South-Western.

Levinson, J. C. (1984) *Guerrilla Marketing: Secrets for Making Big Profits from Your Small Business*. Boston, MA: Houghton Mifflin.

Luckerson, V. (2016) *Bots Are About to Take Over Facebook Messenger*. Available at: http://time.com/4291214/facebook-messenger-bots/ [accessed 12/01/2018].

Mancuso, J. and Stuth, K. (2015) *A Portrait of Modern Media*. Available at: https://www.ama.org/publications/MarketingInsights/Pages/a-portrait-of-modern-media.aspx [accessed 19/07/2016].

Marciniak, R. and Budnarowska, C. (2009) *Marketing approaches to pop-up stores: Exploration of social networking*. Paper presented at the EAERCD Conference, 15–17 July, Guildford, UK.

McKinsey (2010) Beyond paid media: Marketing's new vocabulary. Available at: https://www.mckinsey.com/business-functions/marketing-and-sales/our-insights/beyond-paid-media-marketings-new-vocabulary [accessed 11/09/2017].

Mediakix (2017) *Coachella 2017: Branded experiences, social media stars, & more*. Available at: http://mediakix.com/2017/04/coachella-branded-experiences-social-media-influencers/#gs.DRGioeQ [accessed 09/01/2018].

Mollen, A. and Wilson, H. (2010) 'Engagement, telepresence and interactivity in online consumer experience: Reconciling scholastic and managerial perspectives'. *Journal of Business Research*, 63, pp. 919–925.

Naragon, K. (2017) *Consumers are still email obsessed, but they're finding more balance*. Available at: https://blogs.adobe.com/conversations/2017/08/consumers-are-still-email-obsessed-but-theyre-finding-more-balance.html [accessed 09/01/2018].

Olenski, S. (2016) *How Brands Should Use Celebrities for Endorsements*. Available at: https://www.forbes.com/sites/steveolenski/2016/07/20/how-brands-should-use-celebrities-for-endorsements/#165d13555593 [accessed 02/11/2017].

Pessin, I. and Weaver, K. (2014) *Paid, Owned, Earned: Measuring POE complexity*. Admap at warc.com. Available at: https://www.warc.com/Search/integration/Paid,%20owned,%20earned%20integration?Sort=ContentDate%7c1&DVals=4294638081&RecordsPerPage=25 [accessed 15/11/2017].

Pornpitakpan, C. (2004) 'The persuasiveness of source credibility: A critical review of five decades' evidence'. *Journal of Applied Social Psychology*, 34(2), pp. 243–281.

Prahalad, C. K. and Ramaswamy, V. (2004) 'Co-creation experiences: The next practice in value creation'. *Journal of Interactive Marketing*, 18(3), pp. 5–14.

Ramaswamy, V. and Gouillart, F. (2010) *The Power of Co-Creation*. New York: First Free Press.

Rehman, S. and Ibrahim, S. (2011) 'Integrated Marketing Communication and Promotion'. *International Refereed Research Journal*, 2(4), pp. 187–191.

Reinhard, K., Satow, L. and Fadil, P. (2012) 'Assessing the power of social media marketing'. *Asia-Pacific Journal of Cooperative Education*, 13(1), pp. 39–53.

Ridley, L. (2014) *Patrick Bousquet-Chavanne explains why he moved the M&S media account to Mindshare*. Available at: http://www.campaignlive.co.uk/article/patrick-bousquet-chavanne-explains-why-moved-m-s-media-account-mindshare/1294741 [accessed 10/11/2017].

Safko, L. and Brake, D. (2009) *The Social Media Bible: Tactics, Tools and Strategies for Business Success*. Hoboken, NJ: John Wiley & Sons.

Saunter, L. (2016) *WGSN: Marketing New Authentics: The Rise of Realism in Fashion Marketing*. Available at: www.wgsn.com [accessed 13/12/2017].

Saviolo, S. and Testa, S. (2002) *Strategic Management in the Fashion Companies*. Firenze: Nouva MCS.

Schramm, W. (1955) *How Communication Works. The Process and Effects of Mass Communication*. Urbana, IL: University of Illinois Press.

Scott, D. M. (2017) *The New Rules of Marketing and PR: How to Use Social Media, Online Video, Mobile Applications, Blogs, News Releases, and Viral Marketing to Reach Buyers Directly*, 6th edn. Chichester: John Wiley & Sons.

Shannon, C. and Weaver, W. (1964) *The Mathematical Theory of Communication*. Urbana, IL: The University of Chicago Press.

Shaw, C. and Ivens, J. (2002) *Building Great Customer Experiences (Beyond Philosophy)*. Basingstoke: Palgrave Macmillan.

Singh, S. and Sonnenburg, S. (2012) 'Brand performance in social media'. *Journal of Interactive Marketing*, 26(4), pp. 189–197.

Smith, P. R. and Zook, Z. (2016) *Marketing Communications: Offline and Online Integration, Engagement and Analytics*. London and Philadelphia, PA: Kogan Page.

Strong, E. (1925) *The Psychology of Selling and Advertising*. New York: McGraw-Hill.

SunIdee (2010) *Five types of Co-Creation*. Slideshare: http://www.slideshare.net/sannedekoning/five-types-of-cocreation-3881999 [accessed 05/07/2015].

Theodorson, S. and Theodorson, A. (1969) *A Modern Dictionary of Sociology*. New York: Cassell Education Limited.

Trusov, M., Bucklin, E. R. and Koen, P. (2009) 'Effects of word-of-mouth versus traditional marketing: Findings from an Internet social networking site'. *Journal of Marketing*, 73, pp. 90–102.

UK Chartered Institute of Public Relations (n.d.) Available at: https://www.cipr.co.uk [accessed 02/01/2018].

Valck, K. de, Bruggen, G. van and Wierenga, B. (2009) 'Virtual communities: A marketing perspective'. *Decision Support Systems*, 47(3), pp. 185–203.

Vivek, S. D., Beatty, S. E. and Morgan, R. M. (2011) 'Consumer engagement: Exploring customer relationships beyond purchase'. *Marketing Theory and Practice*, 20(2), pp. 127–145.

Vogue (2016) *Ciao, Milano! Vogue.com's Editors Discuss the Week That Was*. Available at: https://www.vogue.com/article/milan-fashion-week-spring-2017-vogue-editors-chat [accessed 10/11/2017].

WGSN (2016a) *Instagram Ready Retail*. Available at: https://www.wgsn.com/home/ [accessed 13/12/2017].

WGSN (2016b) *Designing for Instagram*. Available at: https://www.wgsn.com/home/ [accessed 13/12/2017].

WGSN (2017) *Social Media Trends: Art Directed Instagram*. Available at: https://www.wgsn.com/home/ [accessed 15/01/2018].

FASHION MERCHANDISE MANAGEMENT

Rosemary Varley and James Clark

INTRODUCTION

In the fashion industry product development is an important and frequent response to strategic opportunity. For some organizations, such as a car company, the development of one new product represents a major strategic move, many years of research, design and prototype production together with a major marketing campaign. For fashion organizations new product introduction takes place on a much more frequent and, in many cases, continual basis with new product variations becoming available to consumers more than once a week. It is therefore important to distinguish between the operational and day-to-day activities associated with the management of merchandise, which bring attractive fashion product offers to the market, and more strategic decisions involving products, categories and brands which support corporate goals. The purpose of this chapter is to examine in more detail how the introduction of product variations and new product ranges, the management of brands and sub-brands, the management of product availability and pricing architecture all play a part in merchandise strategy, which in turn represents a major aspect of a corporate fashion strategy.

This chapter begins by scoping the meaning of merchandise management in the context of a strategic approach to fashion management. It then moves on to consider the concept of product differentiation as a way to achieve sustainable competitive advantage, and the resources required for it. A closer analysis of merchandise management follows, maintaining the strategic viewpoint while discussing product range and category planning. The third part of the chapter focuses on strategic merchandise management in the context of fashion retailing, highlighting the increasingly strategic nature of retail product management roles in response to the changing fashion business landscape.

LEARNING OBJECTIVES

After studying this chapter, you should be able to understand:

- The significance of merchandise management within the context of corporate strategic management for fashion organizations;

- The need for integration between corporate strategy, product strategy and merchandise management;

- Important aspects of strategic merchandise management including assortment planning, pricing architecture, availability and category management;

- The influence of the international and multi-channel context in which strategic merchandise management decisions are made;

- The resource implications associated with merchandise planning, including key personnel and relevant competencies;

- The relationship between merchandise management, branding and supply chain management and the contribution they make to a cohesive product strategy.

MERCHANDISE MANAGEMENT IN THE STRATEGIC CONTEXT

Although merchandise management is often considered to be an operational aspect of fashion management, forces within the external business environment are making merchandise management increasingly strategic (Clark, 2014). 'Fast fashion', for example, has moved over a decade from retail buzz-word to deliberate product strategy to achieve competitive advantage, and while the style-literate and celebrity influenced fashion consumer will continue to be interested in a fast turnaround of garment offer, the environmental and social fall-out from such a strategy is of increasing concern to many commentators and consumers (Fletcher, 2014). Changing consumer lifestyles can affect merchandise management in terms of the growth and decline of particular product categories. For example, the growing interest in wearing more fashionable clothing on frequent visits to a gym has reinvigorated the fashion sportswear market, resulting in a spate of new ranges of performance-oriented sports clothing with a high fashion input to product design, the introduction of a new product category description 'athleisure clothing' and the opportunity to take advantage of a strategic opportunity for brand stretching.

Seasonality, which once dictated much of the fashion world's operation and organizational structure, is now less of an influencing factor on consumer purchasing. Historically, seasons have had a major influence on fashion product offers, being guided by colours, fabrications and silhouettes that reflected outside temperature and cultural events; the outputs of fashion design houses and the ranges on sale in retailers being guided by a seasonal fashion cycle (Birtwistle et al., 2003). Today, when central heating or air-conditioning supplies a consistent moderate temperature and holidays abroad are commonplace, the consumer has a predominantly transitional wardrobe, where swimwear and outerwear can be added at any time of the year depending on travel destination. The immediacy of digital marketing is also having a disruptive effect on the fashion industry, to the point where the seasonal cycle model can appear outdated and problematic (Amed, 2016; Dewintre, 2015). Nevertheless, a commonly heard saying in fashion retailing is 'it's all about the product' and this aspect of strategic management will always

be fundamental to the corporate strategy of the fashion organization. Many of the financial performance indicators introduced in Chapter 5 are dependent ultimately on the sales performance of merchandise, and through the product range companies are able to demonstrate corporate responsibility and build brand equity. It is also worth noting that the CEOs of many successful fashion businesses began their careers as 'merchants'; being able to sense a gap in the market and having an eye for the product to fill it.

THE STRATEGIC MERCHANDISE MANAGEMENT CONCEPT

Planning the range of products to be produced and offered to the customer is at the centre of decision-making for a fashion organization. 'Buying' has been described as a pivotal function (McGoldrick, 2002), which is a useful concept for appreciating the connectivity between product, brand, and company. However, 'buying' is a term used variously in the commercial context for both the narrow function of placing orders and the much wider function that is involved with the successful manifestation of a product range as the outcome of a corporate strategy. Some sources use the term 'product management' and this can be considered synonymous with merchandise management; however, we make the distinction between the term product strategy, which we will use to refer to decision-making concerning brands, consumer markets for products, and new product category development, and the term strategic merchandise management, which we will use to cover decision-making concerning the individual product lines within a range and their availability, the detail of product features including prices and the choices concerning the supplier of that product (see Figure 8.1).

Although the operational processes associated with fashion merchandise management have been well documented (Jackson and Shaw, 2001; Gowerek, 2007; Shaw and Koumbis, 2013; Clark, 2014), less attention has been paid to the relationship between the long-term corporate direction relating to product design and product category representation and the impact on strategic decision-making within merchandise management, as visualized in Figure 8.1.

Corporate Strategy
consolidation, growth, internationalization, positioning, competitive advantage

Product Strategy
products, brand(s), markets, product differentiation, product development

Strategic Merchandise Management
range planning – assortments
pricing architecture
availability
supplier relationships, sourcing
key performance indicators and control

Figure 8.1 *The relationship between corporate strategy and strategic merchandise management*

PRODUCT EXPERTIZE AND DIFFERENTIATION

In Chapter 2 we considered the concept of differentiation to be central to a strategy for fashion companies. As suggested, differentiation in fashion can be achieved via a number of routes but one of the most effective is that of the product itself, with a particular set of features and benefits that appeal to the target customer. In fashion, features such as quality, texture, colours, patterns, and shapes are blended to produce appealing products, but distinctiveness requires a particular recipe, often guided by brand identity and led by a design director. For example, Anya Hindmarch is a British designer who has used humour and quirkiness to differentiate her range of luxury accessories from the more ubiquitous designer handbags that have little more than a logo to enable consumers to tell them apart. Her cereal packet inspired designs launched in 2014 were particularly striking and gained considerable attention in the fashion press. Marimekko, a Finnish company, have bold print designs at the heart of their collection. Some of the prints have been in the collection for decades and are recoloured and applied in different product categories across clothing, accessories and home furnishings as a way to extend the product range. In order to fine-tune and maintain product differentiation, specific resources and competences are required as shown in Table 8.1.

Resources	Competencies
design studio	design knowledge
design/creative director	design talent
designers/teams (e.g. men's wear, women's wear, children's wear)	design expertize and product fit knowledge
product technologists	pattern cutting expertize, fabric and garment construction expertize
product technology laboratory	fabric/material technical expertize
trend forecasting laboratory	trend forecasting interpretation and expertize
quality controllers	fabric expertize and experience, garment production expertize, quality assurance programmes

Table 8.1 *Resources and competencies relevant to product differentiation*

These resources may be permanent in-house facilities, which allow for continual input, or they may be outsourced in order to tap into the expertize and specific competence on a short-term or long-term basis. Frequently suppliers provide these resources, in which case a relationship between a supplier and a fashion organization can in itself be considered a valuable resource and the ability to manage relationships to enable a continuous flow of expertize from suppliers can be a significant competence. A good understanding of one another's competences and synergy in long-term business aims is considered to be vital in the development of positive supply network relationships (see Chapter 9).

One of the reasons why many of the traditional theories associated with strategic management are limited in their application to fashion companies is the changing nature of the product offer. In fashion companies, new products are developed all the time, many organizations no longer restricting themselves to the main seasonal new range introductions but developing and introducing new products on a rolling basis. The idea that Ansoff's 'product development' is a strategic direction fails to be relevant in a purist interpretation of the product/market model (1988) for fashion companies (see Chapter 4). Introducing an entirely new category of merchandise nevertheless can be considered as a strategic development because this may take a brand to new customers and is likely to require additional resources such as a new design team and/or new sections within a retail outlet.

As we saw in Chapter 6, the product–brand relationship must be managed carefully and strategically; according to Kapferer (2012: 249), 'there is no brand without strong internal policing and without a strong external coherence as well'. Brands create a perception of specificity in terms of exclusivity and added value for customers. The repeated experience of customers and the coherence of the branded product range reinforce the brand values through products which may be diverse in terms of the categories but have connections through identity and positioning. This is important given that a fashion brand may be using multi-channel routes to market. The product experience helps to build brand–consumer resonance (Huang et al., 2015) while brand messages transmitted through marketing communications reinforce the strong product–brand coherence externally.

> **Product assortment**
> This refers to the width and depth of a product range offered to customers.

ASSORTMENT STRATEGIES

Coherence within the product offer relies on careful and detailed planning of product ranges. The term 'product assortment' refers to the width and depth of a product range offered to customers and product assortment is an additional factor that blends with the product features and benefits to provide a differentiated product range for a fashion brand. Fashion organizations take different approaches in compiling product ranges in terms of the number of categories covered, and the depth of assortment within the category. There are, for example, specialist shoe brands such as Manalo Blahnik or Russel and Bromley that maintain a single-category approach, whilst mass-market fashion retailer New Look originally built its shoe range as a supplementary category to clothing but is now considered to be a strong player in the UK footwear retailing market (Mintel, 2015). Brand stretching and extending is at the heart of strategic development for fashion companies; however, within a product category fashion companies can choose to be category specialists, offering a deep assortment (large variation) of products within a category, as shown in Figure 8.2. The contrasting approach is to offer a shallow assortment within a category, illustrated in Figure 8.3. A brand that spreads across numerous categories is often described as a lifestyle brand. Lifestyle brands can operate at different levels of the market. For example, Muji is a mass-market Japanese lifestyle brand that embraces many product categories but keeps a stated emphasis on quality materials and simplicity, describing their range of clothing, home products, stationery and food as 'succinct' (Muji.com, 2016). The Armani case demonstrates the strategic importance of brand stretching and rationalization.

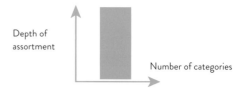

Figure 8.2 *The specialist assortment*

In a specialist assortment the number of product categories is small (narrow) but the variation of assortment within the categories is large (deep). Variety can be introduced by offering many different styles, sizes and fits, quality levels, brands, and prices. Victoria Secrets is an example of a fashion company with a specialist assortment focused on the lingerie category.

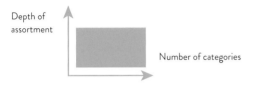

Depth of assortment

Number of categories

Figure 8.3 *The generalist assortment*

In a generalist assortment, the number of product categories is large (wide) but the variation within each category is smaller (shallow). Mass-market retailers such as Marks & Spencer provide a general assortment even though they can have particular category specialisms, such as lingerie, where the variation is deeper than that in other categories.

Although much of the discussion about assortment strategies is set in the context of general retailing, assortment strategies are also highly relevant to fashion companies that produce and/or supply to retailers, as well as fashion retailers themselves. Many well-known producer brands are world famous because of the specialist nature of their product offer, or because of particular experience and therefore relevance in a particular product category. When we think of Levi's, for example, we immediately associate the brand with the product category of jeans; when we think of the brand Burberry we are most likely to think of trench coats; however, these two brands offer many other complementary product categories that have varying relevance for both the customer and the brand. In fact, Levi's has sold trench coats in the past and Burberry offers jeans, but they are not the product categories that have immediate relevance for these brands. Category focus can therefore be a way of differentiating a brand and contributes strongly to a brand strategy. We will return to this idea later on in the chapter.

MERCHANDISE AVAILABILITY STRATEGIES

Availability is an important concept in merchandise management and refers to the extent to which a product is in stock, ready for immediate sale. Availability across sizes adds to the complexity of determining what is an appropriate availability level in fashion organization, in terms of what is offered (size distribution and ratios) and the extent to which each variation (SKU – stock keeping unit) is kept in stock. From a consumer viewpoint, 100% availability is ideal and represents excellent customer service; however, from a retail supply perspective (and further down the supply chain) complete availability of a full range is often an inappropriate strategic aim. For example, as styles lose their appeal due to trend or seasonal changes it is sensible to allow them to run down in stock, allowing for investment of both space and money into new styles.

The widespread adoption of so-called fast fashion (Barnes and Lea-Greenwood, 2006, 2013), which has its roots in the more supply-chain orientated concept of quick-response (Birtwistle et al., 2003), is testament to the preference of many fashion consumers for a high level of product variation rather than a high level of availability. Having said that, a good offer of sizes across the range on offer is an important part of a product service strategy. Availability is therefore the third dimension of a balanced product assortment, along with width and depth.

The omni-shopping behaviour of fashion consumers makes availability an increasingly challenging dimension to manage. Taking into consideration reverse logistics (managing returns, via stores or via post), different availability strategies might be appropriate for more basic items in a range compared with the pieces with a higher fashion or seasonal trend factor. So, for basics that have a demand pattern that is easier to forecast, a higher level of availability is appropriate in order to give a good level of customer service, and efficient supply chains and reverse logistic operations can be set up to match this. With higher fashion items, a different set of suppliers may be used that are flexible enough to supply smaller batches to avert risk but are able to scale up to meet the demand for a 'hot item', while reverse logistics need to react fast to return the product into saleable stock.

> **Availability** The extent to which a product is in stock in all sizes and variations, ready for immediate sale.

PRICING ARCHITECTURE

As we saw earlier, depth in a product range can be increased by offering different price levels, often in conjunction with different quality levels and brands. Pricing architecture is an important dimension of strategic merchandise management because price is so often used as a positioning variable (see Chapter 3). Posner (2011) suggests that pricing architecture normally takes the shape of a triangle, starting at the base with the entry-point pieces (the products in the range with the lowest prices), moving up to the top-of-the-range products, which are most expensive, luxurious and of highest quality. Between these two there is the important middle price-point band where a large number of styles are offered to give customers a good choice within an affordable range. In some assortments a premium band is added to extend the price range upwards or to offer a restricted range of high-end alternatives to the very top prices. Within each band in the hierarchy specific price points can be selected, and a target number of styles set so that a balance for the entire range can be achieved.

> **Category management**
> The strategic management of product groups through trade partnerships, which aims to maximize sales and profits by satisfying consumer needs.

Pricing architecture is often considered when applying vertical (or line) brand extension strategies in the luxury sector; for example, in the introduction of a 'diffusion' sub-brand (Hanslin and Rindell, 2014). The lower price points attract a different, normally wider market segment for a particular brand, positioning it as more accessible in customers' minds.

Moving a pricing structure upwards is a very difficult strategy unless additional benefits are brought to a brand. Mulberry, an upmarket UK-based accessories brand, made a strategic decision in 2013 to reposition as an international luxury brand, raising its pricing architecture to compete with the likes of Loewe and Louis Vuitton. Unfortunately, this alienated many Mulberry customers who felt their bags had become over-priced and out of reach, and sales plummeted accordingly. In 2015 the pricing architecture was revised to the 'almost luxury' positioning Mulberry had previously maintained and in 2016 the company's financial health was in much better shape (Armstrong, 2016).

THE CATEGORY MANAGEMENT CONCEPT AND ITS APPLICATION TO FASHION

It is perhaps the nuanced complexity of range planning for fashion organizations that has prevented the development of strategic management frameworks in this area; however, in general retailing, category management is a well-known merchandise management concept that provides a guide to assortment planning, acknowledging the strategic importance of making appropriate decisions about product ranges. The next section considers this important framework for its applicability within the context of the fashion sector. The Institute of Grocery Distribution defines category management as 'the strategic management of product groups through trade partnerships, which aims to maximize sales and profits by satisfying consumer needs' (IGD, 1999: appendix), highlighting the process as consumer-led, reliant on understanding the consumer relationship with a product type including the level of interest in a product category, shopping process preference, and shopping occasion influence on purchasing behaviour. Category management is normally described as an eight-step process: category definition; establishing category roles; assessing category performance; setting category objectives; devising an overall strategic plan for each category; specifying category tactics; implementing category management; and finally, reviewing the success of the category using performance indicators established in the second step (Aastrup et al., 2007; IGD, 2016).

The objective of the category definition stage is to group similar products that customers expect to see displayed together and in which a meaningful choice can be made. Thus, in the context of fashion end-use, category descriptors such as formal, occasion, relaxed dressing, casual fashion, and outwear are relevant. The second stage of category management also considers the relationship between a product category and an overall retail brand, and the contribution the category makes to the retail brand image in terms of product assortment. The category roles identified for the FMCG (fast moving consumer goods) industry are shown in Table 8.2.

The next three stages in the process involve category planning. The category performance evaluation is not only based on financial measures such as category sales, profits, and markdown, but also on qualitative performance such as a category's ability to generate store loyalty. The category management philosophy encourages retailers and suppliers to undertake collaborative category planning, allowing retailers to benefit from their suppliers' category

Routine	Established categories that a customer comes to regularly. Consistent value provision.
Seasonal/occasional	Categories are linked to a particular time-based demand, or purchase occasion. High profit margins.
Convenience	Categories necessary to complete the full assortment. Stagnant or declining categories. Staple product categories. Competitive with other category providers – low profit margins.
Destination	Growing or well established categories; contains leading brands; deep and wide assortment; considered the best retail offer by target customer.

Table 8.2 *Product category roles*

Source: Varley, R. (2014), *Retail Product Management*, Routledge, Table 3.2, p. 60. By permission of Taylor & Francis.

insight. After the performance evaluation has been completed, strategic category objectives, development plans and an operational category retail marketing mix are drawn up including detailed space allocation plans at SKU (stock keeping unit) level, display plans, and promotional plans. The final two stages of the category management process are implementation, which includes assigning personnel to manage the category; and finally reviewing the performance of the category in the light of the performance evaluation methods previously chosen and the objectives set.

Although category management appears to be a logical conceptual framework and has achieved widespread adoption in the grocery sector (Holweg et al., 2009), its implementation relies on the fine-tuning of a relatively static product range. Dewsnap and Hart (2004) successfully applied category management in the lingerie sector and suggested that the concept could be relevant to other fashion contexts; however, the intrinsic nature of change in the fashion product range means that implementation is problematic because of frequent changes at SKU level. The principle of determining category roles within an overall merchandise assortment nevertheless is an appropriate framework for strategic analysis of fashion product categories whilst providing flexibility for short-term responsive initiatives.

Varley (2013) suggests an interpretation of category management can be a logical and appropriate way to underpin the management of increasingly dynamic fashion assortments (see Table 8.3). In this interpretation, less emphasis is placed on categories as drivers of sales and profits than in previous iterations of category management, while more is placed on the

appropriate management of clothing categories in order to bring good financial performance in the long term. The matrix adopts Kapferer's (2012) notion that the relationship between products and brands can be analyzed using the concepts of the 'distinctive' and 'generic' in terms of product facets, and 'core' and 'peripheral' in terms of brand facets. The distinctive product facets are those that strongly communicate a brand's identity, while the generic product facets are those features that are easily and often replicated by alternative or competitive brands; core brand facets may be considered to be those aspects of a brand that are found in all product category embodiments of the brand, while peripheral facets are those only relevant to a specific category. Combining these concepts with those of the established category management roles outlined in Figure 8.4, four fashion category roles have been developed.

The iconic category maintains all major brand facets in every product and the identity of the brand is distinctive through the category, providing a strong coherence between product and brand. Consumers consider the brand to be a destination for the purchase of this product type. In order to satisfy customers, a deep product assortment is recommended to ensure that most customer needs can be met; for example, a variation in sizes, lengths, fabrication weight, colour and textures. Product detailing can change to ensure updated styling is incorporated, but the essential product type should be recognizable and reassuring. In the case of Burberry, for example, the iconic category would be trench coats (see also the Burberry Case Study, Part 1, in Chapter 10, and Part 2, in Chapter 11 – Case Studies 10 and 11).

The aspirational or occasional category is one where particular brand facets may be included in

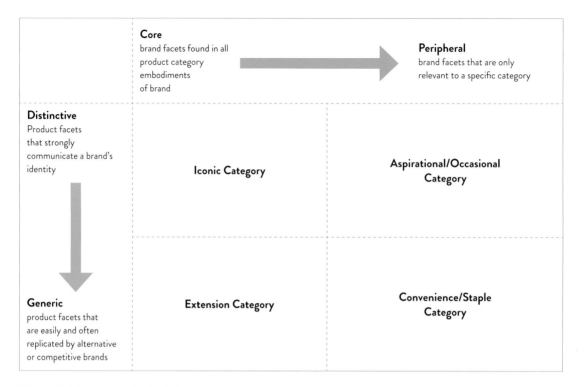

Figure 8.4 *Category roles for fashion assortments*

the product design in order to maintain coherence between the brand and the products; however, there is more freedom here to blend other facets that are more relevant to the specific product category rather than the brand. These facets may be innovative product features, or new styling ideas which add excitement and interest to the product ranges and the brand in general. As the relationship to the brand is apparent and shows the brand/product manifestation moving in a new direction, it is suggested that there needs to be a deep assortment in these categories to demonstrate confidence and commitment to new reincarnations of the brand. For Burberry, handbags could be the aspirational category. Occasional categories are those that have a more temporary or seasonal characteristic, adding interest and excitement to the range, using fashion features. Party dresses, for example, could be an occasional category for Burberry.

An **extension category** would be one that is well established for the brand and represents it in an easily understood way for the consumer, but where there is no really strong coherence between the brand and the product. It is a category that existing customers will be aware of but customers new to the brand may not be. Other brands are seen to have competence and

be competitive in the category. However, this type of category provides a brand with the opportunity to include products within the assortment that are on trend, or in growing markets to capitalize on brand loyalty and/or impulse purchasing. Some of these categories could be considered 'outfit completers' or complementary products. A shallow assortment is therefore recommended, with the potential to deepen should demand grow. Continuing the example, Burberry offers jeans, but only a small number of alternatives.

Convenience or staple categories are those that take the outfit-completing idea further, simply being offered to prevent a customer from having to go to an alternative brand to satisfy this need. Other brands offer this product category, and some may consider them as iconic products of their own. The convenience/staple category may have been one that had stronger brand coherence in the past but is now a stagnant or declining category for the brand, and so a shallow assortment is recommended. For Burberry, the small accessories category has become a staple.

Strategic categories play an important role in international merchandise planning, where iconic categories provide the focus of brand recognition and reinforcement for consumers in new markets, while staple categories provide the opportunity for entry level prices to introduce new customers to the brand in an accessible way.

BRAND ASSORTMENT STRATEGIES

The strategic relationship between fashion brands and product categories cannot really be understated, and although the contribution of brand strategy has been explored in depth in Chapter 6 it is worth highlighting in this chapter the strategic importance of brand choice within the context of a product assortment. In the earlier section on assortment plans we stated that a deep assortment would include many variations or alternatives within a category, and while this might refer to colours, styles, sizes and different fabrications, in a retail context a deep assortment often refers to alternative brand offers within a product category. The choice of brands included within a product assortment can therefore make a significant contribution to how a fashion company is differentiated. For example, Net-a-Porter made its name as a purely online retailer of upmarket and luxury fashion by being able to offer a wide selection of products from well-known brands. Thus, an attractive mix of brands, blended with excellent customer service, positioned Net-a-Porter away from other online fashion retailers who had inferior brand selections and less customer-focused services. One of the ways in which small independent fashion retailers can survive is by offering innovative and unusual brands that are different from those that department stores stock. Wholesale companies can also become differentiated by the brands they represent; in some cases, they build their reputation by focusing on brands in a particular category, such as occasion-wear, whereas other wholesalers spread risk by representing a number of brands that target different markets.

The extent to which manufacturing organizations engage in strategic assortment planning depends on their brand strategy. Many manufacturers work with a selection of different fashion brands, including retailers, and although they can be important to their business customers in terms of resource and expertize, manufacturing companies may not have much control over product design direction or range development activities. Other manufacturers are vertically integrated as part of the fashion company itself, in which case the assortment strategies will be guided by the retail and consumer marketing activities of the brand and their production capabilities. Manufacturing capability sometimes drives product strategy, referring again to the notion of specialism. John Smedley, for example, is a vertically integrated fine knitwear producer and retailer that maintains product and brand integrity by allowing its production of fine-gauge knitwear to drive its product strategy (see Case Study 8 on John Smedley, below).

Online retailing makes it possible and attractive to expand product ranges, including brand offers, almost endlessly. However, range expansion gradually moves a company from a specialist to a generalist stance, and this can result in a weaker positioning in customers' minds about what the brand represents. Therefore, the concepts of targeting and positioning should be borne in mind when making range expansion decisions, to avoid the risk of brand dilution and consumer irrelevance (Reast, 2005; Kapferer, 2012). There are many examples of companies making strategic decisions regarding range rationalization in a brand refocusing exercise, with the well-known online retailer ASOS being one of them; in 2008, ASOS developed a children's range, only to withdraw from the market in 2010.

Table 8.3 outlines the benefits and risks of brand extension. Brand extension decisions are where strategic brand management (see Chapter 6) and merchandise strategy intertwine.

Brand extensions can be referred to as vertical or horizontal. Vertical extension, also referred to as a line extension, is where new lines are launched at new price levels, normally downwards, and may take a new brand name completely. The classic example is the structure of luxury fashion houses with haute couture at the top, diffusion lines at the bottom, and ready-to-wear in between. Each level is aimed at different, or more tightly defined customer segments, with differentiated price points and normally different or new distribution channels. This allows a brand to grow rapidly and reach more customers. There is, however, the risk of weakening the value of the core brand by extending too much at the lower levels. For a fashion brand it is crucial to maintain creativity and excellence at all levels of the market so as not to dilute the brand and lower the appeal of the parent brand. Line extensions can allow for the introduction of diversity and complementary products. In addition to her successful ready-to-wear line, for example, Vera Wang launched a line with David's Bridal, allowing

Benefits of Brand Extension	Risks of Brand Extension
Assists the acceptance of new products by increasing the willingness for trial purchases.	The existing brand needs to give added value to the extension (such as recognition, credibility or quality associations). If it does not, then the extension will be vulnerable to competition.
Increases the effectiveness of marketing communications and other marketing activities.	A strong brand name does not guarantee success – if consumers do not see the connection between the brand and the new product, no value is created.
Reduces the cost for marketing programmes due to synergies created.	The extension needs to transfer a significant added value to the new category.
Provides the parent brand with a positive and enhanced brand image, leading to customer loyalty.	Can create confusion due to possible negative associations; hurting or diluting the parent brand image.
Creates awareness and associations with the parent brand amongst a new group of consumers.	The extension can cannibalize sales of the parent brand.
Updates and renewals create interest for the parent brand; raises the reputation for innovation.	Can diminish identification with the core category/categories.

Table 8.3 *Benefits and risks of brand extension*

Source: Based on Aaker and Keller (1990), and Keller et al. (2008).

Vera Wang White gowns to be available to brides of all income levels and sizes.

Horizontal extension, also known as category extension, is the strategy where a brand launches into other categories whilst maintaining a similar price level. Guided by the parent brand or designer, sub-brands may aim at a different gender or consumption occasion. The extension therefore explores a different category of needs and it faces new competitors. Distribution channels are often the same but may be new or different according to the category extension choice. For example, designer brand cosmetics are often sold in outlets such as department stores that do not carry the clothing categories.

Product and brand strategy in fashion can be finely nuanced, shown in the case of Miu Miu and Prada. There is no obvious difference between these two brands in terms of price point, but the subtle difference in the design approach is explained by Miuccia Prada:

Designing for me is a very complex process. There are many ideas that I want to express in one object, very often contradictory. The creative process in Miu Miu is not as complicated and thought out as Prada. Rather than being young, Miu Miu is immediate. Prada is very sophisticated and considered; Miu Miu is much more naïve. The solution, when I am working on Miu Miu, has to come immediately, instinctively, spontaneously with whatever is available at the moment. If I think three times, I stop. (Miuccia Prada, in Bof, 2014)

Assortments for international markets

Strategic merchandise management requires an understanding of international consumer markets in order to assess the extent to which adaptation of products and/or product ranges is necessary. Chapter 4 introduced the alternative approaches to international market development in terms of the global-local-glocal debate and a selection of examples of adapted responses of fashion brands. Consumers in different geographical locations can differ significantly in their needs and desires for fashion products in terms of sizing and fit, weight of fabric, and cultural referencing in colour and styling.

A modified product can make special connections with particular geographical targeting; for example, many luxury brands develop special ranges heavily featuring the 'lucky' colour red for the Chinese New Year market. Mass-market fashion retailers like Topshop and Warehouse take their best-selling autumn lines in the UK and rework them with lighter-weight fabrics for Southern hemisphere markets, thus retaining the fashion input but adapting for a different climate. Although this type of activity is demanding from a product management (buying and merchandising) resource input, the damage to a brand image of getting the product range wrong is one of a number of strategic risks associated with internationalization. There may be justification for a product range to be specifically designed for a particular international market if viable.

STRATEGIC RETAIL MERCHANDISE MANAGEMENT

Although product and brand management are strategic in nature for all fashion organizations, merchandise management is particularly relevant in a retail context where the category coverage can be wide and the product assortments deep. Fashion retailers are now rarely viewed in their traditional role as intermediaries or distributors but are more often seen as orchestrators or curators of value in terms of product and supply chain (Sorescu et al., 2011). Central to the process of curation of fashion product value are the two key organization roles – the fashion buyer and the fashion merchandiser. Clark (2014: 40) defines buying and merchandising as 'a role that connects the creative and financial product requirements of a fashion brand through strategic range planning and operational trading that optimizes a fashion business opportunity', pointing to the interdependencies of the two functions in the pursuit of common corporate aims.

The strategic role of the buyer

Fashion buying has been considered for many decades as an attractive career. The smart and powerful

Buying and merchandising (B&M) The operation connecting the creative and financial product requirements of a fashion brand through strategic range planning and operational trading to optimize fashion business opportunities.

Buying Strategic and operational product management that translates corporate aims and objectives into tangible and saleable product.

decision-maker, travelling off to all corners of the world to choose products in glamorous showrooms, is an aspirational image for many fashion students. However, what many outside the industry fail to consider is the extent to which buyers are analysts, and the competent buyer acquires and assimilates vast amounts of detailed information. An effective buyer is therefore a hugely valuable resource because their knowledge and experience, while unique to a particular business and product context, is highly transferrable to competition. Buying roles are generally more concerned with the qualitative aspects of merchandise, and buyers often work in collaboration with merchandisers, who are more concerned with the numerical/financial aspects of range planning, and both are supported by a data management system. Fashion buying requires creativity, an appreciation of aesthetics, and technical understanding, as well as knowledge and experience of consumer and supply market dynamics. Product is always central to strategy in fashion organizations, and it is the buyer who bridges strategic and operational management in order to translate corporate aims and objectives into tangible and saleable product.

Buyers need to be trend aware in order to undertake this bridging successfully; not only do they need to have a good understanding of changing fashion trends in terms of colours, styling, fabrications, they also need to have insights into the social and cultural references and changing behaviour of fashion consumers, and they need to be able to assimilate and distil this information in order to interpret it appropriately for a particular target customer and brand. The successful interpretation of trends helps to successfully position a fashion brand. For example, the trend for gender neutral dressing was interpreted in a provocative way at designer brand Gucci, with male models wearing garments such as lace tunics in their Autumn/Winter 2015 collection, while a more commercial interpretation can be seen at upper-mass-market retailer COS, which maintains androgynous casual styling across both men's and women's ranges.

Given the omni-channel nature of fashion brands in today's digital industry, vast amounts of data concerning online shopping behaviour are becoming available within an organization. Analytics are therefore adding to the complexity of sales data analysis to provide the much sharper insights that are necessary in today's fast-moving fashion industry.

Another aspect of a buyer's job which is perhaps less visible, but nonetheless often strategic, is that of supplier selection and management. Curating the product offer from a broad and often global supply base, while orchestrating the value derived from supply chain members, is a core competence of the fashion buyer.

The strategic role of the merchandiser

The merchandiser's role is one that has traditionally been less well known and understood compared with that of a buyer; yet in many fashion organizations, and in particular the large retail companies, merchandising is a function that runs in parallel to buying. Clark (2014) describes the fashion merchandising activity as a financial and detail-minded approach to the product creation process, blended with an involvement with, and understanding of, fashion, its trends and influences. The focus of this role on financial aspects points to the direct link that merchandising has with financial strategy (Chapter 5).

> **Merchandising**
> A financially and numerically detailed approach to the product range planning process, blended with an understanding of fashion trends.

The fashion industry is increasingly volatile and unpredictable, with shortening lifecycles and a high level of impulse purchasing (Sheridan et al., 2006), which makes merchandising in this context particularly challenging. Fashion merchandising is becoming a more strategic role, as it is directly concerned with the implementation of long-term developments such as international and new format development, new product market developments and the use of new channels. For example, online retailing facilitates the opportunity to offer much wider product ranges sourced from a wider supplier base and its immediacy perpetuates the need for frequent injections of stock with a rolling, rather than seasonal approach; thus creating a potentially endless range-planning process, with unit demand decreasing and products increasingly becoming unique (Clark, 2014). ASOS, for example, offered 80,000 products during 2015 – an average of around 220 new products per day (ASOS, 2016). As global opportunities emerge, many fashion markets have a less seasonal, or a different seasonal pattern from those in the traditionally established markets; and so the merchandiser needs to be able to interpret these changes to create balanced financial forecasts and budgets.

As with buyers, experienced merchandisers are major assets to a fashion organization. In large companies, whole teams of buyers and merchandisers support different merchandise departments (such as women's jersey tops, men's casualwear). Junior and assistant buyers and merchandisers work in a supportive role in the departments, whilst gaining the experience and expertize needed to progress into the more responsible role of senior buyer/merchandiser. Highly effective and experienced buying and merchandising personnel can progress to director and board level management positions, where the product and financial planning are predominantly strategic. Nobbs et al. (2014) developed a core competencies framework for retail buying and merchandising (Figure 8.4) summarizing activities that drive the overall buying and merchandising competency within fashion retailing.

Own-brand strategy

Although producer and supplier brands bring expertize, marketing support and often strong consumer recognition and association, the fact that they are unlikely to be exclusive to a retailer means that there is little control over design direction, distribution strategy, and pricing for the retailer. Well-known brands in fact rarely act as differentiators in a retailer's product range but may be really important to drive customer traffic and make a contribution to a particularly well curated collection of brands, which itself is a differentiating factor. Own brands, on the other hand, allow a retailer to gain exclusivity and control over a product offer that is unique to their own outlets, and can be designed and developed specifically for the retailer's customer. Many highly successful fashion retailers sell only own-branded merchandise, from Primark, through Zara to Ralph Lauren. Often a retailer will use a number of owned and controlled sub-brands to segment either by customer or by product area. Table 8.5 illustrates this.

Core Competencies within Buying	Core Competencies within Merchandising
1. Internal and external (competitive) range analysis	1. Sales forecasting and financial range planning
2. Trend prediction and forecasting (colour, silhouette, style, material, prints)	2. Store grading (profiling), model (ideal) stock and size ratios for each style
3. Sourcing and supplier selection and liaison	3. Delivery phasing, stock management and open-to-buy
4. Product selection and range-planning	4. Re-forecasting, markdowns (price reductions) and promotional planning
5. Distribution and allocation strategy	5. Controlling and reporting performance, and budgeting

Table 8.4 *The core competencies within buying and merchandising*

Source: Adapted from Nobbs et al. (2014).

Primark	Zara	Ralph Lauren
Atmosphere	Zara Woman	Polo
Cedarwood State	TRF	Ralph Lauren
B&W	Zara Man	Black Label
Denim Co.	Zara Home	Purple Label
Love to Lounge	Zara Kids	Blue Label
Young Dimension		Club Monaco
No Secret		Chaps
Ocean Club		
Secret Possessions		

Table 8.5 *Sub brands for Primark, Zara and Ralph Lauren*

Source: Retailers' websites, 2016.

Own-brand strategies vary from being quite low key, as in the case of Primark and Zara where the corporate retail brand predominates, to high profile. For example, UK department store Debenhams has developed own-brand ranges under the collective brand name 'Designers at Debenhams'. These are collections of exclusive products across many categories within the store and add long-term value, through customer recognition, to their own-brand ranges. Other companies use short-term collaborations with designers or celebrities to inject short-term interest and excitement (see Chapter 7). McColl and Moore (2011) found that own brand is a strategic marketing tool for fashion companies, requiring centralized control of operational management to ensure consistency, which then brings strength to a corporate retail brand, resulting in competitive advantage and enhanced profitability. Having higher levels of product/brand control also allows a fashion company to react more quickly to market developments.

SOURCING AND SUPPLY CHAIN ACTIVITIES

Although the topic of sourcing is covered in more detail in Chapter 9 (Fashion Supply Chain Management), it is worth mentioning in this chapter that strategic merchandise management cannot be fully implemented in most fashion organizations without the cooperation and collaboration of suppliers. Following the incubation of design and the development of prototypes in the design studio or the buying office, products then have to materialize as tangible merchandise for consumers. Within product management, decisions have to be made concerning, for example, whereabouts in the world a product should be made, how it should be transported to customer outlets and which factory offers the best value in terms of production skills and costs. In particular, pricing strategies and overall financial objectives will be highly influential in guiding these decisions. Sourcing locations can also be tied in to brand identity in terms of country of origin (Rashid et al., 2016) and the choice of producer may be determined by the provision of unique competences. In many fashion companies, sourcing decisions are taken by buyers, merchandisers and product developers, but in some large organizations, a dedicated department may provide additional

expertize to research and negotiate large production programmes, especially for more basic fashion items. Although decisions in this context are likely to revolve around technical detail, the strategic price and quality positioning will provide a framework for them.

Global sourcing; international purchasing

Jonsson and Tolstoy (2014) discuss the two terms 'global sourcing' and 'international purchasing' and suggest that global sourcing is normally used in the context of the strategic coordination and integration of buying activities on a global scale, while international purchasing refers to specific transactional exchanges, which in some contexts may be made within the wider remit of global sourcing. Figure 8.5 demonstrates how international purchasing may progress to global sourcing.

Figure 8.5 *The potential progression from international purchasing to global sourcing*

Relationships between members of a supply network can develop over time to the point where businesses become what is commonly referred to as strategic partners, where dependence is two- or multiple-way, and the companies involved are benefiting from a significant synergistic effect. Sometimes particular production methods and skills are scarce resources, in which case the supply market can exert a considerable competitive force (Porter, 1980). For example, in the manufacturing of luxury leather goods in Italy a network of very small and specialized local companies is used as if they are part of the focal company, with strict control over components and raw materials to ensure the best quality and to prevent the risk of

counterfeiting (Brun and Castelli, 2014). Fernie et al. (2009) discuss the use of the international hub in strategic global sourcing, suggesting that such an organizational structure can help to transition global supply strategies into integrated global supply and demand management.

Some supply markets relevant to fashion are regulated (either self-regulated or legally) to ensure industry standards are maintained, and this can lead to strategic significance. In particular, in the light of the exposure of unacceptable factory conditions there is a call for more transparency in supply chains, and industry standard certifications are a way of reassuring consumers that brands meet certain criteria relevant to environmental and social sustainability. Perry and Towers (2013: 483) argue that 'there is a clear business argument for implementing CSR (corporate social responsibility) in fashion supply chains: as a high-profile consumer industry, poor CSR practices in subcontractor facilities can result in bad publicity, consumer boycotts and loss of retail brand value in the home market'. For further discussion on this topic see Chapters 9 (Fashion Supply Chain Management) and 12 (Managing Fashion Responsibly).

Product lifecycle management (PLM) system The Product Lifecyle Management system is an organizational system, underpinned by information technology, that aims to manage processes and information relating to product development, production and distribution.

senior buyers and merchandisers can become as human resources in the implementation and support of a corporate strategy; however, alongside people, buying and merchandising information management systems have helped to underpin product management. In their ability to facilitate the achievement of strategic goals related to product management, such systems must be considered as a strategic resource and the ability to use them effectively as a strategic competence. In particular, the concept of the **product lifecycle management (PLM) system** has been attractive to large fashion organizations. This is an organizational system, underpinned by information technology, that aims to manage processes and information relating to product development, production and distribution. Supply chain and customer networks have the opportunity to become part of an integrated 'one version' management network that traces a product through its lifecycle. According to www.product-lifecycle-management.com (2016), adopting a PLM system can realize the strategic benefits outlined in Table 8.6.

THE STRATEGIC ROLE OF TECHNOLOGY USE IN MERCHANDISE MANAGEMENT

As noted in Chapter 2, strategic planning is concerned with the management of resources, and earlier in this chapter we discussed how valuable

Resource Optimization	Differentiation
Greater productivity, reduced product cost and greater profitability	Faster time-to-market
Fewer errors, less scrap and rework	Better product quality
Insight into critical processes, better reporting and analytics	Greater design efficiency, decreased cost of new product introduction, improved design review and approval processes
Improved communication and integration, including with extended supply chain.	Standards and regulatory compliance.

Table 8.6 *The benefits of PLM systems*

Source: Adapted from www.product-lifecycle-management.com (2016).

STRATEGIC MERCHANDISE MANAGEMENT PERFORMANCE INDICATION

The central position of merchandise management in producing and/or retailing fashion organizations suggests that monitoring of its performance is vital.

Chapter 5 indicated how important healthy profit generation is to the long-term success of a fashion company. **Product profitability** is therefore fundamental to the process of long-term financial health. Buying and merchandising KPIs (key performance indicators) used to monitor merchandise management include the adherence to planned buying budgets; stock intake margin achievement; optimal stock management to maximize promotional activity; mark-down control; and allocation and replenishment targets to maximize space productivity (Clark, 2014). No amount of quantitative monitoring, however, will help to solve the problem of having the wrong product on offer; therefore from the strategic viewpoint the following qualitative performance indicators should also be regularly reviewed: the balance of the product mix in terms of width and depth of assortment related to locational outlet, and the optimal price/value equation in terms of product/brand benefits in relation to competitors (Varley, 2014).

THE STRATEGIC INFLUENCE OF OMNI-CHANNEL PLATFORMS

Within the fashion industry evidence of the radical transformation of retail distribution by the combination of e-commerce and m-commerce, facilitated by the internet and digital communication technology, is gathering apace. In particular the growing adoption of the role of the 'customer experience champion' at board level is a recognition that anything other than

a fully integrated and proactive customer-focused organization will struggle to survive in this era of transparency and customer review. New business models are developing not only to adapt to 24/7 retailing but to strategically engage the consumer to co-create in the merchandise management process. The online fashion retailer Modcloth (www.modcloth.com, 2014) invited customers to become part of the selection process by asking potential customers to make decisions on proposed designs by clicking on 'pick it' or 'skip it' buttons, while Threadless invites artists to submit their print designs, which are put to the consumer vote, then the successful ones applied to T-shirts, sweatshirts and home-furnishings (www.threadless.com, 2016). The lack of space constraint afforded by online retail allows for innovative, yet low-risk product mixing, yet how to maintain the brand value built in digital media within physical space is a new challenge.

Not so long ago, the way a product was presented to the customer was largely left to the visual merchandisers and the marketing teams. In the omni-channel era, this is not enough. Merchandise managers must be constantly aware of how a product will appear through both online and 'offline' media, and buying decisions are not only influenced by, but led by, marketing activity.

CASE STUDY 8 - John Smedley: UK manufacturing surviving with a vertically integrated approach within a niche premium product category

John Smedley head office and factory, Lea Mills, Derbyshire, UK.

Image Source: B. Alexander, case study author.

John Smedley is an idiosyncratic company within the British fashion industry. Founded in 1784 in Lea Mills, a picturesque part of the Derbyshire,

UK countryside, John Smedley has overcome many external business environment obstacles in its 232-year history to remain 100% British made.

The current Managing Director, Ian Maclean, who is a seventh-generation family member, puts its business longevity down to a number of critical success factors.

The first of these is a fastidious focus on a niche product category. By applying specialization, the company has built a superior level of craftsmanship and a strong reputation and loyal following for its high quality fine gauge knitwear.

The second success factor is that John Smedley has never wavered from its Made in Britain selling point. The history of the brand is the history of knitted garment manufacturing. The company started out spinning cotton and wool into yarn, then started to turn the yarn into garments, beginning with fine knitted cotton underwear, then moving into outer garments, which is the brand focus today. This vertically integrated approach within a niche premium product category, coupled with John Smedley the First's vision to create a brand from the outset (in addition to the manufacturing operation), has given the company a sustainable competitive advantage via a specific value proposition.

The third success factor is the continued private family ownership of the business, which brings a unique kind of morality and culture to fashion management, one based on brand endurance, brand nurturing, and building an 'extended family community' of employees, which drives distinction and high standards.

The fourth factor is that, even in a capital-intensive business such as manufacturing, John Smedley has innovated to remain relevant; investing to strengthen its brand positioning with a resurgence on a design focus. This has included collaborations with external designers and a collection at London Fashion Week.

There has been a systematic strategy of retail growth through multichannel retailing and wholesaling with their commitment evidenced by a second London store opening on Jermyn Street, a mecca for premium and luxury specialist retailers (Hounslea, 2016). The story of John Smedley is one of remaining steadfast to their core brand values of Britishness, design, quality, craftsmanship and community.

Sources:
Alexander, B. (2015) Interview with Ian Maclean, Managing Director and family member, John Smedley. Hounslea, T. (2016) 'John Smedley to open on London's Jermyn street' *Drapers*, 1 March. Available at: https://www.drapersonline.com/news/john-smedley-to-open-on-londons-jermyn-street/7005317.article.

Case Challenge

John Smedley is a heritage brand, differentiated on the basis of product specialization. Identify company resources and competences that contribute to this competitive advantage. Use Table 8.1 to help you.

ONLINE RESOURCES

A longer version of this case study, with additional challenges, can be found on our companion website: https://www.macmillanihe.com/companion/Varley_Fashion_Management.

SUMMARY AND CONCLUDING THOUGHTS

The strategic challenges associated with fashion merchandise management in a multi-channel, multi-market context are huge, and the implications for resource allocation are direct. There is nothing less desirable for fashion consumers than uninteresting or irrelevant products, and reduced stock on rails in a store or heavily promoted on websites is detrimental to a brand image and a clear indication of poor resource management and declining financial health. Merchandise management must therefore take the long-term, strategic view, blending operational short term merchandise performance monitoring with

consideration for the overall product strategy for the corporation. Strategic merchandise management requires the analytical attention to detail of range planning, pricing architecture and determined availability service, applied to the overall blend of brands and differentiated product offerings in relevant markets. This supports the long-term corporate aims relating to performance. Achieving growth through product/market development, or repositioning to consolidate a brand in its market, are all corporate strategies that are dependent on the strategic management of merchandise. From exclusive crafted luxury product to celebrity inspired mass-market fast fashion all merchandise management is supported by specific product-related capability and competence. The loss of creative talent and direction can devastate a product strategy, while the careful orchestration of merchandise-related decision-making helps to maintain the most visible and connective aspect of a competitive fashion strategy; 'You can't be too hot, and you can't be too cold, you just have to be part of the conversation …' (Anna Wintour, Editor of *US Vogue*, referencing advice from designer Ralph Lauren, 2016).

CHALLENGES AND CONVERSATIONS

1. Provide an analysis of the strategic merchandise management of a fashion organization of your choice, referring to the three levels of merchandise management as shown in Figure 8.1.

2. Consider the concept of the product category and analyze the approach to the strategic management of product assortments for two brands that you are familiar with, and that adopt contrasting assortment strategies (for example, a category specialist and a lifestyle brand).

3. Discuss the implications of international growth on product strategy and strategic merchandise management.

4. An own-brand merchandise strategy is common in fashion retailing. Discuss why this might be so, and analyze the resource implication of such a strategy.

5. Analyze and recommend the resources and competences required to achieve a competitive product strategy for:
    a) a low-price fast fashion retailer
    b) a vertically integrated luxury fashion brand
    c) a specialist, trend-led, young fashion brand.

6. Debate the notion that 'products' and 'brands' are of equal value to fashion businesses, using the case of John Smedley as a focus.

7. To what extent do you feel that online 'warehouses' like Amazon, where the product choice is almost endless, have taken the fun out of fashion shopping for consumers? Debate the idea that less is sometimes more in this context.

REFERENCES AND FURTHER READING

Aaker, D. and Keller, K. (1990) 'Consumer evaluations of brand extensions'. *Journal of marketing*, 54(1), pp. 27–41.

Aastrup, J., Grant, D. B. and Bjerre, M. (2007) 'Value creation and category management through retailer–supplier relationships'. *International Review of Retail Distribution and Consumer Research*, 17(5), pp. 523–541.

A. C. Nielson Company (2006) *Consumer Centric Category Management: How to Increase Profits by Managing Categories Based on Consumer Needs.* Princeton, NJ: John Wiley & Sons.

Amed, I. (2016) 'Burberry aligns Runway and Retail Calendar in Game-Changing Shift'. Available at: Businessoffashion.com, 5.2.16 [accessed 05/02/2016].

Ansoff, I. (1988) *The New Corporate Strategy.* New York: John Wiley & Sons.

Armstrong, A. (2016) 'Mulberry triples profits after handbag price cuts'. *Telegraph.* Available at: http://www.telegraph.co.uk/business/2016/06/16/mulberry-triples-profits-after-handbag-price-cuts/ [accessed 16/07/2016].

ASOS.com (2016) 'About Us'. Available at: www.asos.com/about/ [accessed 05/06/2016].

Barnes, L. and Lea-Greenwood, G. (2006) 'Fast fashioning the supply chain: Shaping the research agenda'. *Journal of Fashion Marketing and Management*, 10(3), pp. 259–271.

Barnes, L. and Lea-Greenwood, G. (2013) 'Fast fashion: A second special issue'. *Journal of Fashion Marketing and Management: An International Journal*, 17(2).

Birtwistle, G., Siddiqui, N. and Fiorito, S. S. (2003) 'Quick response: Perceptions of UK fashion retailers'. *International Journal of Retail & Distribution Management*, 31(2), pp. 118–128.

Bof (2014) 'What's the Difference Between Prada and Miu Miu? Miuccia Speaks'. Available at: https://www.businessoffashion.com/articles/intelligence/miuccia-prada-unravels-difference-prada-miu-miu [accessed 20/01/2016].

Brun, A. and Castelli, C. (2014) 'Supply chain strategy in the fashion and luxury industry', in Fernie, J. and Sparks, L. (eds) Logistics and Retail Management, 4th edn. London: Kogan Page, ch. 6.

Clark, J. (2014) Fashion Merchandising: Principles and Practice. Basingstoke: Palgrave Macmillan.

Dewintre, H. (2015) Is the end of the seasonal fashion cycle in sight? Fashion United. Available at: https://fashionunited.uk/news/fashion/is-the-end-of-the-seasonal-fashion-cycle-in-sight/2015030315723 [accessed 05/03/2015].

Dewsnap, B. and Hart, C. (2004) 'Category management: A new approach for fashion marketing?' European Journal of Marketing, 38(7), pp. 809–834.

Fernie, J., Maniatakis, P. A. and Moore, C. M. (2009) 'The role of international hubs in a fashion retailer's sourcing strategy'. International Review of Retail Distribution and Consumer Research, 19(4), pp. 421–436.

Fletcher, K. (2014) Sustainable Fashion and Textiles, 2nd edn. Abingdon: Routledge.

Gowerek, H. (2007) Fashion Buying, 2nd edn. Oxford: Wiley-Blackwell.

Hanslin, K. and Rindell, A. (2014) 'Consumer-brand relationships in step-down line extensions of luxury and designer brands'. Journal of Fashion Marketing and Management, 18(2), pp. 145–168.

Hill, J. and Lee, H.-H. (2015) 'Sustainable brand extensions of fast fashion retailers'. Journal of Fashion Marketing and Management: An International Journal, 19(2), pp. 205–222.

Holweg, C., Schnedlitz, P. and Teller, C. (2009) 'The drivers of consumer value in the ECR category management model. International Review of Retail, Distribution and Consumer Research, 19(3), pp. 199–218.

Hounslea, T. (2016) 'John Smedley to open on London's Jermyn street'. Drapers, 1 March. Available at: https://www.drapersonline.com/news/john-smedley-to-open-on-londons-jermyn-street/7005317.article.

Huang, R., Lee, S. H., Kim H. J. and Evans, L. (2015) 'The impact of brand experiences on brand resonance in multi-channel fashion retailing'. Journal of Research in Interactive Marketing, 9(2), pp. 129–147.

IGD (Institute of Grocery Distribution) (1999) Category Management in Action. Watford: IGD.

IGD (2016) Training Pages. Available at: https://www.igd.com/Training/Category-management-and-shopper-/ [accessed 05/06/2016].

Jackson, T. and Shaw, D. (2001) Fashion Buying and Merchandising Management. Basingstoke: Palgrave Macmillan.

Jonsson, A. and Tolstoy, D. (2014) 'A thematic analysis of research on global sourcing and international purchasing in retail firms'. International Journal of Retail and Distribution Management, 42(1), pp. 56–83.

Kapferer, J. N. (2012) The New Strategic Brand Management, 5th edn. London: Kogan Page.

Keller, K. L., Apéria, T. and Georgson, M. (2008) Strategic Brand Management: A European Perspective, 1st edn. Harlow, England; and New York: Prentice Hall/Financial Times.

McColl, J. and Moore, C. (2011) 'An exploration of fashion retailer won brand strategies'. Journal of Fashion Marketing and Management, 15(1), pp. 91–107.

McGoldrick, P. (2002) Retail Marketing. Maidenhead: McGraw-Hill.

Mintel (2015) Footwear Retailing UK Report, July. Available at: http://academic.mintel.com.arts.idm.oclc.org/display/743780/?highlight#hit1 [accessed 16/07/2016].

Muji.com (2016). Available at: http://www.muji.com/uk/about/ [accessed 12/07/2016].

Nobbs, K., O'Sullivan, J. and Middleton, H. (2014) 'Exploring UK fashion buyers' and merchandisers' job roles'. Proceedings of Global Fashion Conference, Ghent, 2014.

Perry, P. and Towers, N. (2013) 'Conceptual framework development: CSR implementation in fashion supply chains'. International Journal of Physical Distribution and Logistics Management, 43(5/6), pp. 478–500.

Porter, M. E. (1980) Competitive Strategy: Techniques for Analyzing Industries and Competitors. New York: Free Press.

Posner, H. (2011) Marketing Fashion. London: Lawrence King.

Rashid, A., Barnes, L. and Warnaby, G. (2016) 'Management perspectives on country of origin'. Journal of Fashion Marketing and Management, 20(2), pp. 230–244.

Reast, J. D. (2005) 'Brand trust and brand extension acceptance: The relationship'. Journal of Product & Brand Management, 14(1), pp. 4–13.

Shaw, D. and Koumbis, D. (2013) Fashion Buying: From Trend Forecasting to Shop Floor. London: Fairchild.

Sheridan, M., Moore, C. and Nobbs, K. (2006) 'Fast fashion requires fast marketing: The role of category management in fast fashion positioning', Journal of Fashion Marketing and Management, 10(3), pp. 301–315.

Sorescu, A., Frambach, R., Singh, J., Rangaswamy, A. and Bridges, C. (2011) 'Innovations in retail business models'. Journal of Retailing, 87(S1), S3–S16.

Varley, R. (2013) A reassessment of the category management concept for strategic fashion merchandise planning, Proceedings of EAERCD Conference, Valencia, July 2013.

Varley, R. (2014) Retail Product Management: Buying and Merchandising, 3rd edn. Abingdon: Routledge.

Wintour, A. (2016). Available at: http://www.bbc.co.uk/iplayer/episode/b07w1qms/absolutely-fashion-inside-british vogue episode 2 [accessed 20/01/2016].

FASHION SUPPLY CHAIN MANAGEMENT

9

Rosemary Varley and Heather Pickard

⊕ INTRODUCTION

Although fashion is well known as a global industry; with the established structures of international fashion weeks from Paris, New York, and Shanghai to Rio de Janeiro, Budapest and Lagos, and the consumption of global brands such as Zara, H&M, Ralph Lauren, and Burberry across continents, what is less obvious to many is the global network concerned with the production and supply of fashion products and their components. The fashion industry is very much a part of the process of globalization, with the benefits and drawbacks that go with that process. Different international cultures have always had a strong influence on fashion culture and expression; indigenous materials and processes have shaped fashion design directions and international development has embraced the fashion industry as a way to emerge and grow economies, as in China and India. On the other hand, local industry heritage influences the design and use of materials, which become part of a brand's geographical identity; for example, Vivienne Westwood has often used

Tartan and Harris Tweed from Scotland in her British collections, while Issey Miyake's extensive use of pleating makes reference to the Japanese art of folding. The purpose of this chapter is to explore the concept of the supply chain in relation to the strategic management of fashion companies, with particular reference to the notion of competitive advantage.

The chapter starts by scoping the concept of supply chain management, defining key concepts, such as responsiveness and agility, that help to describe supply chains within the context of strategic aims a fashion organization may be pursuing. We then consider the global nature of supply chains, with their historic and social significance, and explore the challenges associated with the global approach. The third part of the chapter focuses on relationships between supply chain entities and considers how they influence strategic decision-making, and we close with a section that sets out the ethical challenges associated with modern supply chain management.

👕 LEARNING OBJECTIVES

After studying this chapter, you should be able to understand:

- The nature of fashion supply chains and supply chain management, and to appreciate the contribution they make to strategic decision-making for fashion organizations;

- Supply chain management characteristics and the applicability of these within different fashion company contexts;

- Motivations for sourcing and the associated global trends;

- The notion of supply chain risk, and how this might be managed;

- How value creation is associated with supply chain management, and the role that supply chain partnerships and information management can play in this process;

- The growing concern for sustainable supply chain strategies, and how these can add to a fashion brand's differentiation.

. Case study, BA (Hons) Bespoke Tailoring. India Heaversedge, BA (Hons) Bespoke Tailoring, London College of Fashion. Photographer Alys Tomlinson. © University of the Arts London.

75

SUPPLY CHAIN MANAGEMENT IN A STRATEGIC CONTEXT

As we saw in Chapter 8 (Fashion Merchandise Management), the broader product management activity has both strategic and operational aspects, but with a focus on the relationship between consumer demand and product range planning. Supply chain management extends this product orientated aspect of a fashion strategy further 'up-stream' into areas of production, logistics and systems design. It is concerned with how the planning of ranges transfers to the manufacture and delivery of the fashion product into retail space, whether a warehouse or a shop. Although these activities are complex in themselves and are often outsourced to organizations that are not owned by the same company, the need to link and integrate supply chain management with the consumer orientated aspects of fashion range planning and product development cannot be overstated. Product strategy and sourcing strategy are therefore interdependent.

> **Supply chain management**
> The planning and management of all activities involved in sourcing and procurement, conversion, and all logistics management activities, including coordination and collaboration with channel partners, which can be suppliers, intermediaries, third party service providers, and customers (CSCMP, 2015).

Supply chain management must be contextualized in order to understand it. Hermès, for example, has a fabled waiting list for its iconic product, the 'Birkin' bag. The scarcity of resources in terms of the high-quality leather as raw material for the bag and the craft skills handed down through generations to construct the bag are perpetuated and add desirability for the discerning luxury customer; but few brands would be able to maintain a business on what in other contexts would appear to be an appalling product availability service. Zara, on the other hand, has built an extraordinarily successful fashion empire, and most observers credit its supply chain strategy as the basis for that success, with the ability to offer a huge range of keenly priced high-fashion products, with new injections of stock on a near to continual basis. Supply chains can therefore have a very strong influence on an overall corporate strategy in a fashion business; whilst corporate aims and strategic directions can dictate the appropriateness of individual supply chain strategies, influencing sourcing, transportation and distribution operations.

THE SUPPLY CHAIN STRATEGY CONCEPT

The Council of Supply Chain Management Professionals (CSCMP) defines supply chain management (SCM) as 'the planning and management of all activities involved in sourcing and procurement, conversion, and all logistics management activities. Importantly, it also includes coordination and collaboration with channel partners, which can be suppliers, intermediaries, third party service providers, and customers' (CSCMP, 2015). Fashion supply chains have been described variously as long, complex, fragmented, volatile and competitive.

Chaudhry and Hodge (2012) visualize the fashion (textile and apparel) supply chain in Figure 9.1.

For many fashion supply companies, however, this diagram is oversimplified. The authors point out that Tier I and Tier II are integrated for products such as knitwear and that further intermediaries may be added between Tier 1 and Buyer. Hines' (2013: 6)

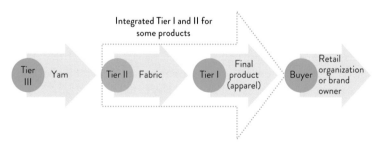

Figure 9.1 *A simplified visualization of a fashion supply chain*

Source: Chaudhry, H. and Hodge, G., 'Postponement and supply chain structure: cases from the textile and apparel industry', *Journal of Fashion Marketing and Management*, 16/1 pp. 64–80, 2012, Emerald Insight. https://doi.org/10.1108/13612021211203032.

illustration of supply chain constituents is more realistic for many fashion supply chains where a plethora of processes including not only yarn, fabric and garment manufacture, but also dying, printing, embellishment application and finishing (e.g. washing and pressing) could be present (see Figure 9.2). The oval shapes represent these processes and/or the organizations that carry them out, demonstrating the complex network of supply chain components or members. This model also captures the integration of logistical (materials and service) information flows and financial flows in supply chains. The model also reflects the definition of a supply chain developed by the Chartered Institute of Procurement and Supply (CIPS): 'The supply chain conceptually covers the entire physical process from ordering and obtaining the raw materials through all process steps until the finished product reaches the end consumer. Most supply chains consist of many separate companies, each linked by virtue of their part in satisfying the specific need of the end consumer' (CIPS, 2015). It is worth noting that fashion supply networks are very often global in nature, where raw material production, garment manufacture and finishing processes may take place on different continents. Whilst the study of supply chains is an academic discipline in its own right, we will concentrate on the contribution that SCM can make to support the corporate strategy of a fashion firm and how supply chains can add value in the supply of fashion products to consumers.

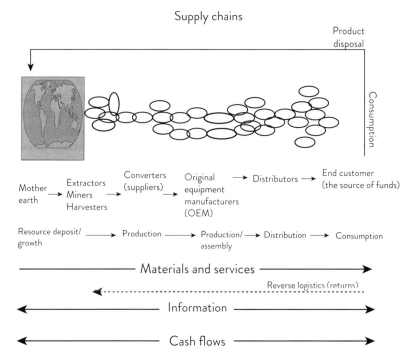

Figure 9.2 *Supply chain constituents*

Source: Supply chain Strategies: Demand Driven and Customer Focused, Hines, T., Copyright © 2013 Routledge, reproduced by permission of Taylor & Francis Books UK.

SUPPLY CHAIN VALUE CREATION AND CHARACTERISTICS

Although the design development focus of product management is central to the creation of desirable and commercial offerings to customers, attributes such as quality (of the components and make) and availability (for example, being able to offer a full range of colours and sizes over a period of time) are entirely dependent on a supply chain. Kim (2013: 217) highlights the contribution that supply chains can make to offering added value to consumers, as follows: 'a supply chain consists of all the activities that must be performed to create value, from procuring raw materials, transforming them into finished products, and delivering those products to the customers'. The activities embraced by the terms 'merchandise management' and 'supply chain management' are therefore interdependent and combine to add value in product-related relevance to consumers. The application of Porter's (1985) seminal concept of a value chain (introduced in Chapter 2) can be seen clearly in the study of supply chains, each component adding in some way to the final overall value to customers, for which they are prepared to pay a price that represents profitability for the fashion organization.

In the following section we introduce some of the important management approaches and operational systems that are used in fashion supply chain configuration and consider how they add value for fashion organizations. More specialized sources are available should a more detailed study of supply chains be required, such as Hines (2013), Christopher (2011) or some of the journals cited in the Reference and Further Reading section.

Responsiveness

The concept of response is an important one for modern fashion supply chains, and in particular the ability to react quickly to a changing business environment has helped the fashion industry to respond to consumer demand changes and ultimately sell more items. Christopher (2011) suggests that responsiveness is one of the guiding principles of supply chain management along with reliability, resilience and relationships (4Rs). **Time-based competitive advantage** has been viewed as a critical success factor in much of the highly time-sensitive fashion industry, with the development of supply chain competences which enable new product ideas to get to market as quickly as possible, to make the most of a trend or an endorsed style. A responsive supply chain should also be able to reduce waste by halting the production of unwanted product. As Kim (2013) notes, however, fashion customer requirements change so fast that product lifecycles are becoming compressed, to the point that achieving an appropriate level of responsiveness has become more challenging. Particular supply chain capabilities therefore become relevant in the pursuit of responsiveness, and these are sometimes referred to as the triple-A capabilities: agility, adaptability, and alignment (Lee, 2004).

> **Time-based competitive advantage** The development of supply chain competences which enable new product ideas to get to market quickly, which is a critical success factor in the highly time-sensitive fashion industry.

Agility

Gligor (2014) summarizes the most common elements found in the various definitions of agility: quick response to sudden changes in supply can demand smooth and efficient handling of disruptions, survival in the face of unprecedented threats in the business environment, the viewing of change as opportunity, flexibility, integration within and across functions and processes, speed, and customer empowerment (including customization). Agility is therefore a multidimensional concept, which reflects the need to be responsive to change. Fashion is an industry where change is intrinsic and therefore to a greater or lesser extent, agile supply chains have been at the heart of all successful fashion companies.

Adaptability

The ability to adapt supply chains in order to change what they produce is an important aspect of a fashion supply chain as firms engage in continuous product development, brand extensions and diversification; 'success in the clothing industry requires a high degree of customer centricity, and firms need to keep production flexible to stay responsive to customers' changing needs and wants' (Jonsson and Tolstoy, 2014: 62).

Alignment

Alignment refers to the practices of coordination and collaboration in resource deployment between supply chain members, where integration of systems and sharing of information helps a supply chain to run smoothly and responsively. Khan et al. (2012) found that it is particularly important in a fashion context to align the design process to the rest of a supply chain because the design of products impacts on the sourcing of components, production and logistics, and retailing. Many fashion retailers align product management teams comprising designers, technicians, buyers, merchandisers, sourcing managers and even key suppliers to improve responsiveness. Gattorna (2010) developed a 'dynamic alignment' framework which demonstrates the link between customers, a company's strategy, the shaping of business processes and leadership style, emphasizing in particular the influence of organizational design and behaviour on effective supply chains. With moves towards smaller orders and even customization for individual customers, design and supply chains need to be aligned in order to achieve reliability and viability.

INTERNATIONAL PURCHASING AND GLOBAL SOURCING

Businesses are motivated to expand into non-domestic markets in two broad directions: first, there is the expansion into geographically dispersed consumer markets in order to increase the opportunities for selling; and secondly, there is the expansion of the supply base in order to include producing or supplying companies that are located further afield. Both of these methods of expansion are strategic decisions; at the very least they require new competences to operate them and the motivations for undertaking them are based on long-term goals and/or the need to respond to business environment opportunities and challenges. For example, to expand into new geographical consumer markets a company will need to become familiar with the legal and regulatory framework of the new country, along with undertaking consumer marketing research to understand growth opportunities, cultural nuances, media preferences and retailing infrastructure. Sourcing internationally requires an accumulation of specialist knowledge and expertize concerning supply markets, production facilities, currency markets and negotiation in different cultural contexts.

Textile and clothing manufacturing is steeped in history and cultural heritage and was one of the very first industries to be engaged in international trade. Hines (2013) refers to the Silk Road, a commercial route linking China, India, Persia, Arabia and North Africa, and finally Europe, which dates back to around 200BC. The concept of international supply chains therefore is not new; however, nowadays they are central to a global industry that is variously estimated to be worth over $1 trillion globally and the choice of where to purchase merchandise is considered to be a key factor when developing a supply chain (Hartman et al., 2012).

The historical and geographical roots of particular types of textile and clothing production can be traced back in many cases to the availability of indigenous materials and traditional skills. For example, the UK's textile and clothing industry was originally built around wool production, based on the climatic preferences of sheep. Historically India has had cotton production and processing at the core of its industry, but also the craft skills of embroidery, beading and other

embellishments have been used to create particular designs. Textiles and clothing is an industry that is often part of national or regional development, where human capital is high and machine and technical capital relatively low. Countries such as China and Bangladesh have developed significant modern textile and clothing production industries with the benefit of comparatively low labour costs. The indigenous production of raw fibres (such as cotton and silk) has been an additional benefit to these industries. The know-how and experience are passed down through generations, which helps the industries maintain their ability to add value and create competitive advantages. The manufacture of fashion product items continues to contribute to the growth and industrial upgrading of emerging economies (Jonsson and Tolstoy, 2014).

Global sourcing for lowest-cost production

With the increased opportunities available through electronic communication, the lowering of 'artificial' barriers to trade (such as import taxes and export quotas) and the reduced impact of natural barriers (such as distance), international supply chains for fashion products have significantly opened up. The worldwide Multi-Fibre Agreement drawn up in 1974 using a system of quotas (which were variable according to specified product categories) had the effect of slowing the amount of exports from so-called developing countries to so-called developed ones. This system came to an end in 2005, paving the way for a much more open global industry (Jones, 2006).

Information technology, data management and improved logistics have underpinned the development of operational systems that have facilitated and quickened the pace of doing business. The configuration of such competences has allowed fashion brands to consistently focus on creating new competitive advantages such as fast fashion and low-cost fashion. In fact, the attraction of flexible fashion production at very low prices has been one of the most significant influencers in changing supply chain management in the last two decades. Supply chain management principles in other industries have also helped to shape fashion supply chains. For example, the JIT (Just-in-time) approach used extensively in car manufacturing helped to promote the benefits of a lean supply

Fast fashion Flexible, responsive and low-cost fashion production based on immediate and detailed sales analysis, rapid trend analysis and the postponement of commitment to styles until the last moment.

chain, only gathering components for a vehicle as they went into production, and production being based on demand (made to order, rather than to keep in stock). Using this principle, garment manufacturing companies postpone the purchasing and delivery of components such as fabric, zips and buttons until the latest possible moment to keep stock holding costs low. Other process organization techniques have been developed in order to allow fashion companies to respond quickly to demand and fashion trend, often referred to as 'quick response' systems (Birtwistle et al., 2006). This type of system relies heavily on having accurate and immediate data exchange to underpin production and logistical planning; digital data allows the real-time exchange and rapid analysis of vast amounts of information. By combining detailed analysis of sales patterns (demand management), rapid trend analysis from copious amounts of digital imagery, and the postponement of commitment to styles until the last moment (supply management), a fashion organization is able to put quick response at the heart of a fast-fashion supply chain strategy.

Although all textile and clothing manufacturing has its roots in labour-intensive operations at all stages of the supply chain, in today's industry much of the fibre, yarn and fabric construction stages are now capital intensive with highly automated modern plants and machinery. Garment manufacturing, however, is still very labour intensive (see Figure 9.3).

This is partly because of the difficulty of producing a sewn-up garment in anything other than a single process and partly because of the demand of the industry for variety, which makes high levels of automation difficult. It follows that with a high level of labour input and therefore cost, in the pursuit of lower selling prices to drive volume or to lower cost prices to enhance profit margins, buying organizations will be attracted to geographical areas or countries where labour costs are at their lowest, thus creating the continual movement of garment and textiles production throughout the world.

According to Jonsson and Tolstoy (2014), Eastern Asia used to be the number one region from which North American and Western European fashion companies imported textiles and clothing. In countries such as Hong Kong, Taiwan and South Korea, the supply market has undergone major developments as suppliers have extended their capabilities and, in some cases, transformed themselves from manufacturers or traders to branded suppliers (Jonsson and Tolstoy, 2014) and/or retailers (Runfola and Guercini, 2013). Li and Fung is one such company and is profiled as a Mini Case Study (9.1).

As wage levels of their domestic workforces have risen, East Asian manufacturers have developed global supply networks of their own to transfer low-wage assembly to other locations such as Western Asia, Africa or Latin America.

Figure 9.3 *A garment production line in a modern factory. Image credit: www.knowtheorigin.com. Reproduced by permission of knowtheorigin.com.*

ONLINE RESOURCES

Another example of a move from supplier to retailer is that of Whispering Smith, which can be found on the companion website: https://www.macmillanihe.com/companion/Varley_Fashion_Management.

 MINI CASE STUDY 9.1 - Li and Fung

The Li and Fung Group has been a force of power behind the global fashion retail industry for decades, but the company's name is not one that most consumers would recognize. Founded in 1906 as a silk and porcelain trading company it is now run by the 4th generation of the Hong Kong Chinese Fung family, employing 22,000 employees. By 2012 the company had grown to encompass four separate business groupings: trading, logistics, distribution and retailing, and in 2014 Li and Fung spun off its wholesale operations, split trading and logistics away from retailing, and formed different business entities.

Although trading is the backbone of the Li and Fung organization, the company played a very important role in helping retail customers (especially in the US and in Europe) to access and source from the rapidly growing fashion manufacturing base in mainland China, as well as other developing supply markets. The company's knowledge, experience and expertize in trading helped to open up and develop quality and ethical standards with these supply sources. Scale is one of the benefits of the organization; according to the Li and Fung website (2017), the strength of the logistics arm of the company lies in scale: managing more than 20 million square feet of warehouse space, and partnering with over 400 other world-renowned logistics companies, the company delivers 100 million units of consumer products every day.

Over time, Li and Fung have acquired retail businesses in both fashion and non-clothing markets and this part of the company is now directed as a separate business unit within the group. Their brand Fung Kids demonstrates the company's ambition to have recognition in consumer markets. In addition, Li and Fung Omni Services connect global brands and retailers to China's online consumers through the development and marketing of stores, online market places and social networks, with Tmall, JD and WeChat as customers.

Since 2015, however, the company's fortunes have changed, with a decline in revenue. Critics suggest the fundamental issue is the company's inability to adapt in an industry where change is thrust upon it by technology. The company is accused of ignoring opportunities to invest in other new business platforms that have changed the balance of power, and they have become vulnerable; according to Guy (2017), Li and Fung refused to invest in Alibaba three times and now finds itself being threatened by irrelevance by this same gigantic e-commerce organization. Nevertheless, with the resources of such a networked and connected organization, the Li and Fung Group will no doubt continue to transform to survive.

Sources:
http://www.funggroup.com/eng/businesses/retailing.php
http://www.scmp.com/business/article/2085456/can-li-fung-recast-itself-catch-internet-age

---

Although labour costs are not the only cost in a garment, they are predominant. Hines' Iceberg Model – the conceptualization of the iceberg in relation to some of the hidden costs of overseas sourcing (Hines, 2013) – continues to be relevant; these include the costs of procurement, factory visits, quality issues and correction costs,

> **Hines' Iceberg Model** This model demonstrates that the hidden costs of overseas sourcing can outweigh attractive low prices quoted per product.

lost sales due to long lead times, lost flexibility due to high minimum quantities, management time, and applicable tariffs (Hartman et al., 2012; Hines, 2013). Some fashion companies have found these non-transparent costs too high to bear (see section on Supply source changes and trends). However, the competitive forces of fragmentation and saturation in consumer markets keep price competition keen and for many of the very successful mass-market brands, such as H&M, Zara and Primark, monetary value in the form of low prices is a strong contributor to a brand's overall value or competitive advantage.

It is not just mass-market fashion companies that use low-cost production countries as a supply source. At one time, China was considered to be a low-cost, low-quality textile and clothing source, but now China has some of the most well-equipped modern factories and is able to produce garments that are made to the highest global standards and is thus used for sourcing luxury clothing production as well as mass market; the rapidly growing domestic consumer market also became of significant interest to these companies. This industrial trading up is a result of pull and push factors: the pull of the expertize and high-quality management systems that result in high-quality outputs at reasonable prices, and the push to replace the business of some of the lower market mass-market fashion companies which have abandoned Chinese production sources to move to countries with even lower labour costs. This practice of chasing the lowest-cost source to the end of the world has been heavily criticized in terms of the ethical implications (see section on 'Ethical issues in supply chain management') but is inevitable for fashion companies pursuing a cost-leadership strategy. Although arguably not fashion, clothing offered by large supermarket retailers such as Wal-Mart (including Asda) and Tesco is also driven by what Porter (1980) described as a cost-leadership approach (see Chapter 2, the section on Strategic choice). For example, in 2007 Asda made national headlines when it sold a washable men's two-piece suit for a promotional price of £19 (Beckford, 2007).

Proximity sourcing
Sourcing goods either closer to home markets or domestically.

Supply source changes and trends

Supply chain value
The contribution to brand value based on supply chain management capability.

As noted earlier, China has been the chief beneficiary of global sourcing trends for the last three decades; at the expense of the contraction of textiles and clothing manufacturing in the US, Europe and Japan. However, as China's economy has risen, labour costs have increased, which has led cost-led fashion companies to source in lower-labour-cost countries such as Bangladesh, Vietnam and India. A more stable political landscape can also be influential

in the development and opening up of countries for trade such as Cambodia and Myanmar (http://www.just-style.com/analysis/myanmar-garment-sector-experiencing-rapid-growth_id124058.aspx). There is also evidence of sub-Sahara Africa becoming a possible import sourcing market in the next five years (see Box 9.1).

Also in evidence is the much-reported trend in both Western Europe (including the UK) and the US to move sourcing closer to home or even back to domestic locations. This is referred to as **proximity sourcing** (near-shoring) or on-shoring. Morocco and Turkey, for example, are often used for sourcing by Western Europe-based fashion organizations, because of their relative proximity and flexible manufacturing capabilities, even though their costs may not be the lowest available globally. South America is being used as a source not only for nearby US, but by other global companies such as Zara; this is because the high import taxes in countries like Brazil can be avoided if products are manufactured in the same country as where they are retailed. Likewise, the Arcadia Group, which includes the brands Topshop, Topman, Miss Selfridge, Evans, Dorothy Perkins, Wallis and Burton Menswear, is working with an increasing number of factories in Turkey and the UK to benefit from shorter lead times, higher flexibility, and better ethical standards through supply chain transparency as well as no import duty for domestic production (Guardian.com, 2014).

Although the cost of labour exerts a strong influence over sourcing and supply chain strategy, this is not the sole consideration. As noted early on in the chapter, supply chains add value in many different ways and much of the academic debate about supply chain management concerns the identification and management of **supply chain value** and the trade-off between factors that raise costs, factors that lower them and factors that add value in other ways. As previously discussed, the value created in a fashion supply chain is not necessarily one that can be evaluated in monetary terms alone. For example, hidden costs in international supply chains include costs incurred if an order is delayed, such as the loss of sales if the product is not available in all sizes and colours and in all outlets, and the hit on profitability should markdowns be necessary because the selling season has been shortened. In the case of high fashion and seasonal products in particular, the selling season may be only a few weeks. Furthermore, a brand's

Box 9.1 - Africa Fashion

In 2015, Ethiopia entered the top ten future sourcing destinations behind the more established locations Bangladesh, Vietnam, India, Myanmar, Turkey and China. Based on research by McKinsey & Company this demonstrates the increasing interest in Africa as a potential location for garment sourcing. Meanwhile, the online news-source The Business of Fashion suggested in 2015 that Africa's fragmented market of 55 countries, and a population of one billion, is set to become a 'lucrative frontier opportunity' for both the production and retailing of fashion. Lagos (Nigeria) Fashion Week is now well-established, but there is a sense that many international brands find the challenges of doing business in Africa somewhat daunting.

As well as Ethiopia, other African countries such as Kenya, Mauritius, Lesotho, Madagascar, Uganda, Tanzania, Botswana, South Africa and Swaziland are gaining interest from global fashion buyers (Berg, Hedrich and Russo, 2015). The main attraction is the low production costs in African countries – for example, wages in Ethiopia are among the lowest in the world and there is potential for the development of local cotton production. Kenya has benefited from a trade agreement with the US (the African Growth and Opportunity Act, AGOA) and has a network of factories making volume orders of basic clothing items. However, issues such as high minimum quantities, low efficiency and long lead times, poor energy infrastructure, corruption, high crime levels and poor social compliance make Kenya a challenging sourcing destination for many.

Young (2015) cites a number of brands that have 'an understanding of how to innovate locally and stimulate consumers and investors globally, while moving Africa up the value chain'. For example, Lisa Folawijo takes local inspiration for pattern, but refreshes print designs with fashionable colours and embellishments, and uses the fabric in trend-inspired silhouettes. Her stunning and original collection was featured in a pop-up store in Selfridges as part of a Lagos Fashion and Design Week celebration in 2013. All products are made in the brand's home country of Nigeria. Solerebels is another brand that uses recycled tyres to make the soles of trendy shoes that are sold around the world in a chain of 18 licensed stores, the name inspired by Ethiopian freedom fighters struggling against colonial occupation (www.solerebels.com). By managing the risks and fostering the originality and creativity of the region, the potential giant that is the African fashion industry can be woken up and put to work.

Design by Lisa Folawijo.

By permission of Jewel by Lisa.

Sources: Based on
Berg, A., Hedrich, S. and Russo, B. (2015) East Africa: The next hub for apparel sourcing? McKinsey & Company. Available at: http://www.mckinsey.com/insights/consumer_and_retail/east_africa_the_next_hub_for_apparel_sourcing [accessed 10/8/2015].
Young, R. (2015) What will it take for Africa to join the global fashion system? Business of Fashion. Available at: http://www.businessoffashion.com/community/voices/discussions/what-will-it-take-for-africa-to-join-the-global-fashion-system [accessed 11/05/2015].

reputation may be damaged by it being out of stock of a key fashion product; this cost is difficult to quantify and may ultimately result in dissatisfied and deserting customers who may never return. Fashion customers are notoriously fickle and are unlikely to remain loyal to brands that do not provide the levels of availability expected. Supply chain value creation is therefore just as much about organizations, systems and management approaches as it is about costing, although the two are very closely connected.

VERTICAL INTEGRATION AND OUTSOURCING; MAKE OR BUY DECISIONS

In some cases, moving a product from the early stages of a design idea to the end result in the form of a desirable fashion item does not involve any process outside of an organization. This type of supply chain is termed one that is vertically integrated. Design, production, finishing and selling is all done 'in house', which allows complete control over all processes, and provides transparency in costing and standards. Vertical integration, however, is not always the most cost-efficient supply chain and often companies 'outsource' some or even all processes in their supply chain to other organizations who have specialist production or logistical facilities or unique capabilities such as information management. Outsourcing allows a company to access outside competences that may cost less than developing them internally, and the accessing of the competence may be carried out on a temporary or permanent basis.

> **Outsourcing** Using external organizations to reach competences that are unavailable or more expensive internally.

> **Supply chain resilience** The ability of a supply chain to remain effective irrespective of external changes.

Strategic decisions to 'make or buy' require a careful consideration of trade-offs, which concern: the cost of the outsourced process (on a short-term and long-term basis); the amount of control over the process in terms of quality and ethical standards; the amount of information known about the process (transparency) and the ability to specialize and provide expertize. 'If we adopt the resource-based view, we could conclude that a firm defines its boundary by vertically integrating those capabilities that are most valuable and difficult to imitate, while outsourcing others' (Kim, 2013). A brand such as Nike, for example, retains control of product development, branding and marketing activities (including some retailing activity) while outsourcing production to a network of suppliers in around 30 countries. This allows the company to tightly control the image of the brand whilst accessing low-cost production facilities, but it has led to challenges in terms of maintaining ethical standards.

SUPPLY CHAIN RISK MANAGEMENT

In spite of better communication, the increasing uncertainty, volatility and turbulence in the business environment continues to put supply chains at risk. Uncertainty and volatility relate to unpredictable consumer reaction and demand, while turbulence relates to exceptional changes that can disrupt normal demand and supply patterns, such as natural disasters or political unrest. Internal disruption can also cause unforeseen risks, as seen in Mini Case Study 9.2.

In order to reduce risk, which is of particular importance to large-scale organizations, supply chain strategies need to reduce aspects that make a company vulnerable. Wieland and Wallenburg (2012) suggest that these strategies can be proactive in order to make supply chains more robust against risk, but that reactive agility (ability to respond quickly to change) is also necessary to reduce risk. They suggest that the importance of robustness, or the ability to withstand adverse events, may have been overlooked because of the interest in reactive agility (particularly prevalent in fashion supply chain research) but that supply chain resilience is really important in terms of creating customer value and improving business performance. A resilient supply chain remains effective irrespective of change and therefore includes factors such as using multiple sources of supply, keeping higher inventory levels at different stages in the supply chain and maintaining control of the design process. These practices help to ensure high levels of availability of product, which is for some fashion brands an important contributor of brand value. It is typical for a major fashion retailer like Topshop, for example, to use more than 10 different suppliers for their basic T-shirts to ensure supply continuity.

MINI CASE STUDY 9.2 - ASOS – testing the resilience of the online retail supply chain

ASOS, the internationally renowned online fashion retailer, has been a major beneficiary of the acceptance of online shopping for clothing and accessories. As an early contender in the 'pure-play' online fashion retail sector, ASOS was the first retailer to offer next day delivery and on the basis of a growing assortment of branded and own brand clothing coupled with highly efficient customer service ASOS started to be known as an online department store and so an attractive route to the online customer market by clothing suppliers.

In June 2014 a fire erupted in an ASOS warehouse in Barnsley, in the North of England.

However, being a modern facility, the technology, automation and structure of the building remained undamaged; only 20% of the stock was lost and the business was out of action for just 3 days. Nevertheless, the scale of the business now is such that this cost the company an estimated £30 million in lost sales. In an effort to have less reliance on the UK distribution centre as a central hub for all operations ASOS have instigated plans to open a network of warehouses overseas, which will add to the resilience of the ASOS supply chain.

Source: Based on http://www.telegraph.co.uk/finance/ 2928953/Asos-fights-back-after-Buncefield-fire.html.

Postponement

Postponement is the practice within a supply chain of delaying commitment to a decision as late as possible in order to reduce the risk of producing or distributing the wrong product. For example, whilst a retailer may choose a particular supplier known for its skill in producing silk blouses and commit to the purchase of the woven silk fabric as the main component months in advance, the colour the silk is to be dyed, and the exact styling details of the garment (e.g. the shape of the collar) are postponed until a later date in order to be able to react to fashion trends, colour preferences and sales histories. Chaudhry and Hodge (2012) studied a variety of postponement forms used in the fashion industry, including those at various stages of manufacture as well as further on in the supply chain, referred to as logistical postponement. They found postponement occurred at different points according to the product type within a fashion brand's assortment and that postponement can contribute to both the agility and robustness of a supply chain (see Table 9.1)

Product Type	Point of Postponement	Management Focus
Fashion	Purchasing postponement. For example, production and fabric booked, but final details of garment confirmed just prior to start of production.	Productivity enhancement and agility. Resilience through commitment in the supply chain, but with ability to react to changes in fashion.
Semi-fashion	Manufacturing postponement. For example, trousers may be made, but garment dyed near season in response to colour order confirmation.	Responsiveness, ability to add fashion value and respond to demand.
Commodity	Logistics/manufacturing postponement. For example, basic T-shirts in non-fashion colours.	Robustness, raw material buying, manufacturing and final movement to warehouses based on forecasts.

Table 9.1 *Postponement possibilities*

Source: Chaudhry, H. and Hodge, G., 'Postponement and supply chain structure: cases from the textile and apparel industry', *Journal of Fashion Marketing and Management*, 16/1 pp. 64–80, 2012, Emerald Insight. https://doi. org/10.1108/13612021211203032.

SUPPLY CHAIN RELATIONSHIPS

In Figure 9.2 the different constituents of a supply chain, represented by oval shapes, were touching or even overlapping. This highlights an important aspect of supply chain management, which concerns the relationship between members and how they operate in connection with each other within the context of satisfying the final fashion consumer. For example, as part of the huge Inditex conglomerate, the international fashion leader Zara is able to rely on a partially vertically integrated company structure as the core of the brand's supply chain, where a considerable portion of the garment manufacturing facilities are owned and locally based. Although more common in up-market fashion brand organizational structures, vertical integration is not the usual set-up for mass-market fashion companies, and supply chains rely on smooth working relationships between different companies. For large fashion companies, where volume sales are key to profitability, dependable supply sources are needed whether they are owned or not. Supply chain relationships and the management of them is therefore an important topic for discussion in SCM.

Supply chain relationships may also be referred to as buyer–supplier relationships, and in the context of the downstream end of the supply chain, retailer–supplier relationships. As such, relationships between two companies in a business to business (B2B) context can vary from being discrete transactions, sometimes referred to as 'one off' or 'arm's length' business exchange episodes, to the opposite end of the spectrum where a fashion company designs, produces and retails their own goods, with no outside involvement at all. Most relationships, however, are made up of a collection of scenarios, where negotiations are carried out, deals are made, and business understanding is built (see Box 9.2).

Box 9.2 - Supply chain relationships: At arm's length or snuggled up?

Charlotte is the owner/buyer of an independent fashion boutique in South-West England. Twice a year she visits the fashion trade show 'Pure' in London to place orders for merchandise for her shop. One of her favourite brands is Superb Fashions because of its popularity with customers, which gives a good sell-through, and because the product styling is in keeping with her shop's image. Each season she peruses the collection, chooses the colours and sizes, and places an order. Until the order is delivered at the boutique there is no further interaction between the buyer and seller. Once the invoice is paid there is no further interaction until the next season's 'Pure'. If, one year, Charlotte didn't like the collection she could quite easily replace the goods with a different supplier as she often finds new brands at Pure, and while Superb may voice some concern, losing Charlotte as a retail customer wouldn't break its business as they have hundreds of customers like Charlotte across Europe.

In complete contrast, Hermès bags are all made in factories owned by Hermès, crafted from high-quality leather processed in a Hermès-owned tannery, and sold in a Hermès retail outlet. In this case, there is no necessity for the role of the 'buyer'. Product developers are able to derive seamless feedback from their discerning customers, who have a guarantee of the integrity and authenticity of the product. In an industry where counterfeiting is rife, this is a valuable asset.

In reality most fashion organizations rely on good relationships with other companies to which elements of the supply chain are 'outsourced'. These relationships build over time, helping operations run more smoothly. The IMP group (2015) have studied marketing relationships between businesses for nearly four decades and have developed the theoretical and practical understanding in this field. In particular they emphasize the interactive nature of a long-term relationship, and that supply and buying firms collaborate and cooperate to overcome challenges and exploit opportunities within a business environment. They also noted that firms interact at many different points and levels within an organization; and that when relationships develop, interdependence grows and strategic aims are shared.

The importance of buyer–supplier relationships in the fashion industry has not been overlooked. For example, in 1985 Marks & Spencer was described as the manufacturer without factories, while its suppliers were described as retailers without stores (Tse, 1985). These descriptions point to the important aspect of the relationships which is a mutual understanding and shared business interests. Given that co-dependence arises when the exchanges between companies involved become large, such relationships are strategic in nature, with much sharing of information and collaborative planning. In the era of fast fashion there has been more attention paid to the management of the design and development stages of the supply chain. Jonsson and Tolstoy (2014), for example, suggest that in fast-fashion supply chains design capabilities work well when they are shared between retailers and suppliers. In the context of different strategic aims, collaborative and trusting relationships were found to have additional benefits in relation to corporate responsibility in the supply chain (Perry and Towers, 2013).

STRATEGIC ALLIANCES

As discussed in Chapter 2, the joining together of distinct competences owned by different organizations for synergistic strategic advantage creates what is often referred to as a strategic collaboration or alliance. The term 'alliance' suggests a longer-term relationship rather than a collaboration, which in fashion could be in place for a season, or less. Nevertheless, such activities are always strategic as the acquiring of the competence has been deemed advantageous to make the additional resource input worthwhile and the outcomes more than a simple uplift in sales. For example, H&M's designer collaborations usually sell out within a matter of hours; however, the continued use of them with different designers reinforces the positioning of H&M as a fashion forward retailer, rather than a discount store. Although many strategic alliances in fashion are designer collaborations, there are other examples of supply chain collaboration, which can involve supply chain members at various stages. In 2004, for example, Nike collaborated with Harris Tweed, a pure wool fabric produced entirely in the Outer Hebrides Islands, off the north coast of Scotland. This collaboration breathed new life into a local industry struggling to survive, while continuing the Nike tradition of collaborative limited-edition ranges to keep its trainer-enthusiast customer interested. Nike also collaborates with Liberty Design Studio to include its famous prints in Nike collections.

Less high-profile strategic alliances may not be apparent to consumers but are nonetheless fundamental to the survival of a particular supply chain. The ultimate strategic alliance is full vertical integration when members of a supply chain are in part or full ownership of one another. Khan et al. (2012) present a case study of a UK mass-market fast-fashion retailer that uses strategic supply partners in Turkey and China to access a close network of suppliers dedicated to design collaboration, sourcing and manufacturing. By aligning product design with the supply chain, the mass-market company was able to reposition from a value retailer to a fast-fashion brand, and after improving profitability based on increased volumes of higher-value product, was able to embark on a programme of international growth. Alliances between different industries can also bring external competences to help to achieve strategic aims; for example, BT Expedite worked with Warehouse (a UK women's fashion retailer) and Thomas Pink (shirt retailer) to develop integrated order and deliver systems to improve multi-channel customer service for non-competing companies (btexpedite.com, 2014).

SUPPLY CHAIN INFORMATION MANAGEMENT SYSTEMS

It is often said that the development of supply chains is dependent on the technologies that underpin them. Fernie and Sparks (2014) suggest that the ability to collect, disseminate and use data through a supply chain and its members has been transformative in supply chain change, while Hines (2013) points to the long-term trend of converging technologies that enable supply chains to improve customer service. Although the scope of this chapter does not allow for a full exploration of supply chain information management (IM) systems, some developments that have been important for fashion SCM are introduced. The need to allocate significant resources to a new IM system (in terms of the cost of the technology itself, the training needed to implement it, and the time involved in the disruption

> **Supply chain collaboration** Two or more supply chain organizations working together for mutual business aims.

caused by its introduction) reinforces the strategic nature of IM adoption decisions.

Enterprise Resource Planning (ERP) systems are information management applications that integrate both internal and external information flows with management functions within and across supply chain members (Shi and Yu, 2013), while Product Life-Cycle Management (PLM) systems tend to focus on information flows through all stages of the supply chain from a product perspective across supply chain participants. Both of these systems attempt to provide relevant information in a standardized form that can be accessed and updated by all those who use it. The aim is for integration and for 'one version/truth' information, to avoid repetition and inaccuracy in data processing. For example, the more times data is transferred between different departments, platforms and so on, the more likely it is that mistakes are made; in addition, without integration, data may be held in different and incompatible formats with different users.

Radio Frequency IDentification (RFID) is a different type of technology which has been used in a number of supply chain operations to improve physical tracking accuracy, and thereby improve transparency and efficiency of the supply chain overall. In particular this is applicable for large organizations because RFID avoids the need for human intervention in data processing, as the system wirelessly 'reads' the presence of product in a location. In the fashion context where product lines, and therefore coded identification, change frequently, a system that makes this information easier to process is of significant value (Azevedo and Carvalho, 2012). RFID also has the potential to improve transparency in a supply chain, by following products through the various locations and processes. Marks & Spencer and Zara have both embedded RFID into their supply chain systems. Recently, blockchain technology has been applied in the fashion supply chain context, particularly in pursuit of a high level of traceability and transparency. Here, supply chain networks contribute factual information about how goods are made in an open and transparent collaborative digital network, which relies on peer-to-peer audit and verification.

In spite of the often-cited drawbacks of high levels of investment and difficulties in associated change management, McAfee and Brynjolfsson (2008) suggested IT enabled processes have the following positive aspects: they are able to include a wide span of contributors and users; implementation results are immediate; they provide precision and consistency and are easily monitored and audited.

For this reason, confidence in organizations that use such systems is generally high (Shi and Yu, 2013) and therefore they may have better opportunity to form strategic supply chain alliances. The growth of online shopping has in particular highlighted the need for IT and supply chain investment. Natalie Massenet, founder of the successful luxury fashion online-only retailer Net-a-Porter, was quoted as saying 'Net-a-Porter is as much a technology company as it is a fashion company' (Massenet, quoted in Amed, 2012), while department store group John Lewis supported its highly successful multi-channel operations by investing over £80 million in its supply chain function and £100 million in IT in 2015 – the latter figure representing five times as much as five years previously (Guardian.com, 2015).

ETHICAL ISSUES IN SUPPLY CHAIN MANAGEMENT

In April 2013 a factory located in a building complex called Rana Plaza in the city of Dhaka, in Bangladesh, collapsed, killing 1135 garment workers and maiming many more for life after they were buried alive. The horror of this disaster, although not the first but perhaps the most dramatic, and certainly the most deadly in terms of lives lost, exposed the dark side of fashion supply chains. The full scale of abuses has been well-documented, but what is shocking for the general public, of whom many will be avid fashion consumers, is that the clothes they happily buy from well-known brands have been made in production centres where working conditions clearly abuse basic health and safety principles. The paradox is that the fashion consumer is what it is because of mass fast-fashion availability. The low-priced and ever-changing fashion garments have fostered a consumption culture that promotes frequent and multiple product purchasing, with rapid replacement, shortened use and high wastage. The vast geographical and psychological distance for most consumers between brand image at retail and its production location at the other side of the globe means that many people are able to ignore the implications of their shopping habits. For an increasing body of consumers, however, the unsustainability of such an industry has become apparent. Sustainability in the fashion industry is discussed further in Chapter 12 (Managing Fashion Responsibly); however, we introduce three important concepts here in the context of achieving the strategic goal of sustainability in the supply chain: compliance, the sustainability index and certifications.

Compliance

In theory, suppliers that comply with legal requirements and codes of conduct should be rewarded with large orders and long-term relationships (Lund-Thomsen and Lindgreen, 2013); however, factors such as corruption and lack of auditing can undermine compliance. In addition, the commercial requirements of fashion buying personnel (such as the need for lower prices or faster deliveries) can conflict with high levels of compliance.

The Sustainability Index

In the pursuit of supporting industries in their efforts to become sustainable there has been increasing attention paid to the concept of a 'sustainability index'. The Sustainable Apparel Coalition, for example, have developed the Higg Index, which is a 'suite of assessment tools that standardizes

the measurement of the environmental and social impacts of apparel and footwear products across the product lifecycle and throughout the value chain' (Sustainable Apparel Coalition, 2015).

Certifications

Certifications are used in supply chains in an attempt to monitor processes and reassure an end user (often the consumer) that a process has been carried out to a particular standard. They are similar in concept to that of quality standards, where the ISO (International Organization for Standardization) provide a worldwide understanding of specific standards for products, services and systems, to ensure quality, safety and efficiency (www.iso.org, 2015). Certifications are used as a way of assuring buyers that goods have been produced in accordance with environmental and social standards, and they are frequently used in an attempt to distinguish sustainably produced fashion. The well-known Fairtrade and Soil Association Organic Standards have been applied successfully to differentiate products and brands in the clothing sector. The pioneering sustainable fashion brand People Tree, for example, follows the principles of Fair Trade in all aspects of its business.

 ONLINE RESOURCES

The companion website provides a more extensive discussion on the subject of sustainable supply chains, at: https://www.macmillanihe.com/companion/Varley_Fashion_Management.

THE 'LAST MILE' IN THE SUPPLY CHAIN

Many sources discuss supply chain management in the context of what happens up until the point that goods enter retail space. At one time this meant receipt at a store; however, online retail means that the boundary between supply chain management and customer relationship management (see Chapter 11) is blurring. Home deliveries, generous and flexible returns policies, 'click and collect' services are all important aspects of the omni-shopping experience, and while fashion organizations may use customer service and/or customer relationship management as a competitive advantage and positioning attribute,

the operational activities associated with the competence to provide good service is based on the capability of the supply chain in the stages that involve the customer. Furthermore, a number of fashion organizations are experimenting with mass-customization as a differentiating device and this has major implications for a supply chain. The logistical ability to receive, sort and make viable a return rate of around 30–50% is a further challenge for the multi-channel fashion retailer.

According to Fernie and Sparks (2014), companies must balance customer convenience, distribution costs and security in the final stage of home delivery. In 2015, John Lewis, the department store famous for high-quality customer service, made the surprise decision to charge customers for click and collect purchases under £30, with the justification that the logistics of dispatching orders of small and inexpensive items such as lipsticks have become overwhelming (Guardian.com 2015).

REVERSE LOGISTICS

The term 'reverse logistics' includes the management of returned goods, which as noted earlier will always be high in fashion online retailing; shoe retailers in particular have high returns rates with 50% or more being the norm. The sooner returned items are received, inspected and returned to saleable stock the

more efficient and profitable the operation. However, the term is used more widely to encompass the recycling and reusing of different types of materials through the supply chain and it is therefore an important concept in the pursuit of more sustainable practices, such as using reusable packaging for transportation (Fernie and Sparks, 2014). In 2012, Marks & Spencer announced that it had achieved its aim of sending no waste to landfill, and it continues to work with suppliers to do the same (greenretaildecision. com, 2013). M&S has also received positive publicity for its 'Schwopping' and donation schemes, which encourage customers to reuse and recycle clothing (see Case Study 12 on M&S, in Chapter 12).

 ## CASE STUDY 9 - H&M: The pursuit of ethical fast fashion

H&M Group is one of the world's largest retailers selling runway fashion at mass market prices. Sustainability is a joint group function, managed by Head of Sustainability Anna Gedda. It makes business sense for such a large player in the global fashion industry to invest in the long-term supply of the natural resources and the stability of the markets they rely on for their sourcing, and as such, H&M's sustainability agenda covers environmental issues, ethics and human rights. H&M has won numerous sustainable business awards including the World's Most Ethical Company® six times. The central mission of H&M's sustainability strategy is to implement a *closed loop* model which sees textiles reused, fair living wages paid by H&M suppliers and increased transparency in the supply chain enabling customers to make informed choices about their fashion purchases.

H&M does not directly own the factories that supply it, instead outsourcing to independent suppliers, whose employees number approximately 1.6 million people. H&M sees working with responsible partners and economic development as key to tackling poverty in countries such as Bangladesh and Cambodia where their suppliers' factories are located. In 2014, H&M implemented a *Fair Wage Method* developed by the Fair Wage Network in three of their *role model* factories, and H&M are part of wider industry collaboration working towards fair living wages across the sector. In 2015, H&M implemented a new partnership approach to assess the sustainability performance of suppliers and to support them better.

H&M launched its own *Conscious Collection* in Spring 2011 to favourable reviews. The first collection featured organic cotton, recycled polyester and a cotton alternative Tencel (derived from Eucalyptus plants). In 2013, H&M launched its Garment Collecting Initiative whereby customers donate unwanted clothing instore and receive a voucher in return. According to the 2016 Sustainability report, since 2013 nearly 39,000 tonnes of garments have been collected instore, equivalent to about 196 million T-shirts. In 2015 1.3 million H&M pieces were made with closed loop materials.

According to the World Wildlife Fund (WWF), 2.7 billion people suffer from water scarcity during at least one month each year, and H&M relies on production based in areas which are or will be considered extreme water scarce by 2025. Denim production in particular has been criticized for its negative environmental impact due to the resources needed to grow cotton and the wash treatments the fabric undergoes during manufacture. H&M's *Conscious Denim* collection was introduced in September 2014 after working with Spanish denim consultants Jeanologia to develop more sustainable materials and processes.

Approximately 36% of a garment's lifetime environmental impact comes from laundering, and H&M encourages consumers to make conscious decisions about how they wash and care for their garment, promoting less frequent and low temperature washing. Since 2013 H&M has formally partnered with WWF to develop a water-stewardship strategy to promote the responsible use of water along a product's lifecycle from field to factory to fashion garment. H&M's mission to provide fashion for conscientious customers is reflected in its position as number one user of certified organic cotton in the world, aiming for 100% of cotton to be either certified organic, recycled or grown under the Better Cotton Initiative (BCI) by 2020.

Sources:
H&M Sustainability (http://about.hm.com/en/sustainability.html).
H&M Sustainability Reports (http://sustainability.hm.com).

Case Author: Natascha Radclyffe-Thomas

Case Challenge
Identify aspects of H&M's supply chain operations that support its aim to make fashion sustainable and sustainability fashionable.

ONLINE RESOURCES

A longer version of this case study, with additional challenges, can be found on our companion website: https://www.macmillanihe.com/companion/Varley_Fashion_Management.

SUMMARY AND CONCLUDING THOUGHTS

With an underlying supply chain strategy being the part of a corporate strategy that is generally unseen by fashion consumers, its importance can sometimes be overlooked. Fashion supply chains are often complex and are increasingly being scrutinized to consider how and why they can add value to the end fashion product and reflect a brand's strategic positioning. The effective coordination of diverse activities and functions in the supply chain therefore has to be one of the top priorities for fashion companies (Kim, 2013). Supply chain management is almost always strategic, because of the distinctive competences provided by supplying organizations and the specialist knowledge and expertize needed to manage activities such as production, sourcing, and logistics, which are in turn driven by product assortment strategy and long-term strategic aims. Drivers of supply chain management such as low cost, quality, delivery timing, and flexibility will increasingly be matched against the need for sustainability considerations, as communication technology allows traceability and transparency to move up the supply chain management agenda.

CHALLENGES AND CONVERSATIONS

1. Outline the various ways that a supply chain can add value to a luxury fashion brand and contrast this with those characteristics that may be required in a mass-market fast-fashion brand.

2. Many fashion organizations have been driven by the priority of low cost in their approach to supply chain management. Why is this the case, and what are the risks involved?

3. Critically review the benefits and drawbacks of vertical integration within a supply chain for fashion companies.

4. There is evidence that the fashion consumer is becoming more conscious of sustainability issues in the supply chain. Give examples of relevant issues and suggest ways that a mid-market fashion company might be able to respond to this trend.

REFERENCES AND FURTHER READING

Accord (2015). Available at: http://bangladeshaccord.org/about [accessed 25/09/2015].

Alliance for Bangladesh Worker Safety (2015). Available at: http://www.bangladeshworkersafety.org/files/Alliance%202015%20AR_Exec%20Summary.pdf [accessed 25/7/2017].

Amed, I. (2012) In Digital London Technology and Fashion Collide. Available at: http://www.businessoffashion.com/articles/fashion-tech/in-digital-london-technology-and-fashion-collide 16/08/12 [accessed 18/09/2015].

Azevedo, S. G. and Carvalho, H. (2012) 'Contribution of RFID technology to better management of fashion supply chains'. *International Journal of Retail and Distribution Management*, 40(2), pp. 128–156.

Beckford, M. (2007) Outfit for the man with a certain style that suits the pocket at £19.00. Available at: http://www.telegraph.co.uk/news/uknews/1539654/Outfit-for-the-man-with-a-certain-style-that-suits-the-pocket-at-19.html [accessed 15/09/2015].

Berg, A. and Hedrich, S. (2014) 'What's next in apparel sourcing?' McKinsey & Company article. Available at: http://www.mckinsey.com/insights/consumer_and_retail [accessed 10/08/2015].

Berg, A., Hedrich, S. and Russo, B. (2015) East Africa: the next hub for apparel sourcing? McKinsey & Company. Available at: http://www.mckinsey.com/insights/consumer_and_retail/east_africa_the_next_hub_for_apparel_sourcing [accessed 10/08/2015].

Birtwistle, G., Fiorito, S. S. and Moore, C. M. (2006) 'Supplier perceptions of quick response systems'. *Journal of Enterprise Information Management*, 19(3), pp. 334–345.

Btexpedite.com (2014). Available at: http://www.btexpedite.com/wp-content/uploads/2014/02/Integrated-Store-Case-Study-Thomas-Pink-and-Warehouse.pdf [accessed 15/09/2015].

Chaudhry, H. and Hodge, G. (2012) 'Postponement and supply chain structure: Cases from the textile and apparel industry'. *Journal of Fashion Marketing and Management*, 16(1). pp. 64–80.

Christopher, M. (2011) *Logistics and Supply Chain Management: Creating Value-adding Networks*, 4th edn. Harlow: Pearson.

CIPS (2015). Available at: https://www.cips.org/Documents/Knowledge/Procurement-Topics-and-Skills/13-SRM-and-SC-Management/POP-Supply_Chain_Management.pdf [accessed 15/09/2015].

CSCMP (Council of Supply Chain Management Professionals) (2015). Available at: https://cscmp.org/about-us/supply-chain-management-definitions [accessed 17/09/2015].

Fernie, J. and Sparks, L. (2014) *Logistics and Retail Management*, 3rd edn. London: Kogan Page.

Fletcher, K. (2014) *Sustainable Fashion and Textiles: Design Journeys*, 2nd edn. Abingdon: Routledge.

Gattorna, J. (2010) *Dynamic Supply Chains: Delivering Value through People*, 2nd edn. Harlow: Pearson.

Gligor, D. M. (2014) 'The role of demand management in achieving supply chain agility'. *Supply Chain Management: An International Journal*, 19(5/6), pp. 577–591.

Greenretaildecision.com (2013). Available at: http://www.greenretaildecisions.com/news/2013/07/11/marks-and-spencer-exceeds-zero-waste-to-landfill-goal [accessed 18/09/2015].

Guardian.com (2014). Available at: http://www.theguardian.com/sustainable-business/sustainable-fashion-blog/returning-fashion-manufacturing-uk-opportunities-challenges [accessed 18/9/2015].

Guardian.com (2015) John Lewis to charge for 'click and collect'. Available at: http://www.theguardian.com/business/2015/jul/01/john-lewis-to-charge-for-click-and-collect [accessed 18/09/2015].

Guy, P. (2017) 'Can Li & Fung recast itself to catch up with the Internet age?' *South China Morning Post*, 7 April 2017. Available at: http://www.scmp.com/business/article/2085456/can-li-fung-recast-itself-catch-internet-age [accessed 10/09/2017].

Hartman, L., Joines, J. A., Thoney, K. A. and King, R. E. (2012) 'The effect speed and replenishment flexibility has on overall costs of sourcing apparel products'. *The Journal of the Textile Institute*, 103(6), pp. 604–621.

Hines, T. (2013) *Supply Chain Strategies: Demand Driven and Customer Focused*. Abingdon: Routledge.

IMP group (2015). Available at: http://www.impgroup.org/about.php [accessed 15/08/2015].

Jones, R. M. (2006) *The Apparel Industry*, 2nd edn. Chichester: Wiley-Blackwell.

Jonsson, A. and Tolstoy, D. (2014) 'A thematic analysis of research on global sourcing and international purchasing in retail firms'. *International Journal of Retail and Distribution Management*, 42(1), pp. 56–83.

Khan, O., Christopher, M. and Creazza, A. (2012) 'Aligning product design with the supply chain: A case study'. *Supply Chain Management: An International Journal*, 17(3), pp. 323–336.

Kim, B. (2013) 'Competitive priorities and supply chain strategy in the fashion industry'. *Qualitative Market Research: An International Journal*, 16(2), pp. 214–242.

Lee, H. L. (2004) 'The triple-A supply chain'. *Harvard Business Review*, 82(10), pp. 102–112.

Lund-Thomsen, P. and Lindgreen, A. (2013) 'Corporate social responsibility in global value chains: Where are we now and where are we going? *Journal of Business Ethics*, 123, pp. 11–12.

McAfee, A. and Brynjolfsson, E. (2008) 'Investing in the IT that makes a competitive difference'. *Harvard Business Review*, July–August, pp. 99–105.

Nike (2010) Nike Releases Environmental Design Tool. Available at: http://news.nike.com/news/nike-releases-environmental-design-tool-to-industry [accessed 15/09/2015].

Perry, P. and Towers, N. (2013) 'Conceptual framework development: CSR implementation in fashion supply chains'. *International Journal of Physical Distribution and Logistics Management*, 43(5/6), pp. 478–500.

Porter, M. E. (1996) 'What is strategy?' *Harvard Business Review*, November–December, p. 60.

Porter, M. E. (1980) *Competitive Strategy: Techniques for Analyzing Industries and Competitors*. New York: Free Press.

Porter, M. E. (1985) *Competitive Advantage*. New York: Free Press.

Runfola, A. and Guercini, S. (2013) 'Fast fashion companies coping with internationalization: Driving the change or changing the model'. *Journal of Fashion Marketing and Management*, 17(2), pp. 190–205.

Shi, M. and Yu, W. (2013) 'Supply chain management and financial performance: Literature review and future directions'. *International Journal of Operations & Production Management*, 33(10), pp. 1283–1317.

Sustainable Apparel Coalition (2015) 'The Higg Index'. Available at: https://apparelcoalition.org/the-higg-index/ [accessed 15/09/2015].

Tse, K. K. (1985) *Marks and Spencer: Anatomy of Britain's Most Efficiently Managed Company*. Oxford: Pergamon Press.

Wieland, A. and Wallenburg, C. M. (2012) 'Dealing with supply chain risks: Linking risk management practices and strategies to performance'. *International Journal of Physical Distribution and Logistics Management*, 42(10), pp. 887–905.

Young, R. (2015) What will it take for Africa to join the global fashion system? Business of Fashion. Available at: http://www.businessoffashion.com/community/voices/discussions/what-will-it-take-for-africa-to-join-the-global-fashion-system [accessed 11/05/2015].

Photograph by Natascha Radclyffe-Thomas. Reproduced by permission of Shanghai Tang.[10]

FASHION RETAIL MANAGEMENT

Rosemary Varley and Mirsini Trigoni

✦ INTRODUCTION

The way fashion products are presented to the consumer is a key strategic consideration for all fashion organizations; the selling environment is a very effective positioning tool and can heavily influence how a consumer perceives and obtains brand value. Decisions regarding those channels employed to reach consumers are becoming more complex as more and more choice is introduced. At one time the retail distribution function was relatively straightforward, but online retailing has opened up new ways of selling and online brand communication enables the blurring of the lines between two fundamental aspects of marketing: the promotion of a brand blending into an instantaneous connection with the selling of it. Managing the retail aspects of fashion brands is therefore of concern for all producers of fashion,

and for fashion brands that classify as retailers, retail strategy is at the core of their corporate strategic planning.

In this chapter, we begin by setting the scene for retail strategy, considering the increasing strategic options offered by diverse physical and digital distribution channels, and how retailing can add value within the overall strategy of a fashion organization. We continue the discussion of international strategy, introduced in Chapter 4, by developing the implications of international growth from the retail viewpoint. In particular we highlight the important role that flagship stores have played in international fashion retail strategy. Finally, the part retail space plays in the strategic positioning of fashion brands is critically evaluated.

👕 LEARNING OBJECTIVES

After studying this chapter, you should be able to understand:

- How to situate retail strategy in the context of the development and growth of a consumer-facing fashion business;

- The complexity of fashion retail strategy in terms of the possible routes to international consumer markets, and the different retail formats available;

- How retailing activity can generate strategic brand value for a fashion organization;

- The strategic importance of the designed retail environment within a contemporary multi-channel retail strategy for a fashion organization;

- The strategic role of the flagship store in fashion retailing, and an appreciation of how flagship stores can underpin a diverse retail strategy for fashion brands;

- The contribution that retailing activity can make to the strategic positioning of a retail brand, and how that positioning may need to evolve within the context of the dynamic business environment.

RETAILING – STRATEGIC OPTIONS

The strategic options in terms of retailing are many; therefore diagrammatic modelling of this variety and citing examples of strategy adoption are perhaps the most efficient ways towards understanding the range of choices. Figure 10.1 shows a number of ways in which fashion products can flow in their demand chain from brand to consumer. The management of supply chains that move product from producing organizations into the domain of the fashion retailer is a different, but connected area of significant strategic concern, covered in Chapter 9. Retailing activity is often carried out by fashion brands that are not classified by governments as retailers; for example, the UK Office of National Statistics classifies a business as a retailer if it gains over half of its income from selling to consumers. It follows therefore that many producing and trading companies that also have significant retailing activities are not classified as retail businesses; Levi's, for example, engages in production, wholesaling and retailing. It is not of any real concern to consumers whether a fashion brand is classified as a retailer or not; what is important to consumers is what is sometimes referred to as the 'servicescape' (Bitner, 1992) that surrounds the product they are buying. This

> **Demand chain** Those operations and entities that move the product from retailer to consumer in response to consumer purchasing and ordering.

> **Servicescape** The selling environment and processes that the consumer experiences in connection with the purchasing process.

> **Retailing** Selling merchandise to a consumer (B2C), for their own or their household's consumption, through one or more type(s) of retail outlet.

term broadly refers to the selling environment and processes that the consumer experiences in connection with the purchasing process. A more modern term is brand engagement in the retail context and it is perhaps more useful therefore to view retail strategy through the lens of retailing activity, rather than retailer activity, given that so many non-retailers are heavily involved in the activity of retailing and that the variations of retail format continue to evolve.

The retailing activity

Retailing is defined (Baker, 1998) as a business selling merchandise to a consumer (B2C), for their own or their household's consumption, as opposed to an organization in a business to business (B2B) context selling merchandise to another company for resale. Baker's definition of retailing additionally refers to the rendering of services incidental to sales, and this is why, even as technology allows producing companies easy virtual access to the final consumer, retailing is still a marketing activity and an industry in its own right. The choices available in retailing activity are so many that it is perhaps more helpful to consider fashion retail strategy in the context of curating retail outlets rather than managing retailers (see Figure 10.1).

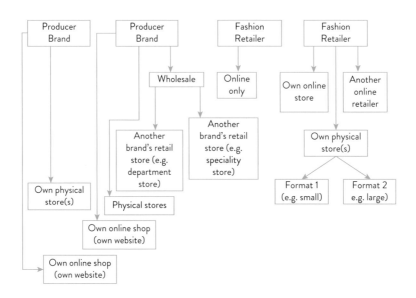

Figure 10.1 *Alternative retail demand chains*

RETAILING – ADDED VALUE

Traditional marketing theory suggests that there are a number of key functional areas associated with retailing. Varley and Rafiq (2014) propose that retail outlets have five distinctive roles over and above the most traditional and fundamental aspect of retailing, which is to buy in larger quantities to break down into smaller quantities for resale. The additional roles are as follows:

Promotion and communication about goods and services, both internally and externally.

Providing advice and guidance, matching consumer needs and desires to specific products that may fulfil them.

Negotiating sales and forming contracts in terms of conforming to the legal requirements of their status as seller to consumers, taking the responsibility for ensuring goods are safe and fit for purpose, for example.

Financial management associated with selling to consumers, such as the provision, and risk management, of credit.

Handling of warranty claims and other aftersales facilities such as home delivery.

Considering the strategic viewpoint of retailing as opposed to the operational context, however, it is perhaps more useful to view the value to the consumer that a well-managed retailing environment can offer. The **value equation** (McGoldrick, 2002: 96) is a useful concept for this purpose, suggesting that consumers require more in terms of product quality, choice and availability, convenience, good service and a pleasing environment, for less of their own time, effort, stress and risk, as well as money. In the context of fashion retailing in the omni-channel era we can build on this concept of consumer value to add some additional relevance.

OMNI-CHANNEL RETAILING

As suggested in Chapter 1, the concept of 'omni-channel retailing' is a development from the longer-established term 'multi-channel retailing'. Multi-channel retailing is a well-understood term that reflects the current situation across most international markets, where a company uses more than one type of retail format to reach and serve consumers. Typically, this means physical store(s) plus online store, but it may also include more formats such as catalogues, or different sizes and variations of store type.

The omni-channel concept refers to the consumer behaviour associated with using more than one retail format/channel/platform during the purchasing process. For example, the sequence of browsing on a mobile app, trying on in a store, then ordering on a personal computer or tablet for home delivery, is an example of omni-channel shopping behaviour, whereas finding an outlet in a shopping centre, going in and buying there and then, is single channel shopping behaviour. The idea that consumers are far more varied in their engagement with different retail platforms or formats offered by a fashion brand is at the heart of the omni-channel concept. It is not a question of choosing one channel or another but the blending of activities that result in customer engagement with a retail brand, however they prefer to shop (see Figure 10.2).

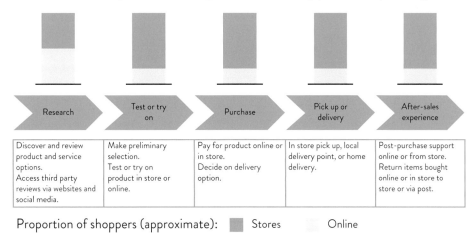

Figure 10.2 *The omni-channel shopping process*

Source: Based on A. T. Kearney, Future of Stores Study, 2013. By permission of Insight @ A. T. Kearney. Available at: https://www.atkearney.com/consumer-goods/article?/a/recasting-the-retail-store-in-today-s-omnichannel-world.

The growth in online fashion sales from around zero in the late 1990s to around 15% currently has resulted in what is often termed a **disruptive change** to the industry. Most organizations do not separate out different retail channels in their sales and profit reporting; therefore it is difficult to know exactly how much online sales contribute to the performance of individual fashion brands. However, in 2015 the well-respected industry commentator Businessoffashion.com suggested that online sales would not grow to more than around 25% of total sales industry-wide. For a traditional fashion retailer, grown via opening stores, this suggests that they cannot expect more than around a quarter of their sales to come via the online route. There are of course highly successful online-only fashion retailers, but recent discussions and events suggest that some of these are considering the opportunity of a physical retail presence as a way to increase awareness and brand engagement. It is difficult to sell profitably online if the price to the consumer is low; the distribution costs associated with single item delivery to a customer's home are relatively high, even though the costs of running a store are high. This is the reason why, at the time of press, Primark still trades without a transactional website. How long this strategy will remain in place is an interesting question, given the intended multi-channel ambitions of Amazon.

The value trade-off for multi-channel retailers and omni-channel shoppers

Consumers will choose to engage with organizations that offer value, as discussed in Chapter 2. Retailing activity occurs in the section of the value chain that is closest to the consumer, and as Porter (1985) suggests, internal value added translates into the ability to generate higher profit margins. Although this relationship between internally generated value and monetary value through profitable sales holds true today in a broad sense, it is important for fashion retailers to avoid the mistake of considering value in the immediate transactional context. As we saw earlier, in the omni-channel context consumer engagement is likely to take place in the form of many different acts that build up into episodes, which in turn, and with sequential behaviour, form a relationship built on various forms of value (Grönroos, 2004). It is also dangerous to assume

that money is the only cost to consumers; indeed, in fashion, what is considered good value is likely to confound the economist. Thus, we expand on the value equation referred to earlier by conceptualizing value in fashion retailing in the era of omni-channel shopping behaviour. This is not an exhaustive **value equation**; however, what is important for a fashion retail strategy is that a fashion brand understands the nature and complexity of what their customers value in the retail context.

More

- *Product choice* including design, trend, style, range, customized and co-created products, associations and endorsements
- *Product quality* including materials, components and manufacture, sustainability aspects, ease of care
- *Product availability* across channels, including sizing, pick-up location, delivery options
- *Enhanced customer service* including sales service, packaging and delivery service, returns service and aftersales advice, customized service
- *Convenience* including store opening and location, online shopping process, returns, payments, proximity to other services, such as eating places
- *Pleasant environment* including both online and physical, design, layout/navigation, atmosphere, visual merchandising, people (staff and customers).

Less

- *Monetary value (price)* including discounts and voucher availability, loyalty schemes, individualized pricing
- *Stress* including lack of enjoyment and frustration
- *Time* including travelling to outlets, and process involved with using outlets
- *Effort* including physical and mental effort in the shopping process
- *Risk* including personal injury, monetary, and psychological risk.

Many fashion stores are realizing that consumers are happy to use retail space for **social and lifestyle engagement** alongside product engagement. This trend will be explored in more detail further on in the chapter; however, one result of it is the growth of the 'fashion café'. These can range from a casual hang-out area serving coffee, to elegant eateries well known in their own right for the dining experience. Fashion-oriented department store Selfridges, for example, has 14 different places where customers can eat and drink. Hospitality outlets are often designed to reflect the strategic positioning of the fashion brand; for example, Shanghai Tang's café in the exclusive heritage shopping development Xintiandi, Shanghai is impeccably and luxuriously styled in keeping with the brand identity (see Figure 10.3 and Case Study 13 Shanghai Tang, in Chapter 13), while the TOMS café areas are laid back and comfortable, blending with the rest of the casual retail identity (see Case Study 14 TOMS, in Chapter 14).

Figure 10.3 *The Shanghai Tang Café, Xintiandi shopping development, Shanghai, Hong Kong. Image credit: Natascha Radclyffe-Thomas. By permission of Shanghai Tang.*

INTERNATIONAL RETAIL STRATEGY

There is a choice of channels, platforms, outlets and locations, which are some of the fundamental areas of decision-making in fashion retail strategy, and it is worth considering retailing choices and decision-making in the context of both national and international strategy. As we saw in Chapter 4, the retail infrastructure was one of a number of aspects that impacted on the level of attractiveness of an overseas market, while an understanding of how different consumers across the world can vary in shopping habits is vital in the fine-tuning of international fashion marketing. Many companies have grown in the past using a particular **retail format** that has evolved as a successful formula in a national market, but which may not be entirely suitable for a modern international market. For example, the '**select store**' is an alternative term for a luxury-orientated multi-brand retailer and is a traditional approach to retailing used in the Far East. However, because of the difficulty in blending products with so many different brand

> **Retail format** A type of retail outlet, defined by physical differences; examples include the department store, the speciality store, the supermarket and the online store.

stories, while not offering the complete ranges, these retailers have become rather dated in their approach, unless they have taken steps to develop a very strong retail brand themselves (see the Shanghai Tang Case Study, Case Study 13).

In Chapter 4 we outlined the range of business models that can be used to access a new geographical market. In addition, there are a number of specialist texts that give a good overview of the different retail options available as a method of entering a new international market so it is not necessary to give an extensive review in this one (see, for example, Alexander and Doherty, 2009). This chapter will therefore focus on a number of variations of retailing that have worked particularly well for international development in the fashion context.

Wholesaling

For many fashion brands that are more involved in producing and/or are not as experienced in retailing activities, the first steps to reaching consumers in non-domestic markets may be through wholesaling activities or simply by taking orders on a domestic online shop and shipping goods overseas. These are simple and low-risk options. However, they may not be very profitable or generate much income. In the case of wholesaling there is the additional risk to a brand of it not being presented in a way that the brand owner would like, but the control to influence this is lost with transfer of ownership. On the other hand, there are many fashion brands that are highly successful in their use of extensive networks of retail customers to reach consumers across the globe and carefully manage their relationships with what are often referred to as retail partners (even though there is no formal, legal or financial partnering) to mutual gain. It is worth noting that although many large retailers have the resources to open their own shops in new international markets this is a costly and risky strategy. Extensive analysis is required to evaluate whether the long-term financial and brand equity gains are likely to outweigh the required resource investment in research, development and operational costs.

Joint ventures

Understanding different retail markets in terms of both consumer preferences and the legal and regulatory framework often requires detailed knowledge and understanding. In particular, the way people like to dress and shop is often deeply ingrained in the cultural identity and psyche of a region. It can therefore be useful to team up with another business organization already operating in that region in order to access expertize and experience that can prevent mistakes and circumvent obstacles. Joint ventures vary enormously in terms of financial and other resource contribution, and control of operations, but in general have proved to be a highly successful formula for international market entry and expansion. Many retail joint ventures take the form of a franchise arrangement whereby control of the brand identity in both product and retailing environment is retained by the franchisor while the day-to-day operations concerning human resources, logistics, customer service and other aspects of retailing are managed by a 'local partner' or franchisee. Running a concession is another form of joint venture, which is a relatively low risk method of retailing, whereby the host store provides not only local expertize but also an established customer market and reputation. When the match-up between brands is good this can create synergy and two-way brand enhancement, but poor match-up or operational difficulties can result in a dilution of brand value. Managing joint ventures is one of the most challenging aspects of an international retail strategy and many fashion brands have found that poorly drawn up contracts between international partners have resulted in a detrimental effect on their brand image and development. In particular, the attraction of fast growth via franchising and/or a licensing agreement that includes retailing has been found to undermine or restrict new directions for fashion brands. Luxury brands Aquascutum, Celine, and Cartier have all suffered from a lack of design control due to licensing arrangements, which has resulted in internal conflict for the organizations.

Organic growth

Organic growth is a straightforward method of internationalizing, whereby the fashion organization locates or increases outlets in non-domestic markets. This strategy is particularly relevant when a company wishes to set up retailing activity in markets that are both geographically and culturally close (Alexander and Doherty, 2009). Organic growth may involve the opening of flagship stores or regular stores and online stores. The difference between this and other methods of entering retail markets is that there is no other organization involved in the retailing activity. The main advantage with organic growth is that control is maintained and for cash-rich companies this is a suitable use of resources. It is also appropriate where markets have been identified that need little change to operations and where a standardized approach to marketing (see Chapter 4) is appropriate.

Flagship stores

The concept of the flagship store is a very important one in terms of international development, and more broadly central to fashion retail strategy (Moore et al., 2010). Flagship stores not only play a key role as distribution outlets for retail brands, but they also make a significant contribution to brand development, communication, and engagement with the consumer.

> **Flagship store** A store that represents a brand as a three-dimensional retail ideal, with strong brand identity in the selling environment and the possibility of additional and exclusive products and services.

In the international context a useful concept is the hub and spoke (visualized in Figure 10.4), which demonstrates the strong base of the flagship store as a central hub supporting the spokes, which point to other alternative aspects of the retail and marketing strategy.

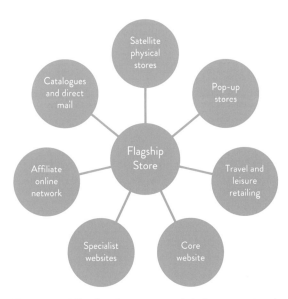

Figure 10.4 *The flagship store as a hub for international retail activity*

In 2013, the CEO of Burberry used the term 'flagship markets' to refer to international markets where flagship stores were central to the retail strategy in that country or area (Ahrendts, 2013). Although a retail strategy is, as suggested earlier, the orchestration of retailing activities through a choice of outlets, in terms of current strategic development the flagship store has taken a central role for many fashion companies and, as such, we devote a section later on in the chapter to an extensive discussion of the characteristics and functions of fashion flagship stores.

Acquisition

In order to take a fast route to expansion, in either a national or international context, a fashion company may find itself in a position to consider buying another one. This may be a way of incorporating a failing company's assets; it may be a way of moving into a new market area, such as a younger market; or it may be a way of acquiring particular retailing expertize such as online retailing. For example, when Edinburgh Woollen Mill (EWM), a knitwear specialist aimed at the mature market, acquired the struggling young fashion retailer Jane Norman, it was to increase EWM's store portfolio rather than to compete in the crowded market for young women's fashion. Whatever the motivation, this is a resource-hungry strategy but could be entirely appropriate for a cash-rich organization wishing to spread risk. 'Acquisition' generally refers to those investments which result in a controlling stake in the acquired company; however, lower profile acquisitions of smaller stakes are common for strategic financial investments and allow the investor some influence in the direction of that organization. As the availability of appropriate companies to acquire is somewhat unpredictable, this is an opportunistic and relatively risky method of international retail market entry; however, it could be a useful way of speeding up retail developments once the market entry has taken place.

Pop-up stores

Although the term 'pop-up stores' is one that is more journalistic than technical or academic, temporary stores have increasingly become an important feature of the retailing landscape and have been used frequently by fashion brands as a way into or as part of international market development.

Picot-Coupey (2014) examined the role of pop-up stores as a means of international market entry, and in contrast to the flagship store, these retail outlets can be more experimental, with much lower investment and therefore less risk. The place of short-term shopping spaces in a retail strategy will also be considered in a more general context later on in the chapter.

FLAGSHIP STORES – CHARACTERISTICS AND FUNCTIONS

Although the term 'flagship' derives from the leading ship in a fleet, the use of the concept in retailing is less prescriptive. In general, a flagship store is one that is representative of 'the best and newest' and therefore an ideal in terms of the way a brand would prefer to see itself. The location of a flagship is important, ensuring that the brand is in contact with high footfall of the target consumer. A flagship store can also be an anchor for a particular retail area or centre development; the footfall it attracts benefiting the centre more generally. With fashion being a so-called high involvement purchase where many alternatives are considered in the shopping process, rubbing shoulders with competing brands is more of an attraction in a location than a disadvantage, with a critical mass of flagships providing a major attraction

as an aspect of a location that creates high footfall. The maintenance of a flagship store in a high-profile location may need to be viewed as an investment that the rest of the retail operational strategy pays for, thus the strategic reinforcement of a brand by flagship stores can be as important as the financial contribution they make (see Figure 10.4).

The flagship store as brand communication

The flagship store is an example of where brand communication and retailing blur boundaries. A flagship store presents a brand, its product offers and its service outputs in a way that brand management idealizes; usually the store is large, enabling the display of a full range of products; the design of the store normally reflects a brand's identity, its heritage and its values; and the flagship space can be used for publicity and brand-engagement events. Nike's flagship stores, for example, not only encourage the trail of products in spacious store layouts but are the base for running clubs and other social activities. One of the first and most impressive fashion retail outlets to gain publicity for built-in social space is the Prada Epicenter in New York, where a section of the store can convert to a music venue by the opening out of the store's display space (see Figure 10.5).

Figure 10.5 *The Prada Epicenter, New York. Image credit: Armin Linke. Reproduced with permission.*

Manlow and Nobbs (2013) highlight the way that luxury flagships in particular are often designed to create an emotional response in consumers, providing pleasure and self-affirmation in the experience of visiting them. The attention paid to the location,

architecture, design, and artistic collaborations contributes to the luxury positioning of brands, while customers determine their own relationship to the brand by experiencing the luxurious branded retail space.

Grand shopping spaces and short-term shopping spaces

Flagship stores enhance the positioning and status of the brand and show the brand as an ideal. They often use prestigious properties and significant or historic buildings as a way to acquire heritage and status. In particular, luxury brand flagships occupy large-scale buildings with plenty of empty space to imply exclusivity and luxury (Moore et al., 2010). 'Star' architects are often commissioned to design the exterior and interior of a flagship store in order to enhance the brand, where design prestige is a powerful enhancement of its image.

> **Third space** Space that is neither home, nor work-space, but is focused on encouraging social interaction and community building, often including retailing actvity.

While these grand shopping spaces are used to communicate a fashion brand's values, short-term shopping spaces are increasingly being used in creative ways to target new or smaller market segments, or to engage more sophisticated customers. Temporary retail spaces are used to quickly target and test new retail concepts and new locations; to launch product lines and excite customers. Innovative technology is often part of the temporary retail spaces concept. For example, the fashion pop-up spaces of Japanese brand Urban Research use virtual changing rooms, while Adidas used interactive displays and video presentations to explain the technology behind the product in its pop-up shop in Seoul (Ng, 2014). Creative visual merchandising techniques often complement the pop-up concept, using theatrical elements reminiscent of set design, to make an emotional appeal.

In temporary retail spaces fashion brands can take the opportunity to focus on local markets. Blending temporary retail with event marketing, and depending on each fashion brand's identity and values, they may incorporate art, cultural exhibitions, book signing, product demonstrations, in-store workshops, short courses, music events, socializing, sports, and food and drinks. For example, Hong Kong retailer Joyce usually uses upscale retail locations; however, the brand has developed a temporary retail space and through collaborations with emerging designers hosts art exhibitions and charity events, placing the pop-up shop into the local community (Ng, 2014). Nike developed a 'permanent pop-up' shop in Helsinki Airport that changes theme every two months, providing a space for travellers to rest, socialize, watch live sports as well as purchase products, appealing to contemporary consumers who are mobile and well-travelled (Rumsey, 2014).

The concept of third space is becoming relevant to retailing, and especially in the fashion and lifestyle sector, where showcasing (with strong online retail support) and the encouragement to engage with a brand is an important part of a strategy. Third space is, according to Oldenburg (2002), space that is neither home, nor work-space but that which is focused on encouraging social interaction and community building. The fashion retailer Kit and Ace, for example, flexed its retail space in the trendy London neighbourhood of Shoreditch to become an art gallery, café and occasional supper club featuring local chefs.

RETAIL INNOVATION, EXPERIMENTATION AND EXPERIENTIAL RETAIL MARKETING

Flagship stores are very often at the forefront of retail innovation, featuring technological applications that enhance the shopping experience and brand engagement in retail space. Retail innovation, however, does not need to be restricted to this particular retail format. There are many retail concepts that are new, innovative, experimental and technology driven but do not conform to the established thinking of the flagship. The term 'concept store' might embrace some of these retail outlets; another might be the 'experiential retailer', and many of the more experimental retail concepts tend to be in the form of temporary pop-up stores.

In-store technology

The use of innovative technology has been associated with fashion stores for many years; for example, the Prada 'Epicenter' flagship store in New York received much press interest for its in-store screens, 360-degree mirrors and its ability to transform into a venue for events, when it opened in 2001 (see Figure 10.5). The cost of many retail technologies has decreased over time, however, leading to an increased and extensive use of technology within retail spaces. Retail brands embrace technology to create a strong and memorable way of shopping and to augment customer service via linkage to an integrated supply. The use of mobile screens in physical retail outlets, for example, allows sales personnel to link to central stock management systems to check availability and offer any alternatives in colours and style that are not in stock in the store. These can then be sent to the shopper's home or ordered for store delivery. The screens can also provide further information about the product, such as its raw materials and how to care for it. Now more than ever retailers with physical outlets need to give a reason to customers to visit their stores, and to provide an excellent experience when they get there. There is some indication that the drift to online shopping is slowing and, according to many commentators, physical stores are more important than ever in the omni-channel world. In addition, some retailers such as lifestyle family fashion brand Boden and young fast-fashion retailer Missguided, who have been trading successfully for years without stores, have moved to a physical retail presence. Retailers need to entertain, excite and even educate customers in fashion stores that become destination attractions, and the embedding of technology in a retail design can assist practitioners to achieve these aims. Burberry's Regent Street store demonstrates how online and physical shopping can be merged, with the whole store having been designed to reflect the company's website (see the Burberry Case Study – Case Study 10, below). There is extensive use of technology in the store, which has helped to attract digitally-informed customers and relate to younger consumers.

Experiential retail marketing

Although there are many exciting new uses of technology in retailing, Pine and Gilmore (1999) provide a useful framework to outline four distinct aspects of experiential marketing and these can be used to analyze store environments in their entirety with reference to the strategic aims of the fashion brand:

Education: digital mirrors (enhancing customers' knowledge about the product and ways of wearing the product); large-scale digital screen (enhancing customers' knowledge on latest products and trends); references to brand heritage, such as exhibits of classic products, images of craftsmanship.

Entertainment: large-scale-screen live fashion shows (entertaining customers, who absorb the performance); sofas and refreshments (encouraging socializing and making shopping a pleasant experience).

Aesthetic: the store environment enhances the visual attraction; customers immerse themselves in the space, enjoying the design of the store as they might an art exhibition.

Escapism: the customer is drawn into a new world with the use of large-scale screens to depict relevant lifestyles, adding to the atmosphere of the store in general; this encourages day-dreaming for aspirational customers and helps to transport the core audience into adopting new trends and styles.

One of the major challenges for retailers is to provide a consistent brand experience across channels. The obvious differences between physical and digital retail space mean that certain elements of the design are not possible or appropriate to replicate; however, similarity in the use of colour themes, typefaces, images, terminology, and layout, all help to build a retailer's multi-channel identity. Although the online shopping process would seem to be more process driven, and physical store shopping driven more by emotional responses to environmental stimuli, Blázquez (2014) suggests that both hedonic and utilitarian aspects of the shopping process should be considered in all channels.

Collaborations

As mentioned in Chapter 6, collaboration with external people and organizations can effectively tap into specific expertize to provide additional competences. As in other areas of a fashion business, collaborations in the creation of the retail environment have become more commonplace. Collaborations between famous architects and fashion brands have resulted in some of the most exciting branded spaces in retailing; the use of a world famous architect helps to elevate a luxury brand in terms of artistic and cultural capital (Moore et al., 2010). In particular the collaboration between architects Frank Gehry and luxury brand Louis Vuitton resulted in the remarkable establishment of the Foundation Louis Vuitton, which in turn inspired window displays to celebrate its opening in September 2014.

Collaborations between designer–fashion brands and department stores have also resulted in exciting retail experiences; for example, Dior collaborated with Harrods to create the Dior Wonderland, which included a café, exhibition, window display and pop-up shop. Through these collaborations retail design practitioners give additional reasons for customers to visit and stay longer in stores. They add interest and fun to the shopping process and provide an opportunity for promotional activity through social and other media. They may also offer something extra to the customer in terms of product, such as a range of limited edition products. The collaborations further educate the consumer about brands, designers and the design and making process.

The strong connection between art and fashion is often communicated in the retail environment, with reference to art made through the window displays, in-store displays and even the blending of fashion retailing and art gallery in common space. In particular, surrealism has often been a source of inspiration for visual merchandising and window display design. For example, in 2013 illustrative artist Kerry Lemon created a surreal scheme for Parisian department store Le Bon Marché.

Art and art collaborations are an effective way used to communicate fashion brand values to sophisticated and elite audiences. Art collaborations can highlight products as high quality and individually made rather than mass-produced. They can add sophistication, status, and thus associate the fashion brand and its products with creativity and originality. For example, Japanese artist Yayoi Kusama collaborated with Louis Vuitton to design both a limited-edition range of products and truly distinctive window displays for stores. The choice of a Japanese artist was a strategic decision to appeal to Louis Vuitton's up-market and sophisticated customers many of whom are from the Far East.

It is likely that retail design will continue to make reference to art at all levels, and in particular art that links with technology in window displays and in-store presentations. Clothing retailer Cos, which is part of the H&M fashion retail group, is a mid-market brand that aligns itself to the art world; on its website a section called 'Studio' links to art exhibitions and artistic projects (cosstores.com, 2016). Artistic collaborative installations can act as an effective eye-catching technique; capturing the attention of customers; encouraging free interpretations and adding a sense of play in the shopping experience. The use of technology in art installations by fashion brands can encourage engagement by young, culturally aware and technology-savvy consumers. Art is an international language appealing to retail tourists, and to internationally well-travelled customers.

CREATIVE DIRECTION IN VISUAL RETAIL

In Chapter 2 we discussed the need and opportunity for fashion companies to use differentiation as a basis for strategy in order to provide unique customer value. As a highly visible aspect of a fashion management strategy, the designed retail environment and the use of visual merchandising is an effective way to achieve differentiation from competitors in a crowded, fragmented market. Rather like the application of design to achieve differentiation in products, the application and use of design principles and design handwriting in visual retail is also very effective in achieving differentiation at brand level. Given the importance of this aspect of retailing for fashion companies, it is not surprising that considerable resources are used to plan and implement visual retail brand strategy. According to Amed (2013), having a strong creative director at the helm of a brand is still important in the digital area, and a fashion business without a clear creative viewpoint is doomed. Winser (2015) concurs and states that the remit of a creative director is about an overall vision that takes into account the marketing and advertising strategy, the retail environments, the format of the catwalk presentations, and the lifestyle that their label is selling.

Creative direction and execution can help to ensure that a structured approach to visual communication is taken and that both human and material resources are used effectively and

> **Design principles** The use of design themes such as repetition, progression and scale to add impact.

> **Design handwriting** The use of colours and design features that by association identify a brand, a designer or a creative director.

responsibly at any market level. A number of retailers use integrated marketing themes that run through media communications and all retail channels. Lifestyle retailer White Stuff uses quirky seasonal themes to add interest to the retail environment and pull together an integrated campaign. Over time, what are sometimes referred to as White Stuff's wrap themes have embraced teapots and coffee cups, squirrels, budgerigars and ice-lollies. An integrated theme provides a cost-effective basis for visual merchandising, online shop presentation and digital marketing communications. The use of the same design theme throughout maximizes the use of expert resources and achieves a coordinated look across all brand touch-points.

THE RETAIL ENVIRONMENT AS A POSITIONING DEVICE

The preceding discussions regarding the designed environment demonstrate how effective retail space can be in sending messages to fashion consumers that reflect the brand identity and values. As we discussed in Chapter 3, strategic positioning is concerned with blending tangible aspects of a brand with emotional aspects to place a brand in a customer's mind in a way that is away from that of competitors but near to what a consumer might consider to be an ideal. The retail environment can play a large part in a positioning strategy as it is visually stimulating and often appeals to our emotive senses. By choosing and blending materials, colours, shapes and motifs that have significance for a target consumer, retail design can be effective in creating a unique appeal (Bailey and Baker, 2014). Figure 10.6 demonstrates the use of various aspects of retail design that help to position three different brands as a value fashion store, a mainstream fashion speciality store and a luxury store.

Sustainability in the retail environment

Positioning a brand on the basis of environmental and/or social responsibility is an increasingly viable, if challenging, option for companies. The retail environment is a place where ethical values can be communicated and reinforced. The preservation of original architectural features, and the use of reclaimed, reused and recycled materials, often result in highly creative and aesthetically interesting retail design, while facilities for repairing and recycling can be incorporated into a store layout. In addition, stores

The value retailer: emphasis on volume display, large price ticketing, banks of checkouts, simple but striking décor.

Image credit: Rosemary Varley. By permission of Primark.

The mass market retailer: emphasis on outfit building, inspirational images, high density visual merchandising in colour themes, lively and fun atmosphere.

Image credit: Valerie Wilson Trower.

The luxury store: emphasis on single product items, with space around them; high quality materials and lighting used in the design.

Image credit: Natascha Radclyffe-Thomas.

Figure 10.6 *Positioning reinforced by the retail environment*

can be designed to be sustainable in terms of energy consumption and waste reduction. US-based retailer Anthropologie is well known for using recycled items and materials creatively in its window and in-store displays, which effectively communicates its values for environmental concern and original design. Outdoor clothing retailers Timberland and Patagonia use reclaimed materials in their store designs and incorporate recycling and repairing facilities into their larger store layouts.

The international dimension to retail positioning

For retailers, the ability to internationalize successfully appears to depend on a retail brand's ability to differentiate. Over time, those retailers that have a more highly differentiated offer in both the product and the retail environment have something that resonates with new customer markets and gives a reason for customers to shop. For example, the three most successful UK-based fashion retailers trading in the US in 2015 were Burberry, Topshop and Boden (Rogers, 2015), all brands with a specific market segment and a differentiated offer, whereas more generalist brands such as Marks & Spencer and Tesco have struggled. However, as well as using differentiation, retailers have sometimes taken the opportunity to adapt their retail environment to international consumer markets to help it be positioned even more attractively. In the Hong Kong Emporio Armani store, for example, a striking red structure doubles up as a catwalk and table in the restaurant; red being a colour that symbolizes luck for Chinese people, and the fluidity of the ribbon-like structure is reminiscent of the shapes of dancing festival dragons (Fuksas, 2004).

 ## CASE STUDY 10 - Burberry, Part One: Brand development and retail

Known today for its digital savviness and innovative marketing practices, Burberry was initially a provider of performance clothing and equipment. Founded in Basingstoke, England, in 1856 by Thomas Burberry, its signature gabardine fabric was introduced in 1879 and the Equestrian Knight logo incorporating the Latin word *prorsum* (forward) was introduced in 1901. Burberry's early patrons included adventurers, polar explorers and the military, who endorsed the functional products fashioned from its water-repellent, tough-wearing fabric. Burberry's Tielocken coat – an overcoat fastened with a buckle belt at the waist and a button at the neck – was patented in 1912 and became popular with the military due to its simple and functional design. This was the precursor to the classic trench coat. The iconic Burberry check – in camel, ivory, red and black – was registered as a trademark and introduced as a lining to the trench coat during the 1920s. The Burberry business is founded on the success of the trench coat and the core image of Burberry, one associated with the English countryside and an upper-class clientele, which was confirmed when Burberry received a Royal Warrant from Queen Elizabeth II in 1955, the same year that the company was taken over by the then retail giant Great Universal Stores (GUS). Burberry opened an overseas outlet in Paris in 1910 but had limited foreign outlets until the GUS takeover, which led to major international expansion through wholesaling, licensing and retailing which vastly increased the brand's presence in the global market.

In 2006, new CEO Angela Ahrendts initiated a repositioning strategy, consolidating brand strengths to deliver a consistent message, in particular to attract the growing global millennial consumer segment. Working with Christopher Bailey as Design Director, the brand identity was established as one combining the quality inherent in its heritage associations and the cool factor of those featured in its marketing campaigns, which featured young British actors and models and the City of London as a backdrop.

Putting its core product – the Burberry trench coat – at the centre of a luxury strategy meant the brand could emphasize its heritage across all brand touch-points. The trench was reimagined in a vast array of new fashionable materials and styles and the communication medium adopted was digital. Burberry launched its latest brand repositioning using digital technologies in innovative ways; positioning Burberry as a young and connected brand and appealing to an online brand community.

As a large-scale business operating inter-nationally, Burberry's retail strategy embraces various store formats, including flagship stores, regular stores, department store concessions and outlet stores. In 2012 a striking new flagship store at 121 Regent Street, London, opened to the acclaim of the global fashion media as well as international shoppers and brand fans. The building had previously been used as a cinema and gallery and these former functions were exploited in the design concept, which preserved the architectural heritage and historic links to film media whilst incorporating new technology to attract younger customers. The original dome in the auditorium space was retained, and a digital screen was installed in a central position where the original cinema screen had been housed, many suggesting the design of the store mimicked the brand's website. The screen, at the time the largest in use in any retail space, was used to show collection videos, showcase brand products and feature associated musical artists.

Materials such as marble and thick carpeting emphasize the luxury experience. Movable walls create flexibility; enabling the creation of more intimate spaces for the elite Burberry customer, and many seating areas are available for customers to relax in, with the 'Thomas' café added in 2015. The fitting room space included toilets for customers, adding to their comfort and encouraging extended visits. The reinvented hero product, the trench coat, was placed at the heart of visual merchandising, with a specific bespoke trench-coat area reflecting the trench-coat customization initiative and archive trench coats featured as instore displays.

Case Author: Natascha Radclyffe-Thomas

Case challenge

Analyze the relationship between Burberry's brand positioning strategy and the retail environment, using information in this case study.

 ## ONLINE RESOURCES

A longer version of this case study, with additional challenges, can be found on our companion website: https://www.macmillanihe.com/companion/Varley_Fashion_Management.

 ## SUMMARY AND CONCLUDING THOUGHTS

Retail strategy is very closely connected to brand strategy; the fashion brand context will drive strategic retail development and certain retail strategies will only be relevant in a particular brand context defined by the size and life-stage of the company, the extent of internationalization, and retail experience. Strategic decisions concerning which retail markets to trade in, the retail formats to use in both existing and new markets, the designing of retailing space to reflect brand values, and the partners to collaborate with in various aspects of the retail strategy to bring in specific competences, are all complex decisions and have long-term implications.

In the fashion industry the branded service environment in terms of how a store looks, feels and makes reference to brand identity, brand heritage and strategic brand values is often a central aspect of retail strategy, and this has had a tendency to be overlooked by more general retail sources, which are more inclined to focus on cost-effective retail operations and strategic growth opportunities in new customer markets. The retail landscape is also the place where a strategy based on differentiation on the basis of service excellence is effectively implemented, and this is explored further in the next chapter.

 ## CHALLENGES AND CONVERSATIONS

1. For an international fashion organization of your choice, provide an overview of their retail strategy in terms of the routes they use to international markets.

2. Choose a luxury fashion flagship store and undertake an analysis of its exterior and interior in order to establish how it reinforces the brand positioning of the fashion company concerned. Continue your analysis of the online retail space of the brand to check for consistencies across retail channels.

3. Using a mass-market fashion company that has a visible retail strategy, consider how brand value is created by its retailing activities. How does this company compare with both domestic and international competitors?

4. Debate the strategic role of physical fashion retail in the era where 24/7 mobile shopping is available to consumers. Is there one?

5. Is the vast expenditure on retail architecture and design ethical? Shouldn't fashion companies save this cost and pass it on to their customers?

REFERENCES AND FURTHER READING

Ahrendts, A. (2013) 'Burberry's CEO on turning an aging British icon into a global luxury brand'. *Harvard Business Review*, January–February. Web, 10 November 2013.

Aiello, G. et al. (2009) 'An international perspective on luxury brand and country-of-origin effect'. *Journal of Brand Management*, 16(5/6), pp. 323–337.

Alexander, N. and Doherty, A.-M. (2009) *International Retailing*. Oxford: Oxford University Press.

Amed, I. (2013) 'Why Creative Directors Matter More Than Ever', The Business of Fashion, 12/06/2013. Available at: http://www.businessoffashion.com/articles/right-brain-left-brain/why-creative-directors-matter-more-than-ever [accessed 13/06/2013].

Bailey, S. and Baker, J. (2014) *Visual Merchandising for Fashion*. London: Bloomsbury.

Baker, M. J. (1998) *Macmillan Dictionary of Marketing and Advertising*, 3rd edn. Basingstoke: Palgrave Macmillan.

Bitner, M. J. (1992) 'Servicescapes: The impact of physical surroundings on customers and employees'. *Journal of Marketing*, 56, pp. 57–71.

Blázquez, M. (2014) 'Fashion shopping in multichannel retail: The role of technology in enhancing the customer experience'. *International Journal of Electronic Commerce*, Summer, 18(4), pp. 97–116.

cosstores.com (2016). Available at: http://www.cosstores.com/gb/Studio/Projects [accessed 9/2/2016].

Dowdy, C. (2008) *One-off: Independent Retail Design*. London: Laurence King.

Fuksas (2004). Available at: http://www.arcspace.com/features/massimiliano-fuksas/emporio-armani/ [accessed 5/2/2016].

Grönroos, C. (2004) 'The relationship marketing process: Communication, interaction, dialogue, value'. *Journal of Business and Industrial Marketing*, 19(2), pp. 99–113.

Kearney, A. T. (2013) 'Recasting the Retail Store in Today's Omnichannel world'. Available at: https://www.atkearney.com/consumer-goods/article?/a/recasting-the-retail-store-in-today-s-omnichannel-world [accessed 11/05/2018].

Kent, T. (2007) 'Creative space: Design and the retail environment'. *International Journal of Retail and Distribution Management*, 35(9), pp. 734–745.

Kent, T. and Brown, R. (eds) (2009) *Flagship Marketing: Concepts and places*. Abingdon: Routledge.

Kotler, P. (1973/1974) 'Atmospherics as a marketing tool'. *Journal of Retailing*, 49(4), pp. 48–64.

Lundqvist, A., Liljander, V., Gummerus, J. and Van Riel, A. (2013) 'The impact of storytelling on the consumer brand experience: The case of a firm-originated story'. *Journal of Brand Management*, 20(4), pp. 283–297.

Manlow, V. and Nobbs, K. (2013) 'Form and function of luxury flagships: An international exploratory study of the meaning of the flagship store for managers and customers'. *Journal of Fashion Marketing and Management: An International Journal*, 17(1), pp. 49–64.

McGoldrick, P. J. (2002) *Retail Marketing*. 2nd edn. Maidenhead: McGraw-Hill.

McIntyre, C., Melewar, T. C. and Dennis, C. (2016) *Multi-Channel Marketing, Branding and Retail Design: New Challenges and Opportunities*. Bingley: Emerald Publishing Group.

Moore, C. M. and Birtwistle, G. (2004) 'The Burberry business model: Creating an international luxury fashion brand'. *International Journal of Retail & Distribution Management*, 32(8), pp. 412–422.

Moore, C. M., Doherty, A. M. and Doyle, S. (2010) 'Flagship stores as a market entry method: Perspectives from luxury fashion retailing'. *European Journal of Marketing*, 44(1/3), pp. 139–161.

Ng, E. (2014) WGSN Retail Trends. Available at: https://www.wgsn.com/en/industries/retail/ [accessed 27/07/2014].

Okonkwo, U. (2007) *Luxury Fashion Branding: Trends, Tactics, Techniques*. New York, NY: Palgrave Macmillan.

Oldenburg, R. (ed.) (2002) *Celebrating the Third Place: Inspiring Stories About the 'Great Good Places' at the Heart of Our Communities*. New York: Marlowe.

Parsons, A. G. (2011) 'Atmosphere in fashion stores: Do you need to change?' *Journal of Fashion Marketing and Management: An International Journal*, 15(4), pp. 428–445.

Phan, M., Thomas, R. and Heine, K. (2011) 'Social media and luxury brand management: The case of Burberry'. *Journal of Global Fashion Marketing*, 2(4), pp. 213–222.

Picot-Coupey, K. (2014) 'The pop-up store as a foreign operation mode (FOM) for retailers'. *International Journal of Retail Distribution Management*, 42(7), pp. 643–670.

Pine, J. and Gilmore, J. (1999) *The Experience Economy*. Boston, MA: Harvard Business School Press.

Porter, M. E. (1985) *Competitive Advantage*. New York: Free Press.

Reddy, M., Terblanche, N., Pitt, L. and Parent, M. (2009) 'How far can luxury brands travel? Avoiding the pitfalls of luxury brand extension'. *Business Horizons*, 52, pp. 187–197.

Rogers, C. (2015) 'The Drapers interview: Johnnie Boden of Boden'. *Drapers*, 7 October 2015.

Rumsey, A. (2014) WGSN Retail Trends. Available at: https://www.wgsn.com/en/industries/retail/ [accessed 06/06/2014].

Sen, S., Block, L. G. and Chandran, S. (2002) 'Window displays and consumer shopping decisions'. *Journal of Retailing and Consumer Services*, September, 9(5), pp. 277–290.

So, J. T., Parsons, A. G. and Yap, S.-F. (2013) 'Corporate branding, emotional attachment and brand loyalty: The case of luxury fashion branding'. *Journal of Fashion Marketing and Management: An International Journal*, 17(4), pp. 403–423.

Varley, R. and Rafiq, M. (2014) *Principles of Retailing*, 2nd edn. Basingstoke: Palgrave Macmillan.

Vecchi, A. (ed.) (2017) *Advanced Fashion Technology and Operations Management*. Advances in Business Information Systems and Analytics. Hershey: ICI Global.

Vecchi, A. and Buckley, C. (eds) (2016) *Handbook of Research on Global Fashion Management and Merchandising*. Advances in Logistics, Operations, and Management Science. Hershey: ICI Global.

Winser, K. (2015) 'Why do luxury brands need creative directors?' *Forbes*, 09/07/2013. Available at: http://www.forbes.com/sites/kimwinser/2013/07/09/why-do-luxury-brands-need-high-profile-creative-directors/ [accessed 20/09/2015].

MANAGING FASHION CUSTOMERS

11

Matteo Montecchi and Francesca Bonetti

INTRODUCTION

According to Paul West, strategy director at Dalziel & Pow, 'today, customers are experiencing new retail ideas, new ways of being served and new ways of engaging with brands – from on-demand, digital services to slower, more indulgent experiences' (Buchanan, 2017). Consequently, in order to be successful and maintain their competitive advantage in an increasingly turbulent sector, fashion companies must invest beyond the realm of the product and provide a wide range of services and memorable experiences tailored to the needs of specific customer groups. The aim is to generate positive and unique emotions which enhance brand favourability and ultimately customer loyalty. As customers are exposed to multiple service encounters, their knowledge of the brand and of its products increases and their attitudes are reshaped. With time, meaningful relationships are formed, which can lead to customers coming back to repeat the purchase and becoming strong advocates of the brand. This is not a simple strategy to implement. It calls for fashion companies to develop a customer-centric culture across the different functions which take part in the process of value creation. Although

most companies have a dedicated customer service department, organizations which develop competitive advantage in this area promote an environment where everyone contributes to offering customers positive and memorable service encounters and experiences.

This chapter will build on Chapter 3 (Fashion Marketing) and Chapter 6 (Fashion Brand Management) to explore the nature, characteristics and functions of the more intangible elements of the fashion market offering. The discussion begins with a review of the concept of service, of its key defining attributes and of how effective customer service management can lead to competitive advantage. The second part of the chapter will focus on the principles of relationship marketing and will explore the supplier/customer relationship stages and the concepts of customer satisfaction and loyalty. The third and final section of the chapter will analyze the principles of Customer Relationship Management (CRM) and discuss how fashion organizations can use CRM systems effectively to manage long-lasting and profitable customer relationships across numerous brand touch-points.

Part 1	Part 2	Part 3
Service: forms and functions	Principles of relationship marketing	Customer Relationship Management

Figure 11.1 *Overview of Chapter 11 structure*

11. 46968 London College of Fashion BA16 catwalk show, June 2016, Nicholls and Clarke building, Shoreditch. Photography by Roger Dean.

SERVICE: FORMS AND FUNCTIONS

Products, services and experiences

Traditionally the term 'product' embodies the tangible elements of a company's value proposition. Marketing scholars generally use the term 'market offering' interchangeably with 'product' to indicate 'a package of tangible and intangible attributes and benefits'

> **Market offering**
> 'A package of tangible and intangible attributes and benefits' (Kotler et al., 2016).

(Kotler et al., 2016). The concept can be further extended to include ideas, people, places and experiences in various combinations. Certain market offerings are primarily tangible (e.g. a bar of chocolate), whilst others are purely intangible entities (e.g. entertainment services). However, most value propositions (including fashion) will fall somewhere in a spectrum of tangible/intangible attributes (Figure 11.2) and will include various combinations of products and services (Baines and Fill, 2014).

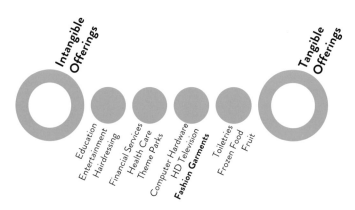

Figure 11.2 *A spectrum of product/service combinations*

Source: Based on Kotler et al. (2016), and Baines, P. and Fill, C. (2014) *Marketing*, 3rd edn. Oxford: Oxford University Press.

Service customization can be used to further differentiate market offerings, but in the long run this approach can lead to price competition and to the service becoming a commodity. For this reason, fashion companies often invest beyond regular products and services to offer bespoke customer experiences. Unlike services, experiences can create 'memorable events' and engage with customers at a more intimate level, thus promoting stronger differentiation of market offerings (Pine and Gilmore, 1998). This approach can lead to fashion companies developing a stronger competitive advantage (Aloysius et al., 2016), as shown in the Rapha Mini Case Study 11.1.

MINI CASE STUDY 11.1 - Customer experience at Rapha

Cycling apparel brand Rapha is the perfect example of the successful combination of the tangible and intangible elements of the fashion value proposition. Rapha has built a strong competitive positioning by establishing meaningful connections with its target customers through a series of initiatives and investments in experience-led stores. According to the founder, Simon Mottram, Rapha's *clubhouses* are more than just stores, but are 'a whole cultural surrounding, mixing content, events, food and drink, all for the person who likes road cycling' (May Johnson, 2013). The company also runs a *Racing Club*, which is designed to foster a 'global community of like-minded, passionate road riders' (Rapha, 2017). Events (the *Rapha Rides*) organized in cities across the world are also aimed at connecting Rapha to its community while at the same time promoting the brand's culture and lifestyle.

Source: Rapha (2017) *Rapha. Company Website*. Available at: https://www.rapha.cc/gb/en/ [accessed 22/10/17]. May Johnson, R. (2013) *Wheels of Fortune: The Rise of Rapha*. Business of Fashion. Available at: https://www.businessoffashion.com/articles/intelligence/wheels-of-fortune [accessed 22/10/17].

Characteristics of service in fashion retailing

Services are complex marketing entities due to their intangible nature. The concept encompasses both the idea of a core value proposition (for example, a fashion public relations agency offering a portfolio of promotional services to fashion retailers) and 'add-ons' to sales (such as additional store services – online customer services offered by fashion retailers to support sales of their products). The American Marketing Association (AMA) definition of service distinguishes between services which *comprise* the product (as an offering in a particular market) and services which *supplement* sales of the product. The AMA's twofold definition of service and of its characteristics is summarized in Table 11.1.

> **Service** A core value proposition together with 'add-ons' to support sales of a product.

Core Element	Services which *comprise* the product (market offering)	Services which *supplement* sales of products
Characteristics	• Intangible (at least to a significant extent); • 'Exchanged directly from producer to user'; • 'Cannot be transported or stored'; • 'Almost instantly perishable'; • 'Often difficult to identify (they come into existence at the same time they are bought and consumed)'; • 'Comprise intangible elements that are inseparable'; • Often involve significant customer participation; • 'They cannot be sold in the sense of ownership transfer'; • 'They have no title'.	• 'Activities performed by sellers and others that accompany the sale of a product and aid in its exchange or its utilization'; • Either pre- or post-sale (generally referred to as customer service); • 'Supplement the product, not comprise it'; • 'If performed during sale, they are intangible parts of the product'.
Example	Fashion PR Agency	Shoe fitting, financing, an 0800 number, 24/7 customer service for online purchases, call-me-back option.

Table 11.1 *Service and its characteristics*

Source: American Marketing Association (no date) *AMA Dictionary*. Services. Available at: http://www.marketing-dictionary.org/Services#cite_note-2 [accessed 10/01/2017]; and Govoni, N. A. P. (2004) *Dictionary of Marketing Communications*. Thousand Oaks, CA: SAGE.

The AMA definition outlined above highlights the fact that intangibility alone is not sufficient to fully understand the nature of service. West, Ford and Ibrahim (2015) identified also heterogeneity, inseparability and perishability as key dimensions or characteristics of services (Figure 11.3). These key characteristics are outlined below.

Intangibility refers to the fact that services cannot be seen, touched or tried on before the purchase. Fashion retailers, for example, can add elements of tangibility to ensure customers recognize the value of the service. This can involve ensuring that customer service staff are dressed appropriately, are trained and knowledgeable about the brand and understand the most effective ways to approach the customer. In-store technology such as portable tablets can also add a further element of tangibility to the service encounter.

Services are *heterogeneous* as they tend to vary each time they are offered, due to different external and internal factors affecting the relationship between the service provider and the receiver. For this reason, fashion companies often implement strict guidelines on how the service should be provided, to ensure consistency. This is particularly crucial in sectors such as luxury retailing as customers will expect an extremely high level of service regardless of the location. Appropriate employee selection is also crucial to ensure consistent delivery of the service provision.

Services as intangible entities cannot be separated from the provider. Fashion companies must understand the importance of the *inseparability* element. Negative service encounters can jeopardize previous marketing efforts, have a negative impact on sales and ultimately affect the brand equity in the long term. Rigorous procedures for dealing with various customers' issues and complaints, scenario planning and constant staff training and motivation (see Chapter 14) are crucial to ensure customers are satisfied each time they encounter the service.

Finally, services are *perishable* and, unlike physical products, cannot be kept or stored. This can cause issues when planning capacity and, in particular, when managing demand peaks and drops in certain periods. Although temporary resources can be brought in relatively easily in the fashion retailing sector, this can increase heterogeneity and the risk of customers being exposed to variable standards of service and inexperienced staff. Technology (such as mobile or self-checkout) can help fashion companies to provide additional and timely services without necessarily increasing the number of people involved.

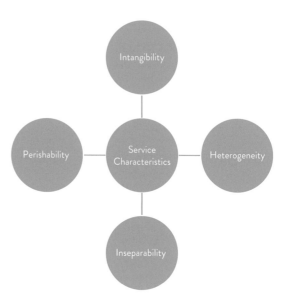

Figure 11.3 *Characteristics of service*

Source: Based on Figure 9.1, p. 293, from West, D. C., Ford, J. and Ibrahim, E. (2015) *Strategic Marketing: Creating Competitive Advantage*, 3rd edn. Oxford: Oxford University Press. By permission of Oxford University Press.

Managing service encounters

Client–supplier relationships, particularly in service industries, can be interpreted as a series of 'episodes or interactions' (Storbacka, Strandvik and Grönroos, 1994; Egan, 2011). In each relationship episode the customer experiences different aspects of the service provision and will be either satisfied or dissatisfied. Storbacka, Strandvik and Grönroos (1994) argue that not all episodes hold the same importance for the client and distinguish between 'routine episodes', which involve 'low level of mental involvement and routine behaviour' (e.g., receiving help to find a product in store), and 'critical episodes', which have a more significant impact on the customer's perception of the service (e.g., dealing with damaged products, late deliveries). The positive or negative evolution of the client–supplier relationship is primarily linked to critical episodes, which in the long run will create (or destroy) a loyal customer base. Each transaction can be considered a relationship episode, which can potentially become critical if the service levels are not met. Missed orders and late deliveries are typical examples of critical events which can lead to the customer being significantly unsatisfied with the service provider unless effective recovery strategies are promptly implemented.

To manage services effectively, fashion companies must understand the nature, frequency and length of service encounters. These are defined as 'a period of time during which

> **Service encounter**
> 'A period of time during which a consumer directly interacts with a service' (Shostack, 1985).

a consumer directly interacts with a service' (Shostack, 1985). Service encounters can involve the company personnel, its physical facilities or other elements such as technological equipment (Bitner, 1990; Baines and Fill, 2014). Service encounters can be classified based on the level and intensity of contact the customers experience, as outlined in Table 11.2.

Contact Level	Explanation
High-contact services	Customers visit the service facility so that they are personally involved throughout the service delivery process (e.g., personal shopping, 'by appointment' services).
Medium-contact services	Customers visit the service facility but do not remain for the duration of the service delivery (e.g., self-service, assisted-service retail, delivery and collecting items for alterations, click-and-collect services).
Low-contact services	Little or no personal contact between customer and service provider. Service is delivered from a remote location, often through electronic means (e.g., customer service support via online chats).

Table 11.2 *Levels of customer contact*

Source: Based on Table 14.2, p. 498, from Baines, P. and Fill, C. (2014) *Marketing*, 3rd edn. Oxford: Oxford University Press. By permission of Oxford University Press.

Technology and customer service management in fashion retailing

Advances in technology have had a considerable impact on the way fashion organizations implement and deliver their customer service strategies. Within the wider retail sector, self-checkout systems or the emergence of the so-called 'omni-channel' business model (Brynjolfsson, Hu and Rahman, 2013; Bell, Gallini and Moreno, 2014), fuelled by consumer 'mixed-mode buying behaviour' (Chaffey and Ellis-Chadwick, 2016), have pushed organizations to re-think the way they provide services and build relationships with increasingly more volatile customers. Piotrowicz and Cuthbertson (2014) provide a comprehensive overview of how technology is reshaping the retail industry, thus significantly affecting the customer experience (Figure 11.4). The themes highlighted have had a significant impact on the way fashion organizations provide customer service and develop effective retail experience offline, online and via mobile channels.

Channel integration and customer service

As we have noted in Chapter 10, customers move freely between offline, online and mobile channels using them interchangeably through the various stages of their purchase, and therefore they expect a consistent level of service and an integrated experience across all the different distribution channels. For example, a customer might visit the physical store to try on a product and check sizing and fitting and then decide to buy the product online – a behaviour generally referred to as 'showrooming' (Rapp et al., 2015). Conversely, customers might visit online stores, compare prices and then visit the physical store to complete the purchase – this practice is known as 'webrooming' (Flavián, Gurrea and Orús, 2016). Regardless of the combination of channels customers decide to use during their purchasing journey, they expect a seamless integration of the different brand-related touch-points and of the customer service elements that connect them. Customers perceive the brand (and not the channels) and expect a holistic experience.

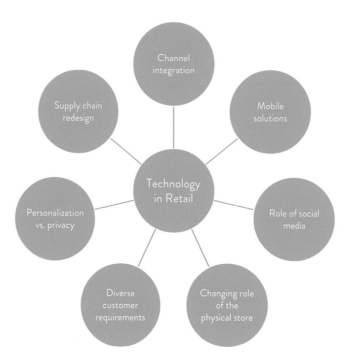

Figure 11.4 *Impact of technology on retail*

Source: Piotrowicz, W. and Cuthbertson, R. 'Introduction to the Special Issue Information Technology in Retail: Toward Omnichannel Retailing', *International Journal of Electronic Commerce*, 18(4), pp. 5–16, 2014, Taylor and Francis, https://doi.org/10.2753/jec1086-4415180400.

Supply chain redesign

The channel integration processes outlined above are not possible without an effective re-design of the fashion supply chain. Different distribution channels are often managed separately and the three main flows, physical, monetary/economic and information, are not connected across the different channel members involved. Nowadays customers demand a mix of online and offline solutions, customized around their perceived needs of convenience, immediacy and access. Click-and-collect services, timed deliveries and 24/7 customer support services are just some of the more obvious manifestations of the impact that the omni-channel business model is having on the fashion supply chain.

Mobile solutions and customer service

Mobile platforms play an increasingly important role in shaping the purchasing experience of fashion customers around the world. The diffusion of smartphones and advances in telecommunication networks offer immense possibilities to create immersive and engaging purchasing experiences. Mobile technology has also had a considerable impact on customer service and relationship building. The mobile device can be

considered a retail platform, as consumers can now purchase products through mobile-optimized sites and retailers' apps. Mobile technology has also had a significant impact on other channels. For example, consumers can now use mobile devices in-store to find additional information about products and services or to complete check-out processes. This creates new challenges of how to balance customer service delivery in-store before, during and after the purchase but it also creates new opportunities for fashion retailers. Recent studies have shown that one-third of customers prefer to find information using their mobile devices in-store rather than asking staff and that in-store mobile users tend to spend between 25% and 50% more than non-users (Swirl, 2014).

Role of social media and customer service

The growth and penetration of mobile technology and the social media revolution have had a powerful effect on the way fashion organizations build a relationship with their customers and deliver customer service. As highlighted by Montecchi and Nobbs (2017), social media can be a powerful tool if effectively integrated with the supply chain and customer service functions within fashion organizations. Customers often use social media as the primary communication channel to get in touch with the brand and to voice concerns and complaints, and they expect a fast, personal and meaningful response (Rubin, 2014).

Diverse customer requirements

It is crucial to remember that different customers will want different levels of interaction with technology. Fashion organizations must identify the characteristics of the segment (or segments) targeted, how customers interact with technology and the best combinations of channels (traditional and digital) to communicate the brand position and deliver the market offering. Ultimately, companies must find a balance between technology-mediated interactions and human interactions. The key is to identify the right combination of technology, staff and store environmental cues to deliver the best possible customer service and experience to a very diverse range of customers.

Personalization vs. privacy in customer service design

Technology enables fashion organizations to collect a vast amount of customer-related data. For example, companies can track customers' purchasing behaviour online by using web-analytics tools (Aloysius et al., 2016) and customers' journeys in-store can be tracked through mobile phones to produce heat-maps, which can be used to optimize the flow of the floor, to boost sales and the overall customer experience. Loyalty programmes and Customer Relationship Management (CRM) systems are also used to collect data to optimize the interaction with the customer, as discussed in the second part of this chapter. Big data companies such as EDITED (https://edited.com) provide fashion companies with intelligence on how to optimize their value proposition and remain competitive.

Changing role of customer service offered in the physical store

The various issues discussed above challenge the role that the physical store will play in the future. Although customers still have the need to touch and feel the product, they might be ready to compromise on this for the 24/7 access and immediacy offered by online channels. Customer service provided by staff will play a key role in re-shaping the future of numerous fashion retail formats. Stores have the opportunity to become brand hubs, where customers can experience various information- and emotion-bearing events designed to reinforce the understanding and perception of brand-related messages.

MINI CASE STUDY 11.2 - Farfetch's store of the future: In-store customer experience with technology

Fashion shopping is about physical retail experience and interaction, and it requires a human element through customer service that a shop assistant or team can provide. This cannot be replaced completely by an online website or a mobile app, according to the founder and chief executive of luxury fashion website Farfetch, José Neves. At the same time, technology and the constant connection with the online world must be part of the experience, to help speed up the service, show stock availability and offer the possibility to order across different channels in-store. Hence, to succeed, fashion retailers need to balance the human touch with technology, within the physical store presence.

At Farfetch, the way-to-go is having physical stores operating and offering customer service through the seamless merging of a unique physical experience with subtle and behind-the-scenes technology. Technological solutions are used to strengthen the service provided in the store, by improving the customer experience. Technology contributes to customer service by helping to deliver a bespoke approach (e.g., by collecting and processing data about each customer across multiple channels in order to address individual requirements in terms of product advice, special deals and an overall personalized message), new and faster ways to order products (e.g., through kiosks, in-store tablets or consumers' smartphones), easier and faster ways to pay (e.g., checkout-free stores, payment through mobile app) and better buy and collect options.

Source: Bearne, S. (2017) *What does the store of the future look like?* The Guardian Online Edition. Available at: https://www.theguardian.com/media-network/2017/jan/25/what-store-future-look-like-retail-technology [accessed: 22/10/2017].

PRINCIPLES OF RELATIONSHIP MARKETING

The relationship marketing concept

Initial conceptualizations of marketing as a discipline and function focused on a transactional approach and were mainly concerned with maximizing single, discrete events between buyers and sellers. Companies concentrated resources on implementing the classic elements of the marketing mix to sell tangible propositions to specific and identifiable target segments at a profit (see Chapter 3).

With markets becoming more competitive and customers becoming more sophisticated in the way they approached selection and purchasing of products and services, marketers soon realized the importance of switching the focus of their efforts from single transactions towards building long-lasting relationships with their customers. This led to the emergence of the relationship marketing approach.

Grönroos defines **relationship marketing** (RM) as a set of practices with the aim to '... *identify* and *establish*, *maintain* and *enhance* and, when necessary, *terminate* relationships with customers and other stakeholders, at a profit so that the objectives of all parties involved are met; and this is done by *mutual exchange and fulfilment of promises*' (Grönroos, 1994). This approach focuses on optimizing buyer–seller relationships, moving away from a classic short-term orientation of the marketing mix approach to a more long-term relationship-building and development approach. Table 11.3 outlines the key differences between traditional transactional marketing (TM) and relationship marketing (RM). RM focuses on the retention of a good quality relationship, using customer service and commitment, to continue contact and development of the relationship over time. This is in contrast to TM, which is orientated towards single sales or short-timescale episodes that are focused on product features meeting immediate customer expectations (Egan, 2011).

The shift in power from producers/ sellers to consumers has also pushed companies to investigate new ways of building long-lasting relationships. Fashion consumers have access to a wider set of knowledge sources (Fernie and Grant, 2015; Verhoef, Kannan and Inman, 2015) and can make sophisticated comparisons between products and brands. Furthermore, today's competitive fashion marketplace is characterized by market offerings that often show limited differentiation. To some extent, this is the result of the continuous growth of competing brands, emergence of online fashion retailers, and value propositions stretching into the same extension categories. If the product or service offered leaves little space for developing sustainable competitive advantage, establishing a relationship with the customer may represent the most effective way of differentiating and standing out from the crowd, building something unique that competitors would find hard to replicate. As discussed in the introduction to this chapter, fashion companies have realized that to be competitive their marketing efforts need to shift from a focus on the products to a focus on the customer and the service offered (Bishop Gagliano and Hathcote, 1994). The RM approach can support organizations in reconfiguring their strategic priorities to achieve this.

RM is based on key *objectives* (such as customer satisfaction, customer loyalty and customer retention), *defining constructs* which characterize the nature of the buyer–seller relationship (for example, trust, commitment, non-opportunistic behaviour, cooperation, communication) and *key instruments* (direct and database marketing and customer relationship management tools) (Lindgreen, 2001). These macro-components of the RM approach are outlined in Figure 11.5 and the key aspects are discussed in the subsequent sections of this chapter.

> **Relationship marketing**
> A practice to '*identify and establish*, *maintain and enhance* and, when necessary, *terminate* relationships with customers' (Grönroos, 1994).

Customer service in relationship marketing

In the RM academic literature, **customer service** is considered a priority for both products and services suppliers, with the aim of establishing a direct and intimate connection with the customer to achieve satisfaction (Innis and La Londe, 1994). Customer service concerns the buyer–seller relationship (Clark, 2000) and aims at building bonds to ensure long-term relationships and mutual advantage for both parties. In order to guarantee high levels of customer service, it is vital to understand customer buying patterns to determine how additional value can be added, to stand out from competitors. It is suggested that the quality of this service is linked to customer satisfaction, which in turn helps strengthen the relationship, results

> **Customer service**
> The building of bonds between buyers and sellers based on the understanding of customer purchasing needs.

in profitability and leads to a stronger competitive advantage (Storbacka et al., 1994). Although this is rather a simplistic model, it represents a valid starting point to understand why customer service is regarded by relationship marketers as a crucial component of the marketing process and why so many resources are invested by practitioners to measure customer service levels.

Figure 11.5 *Breakdown of relationship marketing into objectives, defining constructs and instruments*

Source: Lindgreen, A. 'A framework for studying relationship marketing dyads', *Qualitative Market Research: An International Journal*, 4(2), pp. 75–88, 2001, Emerald Insight, https://doi.org/10.1108/13522750110388572.

In particular, customer service is considered as a key component in the RM process by Christopher, Payne and Ballantyne (1991), who also saw RM as the unifying concept bringing together the elements of marketing and quality. The unification of these elements generates a more effective impact upon the customer. Customer service can be seen at the macro-level as a key component in the effective implementation of RM strategies; at the micro-level, it concerns individual relationships and interactions through the management of an on-going series of meaningful episodes. Fashion companies must understand how to coordinate the meaningful episodes which lead to the purchasing event.

Evolution of customer relationships

Dwyer, Schurr and Oh (1987) identified five general phases through which customer–supplier relationships can evolve (Figure 11.6). This model can be applied to both business-to-consumer and business-to-business relationships and the length of each stage can vary depending on the type and purpose of the relationship.

Figure 11.6 *Evolution of relationships*

Source: Based on Dwyer, F. R., Schurr, P. H. and Oh, S. (1987) 'Developing buyer–seller relationships', *The Journal of Marketing*, pp. 11–27; and Egan, J. (2011) *Relationship Marketing: Exploring Relational Strategies in Marketing*, 4th edn. New York: Financial Times, Prentice Hall.

- *Awareness* – recognition from one party that the other represents a possible exchange party. Interaction has not taken place yet but the parties may seek to enhance each other's attractiveness.

- *Exploration* – period of investigation and testing, where benefits, performances and obligations are considered. Trial purchases may be made. This phase is made of different sub-stages, including attraction, communication and bargaining, development and exercise of power, norm development and expectations development.

- *Expansion* – increasing interdependence. Most transactions take place and trust begins to develop.

- *Commitment* – implicit or explicit agreement to continue the relationship. Both sides have understood roles and goals. Not all relationships reach this phase; some are terminated before, for instance, due to a breach of trust.

- *Dissolution* – this is always an option, and ultimately, will take place unless reinvention is applied to ensure both entities are still gaining from the relationship.

Customer satisfaction

Customer satisfaction can be defined as 'a psychological process of evaluating perceived performance outcomes based on predetermined expectations' (Egan, 2011). Garbarino and Johnson (1999) distinguish between 'overall or cumulative satisfaction', which is a holistic evaluation of the overall purchasing experience with the product/service provider, and 'transaction-specific customer satisfaction', which is an evaluation of performances against set expectations of a specific market offering, and/or a reaction to, and evaluation of, a specific transactional event. It is often argued that customer satisfaction enhances customer retention, which in turn determines customer profitability (Egan, 2011). However, the relationship between these three constructs (satisfaction, retention and profitability) is not always linear and straightforward. According to Storbacka, Strandvik and Grönroos (1994), customer profitability is based on relationship strengths and longevity, which are influenced by satisfaction and quality of service. However, most authors argue that customer satisfaction remains an extremely important relationship driver; it is crucial for any organization to understand the determinants or antecedents of satisfaction and to constantly measure them.

> **Customer satisfaction**
> A psychological state brought about by the evaluation of perceived product and service performance outcomes based on predetermined customer expectations.

Customer retention and loyalty

In a competitive industry like fashion, organizations must recognize the importance of both customer acquisition and customer retention. Customer acquisition is associated with a more traditional or 'offensive marketing approach', which focuses on 'obtaining new customers and increasing customers' purchase frequency' (Storbacka, Strandvik and Grönroos, 1994). Conversely, customer retention is associated with a more 'defensive marketing approach', which aims to reduce customer turnover. By its very nature, RM poses a stronger organizational focus on customer service, relationship development and ultimately customer retention and loyalty.

In order to be successful in difficult economic conditions, for example when a market is saturated and growing slowly, organizations must work towards safeguarding and retaining existing customers while at the same time trying to add new customers to their portfolio. Research has shown that the cost of acquiring a new customer can be significantly higher than the cost of retaining existing customers, particularly in those industries which are characterized by high 'front-end' costs such as retailing (Egan, 2011). Knowing more about customers, their preferences and purchasing behaviours enables companies to create more effective market offerings; for example, loyalty programmes can be used to identify those customers who are more attractive and reward them accordingly.

> **Customer loyalty**
> A behavioural response, expressed over time by a customer with respect to a seller, which is a function of psychological processes that result in commitment to a brand.

Rewards often create switching costs for the customer (costs incurred by the customer if they are not loyal), which help to increase retention rate. It is widely acknowledged that retention has a direct impact on profitability; loyal customers come back, repeat their purchases and this ultimately reinforces the company's market position and competitive advantage.

The concept of customer loyalty is central to RM. Bloemer and de Ruyter (1998) define loyalty in the context of retailing as 'the biased (i.e. non-random) behavioural response (i.e. revisit), expressed over time, by some decision-making unit with respect to one store out of a set of stores, which is a function of psychological (decision making and evaluative) processes resulting in brand commitment'. As a construct, loyalty is often split into two core dimensions: behavioural loyalty and attitudinal loyalty. Behavioural loyalty is based on repeat purchasing. Attitudinal loyalty is demonstrated by costumers' biased preferences and positive attitudes towards a product or brand. Strong brand loyalty is based on both aspects. Lichtlé and Plichon (2008) provide a comprehensive review of the indicators that companies can use to assess both dimensions of loyalty. These are summarized in Tables 11.3a and 11.3b.

Behavioural Measurements	
Proportion of purchases for a given brand, or retention rate	This is based on an arbitrary threshold representing a minimum percentage of purchases of a specific brand or from a specific store, which qualifies the customer as loyal.
Purchase sequence	Based on analyzing the purchase sequence. For example: • No loyalty: ABBACD • Unstable loyalty: AAABBB • Divided loyalty: ABABAB • Perfect loyalty: AAAAAAAA (Brown, 1952, as cited by the authors.)
Repurchase probability	Based on various types of models: stochastic models, probabilistic models and survival analyzes.
Empirical RFM measurements (Recency, Frequency, Monetary value)	Based on the assumptions that the more recent the transaction, the more frequent the customer purchases and the more expensive the purchase, the more loyal the customer will be.

Table 11.3a *Most common measurements of behavioural loyalty*

Source: Based on Lichtlé, M.-C. and Plichon, V., 'Understanding better consumer loyalty', *Recherche et Applications en Marketing (English Edition) (AFM c/o ESCP-EAP)*, 23(4), pp. 121–140, 2008, SAGE Publications.

Attitudinal Measurements		
Customer repurchase intention		Based on the declared intent of the customer to repurchase the brand or to shop at the same store.
Consumer commitment	**Measuring loyalty via its causes**	Based on instrumental form of commitment (economic interests of both partners) and emotional form of commitment (the pleasure from the relationship and sharing common values).
Consumer attachment		Based on the emotional link between the customer and the brand/store. It is a function of dependency and friendship toward the brand/store.
Consumer recommendation	**Measuring loyalty via its consequences**	Based on word-of-mouth.
Positive word-of-mouth or persuasion		Based on customer commitments to convince others to buy the brand (shop from the store) or defend the brand/store (brand advocacy).

Table 11.3b *Most common measurements of attitudinal loyalty*

Source: Based on Lichtlé, M.-C. and Plichon, V., 'Understanding better consumer loyalty', *Recherche et Applications en Marketing (English Edition)* (AFM c/o ESCP-EAP), 23(4), pp. 121–140, 2008, SAGE Publications.

Loyalty can also be measured by using 'composite measurements'. These are a combination of the behavioural and attitudinal measurements discussed above (Lichtlé and Plichon, 2008).

CUSTOMER RELATIONSHIP MANAGEMENT (CRM)

The relationship between fashion producers and sellers and their customers has been the source of interest throughout the history of the industry. In particular, the relationship between haute couture design houses and their prestigious customers has provided intrigue and entertainment. Modern technology, however, has enabled the management of mass customer data, bringing the management of customer relationships to mass-market fashion.

What is Customer Relationship Management (CRM)?

Since the early 1990s consulting firms, academics and information technology vendors have created their

> **Customer Relationship Management** 'The strategic process of selecting customers that a firm can most profitably serve and shaping interactions between a company and these customers' (Kumar and Reinartz, 2012).

own definitions and conceptualizations of **Customer Relationship Management**. These continue to evolve, and a clear consensus has not been reached yet. Kumar and Reinartz (2012) define CRM as 'the strategic process of selecting customers that a firm can most profitably serve and shaping interactions between a company and these customers'. The fundamental goal of CRM is 'to optimize the current and future value of customers for the company' (Kumar and Reinartz, 2012). CRM aims to build long-term competitive advantage by delivering satisfaction and value to the customer. Effective CRM strategies are championed at senior management level and involve multiple organizational functions and departments. CRM can be conceptualized at three levels: strategic, analytical and operational CRM. Effective CRM implementation calls for a fully integrated approach where information and customer-related data are shared across the company and supports strategic decision-making. Technology plays a key role in shaping a CRM strategy. Companies can use technology to strengthen customer relationships by gathering data on purchasing preferences and behaviours and by using analytics tools to generate insights which support the development and promotion of targeted market offerings.

Strategic CRM

CRM as a business strategy and company-wide philosophy has implications for the strategic management of the entire organization. The goal of strategic CRM is to gain deeper understanding of the customer (including their expectations, affiliations and potential switching behaviours). This knowledge is used to shape the relationship and to maximize customer-lifetime value (Venkatesan and Kumar, 2004). A CRM strategy has implications for the entire organization, and requires substantial transformations of business processes, data flows and organizational and technological infrastructures. As outlined by Kumar and Reinartz (2012), a CRM strategy requires four key components as outlined in Figure 11.7.

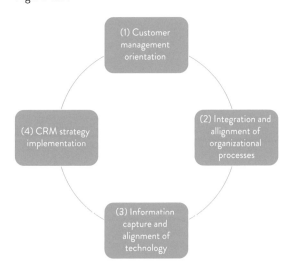

Figure 11.7 *The components of CRM strategy*

Source: Kumar, V. and Reinartz, W., *Customer Relationship Management: Concept, Strategy, and Tools*, 2nd edn, Berlin: Springer, Copyright © 2012.

1. *Customer management orientation*: the set of organizational values and strategic approaches driven by top management believing that the customer is central to the firm's activities and competitive advantage;

2. *Integration and alignment of organizational processes*: systems are created and synchronized to enable the company to implement customer management policies;

3. *Information capture and alignment of technology*: this involves an in-depth analysis of the value offered to target customers;

4. *CRM strategy implementation*: including the relationships with the customer dimension and the management dimension (analytical and operational CRM).

Analytical CRM

Analytical CRM is concerned with collecting, storing, processing, interpreting and using customer-related data and insights. Analysis of customer-related data supports effective management of the relationship lifecycle across multiple stages and customer groups.

A customer database can be built by using both external and internal data sources. Internal data sources include *sales data* (such as purchase history), *marketing data* (such as campaign response, loyalty scheme data, use of consumer-facing technology in-store), *financial data* (e.g., payment history, credit score) and *service data* (for example, contact history). External sources can provide further intelligence – these include geo-demographic and lifestyle databases.

Datasets in corporate databases are structured: data points are stored in a fixed and named field in a record or file and are typically available in relational databases managed by operational units (for example, marketing, sales, finance, customer service and logistics). Unstructured data, also known as 'big data', are datasets that do not fit a pre-defined model. These can take the form of textual (including emails, PowerPoint presentations, PDFs, spreadsheets, and so on) or non-textual files (such as recorded telephone calls, images, videos, digital messages, handwritten notes). Unstructured corporate datasets are increasing massively and their growth and impact are expected to accelerate in the future (Phillips-Wren and Hoskisson, 2015). This creates storage costs and introduces new challenges in relation to privacy, safety of data storage and confidentiality. In particular the EU GDPR (General Data Protection Regulation) introduced in 2016, and legally enforced in May 2018, gives the individual (the data subject) ownership and control of their personal data. From a marketing perspective this means fashion organizations are only allowed to store and use consumers' personal data with the active (opt-in) consent of the consumer.

Analytical CRM has become an essential part of any effective CRM implementation. From the customer's point of view, this approach can deliver timely, customized solutions, thus enhancing satisfaction with the overall customer journey (See Mini Case Study 11.3). From the company's perspective, analytical CRM can increase customer acquisition, retention and ultimately customer loyalty.

MINI CASE STUDY 11.3 - Zara, CRM strategy in the fast-fashion world

International fashion retailers such as Zara understand the advantages of CRM in helping various internal departments to assess the desires of their customers and to develop more relevant market offerings. An effective CRM strategy allows Zara to study the purchasing patterns of their loyal customers to inform the development of new collections. CRM software enables Zara to obtain information about customers' transactions, to understand which products are popular and to identify trends in each of their operating markets. This knowledge supports the decision-making process of various departments. For example, the design team can propose new products which reflect the latest trends in the styles and colours preferred by customers. The buying team is able to choose product styles, sizes and quantities for each market, depending on the local demand, which can be analyzed by using the CRM system.

By implementing an effective CRM strategy, Zara ensure that their brand stays ahead of competitors, and that they present the latest trends to their customers.

Zara's approach demonstrates how analytical CRM systems can be used effectively to enhance product offer and customer services, and to understand customers at a deeper level.

Sources: Based on Expert CRM Software (n.d.) *Zara CRM Case Study*. Available at: http://crmsystems. expertmarket.co.uk/zara-crm-case-study [accessed: 15/01/2017].

Customer value metrics

Analytical CRM allows companies to measure and understand the value of the relationship with customers. This approach helps companies to understand how much prospects or future customer groups could be worth and introduces the notion that not all customers are the same. Some customers have higher potential for the future of the business. Consequently, marketing resources can be allocated differently to individual customers based on their future economic value. Understanding the value that each customer could generate is paramount. To assess this, organizations should constantly monitor several metrics, including:

- *Recency, Frequency and Monetary Value (RFM)* – Recency measures how long it has been since a customer last placed an order with the company / purchased a product. Frequency refers to how often a customer places an order/purchases a product within a defined period. Monetary value is the amount that a customer spends on an average transaction. By combining these three indicators, companies can identify which customers are more likely to respond to marketing campaigns and product offerings. Customers with the highest combined RFM score are more likely to engage.

- *Past Customer Value (PCV)* – The value of a customer is determined based on the total profit contribution of that customer in the past. This modelling technique assumes that future levels of profitability of a specific customer are determined by past performances.

- *Lifetime Value Metrics (LTV)* – The aim is to evaluate the long-term economic value of a customer to the firm. It consists of a multi-period evaluation of a customer's value to the firm at net present value. Operationally, there are numerous ways of calculating LTV. Input factors in the calculation of LTV depend on the nature of the product, data availability and statistical capabilities, and the industry and company context.

- *Customer Equity (CE)* – This refers to the sum of the lifetime value of all the customers of a firm. Conceptually this shows how much a firm is worth at a particular point in time as a result of its customer management efforts.

In addition to these metrics, firms employ different customer selection strategies to identify the right customers to target and to optimally allocate available marketing resources. Finding the right targets for marketing resource allocation is key to a successful CRM strategy. Popular customer selection techniques include: profiling, binary decision trees, and logistic regression. For more detailed discussion of these techniques, see: Kumar and Reinartz (2012, pp. 126).

Data mining

'Data mining' refers to a set of tools and techniques used to interrogate large databases to generate new insights. Data mining gives businesses the ability to make knowledge-driven business decisions, predicting future trends, thus supporting marketing, sales and customer service functions (Finlay, 2014). Data mining can assist in selecting the right target customers and in developing strategies to reach them; for example, as a result of data analysis Marks & Spencer found that more mature customers tend to shop early in the day to avoid crowds (Buttle and Maklan, 2015). A data mining process involves five stages: defining the business objectives, getting the raw data, identifying relevant variables, gaining customer insights, and acting on and monitoring performances. The stages of the data mining process and the key activities involved in each stage are represented in Figure 11.8.

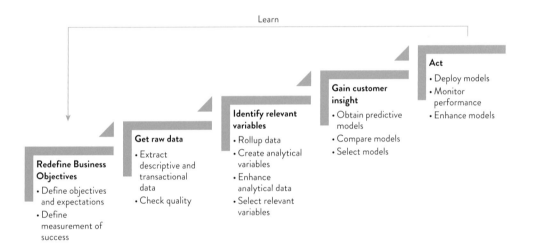

Figure 11.8 *Overview of the data-mining process*

Source: Kumar, V. and Reinartz, W., *Customer Relationship Management: Concept, Strategy, and Tools*, 2nd edn, Berlin: Springer, Copyright © 2012.

Operational CRM

'Operational CRM' refers to services that allow a company to take care of their customers, generating efficiency and operational cost savings. It enables the automation and integration of customer-facing business processes and functions including marketing, sales management and customer service (Buttle and Maklan, 2015). Contact/call centres, websites and data aggregation systems are just a few examples of the operational CRM infrastructure. The major applications of operational CRM can be grouped in the three macro-categories: marketing automation, sales force automation and service automation.

Marketing automation

Marketing automation involves applying technology to marketing processes to support the achievement of marketing-related objectives. It can deliver several benefits, including enhanced marketing efficiency, greater marketing productivity, enhanced responsiveness, better customer experience and higher levels of customer engagement.

Marketing automation includes:

● *Campaign Management*. A marketing campaign is a series of interconnected promotional efforts usually undertaken within a defined timeframe. Campaign management systems allow companies to use customer-related data to select customers or prospects and to develop customized communications and offers that vary at every stage of the customer lifecycle. Campaign management automates the process involved in planning, implementing and measuring communication programmes.

- *Event-based (or trigger) marketing.* This approach involves sending personalized messages and offers to customers at particular points in time. An event such as the customer's birthday, a public holiday or a call to a contact centre triggers the communication or offer.

- *Marketing optimization.* Marketing optimization tools allow companies to set goals (e.g., sales or overall profit margin maximization) and specify all of the constraints of the campaign strategy (e.g., budget, customer contact policy, channels available, etc.). The software then determines which customers should be targeted with what offer and through which channels to ensure the campaign objectives are met.

Real-time marketing automation enables companies to create personalized offers to customers as they interact through different touch-points (e.g., website or consumer-facing technology in retail outlets). Customers' online and offline behaviours generate a vast amount of data that fashion companies can use to predict which market offerings are more likely to succeed, and to adapt their promotional efforts accordingly. For example, tracking and analyzing online visits allows fashion retailers such as Net-a-Porter to continually adapt their website, the display of products, recommendations and offers to create personalized purchasing journeys.

Sales force automation

Sales force automation was considered the original form of operational CRM. It involves the application of technology to support sales management and sales people in the achievement of their objectives. These systems aim to improve and standardize the selling process and are designed to help companies to collect, store, interrogate and analyze customer-related data for sales purposes. SFA software tools can be configured to monitor the different stages of the selling process such as lead generation, needs identification, proposal generation, proposal presentation, handling objections and closing the sale.

Service automation

Service automation helps companies to manage the various customer-service provisions offered through call/contact centres, in-store or online. It enables companies to coordinate customer-related communications across multiple channels.

Tools used in service automation across multiple channels include in-store diagnostic systems; call routing software tools to direct inbound calls to the relevant customer service agent; social media complaints management systems and procedures; live online support through e-chats; and automated self-service channels.

Case Study 11 – Burberry, Part Two: Holistic customer management

As mentioned in Burberry Part One, focusing on targeting millennial customers implied some major changes in marketing strategy with innovative digital technologies being central to the Burberry brand repositioning. Burberry's widely reported increase in digital marketing expenditure went from almost nothing before 2008 to 60% of its marketing budget in 2011 (Baker, 2011). The Burberry website featured emotive brand content, brand history, fashion films, music and heritage brand stories and acted as a way of immersing customers in the brand universe. Burberry has continued its use of young British brand ambassadors, working with British musicians through its Burberry Acoustic platform, featuring young celebrity models Cara Delevingne and Romeo Beckham and actor Emma Watson, whilst maintaining a connection with the young at heart customer by including Kate Moss and Sienna Miller in campaigns. The impact of the Burberry online experience has been extended across all platforms with use of digital technologies in store as well as having technologically enhanced runway shows which are tweeted and live streamed through international social media sites such as Vine, Snapchat and Wechat.

Continuing the application of technology into their customer relationship management strategy Burberry has implemented what they define as a 'single global view' of their customers, investing in customer data and insight in order to get to know, recognize and serve customers better. This allows the company to deliver 'more personalized service and targeted and responsive marketing behaviour' (Chief Creative Officer Christopher Bailey, in Millington, 2015). The focus on customers' centrality in all the firm's acitivities involves Burberry asking their customers to share their purchasing history, shopping preferences and social media profiles online, as part of a strategy called 'Customer 360 programme' (Mitchell-Keller, 2014), in exchange for relevance of offer and a better in-store experience. Sales assistants at any Burberry store can use digital devices to provide personalized recommendations thanks to predictive analytics, such as recommending a clutch bag that will go with a dress previously purchased. The 360 programme also allows the company to send one-to-one personalized communications to customers. This contributed to make customers 50% more likely to return and purchase from Burberry, leading to growth in revenue.

Sources:

Baker, R. (2011) 'Burberry dedicates 60% of marketing spend to digital'. *Marketing Week.* Available at: https://www.marketingweek.com/2011/09/01/burberry-dedicates-60-of-marketing-spend-to-digital/ [accessed 04/07/2018].

Millington, A. (2015) *Burberry looks to a 'fundamentally different' way of using data across its business.* Available at: https://www.marketingweek.com/2015/05/20/burberry-looks-to-build-customer-data-into-the-fabric-of-its-business/ [accessed 24/03/2017].

Mitchell-Keller, L. (2014) Data Helps Burberry Engage Customers Wherever They Are. Available at: http://www.digitalistmag.com/industries/retail/2014/02/14/data-helps-burberry-engage-customers-wherever-01244657 [accessed 24/03/2017].

Case Authors: Matteo Montecchi, Francesca Bonetti and Natascha Radclyffe-Thomas

Case Challenge

The case shows how Burberry embraced technology to augment its appeal to the younger Millennial consumer. To what extent is this a sustainable differentiating factor in terms of enhanced relationships with customers?

ONLINE RESOURCES

A longer version of this case study, with additional challenges, can be found on our companion website: https://www.macmillanihe.com/companion/Varley_Fashion_Management.

SUMMARY AND CONCLUDING THOUGHTS

This chapter has identified the role and importance of the service element in developing value propositions. Services can take the form of core market offerings (services which comprise the actual product) and of 'add-ons' to sales (services which supplement sales – customer services provisions). Core characteristics of service include intangibility, heterogeneity, inseparability and perishability, and fashion organizations must understand the nature, frequency and length of service encounters to develop effective policies to manage service provision across multiple touch-points. Technological advances in fashion distribution and retailing, with the emergence of the omni-channel business model, have had a significant impact on the way fashion organizations implement and deliver customer service strategies. The second part of the chapter outlined the evolution from a transaction-based approach toward a relationship-based approach in marketing. Within this context, customer service plays a key role in the process of developing long-lasting customer relationships. Organizations must understand the link between quality of service, customer satisfaction, loyalty (behavioural and attitudinal) and profitability in order to develop a more sustainable competitive advantage. Customer Relationship Management (CRM) includes the set of procedures, policies and tools which organizations can implement to achieve relationship marketing goals. CRM can be conceptualized at three levels: strategic, analytical and operational. The Zara and Burberry case studies show how elements of an effective CRM strategy enabled fashion companies to develop advanced knowledge of their customers, create more targeted market offerings, and ultimately to increase their competitive advantage.

 ## CHALLENGES AND CONVERSATIONS

1. What are the key dimensions or characteristics of services?

2. Discuss examples of how technology is having an impact on the way fashion companies offer services.

3. Outline the key differences between the transactional marketing (TM) and the relationship marketing (RM) approach.

4. What strategies can fashion companies implement to increase behavioural and attitudinal loyalty?

5. Define Customer Relationship Management (CRM) and outline the components of a CRM strategy.

6. Discuss how fashion companies can use analytical CRM.

7. What are three key applications of operational CRM?

 ## REFERENCES AND FURTHER READING

Aloysius, J. A., Hoehle, H., Goodarzi, S. and Venkatesh, V. (2016) 'Big data initiatives in retail environments: Linking service process perceptions to shopping outcomes'. *Annals of Operations Research*, pp. 1–27.

American Marketing Association (no date) 'Services', in *AMA Dictionary*. Available at: http://www.marketing-dictionary.org/Services#cite_note-2) [accessed 10/01/2017].

Baines, P. and Fill, C. (2014) *Marketing*, 3rd edn. Oxford, United Kingdom: Oxford University Press.

Bearne, S. (2017) 'What does the store of the future look like?' *The Guardian* Online Edition. Available at: https://www.theguardian.com/media-network/2017/jan/25/what-store-future-look-like-retail-technology [accessed 22/10/2017].

Bell, D. R., Gallini, S. and Moreno, A. (2014) 'How to win in an omnichannel world'. *MIT Sloan Management Review*, 56(1), pp. 45–53.

Bishop Gagliano, K. and Hathcote, J. (1994) 'Customer expectations and perceptions of service quality in retail apparel specialty stores'. *Journal of Services Marketing*, 8(1), pp. 60–69.

Bitner, M. J. (1990) 'Evaluating service encounters: The effects of physical surroundings and employee responses'. *Journal of Marketing*, 54(2), pp. 69–82.

Bloemer, J. and de Ruyter, K. (1998) 'On the relationship between store image, store satisfaction and store loyalty'. *European Journal of Marketing*, 32(5/6), pp. 397–513.

Brynjolfsson, E., Hu, Y. J. and Rahman, M. S. (2013) 'Competing in the age of omnichannel retailing'. *MIT Sloan Management Review*, 54(4), pp. 23–29.

Buchanan, V. (2017) *The Future of Service – Part 1.* Available at: https://www-lsnglobal-com.arts.idm.oclc.org/markets/article/20906/the-future-of-service-part-1 [accessed 10/04/2017].

Buttle, F. and Maklan, S. (2015) *Customer Relationship Management: Concepts and Technologies.* London and New York: Routledge.

Chaffey, D. and Ellis-Chadwick, F. (2016) *Digital Marketing*, 6th edn. Harlow: Pearson Education.

Christopher, M., Payne, A. and Ballantyne, D. (1991) *Relationship Marketing.* London: Butterworth-Heinemann.

Clark, M. (2000) 'Customer service, people and processes', in Cranfield School of Management (ed.) *Marketing Management: A Relationship Marketing Perspective.* Macmillan Business. Basingstoke: Macmillan.

Dwyer, F. R., Schurr, P. H. and Oh, S. (1987) 'Developing buyer–seller relationships'. *The Journal of Marketing*, pp. 11–27.

Egan, J. (2011) *Relationship Marketing. Exploring relational strategies in marketing.* Harlow: Pearson Education.

Expert CRM Software (n.d.) *Zara CRM Case Study.* Available at: http://crmsystems.expertmarket.co.uk/zara-crm-case-study [accessed 15/01/2017].

Fernie, J. and Grant, D. B. (2015) *Fashion Logistics: Insights into the Fashion Retail Supply Chain.* London and Philadelphia, PA: Kogan Page Publishers.

Finlay, S. (2014) *Predictive Analytics, Data Mining and Big Data: Myths, Misconceptions and Methods.* London: Palgrave Macmillan.

Flavián, C., Gurrea, R. and Orús, C. (2016) 'Choice confidence in the webrooming purchase process: The impact of online positive reviews and the motivation to touch'. *Journal of Consumer Behaviour*, 15(5), pp. 459–476.

Garbarino, E. and Johnson, M. S. (1999) 'The different roles of satisfaction, trust, and commitment in customer relationships'. *Journal of Marketing*, 63(2), pp. 70–87.

Grönroos, C. (1994) 'From marketing mix to relationship marketing: Towards a paradigm shift in marketing'. *Management Decision*, 32(2), pp. 4–20.

Innis, D. E. and La Londe, B. J. (1994) 'Customer service: The key to customer satisfaction, customer loyalty, and market share'. *Journal of Business Logistics*, 15(1), p. 1.

Kotler, P., Keller, K. L., Brady, M., Goodman, M. and Hansen, T. (2016) *Marketing Management*, 3rd edn. Harlow: Pearson Education.

Kumar, V. and Reinartz, W. (2012) *Customer Relationship Management: Concept, Strategy, and Tools*, 2nd edn. Berlin: Springer.

Lichtlé, M.-C. and Plichon, V. (2008) 'Understanding better consumer loyalty'. *Recherche et Applications en Marketing (English Edition) (AFM c/o ESCP-EAP)*, 23(4), pp. 121–140.

Lindgreen, A. (2001) 'A framework for studying relationship marketing dyads'. *Qualitative Market Research: An International Journal*, 4(2), pp. 75–88.

May Johnson, R. (2013) 'Wheels of Fortune: The Rise of Rapha'. *Business of Fashion*. Available at: https://www.businessoffashion.com/articles/intelligence/wheels-of-fortune [accessed 22/10/17].

Millington, A. (2015) *Burberry looks to a 'fundamentally different' way of using data across its business*. Available at: https://www.marketingweek.com/2015/05/20/burberry-looks-to-build-customer-data-into-the-fabric-of-its-business/ [accessed 24/03/2017].

Mitchell-Keller, L. (2014) *Data Helps Burberry Engage Customers Wherever They Are* Available at: http://www.digitalistmag.com/industries/retail/2014/02/14/data-helps-burberry-engage-customers-wherever-01244657 [accessed 24/03/2017].

Montecchi, M. and Nobbs, K. (2017) *Let It Go: Consumer Empowerment and User-Generated Content – An Exploratory Study of Contemporary Fashion Marketing Practices in the Digital Age*, in Vecchi, A. (ed.) *Advanced Fashion Technology and Operations Management*. Hershey, PA: IGI Global.

Phillips-Wren, G. and Hoskisson, A. (2015) 'An analytical journey towards big data'. *Journal of Decision Systems*, 24(1), pp. 87–102.

Pine, B. J. and Gilmore, J. H. (1998) 'Welcome to the experience economy'. *Harvard Business Review*, 76, pp. 97–105.

Piotrowicz, W. and Cuthbertson, R. (2014) 'Introduction to the Special Issue Information Technology in Retail: Toward Omnichannel Retailing'. *International Journal of Electronic Commerce*, 18(4), pp. 5–16.

Rapha (2017) *Rapha*. Company Website. Available at: https://www.rapha.cc/gb/en/ [accessed 22/10/17].

Rapp, A., Baker, T. L., Bachrach, D. G., Ogilvie, J. and Beitelspacher, L. S. (2015) 'Perceived customer showrooming behavior and the effect on retail salesperson self-efficacy and performance'. *Journal of Retailing*, 91(2), pp. 358–369.

Rubin, E. (2014) Social media: 10 statistics to know now. Available at: www.wgsn.com [accessed 15/04/2015].

Shostack, G. L. (1985) 'Planning the service encounter', in Czepiel, J., Solomon, M. and Surprenant, C. (eds) *The Service Encounter*. Lexington, MA: Lexington Books, pp. 243–254.

Storbacka, K., Strandvik, T. and Grönroos, C. (1994) 'Managing customer relationships for profits: The dynamics of relationship quality'. *International Journal of Service Industry Management*, 5(5), pp. 21–38.

Swirl (2014) *What's Up With Beacons?* Available at: http://sweetiq.com/ whats-up-with-beacons.html [accessed 20/04/2015].

Venkatesan, R. and Kumar, V. (2004) 'A customer lifetime value framework for customer selection and resource allocation strategy'. *Journal of Marketing*, 68(4), pp. 106–125.

Verhoef, P. C., Kannan, P. and Inman, J. J. (2015) 'From multi-channel retailing to omni-channel retailing: Introduction to the special issue on multi-channel retailing'. *Journal of Retailing*, 91(2), pp. 174–181.

West, D. C., Ford, J. and Ibrahim, E. (2015) *Strategic Marketing: Creating Competitive Advantage*, 3rd edn. Oxford: Oxford University Press.

35320 moss dress, Tara Baoth Mooney, MA Fashion and the Environment 2011, London College of Fashion, photography Sean Michael. Image courtesy of Centre for Sustainable Fashion.[12]

MANAGING FASHION RESPONSIBLY

12

Natascha Radclyffe-Thomas and Ana Roncha

⚬ INTRODUCTION

Readers will be aware of recent debates around the social and environmental impact of making and selling fashion. Fashion is an industry with a glamorous image, one that often masks the social and environmental impacts associated with the production of fashion garments. The mass industrialization of fashion production has led to supply chains that stretch across the world, and the development of low-priced fast fashion means consumption of fashion products has increased exponentially. The raw materials and processes required for fashion garment production have massive resource implications and the environmental impact attributed to textile processing has been widely reported. Furthermore, the intensive production methods required to meet cost targets have sometimes led to extremely poor conditions for those working in the factories making fashion. Managing all the processes from textile to garment production and shipping is a huge strategic issue for fashion companies.

This chapter puts a spotlight on the environmental and social responsibilities that the fashion industry is morally bound to engage with and how these relate to managerial and financial strategy. It starts with a review of the structural changes that have impacted production and distribution in the global fashion industry. The concept of business ethics and a detailed review of the area of Corporate Social Responsibility is given as well as examples of strategies to mitigate the negative impacts through management and marketing. The chapter introduces concepts including ethical product lifecycle management, social enterprise business models, cause marketing and radical transparency. The case studies of Kering (in Chapter 2), H&M (in Chapter 9), M&S (in Chapter 12) and TOMS (in Chapter 14) help to demonstrate how fashion companies at different market levels are rising to the challenges of sustainability.

👕 LEARNING OBJECTIVES

After studying this chapter, you should be able to understand:

- The growing concern about the environmental and social impact of the global fashion industry and the relation to business management.

- The dynamic meanings of business ethics and the scope of corporate social responsibility, and the potential benefits associated with their implementation.

- The concept of the three pillars of sustainability and how compliance with these is currently practised in business and management in the fashion industry.

- The meaning of a sustainable fashion brand and its relationship with the socially conscious consumer.

- Relevant brand management and marketing strategies for ethical business and sustainable fashion.

---

12. 35320 moss dress. Tara Baoth Mooney, MA Fashion and the Environment 2011, London College of Fashion, photography Sean Michael. Image courtesy of Centre for Sustainable Fashion.

THE SCOPE OF SOCIAL RESPONSIBILITY IN THE FASHION INDUSTRY

It was in the 1960s that the ready-to-wear fashion industry really took off in Europe and North America, with the birth of the fashion boutique catering for a younger customer and heralding a democratization of the fashion system. The development of lower-cost manufacturing hubs in Asia led to a large volume of offshoring of fashion production as domestic factories could no longer compete on pricing, since when the fashion industry has become global.

The rate of fashion production and consumption has increased exponentially with many designers showing multiple shows per year and stores receiving weekly deliveries of new stock fuelled by the unfettered access to fashion intelligence that digital technologies have enabled through media such as blogs, Instagram and live streaming of fashion shows. Mass-market fashion brands, notably Zara, have built successful business models on translating high fashion runway looks into constantly updated stock of affordable pieces available in-store almost immediately: hence the term 'fast fashion'.

These factors have combined to increase individuals' consumption of fashion, and pressured fashion businesses to pursue low-cost sourcing, sometimes at the expense of social and ethical considerations and environmental impact (see Box 12.1).

> **Fast fashion** Flexible, responsive and low-cost fashion production based on immediate and detailed sales analysis, rapid trend analysis and the postponement of commitment to styles until the last moment.

Box 12.1 - The lifecycle of a garment

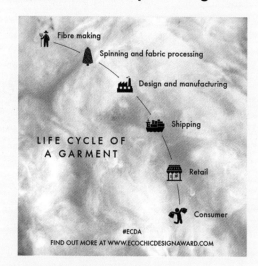

Reproduced by permission of Redress.

environmental and economic impacts of garments

- Garment manufacturing: in cutting, 15–20% of textiles are generally wasted, sewing creates CO_2 emissions, finishing uses water and chemicals, and creates CO_2 emissions

- Transportation (ships, trucks, aircraft, storage): produces CO_2 emissions

- Retail (packaging, point of sales, merchandising): all create plastic and paper waste

- Consumer use (washing, drying, ironing): the largest environmental impact of a garment

- Disposal (end of life): very often in landfill.

Redress, an environmental NGO working to reduce waste in the fashion industry, produces a series of resources for fashion students and designers to inform and inspire imaginative use and re-use of textiles. Each year they hold an international sustainable-design fashion competition, the Redress Design Awards.

The Fashion Lifecycle of a Garment and the points of waste are illustrated above and in a short video available from Redress, available at:

https://www.youtube.com/watch?v=smOXyyqOq7E&feature=share&list=TL_2dVxvoqBRg.

- Textile production (fibre cultivation, farming and harvesting, spinning, weaving, bleaching, dyeing): requires a lot of energy, produces CO_2 emissions, uses water (a diminishing natural resource), uses pesticides and chemicals and produces toxic waste

- Design: sketching, pattern making, sampling and sourcing all influence the waste outcome. Designers influence an estimated 80% of

AN OVERVIEW OF THE SOCIAL RESPONSIBILITY CHALLENGES FACED BY THE FASHION INDUSTRY

For all the glitz and gloss of the runway, fashion is an industry that has attracted bad publicity for poor working conditions and environmental damage. Ever since the Industrial Revolution reorganized labour and machines into factories and production lines, poor working conditions have too often been associated with the textile and fashion industries. The history of fashion is peppered with examples of exploitation, health and safety abuse and industrial accidents. Some of the larger incidents have drawn international attention and led to calls for improvements in workers' conditions; for example, the deaths of 146 workers in a fire at New York's Triangle Shirtwaist Factory in 1911 focused attention on the prevailing sweatshop conditions and the inadequacy of fire inspections. Regrettably, over a hundred years later avoidable large-scale industrial accidents are still occurring, with the Tazreen Fashions factory fire in 2012 in Dhaka, Bangladesh, claiming at least 112 fatalities, and the following year inadequate structural building standards leading to the collapse of the Rana Plaza Factory, also in Dhaka, which resulted in 1134 deaths. A widely-acclaimed documentary *The True Cost* was released in 2015 highlighting the systemic damage resulting from the fast-fashion system, leading to calls for more transparent supply chains and commitments from fashion businesses to hold themselves to higher ethical standards.

The term 'fashion' is synonymous with change and a central strand of fashion marketing is generating consumer needs and wants that drive repeated and continual consumption of fashion products. For most of the twentieth century the fashion industry operated under business models that prioritized profit margins and return on investment without much regard to social and environmental impacts. Fashion buyers were tasked with securing the best-value production, and consumers were generally ignorant of the conditions under which their clothes were made. In a so-called *race to the bottom*, developing economies competed for fashion production contracts by offering lower costs to fashion businesses, which in turn could pass these savings on to consumers in the form of low-priced fashion garments. The extended fashion supply chain is complex and thus hard to monitor and is subject to abuses such as lack of health and safety standards, unreasonable working hours and conditions and the use of child labour (ILO, 2012). Whilst no fashion business would publicly condone such practices, many multinational fashion and apparel companies have been subject to exposés over the years which have revealed that despite claims to the contrary, unethical social and environmental practices are still in existence across the fashion supply chain. More recently, particularly in response to several major industrial accidents, a growing consumer segment is becoming dissatisfied with the built-in obsolescence and disposability of fast fashion (The Future Laboratory, 2016). Fashion businesses are becoming aware of how their Corporate Social Responsibility strategy can translate into competitive business advantage, and the business case for sustainability is becoming apparent.

The Environmental Impact of 'Fast Fashion'		
The number of garments produced annually		
Doubled from 2000 to 2014	Exceeded **100 billion** for the first time in 2014	Represents **14** garments for every person on earth
2015–2025 projected increase in clothing industry's environmental impact		
CO_2 emissions	+ 77%	
Water use	+ 20%	
Land use	+ 7%	

Table 12.1 *The environmental impact of fast fashion*

Source: Based on 'Mapping the benefits of a circular economy' (McKinsey, 2017).

THE ETHICAL SUPPLY CHAIN: CIRCULAR ECONOMIES AND THE CLOSED-LOOP CONCEPT

The textiles and fashion industries have major social and environmental challenges exacerbated by the fact that most industrial production has been linear, whereby resources are sourced and used to create products which are sold to consumers as the end point of a business transaction. Concerns about the high degree of water consumption and textile waste involved in the production of fashion and the impact of waste disposal have made the issue of **product lifecycle management** a key one for fashion businesses.

Although it may seem counterintuitive for an industry built on promoting new trends, encouraging consumption and wardrobe replacement, some fashion industry organizations are looking to closed-loop manufacturing systems to promote a more responsible fashion system the ultimate aim of which is to create a circular and sustainable economy. A circular economy is one which considers and builds in redesign and re-use into procurement, product design, manufacture and end-of-use in order to minimize waste and add value (Weetman, 2016). A closed-loop system for fashion products is one in which the entire lifecycle from design, through manufacture, use and disposal is planned so as to allow resources to circulate for as long as possible. Thus, each stage of the supply chain is analyzed and designed to allow maximum longevity and re-use by considering which materials and processes will allow garments to be mended, and/or disassembled and recycled, thus returning them to the closed-loop system with minimal waste. Closed-loop production also promotes textile recycling, which has the double impact of both reducing landfill and enabling the use of those resources needed to create new textiles.

Although textile recycling and re-use have been evident in smaller eco-fashion businesses, more recently large fashion brands have endorsed closed-loop strategies. For example, in 2013 the sportswear brand PUMA developed its first closed-loop line across clothing, footwear and accessories: InCycle. PUMA's first Environmental Profit and Loss accounts (see Case Study 2 on Kering) produced in 2010 showed that 57% of its environmental footprint had been due to its use of raw materials and their treatments. By reconsidering the materials and production of the InCycle range, PUMA realized a third lower environmental impact by looking for alternative sources: replacing leather, cotton and rubber with biodegradable polymers, recycled polyester and organic cottons.

In fashion production it is the choice of materials that has the most significant effect on the environmental impact of the final product. The Danish Fashion Institute and the sustainability platform NICE created an action plan that positions the challenges of sustainability as a positive design opportunity. The *Five Easy Steps* (see Table 12.2) ask designers to consider the impacts of their design decisions.

> **Product lifecycle management**
> Responsible product lifecycle management considers possible environmental impacts and attempts to lessen these through design efficiencies, re-use and recycling, often described as closed-loop/circular economy, as they seek to minimize waste and keep resources circulating within the production–consumption system.

Reclaim design power	● Know the environmental impacts of design decisions
	● Speak the same language as decision-makers
	● Design for recycling
	● Design for longevity
	● Develop and adopt guidelines
	● Put fashion first avoiding the 'eco look'.
Know the supply chain	● Share information
	● Understand the risks associated with design decisions
	● Keep the supply chain simple
	● Use the Higg Index
	● Adopt best practice in manufacturing.

Choose a focus	• Water
	• Chemicals
	• CO$_2$ emissions
	• Waste
	• Labour and ethics.
Create more, use less	• Know the sustainability impact of different materials and treatments
	• Work with sustainable fabric suppliers
	• Design for zero waste
	• Source through fair trade.
Engage customers	• Promote low-impact garment care
	• Educate sales personnel about your sustainable policies and practices
	• Tell your sustainable story in a way that is appropriate for your brand.

Table 12.2 *Five easy steps to sustainability*

Source: Based on Restart Fashion. Available at: http://www.restartfashion.com.

THE SUSTAINABLE FASHION BRAND

The Ethical Fashion Forum website quotes the 1989 Bruntland Commission's definition of sustainability as '[meeting] the needs of the present without compromising the ability of future generations to meet their own needs'. In the past, the term 'sustainable fashion brand' was often associated solely with textiles, for example the use of organic cotton, but increasingly sustainability is understood as a more holistic concept comprising the three pillars of sustainability: social, environmental and commercial sustainability (see Table 12.3).

Social Sustainability	The human side of fashion production, **social sustainability**, recognizes the contribution of people to business success and considers the well-being of the individuals and communities behind fashion. It also recognizes the link between poverty, exploitation and the long-term viability of the industry.
Environmental Sustainability	**Environmental sustainability** focuses on reducing environmental impacts created along all stages of the supply chain and seeks to increase positive environmental initiatives through investment and awareness raising.
Commercial Sustainability	Financial or **commercial sustainability** recognizes that effective strategies and structures underpin business success and that businesses should focus on developing high-quality products and services meeting needs and wants, and market these fairly.

Table 12.3 *The three pillars of sustainability*

Source: Based on the Ethical Fashion Forum, Sustainability and the triple bottom line (https://www.ethicalfashionforum.com/the-issues/ethical-fashion).

In accordance with this more holistic approach to sustainability, Kapferer and Bastien (2009) define a sustainable brand as one with a long lifespan produced by a qualified human worker, and not by exploited workers in the 'less developed' countries. They also stress the importance of transparency and clarity as two of the major assets of an ethical and sustainable fashion brand (Kapferer and Bastien, 2009) as the more transparency brands can offer in their sourcing, manufacturing and design processes, the more consumers can judge for themselves whether the promises being made are being fulfilled.

Brands understand that being socially responsible can add brand value by improving their image with consumers and business partners (Easey, 2009; Pine II and Gilmore, 2011). We will revisit transparency later in this chapter.

Deloitte (2013) found that many fashion companies are focusing on social issues over environmental ones and that 'Sustainability is becoming a strategic business imperative' with 7 out of 10 businesses risking their short-term profits and medium-term survival by not focusing on the management of natural resources or prioritizing the regeneration of materials (Deloitte, 2013). Environmental sustainability is essential since the Earth's resources are overused and long-term environmental strategies are required to avoid higher future costs due to the scarcity of natural resources (Lovins et al., 2007).

In addition to sourcing and production, Beard (2008) argues that a sustainable brand must furthermore be sustainable in the economic sense, driving consumers to purchase. By moving from involvement to commitment, brands can truly and strategically modify their business models to engage in serious sustainability efforts. One of the debates around sustainable fashion is the extent to which sustainability is communicated to customers, with Beard (2008) suggesting that sustainable practices should be promoted, without being overbearing or over-politicized to avoid alienating customers. The case studies of M&S (Chapter 12), H&M (Chapter 9), TOMS (Chapter 14), Etiko (Chapter 5) and Vigga (Chapter 15) demonstrate alternative approaches in the pursuit of sustainability. 'The problem is there is no cohesion in this space. We're all just doing what we can but, because there's no official anything, no one knows the answer' (Christian Kemp-Griffin, Chief Mission Officer – Edun, in Friedman, 2010).

> **Transparency** The extent to which aspects of a fashion product's supply chain are visible to consumers; often in the form of information available for consumers via Corporate Social Responsibility (CSR) reports on their websites.

> **Corporate Social Responsibility** CSR is a developing area of business practice generally understood to be the method by which a business manages its impact across the environmental, social and financial spheres.

CORPORATE SOCIAL RESPONSIBILITY (CSR) AND BUSINESS ETHICS

Although there is not one single accepted definition of Corporate Social Responsibility (CSR; see Table 12.4), it is a term adopted by businesses to reflect that they have responsibilities extending beyond delivering profits to owners and shareholders.

Because of increased awareness of environmental and social impact, stakeholders, in particular consumers, are increasingly demanding that businesses reduce their negative impacts and increase the positive contributions of doing business, and so have been responsible for changes in business practices (Moisander and Pesonen, 2002). Corporate Social Responsibility is also referred to as corporate citizenship or conscious capitalism (Nielsen, 2014) and adopted by companies willing to make a positive social or environmental impact on society.

Corporate values influence all areas of business operations including management style and investment decisions. Sternberg (2000) proposed a framework for business ethics that encompasses two fundamental ethical principles – distributive justice and decency – intended to guide business governance:

● Distributive justice: that those who contribute to business objectives receive an appropriate share in the returns

● Decency: that business is conducted legally and with honesty, fairness, an absence of physical violence or coercion.

The notion of business concerning itself solely with profits and financial returns on investment has been challenged over the last several decades, and more specifically the worldwide financial crash of 2007 focused attention on the area of business ethics. Organizations such as the United Nations sought to influence future business practice by highlighting that businesses do not operate in a vacuum but are part of a globally interconnected system and that business decisions have the potential to impact people and planet negatively or positively. By questioning the ethics and values of those in management positions who had endorsed decisions that had evidently impacted so negatively on others' lives, the UN also sought to codify global values and business ethics. One outcome was the formation of the UN's Principles for Responsible Management Education (PRME) based on the UN Global Compact's 10 Principles (2007). With this initiative, the UN seeks to influence future business practices through systemic change that integrates

Principles for Responsible Management Education (PRME) A voluntary initiative introduced by the United Nations as a way for those involved in business education to influence future business leaders to adopt sustainable development approaches.

social responsibility education into the business curriculum (see the companion website for further information).

It is not for purely philosophical reasons that businesses are increasingly looking to ensure compliance with ethical business practices; such practices are rewarded by an enhanced reputation and stronger consumer, employee and shareholder relations (Bhattacharya, Korschun and Sen, 2009; Carroll and Shabana, 2010). In their review of CSR practices Ghobadian, Money and

 ONLINE RESOURCES

Further information can be found in the companion website, available at: https://www.macmillanihe.com/companion/Varley_Fashion_Management.

Hillenbrand (2015) report on how businesses are now held to be responsible for actions and impact beyond the financial dimension, and to include the social and environmental dimensions. They also argue that recent changes in the business environment make CSR a central strand of strategy: there is a broad desire from stakeholders for businesses to act sustainably. The availability of information about business practices has led to demands for greater business transparency and multinational businesses are expected not only to act responsibly but to implement social impact projects in the areas in which they are operating internationally (Ghobadian, Money and Hillenbrand, 2015).

Carroll (1979)	CSR is the economic, legal, ethical and discretionary expectations that society has of organizations at a given time.
Kotler (1997)	CSR is defined as being a stakeholder-based, strategically integrated orientation toward ecological and social well-being.
Galbreath (2009)	CSR can be defined by four components: (1) the economic responsibility to generate profits, provide jobs and create products that the consumer wants, (2) the legal responsibility to comply with local, state and relevant international laws, (3) the ethical responsibility to meet other social expectations, (4) the discretionary responsibility to meet additional behaviours and activities that society finds desirable.
Du et al. (2010)	CSR is a commitment to improve [societal] well-being through discretionary business practices and contributions.
International Standards Organization (ISO)	ISO 26000 codifies seven core social responsibilities, which form the basis of most public and private business CSR policies: organizational governance; community involvement and development; human rights; labour practices; the environment; fair operating practices and consumer issues.

Table 12.4 *Definitions of CSR*

Many of the definitions of CSR (see Table 12.4) encompass the internal and external relationships a business has with its stakeholders, comprising the employees, customers, the community, national and international partners and the natural environment. For large businesses especially, the adoption of CSR policies has been used as a way to establish business governance and ethical standards that enhance their reputation externally to drive sales through increased customer loyalty, but also to increase employee well-being and impact on staff performance and retention. Other benefits include allowing customers to better understand the core values of a brand, and thereby produce a competitive edge (see Table 12.5).

CSR can impact directly on various aspects of the value chain (see Chapter 2) in the normal course of business, as shown in Table 12.6.

The business case for adopting CSR and sustainability policies	
Reputation	Increased brand equity from staff, customer and investor loyalty
Governance	Risk management, anticipating regulations and social pressures
Cost saving	Operational efficiencies from supply chain management
Future proofing	Protection of resource supply
Human resources	Lower costs from employee recruitment and retention
Innovation and expansion	Sales and marketing, new markets, products and services.

Table 12.5 *The business case for adopting CSR and sustainability policies*

Support Activities	Firm infrastructure	<ul><li>Financial reporting practices</li><li>Governance and transparency</li><li>Lobbying for policy change</li><li>Stakeholder engagement</li></ul>
	HR management	<ul><li>Education and job training</li><li>Safe working conditions</li><li>Diversity programmes</li><li>Benefits and healthcare</li><li>Layoffs and compensation</li><li>Data protection</li></ul>
	Technology development	<ul><li>Product safety</li><li>Reducing, Re-using and Recycling</li><li>Conservation of raw materials</li><li>Ethical research practices</li><li>Ethical relationships with universities for research and development</li></ul>
	Procurement	<ul><li>Supply chain practices (sourcing practices, ethical standards, compliance and audits)</li><li>Use of natural resources</li></ul>

Primary Activities	Inbound logistics	• Transportation impacts, emissions, energy usage
	Operations	• Emissions and waste
		• Ecological impact of materials used
		• Energy and water usage
		• Worker safety and regulations
		• Hazardous materials handling and disposal
	Outbound logistics	• Packaging reduction, re-using, recycling and disposal
		• Transportation impacts, emissions, energy usage
	Marketing and sales	• Ethical advertising
		• Pricing practices
		• Consumer information and transparency
		• Privacy issues
	After sales service	• Disposal of obsolete products
		• Handling of consumables
		• Customer privacy and data protection

Table 12.6 *The sustainability value chain*

Source: Various, including Porter (1985); McKinsey (2011).

CRITIQUES OF THE CSR CONCEPT

Visser (2010) argues that although CSR strategies have been widely adopted in the business sector and despite the existence of case studies demonstrating successful CSR policies and practices, on a macro-scale they have failed to make any substantial impact on the systems in which they operate. In such critiques, CSR policies are seen at best as inadequate responses to the social, environmental and ethical challenges the world is facing, and at worst as cynical management and marketing tools to avoid public legal sanctions and government censure. CSR may be operationalized as an add-on to improve brand equity through marketing and PR activities or to comply with minimum requirements, with only a very small minority of companies worldwide seeking accreditation for their CSR practices.

AUDITING CSR: HAPPINESS MEASURES AND TRIPLE BOTTOM-LINE (TBL) REPORTING

In order to gain added value from adopting CSR policies and CSR practices businesses need to be able to measure and demonstrate evidence of the results of engaging in them. Stakeholders want to see evidence of the impact of CSR, such as in improved working conditions and better lives, but also to be able to question a business's motivation for getting involved in CSR (Bhattacharya, Korschun and Sen, 2009). CSR policies for fashion businesses naturally often focus on the supply chain but can also extend beyond to include the provision of services and facilities such as educational initiatives and healthcare as well as volunteering programmes. In response to the ethical challenges of production in the fashion industry, guidance and regulatory bodies have been set up which either necessitate or encourage supply chain transparency and compliance. REACH (Regulation Evaluation and Authorization of Chemicals), OHSA (Occupational Health & Safety), and the Higg Index (from the Sustainable Apparel Coalition) are examples of initiatives adopted by fashion companies to mitigate the negative impact of their business operations. A systems approach towards CSR following Elkington's 1997 Triple Bottom Line accounting model recognizes that in addition to accounting for financials (commercial sustainability) and profit margins (profit and loss accounting), businesses should measure their impact on the people and communities that produce fashion (social sustainability) and their entire supply chain (planet accounting).

Triple Bottom Line (TBL or 3BL) The Triple Bottom Line was developed in the 1990s as a way for businesses to account for their social and environmental impact or value as well as their financial results.

Shared value This model highlights how, when business and society goals are aligned, benefits can be more effectively produced for all stakeholders.

Porter and Kramer (2011) propose a shared value business model that goes beyond social responsibility, by engaging in innovative business models that place the amelioration of societal issues at the core of the business. They argue that this approach leads to innovative business solutions and opportunities for competitive advantage to those businesses that formulate themselves as responsive socially responsible organizations. The shared value business offers growth and profit potential through identifying business opportunities that contribute to solving social issues and supporting local economies (see Box 12.2). This approach to business was recognized by Anne Tsui, the President of the Academy of Marketing, in her 2012 Presidential Address in which she advocated for the potential value of a 'virtuous circle' of 'social entrepreneurship: combining doing well with doing good' (Tsui, 2012).

Box 12.2 - Creating shared value (CSV) according to Porter and Kramer (2011)

- **Re-conceiving products and markets** – through seeking out social problems where contributing to a common good and serving consumers can be achieved in parallel;

- **Redesigning productivity in the value chain** – through enhancing the social, environmental and economic capabilities of the supply chain members simultaneously;

- **Building supportive industry clusters at the company's locations** – by enabling local cluster developments, leading to the achievement of various developmental goals in cooperation with suppliers and local institutions.

As such, the principles of CSV are similar to the concept of social entrepreneurship, defined by Mair and Marti in 2006 as 'a process involving the innovative use and combination of resources to pursue opportunities to catalyze social change and/or address social needs'. Moss Kanter (1999) previously defined social innovation as a process where companies take 'community needs as opportunities to develop ideas and demonstrate business technologies, to find and serve new markets, and to solve long-standing business problems'; again, with similar ideas interwoven.

There has, however, been some criticism of the CSV theory. Whilst recognizing its appeal and clear role in promoting responsible behaviour and the ability for CSV theory to be an umbrella for previously loosely connected concepts, Crane et al. (2014) point out that CSV ignores the tensions between social and economic goals, is naïve about the challenges of business compliance and is based on a shallow conception of the corporation's role in society.

THE SOCIALLY CONSCIOUS CONSUMER: CHARACTERISTICS AND KEY DRIVERS FOR MOTIVATION

Fashion is intimately connected to our emotions and is a vehicle to connect our own inner personality with the external world, by the use of external marks such as brands and status symbols (Niinimaki, 2010). Fashion therefore produces symbolic meanings and is a dynamic social process in shaping and building identities, participation in social groups as well as promoting individuality and differentiation from others (Thompson and Haytko, 1997). Consumption of fashion is therefore framed within a growing awareness of sustainable issues. There have been several attempts to explain the meaning and rationale of buying ethical fashion, with most of them pointing out that consumers express willingness to adhere to more conscious behaviours, in order to preserve the environment and protect human and animal rights. Consumers are also becoming more aware of inequality in social conditions across different countries, including sweatshop labour practices (Cowe and Williams, 2000).

The consumerism trend appears to be decreasing in favour of a lifestyle focused on community, connection, affordability and quality. Ethics and sustainability are becoming solidified as the new drivers of mindful consumption – an idea where caring for self, community and nature is balancing out the overconsumption behaviours that dictated the pre-recession age. 'Consumers around the world are saying loud and clear that a brand's social purpose is among the factors that influence purchase decisions' (Amy Fenton, global leader of public development

> **Ethical consumption** This is also called mindful consumption or conscious consumption. It refers to the recent and growing phenomenon by which fashion consumers are increasingly filtering their choices through the lens of sustainability.

and sustainability, Nielsen Press Release, in Nielsen, 2014).

As a consequence, the ethical consumer market is growing rapidly; some consumers who turn to ethical consumption are clearly becoming frustrated with the outcome of 'value' purchases, because garments quickly diminish after the first wash (Cotton Inc., 2013).

Even though ethical philosophies dictate many of the decisions made by ethical consumers (Jackson, 2001; Barnett, Cafaro and Newholm, 2005), a full adoption of these practices still seems inconsistent with patterns and behaviours related to consumption of fast fashion. This may be due to a reluctance to pay high prices, a lack of information, or may be a result of the consumer's own psychographic traits, so understanding the emotional connection between fashion and consumers is important for brands in order to develop strategies to better resonate with consumers. A Nielsen report (Nielsen, 2015) about the characteristics of the global, socially-conscious consumer (defined as those who say they would be willing to pay the extra for products and services from companies that implement programmes that give back to society), revealed that consumers want products that are affordable, healthy, convenient, and environmentally friendly. Some examples of consumer attitudes towards sustainability are shown in Table 12.7.

Brazil	USA	China
'94% of consumers in Brazil believe that brands should take responsibility for their environmental impact.'	'74% of US Baby Boomers say that conscience guides their buying decisions.'	'75% of Chinese consumers will buy a product if it supports a good cause.'

Table 12.7 *Examples of global consumer attitudes towards sustainability*

Source: The Future Laboratory (2016).

SLOW FASHION

We addressed some of the criticisms of fast fashion earlier in this chapter and discussed the most common issues related to overconsumption and low-quality fashion products. In line with the growing social consciousness on a global level, slow fashion has emerged as a quality-

> **Slow fashion** Where all stages of the design, making, delivering and consumption of a fashion product are considered through the lens of sustainability rather than speed.

oriented movement, focusing on the creation of a long-lasting clothing style with a lower turning disposable level (Fletcher, 2014).

Slow consumption movements encourage ethical considerations to be considered by consumers and the slow-fashion movement encompasses these concepts by acknowledging human needs, resourcefulness and maintaining quality and beauty. The recent renaissance of handcrafts, local sourcing, ingredient branding and the interest in heritage, provenance and valuing of artisanal skills can all be seen as evidence of greater consumer engagement with the principles of slow fashion. 'Slow is not the opposite of fast – there is no dualism – but a different approach in which designers, buyers, retailers and consumers are more aware of the impacts of products on workers, communities and ecosystems' (Fletcher, 2007).

Slow fashion is a philosophy of 'attentiveness'; one that is mindful of the impact fashion production has on fashion's different stakeholders: its workers, the environment, and on consumers (Fletcher, 2014). Reversing consumption and adopting an emphasis on quality and longevity is designed to produce a responsive change in businesses and organizations to manage a sustainable work ethic and supply chain, while minimizing waste. Contrary to the perceived continual dissatisfaction produced by fast-fashion consumption, slow-fashion consumption is based on the premises of mindful and well-thought choices that contemplate the way clothing is created. According to Watson and Yan (2013), slow-fashion consumers feel emotionally engaged with their purchases for a longer time, choosing to purchase high quality, versatile clothing that allows them to build a wardrobe based on care and consideration, whereas the fast-fashion consumer chooses to purchase large quantities of trendy, fashion-forward clothing at low prices, which can be replaced frequently.

The increasing importance of consumers as brand ambassadors, co-creators of innovative products and active participants in the creation of value for their favourite brands makes them the central industry player; however, the major disruption needs to come from inside the industry. Ethical brands need to appeal to the consumer's set of values in terms of style *and* sustainability. The next section will shed some light onto the marketing strategies needed to accomplish this.

MARKETING SUSTAINABLE FASHION

Achieving competitive advantage simply by offering an ethical product option is no longer valid in a saturated market like fashion. Brands must look at their target market and at their customers' attitudes towards ethical products alongside fashion design preferences. Marketing strategies hold a major role in creating a positive image of ethical fashion brands, promoting transparency, achieving clarity in their messages, and credibility in order for the differentiation factors to be assimilated by consumers. This commitment to transparency creates competitive advantage, considering that a main aspect of any fashion business is to sell their image as well as their products. Lattimore (2016), writing on the Chartered Institute of Marketing (CIM) blog, argues that marketers hold a key role in moving fashion businesses towards more sustainable positions, as the communication of sustainable practices is vital to improve brand reputation and foster brand loyalty.

Sustainable marketing can be defined as the process of planning, implementing and controlling the development, pricing, promotion and distribution of products in a manner that satisfies the following three criteria (Fuller, 1999):

- Customer needs are met
- Organizational goals are attained
- The process is compatible with ecosystems.

As identified by Ottman (2011) in the book *The New Rules of Green Marketing*, values guide consumers' purchasing; how products are sourced, manufactured, packaged, and how workers are treated, matter in their decision to purchase. Consumers consider both manufacturers' and retailers' reputations and are concerned with their environmental and social standards.

One of the tools that has increased the exposure of fashion business practices is social media. The wide spread of information has enabled customers to connect with their favourite brands across a variety of platforms and to fuel their interest in the brands' stories, share their values and ethical commitments. These actions are often illustrated with catchy images of the recipients of such social sustainability efforts (Radclyffe-Thomas, Roncha and Varley, 2014). Socially conscious consumers are strongly influenced by friends and family and trusted third parties, making word-of-mouth a powerful communication tool (Ottman, 2011). Today's hyper-connected generations of consumers actively use social media as a platform to voice their ethical concerns, express their beliefs, indicate their favorite causes and subvert businesses' usual narratives. Leading brands make use of this behaviour to promote and empower people to act collectively. It allows for the creation of cultural capital, championing sustainability as a trend and bringing more followers/consumers to join the movement. Through consumer involvement, higher loyalty is achieved as well as brand awareness and positive word-of-mouth communications, leading to competitive advantage and the maximization of a sustainable profitability (Storbacka et al., 1994; Yeung et al., 2002).

Strategies embracing sustainability can be reflected in the adoption of what Nicholls and Alexander (2006) call the 3Ps: Process, Product and Place. This framework was developed specifically in the context of fair trade marketing but can be considered as a generic framework for all sustainable brands.

- '**Process**' is a way to build consumer confidence in the authenticity of the process that was adopted by the brand, assuring consumers that messages are in fact genuine and real. It highlights key differences in the (fair) trade process when compared with other brands, and emphasizes individual supplier stories, thus linking the end consumer with the producer and combining the appeal of both an emotional and a rational approach.

- '**Product**' advocates repositioning through a focus on product quality and differentiation, products' development should reflect consumer demands,

including lifestyle characteristics of new market segments.

- '**Place**' empowers consumers to 'act locally' on their ethical concerns by developing specific criteria and achieving fair trade accreditation for a local region, and additionally to increase support for and use of fair trade products in different and relevant locations.

The attachment between consumers and brands that is achieved through the emotional connection advocated by Nicholls and Alexander (2006) and the consumer confidence they promote through authenticity highlight the success of some of the current approaches to branding. Emotional connections are usually mastered by enhancing a particular attribute or story about the company (Silverstein and Fiske, 2003). In this sense CSR becomes a source of opportunity, innovation, and competitive advantage (Porter and Kramer, 2006), acting as a cohesive element of brand strategy, centred on a company's mission, strategic issue, market, customer needs and resources. The competitive advantage generated by incorporating ethical concerns into the business strategy can result in consumer loyalty (Mandhachitara and Poolthong, 2011) as well as improved brand image (Worcester, 2009). See Box 12.3 for a summary of sustainability strategy.

Box 12.3 - Strategy and the social context

McKinsey (2011) states that businesses have to employ a long-term strategic view of sustainability and that the way to capture value lies in three key areas: return on capital, growth and risk management.

- **Return on capital**: reducing operational costs through improved natural-resource management; managing the supply chain; improving employee retention and obtaining higher market share through sustainable product development. For example, Levi's has engaged with open sourcing and collaboration as the route to a sustainable future by adopting revolutionary production methods that will save 50 billion litres of water a year across the sector.

- **Growth**: revising the business portfolio to access the potential impact of trends that could lead to

growth opportunities; reaching new customers and markets and their unmet needs created by sustainability; innovation and new product developments. For example, H&M launched a £787,000 recycling prize for scientists and entrepreneurs who offer innovative solutions to the fashion industry's waste and pollution issues.

- **Risk Management**: detecting operational disruptions from climate change, resource scarcity or community issues; reputation management; regulatory management. For example, TOMS© developed their One-for-one business model to allow for growth into new product areas and new opportunities for giving (see Case Study 14).

Source: McKinsey (2011).

CAUSE MARKETING

Today's ethically conscious consumers require more than compliance with statutory legal requirements, they require that businesses go beyond the minimum legal requirements and include additional society activities as part of their practice (Varley and Rafiq, 2014). This leads to an increased number of businesses attempting to leverage their CSR engagement through various types of cause marketing. Cause marketing allows for the communication of business values beyond financial returns so as to establish legitimacy with various stakeholders – not just customers but society as a whole (Carroll and Shabana, 2010). It stands for a cooperative effort between for-profit and non-profit organizations for mutual benefit and gives stakeholders a chance to take a stand, by raising awareness and at the same time promoting products. By aligning a brand with a cause, profitable and societal benefits are achieved by both parties.

Benefits for for-profit companies:

- Increased brand loyalty
- Higher employee satisfaction
- Increased sales by supporting a worthwhile cause
- Increased engagement with the public
- Creation of social value.

Benefits for non-profit companies:

- Increased funding
- Exposure and reliability by aligning themselves with a trusted brand
- Increased engagement with the public
- Awareness/education to the cause.

Box 12.4, 'Product(RED)', highlights an example of an initiative that adopts cause marketing.

Box 12.4 - Product(RED)

Accentuating the idea that doing good is good business (RED) is a 21st century initiative with sustainable, universal appeal. (www.red.org)

Rock music celebrity Bono and activist Bobby Shriver founded Product(RED) in 2006 as a response to the HIV/AIDS crisis in Africa, announcing the brand's launch at the World Economic Forum in Davos. Product(RED)'s mission was to contribute to the Global Fund which was founded in 2002 to generate private sector funding for prevention and treatment of HIV/AIDS, Tuberculosis and Malaria. According to their website, to date Product(RED) has raised $465m for the Global Fund, impacting over 90m lives.

The (RED) business model

(RED) works with selected brand partners who commit to donating up to 50% of profits from (RED)-branded products and services to the Global Fund. The products developed for the collaboration are distinctively coloured red and use cause marketing by linking promotional materials to their charitable donations in order to motivate consumers. Once purchases are made, the manufacturers send their contributions directly to the Global Fund, that is, (RED) does not receive any of these monies. The Global Fund uses 100% of the monies received from the Product(RED) manufacturers to finance HIV/AIDS programmes currently supporting initiatives in Ghana, Lesotho, Rwanda, South Africa, Swaziland, Tanzania, Kenya and Zambia. Examples of fashion brands that have partnered with (RED) are: GAP (with a line of clothing and accessories); Converse (with a shoe made from African mud cloth); Nike (shoelaces promoted by Didier Drogba), and Giorgio Armani (with a line of Emporio Armani products that include clothes, jewellery, perfume, and accessories).

Other partners of (RED) manufacture products or packaging in African countries, thus generating jobs and opportunities.

Criticisms of (RED)

There has been criticism of (RED) with some arguing its business model is inefficient and does not deliver returns proportional to its advertising spend. Additionally, there has been criticism over the degree of transparency related to the percentage of the purchase price which translates into donations. Labour Behind the Label commended Gap's policy of producing its Product(RED) garments in Lesotho but argued that labour rights are not consistently protected across its partners. In 2008 (RED) introduced a calculator to show how purchases relate to medical treatments.

Source: https://red.org.

SUSTAINABILITY AS BRAND LEADERSHIP

Brand leadership through CSR is aimed at building assets that will result in long-term profitability and, as such, must be supported and linked with action. The notion of a sustainable brand challenges the traditional brand strategy approaches, which tend to focus on primary stakeholders such as customers, shareholders, and business partners (Post et al., 2002) and less on secondary stakeholders, including the social and political actors who support the firm's mission. However, positioning brands according to CSR values entails a 'significant strategic shift in the way the organization thinks about itself and its activities, including communications with a wider range of internal and external stakeholders' (Polonsky and Jevons, 2006: 346). According to Polonsky and Jevons (2006), CSR activities should be aligned with those issues that are salient to brands' stakeholders and be supported by core brand and product attributes; additionally, businesses must make long-term commitments to CSR particularly at senior management level, and ensure sufficient resources and measures are implemented.

In an era where global brands compete in global markets, it is important to consider how value creation relates to multiple stakeholders simultaneously. This understanding requires sensitivity to current pressures and sustainability issues and the identification of entrepreneurial and innovative capabilities. To reinforce a brand's CSR positioning, cross-functional activities must work effectively, such as internal marketing programmes that educate employees about CSR objectives and activities, the brand strategy itself, and the implementation of CSR brand-relevant activities (see Box 12.5)

Box 12.5 - Successful incorporation of sustainability into a brand's strategy

- **Highlight brand trust and commitment to social and environment impact to drive purchases.**

The factors that influence purchasing for nearly two-out-of-three (62%) of consumers globally is brand trust (Nielsen, 2015).

> Brand trust and reputation are paramount. An excellent reputation makes it far more likely a company will be welcomed into new communities; partner with the most respected non-profits working on issues consumers care about most; and be a go-to source for products and services. And what we know for sure is that sustainability is playing an increasingly significant role in consumer decision making. (Carol Gstalder, SVP, Reputation & Public Relations Solutions, in Nielsen, 2015)

- **Have a discerning sustainability strategy; keep regional, category and demographics in mind.**

Although sustainability is a worldwide concern, a study from Nielsen (2015) shows that consumers in developed markets are harder to influence than those in developing markets. Consumers in Latin America, Asia, the Middle East, and Africa are 23%–29% more willing to pay a premium for sustainable offerings and give back to the community. In order to succeed, brands need to demonstrate a credible and relevant social purpose and deliver greater value. Adapting different tactics to various consume groups (based on region, category and age) will increase the effectiveness of such strategies, which should be built according to consumers' expectations and the social drivers that matter the most to them.

- **Focus on the growing interest from Millennials and Generation Z.**

Regarding age, Millennials and Generation Z are more willing to pay extra for sustainable offerings. Brands that are able to hold a reputation for being sustainable will find preference among the power-spending consumers of tomorrow. Baby boomers also demonstrate willingness to pay extra for sustainable products.

- **Support efforts with marketing.**

The marketing of sustainability initiatives needs to be a wider strategy and one that goes beyond using product claims on labels. Communication is regarded as essential to update CSR strategies and intentions and to ensure that those same strategies add to brand image and equity (Jahdi and Acikdilli, 2009). A strong, clear and actionable vision, a focus on outward messaging and consistent cause messaging as well as measurement of outcomes and return on investment are key.

Source: Jahdi and Acikdilli (2009).

GROWTH THROUGH SUSTAINABILITY

As we established earlier in this chapter, adopting responsible social and environmental practices can differentiate products in a saturated market (Aaker and McLoughlin, 2010) and consumers that have stronger brand connections support brands that engage in ethical and environmentally friendly practices (Phau and Ong, 2007), and are willing to pay a price premium for their products (Nielsen, 2014).

A way to demonstrate potential growth through sustainability is to apply **Ansoff's product/market matrix** (introduced earlier in this book, see Chapter 3) to show options for approaching either new or existing markets (see Table 12.8).

	Existing Products	**New Products**
Existing Markets	**Market Penetration** Adopting an ethical positioning that will lead to higher loyalty and consequently to higher market share.	**Product Development** Developing new products that reflect consumers' growing concern and attention to ethical issues.
New Markets	**Market Development** Altering existing products (for example, through changes in the supply chain) to appeal to the growing number of ethical consumers.	**Diversification** Introducing a new ethical range of products that will appeal to the new ethical consumer.

Table 12.8 *Growth options for sustainable brands*

Another way is to collaborate with strategic partners. This allows companies to address competence gaps in various areas (such as sustainable design, energy-saving distribution or ethical supply chain); to gain market knowledge about the ethical consumer; allow for the creation of brand associations leading to higher equity; provide new expertize, as well as to achieve mutual business aims in a more effective manner. Recent examples of this include: EDUN and J. Crew; EDUN+DIESEL, and People Tree and Orla Kiely. Through innovation and creativity, as well as long-term collaboration within and outside the industry, CSR needs to be embedded in all aspects of business practices, building on the notion that all sustainable issues are converging and thus need to be dealt with as interconnected challenges and opportunities.

PEOPLE MANAGEMENT AND SUSTAINABILITY

Consumer brands that haven't embraced sustainability are at risk on many fronts. Social responsibility is a critical part of proactive reputation management. And companies with strong reputations outperform others when it comes to attracting top talent, investors, community partners, and most of all consumers (Carol Gstalder, SVP, Reputation & Public Relations Solutions, in Nielsen, 2015)

It is widely reported that post-industrial millennial employees are less satisfied with long-term career aspirations and are seeking more than just financial rewards from their work. Nielsen (2014) reports that 67% of those surveyed prefer to work for socially responsible companies. Many entering the workplace no longer expect to have one job for life, or even one job at a time, and with employers less able to attract and retain employees through salary and career prospects alone, companies are increasingly providing their staff opportunities to engage in work directly aligned with their personal beliefs and values, whether this is central to the business operations or as part of their CSR policy in practice, such as funding staff to work on volunteering projects. The experience of working for companies with strong ethical values and positive societal and environmental impact creates positive emotional states for employees and stronger employee–employer connections due to enhanced opportunities for 'meeting colleagues, work–life integration, and self-expression at work' (Bhattacharya, Korschun and Sen, 2009: 262). These positive functional and psychosocial benefits result in additional added value through internal brand management, better employee engagement and higher retention rates (Bhattacharya, Korshcun and Sen, 2009; Bloom et al., 2006; Tsui, 2012).

CSR IN THE LUXURY FASHION MARKET

Despite all the recent attention paid to the sustainability agenda, when it comes to the luxury market there is still an image problem to solve. For many consumers, sustainability is still synonymous with less materially satisfying products. Luxury has always been a conduit for new paradigms, progress and innovation, and about driving people towards new possibilities; however, when it comes to sustainability this leadership is not so evident.

The Kering Group, however, is profoundly engaged in making a difference and raising the discussion around sustainable luxury. This luxury conglomerate is no longer solely about the creation of feel-good initiatives but acknowledges that sustainability brings the potential to create and increase business value at the luxury level of the fashion industry (see Box 12.6). According to François-Henri Pinault, Kering's chairman, sustainability is an obligatory part of quality, which luxury brands cannot afford to compromise. It is not a constraint, but rather an impetus to improve performance.

> Sustainability can – and must – give rise to new, highly ambitious business models and become a lever of competitiveness for our brands. (François-Henri Pinault, Chairman of the Kering Group, in Grady, 2011)

Box 12.6 - Kering's EP&L (Environmental Profit & Loss) accounting

The luxury group introduces a financial measure of its environmental footprint

Kering, the luxury fashion and lifestyle group, has developed an in-house accounting system that calculates the costs to society of its environmental impact across the supply chain. Its motivation in so doing was to discover which aspects of its business (location, material, processes, products or technologies) had the most significant environmental impacts, to develop strategy and guidelines for minimizing these. The initiative was implemented as a way of reducing both costs and

risks whilst increasing transparency, stakeholder engagement and business efficiencies.

The EP&L is a means of locating where the environmental impacts are, to inform responsible decision-making. The EP&L measures:

- Carbon emissions
- Water use
- Water pollution
- Land use
- Air pollution
- Waste

Each of these impacts is measured across the value chain:

- Raw materials
- Processing
- Manufacturing
- Assembly
- Operations and retail

The impact of each environmental income is calculated and translated into a monetary value which enables comparisons to be made in different business areas, between different impacts and over time.

Kering published its first EP&L in 2011 for PUMA's 2010 results. Having developed the EP&L methodology, Kering has rolled it out across its brands and as well as reporting on its own brands Kering has made the EP&L methodology an open source in order to positively impact the wider fashion industry.

According to the 2015 EP&L Report, Kering has reduced the group's impact intensity by more than 10% since 2012 as a result of changes in material sourcing, product design and manufacturing. Currently the EP&L focuses on the negative impact of production and does not include either measures of positive impact, or any measures that relate to customer use and product end-of-life, that is, it is described as 'cradle to gate' rather than 'cradle to cradle'.

For more information on Kering's EP&L, see http://www.kering.com/en/sustainability/epl.
See also Case Study 2 on Kering, in Chapter 2.

TRANSPARENCY AND TRACEABILITY AND THEIR IMPACT IN FASHION

In Chapter 9 we introduced the ideas of supply chain transparency and traceability, and according to Nava (1997), promoting and committing to transparency will lead brands to achieve a competitive advantage; when a company is committed to being sustainable and operates at a high transparency level, it creates feelings of reliability amongst consumers, as it makes clear that it is not right all the time (Harris, 2007). Writing in a Euromonitor Analysis Opinion piece, Consumer Trends Consultant Kasriel-Alexander (2012) states that, 'being transparent is the first step to gaining consumer loyalty' and quotes industry insider opinion that 'People appreciate transparency and trust from brands more than good products. Companies that bring social purpose are the ones that will succeed in the long term.'

Earlier we referred to Kapferer and Bastien's (2009) perspective on how brands that address transparency and clarity propose an added value and a way to commit to a more responsible world. There is a growing opportunity in the marketplace for companies whose core values relate directly to sustainable and transparent business models as a key factor to create unique value (see Box 12.7). Supply chain information is seen as an important factor for specific products (Balabanis and Diamantopoulos, 2004; Davidson et al., 2003) and sourcing strategies are also attracting increased attention (New, 2004).

Box 12.7 - Transparent fashion

Provenance

Through the use of blockchain technology, Provenance guarantees the supply chain authenticity to concerned consumers, ensuring the products they have bought are not linked to any unethical factories, and by establishing the global trail from manufacture to sale of products. Accessories brand Elvis & Kresse use Provenance data-tracking in the supply chain of their products, which are made from recycled decommissioned fire hose retrieved from landfill – 50% of the profits from the fire hose collection are donated to the Fire Fighters Charity. For more information, see www.elvisandkresse.com.

Reproduced by permission of Elvis & Kresse.

Honest By, founded in 2012 by Belgian designer Bruno Pieters, has brought change to the industry by developing a business model offering 100% transparency on 'its supply chain products, and displays profit margins online' (Kasriel-Alexander, 2012).

Everlane, founded in 2010 in San Francisco, focuses on delivering beautiful basics through radical transparency. The company shares retail markups by cutting middleman prices and sharing manufacturing information.

Reformation, founded in 2009 in Los Angeles, uses design to make transparency desirable. Every piece on the website displays its carbon footprint, showing, for example, how much water the garment production saves.

Young (2013) suggests that transparency and traceability become more difficult as businesses scale up, with the challenge to achieve the right balance between social and economical benefits. The complexities of running a shared-value business remain an unresolved challenge in today's fashion landscape. The ability to engage with societal issues yet at the same time run a business efficiently has only been mastered by a handful of innovative business models.

CONSUMER EDUCATION INITIATIVES

As discussed earlier in this chapter, sustainable purchasing starts with consumer knowledge and it is up to the educated consumer to drive the necessary change in fashion. Educating consumers to empower them to make the right choices is a key driver for change and has been endorsed by Fletcher (2014) as part of the Slow Fashion movement. Nordic fashion brands have a particular reputation for sustainability which an educational industry project 'NICE' (The Nordic Initiative, Clean and Ethical Fashion) helped to build among young consumers. 'If the fashion industry succeeds in changing the mind-sets of consumers towards sustainable choices, it will have an immense impact not only on the entire industry's focus, but it will also affect other businesses' (Nordic Initiative, Clean and Ethical; in Fashion Futures, 2010).

ONLINE RESOURCES

Our companion website provides more detail about the NICE collaborative project: https://www.macmillanihe.com/companion/Varley_Fashion_Management.

CASE STUDY 12 – Marks & Spencer: No Plan B

Marks & Spencer (M&S) is a UK high street stalwart founded in 1884 and is the UK's biggest clothing retailer by value. The company trades internationally in 55 territories across Europe, the Middle East and Asia and is supplied by approximately 1500 factories across 57 countries, with 50% of production in the Far East, 30–40% made on the Indian subcontinent and 10–15% made in Europe. M&S is the world's only major retailer with carbon neutral operations and the company's efforts in sustainable business have been recognized with over 220 industry awards for sustainability.

M&S's commitment to sustainable business can be seen in its Plan A business plan (http://corporate.marksandspencer.com/plan-a). Plan A (because there is no Plan B) was launched in January 2007 as the central strand of its commitment to ecological and ethical challenges. The decision to invest £200m over three years in such a project was spearheaded by the then chief executive Stuart Rose, who put sustainability at the top of the agenda, for example, by holding a private screening of Al Gore's climate change documentary 'An Inconvenient Truth' for 100 senior M&S executives. Plan A set out measurable targets, timescales and accountabilities, and its adoption represented a huge public commitment to sustainability, by placing sustainability at the core of business strategy for Marks & Spencer. Plan A outlined M&S's commitment to work with customers and suppliers across five 'pillars': the climate, waste, sustainable materials, fair partnership and health, with a bold aim of achieving 100 of their targets by 2012, and to be the world's most sustainable retailer by 2015. Subsequently Plan A was revised in February 2010, with 80 additional commitments and the five pillars renamed to: climate change, waste, natural resources, fair partner, health and well-being. The addition of two extra pillars further extended Plan A: *to involve customers in Plan A* and *to make Plan A how we do business*. Another Plan A refresh in 2014 saw Plan A 2020 adding new commitments and revising the existing ones into 100 commitments that extended across its international business and communicated the M&S core brand purpose: to enhance lives every day, with the ultimate goal of becoming the worlds' most sustainable retailer. At the time, Mike Barry, Director of Plan A, said in a press release: 'Plan A 2020 is a sustainable business plan focused on customer, employee and supplier engagement ... By aligning social and environmental outcomes with our business goals in this way, we believe we can deliver greater value for all ...'.

M&S wanted to distance itself from the disposable mentality of fast fashion and as part of Plan A, M&S committed to help customers recycle over 50 million items of clothing by 2020. In 2008 they launched a clothes exchange whereby clothes donations to anti-poverty charity Oxfam were rewarded with an M&S voucher. This was later developed into a high-profile instore clothes recycling initiative: *shwopping*. Working in partnership with Oxfam and the Ab Fab actress Joanna Lumley as campaign ambassador, M&S invited members of the public to deposit unwanted clothing (not just that bought at M&S) into *Shwop Drop Boxes* by their tills. In return customers received loyalty card points and M&S vouchers. With a commitment that none of the donations would go to landfill, the clothing was sent to Oxfam to sort and resell, reuse or recycle. In October 2012, M&S launched its first closed-loop garment made from recycled *shwopped* clothes – a limited edition, women's wool jacket made entirely from recycled wool, costing £89. To date the M&S–Oxfam *shwopping* partnership has won numerous sustainability awards including a 2013 government-sponsored Big Society Award and the scheme has donated 24 million items to Oxfam raising £16.4m for the charity.

Case challenge

To what extent do you agree that Marks & Spencer is practising its belief, stated in Plan A: '*We believe that sustainability is both a moral and commercial imperative*'?

 ## ONLINE RESOURCES

A longer version of this case study, with additional challenges, can be found on our companion website: https://www.macmillanihe.com/companion/Varley_Fashion_Management.

 ## SUMMARY AND CONCLUDING THOUGHTS

Increasing public concern with the social and environmental impact of the fashion system has led to a situation where the fashion industry itself and its associated business models are being challenged. Consumers have shown support for ethical fashion brands, and there has been a proliferation of social enterprise start-ups in the fashion sector, many of which work with artisans in developing countries to promote indigenous craft skills and support local communities (see the Toms Case Study, Case Study 14).

From these small businesses to the industry monoliths such as H&M or the Kering Group, the sustainability aspects of fashion production will continue to grow in importance. What is unlikely to change is a continued growth in the need for fashion products to be both stylish and ethically produced. Given that strategy encompasses the long-term view and is concerned with the management of resources (Johnson et al., 2012), it is imperative that (in the words of H&M) fashion is sustainable, and sustainability is fashionable.

CHALLENGES AND CONVERSATIONS

1. Explore the concept of the three pillars of sustainability for different market levels in the context of:

    (a) The sourcing of raw materials and components for fashion products,

    and

    (b) The making up of fashion products (for example, manufacturing or finishing).

2. Suggest reasons why different consumer segments may have different attitudes towards sustainable fashion.

3. Some commentators suggest that sustainable fashion is an oxymoron. Critically discuss this viewpoint.

4. Explore how different fashion organizations approach CSR, and critically evaluate the initiatives they each adopt.

5. Find recent examples of fashion companies using sustainability as a brand and marketing strategy; compare the approaches and discuss their effectiveness in terms of delivering against the three pillars of sustainability.

6. Undertake a wardrobe audit and map the lifecycle of your favourite clothes, compare this with those of your classmates and consider cost and value per wear. Discuss any apparent strategic implications of your wardrobe audits for fashion brands.

REFERENCES AND FURTHER READING

Aaker, D. A. and McLoughlin, D. (2010) *Strategic Market Management: Global Perspectives.* Chichester: Wiley.

Balabanis, G. and Diamantopoulos, A. (2004) 'Domestic country bias, country-of-origin effects, and consumer ethnocentrism: A multidimensional unfolding approach'. *Journal of the Academy of Marketing Science*, 32(1), pp. 80–95.

Barnett, C., Cafaro, P. and Newholm, T. (2005) 'Philosophy and ethical consumption', in Newholm, T., Shaw, D. and Harrison, R. (eds) *The Ethical Consumer.* London: Sage.

Beard, N. D. (2008) 'The branding of ethical fashion and the consumer: A luxury niche or mass-market reality?' *Fashion Theory*, 12(4), pp. 447–467.

Bhattacharya, C. B., Korschun, D. and Sen, S. (2009) 'Strengthening stakeholder–company relationships through mutually beneficial corporate social responsibility initiatives'. *Journal of Business Ethics*, 85, pp. 257–272.

Bloom, P. N., Hoeffler, S., Keller, K. L. and Basurto Meza, C. E. (2006) 'How social-cause marketing affects consumer perceptions'. *MIT Sloan Management Review*, 47(2), pp. 49–55.

Carroll, A. B. (1979) 'A three-dimensional conceptual model of corporate performance'. *Academy of Management Review*, 4(4), pp. 497–505.

Carroll, A. B. and Shabana, K. M. (2010) 'The business case for corporate social responsibility: A review of concepts, research and practice'. *International Journal of Management Reviews*, 12(1), pp. 85–105.

Cotton Inc. (2013) *Cotton Incorporated Supply Chain Insights.* Available at: http://www.cottoninc.com/corporate/Market-Data/SupplyChainInsights/Driving-Demand-For-Denim-Jeans/Driving-Demand-for-Denim-Jeans.pdf.

Cowe, R. and Williams, S. (2000) *Who are the Ethical Consumers?* London: The Cooperative Bank.

Crane, A., Palazzo, G., Spence, L. J. and Matten, D. (2014) 'Contesting the value of "Creating Shared Value"'. *California Management Review*, 56(2), pp. 130–153.

Davidson, A., Schroder, M. and Bower, J. (2003) 'The importance of origin as a quality attribute for beef: Results from a Scottish consumer survey'. *International Journal of Consumer Studies*, 27(2), pp. 91–98.

Deloitte (2013) Sustainability: Why CFOs are driving savings and strategy. Available at: https://www2.deloitte.com/content/dam/insights/us/articles/sustainability-why-cfos-are-driving-savings-and-strategy/DUP206_CFO_Insights_Sustainability_Final.pdf [accessed 22/08/2016].

Du, S., Bhattacharya, C. B. and Sen, S. (2010) 'Maximising business returns to corporate social responsibility (CSR): The role of CSR communication'. *International Journal of Management Reviews*, 12(1), pp. 8–19.

Easey, M. (2009) *Fashion Marketing*, 3rd edn. Oxford: Wiley Blackman.

Elkington, J. (1997) *Cannibals with Forks: The Triple Bottom Line of 21st Century Business*. Oxford: Capstone.

Fashion Futures 2025 (2010) *Forum for the future*: Action for a sustainable world. Available at: http://www.forumforthefuture.org/sites/default/files/project/downloads/fashionfutures2025finalsml.pdf [accessed 01/08/2013].

Fletcher, K. (2007) 'Slow fashion'. *Ecologist*. Available at: http://www.theecologist.org/green_green_living/clothing/269245/slow_fashion.html.

Fletcher, K. (2014) *Sustainable Fashion and Textiles: Design Journeys*. Abingdon: Routledge.

Friedman, V. (2010) 'Sustainable fashion: What does green mean?' *Financial Times*. Available at: https://www.ft.com/content/2b27447e-11e4-11df-b6e3-00144feab49a.

Fuller, D. (1999) *Sustainable Marketing, Managerial–Ecological Issues*. Thousand Oaks, CA: Sage.

Galbreath, J. (2009) 'Building corporate social responsibility into strategy'. *European Business Review*, 21(2), pp. 109–127.

Gardner, H., Csikszentmihalyi, M. and Damon, W. (2001) *Good Work: When Excellence and Ethics Meet*. New York, NY: Basic Books.

Gerzema, J. (2011) *Spend Shift: How the Post-crisis Values Evolution is Changing the Way we Buy, Sell, and Live*. San Francisco, CA: Jossey-Bass.

Ghobadian, A., Money, K. and Hillenbrand, C. (2015) 'Corporate social responsibility research: Past–present–future'. *Group and Organization Management*, 40(3), pp. 271–294.

Grady E. (2011) 'PPR Group brings sustainability initiative to Gucci, Stella McCartney and Yves Saint Laurent'. *Treehugger*, 5 April. Available at: https://www.treehugger.com/style/ppr-group-brings-sustainability-initiative-to-gucci-stella-mccartney-and-yves-saint-laurent.html [accessed 01/07/2016].

Harris, N. (2007) 'Corporate engagement in processes for planetary sustainability: Understanding corporate capacity in the non-renewable resource extractive sector, Australia'. *Business Strategy and the Environment*, 16(8), pp. 538–553.

ILO (International Labour Organization) (2012). Available at: https://www.ilo.org/global/lang--en/index.htm [accessed 03/07/2017].

Jackson, J. (2001) 'Prioritizing customers and other stakeholders using AHP'. *European Journal of Marketing*, 35(7/8), pp. 858–871.

Jahdi, K. S. and Acikdilli, G. (2009) 'Marketing communications and corporate social responsibility (csr): Marriage of convenience or shotgun wedding?' *Journal of Business Ethics*, 88(1), pp. 103–113 [accessed 01/07/2016].

Johnson, G., Scholes, K. and Whittingon, R. (2012) *Fundamentals of Strategy*. Harlow, England: Financial Times/Prentice Hall.

Kapferer, J. N. and Bastien, V. (2009) 'The specificity of luxury management: Turning marketing upside down'. *Journal of Brand Management*, 16, pp. 311–322.

Kasriel-Alexander, D. (2012) 'Future watch: Transparency – How the Social Media Age is linking consumers and businesses'. *Analysis Opinion, Euromonitor*, 31 October 2012.

Kotler, P. (1997) *Marketing Management: Analysis, Planning, Implementation and Control*. Upper Saddle River, NJ: Prentice Hall.

Lattimore, P. (2016) 'Nine top business reasons for sustainability'. *CIM Exchange*. Available at: https://exchange.cim.co.uk/blog/nine-top-business-reasons-for-sustainability/ [accessed 01/07/2018].

Lovins, A. B., Lovins, L. H. and Hawken, P. (2007) "A road map for natural capitalism". *Harvard Business Review*, July–August Issue. Available at: https://hbr.org/2007/07/a-road-map-for-natural-capitalism [accessed 01/07/2016].

Mair, J. and Marti, I. (2006) 'Social entrepreneurship research: A source of explanation, prediction, and delight'. *Journal of World Business*, 41(1), pp. 36–44.

Mandhachitara, R. and Poolthong, Y. (2011) 'Brand community'. *Journal of Consumer Research*, 27(4), pp. 412–432.

McKinsey (2011) *The business of sustainability: McKinsey Global Survey results*. Available at: http://www.mckinsey.com/business-functions/sustainability-and-resource-productivity/our-insights/the-business-of-sustainability-mckinsey-global-survey-results.

McKinsey (2017). 'Mapping the benefits of a circular economy'. *McKinsey Quarterly*. Available at: http://www.mckinsey.com/business-functions/sustainability-and-resource-productivity/our-insights/mapping-the-benefits-of-a-circular-economy.

Moisander, J. and Pesonen, S. (2002) 'Narratives of sustainable ways of living: Constructing the self and the other as a green consumer'. *Management Decision*, 40(4), pp. 329–342.

Moss Kanter, R. (1999) 'From spare change to real change: The social sector as Beta site for business innovation'. *Harvard Business Review*, 77(3) (May/June), pp. 122–128.

Nava, M. (1997) *Studies in Advertising and Consumption*. Abingdon: Routledge.

New, S. (2004) 'The ethical supply chain', in New, S. and Westbrook, R. (eds) *Understanding Supply Chains: Concepts, Critiques and Futures*. Oxford: Oxford University Press, pp. 253–280.

Nicholls, A. and Alexander, A. (2006) 'Rediscovering consumer–producer involvement: A network perspective on fair trade marketing in the UK'. *European Journal of Marketing*, 40(11–12), pp. 1236–1253.

Nielsen (2014) *Doing Well by Doing Good Report*. Available at: http://www.nielsen.com/us/en/insights/reports/2014/doing-well-by-doing-good.html.

Nielsen (2015) *The Sustainability Imperative Report*. Available at: http://www.nielsen.com/uk/en/insights/reports/2015/the-sustainability-imperative.html.

Niinimaki, K. (2010) 'Eco-clothing, consumer identity and ideology'. *Sustainable Development*, 18(3), pp. 150–162.

Ottman, J. A. (2011) *The New Rules of Green Marketing: Strategies, Tools and Inspiration for Sustainable Branding*. Sheffield: Green Leaf Publishing.

Phau, I. and Ong, D. (2007) 'An investigation of the effects of environmental claims in promotional messages for clothing brands'. *Marketing Intelligence & Planning*, 25(7), pp. 772–788.

Pine II, B. J. and Gilmore, J. H. (2011) *The Experience Economy*. Boston, MA: Harvard Business Review Press.

Polonsky, M. J. and Jevons, C. (2006) 'Understanding issue complexity when building a socially responsible brand'. *European Business Review*, 18(5), pp. 340–349.

Porter, M. E. (1985) *Competitive Advantage*. New York: The Free Press.

Porter, M. E. and Kramer, M. R. (2006) 'Strategy and society: The link between competitive advantage and corporate social responsibility'. *Harvard Business Review*, 12, pp. 78–92.

Porter, M. E. and Kramer, M. R. (2011) 'Creating shared value'. *Harvard Business Review*, January–February, pp. 62–77.

Post, J. E., Preston, L. E. and Sachs, S. (2002) 'Managing the extended enterprise: The new stakeholder view'. *California Management Review*, 45(1), pp. 6–28.

Radclyffe-Thomas, N., Roncha, A. and Varley, R. (2014) 'Ethical Brand Building and the collaborative fashion brand: Flying the flag for social entrepreneurship –

TOMS a case study'. Conference paper – GAMMA Global Fashion Management Conference.

Silverstein, M. J. and Fiske, N. (2003) 'Luxury for the masses'. *Harvard Business Review*, April.

Sternberg, E. (2000) *Business Ethics in Action*, 2nd edn. Oxford: Oxford University Press.

Storbacka, K., Strandvik, T. and Grönroos, C. (1994) 'Managing customer relationships for profit: The dynamics of relationship quality'. *International Journal of Service Industry Management*. 5(5), pp. 21–38.

The Future Laboratory (2016) Sustainability Summit report, 2016. Available from: https://www.thefuturelaboratory.com/reports/sustainability-summit-report-2016.

The True Cost (2015) [Documentary], Morgan, A. (Director). USA: Life is My Movie Entertainment Company in association with Untold Creative.

Thompson, C. J. and Haytko, D. L. (1997) 'Speaking of fashion: Consumers' uses of fashion discourses and the appropriation of countervailing cultural meanings'. *Journal of Consumer Research*, 24(1), pp. 15–42.

Tsui, A. T. (2012) 'On compassion in scholarship: Why should we care?' Presidential Address. *Academy of Management Review*, 38(2), pp. 167–180.

Varley, R. and Rafiq, M. (2014) *Principles of Retailing*. Basingstoke: Palgrave.

Visser, W. (2010) 'CSR 2.0 and the new DNA of Business'. *Journal of Business Systems, Governance and Ethics*, 5(3), p. 7.

Watson, M. Z. and Yan, R.-N. (2013) 'An exploratory study of the decision processes of fast versus slow fashion consumers'. *Journal of Fashion Marketing and Management*. 17(2), pp. 141–159.

Weetman, C. (2016) *A Circular Economy Handbook for Business and Supply Chains*. London: Kogan Page.

Worcester, R. (2009) 'Reflections on corporate reputations'. *Management Decision*, 47, pp. 573–589.

Young, M. C. H., Ging, L. and Ennew, C. T. (2002) 'Customer satisfaction and profitability: A reappraisal of the nature of the relationship'. *Journal of Targeting, Measurement and Analysis for Marketing*, 11(1), pp. 24–33.

Young, R. (2013) 'Stripped bare: Brands move toward transparency and traceability'. *The Business of Fashion*. Available at: http://www.businessoffashion.com/2013/07/nike-nudie-honest-by-bruno-pieters-stripped-bare-brands-move-toward-transparency-and-traceability.html [accessed 01/08/2013].

MANAGING RISK IN FASHION

13

Liz Gee

 ## INTRODUCTION

The global nature of today's fashion business dictates that a constant monitoring of risk is necessary to ensure strategic advantage is maintained and enhanced. If we assume the simple and arguably most important measurement of performance is through the achievement of profit then it follows that a risk may be defined as any factor that can impact this profit. This of course assumes that the profit objective is the driving force behind the fashion entity and whilst this may not be the sole objective, for example in a Benefit Corporation (see the section on 'A stakeholder perspective'), profit achievement undoubtedly remains important.

A strategy requires detailed analysis, planning and control to ensure sustained performance and profitability. The fashion business, which by its very definition is fast moving and constantly evolving, is subject to fickle consumer demands. Managers are employed to track, monitor, evaluate and act upon factors as wide ranging as changing demographics, global wage fluctuations, and the supply and demand of raw materials in order to trade ranges and products in a profitable way. The close scrutiny of variables, such as costs, retail selling prices, and ultimately margins and gross and net profits, is needed for a fashion business to be sustained, and/or grow both domestically and internationally. This chapter explores both theoretical and practical perspectives of risk as a strategic concept and its impact on the performance of the global fashion business.

 ## LEARNING OBJECTIVES

After studying this chapter, you should be able to understand:

- The concept of risk from a strategic perspective;

- The link between risk events and financial performance;

- How good financial management practices underpin the management of risk;

- Different stakeholder perspectives of risk;

- The specific risks of a globalized fashion business.

RISK AS A STRATEGIC CONCEPT

Arguably the world has not actually got any riskier in recent years, but rather the perception of risk has grown alongside heightened media awareness. Organizational practices are slowly reflecting this 'new normal' and are increasingly focused on risk. For example, there is increased focus of the public company board on matters of Corporate Governance: identifying, assessing, treating and monitoring risks and evaluating the effectiveness of management controls. This originated as a reaction to risk events such as terror attacks, financial market crashes or failed internal control mechanisms further amplified by the media. There is also a trend towards worldwide government regulation using risk-based approaches and internal control

---

13. 46925 London College of Fashion BA16 catwalk show, June 2016, Nicholls and Clarke building, Shoreditch. Photography by Roger Dean.

mechanisms (such as the Sarbanes-Oxley Act introduced in 2002, and the UK Corporate Governance code in 2010). From a fashion perspective, consider the media reaction to a human disaster such as the Rana Plaza factory collapse (see Chapters 8 and 12); searching for blame, recompense and action to ensure it does not happen again, and the ensuing damage to brands from their reaction or indeed lack of response to such a disaster.

In the current dynamic business environment, risk management should not be viewed as a regulatory obligation but as a facilitating driver of strategic success, to help a fashion business avoid potential pitfalls on its journey. Managing risk is an important role for strategic management as it encompasses the art of using lessons from the past to avoid future mistakes and exploit possible opportunities. It is always easier to manage risk where there is a well-planned strategy and equally the process of strategy formulation (see Chapter 2) requires extensive analysis of the business environment, which also serves to highlight the source of potential risks. In

> **Risk** A strategic concept as well as a financial concept underpinning every business venture. Risk is about *uncertainty*, therefore it can be a threat or an opportunity.

> **Risk management** The role of the chief financial officer in preserving business value for its stakeholders. Tools and techniques of financial management can support this aim.

turn, the internal analysis of strategic capabilities demonstrates the ability of the business to deal effectively with any potential risk events.

Is the business environment getting riskier? With increasing focus on cost cutting to provide continual earnings growth especially for public companies (see Chapter 5); with increasing globalization introducing more unknowns of cultural and physical distance; increasing innovation and reliance on technology – it would seem so.

RISK MANAGEMENT

The process of **risk management** can be broken down into four distinct stages as demonstrated in Figure 13.1 and explained in the following sections. Risks need to be identified and their impact evaluated before plans can be put into place to address them through operational monitoring and mitigation. Then it is important to communicate to stakeholders what has been done, to give them confidence in the competence of the management.

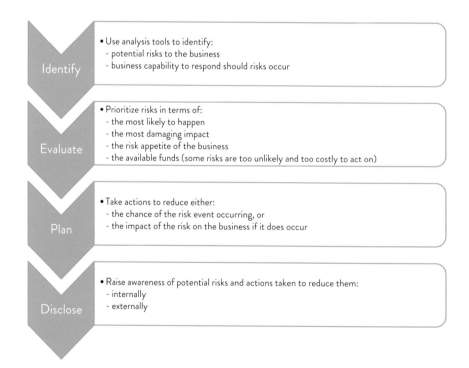

Identify
- Use analysis tools to identify:
  - potential risks to the business
  - business capability to respond should risks occur

Evaluate
- Prioritize risks in terms of:
  - the most likely to happen
  - the most damaging impact
  - the risk appetite of the business
  - the available funds (some risks are too unlikely and too costly to act on)

Plan
- Take actions to reduce either:
  - the chance of the risk event occurring, or
  - the impact of the risk on the business if it does occur

Disclose
- Raise awareness of potential risks and actions taken to reduce them:
  - internally
  - externally

Figure 13.1 *IEPD – a four-stage strategic approach to risk management*

Identify

Risks can be categorized in many ways; using PESTEL factors (introduced in Chapter 2) is a good start and these can be incorporated into a risk management framework to ensure all areas of the business and its environment are considered (see Figure 13.2). The interface of the business with its external environment shows the areas where risks may manifest, and so, where controls are required to mitigate them. This chapter will not cover risk measurement metrics such as Value at Risk (VaR) as that is the domain of the financial services industry and requires a textbook of its own!

Figure 13.2 *Identifying risks in fashion businesses*

Risk management is often considered to be closely related to management accounting and financial control mechanisms but the influence of social, institutional and organizational contexts on strategic risk management cannot be ignored. The human impact of the increasing focus on risk brings with it defensiveness, blame avoidance and fear of sanctions, which are related to organizational culture and employee well-being. It is appropriate to consider here the concept of the Learning Organization (Chapter 2), and corporate risk appetite as a component of business culture, which in turn influences leadership perspectives, executive incentives, employee engagement and talent management (see Chapter 14).

Let us consider strategic risk in the luxury fashion industry context. Luxury is a cost-intensive industry where many costs are fixed at least in the short run, so cannot easily be reduced (for example, collection development, flagship stores, staff, brand communications and so on). Any event that threatens the luxury consumer spend would have an impact on revenues and reduce margins. Economic, political or social factors could influence different luxury customer segments in different ways. For example, the spending propensity of the Chinese consumer may be impacted by a falling stock market or the fiscal actions of their government. The luxury Chinese consumer who traditionally travels to purchase fashion may prefer not to travel following terrorist or health scares. The UK aspirational luxury customer could see economic impacts on their disposable income following interest rate changes. The global nature of the luxury business leaves it open to currency fluctuations, an important issue we will return to later in this chapter. There are risks to the brands of their own making too; in an increasingly crowded global market, over-exposure of the brand can lead it to lose its exclusivity (as happened to the brand Coach). The big luxury players who want to see the market consolidate are also driving risks in acquisition premiums and difficulty realizing synergies in business combinations.

Risks to the strategy of fashion businesses are seemingly endless, so the identification phase requires that you ask 'what if?' questions to drill down and determine the most important risks: those that could affect revenue generation and ultimately the profit of the business (see Figure 13.3). Consider some well publicized risk events that have occurred in fashion businesses:

- What if there was a fire in our distribution centre? (As happened to ASOS in 2014, see Chapter 9.)

- What if a key member of staff is off ill, dies or leaves? (Such as the unexpected death of designer Alexander McQueen, or the departure of Angela Ahrendts from Burberry.)

- What if our main supplier could not supply us or operated in such a way as to damage our reputation? (Such as a main supplier sub-contracting to a factory that was found to be using child labour, as happened to Nike.)

Evaluate and plan

By asking 'what if?' questions a business is trying to determine the worst case scenario: what chain

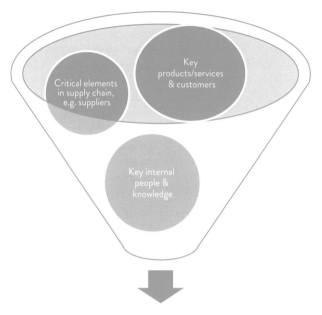

Identify what generates the revenue
and profit of the business

Figure 13.3 *Identifying the key revenue and profit drivers: the risks here matter the most*

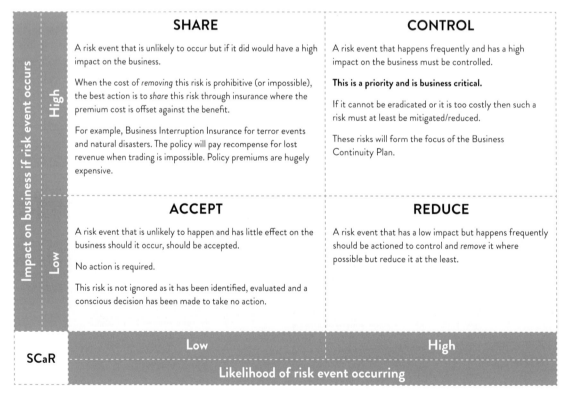

Figure 13.4 *SCaR model: Assess risk likelihood against business impact to determine action required*
Source: Based on Collier (2009).

of events would halt the business completely? The analysis should then consider the *likelihood* of such a catastrophic chain of events, the wide-reaching business impact and how long this would last. This helps to identify the functions and people that are critical to the business so that a plan can be put together to ensure the business can continue. This is the **Business Continuity Plan**, which details who needs to do what, when and where immediately after a major risk event occurs. Mapping the potential impact of an event versus its likelihood, as shown in the SCaR model (Figure 13.4), helps identify where a business should focus its risk reduction efforts and costs.

Disclose

In recognition of the importance of risk to investment decisions, global public companies are obliged to identify and publish their most significant risks within their Annual Report. Ted Baker classifies its risks into the operational, strategic and financial, using a typical risk management framework similar to Figure 13.2, although it could also be argued that all operational risks also have a strategic impact. Reviewing a list of risks can seem anodyne and rather obvious but the process of identification is valuable in itself as it enforces some of the rigour of strategic analysis and planning. This type of disclosure is the statutory minimum and risk-relevant disclosures can be found throughout Corporate Governance Reports, which discuss attitude to risk, internal controls and business continuity plans. These may be separate and lengthy publications; see, for example, those of Next plc or Marks & Spencer plc.

RISK AS A FINANCIAL CONCEPT

In its purest definition risk is the likelihood that returns (profit) will not be as we expect. Why is that a problem when the fundamental premise of business is to put some money such as share capital at risk, in the hope of using it to make more money? As we saw in Chapter 5, there is an important fundamental trade-off between risk and return. If we assume all investors are rational, then they will only accept increased risk if there is a likelihood of increased returns as a result. Also, if the rational investor is forced to accept a degree of risk, they will always choose the option giving the greater return to compensate for this

discomfort. Risk denotes uncertainty and no rational investor, be it a bank, shareholder or private individual, likes uncertainty; investors may have differing levels of tolerance for risk but they will always require that it is compensated for.

The risk universe for a business, as we have seen already, is wide reaching and has many considerations but fundamentally any risk event could result in reduced revenue or increased costs, which in turn would adversely impact profit. Managers need to be aware of the potential risk events in their area, assess their likelihood and judge whether it is worthwhile taking action to minimize the identified risk. From a rather pessimistic viewpoint, risk is generally seen as 'downside'. Sometimes, however, upside risk can be damaging to reputation even though it results in a financial benefit, because it demonstrates management's inability to forecast the opportunity. The issue here underlines a general unease in financial markets arising from any form of unpredictability. Financial risks can be subdivided further as shown in Table 13.1 and we can apply the SCaR model outlined in Figure 13.4 to highlight the actions needed. We saw earlier that Ted Baker chose to highlight operational risks but not to separate out the different elements of financial risk into subcategories. This is fairly standard practice; however, accounting standards require detailed disclosure of financial risk policies and their mitigation within the notes section of the Annual Report and Accounts.

A STAKEHOLDER PERSPECTIVE

Whilst profit is often not the sole objective of a fashion business, it is often the one that the business is most easily measured against. The **UK Companies Act 2006** defines the roles and responsibilities of company directors very widely to ensure they take a stakeholder perspective and promote the success of the company as a whole and not just for the benefit of the shareholders. In performing their duties and making decisions, company directors must consider all stakeholders involved in and impacted by the company (section 172, Companies Act 2006), therefore bearing in mind:

- the likely long-term consequences of their decisions;

- the interests of employees;

Category of Financial Risk	Which means	How can this risk be Shared/Controlled/Reduced (SCaR)?
Liquidity Risk	*The nightmare of the business simply running out of cash*	• Minimize fixed costs – variable costs are easier to 'turn off' in times of cash need. • Diversify sources of funding with regard to availability and costs. • Ensure lending facilities have 'headroom' (a buffer in an overdraft limit in case of bad times). • Staggered maturity timelines ensure lending facilities do not all end at the same time. • Remember, money is always cheaper and more available when you don't need it.
Counterparty/ Credit Risk	*The risk that the counterparties the company does business with cannot fulfil their obligations to the business*	• Spread funding sources across different providers and types in case of banking failure. • Use credit insurance to share the risk of supplier failure (often as a result of their own liquidity risk).
Market Risk	*The risks inherent within the financial markets*	• Very little can be done about unpredictable share price movements, hence the importance of expectation management (see Chapter 5). • Financial instruments can be used to provide some protection ('hedge') against foreign exchange, interest rate and commodity price movements (see the section on 'The great pricing debate').

Table 13.1 *Subcategories of financial risks: Applying SCaR*

- the need to foster the company's business relationships with suppliers, customers and others;

- the impact on the community and the environment;

- the maintenance of high standards of business conduct;

- the need to act fairly [between members].

This is a good point at which to review the work of Alfred Rappaport. An eminent authority on management accounting, Rappaport focuses on the destructive nature of short termism in business, saying: 'Value-creating growth is the strategic challenge. To succeed, companies must be good at developing new, potentially disruptive businesses' (2006: 66). He believes there are key principles to serving the long-term interests of the shareholders in a company, which are summarized in Box 13.1.

Trends in reporting metrics may drive additional focus on, for example, sustainability or international growth, depending on the business model and ownership structure, but fundamentally the focus for all businesses lies on profit and the revenue required to drive a profitable business. This is a good point at which to revisit Chapter 5.

There have been some attempts to redress the balance away from a sole focus on profit as the driver of strategic success in a business. Several authors have devised more holistic approaches to reporting that attempt to consider Environmental, Social and Governance (ESG) factors. John Elkington (1997) coined the term 3BL to represent a Triple Bottom Line of People, Planet and Profit, which he believes businesses should measure to capture the full extent of the impact of their activities. Porritt's (2005) Five Capitals Model takes these ideas further to urge businesses to appreciate how wider environmental and social issues can affect their long-term profitability and competitive advantage. Most would agree with the fundamental principle

BOX 13.1 - Principles of long-term shareholder interest summarized, simplified and interpreted

1. Do not manage profits or provide profit forecasts – instead manage market expectations and provide investors with value-relevant information.

2. Make strategic decisions (such as investments and acquisitions) that maximize expected value, even if it means taking a short-term hit to profit.

3. It follows that you should get rid of assets that do not maximize value even if this results in a hit to profit in the short term.

4. If (and only if) you have no credible value-creating opportunities on which to spend your cash, then return the cash to the shareholders (through share buy-backs).

5. Employee incentives should link reward to long-term value creation – especially for senior managers and Board members – and focus on the value drivers they can influence directly.

6. Board members should be required to bear risks of ownership just as the shareholders do (hence executive share option schemes).

Source: Based on Rappaport (2006).

of measuring the total impact of corporate activity, although no models adequately address the challenge of fair measurement of this impact. A US company is able to formalize this rebalancing of corporate objectives through seeking designation as a Benefit Corporation. Patagonia is an example of such a 'B Corp' which reports on positive impacts it makes from an ESG perspective and the application of its resources to meet wider objectives. Most public companies strive to provide information to some extent on their wider business, adopting a more Balanced Scorecard approach to reporting (Kaplan and Norton, 1996).

MANAGING FINANCIAL PERFORMANCE

Budgets, forecasts and actuals

All businesses will have some form of budget to minimize the risk of running out of cash. The larger the business, the more complex the budgeting process and the greater the resources involved, with armies of management accountants controlling the data and managing the iterative process. Setting the *budget* is often an annual event in the financial calendar and becomes a stake in the ground against which to manage performance. Of course, it rapidly becomes out of date and hence is updated either quarterly or monthly to become a *forecast*. Budgets will be set and monitored for both revenue and capital spend; First we focus on revenue and costs to determine performance.

Actual performance is monitored against the current *forecast*, and exceptions are investigated at cost-centre level using techniques of *variance analysis*. Convention dictates that variances are reported with reference to their impact on profit. A variance that increases profit either by increasing revenue or decreasing cost is known as a *favourable* variance. One that decreases profit by either decreasing revenue or increasing costs is an *adverse* variance. A business will set a variance level, at which investigation would be triggered. In this way variance analysis can be used as an early warning system. Within manufacturing, this type of budgetary control is important. For example, if a production run is budgeted to use a certain volume of material and an adverse usage variance is identified, that could point to a problem with the quality of material used, the maintenance of the machines or the grade of labour-skill employed. A linked analysis of variances might instigate additional quality procedures before the business loses significant revenue, profit or reputation.

Once overall business targets are set, these are filtered down to departmental objectives and become the drivers of performance at product level. It is important that the overall strategic objectives are aligned this way with operational reality. The sales budget must be the first to be considered as this drives the product requirements and ultimately the cash budget. The sales budget has to be owned at department level by the product management teams, who not only know the on-trend designs and colours but hold the relationships with the suppliers, hence are aware of the potential costs of production. The teams weigh this against knowledge of their customers and the prices they will be willing to pay for that product, as discussed a little later. All this knowledge is factored into the product budgets, which are explored in greater detail in Box 13.2.

Costs can also easily erode profit if they are not closely controlled, so here an effective budget setting and monitoring process is important. When setting a budget for a particular cost line it is common practice to use as a starting point the level of actual spend last year. Onto this you may add a general increment for inflation and known additional costs of planned strategic initiatives. For example, a departmental payroll budget where there are three staff costing £50,000 each and recruitment of a new employee is planned at the start of the year:

Payroll

Actual spend in 16/17	£150,000
Add 3% inflationary pay rise/bonus	£ 4,500
Add new post	£ 30,000
Total budget 17/18	£184,500

This total budget would then be split equally over the year at £15,375 per month. Note that reference here is to how much staff cost the business rather than how much they are paid. Employment costs include benefits in kind, employer's National Insurance and pension contributions. As the year progresses it is unlikely that the spend pattern will match the budget; for example, if an employee leaves and a vacancy arises and remains unfilled, spend will be less than budget. Where there is a planned restructuring or redundancy programme, a separate budget would be held centrally for these one-off costs.

If budgets are based on actual spend, such as no bonuses/pay rises in the example above, this amount would be 'lost' from the budget. This leads to a 'use it or lose it' mentality when the pressure to spend when approaching the year end results in new carpet or chairs. Well managed businesses ensure their budgeting discipline does not encourage this wasteful behaviour. The most effective budgeting approach is through justifying each cost line in turn in this way, to minimize the reserve pots (budgetary slack) built in at cost-centre level. It is better for business transparency if there are larger reserves held centrally rather than several smaller pots held in each cost centre. The downside of this zero-based budgeting approach is the time and resource it takes to justify every cost line within every cost centre.

Budgets and behaviours

It is worth considering briefly here the impact of budgets on behaviours within a business. Budgets are often used as motivational tools; their achievement can be linked to executive incentive packages, and the achievement of sales targets is a bonus tool commonly used in retail organizations. Consider perhaps the behaviours that ensue in the drive to achieve individual bonus targets: the effect on teamwork and whether indeed the effect on the company as a whole is positive. Also consider the negative impacts of a manager setting unachievable targets for the team to make them look good and building in financial 'rainy day' funds that are released at the year end to ensure targets are achieved.

Our brains use processing shortcuts when making decisions. These shortcuts are known as heuristics and help us process large amounts of data and analyze complex situations. They are largely unconscious, coined as 'Fast thinking' by Daniel Khaneman (2012) and contrasted against the 'Slow thinking' of deliberate decision-making. His work identifies how we use the most easily available and most recently processed data in making decisions. He terms these phenomena 'The Availability Bias' and 'The Recency Bias'. Further reading of this fascinating subject is highly recommended. Despite these potential downsides, the practice of budgeting is widespread as it prevents overspending and profit erosion through monitoring and authorization of spending levels, providing performance analysis and an early warning system of problems, and ultimately facilitates the achievement of strategic objectives (see Box 13.2).

The risk of getting the forecasts wrong is felt keenly by companies, whose share price can react dramatically to undershooting forecasts and surprises in the market. For example, in April 2012, Supergroup plc, as a newly listed company on the London Stock Exchange, admitted arithmetic mistakes in its accounting. The company lost 40% of its value in response to the profit warning it issued; this was not just a loss of forecast profit but a huge dent to management credibility too.

BOX 13.2 - The product budget in action

On the face of it, blouses, trousers and knitwear seem to have little to do with profit and loss, balance sheets and cash flow. Certainly, customers do not give the financial well-being of a fashion retailer a second thought when choosing what to purchase or when to do so. The two are, however, inextricably linked and so establishing a connection between the two disciplines is vital if strategic goals are to be achieved in the long term.

The connection between finance and product management hinges on the position of the two roles within the value chain (see Chapter 2). The value chain identifies differing activities that when linked together facilitate the creation of optimal value via an efficient use of resources to deliver market suitable products. These activities are divided into two types: primary – those concerned with product supply and delivery; and support – the activities that back up the primary activities in their endeavours. The value chain places product management and finance in differing activity types, with product management clearly a set of primary activities, while finance sits within those defined as support. We could of course critique this view from a funding perspective but that debate is not for this section.

The disparity between product management and financial management is further strengthened if we consider the central role of product within fashion businesses. Product is conceived 'to be a problem solver' (de Chernatony and McDonald 2003: 4), satisfying a particular need. This problem-solving capability could be functional (a winter coat for cold weather), or psychological (a cashmere sweater to give a feeling of status). A second perspective is offered by Brassington and Petitt (2013), who argue that product is a 'physical good, service, idea, person or place that is capable of offering tangible or intangible attributes that individuals or organizations regard as so necessary, worthwhile or satisfying that they are prepared to exchange money, patronage or some other unit of value in order to acquire it' (p. 268). There are parallels with the first perspective but additional concepts are included, importantly the linking of necessary (on trend) product to a unit of value (price paid).

Using these two definitions we can make the case for an explicit link between finance and product management. The finance role by its nature cannot accurately assess the problem-solving capabilities of product in terms of trend interpretation, competing products or the type of decisions that will determine appropriate intangible product benefit. Finance can, however, measure the effectiveness of product unit value to cover the cost of goods sold, overheads and balance sheet requirements. Product management, conversely, can easily understand the problem-solving capabilities and inherent value within product ranges, but it is less likely to be able to translate these into robust strategic financial plans that will enable long-term value creation.

The bridge that connects these two very different business activities is the WSSI (Weekly Sales, Stock, and Intake report) and its use is widespread within fashion businesses.

 ONLINE RESOURCES

Our companion website contains a worked-through example of the WSSI, see https://www.macmillanihe.com/companion/Varley_Fashion_Management.

BUSINESS MODELS AND THEIR FINANCIAL CHARACTERISTICS

Whatever the business model, the good financial manager plays a central role in minimizing risk. First and foremost is the understanding of what the real *key* performance indicators are in the business; both the financial measurements (for example, an interest cover covenant enforced by banking facilities, as discussed in Chapter 5) and non-financial measures dictated by stakeholders. Secondly, there is the use of budgeting and management accounting tools such as variance analysis to monitor how the business is currently performing, both against itself in prior years and against its competition, to inform strategic direction. We have already seen that there will be the need to periodically update the budget to a more realistic forecast to monitor, and use, the variance analysis of exceptions to identify and rectify operational issues before value is destroyed. This in turn may lead to decisions to prune costs, avoiding wasteful or non-essential spend so that cash can be prioritized for strategic purposes. The danger here is of seeking short-term gains at the expense of investment in the long term, but more of that debate later.

Cost profiles and financial risks differ depending on the business model. We can extend an analysis of the financial statements to help us consider risk. In Table 13.2 we can see how it is possible to identify different types of companies and their business model from the features of their accounts, particularly their Statement of Position (Balance Sheet). Remembering of course that this Statement is a snapshot of the business on one day only, its carefully chosen year end date, and that these positions change significantly over the year in a seasonal fashion business, these features give us some idea of the financial risks that need to be controlled, particularly within working capital, the underpinning of many of the key performance indicators.

Operating cost profiles will also differ with business model type and can be seen in the Income Statement. For example, UK retailers saw increasing labour costs as the government policies on the living wage and apprenticeship levy took effect. There are also seemingly upward only trends in the store occupancy costs of rent, rates, utilities and so on.

Understanding manufacturing

Much of what we have talked about so far takes the view of the fashion company being a retail or wholesale distributor of fashion product that has been sourced by the product management teams. How these teams work is explored in Chapter 8. If the product teams have an appreciation of how the manufacturer's business model works they will be better able to develop a longstanding relationship, ultimately resulting in mutually beneficial cost-price negotiations.

It is not appropriate in this text to explore the mechanics of absorption (full) costing versus marginal costing. You can refer to a text such as Jeffrey and Evans (2011) and consider that manufacturers will have systems in place that allow them to calculate the full cost of each garment they produce. Taking the direct costs of producing each garment (fabric and trims), standards are used to add in costs for thread, and labour used to 'cut, make and trim' (CMT) a garment. Further estimates are used to add in costs for overheads of the factory, to ensure a profit is made on each order to sustain the business. Costs of packaging, quality assurance sampling and distribution are also factored in.

The point at which the retailer assumes title (legal ownership) for the manufactured goods is important. This dictates which party manages the risk and hence costs of distribution and insurance. The method of transport chosen will offset its cost against speed of supply and be dependent on distance from the point of sale. The buyer's skilful use of negotiation levers will take into account order size, and the likelihood of repeat business, to reduce cost price and increase intake (profit) margin on product buys.

THE GREAT PRICING DEBATE

If the starting point for every budget is to consider how much revenue can be made, then there is a need to consider how prices are set. There is a limited amount of profit ('intake') margin available in every buy and it is like a tug of war between the customer, retailer and manufacturer to share this out. We saw in Chapter 8 the product manager's view of pricing hierarchies. The fundamental economic concept of price elasticity underpins pricing strategies. In mass-market fashion reality the amount a customer is willing to pay (the market) drives the price that a retailer will be able to charge for a certain item. This price then drives the cost that a retailer is able to pay a supplier; margins are the profit elements shared between the supplier and retailer. The strategic management of these margins is the role of the product manager. Their negotiating skill therefore provides the platform for profitability of the whole fashion business and can be highly complex where global sourcing relationships and corporate social responsibility influence cost structures.

Demand-driven pricing is evident in fashion as some goods can be considered to be commodities. One plain white T-shirt from Topshop is very like one from H&M so the pricing has to be similar as switching costs for customers are low. Customers will only tolerate increased pricing when they perceive they are getting something in exchange for the additional cost, such as better design, better fabric,

Business Model	Relative features of the Statement of Position	Some Specific Financial Risks
Manufacturer	**Fixed Assets (High)** Machinery **Working Capital:** **Stock (High)** Raw materials and finished goods **Creditors (High)** Amounts owing to suppliers for raw materials Amounts owing on debt funding sources **Debtors (High)** Amounts owed to the business from customers **Cash (Low)**	Significant cash tied up in fixed costs of machines that should not be idle. Influences decisions about accepting low-value contracts (refer to marginal costing ideas). Consider the constraints imposed on the business by the funding sources of these investments. Debt collection function is key to generating cash for investment in raw materials. Cash upfront or in stages is an important part of any buying negotiation.
Wholesaler	**Fixed Assets (Low)** **Working Capital:** **Stock (High)** Finished goods to be sold on **Creditors (High)** Amounts owing to suppliers for stock **Debtors (High)** Amounts owed to the business from customers **Cash (Low)**	Minimal fixed costs allows agility. The increasingly obsolete role of the distribution intermediary is about building in time within the fashion system. The wholesaler holds stock from the manufacturer on behalf of the retailer then allows the retailer time to sell it to the end consumer before payment is due. Debt collection practices must be efficient to realize the cash. Often characterized by high overdraft facilities fluctuating seasonally.
Retailer	**Fixed Assets (High)** Bricks & Mortar Stores &/or Website/ IT Infrastructure **Working Capital:** **Stock (Very High)** **Creditors (High)** Amounts owing to suppliers for stock **Debtors (Low)** Amounts owed to the business from customers **Cash (Low)**	Investments depend on channel focus of the retailer. Suppliers may be manufacturers for own-brand stock or wholesale brands. The crux of the retail model is to convert stock to cash as quickly as possible, to free cash for investment in the next trend. The role of the product manager in moving stock through the business quickly using markdown if necessary, is key. Few retailers sell on credit; store-cards are usually run through bank joint ventures.

Table 13.2 *Relating the characteristics of the business model as shown in the statement of position to financial risk*

or better-quality workmanship. Premium and luxury brands justify increased prices in part by better quality materials and production but, in the main, by promising their customer a better buying experience, and overt branding to proclaim their belongingness to an elite group (such as the embroidery of a small polo pony on the T-shirt). This increased profit potential explains the large investment in branding and marketing, although this investment is risky in itself, being subject to the vagaries of customer taste.

Herein lies another example of short-termism; the malaise of discounting in the fashion industry. This is brands engaging in a price war due to the excess of 'me too' products which consumers are not willing to pay full price for. Many brands are overly focused on a race to the bottom; short-term results drive through intake margin battles with suppliers. To stop this, brands need to be brave enough to invest in the long term, in product innovation, design talent and newness, to result in differentiated products customers actually want to buy at full price. With luxury brands, price is a signal (Okonkwo, 2007); if the garment is too cheap it cannot possibly be luxury, which implies elitism, rarity and status.

CURRENCY CALAMITIES

It is quite usual for companies to expend great effort and resource controlling Open-to-Buy (a budgetary planning tool), negotiating intake margins and forecasting demand – then an uncontrollable global event changes exchange rates and wipes out the year's profit! Currency fluctuations and foreign exchange risk become important to even the smallest business once they start to trade overseas in another currency.

Transaction risk

There is a very simple way to eliminate transaction currency risk. A powerful business can force its suppliers to take the risk on its behalf by demanding to trade in its own currency. This logic is flawed, as all that will happen is that the supplier will price into the margin a buffer to allow for currency movements. It is much better therefore to trade in the supplier's currency and for the company to take the risk itself. In that way transparency allows a company to deal with the currency risk separately.

There is no doubt that for globalized fashion businesses currency fluctuations are a big deal and investors need to appreciate the impact. For public companies the currency exposures and the actions taken to control this risk are identified in detail in the notes to the accounts and displayed prominently in the financial statements. It is currently common for a fashion firm's product to be sourced in the Far East, where the usual currency of trade with garment

suppliers is US Dollars, which for a UK/Euro based company yields a transactional exchange risk on every product contract sourced in US dollars. The problem for the fashion industry here arises through time lags. Garment prices are negotiated and contracted well in advance of the delivery and payment. Over that time the exchange rate moves, either in the fashion firm's favour or against it, but what matters is that it moves; the margin changes and it is this unpredictability that is a risk to profit.

Exchange rates are the price of one currency relative to another and in theory reflect the relative attractiveness of a currency pair, with the simple economic principle of expecting money to flow towards a stronger currency. To this end, things such as government economic data releases can affect exchange rates and whilst these can to some extent be predicted, many movements seemingly have no logical cause. Even in a period of relative exchange rate stability there can be significant movements (see, for example, www.ft.com).

Aside from the US dollar there are other significant currencies for the fashion industry: the Euro is particularly relevant for luxury businesses and the value of local currencies in China, Russia, and Brazil impact the viability of localized trade and customer demand. Foreign exchange can also be a significant factor in price setting for overseas brand operations. Fashion brands operating in foreign markets will often charge a considerable premium for their products that exceeds the cost of doing business in the territory, resulting in a substantial benefit to profit levels. This is disclosed in the accounts but can be a factor contributing to the increase in market value (i.e., share price) for an overseas trading company. When exchange rates move against the company and erode this additional profit, the share price and hence the company value can fall. For example, in November 2015 Burberry plc saw a fall in its share price when it announced a profit warning, which was partly due to global currency volatility reducing the expected annual benefit from exchange rate differentials.

Fashion retailers will use a major clearing bank such as HSBC or Barclays to manage their foreign currency requirements and payments alongside their domestic accounts. The use of letters of credit or supply chain finance products may give the retailer financial power in a buying negotiation. In addition, the banks have devised banking products to help reduce or share this currency exchange risk, at a price.

Hedging strategies in a fashion retailer

Using forward exchange contracts is common practice in large fashion companies with significant buy volumes denominated in foreign currencies. This process is called 'hedging'. The advantage of this is clear; the cost is known but the money does not move until the supplier requires payment. There may be factors such as quality issues and shipment delays that mean the contract is not actually required for payment on the date booked. Further contracts can be entered into with the bank to 'swap' the currency movements into subsequent months. Retailers with sophisticated hedging strategies and treasury functions in their finance department will enter into bulk currency contracts on a rolling basis based on the requirements forecast by their product management teams. This allows the retailer to fix a blended 'internal' exchange rate for the product teams to work with each season. This certainty is important considering the incentivization and motivation of these teams. Each product department will forecast the amount of currency required each month to settle supplier payments. These forecasts are rolled up to a total amount of each currency required per month. Treasury will then enter into forward exchange contracts to fix the rate. The retailer will set a policy of how much to fix in advance, allowing some upside benefit and some room for forecasting error. An example of a hedging strategy would be to buy forward contracts covering 50% of the requirement forecast 12–18 months in advance and to top this up to 100% of the forecast requirement between now and 12 months hence. The hedging policy for a public company is detailed in the notes to its accounts and published in its Annual Report and Accounts.

Translation risk

Whilst transaction risk is an issue that directly affects the profit of many fashion businesses, as these businesses grow another type of foreign exchange risk becomes important. Consider the UK-domiciled retailer who sets up a buying office in the Far East to get closer to the suppliers it is transacting with, or perhaps expands into Euro-denominated stores or manufacturing facilities. Now the firm has assets (owned premises) denominated in foreign currency. A requirement to value these assets on the Statement of Position every year introduces translation risk. These currency movements are due to accounting rules and are not real movements of cash until the asset is involved in a transaction (sold) but nonetheless the change in value must be reflected in the accounts. To avoid this risk it is common to finance the foreign asset purchase using a loan denominated in the same currency. In that way the currency movements acting on the equal and opposite asset and liability would cancel each other out.

STRATEGIC INVESTMENT DECISIONS

Aside from the everyday trading of product, fashion businesses invest substantial amounts of money in growth and enhancing their strategic capabilities. They will invest in new stores and branding refreshes at home, fund international expansion, add new web platforms and logistics facilities. These are major investments requiring considerable research to minimize the risk of making expensive mistakes. Approval of such a large spend is usual at Board level following the production of a detailed cost/benefit case.

Building the cost/benefit case

Before a proposed investment can be evaluated a case is needed that weighs the cost outlays against the potential benefits. We introduced the term WACC (Weighted Average Cost of Capital) in Chapter 5, which is relevant here. Needless to say, there are many estimates and forecasts included in such a case but as far as possible the following should be quantified:

1. The initial cost of the investment (capital outlay) and the cost of raising any required finance;

2. The on-going revenue costs of the project such as machinery running costs, or interest on the finance;

3. The estimated life of the investment in the business (and any potential residual value to other businesses once it has finished with it; usually scrap value only); and

4. The forecast returns, which are the income resulting from the investment and the timing of the income.

More complex cases may also consider the opportunity costs, such as interest lost if the project was internally financed, or lost revenue from the alternative projects that cannot be pursued because this one has been chosen, if there is a limit on the funding available.

The returns should be quantified wherever possible; for example a new machine would reduce the costs of quality control rejects at a manufacturer, and these should be valued. Quantified returns expressed in monetary terms are known as 'hard benefits'. There are often 'soft benefits' which cannot easily be quantified and that often form the persuasive argument behind why an investment should be undertaken, such as the effect on reputation and brand image or staff morale.

Evaluating the cost benefit case

Usually there are several investment options to choose between. The analysis of the cost/benefit case follows, using some simple tools of financial analysis. Whilst there is every opportunity for this analysis to get overly complex, simple tools can support common-sense

decisions. The simplest and most intuitive method for evaluating capital projects is by calculating the payback period. Simply, how long does it take to accrue enough benefit to pay off the initial investment? Simplicity is the greatest attraction of this analysis tool but it has its downsides. Payback looks only at cash flows and does not consider the timing of those flows. Why does the timing matter? Now is a good point to introduce an underpinning financial concept.

The time value of money

It is better to have less money today than the promise of more money tomorrow because if you have the money today you have certainty. Remember, a rational investor seeks certainty and with that money today you can choose what to do with it, such as invest it or spend it. There comes a point at which the amount of money promised and how long you have to wait for it start to influence your decision. That influence can be quantified through a process known as discounting (it is important to note that this type of discounting reduces the size of financial flows rather than being directly related to fashion sale events!). Discounting techniques are widely used by corporate financiers, for example in corporate valuations. The concept is simple although the maths may look challenging. Discounting is used in the calculation of the Net Present Value of capital investment projects. This allows projects with different patterns of cash flow to be compared, so that not only the size of the flows but the timing of them is considered.

 ONLINE RESOURCES

A worked-through example of a capital investment appraisal is available on our companion website: https://www.macmillanihe.com/companion/Varley_Fashion_Management, to illustrate these options.

Accounting for risk

Capital investment returns are just like any other forecast, and as estimates, there is an element of risk that they may turn out to be wrong. We could ignore the risk and assume that it will even out over time, with some forecast returns being higher than expected and some lower than expected. The problem is that behavioural factors lead to projects being accepted that more usually under-perform rather than over-perform. Managers are more likely to be over-optimistic in their expectations as a self-serving bias, either minimizing costs or over-forecasting capacity.

Instead of just ignoring risk we could use a Risk Premium Discount Factor to adjust the numbers. Simply put, where the cost of capital is 16%, and experience suggests projects generally only bring in 14% (a 2% shortfall), so all appraisal calculations should be made using a discount rate of 18% to achieve an actual yield of 16%. Using this risk-adjusted discount factor, some projects previously thought to be profitable will now be rejected, but as long as there is a pipeline of new projects this should not be a major problem.

Playing with numbers does not actually avoid risk and may give a dangerous sense of complacency; just because the numbers say something is a good investment, it does not mean we should not still be cautious. The problem with relying on this sort of analysis is the over-emphasis on short-term return. This can be a common problem, in particular for public companies. In minimizing the risk of profit fluctuations so that there is a steady growth in dividend (revenue stream) and share price (capital) as demanded by shareholders, some opportunities may be missed along the way, which could have increased the entity value for the stakeholders as a whole had they been pursued. Herein, as Rappaport (2006) identified, lies the need to balance the strategic requirements of innovation and long-term investment with the rational, risk-averse financial manager's mind-set.

Diversification and portfolios

Investors can reduce their overall investment risk by holding a diversified portfolio. The rational investor looks for investments whose risk profiles complement each other and are as far as possible inversely correlated; for example, a factor like a UK recession may have an adverse effect on a UK investment but may result in a less negative impact on a non-UK exposure. This idea of complementarity works on a corporate portfolio basis too and supports the diversified portfolio of conglomerates (as seen in the Kering Case Study, in Chapter 2). When the luxury brand Moët Hennessy had surplus cash, it sought to use its experience in luxury consumption to invest in other product areas such as Louis Vuitton luxury luggage, with different cost and demand profiles, hence reducing its risk. Risk reduction may not be the driving force behind the business selection within such a conglomerate but it is one consideration. The group does not look to provide a balanced portfolio for the investor as investors can do this for themselves by investing in different sectors and territories. The group can, however, be viewed as an investor itself with elements of risk reduction through diversification in its portfolio of businesses. For example, LVMH can balance the big brands in its stable, such as Louis Vuitton and Christian Dior against the smaller lesser-known brands like Céline and Fendi. The ability to flex their focus across their different brands offers some risk protection.

Corporate financiers express these simple ideas of diversified portfolios in a model known as the Capital Asset Pricing Model (CAPM). We saw how financial management tools can be used to appraise potential investment opportunities in isolation, but CAPM is more useful than these tools as it relates the risk of the potential investment to the risk of the current portfolio (what the company is currently doing). In cases where an investment is risky when viewed in isolation, if it is inversely correlated to the current portfolio its addition will change the risk profile of the whole business. This consideration of new ventures, whether a new business, new store or new machine, and its impact on the risk profile of the existing portfolio is an important lesson from CAPM. Refer to any good corporate finance text for a detailed treatment of this model.

CASH IS ABSOLUTELY EVERYTHING …

Whilst steps can be taken to reduce risk, fashion businesses can and do fail. Fashion retail in particular is vulnerable to cash flow pressures arising from seasonality, as we saw earlier, rendering it a risky game to be in. Stock markets do not like, nor understand particularly well, the risky nature of fashion businesses. The fact that significant investment is required in stock, several months in advance of sales which may or may not actually happen, depending on factors over which you have varying degrees of control, make profitability hard to predict, hence the risk to the business. Have you got your trend predictions right? Will your customer want to buy your product selection? Will the customer feel like spending (effect of weather, economy, global factors)? Not surprisingly, fashion retail in particular has seen many high-profile business casualties. Even seemingly successful businesses may overstretch themselves from a cash flow perspective. A good example of this was seen when Matchesfashion.com wanted to capitalize on their successful business model by rapidly ramping up their store estate. Opening new stores is a great drain on cash resources as significant cash is required for fit-out costs, stock and rent even before any product can be sold. It may take several months to start to turn positive cash flow, meanwhile overheads of staff and premises still have to be paid. Without significant cash backing, overly fast and ambitious expansion plans can see a successful business fall into trouble. We saw in Chapter 5 the importance of the private funders in seeing the potential in fashion brands with cash flow issues, enough to invest in them, restructure their cost base and make them successful. Matchesfashion.com today is a successful largely online retailer but many fashion brands have disappeared over time. The old adage may say 'Cash is King', but for fashion businesses cash is absolutely everything.

... But reputation is important too

Although this is the domain of the branding and marketing professionals, no discussion of risk management can ignore the huge importance of reputation management. The impact of brand equity on company value through its revenue- and profit-generating potential is enormous ... but precarious from a risk perspective.

CASE STUDY 13 - Shanghai Tang: Growing an international brand with a strong Chinese identity

Shanghai Tang was founded in Hong Kong in 1994 by Sir David Tang as a tailoring atelier and developed its clothing offer into a ready-to-wear line primarily aimed at an expatriate and tourist customer who wanted to capture a piece of Hong Kong heritage by buying into a romanticized retro vision of Chinese sartorial style. Key products for Shanghai Tang were the *cheongsam* or *qipao* – the form-fitting dress most widely known in the West as the 'Suzie Wong' dress – for women, and Mandarin collared jackets for men. Subsequent expansions of the brand offer have relied on the cultural connotations of Shanghai specifically and China more generally to inform product development and in 2017 the brand operated in 55 countries globally including 48 boutiques.

With a vision of creating an international Chinese lifestyle brand, Shanghai Tang opened a flagship store on New York's Madison Avenue in late 1997, taking its collection of Chinese classics to the heart of US high fashion retail. Sensing the potential growth opportunities for a Chinese luxury brand both abroad and domestically, with the opening up of the Chinese economy, Richemont acquired a controlling stake in Shanghai Tang in 1998, and bought out the residual share in 2008, the same year the Beijing Olympics turned a spotlight on all things Chinese. However, although the stateside launch garnered much media attention for the brand, sales figures were disappointing and with high rental costs Shanghai Tang was relocated to a store with smaller square footage.

Shanghai Tang store interiors. Image Credit: Natascha Radclyffe-Thomas. Reproduced by permission of Shanghai Tang.

Further financial challenges for the brand were closer to home with the Asian financial crisis which negatively impacted the Hong Kong economy for two years from late 1997. This was followed by the SARS epidemic in 2003 which saw tourist numbers dwindle, although this was ameliorated later in the year when the PRC government relaxed visa restrictions for Mainland Chinese to visit Hong Kong. Sir David Tang had launched Shanghai Tang with a vision to be the first Chinese luxury brand but by the early 2000s it was struggling to communicate its fashion relevance.

The Beijing Olympics of 2008 not only drew attention to Chinese history and culture for an international audience but also instilled Chinese pride in its own heritage. This was seen as an opportunity for Shanghai Tang to capture its share of the growing luxury Chinese customer base. Shanghai Tang had been building its presence in hotels and department stores worldwide. It opened a Kowloon-side Hong Kong store in the repurposed former Marine Police Headquarters luxury retail development, 1881, in 2009 and extended the brand experience by opening a Shanghai Tang café in Xintiandi, Shanghai's exclusive heritage shopping development, in 2010 (see Figure 10.3).

2011 saw the Pedder Building store close and an alternative heritage building was acquired on Hong Kong Island-side; the Shanghai Tang Mansion opened in 2012, a 15,000 square foot four-storey retail space incorporating a restaurant and gallery space on its top floor. The potential for targeting new generations of Chinese luxury consumers and a newfound interest in fugu (retro) informed the rebrand, which saw a focus on new product design and store experience. In addition, Shanghai Tang acquired the historic Cathay Mansion, a 1932 art deco building, for its Shanghai flagship.

2014 was the twentieth anniversary of the brand, celebrated with new initiatives designed to decode the brand vision and attract a younger Mainland Chinese customer. The China Fashion Chic fashion show held in Shanghai showcased the Spring/Summer 2015 see-now-buy-now collection modelled by Chinese supermodels. In the same year, Hong Kong's Pacific Place mall hosted a Shanghai Tang exhibition and at Hong Kong Fashion Week Shanghai Tang partnered with sustainable textile NGO Redress in the annual EcoChic Fashion Awards.

Shanghai Tang has successfully built a brand celebrating Chinese cultural heritage and sought to develop the brand in response to the changing demographic of luxury fashion consumers. Using country-of-origin as a differentiator has added value for European luxury labels but with Richemont's announcement of the sale of Shanghai Tang in July 2017 it seems that the market has not embraced their vision of a global Chinese luxury label, and this sets a strategic challenge for its new owners.

Case Author: Natascha Radclyffe-Thomas

Case Challenge

The case demonstrates some of the risk associated with the expansion of a high-profile fashion orientated brand. Use Figure 13.2 to classify and evaluate the risks presented in this case.

ONLINE RESOURCES

A longer version of this case study, with additional challenges, can be found on our companion website: https://www.macmillanihe.com/companion/Varley_Fashion_Management.

SUMMARY AND CONCLUDING THOUGHTS

Risk is unpredictable by nature and potentially hugely damaging. Figure 13.5 shows that businesses have a choice to either prevent, accept or embrace risk. Fashion by its very nature is all about risk and change, so it follows that fashion businesses should be well placed to embrace risk. With a good awareness of the risks in their business environment and the potential impacts on their operations and performance, fashion businesses can seize opportunities to build and sustain their competitive advantage. Why 'play it safe' and look at risk as a downside to be controlled when risk is really an opportunity to create value adding growth? Risk management is, after all, the art of using lessons from the past to avoid making the same mistakes again and ensure positioning to exploit future opportunities.

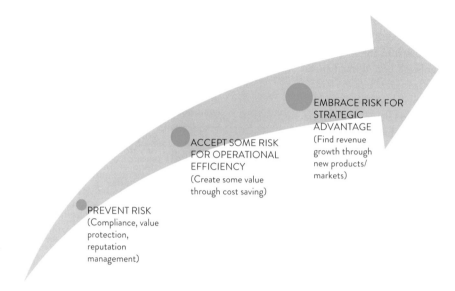

Figure 13.5 *Prevent/Accept/Embrace: A model of risk appetite for strategic advantage*

This guidance can be considered in the context of strategic advantage and the work of Raynor and Ahmed (2013), who performed a vast statistical survey of several hundred companies that have done well enough for long enough to qualify as truly exceptional. Their work discovered that the many and diverse choices that made companies great were consistent with three elementary rules:

1. **Better before cheaper (or compete on differentiators other than price).**

2. **Revenue before cost (or prioritize increasing revenue over reducing costs).**

3. **There are no other rules (so change anything to follow rules 1 and 2).**

This only serves to highlight how long-term success in any industry is rare and difficult to achieve. Finding a workable strategy that stays within these rules requires creativity, flexibility and, above all, the willingness to take a risk.

CHALLENGES AND CONVERSATIONS

1. For a fashion business of your choice, use some of the analysis tools (such as Figures 13.2 and 13.4) to perform a risk mapping exercise.

    ● What are the most important risks in today's global fashion industry?

    ● What is their likelihood of occurrence and what is their impact on your chosen business should they occur?

    ● Is the risk universe the same for different types of fashion company, for example a global luxury brand versus a pureplay e-tailer?

2. Look at the reports of some public fashion companies and the level of detail of their risk disclosure. For example, compare Marks & Spencer plc with Supergroup plc. What do you think the risk appetite of these companies is? Can you find examples of fashion companies which use alternative reporting approaches?

3. Compare and contrast the principles suggested by Alfred Rappaport (2006) with Raynor and Ahmed's (2013) conclusions. How can you reconcile these two seemingly opposite theoretical positions?

REFERENCES AND FURTHER READING

Atrill, P. (2014) *Financial Management for Decision Makers*. 7th edn. Harlow: Financial Times/Prentice Hall.

Brassington, F. and Petitt, S. (2013) *Essentials of Marketing*, 3rd edn. Harlow: Pearson Education.

Collier, P. (2009) *Fundamentals of Risk Management for Accountants and Managers*. London: Taylor & Francis.

de Chernatony, L. and McDonald, M. (2003) *Creating Powerful Brands*. Oxford: Butterworth-Heinemann.

de Chernatony, L., McDonald, M. and Wallace, E. (2010) *Creating Powerful Brands*, 4th edn. Abingdon: Routledge.

Elkington, J. (1997) *Cannibals with Forks: The Triple Bottom Line of 21st Century Business*. North Mankato. MN: Capstone.

Hillier, D., Ross, S., Westerfield, R., Jaffe, J. and Jordan, B. (2016) *Corporate Finance*, 3rd edn. Maidenhead: McGraw Hill.

Hopkin, P. (2012) *Fundamentals of Risk Management*, 2nd edn. London: Kogan Page.

Jeffrey, M. and Evans, N. (2011) *Costing for the Fashion Industry*. Oxford: Berg.

Kaplan, R. and Norton, D. (1996) *The Balanced Scorecard: Translating Strategy into Action*. Boston, MA: Harvard Business School Press.

Khaneman, D. (2012) *Thinking, Fast and Slow*. London: Penguin.

Koller, T., Lovallo, D. and Williams, Z. (2012) *Overcoming a bias against risk*. Available at: http://www.mckinsey.com/business-functions/strategy-and-corporate-finance/our-insights/overcoming-a-bias-against-risk [accessed 10/04/2018].

Okonkwo, U. (2007) *Luxury Fashion Branding: Trends, Tactics, Techniques*. Basingstoke: Palgrave Macmillan.

Porritt, J. (2005) *Capitalism: As If the World Matters*. London and Sterling, VA: Earthscan.

Rappaport A. (2006) '10 ways to create shareholder value'. *Harvard Business Review*, 84(9), pp. 66–77.

Raynor, M. and Ahmed, M. (2013) 'Three Rules for Making a Company Really Great'. *Harvard Business Review*, 91(4), pp. 108–117.

The Institute of Risk Management (n.d.). Available at: https://www.theirm.org/media/885907/Risk_Culture_A5_WEB15_Oct_2012.pdf and https://www.theirm.org/media/1454276/IRM_Operational-Risks_Booklet_hi-res_web-2-.pdf [accessed 10/04/2018].

Watson, D. and Head, A. (2013) *Corporate Finance: Principles and Practice*, 6th edn. Harlow: Pearson.

PEOPLE MANAGEMENT IN FASHION

Lisa Henderson

 INTRODUCTION

We have noted in previous chapters the huge scale of employment within the global fashion industry; as a focus, 555,000 people work across the fashion and textiles industry in the UK and 1.8 million in the US (Fashion United, 2017). Organizations are becoming more aware of the link between people and organizational success and they are investing more readily in the asset that is human capital. Within the fashion environment, the nature of the industry is forward thinking and service driven, which places the workforce as crucial components of organizational success. In chapter 2 we classified strategic capability as the 4M's (men, money, machines, and minds). Here we concentrate on people (men) and their mental characteristics (minds).

Originally classed as an administrative support function (Porter, 1985), Human Resources (HR) now offers strategic management input and structured development for organizations to enable competitive advantage to be gained through the workforce employed. The rise of the HR director onto the senior board has continued to develop along with the development of the strategic nature of the department and its role within organizations; however, as fashion organizations and working environments develop at a pace, agility and flexibility are required to provide the workforce needed to support the strategic aims of a business. HR is being challenged not just to work strategically within the business for answers but also to look outside the organization to find the methods, solutions and resources needed, bringing a far broader and more complex element to the function (Ulrich and Dulebohn, 2015).

Human Resources Management (HRM), Human Resource Development (HRD) and Strategic Human Resource Management (SHRM) are all explored in this chapter, highlighting the key elements needing consideration in fashion businesses today. The complexity of how these sections connect and interrelate needs to be considered throughout.

 LEARNING OBJECTIVES

After studying this chapter, you should be able to understand:

- The key principles and elements of Human Resources Management, Human Resource Development and Strategic Human Resource Management;

- Various models and theories of Human Resources and its management within the fashion industry;

- The link between the corporate strategic aims and the people within a fashion organization;

- The importance of the employee in the organization and the factors that affect satisfaction, performance and engagement;

- The potential future challenges of Human Resources in a changing business environment.

---

14. Photograph by Valerie Wilson Trower.

THE DEVELOPMENT OF HUMAN RESOURCES: FROM AN ADMINISTRATIVE TO A STRATEGIC FUNCTION

In its original form the personnel department, as it was called then, was responsible for the administration of all people matters such as payroll, employment contracts and general paperwork. As business practices have developed to be more strategically led, the thinking around the workforce and what it could bring to the organization as a resource has also changed. Through development of processes and practices to give standardized expectations and requirements for the workforce, the people agenda has slowly become more recognized for the unique value it brings.

Strategic thinking in organizations has developed to ensure all areas of a business are providing high performance and where possible an advantage, and people have become a key part of the agenda. For HRM, the requirement is now to ensure that the selection, skills and knowledge of the workforce are the best they can be to support and provide success. People have become less of a resource and are now being seen as an asset that fashion organizations need to nurture and care for, to protect their investment.

Strategic Human Resource Management (SHRM)

With the integral part people play in fashion organizations' success, the HR function has had to become more adaptable to align itself with the overall corporate strategy. Academic research in the 1980s was able to look at the methods in which HRM was being used within organizations and apply behavioural science theories to make sense and suggest how a more strategic focus could be placed on HRM (Guest, 1987; Purcell, 1989; Greer, 1995) and by the 1990s Strategic Human Resource Management was a focused area for most organizations.

Much of the research showed that, if considered, HR could positively contribute to the management of the workforce and the performance of the teams within it, rather than just

being the hiring and firing element of the business. Strategically focused HRM offers an opportunity to support competitive advantage in organizational culture and ensure that there is a longer-term, senior level focus towards people, which is beneficial particularly within the complexity of global fashion businesses.

The greater the level of integration and responsibility for HRM given to leaders and line managers, the more likely it is that the people agenda will be in the focus of the whole business. SHRM is therefore the framework that shapes the delivery of the individual HR strategies that will link people to the broader organizational strategy.

Workforce planning is a core element of SHRM, informing what the skills and capabilities of the workforce are, and understanding the gaps and needs to deliver the business strategy. With the pace of change ever increasing in the fashion sector, this planning is an important part of ensuring that the long-term organizational goals can be achieved (see Box 14.1).

Human capital

The individuals in the workforce along with the skills, knowledge, abilities and capacities they have to innovate and develop are the resource of organizations and can also be known as 'human capital (HC)'. HR is the enabler of maximizing this in the workforce. The management of human capital ensures that people are treated as an asset in a business and not as a cost. It is recognized that human capital is an important part of a fashion organization's intangible assets alongside elements such as brand and reputation.

Within the workplace, human capital can be split into three knowledge bases that an individual brings, which can then support and inform future development of both HRM and organizational strategies.

- **Intellectual capital** – the intangible knowledge and skills that an individual brings to a role, having high value as it is unique to the individual.

- **Social capital** – the internal and external relationships and networks that individuals build into roles, learnt from the cultural and individual experiences that a person is exposed to.

> Strategic Human Resource Management SHRM is the linking of people in all levels of an organization strategy, which allows for the integration of HRM strategy into the broader business strategy.

Box 14.1 - Shifting roles in the fashion industry

15 years ago a Marketing team within a fashion organization was a simple function with the core aim of promoting the brand visually in stores and with in the press. It would have included a limited number of roles including:

Marketing Director, Marketing Manager, Marketing Coordinator, Graphic Designer, VM and/or Creative Manager, PR Manager.

As data became more available through technological development, customer relationship management (CRM) became a required part of the team with the addition of CRM Managers and Analysts. The development of e-commerce and social media then rapidly changed the shape and roles of this department beyond recognition. Marketing departments now contain a huge variety of roles, along with the more traditional ones above, that support global brand messages (the DNA), brand communications to various global markets and digital marketing where there are no boundaries. Insights into consumers are greater than ever; the data that can be obtained is vast and when utilized effectively can bring advantages. The result of this is that more specialist roles that didn't exist a few years ago are now being seen in many global fashion brands.

A sample of roles that now exist under the marketing banner include:

Online Marketing and Content Manager, PR & Social Media Manager, Email and Retention Marketing Executive, Customer Experience Manager, UX Manager, Customer Insight and Data Analyst, eCRM Executive, Affiliate Marketing Specialist, Social Impact and Communications Manager, Global SEO Manager, Community Manager, Editorial Project Executive.

- **Organizational capital** – the business property and systems that an individual uses within their role, including initial skills and required learning of the role.

By adopting integrated and strategic approaches, management can obtain, analyze and report on data that support how people can bring added value to an organization. Producing a specific measurement of the overall value of a workforce as an asset is challenging given the complexity of people and so the emphasis has focused on looking at context-specific areas that can help to inform decision-making at a senior level. Measures that are often used in fashion organizations are pay and rewards, retention levels, employee surveys and workforce composition.

The impacts of measuring human capital will vary depending on the stakeholders involved and the structure of the organization.

- Leaders — want to see high levels of performance and value from the teams they have along with seeing how sustainable they are – *are they on the journey?*

- Managers — want to understand what the performance levels are and what needs to be done to improve this – *is the job being done?*

- Employees — want to know they have stability and clarity in their roles and the development they will be getting in order to progress – *what's in this for me?*

- Customers — want to be getting the experience and service they expect from a brand – *is this what is expected?*

- Investors — will want to see how the long-term plans will affect the workforce through growth and development to support the organizational aims – *will investing in people add value in the long term?*

- Stakeholders — will want to see that they are getting value for money from the investments they are making in people and that performance levels are high and positively impacting financial performance – *why are we investing and is it worth it?*

- Policy Makers — want to understand that the processes and actions being taken are ethical and support corporate governance – *are we being moral and ethically correct?*

Human Resource Management theory

There are many theories and models that support HRM; however, many are focused on the areas of commitment, motivation and organizational design and the overall impacts they have on performance.

The approaches of 'hard' and 'soft' HRM have been established for many years and support the basic significance that people have within an organization. Research by Truss et al. (1997) gave insights into how both approaches are relevant and how they can be used within fashion organizations, depending on the internal and external factors that can influence the environments in which HRM operates. It is a choice between best fit and best practice to suit the strategic objectives.

Soft models of HRM such as the Harvard Framework (Beer et al., 1984) gain the controls needed in an organization through a more human approach of commitment, motivation and leadership, which in turn bring success. They tend to be more flexible in their approaches, incorporate responsibilities across the workforce and allow adaptability for an organization.

Hard models of HRM, such as the Michigan (or matching) approach (Fombrun et al., 1984), emphasize a tight strategic control over the fit and costs associated with delivering the overall corporate strategy. HRM is a resource and, as such, systems will ensure effective implementation of the people requirements. The strategy of an organization will dictate the structure and HR approaches used. It has been argued that this approach is too tight and lacks the flexibility that strategic organization may need, ignoring the 'human' aspects of business needs.

Shape and systems of HRM in organizations

Over time, with the understanding of the true resource a workforce can be, there has been a growing complexity and broader range of HRM areas that have been introduced to support and influence positive performance (see Figure 14.1).

Figure 14.1 *The HR System*

As the breadth of the HRM function has grown, so have the roles required to deliver the requirements of HRM to fashion organizations. Much of the structure is based on the size of the business itself and the importance that the board place on human capital within the organization. Within this, roles can be generalist or more focused and specialized.

The three-legged stool model put forward by Ulrich (1997) gives a view of how HR can work in organizations, proposing that the HR function is made of three key components: shared services, business partners and centres of excellence, and that these support the organization fully.

Shared Services: There is a requirement for the sharing of administrative or transactional support functions such as payroll, recruitment and leavers/absence administration that are fundamental tasks that need to be actioned for the organization and its employees. Some areas of shared service can be outsourced, such as payroll. Within many fashion retail groups there will be a shared services role or team that goes across all brands.

Business Partners: The strategic part of the function supporting the business strategy. It is seen through business partner roles offering support alongside department leaders in planning, shaping and implementing the changes needed in an organization's strategic aims and objectives. Given the changing nature of roles and departments within fashion organizations, this role is key to developing the roles needed for the future.

Centres of Excellence: The specialist roles which support, develop and improve on the skills, qualities and behaviours of the workforce – working across all levels of an organization, through a variety of means that ensure that people are motivated, operationally strong and can deliver to the needs of the organization. Delivered through subject area experts (such as for reward, learning and development, and talent) to provide innovative solutions to create and support competitive advantage and help to protect the human capital.

Structure and roles of HR within organizations

The size and scale of a fashion organization will dictate the functional set-ups of HR and the roles that are in place (see Figure 14.2). Larger organizations can build teams based on functional focuses and specialisms. For SMEs the focuses tend to combine these into either HR or learning and development (L&D) streams, with individuals often taking roles that cover various aspects (for an example, see Mini Case Study 14.1).

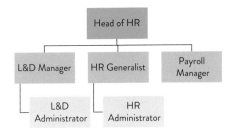

SME (Small and Medium sized Enterprise) example

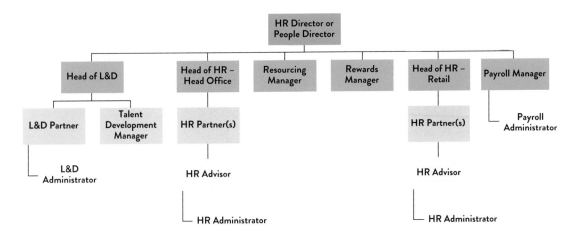

Large organization example (retail)

Figure 14.2 *Small and large scale organizational structures*

MINI CASE STUDY 14.1 - Introducing the HR Director: Superdry

Since being founded in 1985, Superdry has been a true British retail success story. With its first store opening in 2004 and rapid growth, it has become a global brand operating over 400 stores (both owned and franchised) along with wholesale and licence agreements. In 2012, with serious plans to grow the brand across the globe, the holding company Supergroup decided to bring in an HR Director to the senior management team. By 2015 they had over 4000 employees across 15 countries globally.

The organic culture of the company had been a key to the passion of people within the organization, with HR being very much an administrative role. With entrepreneurial leadership, those being hired need to fit with the values of the owners; however, with the lack of expertize in the broader HR area, the people aspects of the business remained transactional rather than developmental and transformational.

Not uncommon in founder-led businesses, having HR as part of the senior team was seen as the dampener of innovation and creativity that would stop the risk elements that have often made these businesses successful. The growing business needs and the lack of infrastructure and systems, combined with the understanding of the benefits of more strategic people management, however, became a reality for Superdry. Lack of clarity around roles, succession planning and development programmes all hindered the workforce, and with global expansion the complexity of differing employment needs and leaders to take the business forward supported the hiring of an HR Director.

Understanding the workforce and how it is changing, the needs of individuals in their own growth and development along with what the business is going to need were all priorities. Influencing and educating the founders and senior teams on the positive impacts of HR were key to the success of the role, within a brand with such strong culture and values. The introduction of the Directorship allowed HR to be recognized as a function that supports and enables success through ensuring the people within the business have the purpose, capability and drive to achieve.

Working with the culture of the business has allowed effective and innovative approaches including employee engagement, reward and recognition, and organizational effectiveness. Global growth has been successful and the agility of the business allows Superdry to be ready for the next challenge.

Source: Various secondary sources.

THE BACKBONE OF HR IN FASHION ORGANIZATIONS

HR or People strategy

The focus of any HR or People strategy is to be looking forward, having the resources needed and the right strategic fit to the organizational goals. It is the driver of what you do in relation to people in your fashion organization (see Mini Case Study 4.2). For HR to achieve its goals of having high-performing, engaged and knowledgeable employees, the HR strategy should consider the aspects shown in Figure 14.3.

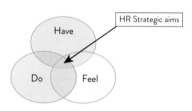

Figure 14.3 *HR strategy*

- *Have* – the skills, competencies and abilities, for individuals;

- *Feel* – commitment, engagement and motivation, for those in your organization;

MINI CASE STUDY 14.2 - Adidas's people strategy

Adidas have long taken the belief that you start with the people to define your strategic journey. They have developed a new people strategy to support the new corporate strategy of 'creating the new' that will run from its launch in 2015 through to 2020. They have been champions of culture for many years and this takes the next step in developing the people philosophy to ensure agility to adapt to the changing workforce. Adidas's people strategy is a large part of the corporate five-year business plan. This has made the people agenda part of every leader's agenda across the business. For true success, they are ensuring people sit level with product and brand. The four key pillars of the people strategy have been developed to ensure that the right people are in the right roles at the right time. They are:

- Meaningful reasons to join and stay
- Role models who inspire
- Bringing forward fresh and diverse perspectives
- Creative climate to make a difference.

This people strategy promotes innovation, performance and diversity in an environment that stimulates teamwork and engagement through a culture that is passionate and has integrity.

Source: Various secondary sources.

- *Do* – purpose in role, loyalty, productivity and achievement, for the individuals.

Culture

Since the 1980s culture has become a more and more important requirement for organizations and is now a critical part of how senior leaders want the workforce and consumer to see and understand a fashion brand. HR has a key role and is often seen to be the guardian in ensuring that culture is defined, understood and maintained in an organization.

Organizational culture allows for individuals in a fashion organization to have shared perceptions, through meanings, norms and values that give guidance on social interactions and shape the patterns of beliefs and expectations of individuals.

The Culture Iceberg, as used by Hall (1976), explains that formal and informal elements impact the organizational culture, and is supported by Schein's Cultural Theory (Schein, 2017). Both distinguish that there are observable and unobservable elements that make up culture within a fashion organization (see Figure 14.4).

> **Culture** The way that things are done in an organization, seen through shared meanings, beliefs and objects; culture will condition how an organization achieves its strategic aims and objectives.

- The visible elements are often the ways in which a business says things will be done – strategy, structures and policies.
- The invisible elements are more psychologically based with feelings, stories and norms all shaping the understanding of how things are actually done.

Organizational culture influences and links to most of the processes and issues of HR. The structure a fashion organization chooses to take should support the culture through the social interaction required to accomplish the goals. This structure can grow organically, where culture influences the strategy, or systematically when strategy influences the culture.

Change management

Even though change is a constant part of businesses today, it is often difficult to manage successfully.

Historically, any organizational change had been focused on the harder elements of the business – systems and structures; however, more recently the

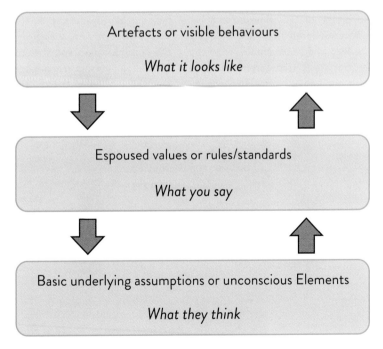

Figure 14.4 *The 3 levels of culture*
Source: Adapted from Schein (2017).

longer-term, softer impacts of change programmes have been considered. Failure of any change programme can have damaging effects on many areas of the business including loss of key employees, and reduced engagement levels.

Change management is a specialized area, which requires a deep understanding of how any change affects a business across all elements. HRM teams are often a key part of any change programme, taking on the role of a change agent focused on the people in the organization, and will initiate, advise on, and deliver many areas of transformation across a business to support and communicate implementations being actioned. In order to support successful management, various change models are available in order to explain (Burke and Litwin, 1992), understand (Lewin, 1947; Kubler-Ross, 1969), identify (Johnson et al., 2008), plan (McKinsey 7S – see Peters and Waterman, 1982) and implement (Kotter, 1996) change, and used in combination can support an organization effectively.

There are a variety of reasons for change to be resisted including fear of the unknown, lack of trust, shifts in power or influence, removal from ones' comfort zone and dislike of the imposed change. Communication is considered key to reducing resistance and leaders should maintain trust by ensuring that the process is transparent and well communicated with the organization. The change agents and leaders of organizations not only have

Change management A systematic approach to ensure that an organization has the skills, knowledge and confidence needed so that change and its impacts on people is managed effectively, by considering, designing and applying the right processes to ensure success.

Leadership The 'capacity to influence people, by means of personal attributes and/or behaviours, to achieve a common goal' (CIPD, 2016).

to be clear on the requirements and impacts of change but need to be able to impart a clear vision of the future and to gain commitment and buy-in.

Leadership

Leadership has been a subject of much research and discussion since the mid-1800s. The original concept of 'The Great Man' acknowledged that great leaders (and at that time only men) were born with talent and skill. As time and research has progressed, the subject of leadership has become more scientific in its approach and is now deeply positioned within psychology, philosophy, sociology and most recently neuroscience interests. As a complex area of academic research, it explores the skills and characteristics of leaders in order to deliver results and make things happen in organizations.

Within fashion organizations, leadership is now more than a competency for senior players, with the changing of roles and responsibilities requiring people at all levels of a business to act as leaders in different capacities. The traits and behaviours that an individual has in their leadership approach impacts on the overall effectiveness, especially when considered with the culture, values and structure of an organization. Various leadership theories have developed over the years, bringing the relationship between leader and follower to be fully explored in both directions.

Theory of Leadership	Decade	Key Components
Great Man	1840s	Great leaders are born
Trait	1930s	Individuals have specific qualities – psychometric measures
Behavioural	1950s	Behaviours required can be taught
Contingency	1960s	Adaptable approach combining styles to suit the situation – situational, path goal
Relational/Transactional	1970s	Exchange between follower and leader
Transformational	1980s	Developing the transactional to focus on follower–leader and the organization's outcomes.

Table 14.1 *The development of leadership theories*

Leadership Style	Elements of the Style	Examples of Style
Charismatic	Relies on self-belief and charisma to gain followers, and leaders are the 'face' of an organization.	Phillip Green – Arcadia Mike Ashley – Sports Direct George Davies – Next
Visionary	Create positive vision for followers towards the goal, allowing follower development to naturally evolve.	Steve Jobs – Apple Mark Parker – Nike Nick Robertson – Asos
Ethical	Focused on the moral basis of leadership – do the right thing, for the greater good.	Blake Mycoskie – Toms Rose Marcario – Patagonia Anita Roddick – Body Shop
Authentic	Focused on followers' development of authenticity and is delivered through being authentic with self, value and goals.	Howard Schulz – Starbucks Simon Wolfson – Next Peter Ruis – Anthropologie

Table 14.2 *Common leadership styles within the fashion industry*

Transformational leadership took this a step further, incorporating the interests of the organization into the thinking.

Since then, academic and professional studies have explored leadership styles, the traits that they have, and the benefits they can bring to organizations. These styles reflect the culture and values of the organization and can help to provide a consistent internal and external view of a brand. As fashion organizations become more agile and flexible to respond to global competition through globalization, leadership and its links to employee engagement, motivation and performance are important to get right.

Leadership is a continuous focus for many senior teams and is often the number one concern for organizations in industry surveys including fashion. With this in mind, development of individuals to become the next leaders should focus on the approaches, behaviours and characteristics needed to respond to disruptive and complex business environments.

Leadership vs. management

Although they are closely related and complement one another, leadership is different from management.

- Leadership is about *inspiring and sharing vision to support the goals that need to be achieved.*

- Management is about *the planning, developing and delivering of the strategies and goals.*

An understanding of the differences between the two is important, even though they may both be required in a role.

Leaders
Influencing people and coping with change through setting direction, aligning the workforce and motivating through vision

Managers
Directing people and coping with complexity through planning, budgeting, organizing and staffing effectively, controlling situations and problem solving

Figure 14.5 *Leaders vs. Managers*

Corporate Social Responsibility (CSR)

As we saw in Chapter 12, CSR refers to an organization's ability to perform in line with the principles of sustainability, responsibility, accountability and transparency, and in the context of human resources through its internal organizational leadership, values, culture, capabilities and communications. Business ethics scandals continue to be headline news stories across many sectors including fashion, concerning obstruction of justice, misrepresentation of information, fraudulent behaviour or abuse of rights and privileges. Conducting business is no longer a private matter in a technological and global environment where information is far more accessible than ever. Having an ethical approach that aligns the corporate strategy with HR practices, culture and values is a current challenge for many HR departments.

The guidelines that HR implements in fashion organizations to support this area are the processes and practices surrounding employees. They ensure that the 'ways things are done' are fair, so that employees and the environment are treated well and that sustainable approaches are instilled in the culture of the business rather than for a greenwashing effect. In a global fashion retail business, for example, that could mean ensuring that health and safety and working practices in suppliers' factories overseas are complying with legal standards, or ensuring that basic recycling is available in the head office.

with a clear understanding of the meaning of the business and its role in society.

Those that take this approach to business may focus on the higher purpose of providing great service, being environmentally sustainable, having safe workplaces, or placing purpose over profit (see the TOMS Case Study, below).

Four basic principles can help fashion organizations to achieve this – Purpose, Stakeholder, Leadership and Culture.

- *Purpose* identifies that a business is not just about making money but also how it focuses, inspires and energizes its stakeholders.

- *Stakeholder* recognizes that value is important to the people in the business.

- *Leadership* creates and guides the journey in an organization, and so, when creating the purpose, value and culture, it has a role in bringing harmony to the process.

- *Culture* is the underlying ways in which we do things and the values we hold in an organization, which connects stakeholders and supports purpose.

Conscious business practices

A conscious business practice will recognize that trust, compassion and collaboration will bring value to the employees and stakeholders (anyone who interacts with the business on any level). This is achieved by creating a mind-set to support a conscious system of working within an organization. With this approach, organizations offer an environment that supports personal growth and professional fulfilment along

> **Conscious business practice** A way of doing business that elevates the human element, where the outcome is not focused on profits but on making a positive impact on the world.

Diversity

Diversity recognizes and values the differences that individuals have regardless of shared characteristics and consists of both visible and non-visible factors, with the main areas of discussion being demographic, and involving cognitive ability, personality, attitudes, beliefs and values. Discrimination laws

---

MINI CASE STUDY 14.3 - Patagonia

Patagonia's mission:

   'Build the best products, cause no unnecessary harm, use business to inspire and implement solutions to the environmental crisis.'

   Through clear vision, leadership and purpose, the brand ensures that corporate responsibility is at the heart of what they do. These are the values that the brand has encouraged individuals to strive to achieve in the mission and are embedded into the operations and activities in everyday working. To support this, the environment in which business runs focuses on how to get the best from the workforce through

encouraging innovation and creativity, supporting this with childcare, flexible working and well-being activities and by developing and encouraging people to grow within their roles. Work–life balance is important across all areas of the business. This approach is also seen through the attention given to ensuring manufacturing and supply chain observe global ethical standards, with fair labour and workplace conditions all satisfying stakeholder groups, and to showing that people are an important part of staying true to the Patagonia mission.

Source: Patagonia.com, various dates.

protect individuals from unfair treatment due to personal characteristics such as age, gender, religion and disability. In other responses to this, voluntary quotas exist in countries to encourage greater diversity in the workplace, such as having women in senior positions. HR has an important and growing responsibility in ensuring that diversity is managed effectively in fashion organizations (see Box 14.2). The challenge of unconscious bias remains though and for HR this is where adopting the right and fair approaches to processes and systems will minimize the negative impacts of this.

When full diversity exists in a business, it supports CSR by providing an ethical approach, which creates a positive connection to the psychological contract of individuals internally and externally along with making people feel valued in a workforce. It supports building respect and trust within the organization along with promoting a harmonized working environment where harassment, bullying and stereotyping are not acceptable behaviours. A recent research report by Deloitte (2016) found that the majority of millennials,

brought up in the surroundings of diversity and with open dialogue about it, walked into the workplace expecting to find a diverse workforce.

Cross-cultural management

National culture shapes the values, behaviours and attitudes of the individuals within society and therefore has an impact on the way people work. It can influence the structures of organizations, processes in place and decision-making impacting the relationships between management and employees. Awareness is therefore needed when taking a fashion business global and looking at how national cultures can affect the organizational culture and working practices of an organization.

The national cultures across the globe offer differences based on political, economic, religious and social conditions. In a globalized business world, the understanding and acknowledgement of this is core to aligning a fashion brand in multiple locations. Organizations, working with HR, need

---

BOX 14.2 - Women on the board – a continuing diversity challenge

In an industry that has a higher than average proportion of female workforce at 60%, it appears strange that when we look to the top levels of boardroom executives, the patterns reflect that of a male dominated industry, with only 20% of females in top roles.

With UK government quotas in place to ensure that at least 25% of board members are women, what we still see is that most key positions are being held by men and the quotas are being achieved by the less operational non-executive director roles.

It had been a slowly improving area of balance; however, in 2015 the share of female CEOs in the fashion industry fell from 25% to 15% . The question we all need to understand is: why?

In Drapers 2016 top 100 influencers, we find that in the top 20 only four women are mentioned. Look at the whole 100 and twenty-nine are mentioned. Reviewing these influencers further finds there is a lack of ethnic diversity too.

Source: Women in Retail and Elixirr (2016).

Flat structures	-Dimension+ Power Distance	Hierarchal Structures
Team	Individualism	Individual
Nurture	Feminine/Masculine	Power
Comfortable with ambiguity	Uncertainty Avoidance	Ambiguity creates anxiety
Short-term first	Long-term Orientation	Long-term first
Happiness is bad	Restraint/Indulgence	Happiness is good

Table 14.3 *Cultural Dimensions*

Source: Based on Hofstede, Hofstede and Minkov (2010).

to decide on whether to adapt or adopt policies and practices based on the understanding of these national cultures.

Hofstede (2001) and House et al. (2004) have developed an understanding of dimensions of national cultures that supports organizations to evaluate the variations occurring in different countries. Approaches to working across boarders can then be adopted. However, with use of the results, there needs to be an awareness of the stereotyping that can influence the decisions made.

CORE COMPONENTS OF HRM IN FASHION ORGANIZATIONS

In order to provide fashion organizations with the support, vision and focus needed, various components of HRM can be understood, developed and used for reviewing and delivering capabilities of individuals and teams, although the use of these varies from business to business. These are performance management, learning and development, succession planning, leadership development and talent management.

 ONLINE RESOURCES

Our companion website provides a fuller description of the core components of HRM, see: https://www.macmillanihe.com/companion/Varley_Fashion_Management.

Performance management

In its simplest form, as described in the AMO model (Boxall and Purcell, 2003), without these three elements performance is likely to be compromised.

Ability – is the basic possibility that a person can do the job or task required, and this can be supported through learning and development, leadership and organization design.

Motivation – is about the desire to do the job or task, and can be influenced through a variety of extrinsic and intrinsic motivators such as reward management and employee voice.

Opportunity – is where a person is positioned in the right place at the right time to take on the job or task, and this can be supported through resourcing, succession planning and talent management.

Performance management in a retail business is critical to the success of a brand in producing high-performing teams, through processes that support and align with the aims and goals of the organization. The processes need to be strategic to support the broader issues and longer-term goals and they need to flexibly integrate various aspects of the business process and people together. It has been thought of as just performance improvement; however, more recently the need for continuous development of the workforce and encouragement of behaviours to support the culture of an organization has changed this position.

Performance management is a cyclical process incorporating planning, performing, reviewing

> **Performance management** The process of reviewing, focusing and improving the performance of individuals and teams with the goal of achieving high levels of performance and success.

and rewarding the performance of individuals and groups. It allows leaders and line managers to be clear on the expectations, support and resources required to do their job and to engage individuals around the business strategy. Regular and clear communication, along with feedback, support both employee and employer in this process. It also supports a culture where taking ownership of development and improvement to working practices is part of every employee's role and one that behaviours reflect accordingly.

Learning and development (L&D)

Learning and development is the function responsible for assessing, reviewing and providing development and learning to individuals and teams to ensure that the right skills and knowledge required are within a fashion organization at the right time. Skills development is a challenge facing L&D and as the people agenda has grown in business leaders' minds so have the requirements of this function in delivering a workforce with the right skills and capabilities to do the job. Originally focused on vocational training programmes and the delivery of them, the addition of psychology and social sciences to develop the understanding of people as employees, and connecting it with the strategic nature of businesses, this is a function with a broad remit. It is also supporting the view of lifelong or continuous learning as a response to the pace and change of the working environment.

The fundamental basic requirements of learning and development are at the heart of the function; however, it is far more developed and complex in its make-up now to ensure competencies, capabilities and skills are delivered to support sustainable business success. With this in mind, some larger fashion organizations are taking the position of this function to sit alongside the already vast function of HRM as a separately focused area of HRD (Human Resource Development).

L&D now encompasses supporting strategic goals and championing longer-term objectives such as leadership and management development, change management and knowledge management to support individual and organizational development. When applied successfully it can support the organizational strategy and human capital approach along with giving vision to change, supporting performance, engagement and motivation of individuals, and aiding retention of the workforce.

> **Succession planning**
> The identification and planning for the replacement of employees who leave a position, to support the needs of the business in both the short and long term.

growth and ensures that organizations are ready for the future and what it brings in relation to changes in the workforce.

Succession planning can identify the needs of key senior and strategic roles or can be adopted across the whole organization in a more inclusive approach. Working with HR as a facilitator, it allows for line managers or senior leaders to have an internal recruitment support that ensures that individuals are not overlooked. Where completed it allows successors to be highlighted for key or new roles and enables the support and development to be put into place prior to the role becoming 'live'. This allows for a smooth transition for an individual when a role becomes available. It does, however, need to be a transparent and open process for the workforce to buy in to it. This also supports the growing trend of individuals taking responsibility for their own growth and development.

For the workforce, succession planning supports the motivation and engagement as individuals learn about the potential to grow, what their next role could be, and gives them the security that they have a future in an organization. Through management training, developmental activities and work experiences individuals can build their capabilities. Leadership development and talent management connect very closely to succession planning by providing the activities needed to prepare internal

Succession planning

The actions that a fashion organization takes to ensure a flow of developed individuals within the workforce can be highly effective in providing a stable workforce and overall improved performance and success. It supports strategically designed

---

 ## MINI CASE STUDY 14.4 - Stepping up: The journey of Sarah Burton

The dream of most designers is to one day be at the helm of a brand where all the creativity and passion they have can be shown on a catwalk each season. Traditionally, succession within designer brands is not often seen, and the departure of a creative name will often result in a search for another high-profile designer to replace them rather than promoting internally. In the extraordinary case of Alexander McQueen, however, internal succession saved the brand.

Sarah Burton started to fulfil her dreams by graduating from Central St Martins in 1997 and working at the design studio of the moment, Alexander McQueen. Over the next decade she continued to learn and develop her skills, being

mentored and supported by the senior design teams within the brand including McQueen himself. Burton was eventually promoted to Head of Womenswear in 2000, where she was able to lead a team in designing and developing the handwriting of the brand alongside its creative mind-set.

In 2010, the unexpected and sudden death of McQueen left a creative void. With the loyalty and development that Burton had gained she was able to successfully take the helm and continue steering the heritage, vision and feel of the brand. In spite of the untimely departure of a brand figure-head, personal development can prepare an individual for the next steps whenever they arise.

individuals for the transition into more senior and strategic roles.

Leadership development

With the complexity surrounding what makes a good leader and the varying traits and behaviours that a person can have, leadership development is open to much discussion and a variety of approaches.

There is still support for there being a natural ability when it comes to leadership; however, some skills can be developed through formal and informal training.

The natural journey of an employee is to build and gain experience as they progress into roles that are more senior where the responsibilities and opportunities to lead become greater. The challenge for many fashion industry employers is that those rising through the ranks will often be promoted due to technical skills and abilities with little consideration for the leadership skills they may need in later roles.

For fashion organizations to support the leadership requirements, individuals' capabilities need identifying and developing to provide them with the skills they need to lead others successfully. The earlier that leadership opportunities are identified through succession planning, the better a position the business will be in, to ensure it does not have a skills gap that is difficult to fill.

For leaders to be successful, not only the leadership style they apply but individual elements such as personality, emotional intelligence and communication skills should be reflected upon and developed by organizations, HR and the individual.

Talent management

The need for talent development was first established as a strategic need of businesses in the 1990s within a research report by McKinsey (Chambers et al., 1998) that brought us the phrase 'war for talent'. From this point, organizations started to focus on this as a key area for achieving success, developed

> **Leadership development** The ways in which an individual is prepared for and developed to be an effective leader in their organization, considering their traits and behaviours along with the organizational culture and values.

> **Talent management** 'The systematic attraction, identification, development, engagement, retention and deployment of those individuals who are of particular value to an organization, either in view of their "high potential" for the future or because they are fulfilling business critical roles' (CIPD, 2015).

by HR through core recruitment activities and succession planning. The growing needs of the business required identification and development of high achievers at a faster rate to ensure that talent could be delivered to the most strategical levels of an organization, as it was needed. This is a need that has continued to gather pace along with the pace and change of business and is often one of the most pressing priorities for CEOs to be discussing with HR and L&D. Focusing on your talent is investing in the asset of human capital.

More strategic than succession planning and more rounded than leadership development, talent management applies the norms of development alongside additional activities of coaching, networking and profile raising to support an individual's longer-term learning journey. This is part of the responsibilities of L&D and should be handled in much the same way as succession planning in ensuring that the needs are known, there is transparency and that it delivers success and results.

Talent management is a way of gaining competitive advantage for fashion organizations. The value of a strategically aligned talent programme can be measured as part of human capital in being an employer of choice, having strong employee engagement, delivering high performance outcomes, and in supporting diversity (see Box 14.3).

The scope of talent management's remit has, like many other HR functions, changed to now look deeper at the area and not just at how talent is identified but at how to bring talent to the surface when not obvious. Two schools of thoughts now exist in the business world.

1. Identify talented people and focus on their development, preparing them for the bigger roles and ensuring that the talent needs of the business are met.

2. Take talent across the business as part of the culture, encouraging people to become better at what they do and offering support through their employee journey with you.

BOX 14.3 - When the talent pipeline is empty what do you do?

There are moments when the demand for certain roles cannot be fulfilled within a business and this can result in increased recruitment costs. Take the example of buyers and merchandisers in a growing business. As a business grows, the challenges and pace of change mean more experienced, strategic individuals will be needed to operate at more senior levels. The skills of individuals within the business may not have naturally been built over the time of growth and so there may not be skilled individuals ready for the next step up.

Having a talent pipeline in place that supports these changes, especially given the pace of the fashion industry, requires designing and developing an accelerated development programme to ensure individuals are being equipped in advance with the skills they will later require in more senior roles.

The objective of such a programme is to provide a pool of buying and merchandising talent that is available for promotion when roles become live within the business. Often these development programmes involve leadership, strategic thinking and influencing skills. This supports the transition, ensures greater productivity and allows for the change process to be managed more effectively.

The impacts of talent management support the broader business, particularly with the culture and values. Having a focused programme also allows for transparency and visibility for the high-potential individuals who are looking for progression within a business, supporting engagement and commitment for individuals concerned. It also reduces the need for external resourcing.

THE EMPLOYEE

Employee relations

Employee relations have become an important part of the HR function within fashion organizations. It ensures that the relationship between the employer and employee develops trust and delivers involvement, commitment and engagement from all parties. The relationship with trade unions is within this area, although fashion companies are not known for high levels of unionization.

The employee relationship is strongly influenced by HR in organizations. The main focus is on ensuring people are treated well and fairly, ensuring that individuals are clear in the role and outcomes expected of them in doing their jobs. High levels of communication within organizations support the processes and policies within an organization and allow for dialogue to flow surrounding the practices in place. This level of dialogue can encourage positive and proactive problem solving and supports the traditional approaches of collective bargaining, which does still exist in many organizations. Strong employee relationships tend to create high levels of trust in organizations where managerial behaviours support clarity of understanding.

> **Employee relations**
> Ensuring the employee relationship is healthy and productive for the organization and ensuring that any policies and plans take into account the impacts on employees.

Employee behaviours

'Employee behaviours' refers to the way in which employees' behaviours are seen, in a fashion organization, through levels of motivation, satisfaction, commitment and engagement. Focusing on the elements of employee behaviours supports organizational success and provides a workforce with enhanced levels of performance and well-being.

Engagement can be achieved and assist in achieving success through delivering strategic aims and goals for the individual and the organization. Fully motivated, committed and engaged individuals are likely to perform to a level that achieves the planned aims. Individuals will often be more likely to take on additional tasks and responsibilities in order to help achieve greater organizational success, showing higher levels of loyalty. This is also seen in improved levels of innovation and creativity as interest levels are increased, which, given the nature of the fashion industry, can be highly impactful and important to organizations.

Psychological contract

Formed through a series of beliefs that an employee and employer have towards what is expected from them, the **psychological contract** is a key part of the employee relationship and underpins the behaviours that are seen.

The relationship for the employee will include expectations of how they are treated, how secure they feel in a role, what the developmental opportunities are, how much involvement and influence they have and importantly the trust they have in the management to keep promises (see Figure 14.6).

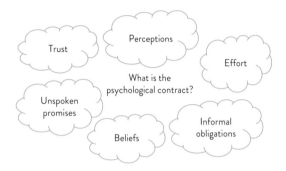

Figure 14.6 *The psychological contract*

The employer expectations are more in line with competence, commitment and efforts that an individual will put into the role they are doing. Rousseau (1989) offers a deeper insight into this area. The employee (and at times the employer) will often not be 100% sure of the expectations they have and so this concept becomes highly flexible and adaptable as knowledge changes.

However, if these expectations are misaligned or fail then there is a high probability that the psychological contract will be broken and the relationship will become strained and there is potential for either party to cease the relationship. Avoidance of this can come through clear expectations and open communication by both parties.

The psychological contract supports organizations' approaches towards clarity of communication, culture, and strategy in order to give the employees clearer expectations, especially surrounding fairness, security and involvement.

> **Employee voice** 'The term increasingly used to cover a whole variety of processes and structures which enable, and sometimes empower employees, directly and indirectly, to contribute to decision making' (Boxall and Purcell, 2003).

> **Employee engagement** 'An individual employee's cognitive, emotional and behavioural state directed toward desired organizational outcomes' (Shuck and Wollard, 2010).

Employee voice

The **employee voice** facilitates a two-way communication within a fashion organization, which ensures that the employees have the ability and potential to influence outcomes that affect them as a workforce, both positively and negatively. In turn, these have an impact on and support the outcomes of employee engagement.

The levels of employee voice within an organization will vary depending on the style and control level of management at the top. Armstrong (2016) refers to four levels of employee voice within an organization – job, management, policy-making and ownership level – which also can vary depending on the organizational set-up. As with employee engagement, employee voice can have a positive impact on the performance, retention levels and well-being of employees if used in appropriate ways.

Employee engagement

For fashion organizations to have fully engaged individuals they need to ensure that a person is not just satisfied but is willing to go above and beyond. Engagement is about winning both the hearts and minds of individuals through mutual commitment.

To encourage and support **employee engagement** there needs to be awareness of how culture, values, development, job design and progression opportunities, rewards and recognition all influence the decisions and feelings an employee can have.

An organization can provide all the environmental, emotional and physical elements to deliver a positive, engaging workplace; however, the final piece is how that individual then processes that in a deeper psychological way.

Kahn's (1990) research helps us to understand what can have an impact on an individual's engagement through three simple areas of psychological understanding – **meaningfulness**, **availability** and **safety**. Without these being considered for an individual then engagement is unlikely to fully develop and can affect performance and success for a fashion organization. The individual assesses each of these conditions and makes decisions about to what extent they will then engage themselves in a role.

Engagement levels of the workforce have a link to the success and performance achieved by an organization. Tools such as employee surveys help us to understand how individuals are feeling in relation to their role, their team and the bigger organization. When looking at the make-up of the workforce, several studies point to show us that engagement levels increase through the generations and in the seniority of roles.

Building an engaged workforce is therefore an important role to be fulfilled and can be done through a variety of ways including providing challenge in job roles, giving individuals the autonomy to deliver outcomes, providing variety in the day-to-day role, giving feedback regularly, ensuring those recruited fit the culture of the organization, providing development opportunities and giving recognition and reward for good performance. Enhance this with strong leadership and management, ensuring the employees have a voice, with flowing communication, a clear culture and values, and organizations can maximize the opportunity of an engaged workforce, the benefits of which include increased creativity and innovation, higher performance levels, better retention levels and loyalty, and being an employer of choice.

Disengaged employees can be damaging to an organization in two ways. Firstly, through individual performance as they are unlikely to be high performers if disengaged. Secondly, the negative behaviours they display will impact on others, potentially leading to others' dissatisfaction and reducing performance levels.

MANAGING HUMAN RESOURCES: POLICIES AND PROCEDURES

Policies set out how various aspects of HRM are approached by fashion organizations and offer guidance on how they should be applied. They support the values of the organization through showing how people should be treated and what the expectations are for employees, helping to build the psychological contract. They also support line managers when dealing with HR issues.

In general, organizations will have an overarching HR policy that expresses the core values of how people should be treated. Armstrong (2016) refers to HR policy supporting the concepts of equity, organizational learning, performance through people, quality of working life, and working conditions.

To further support the organization, specific HR policies are developed by HR to address the key issues identified. Once the policies are written, implementation needs to be clear and wide reaching, ensuring all employees are aware of them and that they will be implemented in a fair and consistent way. Within the fashion context this could include the policies surrounding holidays and sickness.

Procedures are the actual actions that are expected to be taken in dealing with a situation and are the key tools in managing major employment issues such as grievance, disciplinary matters and performance. Within the fashion context this could include the procedures expected in retail stores, such as processing deliveries or weekly paperwork and banking.

Legal compliance

The legal compliance in connection with employees is a responsibility that firmly sits with the HR function. Awareness of basic legal changes is core to any fashion organization. Many of the legal requirements that need to be known within businesses are surrounding the areas of working practices, regulations and conditions, which are in place to protect both the employee and employer. Examples include minimum wage levels, changes to legislation on well-being issues such as maternity or paternity allowances, and regulations for foreign employees.

With many fashion businesses operating globally, this puts an additional requirement on HR to have international knowledge and expertize, and so many organizations choose to outsource legal compliance to external specialists for support.

Analyzing the data

Part of becoming a more strategic function means HR needing to analyze the value of people and the impacts of the actions they are delivering on improving performance and outputs. Technology has helped to develop this area, with most administration functions now being automated to some level. This allows HR to draw on a variety of data to bring credibility to the previous non-tangible context of people.

Employee surveys have become a great source of information and data about how the people in the business feel and see the organization, the roles they perform and what the future holds. This has become a key tool in many fashion organizations for getting a temperature check on how the workforce are feeling and what can be done to improve things to support positive business performance.

Retention figures, sickness levels and progression statistics can indicate motivation, engagement and commitment levels within a business, which can be reviewed in line with employee surveys or at specific touch-points throughout a trading year.

Payroll gives a value to the people and their performance levels as a cost to a business and, as such, is a high-risk area when performance is down and costs are too high. People are often seen as the easy route to saving money but service or performance levels of organizations can suffer when people are removed. In a recession period, the numbers of front-facing shop floor staff tend to be the first to be reduced in fashion retail organizations, yet this may go against a strategic move to improve service to customers (see Chapter 11).

 ## CASE STUDY 14 - TOMS: Tomorrow's shoes

Social enterprises are often started when an entrepreneur becomes aware of a social or environmental problem that they believe they can alleviate through a business solution. In 2006 TOMS' founder Blake Mycoskie was holidaying in Argentina when he came across a charity group donating shoes for local shoeless children. His response was to found a shoe company which would sell shoes in order to finance a sustainable supply of shoe donations.

The TOMS' story and its simple buy-one-give-one business concept had immediate marketing appeal and the brand was picked up by retailers and press. TOMS sold through its own website and local Los Angeles stores, Hollywood stars were spotted wearing TOMS and with features in *US Vogue* and *TIME*, TOMS was soon stocked by established national retailers such as Nordstrom. With footwear being a high margin product, TOMS was able to sell a reasonably priced shoe, cover the costs of shoe drops and return a profit. TOMS' founder Blake Mycoskie was a charismatic spokesman for the brand and for this new way of doing business and the initial sales exceeded expectations, passing the initial target of selling 10,000 pairs of shoes in its first year and providing the money to finance the first TOMS' shoe drop back in Argentina.

Early on, founder Blake Mycoskie realized that the buy-one-give-one model had the potential to address other social needs and the first TOMS brand extension into eyewear was launched in 2011. In return for purchases of TOMS eyewear, medical treatment, prescription glasses or sight-saving surgery would be funded. TOMS works with a network of giving partners and its own impact team to assess the benefits derived from their giving and to develop new opportunities for the business, and subsequently TOMS has extended its giving so that it now covers four main areas: shoes, sight, safe water and safe birth, each funded from the sales of different product categories. Interest in this innovative business model led Blake to write a book in 2011 explaining why and how he started TOMS; *Start Something that Matters* became a *New York Times* bestseller.

Social media has enabled brands and consumers to co-create value and TOMS is present across platforms. Its products and Giving Trips provide visually appealing images for brand content as well as showcasing the wider TOMS community through encouraging consumer interaction. TOMS' most high-profile awareness raising event was their annual One Day Without Shoes (ODWS), when the brand encouraged everyone to spend a day shoeless. The idea was inspired by Pepperdine University's TOMS campus club shoeless walk and each year TOMS has organized events to raise awareness of the issues that inspire its giving mission, working from Toms' own stores and with stockists, members of the TOMS community were encouraged to spend a shoeless day and to share their experiences via social media.

Currently TOMS works with over 100 non-profit humanitarian giving partners in over 70 countries. The company has its own Director of Social Innovation and Impact; by undertaking research into how and where TOMS give, product development ensures that the giving shoes are suitable for specific climates and terrains. Other employees have also had the opportunity to go on giving trips to experience for themselves the impact of the donations on communities.

TOMS London 'Community Outpost' (Store), interior and VR Space. Images courtesy of TOMS. Reproduced by permission of TOMS.

TOMS has developed an innovative experiential 360-degree Virtual Reality Giving Tour which enables customers to experience a TOMS Giving Trip through the VR headset in store.

Source: Mycoskie, B. (2012) Start Something That Matters. London: Virgin Books.

Case Author: Natascha Radclyffe-Thomas

Case Challenge

Use Figure 14.4 to analyze the organizational culture of TOMS using the information in the case study.

ONLINE RESOURCES

A longer version of this case study, with additional challenges, can be found on our companion website: https://www.macmillanihe.com/companion/Varley_Fashion_Management.

SUMMARY AND CONCLUDING THOUGHTS

The world is changing at an accelerated rate and the impacts of progression are challenging for organizations. Disruption by technical development, rapid urbanization, social and demographic changes and changes in global economics are all having an impact on the workforce of fashion organizations. With many of those businesses looking at international activities as the norm (see Chapter 4), HR departments need to become experts not just in their own country but also in those where expansion opportunities exist, because people remain one of the costliest resources. The management of HRM and SHRM in an international context adds complexity and challenge to many well set up functions within stable businesses; however, with planning and acceptance of the differences that will inevitably be found, the transition can be managed successfully and organizations can achieve success.

When organizations go global, there are two areas of thought on how it can be planned; the structure will determine the strategy (who we have) or the strategy will determine the structure (how we can do it). In both cases, the choice of people to take an international strategy forward is an integral part of globalization. Cultural differences and cross-cultural management are a core part of successful growth. Hofstede's cultural dimensions (1980) and the GLOBE study (House et al., 2004) allow us to initially understand the differences between nations on selected dimensions of culture. Understanding the differences of national values, attitudes and working norms is required to decide on whether to adapt or adopt HR practices for that market.

Comparative HRM reviews allow institutional, cultural and legal requirements to be assessed by an organization in an international context. HR needs to be responsive to the needs of each location, making recommendations that reflect the right practices with a strategic approach of maintaining cost-effective management practices and managing people across borders. There are often multiple relationships that need to be managed, including additional head offices, subsidiaries, trade unions, legislative and local communities.

The make-up of the workforce is now venturing into a situation where five generations can be found in organizations, with the youngest generations growing in numbers and having different values, cultures and social norms from those of the older generations. The way that different generations work within organizations affects learning styles, position on power and authority, along with the expectations of basic roles. Fashion organizations will need to consider how this affects their culture and strategies and how they can use all generations to fill growing workforce gaps. In particular, fashion organizations need to attract and retain high-performing millennials and Generation Z individuals. They will also need to develop managers and leaders with the skills to work with differing engagement, development and behaviours, to ensure that talent across a business is fully optimized.

Employers and employees are both growing more aware of the importance of having a mentally and physically strong workforce, given that individuals spend the greater part of a working day with an organization. From an employer's viewpoint, positive well-being of employees supports retention, development, culture and strategic intentions. It drives better engagement levels, lowers sickness rates and improves performance levels. From an employee's viewpoint, well-being initiatives and practices support a feeling of being valued, allow for growth and development of an individual and create a positive working environment. Recognizing the signs of the impacts of well-being is a key part of the organizational effectiveness and a focus for the management and leadership teams within organizations, and therefore will become an increasingly important part of the behaviours and values of organizational culture.

CHALLENGES AND CONVERSATIONS

1. Outline the main components that senior teams within fashion organizations should consider when planning their HR strategy.

2. Discuss why culture is so important to organizations and employees. How can a fashion organization ensure it is understood?

3. Provide an analysis of a good leader in a fashion organization. Use examples to justify your points.

4. Suggest practices that can engage employees within organizations. Suggest why this is important in the contemporary fashion industry.

5. Discuss how fashion companies might work to maximize their human capital in the future.

6. Debate how innovation, creativity and progression impact people and the associated processes in fashion organizations.

REFERENCES AND FURTHER READING

Armstrong, M. (2016) *Armstrong's Handbook of Strategic Human Resource Management.* 6th edn. London: Kogan Page.

Beer, M., Spector, B., Lawrence, P. R. and Mills, D. Q. (1984) *Managing Human Assets: The Groundbreaking Harvard Business School Program.* New York, NY: Free Press.

Boxall, P. and Purcell, J. (2003) *Strategy and Human Resource Management.* London: Palgrave Macmillan.

Burke, W. and Litwin, G. (1992) 'A causal model of organization performance and change'. *Journal of Management*, 18(3), pp. 523–545.

Chambers, E., Foulton, M., Handfield-Jones, H., Hankin, S. and Michaels III, E. (1998) 'The war for talent', *McKinsey Quarterly*, 3, pp. 44–57.

CIPD (Chartered Institute of Personnel & Development) (2015, 2016). Available from: https://www.cipd.co.uk/.

Deloitte (2016) The Six Signature Traits of Inclusive Leadership. Available at: https://www2.deloitte.com/content/dam/Deloitte/au/Documents/human-capital/deloitte-au-hc-six-signature-traits-inclusive-leadership-020516.pdf [accessed 26/09/2016].

Fashion United (2017). Available at: https://fashionunited.uk/.

Fombrun, C. J., Tichy, M. M. and Devanna, M. A. (1984) *Strategic Human Resource Management*. New York: Wiley.

Greer, C. R. (1995) *Strategy and Human Resources*. Englewood Cliffs, NJ: Prentice Hall.

Guest, D. E. (1987) 'Human resource management and industrial relations'. *Journal of Management Studies*, 24, pp. 503–521.

Hall, E. T. (1976) *Beyond Culture*. Garden City, NY: Anchor Press.

Hofstede, G. (2001) *Culture's Consequences*, 2nd edn. Thousand Oaks, CA: Sage Publications.

Hofstede, G., Hofstede, G. J. and Minkov, M. (2010) *Cultures and Organizations: Software of the Mind*, 3rd edn. New York: McGraw-Hill.

House, R. J., Hanges, P. J., Javidan, M., Dorfman, P. W. and Gupta, V. (eds) (2004) *Culture, Leadership, and Organizations: The GLOBE Study of 62 Societies*. Thousand Oaks, CA: Sage.

Johnson, G., Scholes, K. and Whittington, R. (2008) *Exploring Corporate Strategy: Text and Cases*. Harlow: Pearson Education.

Kahn, W. A. (1990) 'Psychological conditions of personal engagement and disengagement at work'. *Academy of Management Journal*, 33(4), pp. 692–724.

Kotter, J. P. (1996) *Leading Change*. Boston, MA: Harvard Business School Press.

Kubler-Ross, E. (1969) *On Death and Dying*. New York: Touchstone.

Lewin, K. (1947) 'Frontiers in group dynamics', in Cartwright, D. (ed.) (1952) *Field Theory in Social Science*. London: Social Science Paperbacks.

McClelland, D. C. (1985) *Human Motivation*. Glenview, IL: Scott, Foresman.

Peters, T. and Waterman, R. H. (1982) *In Search of Excellence: Lessons from America's Best-Run Companies*. London: Harper and Row.

Porter, M. E. (1985) *Competitive Advantage*. New York: Free Press.

Purcell, J. (1989) 'The impact of corporate strategy and human resource management', in Storey, J. (ed.) *New Perspectives on Human Resource Management*. London: Routledge, pp. 67–91.

Rousseau, D. M. (1989) 'Psychological and implied contracts in organizations'. *Employee Responsibilities and Rights Journal*, 2, pp. 121–139.

Schein, E. H. (2017) *Organizational Culture and Leadership*, 5th edn. Hoboken, NJ: John Wiley & Sons.

Scholes, K., Regner, P., Johnson, G., Whittington, R. and Angwin, D. (2013) *Exploring Strategy: Text and Cases*, 10th edn. Harlow: Pearson Education.

Shuck, B. and Wollard, K. (2010) 'Employee engagement and HRD: A seminal review of the foundations'. *Human Resource Development Review*, 9(1), pp. 89–110.

Truss, C., Gratton, L., Hope-Hailey, V., McGovern, P. and Stiles, P. (1997) 'Soft and hard models of human resource management: A reappraisal'. *Journal of Management Studies*, 34(1), pp. 53–73.

Ulrich, D. (1997) *Human Resource Champions: The Next Agenda for Adding Value and Delivering Results*. Boston, MA: Harvard Business School Press.

Ulrich, D. and Dulebohn, J. H. (2015) 'Are we there yet? What's next for HR?' *Human Resource Management Review*, 25(2), pp. 188–204.

Women in Retail & Elixirr (2016) The commercial advantage of more women in the boardroom, June 2016. Available from: https://www.elixirr.com/2016/06/commercial-advantage-of-more-women-in-the-boardroom/.

FASHION FUTURES

15

Ana Roncha

INTRODUCTION

The fashion landscape is constantly challenged by new market ecosystems and within the creative economy management requires different ways of organizing and coordinating work, different values and different ways of communicating (Denning, 2013). Consumers are demanding greater levels of personalization in their consumption experience, resulting in companies having to re-assess their business models in order to become more responsive to consumer needs and demands. The new premises are based on collaboration, co-creation and innovation in order to create organizational and shared value. The driver of this dramatic shift is the rising power of technology and its influence in building consumer–brand relationships. The virtual brand landscape is today a powerful and interactive engagement platform for consumer-to-consumer recommendations; the use of technology has facilitated a level of exposure and customer engagement well beyond what was previously possible. By using social media platforms, brands have the power to develop a meaningful connection and provoke conversations with actively engaged audiences and this has led to the formation of brand communities, where members share a common interest and bond, and the opportunity to critique.

In this environment, where consumers are constantly informed, have the power to create products themselves and contribute to the generation of new business models, questions regarding the relevance of traditional business models arise. The last few years have resulted in an increasingly changing competitive landscape for fashion with more brands, more channels, more retailers and with more complex consumers. This last chapter intends to uncover some of the main changes that have recently taken place in the industry and also to identify the emerging and disruptive trends that will transform the industry in the next decade.

LEARNING OBJECTIVES

After studying this chapter, you should be able to understand:

- The changing marketplace for fashion and the current challenges for brands;

- The changes in values and demands of the new consumer;

- The role of technology as well as its potential for disruption;

- The growing importance of co-creation and collaborative networks;

- The existence of touch-points across the physical and digital environment for brands;

- New technology developments that have a potential impact on the fashion industry;

- How fashion organizations can apply new business models to generate increased value.

---

15. Photograph by Valerie Wilson Trower.

THE CHANGING MARKETPLACE

A common theme throughout this book has been acknowledgement of change within the fashion industry and how this has led to a highly competitive environment and resulted in a more informed and demanding consumer. The value chain is no longer the onus of the company; value is being created with consumers at various stages of consumption, thanks to their growing involvement and participation. The factors contributing to this change include societal impacts, changing consumer behaviour and technology adoption; dimensions that have given rise to new business models that disrupt the current context and lead to a more exciting and innovative industry.

- **Societal impacts** – This includes aspects related to the environment, urban layout and workforce flexibility. According to a UK 2017 report by investment management company Investec Click & Invest, 32% of the people surveyed are planning a major life change in the next 5 years such as turning a hobby into a profitable business (the 'hobbypreneurs'). We are also witnessing the rise of global online talent exchange, a factor that can impact largely on the industry, redefine barriers and impose flexibility across the sector.

- **Consumer behaviour** – Consumer demand and consumption patterns are changing rapidly, leading to a need to redesign how businesses interact with consumers. In particular, consumer demand for 24/7 fast fashion and more recently sustainable fashion are conflicting but nonetheless significant industry trends.

- **Technology adoption** – At the heart of technology adoption is the need to embrace consumer centrality and to redesign the omni-channel experience to focus on the changing consumer decision journey. Also of interest is the evolution of AI, 3D printing, VR and AR as well as conversational commerce.

These three key factors have led to the emergence of new business models, with companies continuously assessing how they engage with consumers, determine their product/service mix, prioritize channels and capture value. These new operating models need to be accompanied with different capabilities and resources so as to manage and grow them more effectively (see Figure 15.1).

Agility and innovation allow for increased engagement with the empowered and tech-literate consumer as they are central to shaping the direction of the industry. Business models of the future have to accommodate these advances and evolutions and accommodate both the physical and digital world into one unified experience.

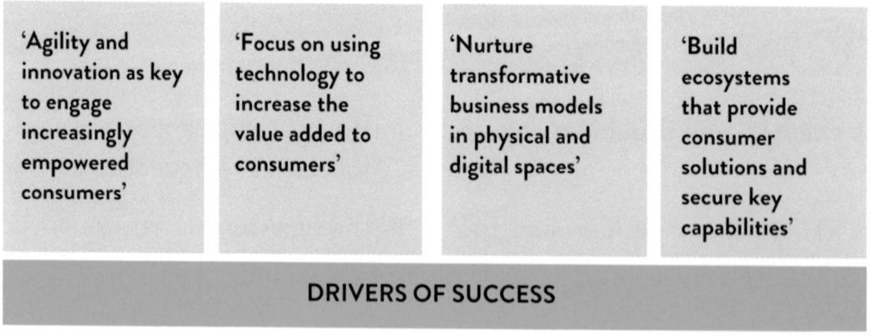

> **Agility** A company's ability to make changes according to both consumer demands and changing environments. Requires rapid decision-making and a responsive approach to change. Here 'agility' refers to the ability of fashion entities to use technology developments to increase and sustain consumer–brand engagement.

'Agility and innovation as key to engage increasingly empowered consumers'	'Focus on using technology to increase the value added to consumers'	'Nurture transformative business models in physical and digital spaces'	'Build ecosystems that provide consumer solutions and secure key capabilities'
DRIVERS OF SUCCESS			

Figure 15.1 *Drivers of success for consumer industries*
Source: Adapted from WEF (2017).

Change in the modus operandi within the fashion system

Prompted by easy and frequent access to fashion brands, the technical changes are leading to major consequences for the traditional calendar for fashion weeks and collection drops. The fashion calendar as we know it is currently under debate, and some brands have started to find alternative ways of presenting their collections to customers. The CFDA (Council for Fashion Designers of America), for example, made changes to turn New York Fashion Week into a consumer-facing event as a way to increase engagement. 'We have designers, retailers and everybody complaining about the shows. Everything needs to be rebooted' (Diane von Furstenberg, in Conlon, 2015).

The growing importance of pre-collections has also had a profound effect on the way brands and retailers work. Pre-shows from Dior, Chanel and Gucci have been taking place in remote and highly attractive locations, with content tailored specifically to encourage social media activity. The 'see now, buy now' (SNBN) phenomenon also capitalized on the social media buzz surrounding the industry. The traditional fashion system relies on shows during fashion weeks to showcase a new collection to key buyers and press. After the buyers placed orders, brands would then start coordinating styles to be put into production with suppliers, and at the same time, the fashion press would request sample pieces to feature in their publications. The whole process would take around six months to get product to stores, during which time fast-fashion brands would produce similar items and saturate the market with close interpretations of designer collections. The SNBN model emerged to counteract this, with brands showing their runway pieces and making these available to consumers straight after, responding to their rising need for instant gratification. 'There is a definite appetite from some of our customers for the immediacy and practicality of see now buy now. These customers tend to be very social media savvy and natural purchasers of pre-collections and fast fashion lines in general. Our offering of See Now/ Buy Now collections will continue to be explored and expand' (Heather Gramston, Selfridges Womenswear Buying Manager, in Salonga, 2017).

Burberry has been an enthusiastic adopter of the SNBN model, live streaming the show on their website, and partnering with Facebook and Snapchat (Arthur, 2016a). The brand has also used WeChat as a selling tool, allowing users to buy two exclusive editions of the Bridle bag from the collection. 'The changes we are making will allow us to build a closer connection between the experience that we create with our runway shows and the moment when people can physically explore the collections for themselves' (Christopher Bailey, Burberry chief creative officer and chief executive officer, in BoF (Business of Fashion), 2016).

The SNBN strategy, however, requires extreme agility, rapid decision-making and a more responsive approach to change. This is not necessarily in line with hierarchical business structures; for the SNBN model to work, trends and designs need to be agreed and implemented quickly and that is only possible if businesses in the supply chain operate in a more transparent and collaborative manner to replace competitive advantage by transient advantage (as discussed in Chapter 2).

Already some designers have tried and dropped this model; Tom Ford, for example, tried the SNBN but stopped it the season after. 'The store shipping schedule doesn't align with the fashion show schedule ... you can't have a show with clothes that have been on the selling floor for a month. (...) We lost a month of selling. We had merchandise sitting in stockrooms all over the world' (Tom Ford, in Foley, 2017). Currently the see now, buy now model appears to be an attention raiser rather than a sales motivator and the debate about its future remains contentious.

The overarching theme of the introduction of capsule, resort collections or the SNBN model is the need to adapt to the rapid demands from an increasingly informed consumer and trend- and brand-literate consumer. In fast fashion, for example, brands develop their collections with a breakdown of basic or seasonal lines influenced by the need to develop more trend based limited editions and short production-run styles that reflect the trends of the moment. Some of the most common speed-to-market based models are indicated in Figure 15.2.

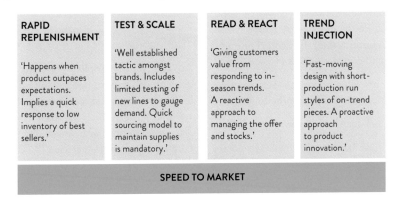

RAPID REPLENISHMENT	TEST & SCALE	READ & REACT	TREND INJECTION
'Happens when product outpaces expectations. Implies a quick response to low inventory of best sellers.'	'Well established tactic amongst brands. Includes limited testing of new lines to gauge demand. Quick sourcing model to maintain supplies is mandatory.'	'Giving customers value from responding to in-season trends. A reactive approach to managing the offer and stocks.'	'Fast-moving design with short-production run styles of on-trend pieces. A proactive approach to product innovation.'

SPEED TO MARKET

Figure 15.2 *Speed models*

Source: Adapted from Kurt Salmon (2017).

Consumer changes

The moving landscape of the fashion industry can be categorized into three dimensions that sum up the change in consumer profiles:

- **Expectations**: The rise of the 'right now' economy demonstrated by fashion brands doing same-day delivery (for example ASOS) and even 90-minute deliveries (for example, Gucci at Farfetch) has raised expectations across categories and consumer-market segments.

- **Empowerment**: The sharing and influencing abilities of consumers now have the power to make or break a brand or product. Consumers take on a more powerful role than before in their relationships with brands.

- **Engagement**: Brands can build a closer connection with their target audience with the opportunity to drive loyalty and trust.

Throughout this book, it has become evident that consumer interest now goes beyond product utility and quality, to the story behind it, whether it be the integrity of design, the source of the fabric, innovation, exclusivity, value or trend. By combining rational and emotional bonds and aligning with Schmitt's (1999) experiential marketing-concept approach, brands are seen as an integrated holistic experience, created through an affective relationship, and through the association of a specific lifestyle.

A study from *Harvard Business Review* (*HBR*, 2016) highlights four types of needs relevant to today's independent, involved and informed individuals.

- **Functional**: Saves time, simplifies, makes money, reduces risks, organizes, integrates, connects, reduces effort, avoids hassles, reduces cost, offers quality, variety, sensory appeal, and informs.

- **Emotional**: Reduces anxiety, rewards me, offers nostalgia, design/aesthetics, badge value, wellness, therapeutic value, fun/entertainment, attractiveness, and provides access.

- **Life changing**: Provides hope, self-actualization, motivation, heirloom and affiliation/belonging.

- **Social impact**: Self-transcendence.

This model can be seen as a contemporary interpretation of Maslow's Hierarchy of Needs model (1943) with *HBR* suggesting that the more the types of needs satisfied, the greater customers' loyalty. Another interesting new take on value was developed by the World Economic Forum in 2017, exploring the new dimensions of the value equation. Whereas the traditional value was driven by cost, choice and convenience (as discussed in Chapter 3) the new equation adds two new elements; control and experience (Figure 15.3).

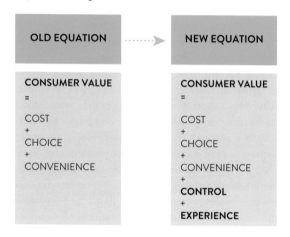

Figure 15.3 *An updated equation on consumer value*
Source: Adapted from WEF (2017).

Control relates to consumers' need to influence and shape their own purchasing journey, powered by digital channels, and experience represents the addition of all interactions into one unified and consistent experience across touch-points.

Change in value leading to the creation of new channels

Increasingly consumers, millennials in particular, value experiences over products (Solomon, 2017), and brands are finding alternative and innovative ways to engage in brand activation, leading to a reassessment of the channels used to interact with consumers.

The fashion travel and tourism experience

As the world shrinks, travelling experiences are growing in importance, resulting in the creation of experiences that consumers will want to share via social networks. In response, fashion brands are collaborating with travel companies to launch curated experiences (see Box 15.1). There is a growing awareness that consumers do not need brands they interact with to be everywhere, all the time, but they value brands that use new channels and innovative contexts.

Box 15.1 – The curated fashion-travel experience

Net-a-Porter and Cathay Pacific	Net-a-Porter's collaboration with Hong Kong-based airline Cathay Pacific in 2016 where passengers have the opportunity to shop online via the brand's e-commerce platform available during the flight. '*Net-A-Porter and Mr Porter's partnership with Cathay Pacific is the meeting of two global, luxury brands known for innovation and service*' (Sarah Rutson, vice-president of global buying at Net-a-Porter, in Hendriksz, 2016).
West Elm	West Elm is expanding its business into boutique hotels, due to open in 2018 as the first of five planned hotels across the US. The innovation in this concept lies in it being a 100% shoppable hotel brand, acting as a living showroom allowing consumers to try out the products before purchasing them. The retailer has explored a close connection to community-based retail by decorating each hotel with products and artwork from their communities and even changes its restaurant menus according to locations. Therefore, each hotel is planned to be different according to the location it serves. '*Everything is about that guest experience. Our tag line has been whole-hearted hospitality*' (David Bowd, Principal at West Elm Hotels, in Brady, 2017).
Canada Goose	Canada Goose Adventure tours. The luxury outwear brand has entered into the travel business by developing a partnership with Canadian luxury active travel company Butterfield & Robinson. They have curated three adventure tours (Iceland, Newfoundland and British Columbia) so as to bring to life both companies' shared values of luxury and exploration by allowing 16 people the opportunity to explore these destinations, enjoy kayaking, snorkelling and snowmobiling, and experience Canada Goose products.
Kit and Ace	Kit & Ace: The Carry-on pop-up. The rising travelling consumer has been the focus of the brand with its collection of travel-friendly, wrinkle-free clothing presented at pop-ups in various hotels. Apart from the collection, the brand also developed online travel guides for each city, with curated suggestions from local influencers. The Carry-on took place in San Francisco, Los Angeles, Melbourne, London, Sydney and New York. '*We wanted to create a multi-platform experience where people could shop travel essentials and explore cities around the world at the same time*' (JJ Wilson, co-founder and head of brand at Kit & Ace, in Jordan, 2016).

With the rising number of international travellers, airports are now commercial spaces in their own right, and are providing opportunities for fashion brands to design shopping experiences to suit the various needs of increasingly diverse travellers. Technology developments such as beacon applications and mobile wallets allow for personalized offers using flight data and location services. As a successful example of this evolution, Alibaba's Alipay allows Chinese consumers to take advantage of digital payments at selected airports around the world.

The mobile channel strategy

'39% of millennials say they interact more with their smartphone than they do with their significant others – parents, friends, children or co-workers' (Bank of America, June 2016).

Modern experiences are the ones where multiple devices are connected, where there is human-centred design, where content, commerce and advertising converge, which are highly personalized and where mobile is the first screen. Online retailers such as Mr Porter have led the way into a successful integration of m-commerce with editorial-styled content. Not only does the brand sell the products but it establishes a conversation with customers in a personalized manner, with content such as branded how-to guides, information, inspiration and style advice.

Another impact on mobile channel strategy is the so called 'Uber' effect, paving the way to the 'right-now' economy, which aims to provide immediate supply of goods or services to consumers, merging mobile, social, cloud and big data. UberRush, Etsy ASAP and Everlane Now are amongst those offering same-day fashion delivery via online orders. Time-saving has become the new luxury (WGSN, 2016a). Founded in 2012, Deliv has partnered with over 250 retailers including Macy's and Footlocker to provide crowdsourced, same-day delivery between retailers and consumers. 'Today's consumers want the convenience of picking exactly when their packages will arrive. It's no surprise we've experienced an organic growth increase of 800% in the first half of this year compared to the same period last year' (Daphne Carmeli, Deliv CEO, in Chain Storage (2015).

The digital ecosystem has also allowed for developments that tackle one of online fashion's biggest concerns – the fit, and consequent returns. Various start-ups have used the 'try before you buy' model (WGSN, 2016c). Try.com, for example, developed a system that can be integrated into websites. Instead of the 'Buy' button, consumers can select 'Try' instead, giving seven days to try it on before returning it or keeping it and paying. The app hosts the try cart and carries out data analytics to assess a customer's credit worthiness and purchase intent. If the goods are returned properly and within the right time, this profile is saved and they will be able to try more items next time. Nike, Zara and COS have used this application.

Mobile is an increasingly important payment technology with Gartner (2016) predicting that 50% of consumers in mature smartphone markets will use phones or smartphones for mobile payments by 2018. In 2016, Topshop launched a range of accessories that incorporate Barclaycard's bPay contactless payment technology, enabling shoppers to make tap and go payments at 300,000 contactless terminals. Users remove the chip from the card and insert it into the accessory, download the bPay app to activate, add money and track spending.

Net-a-Porter has also been using the messaging platform WhatsApp to engage in one-to-one conversations with consumers and allow them to purchase directly on the platform. The luxury retailer has also been using a try-on-at-home concierge service that lets customers try on the clothes they have ordered while personal stylists wait to take back any unwanted items.

> **Co-creation**
> A collaborative process implying that customers actively participate in the production and marketing process using tools such as user-generated content or crowdsourcing. Co-creation allows for a two-directional conversation between businesses and consumers.

CO-CREATION AS THE DRIVING FORCE FOR COLLABORATION

Co-creation has emerged as a new business paradigm, with customers actively participating in the production and marketing process. We introduced this concept earlier in the book when discussing models of communication using user-generated content (UGC). Today's consumers share experiences with products and services with their peers and have an increased will to participate in designing the products and services that they use, providing an on-going and two-directional conversation between businesses and consumers.

As we saw in Chapter 7, there are five types of co-creation: co-creation workshops, crowdsourcing, open sourcing, mass customization, and user-generated content. Gouillart (2014) adds community or social marketing to this typology. Crowdsourcing and mass customization are specifically relevant to recent developments within the fashion industry, so we will explore them in more detail in the next sections.

Crowdsourcing

Crowdsourcing was initially referred to in an article by journalist Jeff Howe in a *Wired* article 'The Rise of Crowdsourcing' (2006) and was explained as the practice of companies making an open call to solve a problem, either through competition or collaboration, and quickly became a major trend in a number of industries. The closely related concept of crowdfunding which relates to the raising of finance was discussed in chapter 5. In the fashion world, 'crowdsourcing' refers to user-generated clothing designs or user participation in the selection of such designs, allowing for consumers to be directly involved with a brand and helping to shape its identity. One of the first examples of crowdsourcing in the fashion

MINI CASE STUDY 15.1 - Threadless

Threadless was founded in 2006 as a web-based T-shirt company that crowdsources the design process for their shirts through an ongoing online competition. Members of the community can submit their designs and vote on what they intend to be the winning design. All designs are scored and the new designs become available to the community. Designs remain available for voting for two weeks, and the highest-scoring designs are selected by Threadless staff to be printed and made available for sale on the website. Winning designs receive money prizes as well as gift certificates. Threadless also rewards its members with purchasing credits in return for referring sales by linking to the website or by submitting photos of themselves wearing Threadless shirts.

At Threadless.com, the process also continues following purchase. According to the company, they do not advertise, but all their efforts are directed towards word of mouth. They give upcoming designers the chance to promote their own work through creating tools that allow them to spread the message: banners, sending mass e-mails and newsletters.

They have also created three additional platforms:

- Tattoodo – a social marketplace for tattoo designs where visual artists are inspired and can submit new tattoo ideas.

- Creative Market – a platform for handcrafted and independent creative designs around the world.

- Open Me – a greeting cards platform that allows for customization and personalized delivery options.

---

industry was the website Threadless.com (see Mini Case Study 15.1)

Crowdsourcing can also be used for feedback on specific pieces from designers and to fund the production of items via pre-ordering. According to Humphreys and Grayson (2008), participants in crowdsourcing projects can be identified as prosumers, engaging in 'the novelty of asking individuals to simultaneously play the role of consumer and producer'. They are motivated by the enjoyment of participating in the project and have a desire to create and use consumption in order to express themselves.

Crowdsourcing works on the premise of a two-directional flux: D2C (designer to consumer) and C2D (consumer to designer). The added value is that brands and designers are able to track data about who their users/consumers are and how they interact with the fashion process; they can enable more accurate product development and reduce sampling costs. By collecting brand community member feedback and suggestions, ideas are generated that are clear representations of consumer needs and desires. Positive attitudes towards the product are shared as well as subsequent purchase intentions, willingness-to-pay, and referrals. Higher awareness also stimulates faster diffusion, improving the likelihood of success.

Apart from providing engagement benefits, crowdsourcing platforms are creating socially driven experiences. It is an open-ended ecosystem where anyone can assume a key role, leading to a business model that is changing the boundaries of traditional fashion formats. Rebecca Minkoff, for example, ventured into the crowdsourcing arena in 2011 through collaboration with Polyvore.com, a photo-sharing-based fashion community website, in a contest that set out to look for designs for a 'morning after' clutch that would debut during the Designers Show at the Fall 2011 New York Fashion Week. The designer's team selected the top creations for public voting and the design with the most votes won a trip to New York Fashion Week as well as the bag design being named after them (Wang, 2010). In 2012, Oscar de la Renta also took part in a crowdsourcing venture, launching 'The Board' on Pinterest – a digital pinboard of inspirations and ideas for his brand. The submissions were used to guide the creative process of the conception of the spring/summer 2013 collection. By involving consumers/fans in the creative process, the designer increased public interest in the runway show and subsequently in retail stores (Cain, 2013). More recently in 2017, J. Crew used Instagram Stories to gather feedback from consumers about its Chateau Parka. Consumers could choose between three colour options and the one with the most votes would go into production.

Mass customization (MC)

In 1989, Kotler defined mass customization as 'a kind of scope economies application, through single manufacturing process modularization, providing tremendous variety and individual customization at prices and time comparable to standard goods and service'. In more recent years, MC is still characterized by the ability to provide a customized product or service, designed, produced and delivered to meet the specific demands of consumers. Although a similar concept in scope to crowdsourcing, MC differs from the first as its premises are based on interacting with a product that will ultimately be mass produced yet is available to personalize, as opposed to participating in the full process.

When Nike introduced customization back in 1999, it contributed towards a 20% increase in annual revenues (Forbes, 2016). In terms of consumers, their satisfaction is increased, hedonic benefits are tapped into as customization becomes an enjoyable and entertaining experience and one where customers can express their creativity (Kaplan and Haenlein, 2010). MC therefore strengthens brand–consumer relationships and brand attachment, which leads to further customer loyalty.

From a customer's perspective, the key success factors are (Altonen, 2011):

- Meeting the needs of each individual consumer,
- Customer co-design and integration,
- Technology – ability to produce within a fixed solution space,
- Producing within tolerable cost and price levels.

Unmade (UMD) is a London-based company that is revolutionizing knitwear through the use of cutting edge technology that allows the production of one-off pieces: 'Unmade is building the next level of customisation where colours can be changed, patterns can be broken apart and monograms are seamlessly integrated into the very fabric of each piece of bespoke knitwear' (Hal Watts, Unmade CEO, in Roberts, 2016). Footwear brand Josefinas is another example of mass customization, allowing consumers to add their initials or other words to the back of the shoe (see Figure 15.4)

Figure 15.4 *Josefinas ballet-pumps, an example of mass customization. Image courtesy of Josefinas. Reproduced with permission.*

Collaborative networks

The premises upon which both crowdsourcing and mass customization are built make full sense in the sharing economy, which is all about exchanging ideas and being part of a collaborative process. This new model paves the way to bridge the gap between consumers and designer, providing benefits for both

> **Collaboration** A relationship where all parties choose to take part to accomplish a shared outcome. The use of collaboration fosters innovation and agility as well as efficiency.

parties, which are unavailable within traditional retail models. The biggest precursor of change was when social media channels began morphing into new channels for collaboration and innovation (Moore and Neely, 2011). Collaboration can be defined as 'a purposeful relationship in which all parties strategically choose to cooperate in order to accomplish a shared outcome' (Rubin, 2009).

Collaborative communities

Many successful brands have been using social media to ask their communities to participate in brainstorming, leading to the development of better products and services, and to support the values and issues of the community. We have witnessed growing disruptions in the market that allow for product development, innovative delivery systems, a distinctive supplier network, the possibility of customization, and apps and platforms for enhanced consumer engagement. In sum, a whole new array of possibilities that changed the traditional way of doing business (Denning, 2014). Collaborative communities are expected to foster not only innovation and agility but also efficiency and scalability (Adler et al., 2011). The greatest consequence of collaboration is the ability to implement ideas and push the boundaries in a way that would not be possible for a single party.

From collaborative to sharing economy

Specifically, in the fashion industry, the collaborative economy is driven by a convergence of numerous factors including the global economic slowdown, and the growing environmental consciousness. The sharing economy, once an underground movement, is becoming mainstream. Temporary or leased ownership of products is not necessarily a new method but has been rare in the fashion industry; however, its potential is demonstrated by Rent the Runway (RTR). This company has recently added another service, Unlimited, where the idea is to create a 'closet in the cloud'. A monthly charge is made for three dresses, sweaters, handbags, and/or coats at a time. As a result of data sharing between Rent the Runway and Marchesa (a well-known 'red carpet' dress brand) which indicated an increase in demand for blouses, the two companies collaborated to launch a range of Marchesa tops exclusively through the RTR platform (Biron, 2017).

BRAND TOUCH-POINTS IN THE ERA OF DIGITAL DISRUPTION

In the current era of digital advancement and the move towards omni-channel, the unified customer experience should be possible. Consumers' interaction is now with the brand and not with channels and hence the importance and relevance of this approach. 'The bottom line is, we're indifferent to whether she converts in the store or online. We just want her to shop with Macy's' (Jennifer Kasper, Group Vice President, Digital Media & Multi-cultural Marketing, in Think with Google, 2014). This activity has been further categorized into three types of shopping behaviour:

- **Showrooming**
  Consumers research in-store but complete purchase online.
  Motivation: Get the best price and convenience.

- **Webrooming**
  Consumers research online but complete purchase in-store.
  Motivation: See, feel and try on product.

- **Boomerooming**
  Consumers research online, go to store to feel and touch and return online to complete purchase.
  Motivation: See, feel and try on product and get the best price and convenience.

In order for Omni-channel to be successfully implemented, brands need to address the following challenges:

- **Achieving a seamless fulfilment process** – as all channels are managed together, the perceived interaction is not with the channel but with the brand.

- **Understanding the changing role of physical stores** – and develop skills to leverage their new potential.

- **Reconstruction of the supply chain** – to include a more strategic management of the customer's journey.

- **Channel integration** – offering the customer the choice to move freely between channels during the shopping journey.

- **Impact of mobile technologies** – achieving a balance between data privacy, ethical restrictions and personalization of messages.

- **Ability to respond to the need for transparency** on both price and product offers.

- **Consistency on brand image and service** – creating a similar message across all channels and touch-points and being immersed in a consistent brand experience.

- **The need for authentic and engaging brand stories** – rather than being present across all platforms at all times.

With this approach, the relevance and importance of physical stores is regained. In fact, as reported by retail property group British Land in 2017, a physical store increases local online traffic to a retailer's website by an average of 52%. Physical stores can then be an engine of online growth, with consumers being able to choose the channels that best align to their lifestyle and values. 'Blending channels is increasingly common, pure-plays are still moving to physical, and click & collect, an increasingly important link between physical and online, is continuing to take ground' (Ben Dimson, British Land head of retail business development, Retail Design World, 2017). The store is no longer the place to complete the purchase but has acquired a whole new set of functions (Figure 15.5).

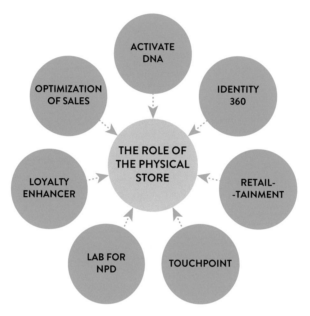

Figure 15.5 *The new role of physical stores*
Source: Adapted from Kurt Salmon (2017).

- **Activate DNA** – The store is used to educate current and potential partners about the brand in terms of its position in the market, differentiate the brand's image and message values (Riewold, 2002) and showcase its unique DNA. For example, Nike Lab stores (a total of 8 worldwide) promise an immersive experience, full engagement, and feature exclusive collections. The stores also host special launches and stock exclusive collaborations (for example, the 'Ten Nike Icons' by Virgil Abloh).

- **Identity 360** – The physical space allows consumers to experience the brand in a fully immersive 360. We have mentioned atmospherics in Chapter 6 and through the use of technology, interactive features, highly trained staff and visual displays, consumers are able to experience the brand in a way that is not possible online.

- **Retail-tainment** – When elements of entertainment are merged in the store space. The aim of retail-tainment is not just about entertainment, the aim is to create a relevant emotional connection with the brand's values. For example, Burberry hosting music concerts in the London flagship stores, or Sweaty Betty Yoga classes.

- **Touch-point** – In the Omni-channel world, the perceived interaction is with the brand and not the channels and hence physical stores become a showroom and point of inspiration. Also, with more and more brands adopting 'click and collect' and ship from store, the store becomes a collection point and stock centre for all channels.

- **Lab for NPD** – The store becomes a place to test new products and services; consumer's feedback leading to new product development (NPD) as brands capture interactions with consumers. This also involves mass customization in-store (for example, Adidas and Nike).

- **Loyalty enhancer** – The store as a focal point to forge relationships and enhance brand loyalty.
- **Optimization of sales** – The physical space allows for personal interactions that will have a direct impact on sales conversions with engaged consumers.

In spite of this, mobile commerce reflects the increased time consumers spend in transit, commuting to work in major cities. These so-called 'transumers' offer new targeting opportunities to brands, with more than a fifth of UK online shopping sales now taking place during people's daily commutes (Skeldon, 2015) and with clothing topping the list of purchases. In summary, three types of touch-point are emerging (see Table 15.1): owned, tenanted and third-party.

Brands' owned touch-points	Tenanted touch-points	Third-party touch-points
Channels such as website, stores and email – the ones where brands have complete control.	Those where customers connect with the brand and where the brand has control of the content but not necessarily the platform – social-media channels, for example.	Where brands have no control. For example, Google's search results, where it is Google that decides how the content about the brand is displayed, and the brand has no control over this.

Table 15.1 *A typology of touch-points*

Creative Phygital

The expression 'creative phygital' has evolved from the digital vs physical debate and adds an element of creativity in terms of how brands are experimenting with digital technologies. Creative phygital is therefore a way to turn production processes into theatre, or to immerse consumers in a particular ethical stance (LSN Global, 2016). While the term 'phygital' refers to the merging of the physical and the digital experience, creative phygital can be defined as a playful synergy of physical and digital systems which aims to inspire, intrigue and entertain consumers as they shop. An example of this was Kenzo's attempt to raise awareness about the environment with its digital pop-up shop in Paris as part of the brand's No Fish No Nothing range. The virtual fish swimming around the aquarium would gradually disappear until someone bought an item, when they would reappear to represent the fact that money from the purchase would help protect the marine environment.

Understanding the full and increasingly complex customer journey requires new skills from marketers that are now looking to integrate digital creativity into wider communications and viewing the customer experience more holistically, within the six stages of the consumer decision journey: consider, evaluate, buy, experience, advocate and bond (McKinsey, 2016).

TECHNOLOGY: NEW HORIZONS FOR FASHION

In addition to the developments discussed above, there has been much attention recently on three key innovations: virtual reality (VR), augmented reality (AR) and artificial intelligence (AI).

Virtual reality (VR) allows consumers to have an immersive shopping experience, built on industries such as gaming, entertainment and beauty. According to data from Statista (2015), the number of VR users is expected to reach 171 million by 2018. In the fashion industry there have been several attempts to introduce VR as an experiential tool, such as the partnership between Google Cardboard and outdoor brand North Face. Most of the applications are connected to bringing products and events to life but they can expand to create direct marketing and sales opportunities. Luxury retailer The Apartment (New York) has used Samsung Gear VR HMD combined with a Galaxy Note 4 phone to create a remote shopping experience enabling users to walk around the store and focus on hotspots to approach furnishings. With audio-info and the cost displayed, with a tap in the headset the product is then added to a virtual shopping cart.

Augmented reality (AR) has been trialled within the fashion retail environment a number of times, with limited success. Some of the latest applications in facial recognition technology are being trialled by beauty brands: Sephora, Charlotte Tilbury, Estée Lauder and L'Oréal have all launched apps with virtual try-on. ModiFace, a leading technology provider of the above technology, claims its application can increase time spent on mobile six times over and double conversions (Milnes, 2017c). These apps also allow for the collection of consumer data, better shopping experiences and improved performance in terms of advice and service. It also opens up a new world of possibilities – by knowing what products get tried on the most, which ones convert to purchase, or even trends by region. Product development teams can then respond accordingly and increase effectiveness.

Artificial Intelligence (AI) is the technology capable of performing tasks that usually require human intelligence and its impact can be seen largely in how it is transforming the consumer journey. IBM predicts that by 2020, 85% of all interactions will be done without a human agent (Sim, 2017). AI has the potential to improve the retail experience, basing this on data on past purchases and consumer profiles and preferences. At the other end of the supply chain, companies such as EDITED and INstock by WGSN are using retail analytics to predict bestsellers and trends. The impact of Artificial Intelligence (AI) is said to be largely down to its ability to transform the experience from mass to individualized across a variety of touch-points (Euromonitor, 2017). Examples include:

- **Empowering store associates** – Driven by a desire to incorporate technologies into the physical space, retailers are looking at the possibility of using automated robots to greet and guide consumers in-store, freeing up store associates to engage in more meaningful interactions.

- **Improving recommendations** – The use of data allows brands to offer more personalized recommendations as well as predict consumer behaviour, which will result in a more personalized shopping experience. For example, Starbucks launched 'My Starbucks Barista', allowing consumers to place orders with voice command or messaging, and is looking to use AI to analyze its data so as to deliver unique suggestions (Evans, 2017).

- **Providing a personal touch** – Through the use of improved Chatbots, revolutionizing the role and impact of digitally empowered assistants.

This enables the building of an experience for the individual and, with a rising momentum, for conversational commerce, rooted in machine learning and natural language processing. These are evolving from multiple-choice answers to natural language conversations.

'We will chat to them about the best products, style ideas and offers, and help them select what's right for them' (Alex Baldock, CEO Shop Direct, in Baldwin, 2016). Consumers are increasingly adopting this technology, mostly due to the success of artificially intelligent devices such as Amazon's Alexa. These 'Always-on' listening devices have helped to create a sense of familiarity with the technology that allows for other applications to be created.

- **Enabling a more powerful search** – A movement towards making e-commerce search engines think the way consumers do by improving the context. This involves image, voice and video recognition by leveraging machine learning. In fact, Gartner (2016) has estimated that by 2020, 30% of web browsing sessions will be done without a screen. As an example, ASOS launched a visual search technology in 2017, allowing users to take a photo of a desired item, identifying the shape, colour and pattern, and cross-referencing its own inventory so as to come up with the most relevant suggestion.

Artificial intelligence is at the beginning of its application and is controversial not only in the fashion industry, because of the potential for privacy intrusion and its ability to replace the human workforce.

Wearable technology

By 2020, the global wearable tech market is expected to be worth $80 billion (WGSN, 2016b). According to Credit Suisse, wearable technology is 'a mega trend that has hit an inflection point in market adoption and one that will have a significant and pervasive impact on the economy'. Wearable technology can be defined as 'the electrical engineering, physical computing, and wireless communication networks that make a fashionable wearable functional' (Seymour, 2009: 15). This segment is moving towards total integration where 'wearables will simply be known as clothes' (WGSN, 2016b).

Wearable technology combines practical benefits, such as being linked to physical, emotional or mental health, with clothes that are comfortable and desirable. Beecham Research (2015) noted that unobtrusive patient monitoring, such as detecting vital signs for diabetes care, remote ECG care monitoring and so on (see Mini Case Study 15.2), can hold high potential within the fashion sector. Another application is the use of conductive fibers embedded in shirts, running socks and sports bras to track metrics associated with physical activity, as used by start-ups OmSignal and Sensoria (Higginbotham, 2015). Table 15.2 gives other examples of wearable technology.

Category	Brands
Smart watches	Apple watch; LG Watch Style; Fitbit Ionic
Eyewear	Google glasses; Solos; Vuzix Blade; Sony SmartEye; Snap Spectacles
Smart Jewelry	Motiv; Kate Spade Bangle Tracker; Ringly; Tori Burch x Fitbit Flex 2
Smart Clothing	Spinali Design smart bikini; Owlet Smart Sock; Levi's and Google Project Jacquard; Samsung NFC Suit
Fitness wear	NikeFlex; Fitbit; Jawbone; Wearable Xs Nadi X pants; Supa Powered Sports bra

Table 15.2 *Examples of wearables in fashion*

MINI CASE STUDY 15.2 - Kokoon

Image courtesy of Kokoon, reproduced with permission.

Kokoon's project sits at the intersection of two highly competitive industries – technology and fashion; both propelled towards new developments. Kokoon's headphones combine hidden electroencephalographic (EEG) sensors with pioneer acoustic expertize to actively improve sleep. The brain-state sensing with the embedded EEG sensors monitors brain activity and determines the sleep state. Data from the EEG sensors can then be used to adapt the user's audio and enhance sleep. Tim Antos, founder and CEO of Kokoon, explains: 'the headphones are designed to help you sleep anytime, anyplace, and anywhere. They'll do this by helping you relax and switch off using audio, then protecting your sleep from disturbances then at the right time for your natural sleep cycle wake you up.' This level of insight enables Kokoon to become truly intelligent. It adjusts audio volume and equalization as the wearer falls asleep, and it blocks out external noises.

Source: Conversation between Ana Roncha and Tim Antos, CEO Kokoon

ONLINE RESOURCES

A longer version of this case study can be found on our companion website, at: https://www.macmillanihe.com/companion/Varley_Fashion_Management.

Data activation and personalization

The potential in the use of customer data is the ability to build improved insights. Companies that are able to learn, organize and leverage volumes of data have the ability to capture consumers' preferences. Knowing what customers own and what they can access will allow retailers to more comfortably navigate options and to increase their knowledge of consumers' end-to-end purchase journey. Capturing, owning and working with this data requires a new set of management skills.

The advantages of collecting data has had a profound effect in the organizational structure of various fashion companies. We have witnessed a shift from the front to the back end of the business in an attempt to drive sales by improving customers' experiences. According to Marian (2015), the three main areas of potential application are:

- **Optimizing in-store operations** – Using in-store analytics systems powered by consumer Wi-Fi on smartphones, brands are able to capture a consumer's movements and dwell times.

- **Personalizing the retail experience** – Investing in improving the user's experience through personalizing homepages (at the time of writing, Mr Porter and Very.co.uk are good examples) as well as sending unique promotional messages linked to consumers' own profiles and viewings.

- **Predicting demand for product** – Aiming to connect the right consumer at the right moment and place with the right product. Using data from relevant social feeds, locations and feedback, retailers are able to predict potential demand for products.

Another benefit of big data is its ability to identify the most valuable customers and build a meaningful relationship with them. Examples of this include:

- **Asos A-List** loyalty programme – offering members different rewards and events based on their spending. For example, when customers spent more than £600 in a 12-month period, they were granted access to Asos Headquarters for a special catwalk event and to meet the brand's in-house team.

- **Revolve's social club** in Los Angeles – targeting its highest spending customers, VIPs, influencers and celebrities. In this location, the brand is able to offer personalized private shopping curated for members through its data-driven merchandising algorithms and the brand's stylists.

Not only is data valued by brands but consumers themselves are starting to realize the value of giving away (or not) their personal details. Recent developments in data protection legislation will make it harder for organizations to exploit consumer data and will give the consumer more rights in respect of the information held about them.

Frictionless experiences in-store

The checkout process lies at the centre of most retailers' concerns about improving the in-store experience, with most brands trying to mimic the online experience and ease of payment. In 2016, Amazon Go launched a pilot grocery store in Seattle in the US, which raised the bar for frictionless experiences. Consumers scan an app on the way in, select and place items into a bag and are then able to walk out without having to stop, due to a combination of computer vision, sensor fusion and deep learning. A fashion brand leading the way in terms of technology integration is Rebecca Minkoff, who have installed self-checkouts in their New York Store. 'More and more we are seeing millennials want to be in complete control of any and all of their shopping, and that includes payment. Long gone are the days where you needed to depend fully on a sales assistant to request new sizes or to ring you up' (Uri Minkoff, CEO at Rebecca Minkoff, in Arthur, 2016c).

Apart from payment processes, other innovations are aiming at reducing the interaction between staff and consumers while enhancing the service experience. In the US, Zara has been using tablets in the dressing rooms that are connected to Radio Frequency Identification (RFID) tags on the garments, which allow customers to have access to product information and the availability of sizes and colours, mirroring the experience of shopping online. Customers can also request further options to be brought into the fitting room via the tablet.

In-store digital technology is no longer simply a tool for seamlessly managing sales and stock control. Consumer expectation and higher digital proficiency are driving retailers to equip their stores with similar functionalities to those offered online. 'While many of the latest innovations such as magic mirrors, in-aisle payments and online sizing tools can improve the in-store and online shopping experience, it is important for retailers to focus on technologies that resonate with their target customer' (Mintel, 2016, *Fashion: Technology and Innovation – UK*).

THE INTERNET OF THINGS (IOT)

'Manus x Machina: Fashion in the age of technology' was the motto for the 2016 Met Ball, one of the key events in the US fashion calendar. Exploring how technology is shaping fashion was the underlining theme and served as a way to officially show how fashion companies are starting to understand that connected clothing and the Internet of Things (IoT) is a reality that can be applied to fashion pieces.

We discussed earlier in this chapter how today's consumers are driven by experiences over things and value over price. In the age of the IoT, what matters the most is the experience and the data associated with it. The underlining principle of the IoT is that all products we interact with on a daily basis are interconnected and they should exist to make our life easier and reflect our lifestyle. This could be in the form of Radio Frequency Identification (RFID) or using embedded sensors or QR (Quick Response) codes. For fashion brands, this represents a shift, allowing them to use real-time data collected through non-intrusive means with the aim of creating better and more purposeful products, more responsive and agile supply chains and better shopping experiences, both on and offline.

RFID was first introduced to enable product tracking in the supply chain but nowadays it is being used to understand how people interact with pieces and what they do with them. What the IoT ultimately allows is for objects around us to be smarter and have the ability to create new data streams that enable powerful insights, which have the potential to drive cost and operational efficiencies and provide a higher level of customer engagement. For example, brands could target consumers with purchase incentives after a certain period of time, or number of miles run, or to assess how a product has performed with regards to its brand promise. This should result in better products with enhanced performance as well as new levels of retail service personalization. Digital identities allow the creation of data to use in loyalty programmes or programmatic re-targeting campaigns. Through giving physical items a digital identity in the cloud, real-time software, apps and analytics can tap into this data and enable it to be part of a digital ecosystem.

An example of this is the platform EVRYTHNG, which allows clothes and footwear to be 'born digital'. Here consumers can scan their garments and receive style suggestions, recommendations and rewards/benefits based on what they already own (Hobsbawm, 2017). EVRYTHNG and Avery Dennison have established a partnership in 2016 that intends to introduce products with these unique digital identities (brands such as Hugo Boss and Nike were early adopters) through smart labels, apps and software in the cloud (Arthur, 2016b).

Another advantage of connected clothing is to allow for brand authenticity to help prevent counterfeiting and enhance transparency in the supply chain. Having a digital identity enables monitoring of the lifecycle of a product to identify re-use and recycling. Within the wearables category and its connected systems, this is taken further with pieces being able to detect changes in the environment and react to stimuli from the wearers' bodies. For example, a jacket can allow access to an event or club and your sweater can tell you its carbon footprint or how to recycle it.

Some of the applications of the IoT for brands include delivering personalized content, service, and even pricing (when linked to purchase history). The IoT allows the creation of a new ecosystem in fashion, one powered by technology, and is highly interactive, informative and individualized for consumers. 'Our belief is data is the new oil. You think it's a coincidence Google or Amazon is who you'd bet on? The companies that win are those using math' (Kevin Plank, founder and CEO Under Armour, in EVRYTHNG, 2017).

DISRUPTIVE INNOVATION AND NEW BUSINESS CREATION

> **Innovation** Innovation implies the development of new outputs whether a new product, method of production, new market or business model. It implies the commercialization of ideas and their consequence as a component of economic growth.

Innovation is a term often used as a replacement for creativity, knowledge, or change (Crossan and Apaydin, 2010) but has recently been defined by the World Economic Forum (2015) as 'the successful commercialization of novel ideas, including products, services, processes and business models' and represents 'a critical component of economic growth'.

In addition to

- **product innovation,**
- **process innovation,**
- **business model innovation,**

innovation can also come in the form of

- **management innovation,**
- **technological innovation.**

Technological innovation considers the involvement of a new product or service, and processes to produce and deliver them (Volberda et al., 2013), and can also be defined in terms of its novelty degree; incremental or radical.

Creating an environment that stimulates innovation is a major competence; internal capabilities do not always match the desired requirements to achieve innovation, so companies are increasingly collaborating with external parties (OECD, 2013) and are moving towards open forms of innovation. By doing so, companies accelerate innovation and create more competitive market positions as opposed to those that are more internally focused with slower time-to-market and higher development costs (Engel et al., 2015).

From the typology of innovation above, we will look further into business model innovation, as this is a crucial outcome of this chapter and summarizes some of the key concepts discussed earlier (see Figure 15.6).

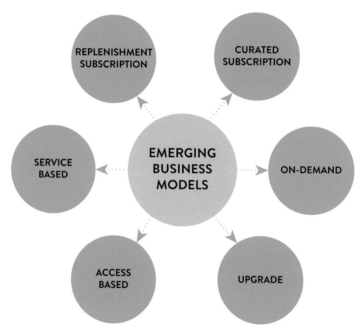

Figure 15.6 *Business models driving change in the fashion industry*
Source: Adapted from WEF (2017).

Replenishment subscription – Within these models, products are automatically ordered and delivered on a consistent schedule. Examples include subscription boxes that allow users to receive the same products, such as the Gillette Shave Club.

Curated subscription – Similar to the first in principle, but products are expertly curated based on an individual's preferences, supplied when signing in. Consumers enjoy a sense of discovery and surprise when opening the box (see Figure 15.7). For this to work, retailers need to understand the variables, price points and most importantly the receiving value and benefits from month-to-month consumers. A good feature to have is the ability to upgrade or downgrade the level of subscription so consumers can find the right level of subscription for them. The case study company VIGGA, below, uses this model.

On-demand – Anchored in the IoT and rising applicability of data to items, this model works with sensors that gauge supply level and automatically reorder when supply is low, such as the Amazon Dash button. Through AI and machine learning as well as IoT connectivity, this works mostly for low-engagement products but serves as a footprint for future developments.

Upgrade – This allows brands to offer upgrades to the newest model based on a fee or trade-in model. A good example of this in the fashion industry is Nudie Jeans' repair shop, offering consumers the chance to repair their pieces. Pepe Jeans also offers an in-store customization service, allowing consumers the opportunity to upgrade a style they already own, by adding new features such as patches or laser imprints.

Figure 15.7 *Curated subscription brand Birchbox. Image courtesy Birchbox, reproduced with permission.*

Access based – The access-based model relates closely to the sharing economy and is based on consumers opting for access instead of ownership of a piece, as seen above in the case of Rent the Runway. Another example is Mud Jeans creating a programme entitled 'Lease a Jeans', where consumers can rent their jeans for a deposit and a small regular sum for each month of use. After a year's lease, consumers can opt to swap for a new pair, purchase, or return.

Service based – This includes models where consumers pay for a service. For example, Boon + Gable is a US-based styling service that uses expertize as a point of differentiation. Stylists come to your home with a personalized selection of pieces you might like (based on data provided previously) and help you choose. Another example is Glamsquad, an in-home beauty service that provides hair, make-up and nail services.

CASE STUDY 15 - VIGGA™: A new business model for those new to the world in Denmark

VIGGA is a Danish brand which is a subscription-based leasing concept for baby and children's wear. Vigga and Peter Svensson founded the company in 2014 with the ambition of changing the usage of baby's clothing to be more sustainable. As babies outgrow clothes quickly, the couple saw

An Example of a VIGGA Package. Image: Courtesy of Vigga – www.vigga.us. Reproduced by permission of Vigga.us.

the opportunity to offer a basic wardrobe package (see Figure) that could be exchanged for a larger size when the clothes become too small. The items are made in organic and GOTS certified cotton, which means they are free from harmful chemicals. During the subscription period the child receives up to 11 packages of organic clothing (VIGGA, 2017).

Vigga Svensson had previously built up the popular children's brand Katvig, which also focused on a sustainable production. Through the experience of Katvig, she realized that most baby's clothing ends up in wardrobes or attics, often only worn 5–10 times before it becomes too small. Even though the production of the clothing was sustainable, it did not have enough effect when the way the customers were using the product was not sustainable (Meinecke, n.d.). This was an opportunity for Vigga Svensson and her husband to re-think the business model for their new company. A circular concept was the answer to the issue of the buy-and-throw-away culture and offered a means of sustainable consumption along with sustainable production. Another benefit from the subscription-based concept was a more stable cash flow compared with the more traditional seasonal structure in a wholesale-focused fashion company, which had been the case with Katvig (Johnston, 2015).

VIGGA offers the customer convenience, saving time and ensuring that the child is dressed in quality products with appealing design and manufactured from non-harmful textiles. VIGGA (2017) suggests that during the first two years of a child's life, it will grow through 8 different wardrobes. With that in mind the subscription-based concept is a cost-saving choice and adheres to the megatrend of moving towards a sharing economy (Steensgaard, 2015).

Ambitions are high, and the turnover of the start-up company is expected to reach 25 million DKK (approx. £2.8 million) in 2018 (Steensgaard, 2015). VIGGA was awarded 'most sustainable solution within the fashion industry' in 2015 by Sustainia at COP21 (VIGGA, 2017), which highlights the achievements from a sustainability perspective. This is, however, an example not just of incorporating sustainability, but of how a company has used an innovative business model to respond to a new way of consuming based upon sharing and circulating high-quality products.

Sources:
VIGGA (2017). Available at: www.vigga.us [accessed 20/04/2017].
Meinecke, S. (n.d.). Available at: https://groenforskel.dk/feature/vigga-baeredygtigt-boernetoej/ [accessed 25/04/2017].
Steensgaard (2015). Available at: http://www.business.dk/vaekst/vigga-vil-vende-boernetoejsbutikken-paa-hovedet [accessed 20/04/2017].
Johnston, S. (2015). Available at: http://www.wearesalt.org/vigga-turning-childrens-clothing-circular-one-babygrow-at-a-time/ [accessed 20/04/2017].

With thanks to Jeanne Rye Nielsen who authored this case study.

Case Challenge

To what extent do you think subscription business models have a place in the fashion industry of the future? Debate whether they are just a fad, or whether they can contribute to a sustainable future for the fashion industry.

ONLINE RESOURCES

A longer version of this case study, with additional challenges, can be found on our companion website: https://www.macmillanihe.com/companion/Varley_Fashion_Management.

SUMMARY AND CONCLUDING THOUGHTS

Today's brands have to continually reinvent themselves in order to adapt to the dynamic market reality. The underpinning reason for this is that demanding consumers want greater levels of personalization in their consumption experience and brands need to provide them with more effective responsiveness. Strong brands are the ones able to offer emotional benefits that go beyond functional attributes so as to establish a lasting connection with their customers, adopting the consumer-first mentality where companies have the consumer as the focus of their business strategy.

In the age of the Internet of Things, relationships between consumers and brands have evolved to a high level of intimacy and disclosure, with connectivity allowing brands to adopt service-oriented business models. IoT will bring new opportunities for fashion retailers, as the technology matures and becomes less costly. It allows brands to have a deeper understanding of their consumers and to improve investment targeting more effectively for higher returns. The focus must be on providing the most relevant content without being too intrusive, and on choosing messages to display according to social behaviour and information collected.

A consequence of digital disruption is the move towards more agile operating models with improved capabilities and resource deployment that differ largely from those in the past. Strategic fashion management is now about adopting a collaborative mind-set and new capabilities that will better understand the needs and demands of the consumer within the digitally empowered ecosystem. The speed at which companies are able to do this will be crucial to success; developing or acquiring consumer-focused capabilities to remain competitive in the marketplace will be vital.

It's not about that store of the future, it's about the customer of the future. (Scott Emmons, Head of Innovation at Neiman Marcus, in Milnes, 2017b)

 ## CHALLENGES AND CONVERSATIONS

1. Select a fashion brand of your choice and evaluate the extent to which it appears to be ready to face the challenges of the future in terms of technological innovations.

2. In a hyper-competitive market like fashion, to what extent do you believe trends like co-creation, collaboration and the sharing economy really support future strategic development for fashion organizations?

3. For a fashion retailer of your choice, suggest conceptual elements that might be built into the store of the future for this brand. Use the diagram in Figure 15.5, 'The new role of physical stores', to help you with this task.

4. Debate the motion 'within the context of the fashion industry, VR, AR and AI are all promotional gimmicks rather than the underpinning of further disruptive changes'.

5. The content of this chapter suggests that fashion brands will increasingly differentiate on the basis of customer experience and personalized service. Will these factors ever replace product-based differentiation in strategic fashion management?

6. Restricting your analysis to one level of the fashion market (for example, luxury, bridge, mass market), suggest what will be important for the 'customer for the future', and how strategically managed fashion companies should approach the challenge of remaining relevant to this customer.

 ## REFERENCES AND FURTHER READING

Adler, P., Heckscher, C. and Prusak, L. (2011) 'Collaborative enterprise: Four keys to creating a culture of trust and teamwork'. *Harvard Business Review*, July–August, pp. 1–9.

Altonen, A. (2011) *Success factors of mass customization – Cases: Chocri and Shoes of Prey*. MBA Thesis. Available at: https://aaltodoc.aalto.fi/handle/123456789/692 [accessed 20/05/2016].

Arthur, R. (2016a) *Burberry is also experimenting with chatbots for London fashion week*. Available at: https://www.forbes.com/sites/rachelarthur/2016/09/17/burberry-is-also-experimenting-with-chatbots-for-london-fashion-week/#38cf8381ffd4 [accessed 02/05/2017].

Arthur, R. (2016b) *10 Billion Items of Connected Clothing: The Internet of Things Just Became a Lot More Fashionable*. Available at: https://www.forbes.com/sites/rachelarthur/2016/04/21/10-billion-items-of-connected-clothing-the-internet-of-things-just-became-a-lot-more-fashionable/#35eef8a05f8f [accessed 26/10/2017].

Arthur, R. (2016c) *The Automated Future of the Fashion Store: Where Self-Checkouts and Human Touch Collide*. Available at: https://www.forbes.com/sites/rachelarthur/2017/02/01/the-automated-future-of-the-fashion-store-where-self-checkouts-and-human-touch-collide/#576c859c5d6c [accessed 26/10/2017].

Baldwin, C. (2016) *Shop Direct introduces chat bots to Very app*. Available at: http://www.essentialretail.com/news/article/5825c4fd9c1e8-shop-direct-introduces-chat-bots-to-very-app [accessed 30/11/2017].

Bank of America (2016) *Trends in Consumer Mobility Report*. Available at: http://newsroom.bankofamerica.com/files/press_kit/additional/2016_BAC_Trends_in_Consumer_Mobility_Report.pdf [accessed 22/12/2016].

Beecham Research (2015). Available at: http://www.beechamresearch.com [accessed 08/05/2016].

Biron, B. (2017) *Marchesa is using Rent the Runway to test a new collection of blouses*. Available at: http://www.glossy.co/evolution-of-luxury/marchesa-is-using-rent-the-runway-to-test-new-collection-of-blouses [accessed 03/02/2018].

BoF (Business of Fashion) (2016) *How Burberry is operationalizing See now Buy now*. Available at: https://www.businessoffashion.com/articles/intelligence/how-burberry-is-operationalising-see-now-buy-now [accessed 03/03/2017].

BoF (Business of Fashion) and McKinsey (2016) The state of fashion. Available at: https://www.mckinsey.com/industries/retail/our-insights/the-state-of-fashion [accessed 03/03/2017].

Brady, P. (2017) *8 Ways West Elm Hotels is Revolutionizing the Hotel Industry*. Available at: https://www.cntraveler.com/story/west-elm-hotels-is-revolutionizing-the-hotel-industry [accessed 17/09/2017].

Cain, S. (2013) *What Crowdsourcing 'Says About Big Data'*, Edited. Available at: https://edited.com [accessed 11/05/2016].

Chain Storage (2015). Available at: https://www.chainstoreage.com/article/instacart-deliv-turn-heat-delivery-wars/ [accessed 09/05/2016].

Click & Invest (2017). Available at: https://www.clickandinvest.com [accessed 24/01/2018].

Conlon, S. (2015) 'All change at NYFW'. Available at: http://www.vogue.co.uk/article/new-york-fashion-week-cfda-research-consumer-event [accessed 17/09/2017].

Credence Research (2016) *Airport Retail Market*. Available at: https://www.credenceresearch.com/report/airport-retail-market [accessed 03/02/2018].

Crossan, M. and Apaydin, M. (2010) 'A multi-dimensional framework of organizational innovation: A systematic review of the literature'. *Journal of Management Studies*, 47(6), pp. 1154–1191.

Denning, S. (2013) 'Masterclass: The management revolution's growing army of rebel voices'. *Strategy and Leadership*, 41(5), pp. 23–33.

Denning, S. (2014) 'Navigating the phase change to the creative economy'. *Strategy and Leadership*, 42(2), pp. 3–11.

Engel, K., Dirlea, V. and Graff, J. (2015 *Masters of Innovation: Building the Perpetually Innovative Company*. London: LID Publishing.

Euromonitor (2017) *Mega trends: Connected consumers*. Available at: http://www.euromonitor.com/megatrends [accessed 25/01/2018].

Evans, M. (2017) *Why Commerce Players Must Invest in Artificial Intelligence Today*. Available at: https://www.forbes.com/sites/michelleevans1/2017/03/23/why-commerce-players-must-invest-in-artificial-intelligence-today/#2cc07a634283 [accessed 07/02/2018].

EVRYTHNG (2017) *The internet of clothing: How smart products will transform fashion*. Available at: https://evrythng.com/the-internet-of-clothing-how-smart-products-will-transform-fashion/ [accessed 14/01/2018].

Foley, B. (2017) *Bridget Foley's Diary: Tom Ford, Coming Home*. Available at: http://wwd.com/fashion-news/fashion-features/bridget-foley-diary-tom-ford-coming-home-10846206/ [accessed 12/12/2017].

Forbes (2016) Here's How Nike is Innovating to Scale Up Its Manufacturing. Available at: https://www.forbes.com/sites/greatspeculations/2016/05/18/heres-how-nike-is-innovating-to-scale-up-its-manufacturing/#1e93cc0d1497 [accessed 02/05/2017].

Gallace, A. and Spence, C. (2014) *In Touch with the Future: The Sense of Touch from Cognitive Neuroscience to Virtual Reality*. Oxford: Oxford University Press.

Gartner (2016). Available at: https://www.gartner.com/newsroom/ [accessed 26/11/2017].

Gouillart, F. J. (2014) The race to implement co-creation of value with stakeholders: Five approaches to competitive advantage. *Strategy & Leadership*, 42(1), pp. 2–8.

Gouillart, F. and Ramaswamy, V. (2010) *The Power of Co-Creation*. New York: First Free Press.

Harvard Business Review (*HBR*) (2016) The elements of value: Measuring what consumers really want. Available at: https://hbr.org/webinar/2016/07/the-elements-of-value-measuring-what-consumers-really-want [accessed 03/09/2017].

Hendriksz, V. (2016) *Net-a-Porter joins forces with Cathay Pacific for exclusive inflight shopping*. Available at: https://fashionunited.uk/news/business/net-a-porter-joins-forces-with-cathay-pacific-for-exclusive-inflight-shopping/2016081521415 [accessed 15/09/2017].

Higginbotham, S. (2015) *Google's Project Jacquard wants to make wearables truly wearable*. Available at: http://fortune.com/2015/05/29/googles-project-jacquard/ [accessed 29/05/2017].

Hobsbawm, A. (2017) *Making Clothing Part of the Internet of Things*. Available at: https://disruptionhub.com/making-clothing-part-internet-things/ [accessed 12/12/2017].

Howe, J. (2006) 'The rise of crowdsourcing'. *Wired Magazine*, 14(6), pp. 1–6.

Humphreys, A. and Grayson, K. (2008) 'The intersecting roles of consumer and producer: A critical perspective on co-production, co-creation and prosumption'. *Sociology Compass*, 2, pp. 963–980.

Jordan, A. (2016) *Travel Essentials*. Available at: https://www.lsnglobal.com/briefing/article/19316/travel-essentials [accessed 05/03/2017].

Kaplan, A. M. and Haenlein, M. (2010) 'Users of the world, unite! The challenges and opportunities of social media'. *Business Horizons*, 53(1), pp. 59–68.

Kotler, P. (1989) 'From mass marketing to mass customization'. *Planning Review*, 17, pp. 10–13.

Kurt Salmon (2017) *See now buy now – How ready are you?* Available at: https://www.accenture.com/t00010101T000000Z__w__/gb-en/_acnmedia/PDF-53/Accenture-Strategy-DD-See-Now-Buy-Now.pdf#zoom=50 [accessed 10/01/2018].

LSN Global (2016). Available at: https://www.lsnglobal.com/micro-trends/article/15940/creative-phygital [accessed 03/03/2017].

Marian, P. (2015) '3 ways retailers are using big data to drive sales and improve margin'. Available at: www.wgsn.com [accessed 19/12/2017].

Maslow, A. H. (1943) 'A theory of human motivation'. *Psychological Review*, 50(4), pp. 370–396.

McKinsey (2014) *Digitizing the consumer decision journey*. Available at: https://www.mckinsey.com/business-functions/marketing-and-sales/our-insights/digitizing-the-consumer-decision-journey [accessed 23/06/2017].

McKinsey (2016) *Demystifying social media*. Available at: https://www.mckinsey.com/business-functions/marketing-and-sales/our-insights/demystifying-social-media [accessed 17/09/2017].

Milnes, H. (2017a) *In the Amazon era, debating the store of the future*. Available at: http://www.glossy.co/store-of-the-future/in-the-amazon-era-debating-the-store-of-the-future [accessed 28/12/2017].

Milnes, H. (2017b) *5 years in what Neiman Marcus has learned from its innovation lab*. Availabe at: http://www.glossy.co/store-of-the-future/5-years-in-what-neiman-marcus-has-learned-from-its-innovation-lab [accessed 28/12/2017].

Milnes, H. (2017c) *Modiface is becoming the go to provider of augmented reality to beauty brands*. Available at: http://www.glossy.co/new-face-of-beauty/modiface-is-becoming-the-go-to-provider-of-augmented-reality-to-beauty-brands [accessed 27/12/2017].

Milnes, H. (2017d) *Yoox Net-a-Porter's new 'temple of innovation' focuses on AI and mobile commerce*. Available at: http://www.glossy.co/ecommerce/yoox-net-a-porters-new-tech-hub-focuses-on-ai-and-mobile-commerce [accessed 29/12/2017].

Mintel (2016) *Fashion: Technology and Innovation – UK*. Available at: http://academic.mintel.com/display/748743/ [accessed 12/02/2018].

Moore, K. and Neely, P. (2011) *From Social Networks to Collaboration Networks: The Next Evolution of Social Media for Business*. Forbes, available at: http://www.forbes.com/sites/karlmoore/2011/09/15/from-social-networks-to-collaboration-networks-the-next-evolution-of-social-media-for-business/ [accessed 09/05/2016].

OECD (2013) *Science, Technology and Industry Scoreboard*. Available at: http://www.oecd-ilibrary.org/science-and-technology/oecd-science-technology-and-industry-scoreboard-2013_sti_scoreboard-2013-en [accessed 07/05/2016].

Peterson, J. (2016) 'The co-design process in mass customization of complete garment knitted fashion products'. *Journal of Textile Science and Engineering*, 6, p. 270.

Qmatic (2017). Available at: http://www.qmatic.com [accessed 28/02/2018].

Retail Design World (2017) *Physical stores 'an engine of online growth' finds research*. Available at: http://www.retaildesignworld.com/59a52dc0afef9-lack-of-in-store-tech-puts-off-shoppers-finds-research/article/598823550f7fc-physical-stores-an-engine-of-online-growth-finds-research [accessed 19/12/2017].

Riewold, O. (2002) *Brandscaping: Worlds of Experience in Retail Design*. Basel, berlin Boston, MA: Birkhauser Verlag AG.

Roberts, L. (2016) *Customizable Opening Ceremony X UMD capsule launches on Farfetch*. Available at: http://www.theindustrylondon.com/customisable-opening-ceremony-x-umd-capsule-launches-farfetch/ [accessed 12/02/2018].

Rubin, H. (2009) *Collaborative Leadership: Developing Effective Partnerships for Communities and Schools*. Thousand Oaks, CA: Sage.

Salonga, B. (2017) *Burberry's 'See Now Buy Now' Fashion Show Revolutionizes the Pace of Luxury Retail*. Available at: https://www.forbes.com/sites/biancasalonga/2017/02/28/burberrys-buy-now-see-now-february-show-revolutionizes-the-pace-of-luxury-retail/#1006025255ae [accessed 03/03/2017].

Schmitt, B. (1999) *Experiential Marketing*. New York, NY: The Free Press.

Seymour, S. (2009) *Fashionable Technology: The Intersection of Design, Fashion, Science and Technology*. Vienna: Springer Vienna Architecture.

Sim, H. R. (2017) *The Fashion Industry is Learning More and More about How You Spend, Thanks to AI*. Available at: https://www.forbes.com/sites/herbertrsim/2017/10/06/the-fashion-industry-is-quickly-learning-more-and-more-about-you-thanks-to-artificial-intelligence/#4a792d727395 [accessed 12/02/2018].

Skeldon, P. (2015) Consumers to spend £9.3bn shopping on mobile while they commute, study finds. Available at: https://internetretailing.net/themes/themes/consumers-to-spend-93bn-shopping-on-mobile-while-they-commute-study-finds-12619 [accessed 27/08/2016].

Solomon, M. (2017) 'How Millennials will Reshape the Luxury Market'. Available at: https://www.forbes.com/sites/msolomon/2017/06/20/how-millennials-will-reshape-the-luxury-goods-market-bain-luxury-report-2017/#5db9ddf12f86 [accessed 12/02/2018].

Statista (2015) *Number of active virtual reality users worldwide from 2014 to 2018 (in millions)*. Available at: https://www.statista.com/statistics/426469/active-virtual-reality-users-worldwide/.

Think with Google (2014). Available at: http://apac.thinkwithgoogle.com/interviews/macys-goes-omni-channel.html [accessed 09/01/2018].

Thomasson, E. (2017) *Adidas takes the sweat out of sweater shopping with in-store machine*. Available at: http://www.reuters.com/article/us-adidas-manufacturing/adidas-takes-the-sweat-out-of-sweater-shopping-with-in-store-machine-idUSKBN16R1TO [accessed 12/02/2018].

Toffler, A. (1970) *Future Shock*. New York: Bantam Books.

VIGGA (2017). Available at: www.vigga.us.

Volberda, H. W., Van Den Bosch, F. A. J. and Heij, C. V. (2013) 'Management innovation: Management as fertile ground for innovation'. *European Management Review*, 10, pp. 1–15.

Wang, C. (2010) Polyvore Taps Its Users to Design the Next Rebecca Minkoff Clutch. Available at: https://www.refinery29.com/polyvore-taps-its-users-to-design-the-next-rebecca-minkoff-clutch [accessed 11/05/2016].

Warc (2014) *UK shoppers now 'boomerooming'*. Available at: https://www.warc.com/NewsAndOpinion/news/UK_shoppers_now_boomerooming/2ce6181c-8380-400f-af35-44c26af585cf [accessed 09/05/2016].

WGSN (2016a) *Future Consumer 2016*. Available at: wgsn.com [accessed 07/02/2018].

WGSN (2016b) *Smart Clothes*. Available at: wgsn.com [accessed 16/10/2017].

WGSN (2016c) *Try before you buy*. Available at: wgsn.com [accessed 03/02/2018].

WGSN (2016d) *Modern Retail Marketing*. Available at: wgsn.com [accessed 19/12/2017].

World Economic Forum (WEF) (2015) *Collaborative Innovation – Transforming business, driving growth*. Available at: http://www3.weforum.org/docs/WEF_Collaborative_Innovation_report_2015.pdf [accessed 07/05/2016].

World Economic Forum (WEF) (2017) *Shaping the Future of Retail for Consumer Industries*. A World Economic Forum project in collaboration with Accenture. Available at: http://www3.weforum.org/docs/IP/2016/CO/WEF_AM17_FutureofRetailInsightReport.pdf [accessed 28/12/2017].

INDEX